SIXTH EDITION

BEHAVIOR MODIFICATION
What It Is
and
How to Do It

Garry Martin
Joseph Pear

University of Manitoba

Pearson
Education

Prentice Hall, Upper Saddle River, New Jersey 07458

Library of Congress Cataloging-in-Publication Data

Martin, Garry
    Behavior modification : what it is and how to do it / Garry
Martin, Joseph Pear. — 6th ed.
        p.   cm.
    Includes bibliographical references and indexes.
    ISBN 0-13-080742-7
    1. Behavior modification   I. Pear, Joseph   II. Title.
BF637.B4M37   1999
    155.2'5—dc21   97-52698
                                                          CIP

Editor-in-chief: Nancy Roberts
Executive editor: Bill Webber
Assistant editor: Jennifer Hood
Editorial assistant: Tamsen Adams
Production liaison: Fran Russello
Editorial/production supervision: Bruce Hobart
    (Pine Tree Composition)
Cover director: Jane Conte
Cover designer: Bruce Kenselaar
Cover photo: Bharati Chaudhuri (1951) Indian.
    Untitled, 1994, SuperStock, Inc.
Prepress and manufacturing buyer: Lynn Pearlman
Marketing manager: Michael Alread
Director, Image Resource Center: Lori Morris-Nantz
Photo Research Supervisor: Melinda Lee Reo
Image Permission Supervisor: Kay Dellosa
Photo Researcher: Beth Boyd

Photo Credits: Page 19, John Henley/The Stock
Market; p. 31, Laimute E. Druskis/Photo Researchers, Inc.; p. 81 (top left) Dennis MacDon-
ald/PhotoEdit; (top right) Laura Dwight/Pho-
toEdit; (bottom left) Will Faller; (bottom right)
Elizabeth Crews Photography; pp. 102, 127, 178,
196, 209, 225, 238, & 291, Garry L. Martin; p. 372,
Spencer Grant/Photo Researchers, Inc.

This book was set in 10/12 Palatino by Pine Tree Composition, Inc.,
and was printed and bound by RR Donnelley Company & Sons.
The cover was printed by Phoenix Color Corp.

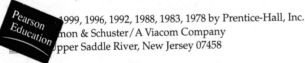

© 1999, 1996, 1992, 1988, 1983, 1978 by Prentice-Hall, Inc.
Simon & Schuster/A Viacom Company
Upper Saddle River, New Jersey 07458

Printed in the United States of America
10 9 8 7 6 5 4

ISBN 0-13-080742-7

Prentice-Hall International (UK) Limited, London
Prentice-Hall of Australia Pty. Limited, Sydney
Prentice-Hall Canada Inc., Toronto
Prentice-Hall Hispanoamericana, S.A., Mexico
Prentice-Hall of India Private Limited, New Delhi
Prentice-Hall of Japan, Inc., Tokyo
Simon & Schuster Asia Pte. Ltd., Singapore
Editora Prentice-Hall do Brasil, Ltda., Rio de Janeiro

To
Jack Michael, Lee Meyerson, Lynn Caldwell,
Dick Powers, and Reed Lawson, who taught us so
much and made learning so enjoyable
and
Toby, Todd, Kelly, Scott, Tana, and Jonathan
who live in a better world because of such
dedicated teachers

Contents

PART II   BASIC BEHAVIORAL PRINCIPLES AND PROCEDURES

3   GETTING A BEHAVIOR TO OCCUR MORE OFTEN WITH POSITIVE REINFORCEMENT

4   DECREASING A BEHAVIOR WITH EXTINCTION

Contents

Contents

Contents

Preface

This sixth edition of *Behavior Modification: What It Is and How to Do It,* like its predecessors, assumes no specific prior knowledge about psychology or behavior modification on the part of the reader. Those who want to know how to apply behavior modification to their everyday concerns—from helping children learn life's necessary skills to solving some of their own personal behavior problems—will find the text useful. Mainly, however, this book is addressed to two audiences: (a) college and university students taking courses in behavior modification, applied behavior analysis, behavior therapy, the psychology of learning, and related areas; and (b) students and practitioners of various helping professions (such as education, counseling, clinical psychology, medicine, nursing, psychiatry, psychiatric nursing, social work, speech therapy, sport psychology, physiotherapy, and occupational therapy) who are concerned directly with enhancing various forms of behavioral development.

From our separate experiences over the past 30 years in teaching members of both groups, we are convinced that both groups learn the principles of behavior and how to apply them most effectively when the applications are explained with reference to the underlying behavior principles on which they are based. For this reason, as our title implies, this book deals equally with both the principles and the tactics (i.e., the rules and guidelines for specific applications) of behavior modification.

Our goals, and the manner in which we have attempted to achieve them, can be summarized as follows:

1. To teach the elementary principles and procedures of behavior modification. Thus, we begin with the basic principles and procedures, illustrate them with numerous examples and applications, and increase the complexity of the material gradually. Study Questions at the end of each chapter promote the reader's mastery of the material and ability to generalize to situations not described in the text. These questions can also be used for examination purposes in formal courses.

2. To teach practical how-to skills, such as observing and recording; recognizing instances of reinforcement, extinction, and punishment and their likely long-term effects; interpreting behavioral episodes in terms of behavioral principles and procedures; and designing, implementing, and evaluating behavioral programs. To accomplish this, we provide Application Exercises Involving Others, which teach the reader about analyzing, interpreting, and developing programs for the behavior of others; Self-Modification Exercises, which encourage the reader to analyze, interpret, and develop programs for his or her own behavior; and guidelines for specific applications.

3. To provide advanced discussion and references to acquaint readers with some of the empirical and theoretical underpinnings of the field. This material is presented in the Notes and Extended Discussion section at the end of each chapter. These sections, which contain numerous references to relevant articles and books, can be omitted without harm to the continuity of the text. Separate study questions on the notes are provided for those instructors who wish to use them and as aids for students wishing to broaden their understanding of behavior modification. The information given in the extended discussion sections can also be used by instructors as springboards for lecture material.

4. To present the material in such a way that it will serve as an easy-to-use handbook for practitioners concerned with overcoming behavioral deficits and excesses in a wide variety of populations and settings.

The book is divided into six parts:

Part I (Chapters 1 and 2) introduces the behavioral orientation of the book and describes major areas of application of behavior modification techniques for improving a wide variety of behaviors of individuals in diverse settings.

Part II (Chapters 3–15) covers the basic principles and procedures of behavior modification. Each of the chapters, except for Chapter 15, begins with a case history drawn from the fields of child development, developmental disabilities, childhood autism, early education, coaching, or normal everyday adult adjustment. Numerous examples of how each principle operates in everyday life and how it can operate to the disadvantage of those who are ignorant of it are also given.

Part III (Chapters 16 and 17) covers no new principles, but rather discusses more sophisticated ways in which to combine and apply the basic principles and procedures discussed in Part II.

Part IV (Chapters 18–21) presents detailed procedures for assessing, recording, and graphing behavior. Methods for conducting functional assessments and behavioral research are also described. Many instructors prefer to present much of this material quite early in their courses—sometimes at the very beginning. Therefore, we have written these chapters so that they can be read independently of the rest of the book; they do not depend on any of the other material. We recommend that students be required to read these chapters prior to carrying out any major projects for their courses.

Part V (Chapters 22–27) deals with how the basic principles, procedures, and assessment and recording techniques are incorporated into effective programming strategies. In keeping with the rigorously scientific nature of behavior modification, we have placed heavy emphasis on the importance of empirically validating program effectiveness. After describing general guidelines applicable to nearly all behavior modification programs, we describe the details of developing token economies in a wide variety of settings. Then, the chapters on self-control and self-desensitization expand on the self-modification exercises of the previous chapters and discuss recent applications to important clinical problems. The chapter on cognitive behavior modification attempts to show that the same behavioral approach that is so effective with public (overt) behavior is also applicable to private (covert) behavior. The final chapter in this section provides an overview of behavior therapy treatments with some of the most common clinical problems with outpatients.

Part VI (Chapters 28 and 29) expands the reader's perspective of behavior modification. It presents an overview of the history of behavior modification and contains a discussion of the ethical issues in the field. Although some instructors might think that these chapters belong near the beginning of the book, we believe that the reader is more prepared to fully appreciate this material after obtaining a clear and thorough knowledge of behavior modification. We placed ethical issues at the end of the text not because we believe that this topic is less important than the others. On the contrary, we stress ethical issues throughout the book, and, thus, the last chapter provides a reiteration and elaboration of our views on this vital subject. We hope that after reading the concluding chapter, the reader will be fully aware that the only justification for behavior modification is its usefulness in serving all humanity in general and its recipients in particular.

Changes in the Sixth Edition

Many chapters have received considerable revision in accordance with reviewers' comments and recent developments in this rapidly expanding field. To Chapter 2 we added sections on parenting and gerontology. In Chapter 3 we added material on establishing operations (previously relegated to a note) to the body of the chapter. To Chapter 6 we added information on concurrent schedules and the matching law to better reflect the increasing theoretical influence of the matching law on the field of behavior modification. To Chapter 7 we added additional examples to help alleviate difficulties many students have in distinguishing between the reinforcement schedules for reducing behavior: DRL, DRO, and DRI. We rewrote critical portions of Chapter 8 to alleviate difficulties some students had with the concept of stimulus control, particularly discriminating between S^Ds and S^As, and in discriminating between rule-governed and contingency-shaped behavior. To Chapter 11 we added information on teaching independent use of prompts in chaining procedures. To Chapter 12 we added substantial new material on conceptual behavior, equivalence classes, and behavioral momentum, thus reflecting the importance these topics have come to have in behavior analysis and behavior modification. To Chapter 14 we added numerous examples and discussion to help students better understand the nature of escape and avoidance conditioning. To Chapter 15 we added a section on the causes of emotions. Chapter 18 has been completely reorganized based on suggestions by reviewers. We added information to Chapter 20 to clarify the distinction between functional assessment and experimental functional analysis. To Chapter 27 we added a section on the treatment of habit disorders.

Throughout the book we have added *examples to better illustrate the application of behavior principles in everyday life.* We have trimmed much of the material in the previous edition and added many new references to reflect recent developments in the field. In particular, we updated Chapter 27 to describe the latest research findings on treatments of choice for problems and disorders commonly seen by behavior therapists.

Acknowledgments

The writing of the six editions of this book was made possible by the help of many individuals. We gratefully acknowledge the cooperation and support of the staff at the Manitoba Developmental Centre and Dr. Carl Stephens and the staff at the St. Amant Centre. Much of the material in this volume was generated while the authors were involved in these institutions; without the support of these staff members this book would not likely have been written.

Grateful acknowledgment is due to our many students and to Joan Lumsden, Lyle Wray, and Michael LeBow for their constructive feedback on earlier editions; to Linda McDonald, who helped to gather some of the material for the guidelines sections; to Jim Rennie, for contributing a number of study questions; and especially to Jack Michael, Rob Hawkins, Bill Leonhart, and Iver Iversen and his students for their many excellent suggestions for improvements. We also wish to thank Leila Krumm, Barb Roscoe, Beryl Lagassi, Vikki Wood, Daryla Christie, and Claudia Milton-Harris for their cheerful and efficient typing of various editions and drafts of this text.

We are grateful to the following reviewers whose helpful criticism improved this sixth edition: Dr. Rita Curl, Minot State University; Dr. Raymond G. Romanczyk, Binghamton University; Dr. John M. Grossberg, San Diego State University; Dr. Sandra Squires, University of Nebraska at Omaha; and Dr. David A. Wittrock, North Dakokta State University.

Finally, we express our appreciation to the very capable editorial and production team at Prentice Hall. In particular, we want to thank Jennifer Hood, our editor, and Bruce Hobart, our production editor.

Completion of this book was facilitated by a research grant from the Medical Research Council of Canada (Grant No. MT-6353) to G. L. Martin.

To the Student

This book is designed to help you learn to talk about and apply behavior modification effectively. You need no prior knowledge about behavior modification to read and understand this text from beginning to end. We are confident that students at all levels—from beginners to advanced—will find the text informative and useful.

Behavior modification is a broad and complex field, with many ramifications. Realizing that some students will require or want a deeper knowledge of behavior modification than others, we have separated the more elementary material from the material that demands more thought and study. The former material is presented in the main body of the text. The latter material is presented at the end of each chapter under the heading Notes and Extended Discussion. The numbers in the margin of the main text refer you to the corresponding numbered passages in Notes and Extended Discussion sections. How you use these sections is up to you and your instructor. You can ignore them altogether and still obtain a good working knowledge of the principles and tactics of behavior modification, because the main text does not depend on the material in the Notes and Extended Discussion. We believe, however, that many students will find these sections very informative and that many teachers will find the material useful in stimulating class discussion and imparting additional background information.

Another major way in which we have attempted to help you learn the material is by providing guidelines on the use of all the behavior modification methods discussed in the text. These guidelines should prove useful as summaries of the material as well as in helping you to actually apply the methods described in the text.

Numerous study questions and application exercises (including "self-modification" exercises) are also presented in most chapters. The study questions are intended to help you check your knowledge of the material when preparing for quizzes and exams. The application exercises and self-modification exercises are intended to help you develop the practical skills you will need to carry out behavior modification projects effectively.

To help make your study productive and enjoyable, we progress from the simpler and more intrinsically interesting material to the more difficult and complex material. This is also true of the writing style. But a word of caution: *Do not be misled by the seeming simplicity of the earlier chapters.* Students who conclude that they are skilled behavior modifiers after they have learned a few simple behavior modification principles unfortunately end up proving the old maxim that "a little knowledge is a dangerous thing." If we personally had to pick the most important chapter in this book, in terms of the knowledge and skills that define a competent behavior modifier, it would probably be Chapter 22. We therefore strongly suggest that you reserve judgment about your abilities as a behavior modifier until you have mastered Chapter 22 and all the preliminary material on which it is based.

With that word of caution, we wish you much success and enjoyment as you pursue your studies in this exciting and rapidly expanding field.

G.L.M.

J.J.P.

Introduction

What is the common element in situations involving the withdrawn behavior of a nursery school child, tardiness in a special education classroom, littering, ineffective studying, writing a novel, speeding, a phobia, migraine headaches, and staff management? Before attempting an answer, let's look at an example of each of these situations.

1. *Withdrawn Child*. A class of nursery school youngsters is in the playground. Some of the children are playing tag; others are swinging vigorously on the swings; a few are taking turns going down the slide; and several are climbing on the monkey bars. But one little boy sits quietly by himself, making no effort to join in the fun. A teacher tries conscientiously, as he has many times before, to coax this child into playing with the others. But the boy steadfastly maintains his social isolation from the other children.

2. *Tardiness*. Cathy is a seven-year-old girl with very poor visual-motor coordination. She attends a school for developmentally disabled children. Although she is able to take off her coat and boots and put them in their proper place each morning, she takes a great deal more time than is necessary to perform these simple functions. She has been known to spend as much as an hour in the cloakroom. Her teachers fear that this arrangement is interfering with Cathy's development of self-reliance. However, they are at a loss as to what to do about the situation, since all their urgings do not make the child move any faster.

3. *Littering*. Tom and Sally have just arrived at the place where they intend to set up camp and are looking in disgust and amazement at the litter left by previous campers. "Don't they care about the environment?" asks Sally. "How can they enjoy nature and

not want to let others enjoy it too?" "If people keep this up," Tom says, "there won't be any nature left for anyone to enjoy." Sadly they tell each other that something should be done about the problem, but neither can say what would solve it.

4. *Ineffective Studying*. With two term papers due next week and a midterm exam at the same time, Sam is wondering how he is ever going to make it through his first year at the university. "Why didn't I start working on this stuff sooner?" he mutters over and over while sitting at his cluttered desk. The week before the exam he gets practically no sleep because of cramming every night, and just barely manages a C-minus on the test. But neither term paper is finished, and he is almost sure to lose marks for lateness even if his professors accept his overdue papers.

5. *Writing a Novel*. Karen works in a bank, but her real ambition is to write a novel. Although most of her evenings and weekends are relatively free, she has not yet begun to write. Instead she spends all her spare time watching television, sewing, cooking, visiting friends, and going out on dates. A box of sharpened pencils and a blank pad of paper lie on her desk in preparation for that important day when Karen will be inspired to write. Unfortunately, it is becoming more and more apparent that Karen's ambition will never be realized.

6. *Speeding*. Accidents frequently occur on the highway approach into Pleasant City. Despite clearly posted signs to reduce speed, many motorists fail to slow down until they are well within the city limits. This is especially dangerous because a large number of children live in Pleasant City, and there have been quite a few close calls in which cars speeding into the city have just narrowly missed a child. If this continues, eventually some child is going to be hurt seriously or killed.

7. *A Phobia*. Albert is a normal, healthy young man, but he has one quirk: he is terrified of airplanes. If you were to ask him why he is afraid of airplanes, he would not be able to tell you. Rationally, he knows that it is unlikely that anything bad will happen to him when he is in one. Nevertheless, he cannot force himself to get in one. Not only is his airplane phobia inconvenient, but it is also very embarrassing since his friends do not seem to understand why he will not ride in an airplane to go on vacation with them.

8. *Migraines*. While preparing dinner for her family, Betty was vaguely aware of an odd, yet familiar, feeling creeping up on her. The odd feeling intensified. Then, all at once, she felt nauseous. She looked around fearfully, knowing from past experience what to expect. "Tom, Jack," she called to her sons watching TV in the living room, "you'll have to finish fixing dinner for yourselves and your father—I'm having another attack." She then rushed up to the bedroom, quickly drew the blinds, and lay down on the bed. A throbbing sensation in her right temple gradually intensified until it seemed that the whole right side of her head was about to explode. Finally, after about six hours of almost unbearable pain, her symptoms subsided and she was able to rejoin her family. But the threat of "another one of Mom's migraines" that could occur again unpredictably at any time still hung over the heads of Betty's family.

9. *Staff Management*. Jack and Brenda were having coffee one morning at the Dairy Queen restaurant they owned. "We're going to have to do something about the evening staff," said Brenda. "When I came in this morning, the ice cream machine wasn't properly cleaned and the cups and lids weren't restocked." "That's only the tip of the iceberg," said Jack. "You should see the grill! And the tables and both bathrooms could use a good scrubbing. Maybe we need some kind of a staff motivation program. We need something!"

Now, let us consider our initial question. What do the nine situations involving the withdrawn behavior of a nursery school child, tardiness in a special education classroom, littering, ineffective studying, writing a novel, speeding, a phobia, migraine headaches, and staff management have in common? It might seem at first that they are too diverse to have anything in common. Closer inspection, however, shows that each is concerned with some sort of human behavior. Together, they illustrate the range of problems with which specialists in behavior modification are trained to deal. In fact, if you read this book very carefully, you will find each of these types of behavioral problems discussed somewhere in the following pages, in terms of how it might be treated by means of behavior modification. Many other types of cases will also be discussed. Behavior modification, as you will see, is applicable to virtually the entire range of human behavior.

WHAT IS BEHAVIOR?

Before we can talk about behavior modification, we must first ask, what do we mean by **behavior**? Some commonly used synonyms include "activity," "action," "performance," "responding," "response," and "reaction." Essentially, behavior is anything that a person says or does. Is the color of someone's eyes behavior? Is blinking behavior? Are the clothes someone is wearing behavior? Is dressing behavior? If you said no to the first and third questions and yes to the second and fourth, we are in agreement. One of the goals of this book is to encourage you to begin thinking and talking very specifically about behavior.

How about getting an "A" in a behavior modification course, or losing 10 lbs.; are those behaviors? No. Those are *outcomes or products of behavior.* The behavior that produces an "A" is studying effectively. The behaviors that lead to weight loss are eating less and exercising more.

Walking, talking out loud, throwing a baseball, yelling at someone—all are *overt* (visible) behaviors that could be observed and recorded by an individual other than the one performing the behavior. As will be discussed further in later chapters, the term *behavior* can also refer to *covert* (private, internal) activities that cannot be readily observed by others. For example, just before stepping onto the ice at an important competition, a figure skater might think, "I hope I don't fall," and he or she is likely to feel nervous (increased heart rate, etc.). Thinking and feeling are private behaviors, and are discussed further in Chapters 15 and 26. Both overt and covert behaviors can be influenced by techniques of behavior modification.

While it is true that we have all learned to talk about behavior in various ways, we often do so in quite general terms. Terms like "honest," "carefree," "hardworking," "unreliable," "independent," "selfish," "incompetent," "kind," "graceful," "unsociable," and "nervous" are summary labels for human actions, but they do not refer to specific behaviors. If, for example, you were to describe a man as nervous, others might know generally what you mean. But they would not know if you were referring to that person's tendency to chew his fingernails frequently, his constant fidgeting when sitting in a chair, the tendency for his left eye to twitch when talking to someone of the opposite sex, or some other behavior. In later chapters we discuss specific dimensions of behavior that can be measured accurately.

Traditional helping specialists often use general summary terms such as *intelligence, attitudes, motivation,* and *creativity.* Behavior modifiers, however, generally try to talk more precisely about behavior.

What do we mean when we say that a person is intelligent? To many people, intelligence is something that you are born with, a sort of "inherited brain power" or innate capacity for learning. But we never observe or directly measure any such thing. On an intelligence test, for example, we simply measure people's behavior—their answers to questions—as they take the test. The word *intelligent* is best used in its adjective form (e.g., "he is an *intelligent* speaker," "his speech is *intelligent,*") or its adverb form, (e.g., "she writes *intelligently,*") to describe how people behave under certain conditions, such as taking a test, not as a noun for some "thing." Perhaps a person described as intelligent readily solves problems that others find difficult, performs well on most course examinations, reads many books, talks knowledgeably about many topics, or scores well on an intelligence test. Depending on who uses the word, *intelligence* can mean any or all of these—but whatever it means, it refers to ways of behaving. Therefore, in this book we avoid using the word "intelligence" as a noun.

What about an *attitude*? Suppose that Johnny's teacher, Ms. Smith, reports that he has a bad attitude toward school. What does Ms. Smith mean by this? Perhaps she means that Johnny frequently skips school, refuses to do his classwork when he does attend, and swears at the teacher. Whatever she means when she talks about Johnny's "bad attitude," it is clearly his behavior with which she is really concerned.

Motivation and *creativity* also refer to the kinds of behavior in which a person is likely to engage under certain circumstances. The highly motivated student spends a great deal of time studying. The creative individual frequently emits behaviors that are novel or unusual and that, at the same time, have desirable effects.

Other psychological terms, such as *developmental disabilities*[1], *learning disabilities, autism,* etc. also are labels for certain ways of behaving. They do not refer to invisible mental abnormalities. How do psychologists and other helping specialists decide that someone is severely developmentally disabled? They make the decision primarily because they might observe that the person, at a certain age,

> cannot tie shoelaces;
> is not toilet-trained;
> eats only with the fingers or a spoon;
> performs on psychological tests in such a way that the combined answers yield an IQ score of 35 or less.

How do specialists decide that a school-age child has a learning disability? They make the decision on the basis of certain behaviors that they observe, such as

> attending to a task for only a few seconds or minutes (typically labeled a *short attention span*);

---

[1]Although the American Association on Mental Retardation (1992) continues to use the term "mental retardation," we prefer the increasingly popular term, "developmental disabilities."

staring at an item for many minutes (typically labeled *perseveration*);

moving frequently from one position, location, or task to the next (often labeled *hyperactivity*);

confusing words while speaking, such as "thumb" for "tongue" (labeled *speech disability*);

inverting words while reading, such as "saw" for "was" (labeled a *reading disability* or *dyslexia*).

How do specialists decide that a child is autistic? They make this decision on the basis of certain behaviors that they observe. For example, they might observe that a child

frequently mimics particular questions rather than answering with an appropriate statement;

engages in various self-stimulatory behaviors, such as rocking back and forth, twirling objects with the fingers, or fluttering the hands in front of his or her eyes;

when called, does not respond, or moves away from the person doing the calling (more generally, shows antisocial behavior);

performs much below average on a variety of self-care tasks, such as dressing, grooming, and feeding.

Why are summary terms or labels for behavior patterns so frequently used in psychology and in everyday life? First, they may be useful for quickly providing general information about how a labeled individual might perform. A ten-year-old child who has been labeled as severely developmentally disabled, for example, will not be able to read even at the first-grade level. Second, the labels may imply that a particular treatment program will be helpful. Someone experiencing problems with frequent anger might be encouraged to take an anger management program. Someone who is unassertive might benefit from an assertiveness training course. However, the use of summary labels also has disadvantages. One is that they may lead to pseudoexplanations of behavior (*pseudo* means false). For example, a child who inverts words while reading, such as "saw" for "was," might be labeled as dyslexic. If we ask why the child inverts words, and we are given the answer, "Because he is dyslexic," then the summary label for the behavior has been used as a pseudoexplanation for the behavior. (Another name for *pseudoexplanation* is circular reasoning.) A second disadvantage of labeling is that labels can negatively affect the way an individual might be treated. Teachers, for example, are less likely to encourage children to persist in problem solving if the children have been labeled as *sexually abused* or *mentally retarded* (Bromfield, Bromfield, & Weiss, 1988; Bromfield, Weisz, & Messer, 1986). Another disadvantage of labeling is that it may influence us to focus on an individual's problem behaviors rather than on his or her strengths. Suppose, for example, that a teenager consistently fails to make his bed, but reliably mows the lawn and places the garbage cans on the street on pickup days. If the parents describe their son as "lazy," that label may cause them to focus more on the problem behavior than to praise the positive behaviors.

In this book, we strongly stress the importance of defining all types of problems in terms of *behavioral deficits* (too little behavior of a particular type) or *behav-*

ioral excesses (too much behavior of a particular type). We do so for several reasons. First, we want to help you to avoid the problems of using general summary labels discussed earlier. Second, regardless of the labels attached to an individual, it is *behavior* that causes concern—and behavior that must be treated to alleviate the problem. Certain behaviors that parents see and hear often cause them to seek professional help for their children. Certain behaviors teachers see and hear often prompt them to seek professional help for their students. Certain behaviors that can be seen or heard cause governments to set up institutions, clinics, community treatment centers, and special programs. And certain behaviors that *you* emit might cause you to go on a self-improvement program. Third, specific procedures are now available that can be used in school, in the workplace, in home settings—in fact, just about anywhere that there is a need to overcome behavior problems and to establish more desirable behaviors. These techniques are referred to collectively as *behavior modification*. Two terms that are closely related to behavior modification are *behavior therapy* and *applied behavior analysis*. In our view, the term *behavior modification* has acquired a broader meaning than these other terms, and that is the term that we generally use throughout this book. (The historical use of these and similar terms is discussed in Chapter 28.)

The main purpose of this book is to describe behavior modification techniques in an enjoyable, readable, and practical manner. Since it has been written for people in various helping professions as well as for students, we intend to help readers learn not merely about behavior modification but also how to use it to overcome behavioral deficits and excesses in whatever field of specialization they may engage.

"Wait a minute," you may say. "From many of your examples it sounds as if this book is intended primarily for people concerned with observable behavior of severely handicapped individuals." In answer to such an observation, we wish to point out that the behavior modification procedures described in this volume can be used to solve any individual's behavior problems. Even people who are normal or average in most respects usually have some behavior that they would like improved. Behavior that someone would like to improve can be classified as either behavioral deficits or behavioral excesses, and can be overt or covert. Here are examples of each type.

Examples of behavioral deficits

1. A child does not pronounce words clearly and does not interact with other children.
2. A teenager does not complete homework assignments, help around the house, work in the yard, or discuss problems and difficulties with her parents.
3. An adult does not pay attention to traffic regulations while driving, thank others for courtesies and favors, or meet his or her spouse at agreed-upon times.
4. A basketball player, encouraged by the coach to visualize the ball going into the net just before a foul shot, is unable to do so.

Examples of behavioral excesses

1. A child frequently gets out of bed and throws tantrums at bedtime, throws food on the floor at mealtime, and plays with the controls for the television set.

2. A teenager frequently interrupts conversations between his parents and other adults, spends hours talking on the telephone in the evening, and uses abusive language.
3. An adult watches television continuously, frequently eats candies and other junk food between meals, smokes one cigarette after another, and bites his or her fingernails.
4. A golfer often thinks negatively (e.g., "If I miss this one, I'll lose!") and experiences considerable anxiety (i.e., heart pounding, palms sweating) just before important shots.

To identify a behavior as excessive or deficient, we must consider the context in which it occurs. For example, a child drawing on paper is showing appropriate behavior, but if the child repeatedly draws on the living room wall, most parents would regard that as a behavioral excess. A normal teenager might interact appropriately with members of the same sex, but be extremely embarrassed and have difficulty talking to members of the opposite sex (a behavioral deficit). Some behavioral excesses—for example, self-injurious behavior—are inappropriate no matter what the context. In most cases, however, the point at which a particular behavior is considered deficient or excessive is determined primarily by the practices in our culture or by the ethical views of concerned individuals. The relationship between cultural practices, ethics, and behavior modification is discussed in detail in Chapter 29.

CHARACTERISTICS OF BEHAVIOR MODIFICATION

We conclude this introduction by identifying some defining characteristics of behavior modification. The most important characteristic of behavior modification is *its strong emphasis on defining problems in terms of behavior that can be measured in some way, and using changes in the behavioral measure of the problem as the best indicator of the extent to which the problem is being helped.*

Another characteristic of behavior modification is that *its treatment procedures and techniques are ways of altering an individual's environment* to help that individual function more fully in society. The term **environment** refers to the people, objects, and events currently present in one's immediate surroundings that impinge on one's sense receptors and that can affect behavior. The people, objects, and events that make up a person's environment are called **stimuli** (plural of **stimulus**). For example, the teacher, chalkboard, other students, and the furniture in a classroom are all potential stimuli in a student's environment in a classroom setting. An individual's own behavior can also be a part of the environment influencing that individual's subsequent behavior. When hitting a forehand shot in tennis, for example, both the sight of the ball coming near *and* the behavior of completing your backswing provide stimuli for you to complete the forehand shot and hit the ball over the net. Behavior modification procedures deal with stimuli in a person's environment and do *not* involve such procedures as psychosurgery, electroconvulsive therapy, or the use of drugs.

A third characteristic of behavior modification is that *its methods and rationales can be described precisely*. This makes it possible for behavior modifiers to read descriptions of procedures used by their colleagues, replicate them, and get essentially the same results. It also makes it easier to teach behavior modification procedures than has been the case with many other forms of psychological treatment.

As a consequence of the third characteristic, a fourth characteristic of behavior modification is that *the techniques of behavior modification are often applied by individuals in everyday life.* Although, as you will read in Chapters 2, 27, and 29, appropriately trained professionals and paraprofessionals use behavior modification in helping others, the precise description of behavior modification techniques makes it possible for individuals such as parents, teachers, coaches, and others to apply behavior modification to help individuals in everyday situations.

A fifth characteristic of behavior modification is that, to a large extent, *the techniques stem from basic and applied research in the psychology of learning in general, and the principles of operant and Pavlovian conditioning in particular.* Therefore, in Part II we cover these principles in considerable detail and show how they are applicable to various types of behavior problems.

Two final characteristics are that *behavior modification emphasizes scientific demonstration that a particular intervention was responsible for a particular behavior change,* and *it places high value on accountability for everyone involved in behavior modification programs*: client, staff, administrators, consultants, etc.[2]

THE APPROACH OF THIS BOOK

Note 1   To summarize, the behavior modification approach focuses primarily on behavior and involves environmental (as opposed to medical, pharmacological, or surgical) manipulations to change behavior. Individuals who are labeled developmentally disabled, autistic, schizophrenic, or neurotic, for example, are individuals who show behavioral deficits or excesses. Similarly, individuals who are labeled lazy, unmotivated, selfish, incompetent, or uncoordinated are also individuals who show behavioral deficits or excesses. Behavior modification consists of a set of procedures that can be used to change behavior so that these individuals will be considered less of whatever label has been given them. Some traditional psychologists have shown an excessive concern for labeling and classifying individuals. Regardless of the label given, the individual's behavior is still there and is still being influenced by the individual's immediate environment. The mother in Figure 1–1, for example, is still concerned about what to do with her child and how to handle the problem. That is where behavior modification comes in.

After the overview in the next chapter, Part II (Chapters 3 to 15) describes the principles and procedures of behavior modification. In essence, principles are procedures that have a consistant effect and are so simple that they cannot be broken down into simpler procedures. Principles are like laws in science. Most procedures used in behavior modification are combinations of the principles of behavior modification. These principles are almost never used in isolation from

---

[2]We thank Rob Hawkins for bringing these last two points to our attention.

other principles in practical applications, especially with highly verbal individuals. Therefore, to better illustrate the principles under discussion, we have selected relatively simple lead cases for the chapters in Part II. After illustrating the principles involved in such cases, we elaborate on how these principles are used with other types of problems. We also give numerous illustrations of these principles from normal behavior in everyday life. Later parts of the book show how highly complex programs are built from the principles and procedures introduced in Part II. In addition to these detailed programming strategies, ethical issues in their use are described. We hope that this book provides satisfactory answers to teachers, psychiatric nurses, students, teenagers, fathers, mothers, and others who say, "Thank you, Ms. or Mr. Expert, but what can I do about it?" (This is the question asked by the mother in Figure 1–1.) We hope also that the book will give introductory students of behavior modification an understanding of why the procedures are effective.

Figure 1–1   The experts "helping" mother with her child?

STUDY QUESTIONS

1. What is behavior? Give three synonyms for behavior.
2. Distinguish between behavior and outcomes (or products) of behavior. Give an example of a behavior and an outcome.
3. Distinguish between overt and covert behaviors. Give two examples of each.
4. From a behavioral point of view, what is intelligence? creativity?
5. What other terms are closely related to *behavior modification*?
6. What are three disadvantages of using summary labels to refer to individuals or their actions?
7. What is a behavioral deficit? Give two examples.
8. What is a behavioral excess? Give two examples.
9. Why do behavioral psychologists describe behavioral problems in terms of specific behavioral deficits or excesses?
10. What do behavior modifiers mean by the term *environment*? Give an example.
11. What are stimuli? Describe two examples.
12. Describe seven defining characteristics of behavior modification.

APPLICATION EXERCISES

In most of the chapters of this book, we provide you with exercises to apply the concepts you learned in the chapters. Generally, we present two types of application exercises: (a) exercises that involve the behavior of others, and (b) self-modification exercises in which you apply the behavior modification concepts you have learned to your own behavior.

A. Exercise Involving Others

Consider someone other than yourself. From your point of view, identify:
1. two behavioral deficits for that person to overcome
2. two behavioral excesses to decrease.

For each example, indicate whether you have described:
a) a specific behavior or a general summary label
b) an observable behavior or a covert behavior
c) a behavior or the outcome of a behavior

B. Self-Modification Exercise

Apply the above exercise to yourself.

NOTES AND EXTENDED DISCUSSION

1. Because of this emphasis on the environment, behaviorists are often accused of denying the importance of genetics in determining behavior. This mistaken impression may stem in part from the writings of John B. Watson (1913), who, dissatis-

fied with the introspective psychology of his day, argued that the correct subject matter of psychology was observable behavior and only observable behavior. Watson also advocated an extreme form of environmentalism, summarized in the following famous (or infamous) claim:

> Give me a dozen healthy infants, well-formed, and my own specified world to bring them up in and I'll guarantee to take any one at random and train him to become any type of specialist I might select—doctor, lawyer, artist, merchant-chief, and, yes, even beggarman and thief, regardless of his talents, penchants, tendencies, abilities, vocations, and race of his ancestors. (Watson, 1930, p. 104)

However, Skinner (1974) pointed out that Watson himself admitted that this claim was exaggerated, and he did not disregard the importance of genetics. An appreciation by behavior modifiers of the importance of genetics was indicated by the publication of a miniseries on behavioral genetics in the journal *Behavior Therapy* (1986, Vol. 17, No. 4). Included in the miniseries were articles on cardiovascular stress and genetics, childhood obesity and genetics, smoking and genetics, and alcoholism and genetics (also see Turner, Cardon, & Hewitt, 1995). However, even though the influence of heredity may increase the susceptibility of an individual to certain behavioral problems, such as obesity or alcoholism, an individual's environment still plays a major role in the development and maintenance of behaviors that lead to such problems.

Study Questions on Notes

1. Do behavior modifiers deny the importance of genetics? Discuss.

Areas of Application:
An Overview

The value of behavior modification techniques for improving a wide variety of behaviors has been amply demonstrated in thousands of research reports. Successful applications have been documented with populations ranging from the profoundly learning disabled to the highly intelligent, with the very young and the very old, both in controlled institutional programs and in less-controlled community settings. The behaviors have ranged from simple motor skills to complex intellectual problem solving. Applications are occurring with an ever-increasing frequency in such areas as education, social work, nursing, clinical psychology, psychiatry, community psychology, medicine, rehabilitation, business, industry, and sports. This chapter briefly describes major areas of application in which behavior modification has a solid foundation and a promising future.

PARENTING AND CHILD MANAGEMENT

Being a parent is a tremendously challenging job. In addition to meeting a child's basic needs, parents are totally responsible for their child's initial behavioral development, and they continue to share that responsibility with teachers and others as the child matures through the early school years, adolescence, and into adulthood. There are numerous applications of behavior modification to teach parents methods to improve their childrearing practices. Behavioral techniques have been applied to help parents more effectively teach their children to walk, develop initial language skills, provide effective toilet training, and influence their children to do household chores (Bijou, 1993; Meadows, 1996). Parents have also been taught behavioral strategies for decreasing problem behaviors, such as nailbiting, temper tantrums, aggressive behaviors, ignoring of rules, failure to comply with parents' requests, and frequent arguing (Hembree-Kigin & McNeil, 1995; Serketich & Dumas, 1996; Schlinger, 1995). Some child and adolescent behavior problems are complex enough that, in addition to helping parents work with their children, behaviorally oriented clinical psychologists treat the problems directly (Ammerman & Hersen, 1995; Blum & Friman, 1998; Watson & Gresham, 1997).

EDUCATION: FROM PRESCHOOL TO UNIVERSITY

Since the early 1960s, behavior modification applications in classrooms have progressed on several fronts. Many applications in grade school were designed to change student behaviors that were disruptive or incompatible with academic learning. Out-of-seat behavior, tantrums, aggressive behavior, excessive socializing—all have been successfully dealt with in classroom settings. Other applications have been concerned with modifying academic behavior directly, including oral reading, reading comprehension, spelling, handwriting, mathematics, English composition, creativity, and mastering science concepts. Considerable success has also been achieved in applications with individuals with special problems, such as learning disabled and hyperactive children.

Inroads have also been made in the use of behavior modification in physical education. The progress that has been made includes: (a) development of reliable observations for monitoring the behavior of physical education teachers and students so as to provide usable information on "what's happening in the gym?"; (b) increased acceptance of behavioral teaching skills as important components for teacher preparation programs; and (c) increased acceptance of behavioral strategies to help physical educators manage a variety of behavioral difficulties of students (Martin, 1992; Siedentop & Taggart, 1984).

An important innovation in behavioral approaches to teaching is the *Personalized System of Instruction (PSI)*. PSI was developed by Fred S. Keller and his colleagues in the United States and Brazil in the 1960s as a behavior modification approach to university teaching (Keller, 1968). Since then it has spread to a wide variety of subject matters and levels of instruction (Keller & Sherman, 1982). The approach has a number of distinctive characteristics that make it possible for teachers to effectively use principles of behavior modification in improving classroom instruction. In particular, PSI (also known as the *Keller Plan*):

1. identifies the target behaviors or learning requirements for a course in the form of study questions, such as the questions at the end of each chapter in this book;
2. requires students to study only a small amount of material before demonstrating mastery, such as the amount of material in one or two chapters that might be studied in a week or two;

3. has frequent tests (at least once every week or two) in which students demonstrate their knowledge of the answers to the study questions;

4. has mastery criteria so that students must demonstrate mastery at a particular level before going on to the next level;

5. is nonpunitive, in that students are not penalized for failing to demonstrate mastery on a test but simply restudy and try again;

6. uses a number of student assistants (called proctors) to immediately score tests and provide feedback to students concerning test performance;

7. incorporates a "go-at-your-own-pace" feature in which students are allowed to proceed through the course material at rates that suit their own particular abilities and time demands;

Note 1

8. uses lectures primarily for motivation and demonstration, rather than as a major means of presenting new information.

As originally conceived by Keller, PSI courses can require a good deal of labor to administer, especially with large classes, because of the extensive record keeping that PSI requires. With the rise of computer technology, some instructors have begun to automate much of the PSI procedure to make it more efficient. Moreover, some instructors have added electronic backup components, such as videotapes, interactive videodiscs, and computer-delivered tutorials to increase the efficiency of PSI (Crosbie & Glenn, 1993; Crowell, Quintanar, & Grant, 1981; Hantula, Boyd, and Crowell, 1989; A. Rae, 1993). In addition, computers that are part of networks have built-in telecommunications capabilities (e.g., electronic mail) that enable students to write and submit tests for marking, and that allow instructors and proctors to mark tests and provide rapid feedback, without the instructor, proctors, and students having to be at the same location or working on the course at the same time. This can be of great benefit to students who are unable to attend classes because of where they live, their job, or a disability. At the University of Manitoba, where it has been used for a number of years in several psychology courses, computer-aided PSI has been very popular with both on-campus and off-campus students (Kinsner & Pear, 1988; Pear & Kinsner, 1988; Pear & Novak, 1996).

Excellent "how-to-do-it" descriptions of behavior modification techniques for teachers have been published by Alberto and Troutman (1990), Becker (1986), and Cangelosi (1997). Reviews of research in behavior modification and education can be found in Evans and Matthews (1992), and Walker, Greenwood, and Terry (1994). Descriptions of PSI and its research foundation are contained in Keller and Sherman (1982), and Sherman, Ruskin, and Semb (1982). Behavioral approaches to college teaching were discussed by Austin (1998). A special section on behavior analysis in school psychology was published in Vol. 17 (1994) of the *Journal of Applied Behavior Analysis*.

SEVERE PROBLEMS: DEVELOPMENTAL DISABILITIES, CHILDHOOD AUTISM, AND SCHIZOPHRENIA

Beginning in the 1960s, some of the most dramatic successes of behavior modification have occurred with applications to individuals with severe behavioral handicaps.

Developmental Disabilities

In 1992, the American Association on Mental Retardation (AAMR) decided to retain the term *mental retardation*. In this book, we use the term *developmental disabilities* in the sense of AAMR's new definition, which states,

> Mental retardation is characterized by significantly subaverage intellectual functioning, existing concurrently with related limitations in two or more of the following applicable adaptive skill areas: communication, self-care, home living, social skills, community use, self-direction, health and safety, functional academics, leisure, and work. Mental retardation manifests before age 18. (AAMR, 1992, p. 5).

Limited intellectual functioning is defined as an IQ score of approximately 70 to 75 or below, which includes approximately 2.3% of the population. With the new classification system, AAMR proposed that the previously used categories of mild, moderate, severe, and profound mental retardation no longer be used. Instead, they proposed that individuals be classified according to the intensity and pattern of support that they require (intermittent, limited, extensive, or pervasive). Clearly, the new definition places a greater emphasis on assessing and improving an individual's adaptive behavior than did past definitions. This changed emphasis is a result of several developments during the past four decades.

Until approximately the 1960s, treatment and training programs for all levels of developmental disabilities were minimal, and they were the most limited for the severe and profound levels. Fortunately, three forces materialized in the 1960s that, collectively, revolutionized the education of developmentally disabled persons. One force was represented by normalization advocates, such as Wolfensberger (1972), who argued that developmentally disabled persons should be helped to lead the most normative lives possible, and that the traditional, large institutions were simply not normative. This led to a deinstitutionalization movement and the development of community living options for developmentally disabled persons. The second force was represented by civil rights advocates and parents of the developmentally disabled who successfully secured the legal right of the severely handicapped to receive an education. This meant that education programs for developmentally disabled persons had to be developed. The third force came primarily through the efforts of behavior modifiers who developed a technology that made it possible to demonstrate changes in the behavior of severely and profoundly developmentally disabled persons that experts in the field would have said were impossible just a few short years before.

During the past four decades, many studies have successfully demonstrated the applicability of behavioral techniques for teaching developmentally disabled persons such behaviors as toileting, self-help skills (feeding, dressing, and personal hygiene), social skills, communication skills, vocational skills, leisure-time activities, and a variety of community survival behaviors. Reviews of the literature can be found in such sources as Konarski, Favell, and Favell (1997), Matson (1990), and Whitman (1994), and in issues of *Research in Developmental Disabilities*.

Childhood Autism

Children diagnosed as autistic show some behaviors similiar to children diagnosed as developmentally disabled in that they score much below average on a variety of self-care tasks, such as dressing, grooming, and feeding. However, they are also likely to show some combination of asocial behavior (e.g., not showing distress when their mother leaves the room), echolalia (repeating words or phrases without indicating that the words convey any meaning), under- or overresponsiveness to sensory contact, a flat or inappropriate emotional affect, abnormal play behaviors, and repetitive self-stimulatory behaviors (e.g., spinning objects in front of their eyes).

Beginning in the 1960s, and continuing through to the present, Ivar Lovaas (1966) and others have developed behavioral treatments for autistic children. Using behavior change techniques, Lovaas focused on strategies to teach social behaviors, eliminate self-stimulatory behaviors, and develop language skills (Lovaas, 1977). When his intensive treatment programs have been applied to autistic children less than 30 months old, 50 percent of those children have been able to enter a regular classroom at the normal school age (Lovaas, 1982), and the behavioral treatment produced long-lasting gains (McEachin, Smith, & Lovaas, 1993). No alternative treatment for autistic children has been shown to be as successful as behavior modification (Celibverti, Alissandri, Fong, & Weiss, 1993; Ghezzi, 1998; Lovaas, 1993; Lovaas & Smith, 1988, 1989; Schopler & Mesibov, 1994; Schreibman, 1994).

Schizophrenia

Beginning with a few case studies in the 1950s, major attention was directed toward schizophrenia by behavior therapists in the 1960s and early 1970s (Kazdin, 1978). During the late 1970s and early 1980s, however, interest in this area decreased and only a small number of behavioral articles were published (Bellack, 1986). There is, nevertheless, clear evidence of the success of behavior modification treatments with this population. Because they are a prime contributor to the poor quality of life experienced by people with schizophrenia, inadequate social relationships have been one of the behaviors targeted for change in behavior modification programs. Available research indicates considerable success in teaching patients social skills, communication skills, assertiveness skills, and job-finding skills (Bellack & Hersen, 1993b; Bellack & Mueser, 1990; Bellack, Mueser, Gingerich, & Agresta, 1997). Cognitive behavioral techniques have also been used effectively to reduce or eliminate hallucinations or delusions in schizophrenia patients (Bouchard, Vallieres, Roy, & Maziade, 1996). Such findings led Bellack and others to argue strongly that behavior therapy can make a significant contribution to the treatment, management, and rehabilitation of schizophrenic patients (Bellack & Hersen, 1993b; Wong & Liberman, 1996).

CLINICAL BEHAVIOR THERAPY

Behavioral treatment of people who are treated by therapists in office settings has come of age (Forsyth & Eifert, 1996; Hayes, 1998; Hayes, Strosahl, & Wilson, 1997; Kohlenberg, Tsai, & Dougher, 1993). In Chapter 27, we provide a detailed discussion of the treatment of such clinical problems as anxiety disorders, obsessive-compulsive disorders, stress-related problems, depression, obesity, marital problems, sexual dysfunction, and personality disorders. More detailed discussion of these and other areas of clinical treatment can be found in Bellack and Hersen (1993a), Bellack, Hersen, and Kazdin (1990), Turner, Calhoun, and Adams (1992), and Van Hesselt & Hersen (1996).

How common is behavior therapy among practicing psychologists? By the early 1980s, surveys indicated that at least half of clinical child psychologists followed a behavioral orientation, and that behavior therapy had become one of the top two orientations (about on par with the psychodynamic orientation) for psychologists treating adults (O'Leary, 1984). While many behavioral psychologists today are likely to describe their orientation as "cognitive behavioral" (Association for Advancement on Behavior Therapy [AABT], 1994; cognitive behavior modification is discussed in Chapter 26), the behavioral orientation in general continues to grow (Eysenck, 1994).

How effective is behavior therapy with clinical populations? Many studies have demonstrated that there are clear problem areas (e.g., phobias, obsessive-compulsive disorders) in which specific behavior therapy procedures are demonstrably superior to existing psychotherapeutic alternatives (e.g., see Eysenck, 1994; Giles, 1990, 1993). In some cases, the treatment of choice may be a combination of behavior therapy and medical treatments (such as drugs). The current treatments of choice for a variety of clinical disorders are discussed further in Chapter 27.

SELF-MANAGEMENT OF PERSONAL PROBLEMS

Recall some of the problems described in Chapter 1. Sam had difficulty studying and finishing his term papers on time. Karen was not able to get started on that novel she wanted to write. And then there was Albert and his phobia of riding in airplanes. Many people would like to change something about themselves. How about you? Would you like to lose a few pounds? Get into an exercise program? Become more assertive? Are there skills you can learn to help you to modify your behavior? A great deal of progress has been made in the area referred to as self-management, self-control, self-adjustment, self-modification, or self-direction. Successful self-modification requires a set of skills that can be learned. The skills involve ways of rearranging your environment to control your own subsequent behavior. Hundreds of successful self-modification projects directed at problems such as saving money, increasing exercise behavior, improving study habits, and controlling excessive gambling have been reported in the psychological literature (Logue, 1995). Self-modification for personal adjustment is described in more detail in Chapter 24. Extensive discussion of this topic can be found in Martin and Osborne (1993) and D. L. Watson and Tharp (1997).

MEDICAL AND HEALTH CARE

Traditionally, if a person suffered from chronic headaches, a respiratory disorder, or hypertension, that individual would see a physician. In the late 1960s, however, psychologists working with physicians began using behavior modification techniques to directly treat these and other medical problems—such as seizure

18   2   Areas of Application: An Overview

disorders, chronic pain, addictive disorders, and sleep disorders (Doleys, Meredith, & Ciminero, 1982). This launched the discipline that came to be known as **behavioral medicine,** a broad interdisciplinary field concerned with the link among health, illness, and behavior. Behavioral psychologists practicing behavioral medicine work in close consultation with physicians, nurses, dieticians, sociologists, and others on problems that, until recently, have been considered to be of a purely medical nature. Within the interdisciplinary field of behavioral medicine, **health psychology** considers how psychological factors can influence or cause illness, and how people can be encouraged to practice healthy behavior so as to prevent health problems such as heart disease (DiClemente, Hansen, Ponton, 1996; Goreczny, 1995; Sarafino, 1994). Health psychologists have applied behavioral principles in five major subareas.

Direct Treatment of Medical Problems   Do you suffer from migraine headaches, backaches, or stomach problems? At one time it was thought that such problems were purely of a medical nature. But sometimes such problems have a psychological cause. Health psychologists are continuing the trend of the late 1960s of developing behavioral techniques to directly treat symptoms such as these (Sarafino, 1994; Rowan & Andrasik, 1996). Behavioral treatments are also being applied to ameliorate symptoms of other medical problems, such as improving motor skills and decreasing tremors characteristic of Parkinson's disease (Mohr et al., 1996), and conducting brain injury rehabilitation (Jacobs, 1998).

Establishing Treatment Compliance   Do you always keep your appointments with the dentist? Do you always take medication exactly as described by your doctor? Many people do not. But a drug that is 100 percent effective in curing a particular disease will be ineffective if the patient fails to take it as directed. Thus, an important part of health psychology is establishing treatment compliance with prescribed medical regimens. Because drug taking is a behavior, promoting compliance with medical prescriptions is a natural for behavior modification (Sarafino, 1994).

Promotion of Healthy Living   Do you exercise at least three times per week? Do you eat healthy foods and minimize your consumption of fat, cholesterol, and salt? Do you limit your consumption of alcohol, say, to no more than five drinks a week? Do you say no to nicotine and other addictive drugs? If you can answer yes to these questions, and if you can continue to answer yes as the years go by, then you can considerably lengthen your life span (Figure 2–1). An important area of behavior modification involves the application of techniques to help people stay healthy, such as eating well-balanced meals and getting adequate exercise (Williamson, Champagne, Jackman, & Varnado, 1996).

Management of Caregivers   Health psychologists are concerned not only with the behavior of the client or patient, but also with the behavior of those who have an impact on the medical condition of the client. Thus, health psychologists deal with the behavior of the client's family or friends as well as with various medical staff. Changing the behavior of physicians, nurses, psychiatric nurses, occupational therapists, and other medical personnel to improve service provided to patients is receiving increased attention (e.g., see Hrydowy & Martin, 1994; Neef, 1995).

Figure 2–1 Behavioral strategies have been used effectively to help people to persist in physical fitness programs.

Stress Management Like death and taxes, stress is one of the things that you can be sure of encountering in life. Stressors are conditions or events, such as excessive smog, a death in the family, pending examinations, large debts, and lack of sleep, that present coping difficulties. Stress reactions are the physiological and behavioral responses, such as fatigue, high blood pressure, and ulcers, that are brought on by stressors. An important area of health psychology concerns the study of stressors, their effect on behavior, and the development of behavioral strategies for coping with stressors (e.g., see Martin & Osborne, 1993). Some of these strategies are described in later chapters.

Although the broad interdisciplinary field of behavioral medicine and the subfield of health psychology are very young, they have the potential to make a profound contribution to the efficiency and effectiveness of modern medicine and health care. For additional reading in this area, see issues of *The Journal of Behavioral Medicine*, the book by Sarafino (1994), and a special issue on behavioral medicine in the *Journal of Consulting and Clinical Psychology* (1992, Vol. 60, No. 4).

GERONTOLOGY

Do you want to know what it's like to be old? Then "you should smear dirt on your glasses, stuff cotton in your ears, put on heavy shoes that are too big for you, and wear gloves, and then try to spend the day in a normal way" (Skinner & Vaughan, 1983, p. 38). As an increasing percentage of the population is made up of the elderly, more and more individuals must deal on a daily basis with the loss of skills and ability to function independently that occurs with old age or with chronic illness.

Once again, behavior modification can make a positive contribution. For example, habitual ways of performing daily routines at home or at work may no longer be possible. New routines must be developed and learned. Anxiety or fear about the possibility of failing to cope also might have to be dealt with. And new relationships might have to be developed with professional care staff. Behavioral techniques are being used increasingly to help the elderly and chronic-care patients to solve such problems (Wisocki, 1991; Wisocki & Powers, 1997).

BEHAVIORAL COMMUNITY PSYCHOLOGY

As you will read in Chapter 28, which gives a brief history of behavior modification, the bulk of the early (1950s) applications were done with individuals (such as developmentally disabled persons and psychiatric patients) who experienced severe problems, and took place in institutional or highly controlled settings. By the 1970s, however, important behavior modification projects were occurring in such areas as controlling littering in public campgrounds, increasing recycling of returnable soft drink containers, helping community boards to problem solve, promoting energy conservation by increasing bus ridership, encouraging welfare recipients to attend self-help meetings, and helping college students live together in a cooperative housing project (for reviews of the early research in these areas, see Geller, Winett, & Everett, 1982; Martin & Osborne, 1980). The scope of behavior modification had clearly expanded from individual problems to community concerns. One of the early studies in this area defined **behavioral community psychology** as "applications to socially significant problems in unstructured community settings where the behavior of individuals is not considered deviant in the traditional sense" (Briscoe, Hoffman, & Bailey, 1975, p. 57).

   Glenwick (1990) identified five trends in behavioral community applications. The first is greater involvement of the target populations in all aspects of the intervention process. If, for example, a goal is to increase glove wearing by nurses in an AIDS treatment program (e.g., DeVries, Burnett, & Redmon, 1991), then the nurses would be fully involved in selecting goals, choosing an intervention, and monitoring the results. Second, there is increased fostering of the target individual's personal control (vs. control by professionals). In the project with nurses, there might be an emphasis on self-control techniques (described in Chapter 24) to increase their glove wearing, rather than relying on their being told to do so by the head nurse. Third, there is increased inclusion of subjective assessments when evaluating treatment outcomes. Objectively, one might assess whether or not the nurses are wearing gloves more often. Subjectively, we would want to know how they feel about the overall program (subjective assessment is discussed further in Chapter 21). Fourth, there is increased emphasis on antecedent events (the intervention with the nurses might rely on posted reminders and the example of senior staff wearing their gloves) versus consequent events (such as praising the nurses for wearing their gloves). (Issues regarding antecedent and consequent events are discussed in Chapters 8 and 16.) Finally, there is greater interdisciplinary collaboration among professionals. For additional reading in this area, see the special section on Behavioral Community Intervention in the *Journal of Applied Behavior Analysis* (1991, Vol. 24).

BUSINESS, INDUSTRY, AND GOVERNMENT

Behavior modification has also been applied to improve the performance of individuals in a wide variety of organizational settings. This general area has been referred to as **organizational behavior management (OBM),** which has been defined as the application of behavioral principles and methods to the study and control of individual or group behavior within organizational settings (Frederiksen & Lovett, 1980). Other labels used interchangeably with organizational behavior management include "performance management," "industrial behavior modification," "organizational behavior modification," "organizational behavior technology," and "organizational behavior analysis." Like all areas of application in this overview, organizational behavior management is data oriented. It emphasizes specific activities of staff that characterize successful performances and/or produce successful results. It also emphasizes frequent feedback and rewards for employees who show desirable behaviors. Examples of the types of organizations involved range from small businesses to large corporations, and from small community centers (note the overlap with behavioral community psychology) to large state hospitals. Thus, OBM is concerned with organizations both small and large, and both private and public.

One of the earliest studies in what was to become the field of OBM was carried out at the Emery Air Freight Company. According to an article entitled "Conversations with B. F. Skinner" in the 1973 issue of *Organizational Dynamics*, the desired behavior—employees' placement of packages in special containers—was increased from 45 percent to 95 percent through the use of positive reinforcement in the form of praise from supervisors.

Other studies since then have used behavioral techniques to change behavior in ways that improve productivity, decrease tardiness and absenteeism, increase sales volume, create new business, improve worker safety, reduce theft by employees, reduce shoplifting, and improve management-employee relations (Austin, 1998; Hayes & Adams, 1998; Poling, Dickinson, & Austin, 1998; Reid, 1998). For additional reading in this area, see issues of the *Journal of Organizational Behavior Management*, as well as books by Daniels (1994), and Redmon & Dickinson (1990).

SPORT PSYCHOLOGY

Since the early 1970s, there has been a growing desire on the part of coaches and athletes for more applied sport science experimentation, particularly in the area of sport psychology. *Applied sport psychology* has been defined as the use of psychological knowledge to enhance the development of performance and satisfaction of athletes and others associated with sports (Blimke, Gowan, Patterson, & Wood, 1984). Behavior modification has made a number of contributions to this rapidly growing area (Martin, 1992, 1997).

Techniques for Improving Skills of Athletes   What is the most effective way to help an athlete learn new skills, eliminate bad habits, and combine simple skills into complex patterns of execution? Considerable research has examined behavior modification techniques for effectively improving athletes' skills (Martin & Tkachuk, 1998) and practical strategies for applying these techniques have been described (Martin, 1997).

Strategies for Motivating Practice and Endurance Training   How can a coach effectively improve attendance at practices, motivate athletes to get the most out of practice time, organize practices so that there is very little downtime in which athletes are inactive? Techniques for solving these types of problems include goal-setting strategies, reinforcement (or reward) strategies, self-recording and self-monitoring by individual athletes, and team-building sessions (Martin, 1997). All of these motivational techniques are based on principles described in later chapters of this book and can readily be learned by coaches.

Changing the Behavior of Coaches   Coaches have a very difficult job. From a behavior modification perspective, a coach must effectively instruct, set goals, praise, reprimand, and perform other activities that, collectively, determine his or her effectiveness as a behavior modifier. Numerous research studies have been conducted in this area (Martin & Tkachuk, 1998).

"Sports Psyching" to Prepare for Competition   We have all heard expressions such as "The reason the team lost was that they were psyched-out," or "If you want to do your best, you have to get psyched-up." While we may have some general ideas as to what these kinds of phrases mean, knowing generally what they mean and learning how to teach psychological coping skills to athletes are two different things. A number of behavioral strategies have been described for helping athletes prepare for serious competition in sport (see recent issues of *The Sport Psychologist*, and books by Martin, 1997; Martin, Toogood, & Tkachuk, 1997).

BEHAVIORAL ASSESSMENT

Behavioral assessment began to emerge during the 1960s as an alternative to traditional psychodiagnostic assessment. Psychoanalytic approaches to abnormal behavior originated with Freud and others who viewed abnormal behavior as a symptom of an underlying mental disturbance in a personality mechanism. A major purpose of traditional psychodiagnostic assessment was to identify the type of mental disorder assumed to underly abnormal behavior. In contrast, behavioral assessment is concerned with obtaining a description of the problem behavior, identifying possible environmental causes of the behavior, selecting an appropriate behavioral treatment strategy to modify the behavior, and evaluating treatment outcome. One type of behavioral assessment that has become especially important is termed *functional analysis*. Essentially, this approach (discussed in Chapter 20) involves isolating through experimentation the causes of problem behavior and removing or reversing them. As the interest in behavior therapy and behavior modification has expanded during the past three decades, so has the demand for guidelines for conducting behavioral assessments. For more information, refer to Chapters 18, 19, and 20 of this text; the *Journal of Psychopathol-*

ogy and Behavioral Assessment; or the books by Bellack and Hersen (1997), Ninness, Glenn, and Ellis (1993), and Van Houten and Axelrod (1993).

CONCLUSION

The meteoric rise of behavior modification as a successful approach for dealing with a wide range of human problems has been remarkable. Books and journal articles describe behavioral procedures and research ranging from child raising (Bijou, 1993) to coping with old age (Lundervold & Lewin, 1992; Skinner & Vaughan, 1983), and from work (Daniels, 1994) to play (R. L. Williams & Long, 1982). It has been used both with profoundly handicapped persons (Whitman et al., 1983) and with gifted students (Belcastro, 1985), for self-improvement (Watson & Tharp, 1997), and to preserve the environment in which we live (Geller et al., 1982). By 1984, over 850 books had been published concerning basic, applied, and theoretical issues in behavior modification (Rutherford, 1984). A total of 26 journals are predominantly behavioral in their orientation. Examples of applications in many of **Note 2** these areas are described and illustrated in the following chapters.

STUDY QUESTIONS

1. List at least five areas in which behavior modification is being applied.
2. List at least four behaviors of children that have been improved by the application of behavior modification by parents.
3. List at least four behaviors in education that have been modified with behavior modification.
4. What is PSI, and who was its founder? State eight characteristics of PSI.
5. Briefly describe how PSI has made use of computer technology. State two benefits of this use of computer technology.
6. Name and briefly describe the three forces that have revolutionized the education of developmentally disabled persons since the 1960s.
7. List at least four behaviors that have been modified by behavior modification with developmentally disabled persons.
8. List at least four behaviors that have been modified by behavior modification with children with autism.
9. List at least three behaviors that have been modified by behavior modification with people with schizophrenia.
10. How effective is behavior therapy with clinical populations? Discuss.
11. List at least four behaviors that have been modified by behavior modification in the area of self-management of personal problems.
12. What is health psychology? Describe five areas of application within health psychology.
13. List at least four behaviors of elderly persons that have been improved with behavior modification.
14. What is behavioral community psychology?
15. List five current trends in behavioral community applications.

16. List at least four behaviors that have been modified by behavior modification in the area of behavioral community psychology.
17. Define organizational behavior management.
18. List at least four behaviors that have been modified by behavior modification in business, industry, or government. (Be sure that you are referring to actual behaviors, and not just products of behavior.)
19. List four general areas in which behavior modification has been applied in the area of sport psychology.
20. Distinguish between psychodiagnostic assessment and behavioral assessment.

NOTES AND EXTENDED DISCUSSION

1. Lecturing (in combination with two or three exams per semester) continues to be the overwhelming method of choice for teaching undergraduates in most institutions (Terenzini & Pascarella, 1994). How effective is this conventional approach in comparison to PSI? A number of studies have consistently demonstrated that PSI is more effective in enhancing learning of the subject matter than is the more traditional approach (Kulik, Kulik, & Bangert-Drowns, 1990). In fact, PSI has produced a statistically significant average learning advantage of 19 percentile points over traditional approaches (Pascarella & Terenzini, 1991). How do students feel about a system that involves frequent tests or exams? Course evaluations indicate that most students strongly praise such a system and identify frequent exams as being responsible for generating extensive and well-paced study (Michael, 1991). Perhaps, as expressed by Terenzini and Pascarella (1994), "It is time we put to use what we know with some confidence about what constitutes effective teaching and learning and put to rest educational myths that have outlived their usefulness."

2. Wyatt, Hawkins, and Davis (1986) critiqued the claim by some nonbehavioral psychologists that behaviorism—the philosophy behind behavior modification—is dead. Wyatt and others argued that it is very much alive, vital, and growing. A part of the evidence in support of their argument is the abundance of journals that are primarily behavioral in orientation, including the following: *Behavior Analysts for Social Action* (1980–), originally *Behaviorists for Social Action; Behavior and Social Issues* (1991–); *Behaviour Change* (1984–), the official journal of the Australian Behavior Modification Association, which changed its name in 1995 to the Australian Association for Cognitive and Behavior Therapy; *Behavior Modification* (1977–); *Behavior Research and Therapy* (1963–); *Behavior Therapy* (1970–); *Behavioral and Cognitive Psychotherapy* (1973–), originally *Behavioral Psychotherapy; Behavioral Counselling Quarterly* (1981–); *Behavioral Interventions* (1986–); *Behavioral Processes* (1981–), originally *Behavior Analysis Newsletters; Behavioral Residential Treatment* (1986–); *Child and Family Behavior Therapy* (1979–), originally *Child Behavior Therapy; Education and Treatment of Children* (1969–), originally *School Applications of Learning Theory; Japanese Journal of Behavior Therapy* (1976–); *Journal of Applied Behavior Analysis* (1968–); *Journal of Behavior Therapy and Experimental Psychiatry* (1970–); *Journal of Behavioral Education* (1991–); *Journal of the Experimental Analysis of Behavior* (1958–); *Journal of Organizational Behavior Management* (1978–); *Journal of Psychopathology and Behavioral Assessment* (1979–), originally *Journal of Behavioral Assessment; Journal of Rational-Emotive and Cognitive Behavior Therapy* (1983–); *La Technologie du Comportement* (1977–);

Mexican Journal of Behavior Analysis (1975–); *Research in Developmental Disabilities* (1987–) (in 1987, *Applied Research in Mental Retardation* (1980–86) and *Analysis and Intervention in Developmental Disabilities* (1981–1986) were collapsed into one journal); *Scandanavian Journal of Behavior Therapy* (1972–); *The Behavior Analyst* (1978–); *The Behavior Therapist* (1978–).

Study Questions on Notes

1. Which is more effective for teaching undergraduates, the traditional lecturing approach or PSI? Justify your choice.
2. What is behaviorism? Is it dead, sleeping, or very much alive? Justify your answer.

3

Getting a Behavior to Occur More Often with Positive Reinforcement

"Do you want to sit here, Mommy?"

REINFORCING DARREN'S COOPERATIVE BEHAVIOR

   Six-year-old Darren was extremely uncooperative with his parents.[1] In the hope of learning how to deal more effectively with his excessive commanding behavior, Darren's parents took him to the Gatzert Child Developmental Clinic at the University of Washington. As his parents put it, Darren virtually "ran the show," deciding when he would go to bed, what foods he would eat, when his parents could play with him, and so on. To obtain direct observations of Darren's behavior, both cooperative and uncooperative, Dr. Robert Wahler asked Darren's mother to spend some time with Darren in a playroom at the clinic. The playroom was equipped with adjoining observation rooms for data recording. During the first two 20-minute sessions (called a baseline phase[2]), Darren's mother was instructed: "Just play with Darren as you might at home." Darren's commanding behavior was defined as any verbal or nonverbal instructions to his mother, such as pushing her into a chair or saying such things as "You go over there and I'll stay here," or "No, that's wrong. Do it this way." Cooperative behavior was defined as any nonim-

---

[1]This example is based on an article by Wahler, Winkel, Peterson, and Morrison (1965).

[2]A baseline phase (discussed further in Chapters 18 and 21) is a measure of behavior in the absence of a treatment program.

perative statements, actions, or questions, such as, "Do you want to sit here?" while pointing to a chair. To illustrate the consistency of Darren's behavior, Figure 3–1 is a graph of the data collected in consecutive 10-minute intervals. As can be seen, Darren showed a very low rate of cooperative behavior during the baseline sessions. His commanding behavior (not shown in the figure), on the other hand, occurred at an extremely high rate. Following the baseline sessions, Darren's mother was asked to be very positive and supportive to any instances of cooperative behavior shown by Darren. At the same time, she was instructed to completely ignore his commanding behavior. Over the next two sessions, Darren's cooperative behavior steadily increased. (During the same time, his commanding behavior decreased to near zero.) Further experimentation was done by Dr. Wahler and his colleagues to demonstrate that Darren's improvement resulted from the positive consequences provided by his mother following instances of Darren's cooperative behavior (in conjunction with her ignoring of commanding behavior).

POSITIVE REINFORCEMENT

A **positive reinforcer** is an event that, when presented immediately following a behavior, causes the behavior to increase in frequency (or likelihood of occurrence). The term *positive reinforcer* is roughly synonymous with the word **reward.** Once an event has been determined to function as a positive reinforcer for a particular individual in a particular situation, that event can be used to strengthen other behaviors of that individual in other situations. In conjunction with the concept of positive reinforcer, the principle called **positive reinforcement** states that *if, in a given situation, somebody does something that is followed immediately by a positive reinforcer, then that person is more likely to do the same thing again when he or she next encounters a similar situation.*

Although everyone has a commonsense notion of rewards, very few people are aware of just how frequently they are influenced by positive reinforcement

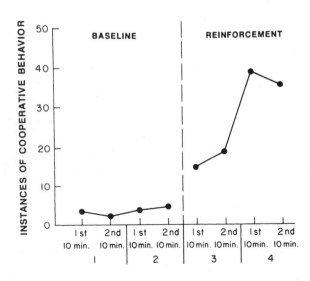

Figure 3–1 Darren's cooperative behavior. Each data point (dot) represents the total instances of Darren's cooperative behavior during a 10-minute interval within a session. Baseline refers to the observation phase prior to the reinforcement program. (*Note:* Replotted from "Mothers as Behavior Therapists for Their Own Children," by R. G. Wahler, G. H. Winkel, R. F. Peterson, and D. C. Morrison, 1965, *Behavior Research and Therapy,* 3, Figure 1, p. 117.)

TABLE 3–1   EXAMPLES OF INSTANCES OF REINFORCEMENT OF DESIRABLE BEHAVIORS

Situation	Response	Immediate consequences	Long-term effects
1. Mother is busy ironing in the kitchen.	Her 3-year-old daughter begins playing with baby brother.	Mother has just completed her ironing and sits down to play with daughter and baby brother for a brief period.	In the future, the daughter is more likely to play with baby brother when mother is ironing because of the attention given when she began playing with her baby brother.
2. While you are waiting in a long line of cars for the light to change at a busy intersection, a car stops in the alley on your right.	You wave to the driver in the alley to pull into the line of traffic in front of you.	The driver nods and waves thanks to you and pulls into the line of traffic.	The pleasant feedback from the driver increases the likelihood that you will be courteous in similar situations in the future.
3. The students in a third-grade class have been given an assignment to complete.	Suzy, who is often quite disruptive, sits quietly at her desk and works on the assignment.	The teacher walks over to Suzy and pats her gently on the shoulder.	In the future, Suzy is more likely to work on the assignments given to her in class.
4. Father and child are shopping in a department store on a hot afternoon and both are very tired.	The child (uncharacteristically) follows father around the store quietly without complaining.	Father turns to the child and says, "Let's go and buy an ice cream cone and sit down for a while."	On future shopping excursions, the child is more likely to follow father quietly.
5. A woman has just tasted a batch of soup she made, and it tasted very bland.	She adds a little Worcestershire sauce.	"It tastes very tangy, just like minestrone soup," she says to herself.	There is an increased likelihood that, in similar situations in the future, she will add Worcestershire sauce to her soup.
6. A husband and wife are undressing and getting ready for bed.	The husband picks up his wife's underthings and places them in the laundry hamper.	His wife pats him and murmurs her thanks.	In future evenings, the husband is more likely to put her underwear in the laundry hamper.
7. One of the authors of this book is attempting to dictate some material into the tape recorder, but the tape recorder is not working.	The author jiggles one of the wires attached to the microphone.	The tape recorder starts working.	The likelihood of wire jiggling increases in similar situations in the future.

during every day of their lives. Some examples of instances of positive reinforcement are shown in Table 3–1. (The terms *positive reinforcement* and *reinforcement* are often used interchangeably.)

The individuals in each of the examples in Table 3–1 were not consciously using the principle of reinforcement; they were just "doing what comes naturally." In each example, it might take several repetitions before there would be any really obvious increase in the reinforced response (that is, an increase that would be noticeable to a casual observer). Nevertheless, the effect is still there. Every time we do something, no matter what it is, there are consequences that "turn us on" or "turn us off" or don't affect us one way or the other. Think about some of your behaviors during the past hour. Were any of those behaviors followed immediately by reinforcing consequences?

Behaviors that operate on the environment to generate consequences, and are in turn influenced by those consequences, are called **operant behaviors** (or **operant responses**). Each of the responses listed in Table 3–1 is an example of operant behavior. Operant behaviors that are followed by reinforcers are strengthened, while operant behaviors that are followed by punishers (see Chapter 13) are weakened. A different type of behavior—reflexive behavior—is discussed in Chapter 15.

It is helpful to think about behavior in the same way that we think about other aspects of nature. What happens when you drop your shoe? It falls toward the earth. What happens to a lake when the temperature drops below 0° C? The water freezes. These are things that we all know about and that physicists have studied extensively and formulated into laws, such as the law of gravity. The principle of positive reinforcement is also rapidly approaching the status of a law. Scientific psychology has been studying this principle in great detail since the 1930s, and we know that it is an extremely important part of the learning process. We also know of a number of factors that determine the degree of influence the principle of reinforcement will have on behavior. These factors have been formulated into guidelines to be followed when using positive reinforcement to strengthen desirable behavior.

FACTORS INFLUENCING THE EFFECTIVENESS OF POSITIVE REINFORCEMENT

1. Selecting the Behavior to Be Increased

The behaviors to be reinforced must first be identified specifically. If you start with a general behavior category (e.g., being more friendly), you should then identify specific behaviors (e.g., smiling) that characterize that category. By being specific in this way, you (a) help to ensure the reliability of detecting instances of the behavior and changes in its frequency, which is the yardstick by which one judges reinforcer effectiveness; and (b) increase the likelihood that the reinforcement program will be applied consistently.

2. **Choosing Reinforcers ("Different Strokes for Different Folks")**

Some stimuli are positive reinforcers for virtually everyone. Food is a positive re-inforcer for almost every person who has not had anything to eat for several hours. Candy is a reinforcer for most children.

On the other hand, different individuals are frequently turned on by differ-ent things. Consider the case of Dianne, a 6-year-old developmentally disabled girl who was in a project conducted by one of the authors. She was able to mimic a number of words, and we were trying to teach her to name pictures. Two rein-forcers commonly used in the project were candy and bites of the child's supper, but neither of these proved effective with Dianne. She spat them out about as of-ten as she ate them. After trying many other potential reinforcers, we finally dis-covered that allowing her to play with a toy purse for 15 seconds was very rein-forcing. As a result, after many hours of training she is now speaking in phrases and complete sentences. For another child, listening to a music box for a few sec-onds turned out to be an effective reinforcer after other potential reinforcers failed. These stimuli might not have been reinforcing for everyone, but that is not important. The important thing is to use a reinforcer that is effective with the in-dividual with whom you are working.

It is important to keep in mind that positive reinforcers are events that strengthen a response when they are introduced or added following the response. The removal of an event following a response may also strengthen that response, but this is not positive reinforcement. For example, a parent might nag a teenager to do the dishes. When the child complies, the nagging stops. Although the cessa-tion of nagging when dishwashing occurs may strengthen the dishwashing re-sponse, it was the nagging's *removal* (not its introduction) following the response that strengthened it. (This process, which is referred to as *negative reinforcement* or *escape conditioning*, is discussed further in Chapter 14).

Most positive reinforcers can be classified under five somewhat overlapping headings: *consumable, activity, manipulative, possessional,* and *social.* Consumable re-inforcers are items that one can eat or drink (i.e., consume) such as candy, cookies, fruit, and soft drinks. Examples of activity reinforcers are the opportunities to watch television, look at a picture book, or even stare out of a window. Manipula-tive reinforcers include the opportunities to play with a favorite toy, color or paint, ride a bicycle, surf the Internet, or tinker with a tape recorder. Possessional rein-forcers refer to the opportunities to sit in one's favorite chair, wear a favorite shirt or dress, have a private room, or enjoy some other item that one can possess (at least temporarily). Social reinforcement includes affectionate pats and hugs, praise, nods, smiles, and even a simple glance or other indication of social attention. At-tention from others is a very strong reinforcer for almost everyone (Figure 3–2).

In choosing effective reinforcers for an individual, it is often helpful to ex-amine a list of reinforcers used by others (see Table 3–2) or to complete a rein-forcer survey. An example of such a survey is shown in Figure 3–3.

A considerable amount of trial and error may be involved in finding an ap-propriate reinforcer for a particular individual. Another method is simply to ob-

Figure 3–2   Praise is a powerful positive reinforcer for strengthening and maintaining valued behaviors in everyday life.

serve the individual in everyday activities and note those activities engaged in most often. This method makes use of a principle first formulated by David Premack (1959), which states that the opportunity to engage in a behavior that has a high probability of occurring can be used to reinforce a behavior that has a lower probability of occurring. For example, W. G. Johnson (1971) used this principle to help a depressed 17-year-old college student increase the frequency of positive self-statements. The student was asked to imagine a positive thought (a low-probability behavior) as prompted from a statement on an index card just before each instance of urinating (the high-probability behavior). After a few days, the student spontaneously thought the positive self-statements just before urinating without the necessity of reviewing the index card. After two weeks of this procedure, the student reported that the positive thoughts were occurring at a high rate (and that the depressive thoughts had completely disappeared).   **Note 1**

It is often quite effective to allow an individual to choose among a number of available reinforcers (DeLeon & Iwata, 1997). Variety is not only the spice of life; it is also a valuable asset to a training program. For example, in a program for a developmentally disabled person, a tray containing sliced fruits, peanuts, raisins, and diet drinks can be presented with the instruction to take one item.

TABLE 3–2   REINFORCERS FOR EMPLOYEES IN A VARIETY
OF WORK SETTINGS

SPECIAL ATTENTION REINFORCERS	MONETARY REINFORCERS
Praise	Promotion
Praise in front of others	Paid days off
Special work assignments	Company stock
Reserved parking space	Company car
Choice of office	Pay for sick days not taken
Selection of own office furnishings	Pay for overtime accumulated
Invitation to higher level meetings	Tickets to special events
Choice of work attire	Free raffle or lottery tickets
Social contacts with others	Extra furnishings for office
Solicitation of opinions and ideas	Gift certificates
Choice of work partner	Dinner for family at nice restaurant
Flexible job duties	Personalized license plate
	Personalized gifts
COMPANY TIME REINFORCERS	Desk calculator or computer terminal
Time off for work-related activities	Business cards
Time off for personal business	Expense account
Extra break time	
Extra meal time	PARTICIPATION REINFORCERS
Choice of working hours or days off	Voice in policy decisions
	Help set standards
	More responsibility
	Opportunity to learn new skill

Note: From *Turning Around: The Behavioral Approach to Managing People* (p. 45) by Beverly Potter. All rights reserved. New York: AMACOM, a division of American Management Association. Copyright 1980. Reprinted with permission.

The advantage of this is that at least one reinforcer among the selection is likely to be strong. If the individual can read, the reinforcers can be listed in the form of a "reinforcer menu," and the preferred reinforcers can be chosen in the same way that one would order a meal at a restaurant.

No matter how you have selected a potential reinforcer for an individual, it is always the individual's performance that tells you whether or not you have selected an effective reinforcer. When you are not sure if a particular item is reinforcing, you can always conduct an experimental test that involves *going back to the definition of **reinforcer** given at the beginning of this chapter*. Simply choose a behavior that the individual emits occasionally and that does not appear to be followed by any reinforcer, record how often the behavior occurs without reinforcement over several trials, and then present the item following the behavior for a few additional trials and see what happens. If the individual begins to emit that behavior more often, then your item is indeed a reinforcer. If the performance does not increase, then you do not have an effective reinforcer. In our experience, not using an effective reinforcer is a common error of training programs. For example, a teacher may claim that a particular reinforcement program that he is trying to use is failing. Upon examination, the reinforcer used may turn out not to be a reinforcer for the student. You can never really be sure that an item is a reinforcer for someone until it has been demonstrated to function as such for that per-

This questionnaire is designed to help you find some specific activities, objects, events, or individuals that can be used as reinforcers in an improvement program. Read each question carefully and then fill in the appropriate blanks.

A   Consumable reinforcers: What does this person like to eat or drink?
   1   What things does this person like to eat most?
      a   regular meal-type foods _____
      b   health foods—dried fruits, nuts, cereals, etc. _____

        _____
      c   junk foods—popcorn, potato chips, etc. _____
      d   sweets—candies, ice cream, cookies, etc. _____
   2   What things does this person like to drink most?
      a   milk _____   c   juices _____
      b   soft drinks _____   d   other _____

B   Activity reinforcers: What things does this person like to do?
   1   Activities in the home or residence
      a   hobbies _____
      b   crafts _____
      c   redecorating _____
      d   preparing food or drinks _____
      e   housework _____
      f   odd jobs _____
      g   other _____
   2   Activities in the yard or courtyard
      a   sports _____
      b   gardening _____
      c   barbecue _____
      d   yardwork _____
      e   other _____
   3   Free activities in the neighborhood (window shopping, walking, jogging, cycling, driving, swinging, teeter-tottering, etc.) _____

      _____
   4   Free activities farther away from home (hiking, snow shoeing, swimming, camping, going to the beach, etc.) _____

      _____
   5   Activities you pay to do (films, plays, sports events, night clubs, pubs, etc.) _____

      _____
   6   Passive activities (watching TV, listening to the radio, records, or tapes; sitting, talking, bathing, etc.) _____

      _____

C   Manipulative reinforcers: What kinds of games or toys interest this person?
   1   Toy cars and trucks _____
   2   Dolls _____
   3   Wind-up toys _____
   4   Balloons _____

(Continued)

Figure 3–3   A questionnaire to help an individual identify reinforcers.

    5 Whistle _____

    6 Jump rope _____

    7 Coloring books and crayons _____

    8 Painting kit _____

    9 Puzzles _____

   10 Other _____

D Possessional reinforcers: What kinds of things does this person like to possess?

    1 Brush _____

    2 Nail clippers _____

    3 Hair clips _____

    4 Comb _____

    5 Perfume _____

    6 Belt _____

    7 Gloves _____

    8 Shoelaces _____

    9 Other _____

E Social reinforcers: What kinds of verbal or physical stimulation does this person like to receive from others? (specify who)

    1 Verbal stimulation

       a "Good girl (boy)" _____

       b "Good work" _____

       c "Good job" _____

       d "That's fine" _____

       e "Keep up the good work" _____

       f other _____

    2 Physical contact

       a hugging _____

       b kissing _____

       c tickling _____

       d patty-cake _____

       e wrestling _____

       f bouncing on knee _____

       g other _____

Figure 3–3 (*Continued*)

son. In other words, an object or event *is defined as a reinforcer only by its effect on behavior.*

3. Establishing Operations

Most reinforcers will not be effective unless the individual has been deprived of them for some period of time prior to their use. In general, the longer the deprivation period, the more effective the reinforcer will be. Sweets will usually not be reinforcing to a child who has just eaten a large bag of candy. Playing with a purse would not have been an effective reinforcer for Dianne had she been allowed to play with one prior to the training session. We use the term *deprivation* to indicate the time, prior to a training session, during which an individual does not experience the reinforcer. The term *satiation* refers to that condition in which the individual has experienced the reinforcer to such an extent that it is no longer reinforcing. "Enough's enough," as the saying goes.

Events or conditions—such as deprivation and satiation—that (a) temporarily alter the effectiveness of a reinforcer, and (b) increase the frequency of behavior reinforced by that reinforcer, are called **establishing operations (EOs)** (Michael, 1993). Thus, food deprivation not only establishes food as an effective reinforcer for the person who is food deprived, it also momentarily increases various behaviors that have been reinforced with food. As another example, feeding a child very salty food would be an EO. It would momentarily increase the effectiveness of water as a reinforcer for that child, and it would also evoke behavior (e.g., asking for a drink, turning on a tap) that had previously been followed by water. An EO might be thought of as a **motivational variable**—a variable that affects the likelihood and direction of behavior. Because it is genetically determined (i.e., not learned) that food deprivation increases the effectiveness of food as a reinforcer and salt ingestion increases the effectiveness of water as a reinforcer, these events are called **unconditioned** EOs. In Chapter 8, we will introduce you to the notion of conditioned EOs. In general terms, establishing operations might be thought of as motivators. In everyday life, people might say that depriving one of food motivates that individual to seek food. Similarly, they might say that giving an individual salted peanuts motivates the individual to find something to drink.

4. Immediacy

For maximum effectiveness, a reinforcer should be given immediately after the desired response. Recall that Darren's mother followed this rule closely when working with him. A positive reinforcer strengthens any response that it immediately follows.

Sometimes it is possible to get an individual (who can follow instructions) to work for delayed reinforcement. Telling a child that if she cleans up her room in the morning her father will bring her a toy in the evening is sometimes effective. Moreover, some people do work toward very long-delayed goals, such as college degrees. But it is a mistake to attribute such results to the direct effects of the principle of positive reinforcement. A reinforcer is not likely to have much direct effect on a behavior that precedes the reinforcer by anything much longer than 30 seconds with animals (Chung, 1965; Lattal & Metzger, 1994; Perin, 1943), and we have no reason to believe that humans are any different (Michael, 1986).

Knowing this can help prevent misinterpretations of causes of behavior change. Consider the case of Fernando. Fernando worked in an American-owned factory located in the outskirts of Mexico City.[3] He was one of a group of twelve workers who had a chronic problem—they were frequently late for work. Annual bonuses given by the factory to the forty workers who had the best attendance

---

[3]This example is based on an article by Hermann, Montes, Dominguez, Montes, and Hopkins (1973).

records had no effect on Fernando. Likewise, disciplinary interviews and one-day suspensions without pay failed to increase the frequency with which he arrived on time. In fact, over a 12-week period while the latter condition was in effect, Fernando arrived on time less than 80 percent of the working days (see Figure 3–4, baseline phase). Jaime Hermann, with the support of managers at the factory, decided to implement a treatment program involving positive reinforcers. Jaime explained the procedure individually to Fernando and the other workers who participated in the program. Each day that Fernando punched in on time, he was immediately given a slip of paper indicating that he had earned approximately 2 pesos (which had considerable value for Fernando at the time that the study was conducted). At the end of each week, Fernando exchanged his slips for cash. As can be seen in Figure 3–4, the program had an immediate effect. Fernando arrived at work on time every day during the first eight weeks of the program. The program had a similar positive effect on the other eleven workers who had also frequently been late for work. Moreover, additional experimental phases demonstrated that the improvement was due to the treatment.

At first glance, Fernando's improvement may appear to represent a straightforward case of the direct effects of positive reinforcement. A closer analysis reveals the necessity for an alternative interpretation (Michael, 1986). The response that made it possible for Fernando to arrive on time was leaving for work a half-hour earlier in the morning, but that response preceded his receiving the slip of paper (indicating 2 pesos) by much longer than 30 seconds. Thus, although the reinforcer influenced Fernando's behavior, it could not have directly done so because it did not immediately follow the critical behavior. So how did it work? Perhaps just after awaking, Fernando said to himself, "I'm going to leave for work a half-hour early to make sure that I earn two extra pesos," and these self-statements may have directly influenced the critical behavior. Although the positive effects of the program were due to the treatment, the treatment was more

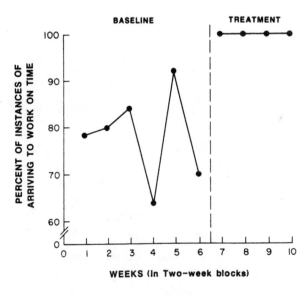

Figure 3–4   Fernando's instances of arriving at work on time. Each data point (dot) represents the percentage of total instances that Fernando arrived at work on time during a 2-week period. (*Note:* Replotted from "Effects of Bonuses for Punctuality on the Tardiness of Industrial Workers," by J. A. Hermann, A. I. Montes, E. Dominguez, F. Montes, and B. L. Hopkins, 1973, *Journal of Applied Behavior Analysis*, 6, Figure 2, p. 568.)

complex than that of a positive reinforcer increasing the frequency of a response that immediately preceded it.

The **direct-acting effect** of the principle of positive reinforcement is the increased frequency of a response because of its immediate reinforcing consequences (within approximately 30 seconds). The **indirect-acting effect** of positive reinforcement is the strengthening of a response (such as Fernando leaving for work earlier) that is followed by a reinforcer (earning 2 pesos) even though the reinforcer is delayed. Delayed reinforcers may have an effect on behavior because of instructions about the behavior leading to the reinforcer, and because of self-statements (or "thoughts") that intervene between that behavior and the delayed reinforcer. On the way to work, for example, Fernando may have been making self-statements (i.e., "thinking") about how he would spend his extra pesos. **Note 2** (Other explanations of indirect-acting effects of positive reinforcement are presented in Chapter 16.)

The distinction between direct- and indirect-acting effects of reinforcement has important implications for practitioners. If you can't present a reinforcer immediately following the desired behavior, then provide instructions concerning the delay of reinforcement.

5. Instructions: Make Use of Rules

For reinforcement to increase an individual's behavior, it is *not* necessary that that individual be able to talk about or indicate an understanding of why he or she was reinforced. After all, the principle has been shown to work quite effectively **Note 3** with animals that cannot speak a human-type language. Nevertheless, instructions should generally be used.

Instructional influences on behavior will be easier for you to understand after reading Chapters 8 and 16. But for now, let's view instructions as specific rules or guidelines that indicate that specific behaviors will pay off in particular situations. For example, your instructor might suggest the rule, "If you learn the answers to all of the study questions in this book, you will receive an *A* in the course."

Instructions can facilitate behavioral change in several ways. First, specific instructions will speed up the learning process for individuals who understand them. For example, beginning tennis players practicing backhand shots showed little progress when simply told to "concentrate." But they showed rapid improvement when told to vocalize the word "ready" when the ball machine was about to present the next ball, the word "ball" when they saw the ball fired from the machine, the word "bounce" as they watched the ball contact the surface of the court, and the word "hit" when they observed the ball contacting their racquet while swinging their backhand (Ziegler, 1987). Second, as indicated earlier (and discussed further in Chapter 16), instructions may influence an individual to work for delayed reinforcement. Getting an *A* in the course for which you are using this book, for example, is delayed several months from the beginning of the course. Daily rehearsing of the rule, "If I learn the answers to the questions at the end of each chapter, I'll likely get an *A*," may exert some influence over your study behavior. Third (as discussed further in Chapter 8), adding instructions to reinforcement programs may help to teach individuals (such as very young children or developmentally disabled persons) to follow instructions.

6. Contingent Versus Noncontingent Reinforcement

When a behavior must occur before a reinforcer will be presented, we say that the reinforcer is **contingent** upon that behavior. If a reinforcer is presented at a particular time, irrespective of the preceding behavior, we say that the reinforcer is **noncontingent.** To illustrate the importance of this distinction, consider the following example.[4] Coach Keedwell watched her young swimmers swim a set during a regular practice at the Marlin Youth Swim Club. (A set is several lengths of a particular stroke to be swum within a specified time.) She had frequently tried to impress upon them the importance of practicing their racing turns at each end of the pool and swimming the sets without stopping in the middle. Following the suggestion of one of the other coaches, she had even added a reward to her practices. During the last ten minutes of each practice, the swimmers were allowed to participate in a fun activity of their choice (swimming relays, playing water polo, etc.). But the results were still the same. The young swimmers continued to show a high frequency of improper turns and unscheduled stops during sets.

The mistake made by Coach Keedwell is common among novice behavior modifiers. Incorporating a noncontingent fun activity into practices might increase attendance, but it's not likely to have much effect on practice behaviors. Educators frequently make the same mistake as did Coach Keedwell. They assume that creating a pleasant environment will improve the learning of the students in that environment. But reinforcers must be contingent upon specific behaviors in order for those behaviors to improve. When this was pointed out to Coach Keedwell, she made the fun activity contingent upon desirable practice behaviors. For the next few practices, the swimmers had to meet a goal of practicing a minimum number of racing turns at each end of the pool and swimming their sets without stopping in order to earn the reinforcer at the end of practice. As a result, the swimmers showed approximately 150 percent improvement. Thus, to maximize the effectiveness of a reinforcement program, be sure that the reinforcers are contingent upon specific behaviors that you want to improve.

7. Weaning the Student from the Program and Changing to Natural Reinforcers

The previous factors influence the effectiveness of positive reinforcement while it is being applied in a program. But what happens to the behavior when the reinforcement program terminates and the individual returns to his or her everyday environment? Most behaviors in everyday life are followed by reinforcers even though no one specifically or deliberately programmed the reinforcers to increase

---

[4]This example is based on a study by Cracklen and Martin (1983).

or maintain them. Reading signs is frequently reinforced by finding desired objects or directions. Eating is reinforced by the taste of food. Flipping on a light switch is reinforced by the increased illumination in the room. Turning on a water tap is reinforced by the flow of water. Verbal and social behaviors are reinforced by the reactions of other people. Such consequences may be manipulated deliberately by psychologists, teachers, and others in behavior modification programs, and in such cases they would be referred to as arbitrary, contrived, or programmed reinforcers. Unprogrammed reinforcers that occur in the normal course of everyday living are called **natural reinforcers,** and the settings in which they occur are called the **natural environment.**

After we have strengthened a behavior through proper use of positive reinforcement, it may then be possible for a reinforcer in the individual's natural environment to take over the maintenance of that behavior. For example, sometimes it is necessary to use reinforcers such as edibles to strengthen object naming in developmentally disabled children. However, when the children leave the classroom and return to their homes, they often say the words that they have learned and receive a great deal of attention from their parents. Eventually, the edibles may no longer be needed to reinforce the children for saying the names of objects. This, of course, is the ultimate goal of any training program. The teacher[5] should always try to ensure that the behavior being established in a training program will be reinforced and maintained in the natural environment. One thing that you can count on with certainty is that if a behavior that has been strengthened in a reinforcement program is no longer reinforced at least occasionally (either by arbitrary or natural reinforcers), then the behavior will return to its original level. Because the problem of maintaining desirable behaviors is so important, it is discussed in much more detail in Chapters 5, 6, and 12.

PITFALLS OF POSITIVE REINFORCEMENT

Those who are aware of the principle of positive reinforcement can use it to bring about desirable changes in behavior. The principle operates equally well for those who are not aware of it. Unfortunately, those who are not aware of it are apt to use it unknowingly to strengthen undesirable behavior. Table 3–3 presents some examples of how positive reinforcement may work against us in the long run.

In our experience, many undesirable behaviors are due to the social attention that such behavior evokes from aides, nurses, peers, teachers, parents, doctors, and others. This may be true even in cases where one would least expect it. Consider, for example, children who exhibit extreme social withdrawal. One behavioral characteristic of such children is that they avoid looking at a person who is talking to them.

---

[5]Throughout this book, the word *teacher* is sometimes used to refer to the individual (parent, teacher, therapist, nurse, aide) who is helping someone to overcome a behavioral problem. The word *student* is frequently used to refer to the individual who has the problem. Unless prompted otherwise, do not think just of a typical classroom situation when you read about teachers and students in this book. The word *client* is also often used interchangeably with the word *student* to refer to the person with the problem.

TABLE 3–3   EXAMPLES OF POSITIVE REINFORCEMENT FOLLOWING UNDESIRABLE BEHAVIOR

Situation	Response	Immediate consequences	Long-term effects
1. A 3-year-old child who has been playing with her coloring book gets up and looks around the living room.	The child goes over to the TV and begins fiddling with the dials.	Mother immediately comes over to her and says "I guess you're tired of playing by yourself; let's go for a walk."	The chances of the child fiddling with the TV dials in the future increases because of the attention from mother.
2. While getting ready for work in the morning, a man cannot find his clean shirt.	He hollers loudly, "Where in the hell is my shirt?"	The wife immediately finds the husband's shirt.	In the future, the husband is more likely to holler and swear when he can't find his clothes.
3. A father is busy ironing, and his two young children are playing quietly.	One child hits his little brother over the head with a toy truck.	Father stops ironing and sits down to play with the child for a while.	The child is more likely to belt his little brother in the future to gain father's attention.
4. Mother and child are shopping in a department store.	Child begins to whine, "I want to go home; I want to go home."	Mother is embarrassed and leaves the store immediately with the child before making her purchases.	Child is more likely to whine in a similar situation in the future.
5. Severely developmentally disabled residents are eating their meal in the dining room at a group home.	One girl holds up her empty glass and grunts loudly, "Mmmmm, mmmmm, mmmmm."	One of the staff members immediately comes and fills the glass with milk.	The girl is likely to hold up her glass and make similar noises in future situations when she wants milk.
6. Father is watching a Stanley Cup playoff hockey game on TV.	Two of the children are playing in the same room and are being extremely noisy.	Father gives them each a dollar so that they will go to the store and not interfere with his TV watching.	The children are more likely to play very noisily when father is watching TV in similar situations in the future.
7. At a party, a husband becomes sullen when his wife is dancing flirtatiously with another man.	The husband shows signs of jealousy and angrily leaves the party.	The wife immediately follows him and showers him with attention.	The husband is more likely to leave parties in similar situations in the future.

Frequently, they move away from approaching adults. We might conclude that they don't want our attention. Actually, the withdrawn child's behavior probably gains him or her more social attention than would have been obtained by looking at the adult. In such cases it is only natural for adults to persist in attempting to get a child to look at them when they speak to the child. Unfortunately, this behavior is likely to reinforce the child's withdrawal behavior. The tendency to shower attention is sometimes maintained by the theory that social interaction is needed to "bring the child out of his or her withdrawn state." In reality, an appropriate treatment might involve withholding social attention for withdrawal behavior and presenting it only when the child engages in some sort of social-interaction behavior—such as looking in the direction of the adult who is attempting the interaction. The hard work of one aide or nurse using appropriate behavior techniques can be greatly hindered, or completely undone, by others who are reinforcing the wrong things. For example, an aide who attempts to reinforce eye contact in a withdrawn child is probably not going to have much effect if other people who interact with the child consistently reinforce looking-away behavior.

In Chapter 20 we discuss methods for assessing whether a problem behavior is being maintained by positive reinforcement and how to treat it if it is.

GUIDELINES FOR THE EFFECTIVE APPLICATION OF POSITIVE REINFORCEMENT

The following guidelines are offered for the use of parents, teachers, nurses, therapists, and others who wish to utilize positive reinforcement to increase occurrences of a particular behavior.

1. *Selecting the behavior to be increased.* As we indicated earlier in this chapter, the behavior selected should be a specific behavior (such as smiling) rather than a general category of behavior (such as socializing). Also, if possible, select a behavior that will come under the control of natural reinforcers after it has been increased in frequency. Finally, as shown with Darren's case, to judge the effectiveness of your reinforcer accurately, it is important to keep track of how often the behavior occurs prior to your program.
2. *Selecting a reinforcer.*
   a. If possible, complete the reinforcer survey presented in Figure 3–3 and select strong reinforcers that
      (1) are readily available.
      (2) can be presented immediately following the desired behavior.
      (3) can be used over and over again without causing rapid satiation.
      (4) do not require a great deal of time to consume (if it takes a half-hour to consume the reinforcer, this minimizes the training time).
   b. Use as many reinforcers as feasible, and, where appropriate, use a reinforcer tray or menu.
3. *Applying positive reinforcement.*
   a. Tell the individual about the plan before starting.
   b. Reinforce *immediately* following the desired behavior.

    c. Describe the desired behavior to the individual while the reinforcer is being given. (For example, say "You cleaned your room very nicely.")

    d. Use lots of praise and physical contact (if appropriate and if these are reinforcing to the individual) when dispensing the reinforcers. However, to avoid satiation, vary the phrases you use as social reinforcers. Don't always say "Good for you." (Some sample phrases are "Very nice," "That's great," "Super," "Tremendous.")

4. *Weaning the student from the program* (discussed more fully in Chapter 12).

    a. If, during a dozen or so opportunities, a behavior has been occurring at a desirable rate, you might try to gradually eliminate tangible reinforcers (such as treats and toys) and maintain the behavior with social reinforcement.

    b. Look for other natural reinforcers in the environment that might also maintain the behavior once it has been increased in frequency.

    c. To ensure that the behavior is being reinforced occasionally and that the desired frequency is being maintained, plan periodic assessments of the behavior after the program has terminated.

STUDY QUESTIONS

1. What is a positive reinforcer?
2. What is the principle of positive reinforcement?
3. What is operant behavior? Describe an example, and indicate how the example fits the definition of operant behavior.
4. In what way is positive reinforcement like gravity?
5. Why is it necessary to be specific when selecting a behavior for a reinforcement program?
6. After dinner, a teenager begins washing dishes, with the consequence that the teenager's parent stops nagging the teenager to do so. Is that an example of positive reinforcement? Explain why or why not, in terms of the definition of positive reinforcement.
7. Describe the Premack Principle. Give an example.
8. Using the definition of positive reinforcer, describe the steps to test if a particular item is a reinforcer for someone. Illustrate with an example.
9. What is an establishing operation? Describe two examples, one of which was not in this chapter.
10. What is a baseline? Give an example.
11. Distinguish between the direct-acting and indirect-acting effects of reinforcement.
12. Should you tell an individual with whom you are using reinforcement about the reinforcement program before putting it into effect? Why or why not?
13. When Coach Keedwell required young swimmers to show improved performance in order to earn a fun activity at the end of practice, their performance improved dramatically. Was this a direct-acting or an indirect-acting effect of reinforcement? Justify your choice.
14. Describe an example of contingent reinforcement.
15. Describe an example of noncontingent reinforcement.
16. What do we mean by the *natural environment*? By *natural reinforcers*?
17. Describe three behavioral episodes in this chapter that involved natural reinforcers. Justify your choices.
18. Briefly describe the seven factors that influence the effectiveness of reinforcement.
19. Is it correct to conclude that a withdrawn child does not like attention from other people? Explain.

20. Using the definition of positive reinforcer, how might you conduct a test to determine if the social attention of a particular adult is or is not reinforcing for a withdrawn child?
21. Ideally, what four qualities should a reinforcer have (besides the necessary quality of functioning as a reinforcer)? (see p. 41)
22. Describe two examples of positive reinforcement that you have encountered, one involving a desirable behavior and one involving an undesirable behavior. For each example, identify the situation, behavior, immediate consequence, and probable long-term effects (as shown in Tables 3–1 and 3–3). (The examples should not be from the text.)
23. What is plotted on the vertical axis in Figure 3–1?
24. What is plotted on the horizontal axis in Figure 3–1?

APPLICATION EXERCISES

A. Exercises Involving Others

1. During an hour that you spend with children, how many times do you dispense social approval (nods, smiles, or kind words)? How many times do you dispense social disapproval (frowns, harsh words, etc.)? Ideally, your social approval total at the end of the hour will be four or five times the social disapproval total. We would encourage you to continue this exercise until you have achieved this ratio. Several studies have shown this ratio of reinforcers to reprimands to be beneficial (e.g., Madsen & Madsen, 1974; Stuart, 1971).
2. List ten different phrases that you might use to express your enthusiastic approval to an individual. Practice varying these phrases until they come naturally to you.
3. Are you aware of how your gestures, expressions, posture, and body language in general affect those around you? Briefly describe five different examples of one or more of these behaviors that you might show when expressing your approval to an individual.

B. Self-Modification Exercises

1. Be aware of your own behavior for five 1-minute periods while behaving naturally. At the end of each minute, describe a situation, a specific behavior, and the immediate consequences of that behavior. Choose behaviors whose consequences seemed pleasant (rather than neutral or unpleasant).
2. Complete the reinforcer questionnaire (Figure 3–3) for yourself.
3. Assume that someone (your husband, wife, friend, etc.) is going to reinforce one of your behaviors (such as making your bed daily, talking in conversation without swearing, or reading pages of this book). Select the two reinforcers from your completed questionnaire that best satisfy the above guidelines given previously for *selecting a reinforcer* (p. 41). Indicate how the guidelines have been satisfied.

NOTES AND EXTENDED DISCUSSION

1. Timberlake and Farmer-Dougan (1991) point out several limitations of the Premack Principle: (a) it is often difficult to measure the probability of one behavior relative to another; (b) the reinforcing behavior must always be of a higher probability than the response it is to reinforce; and (c) the principle is not conceptually well integrated with other behavior principles. To overcome these limitations, Timberlake and Farmer-Dougan encourage applied workers to adopt a "response-disequilibrium" approach (based on earlier research by Timberlake & Allison, 1974). According to the response-disequilibrium approach, the opportunity to engage in *any* behavior that normally occurs at some level greater than zero can be used to reinforce any other behavior, provided that the reinforcing behavior (before reinforcement) is below its usual level. For example, even if a child normally does more writing than arithmetic, the opportunity to do arithmetic can be used as a reinforcer to increase the child's writing—provided that the child normally does at least some arithmetic and the child's arithmetic behavior prior to reinforcement is at a level of occurrence below that at which it normally occurs.

2. Michael (1986) has identified three clues for deciding if a behavior change is due to indirect-acting (vs. direct-acting) effects: (a) the critical response precedes the reinforcer by more than 30 seconds (such as in the case of Fernando, where the critical response was leaving for work earlier than usual); (b) the behavior that is measured shows some increase in strength prior to the first occurrence of the consequence (such as Fernando arriving for work on time the very first morning of the program before he had even received the 2-peso consequence); and (c) a single occurrence of a consequence produces a large change in behavior (such as Fernando maintaining 100 percent on-time from the onset of the treatment). In Chapter 16, we will discuss in more detail strategies that teachers can follow to increase the chances of obtaining indirect-acting effects with procedures that involve positive reinforcers.

3. Although it may seem strange to think of people learning without understanding, or being reinforced for emitting a certain behavior without being aware of it, this is much easier to understand when we consider the following observations: First, from everyday experience as well as from basic experiments, it is obvious that animals can learn even though they are not able to verbalize an understanding or an awareness of their behavioral changes. Similarly, the behavior of the most profoundly developmentally disabled individuals who cannot speak has been shown to be strengthened by reinforcement (see Fuller, 1949). Finally, a number of experiments have demonstrated that normal adult humans can be influenced by reinforcement to show behavioral changes even if they are unable to verbalize them. For example, university students in an experiment were instructed to say words individually and not use sentences or phrases. When the experimenter nodded and said "Mmm-hmm" following particular types of words (such as plural nouns vs. adjectives), the students showed an increased frequency of saying that particular type of word. And yet, when questioned after the experiment, the students were unaware that their behavior had been influenced (Greenspoon, 1951).

Study Questions on Notes

1. State three limitations of the Premack Principle. Describe how the response-disequilibrium approach differs from the Premack Principle.
2. What are three clues for deciding if a behavior change is due to indirect-acting versus direct-acting effects?
3. Discuss evidence that people's behavior can be modified without their being aware of it.

Decreasing a Behavior
with Extinction

"Louise, let's get rid of your migraines."

LOUISE'S CASE

When Louise was 13 years old, she began complaining about headaches.[1] Over the next few years, she received inordinate amounts of parental, social, and professional attention for her headaches, including comments such as, "You poor dear, that must really hurt," "Let me give you a hug, that might make you feel better," and "I'm so sorry your head aches. Is there anything I can do to help?" In addition, Louise's complaints about headaches often led to her being allowed to stay home from school. All of these consequences may have contributed to positive reinforcement of the problem. At 26 years of age, Louise experienced debilitating headaches almost daily. These headaches had typical migraine characteristics—some visual effects (seeing "silver specks"), followed by throbbing pain over her temples, nausea, and occasional vomiting. Various treatments had been tried unsuccessfully, including medication, acupuncture, chiropractic, psychotherapy, and electroconvulsive shock. Demerol injections, which she received from her physician approximately three times per week, appeared to provide temporary relief.

Several medical examinations failed to identify an organic basis for Louise's headaches. Following extensive assessment by behavior therapist Dr. Peter Aubuchon, Louise agreed that her migraines may have been learned, and said she would try a behavioral treatment program. First, Louise understood that her physician would no longer provide Demerol under any circumstances. Second, Louise and her husband agreed that her husband would record Louise's pain

---

[1]This case is based on one reported by Aubuchon, Haber, and Adams (1985).

behaviors (which were identified as complaints, going to bed, and putting cold compresses on her head). The actual headaches were not recorded. Third, Louise's parents, husband, physician, and nurses at the clinic that she regularly visited all agreed to completely ignore all pain behavior exhibited by Louise. Moreover, these same individuals provided praise and other reinforcers for "well" behaviors (such as exercising and performing domestic duties). To ensure her commitment to the program, Louise signed a statement (called a behavioral contract, discussed more in Chapter 24) outlining the treatment components. The results of this program are shown in Figure 4–1.

EXTINCTION

The principle of **extinction** states that: (a) If, in a given situation, an individual emits a previously reinforced response and that response is not followed by a reinforcing consequence, then (b) that person is less likely to do the same thing again when he or she next encounters a similar situation. Stated differently, if a response has been increased in frequency through positive reinforcement, then completely ceasing to reinforce the response will cause it to decrease in frequency.   **Note 1**

Discussions with Louise had indicated that she received a lot of attention for talking about her headaches. It is possible that this attention was a positive reinforcer in maintaining the high frequency of her pain behaviors. In the program described, Louise's pain behaviors no longer received attention, and their frequency decreased to a very low level. Although extinction was an effective treatment for   **Note 2** Louise's pain behaviors, we don't mean to imply that all pain behaviors are maintained by attention from others. For an evaluation of other factors that may influence pain behaviors of chronic pain patients, see Turk and Okifuji (1997).

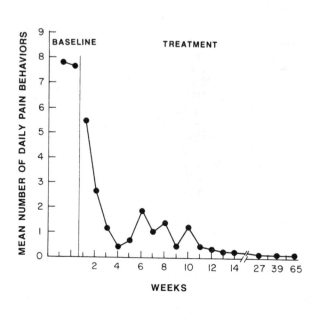

Figure 4–1   Mean number of daily pain behaviors as reported by spouse. (*Note:* Reprinted from *Journal of Behavior Therapy and Experimental Psychiatry, 16,* "Can migraine headaches be modified by operant pain techniques?" by P. Aubuchon, J. D. Haber, and H. E. Adams, p. 262. © 1985, with permission of Elsevier Science Ltd., The Boulevard, Langford Lane, Kidlington OX5 1GB, UK.)

As with positive reinforcement, very few of us are aware of just how frequently we are influenced by extinction during every day of our lives. Some examples of extinction appear in Table 4–1. In each example in this table, the individuals are simply doing what comes naturally in their daily activities. In each example, it might take several repetitions of the behavior occurring and not being reinforced before there would be any really obvious decrease in its frequency.

TABLE 4–1   EXAMPLES OF EXTINCTION

Situation	Response	Immediate consequences	Long-term effects
1. A four-year-old child is lying in bed at night while the parents are sitting in the living room talking to guests.	The child begins to make loud animal noises while lying in bed.	The parents and guests ignore the child completely and continue to talk quietly.	The child is less likely to make animal noises in future situations of that sort.
2. The next evening, the same child and parents are having dinner at the dining room table. The child has just finished the main course.	The child holds up her empty plate and yells loudly, "Dessert! Dessert! Dessert!"	The parents continue talking and ignore the child's loud demands. After the child sits quietly for a brief period, the mother serves dessert.	The behavior of demanding dessert is less likely to occur in similar situations in the future, and the behavior of waiting quietly until dessert is served is more likely to occur in similar situations in the future.
3. A husband is standing in the kitchen and begins to complain to his wife about the traffic on his way home from work.	The husband continues to stand in the kitchen and complain about the traffic.	The wife goes about the business of preparing supper and does not pay attention to any of his comments.	Continual (and probably unproductive) complaining by the husband is less likely to occur in the future.
4. A child in a third-grade classroom has just finished an assignment and raised his hand.	The child begins to snap his fingers.	The teacher ignores the child and responds to those children who raised their hand and are not snapping their fingers.	The child is less likely to snap his fingers in similar situations in the future.
5. A three-year-old child working on a plastic puzzle is attempting to put a piece in the wrong place.	The child rotates the piece to try to make it fit.	The piece still doesn't fit, no matter how many times it is rotated.	The likelihood of the child attempting to insert that piece in that position decreases.

Nevertheless, the effect is still there. Over a number of trials, behaviors that no longer "pay off" gradually decrease. Of course, this is highly desirable in general, for if we persisted in useless behavior, we would quickly disappear as a race.

Extinction, like the principle of positive reinforcement, has been studied extensively by experimental psychologists over several decades, and we are able to describe a number of factors that influence its effectiveness. These are discussed now.

FACTORS INFLUENCING THE EFFECTIVENESS
OF EXTINCTION

1. Controlling Reinforcers for the Behavior
That Is to Be Decreased

Consider the case of a 4-year-old girl, Susie, who has developed a great deal of whining behavior, especially in situations in which she wants something. Her mother has decided to ignore this behavior in the hope that it will go away. On three occasions during an afternoon, mother ignored the whining behavior until it ceased, and then, following a brief period of no whining, provided Susie with the item she desired. Things seemed to be progressing well until early evening, when father came home. While mother was in the kitchen, Susie approached mother and in a whiny tone asked for some popcorn to eat while watching TV. Although mother completely ignored Susie, father entered the room and said, "Mother, can't you hear your child? Come here, Susie, I'll get your popcorn." We are sure that you can now predict the effect this episode will have on Susie's whining behavior in the future (not to mention mother's anger toward father).   **Note 3**

2. Extinction of a Behavior Combined with Positive
Reinforcement for an Alternative Behavior

Extinction is most effective when combined with positive reinforcement for some alternative behavior (Lerman & Iwata, 1996). Thus, not only were Louise's pain behaviors ignored (extinction), but alternative behaviors (exercising, performing domestic duties, etc.) were positively reinforced. The combination of the two procedures probably decreased the frequency of the undesirable behavior much faster (and possibly to a lower level) than would have been the case had the extinction procedure been used alone.

Suppose that you want to combine extinction of a child's inappropriate crying with positive reinforcement for a desirable alternative behavior. It is often impractical to reinforce a child every few seconds for engaging in some desirable behavior (such as playing quietly) in place of disruptive behavior. It is possible, however, to begin with short intervals of desirable behavior and gradually increase them to longer, more manageable intervals. For example, a child who is engaging in inappropriate crying could be ignored until he had stopped crying for a period of 10 seconds. At the end of the 10-second interval, he could be reinforced with praise. On subsequent trials, the teacher could require successively longer periods of silence—15 seconds, then 25, then a minute, and so on—before presenting reinforcement. It is important that the increase in the requirement be very gradual; otherwise, the undesirable behavior will not decrease very rapidly. Also, care must be taken not to present the reinforcer immediately after the crying ceases, as this would tend to reinforce the crying, thereby increasing rather than reducing it.

Reinforcers presented by other people or by the physical environment can undo your good efforts at applying extinction. Unfortunately, it is often difficult to convince others of this if they are not familiar with the mechanics of positive reinforcement and extinction. For example, if several nurses are ignoring a child's tantrumming behavior and another psychiatric nurse enters and says, "Oh, I can get this child to stop crying—here, Tommy, have a candy," then Tommy is likely to stop crying at that moment. But in the long run his crying may increase in frequency because of that reinforced trial. Since the nurse did get Tommy to stop crying, however, it would probably be difficult to convince her of the importance of extinction. In such cases, it is necessary either to control the behavior of these other individuals in some fashion or to carry out the extinction procedure in their absence.

It is also important during the application of extinction to ensure that the reinforcers that you are withholding are the ones that were actually maintaining the undesirable behavior. Failure to do this, technically, would not meet the definition of extinction, and the undesirable behavior would not likely decrease, as shown in Figure 4–2.

Figure 4–2   An extreme example of why attempts to apply extinction often fail. The actual reinforcer for the behavior must always be withheld.

Extinction is sometimes criticized on the grounds that it is cruel to deprive people of social attention during their time of need (this criticism usually assumes that an individual who is crying, whining, or showing various other behaviors that commonly evoke attention is in a time of need). In some cases, this might be a valid criticism. In many situations crying does indicate injury, emotional distress, and other forms of discomfort. We suggest that any behavior must be examined closely in terms of the desirability of decreasing it. If a decrease is desired, then extinction frequently provides the right route to travel.

3. The Setting in Which Extinction Is Carried Out

As indicated previously, one reason for changing the setting in which extinction is carried out is to minimize the possibility that other people will reinforce the behavior you are trying to decrease. There is another reason for considering the setting. It would probably be unwise, for example, for a mother to initiate extinction of her child's temper tantrums in a downtown department store. The child is likely to display behavior in the department store such that the nasty looks from other shoppers and store clerks would decrease the chances of mother carrying through effectively. In other words, it is important to consider the setting in which extinction will be carried out, to (a) minimize the influence of alternative reinforcers on the undesirable behavior to be extinguished and (b) maximize the chances of the behavior modifier persisting with the program.

4. Instructions: Make Use of Rules

Although it is not necessary that an individual be able to talk about or understand extinction, it will probably help to speed up the decrease in behavior if the person is initially told something like this: "Each time you do X, then Y [the reinforcing item] will no longer occur." Consider, for example, the third case described in Table 4–1. The husband, upon arriving home from work each day, complains excessively about the slow traffic. His wife would be adding instructional control to extinction if she said something like, "George, the traffic is the same each day, and it doesn't do any good complaining about it. I love to talk to you about other things. But each time that you come home and complain excessively about the traffic, I'm just going to ignore it." This should cause George's complaining to decrease rapidly, although it may take a few trials. But remember that this procedure is more complex than simple extinction. (Instructional control is discussed further in Chapter 16.)

5. Extinction May Be Quicker After Continuous Reinforcement

Let's take another look at the case concerning Susie's whining behavior with mother. Before mother decided to introduce extinction, what happened when Susie was whining? Sometimes nothing would happen, because mother would be busy with other things, such as talking on the telephone. But at other times (often after five or six instances of whining), mother would attend to Susie and give her what she wanted. This is typical of many reinforcement situations in that Susie was not reinforced following each instance of whining. Rather, she was reinforced occasionally, following several instances of whining. This type of situation is referred to as *intermittent reinforcement,* as opposed to continuous reinforcement, and is discussed in detail in Chapters 6 and 7. It is necessary to mention these two schedules of reinforcement here because the schedule can influence the effectiveness of extinction.

The influence of the reinforcement schedule on extinction can easily be imagined if you consider a little problem that you may have encountered. Suppose you are writing with a ballpoint pen that suddenly stops. What do you do? You probably shake it up and down a couple of times and try to write with it a few more times. If it still doesn't write, you throw it away and get another pen. Now suppose that you are writing with another ballpoint pen. This second pen occasionally skips. You shake it a few times and write some more, and then it misses some more. Each time you shake it, it writes a little more. Now comes the question: In which situation are you likely to persist longer in shaking and attempting to use the pen? Obviously, the second, because the pen occasionally quits but it usually writes again.

When a behavior has always been reinforced and then is never reinforced (such as when a pen quits suddenly), behavior extinguishes fairly quickly. When intermittent reinforcement has maintained a behavior (such as a pen writing after shaking it), that behavior is likely to extinguish more slowly than after continuous reinforcement, although this phenomenon is quite complex and depends (in part) on how you measure behavior during extinction. If you measure behavior during extinction as a percentage of responding before extinction, then behavior generally does not extinguish more slowly after intermittent reinforcement because individuals tend to respond with higher frequency during intermittent than during continuous reinforcement. Behavior that extinguishes slowly is said to be *resistant to extinction.*

Note 4

Now let us take a look at Susie's whining. It will likely take longer for extinction to eliminate her whining completely if it sometimes paid off and sometimes did not than if it always paid off before being completely ignored. In other words, extinction is often quicker after continuous reinforcement (in which each response was reinforced) than after intermittent reinforcement (in which reponses were reinforced only occasionally). If you try to extinguish a behavior that has been reinforced intermittently, you must be prepared for extinction to take longer.

6. Behavior Being Extinguished May Get Worse Before It Gets Better

During extinction, behavior may increase before it begins to decrease. That is, things may get worse before they get better. An increase in responding during extinction is commonly referred to as an *extinction burst.* Suppose that a child in the classroom is constantly raising her hand and snapping her fingers to gain the teacher's attention. If the teacher were to keep track of the frequency of finger snapping for a while, and then introduce extinction (that is, completely ignore the finger snapping), she would probably observe an increase in finger snapping during the first few minutes of extinction before the behavior gradually began to taper off. Why? Most of us have learned that if something is no longer paying off, a slight increase in the behavior may be sufficient to again bring the payoff. An examination of the prevalence of the extinction burst in applied research found that initial increases in response frequency occurred in 24 percent of 113 sets of extinction data (Lerman & Iwata, 1995). Thus, extinction bursting is something that everyone who attempts to apply an extinction procedure should know. If the teacher decided to introduce extinction following finger snapping, and then observed an increase in this behavior during the next few minutes, she might erroneously conclude that extinction wasn't working and give up in the middle of the program. The effect of this action would be to reinforce the behavior when it gets worse. The rule to follow here is this: if you introduce extinction, keep with it. Things usually get worse before they get better, but hang in there; doing so will pay off in the long run.

7. Extinction May Produce Aggression That Interferes with the Program

Another unexpected difficulty of extinction is that the procedure may produce mild aggression. Again, we have all experienced this. Probably all of us have performed the act (or at least had the desire) of pounding and kicking a vending machine that took our money and did not deliver the merchandise. If we reconsider the finger-snapping example, we might see some mild aggression. If a teacher ignores a child's finger snapping, the child might start snapping her fingers louder and louder and perhaps banging on the desk and hollering "Hey!" This characteristic of extinction has also been studied extensively in laboratory situations, it has been anecdotally (i.e., informally) reported in human applications of extinction, and three applied research studies demonstrated increases in aggression during extinction (Lerman & Iwata, 1996). Considering that there have been relatively few reports of extinction-induced aggression in applied research, our advice is that the teacher be prepared to wait it out if it occurs. If an extinction procedure produces mild aggression, then giving up in the middle will not only reinforce the undesirable behavior on an intermittent schedule, it will also reinforce additional undesirable mild aggression.

8. Extinguished Behavior May Reappear after a Delay

An additional difficulty of extinction is that a behavior that has completely disappeared during an extinction session may reappear, after some time has passed, at the next opportunity for the behavior to occur. This reappearance of an extinguished behavior following a rest is called **spontaneous recovery.** Typically, the amount of behavior that recovers spontaneously is less than the amount that occurred during the previous extinction session. After several additional extinction sessions, spontaneous recovery is usually not a problem. Although these characteristics of spontaneous recovery are well documented in basic research, it has not been formally studied in applied research, and there are very few anecdotal (i.e., informal) reports of spontaneous recovery occurring in applications of extinction (Lerman & Iwata, 1996). If spontaneous recovery should occur, our advice is that the teacher be prepared to continue with the extinction program.

To oversimplify this and the preceding chapter, we suggest that if you want behavior to happen more often, reinforce it; if you want behavior to happen less often, ignore it. But beware. There is much more to positive reinforcement and extinction than first meets the eye. For maximal effectiveness in the application of positive reinforcement and extinction, one should be aware of their pitfalls as well as the guidelines for the effective application of the two principles.

PITFALLS OF EXTINCTION

As with the law of gravity, the principle of positive reinforcement, and other natural laws, the principle of extinction operates whether or not we are aware of it. Unfortunately, those who are not aware of extinction are apt to apply it unknowingly to the desirable behavior of friends, acquaintances, family, and others. Table 4–2 presents some examples of how extinction may, in the long run, work to decrease desirable behavior. As these examples indicate, no one can escape the effects of extinction.

Even when some individuals are knowledgeably applying behavior modification in an effort to help behaviorally deficient individuals, their good works may be undone by others who are not knowledgeable about extinction. Suppose, for example, that a child in a program for developmentally disabled persons has been reinforced by an aide for dressing himself. Suppose, further, that this aide has been transferred or has gone on vacation and is replaced by an aide who is not familiar with the principles of positive reinforcement and extinction or with the particular program for the child. Confronted with a child who dresses himself and many children who do not, the new aide will quite likely spend a great deal of time helping the latter children but giving very little attention to the one child. It is a common human tendency to give plenty of attention to problems and to ignore situations in which things seem to be going well. It is easy to rationalize this selective attention. "After all," the aide may say, "why should I reinforce Johnny for doing something that he already knows how to do?" Despite this seemingly justifiable rationalization, we know that if the child's self-dressing behavior is to be maintained after it has been established, it must occasionally be reinforced. Strategies to maintain desirable behavior (and thereby prevent unwanted extinction) are described in Chapter 12.

GUIDELINES FOR THE EFFECTIVE APPLICATION
OF EXTINCTION

The following rules are offered as a checklist for individuals who wish to utilize extinction to decrease a particular undesirable behavior. As with the guidelines for positive reinforcement in Chapter 3, these rules assume that their user is a

TABLE 4–2 EXAMPLES OF UNDESIRABLE INSTANCES OF EXTINCTION

Situation	Response	Immediate consequences	Long-term effects
1. You ask a friend to call you on the telephone on a particular evening.	Your friend dials your number several times.	Each time the phone rings, you ignore it and continue reading your novel.	Your friend is less likely to attempt to call you when requested to do so.
2. Two staff members are talking to each other in a special education classroom and a student approaches and stands nearby.	The student stands and waits patiently beside the two staff members for several minutes. Finally, the student interrupts.	The staff members continued talking while the student waited patiently, and stopped talking and listened after the student interrupted.	The response of standing beside the staff and waiting patiently is less likely to occur in the future, and the response of interrupting staff is more likely to occur in the future.
3. A man carrying several parcels is walking toward the exit door of a department store. A woman standing by the door waiting for the bus sees the man coming.	The woman opens the door for the man.	The man rushes out without saying a word.	The chances of the woman opening the door in similar situations in the future are decreased.
4. A three-month-old baby is lying quietly in the crib just before feeding time.	The baby begins making cooing sounds (which, might be interpreted by eager parents as "mama" or "dada").	The mother, busily preparing a bottle, ignores the child. When the child is picked up later she is again quiet (or, more likely, crying).	The mother has just missed an opportunity to reinforce noise making that approximates speech. Instead, she reinforced lying quietly (or crying). Therefore, cooing is less likely to occur in the future.

parent, teacher, or some other person who is working with individuals with behavior problems.

1. *Selecting the behavior to be decreased.*
    a. In choosing the behavior, be specific. Don't expect a major character improvement to take place all at once. For example, do not try to extinguish all of Johnny's trouble-making behavior in a classroom. Rather, choose a particular behavior, such as Johnny's finger snapping in the classroom.
    b. Remember that the behavior may get worse before it gets better and that aggressive behavior is sometimes produced during the extinction process. Therefore, make sure that the circumstances are such that you can follow through with your extinction procedure on the behavior chosen. For example, be very careful if the behavior is destructive to the individual or others. Will it be harmful for you to persist in your extinction program if the behavior gets worse? You should also consider the setting in which the behavior that you have selected is likely to occur. It may be impractical to extinguish temper tantrums in a restaurant, because of obvious social pressures that you may be unable to resist. If you are concerned with decreasing a particular behavior but you cannot apply extinction because of these considerations, do not despair. We will describe other procedures for decreasing behavior in Chapters 7, 13, and 20.
    c. Select a behavior for which you can control the reinforcers that are currently maintaining it.
2. *Preliminary considerations.*
    a. If possible, keep track of how often the undesirable behavior occurs prior to your extinction program. During this recording phase, do not attempt to withhold the reinforcer for the undesirable behavior.
    b. Try to identify what is currently reinforcing the undesirable behavior so that you can withhold the reinforcer during treatment. (If this is not possible, then, technically, the program does not have an extinction component.) The reinforcement history of the undesirable behavior might provide some idea of just how long extinction will take.
    c. Identify some desirable alternative behavior in which the individual can engage.
    d. Identify effective reinforcers that can be used for desirable alternative behavior by the individual.
    e. Try to select a setting in which extinction can be carried out successfully.
    f. Be sure that all the relevant individuals know before the program starts just which behavior is being extinguished and which behavior is being reinforced. Be sure that all who will be coming in contact with the individual have been prompted to ignore the undesirable behavior and to reinforce the desirable alternative behavior.
3. *Implementing the plan.*
    a. Tell the individual about the plan before starting.
    b. Regarding the positive reinforcement for the desirable alternative behavior, be sure that the rules in Chapter 3 for putting the plan into effect are followed.
    c. After initiating the program, be completely consistent in withholding reinforcement after all instances of the undesirable behavior and reinforcing the desirable alternative behavior.
4. *Weaning the student from the program* (discussed in more detail in Chapter 12).
    a. After the undesirable behavior has decreased to zero, there may be occasional relapses, so be prepared.

b. Three possible reasons for the failure of your extinction procedure are:
   (1) the attention you are withholding following the undesirable behavior is not the reinforcer that was maintaining the behavior.
   (2) the undesirable behavior is receiving intermittent reinforcement from another source.
   (3) the desired alternative behavior has not been strengthened appropriately.
   Examine these reasons carefully if it is taking a long time to complete the extinction procedure successfully.
c. Regarding the reinforcement of the desirable alternative behavior, try to follow the rules in Chapter 3 for weaning the child from the program.

STUDY QUESTIONS

1. What are the two parts to the principle of extinction?
2. If you tell someone to stop eating candies and the person stops, is that an example of extinction? Explain why or why not on the basis of the definition of extinction.
3. If a parent ignores the behavior of a child, is that an example of extinction? Explain why or why not, on the basis of the definition of extinction.
4. Why did the mother's attempt to extinguish the child's cookie eating fail (refer to Figure 4–2)?
5. Describe a particular behavior you would like to decrease in a child with whom you have contact. Would your extinction program require a special setting? Why or why not?
6. Why is it necessary to consider the setting as a factor influencing your extinction program?
7. If a behavior that was maintained by positive reinforcement is not reinforced at least once in a while, what will happen to it?
8. What is an extinction burst? Describe an example.
9. What is spontaneous recovery? Describe an example.
10. Briefly describe eight general factors influencing the effectiveness of extinction.
11. If you were recording some observations of an undesirable behavior prior to introducing an extinction program, what five things would you be looking for?
12. What are three possible reasons for the failure of an extinction program?
13. Extinction should not be applied to certain behaviors or in certain situations. What types of behaviors and situations would these be? Give an example of a behavior to which extinction should not be applied. Give an example of a situation in which extinction should not be applied.
14. Describe two examples of extinction that you have encountered, one involving a desirable behavior and one involving an undesirable behavior. For each example, identify the situation, behavior, immediate consequence, and probable long-term effects, as is done in Tables 4–1 and 4–2. (Your examples should not be from the text.)
15. Briefly describe a pitfall of extinction. Give an example.
16. Examine Table 4–1. Which of those examples involve positive reinforcement for an alternative response? For those that do not, indicate how positive reinforcement for an alternative response might be introduced.

APPLICATION EXERCISES

A. Exercise Involving Others

Choose a situation in which you will be able to sit and watch an adult interact with one or more children for approximately a half-hour. During this half-hour period, mark down the number of times that the adult pays attention to desirable behaviors of the children and the number of times the adult ignores specific desirable behaviors. This will give you some idea of how often we miss opportunities to reinforce desirable behaviors of those around us.

B. Self-Modification Exercises

1. Think of something you did today that did not pay off. Give a specific, complete description of the situation and behavior, following the examples in Table 4–1.
2. Select one of your behavioral excesses (perhaps one that you listed at the end of Chapter 1). Outline a complete extinction program that you (with a little help from your friends) might apply so as to decrease that behavior. Make sure that your plan follows the guidelines given for the effective application of extinction.

NOTES AND EXTENDED DISCUSSION

1. Extinction is but one way in which a behavior can be weakened. The reader should be careful not to confuse it with punishment or with forgetting. In punishment, a behavior is weakened by the presentation of an aversive event following the behavior. In forgetting, a behavior is weakened as a function of time following the last occurrence of the behavior. (For a behavioral interpretation of memory, see Palmer, 1991.) Extinction differs from both of these in that in extinction, behavior is weakened as a result of being emitted without being reinforced.

2. Louise's case raises some intriguing questions. Was it simply her reports of pain that decreased? Did her "feelings" of pain—the actual headaches—also decrease? Although there was no self-monitoring of headache frequency, Louise reported at a 12-month follow-up that she had experienced only two headaches over the previous several months. Her other behaviors tended to support this in that she was able to perform a variety of activities (domestic chores, work, etc.) that she had not been able to do in the past, and she and her husband reported that their marital relationship had greatly improved. As discussed further in Chapters 24 and 26, private behaviors are assumed to be affected by behavioral techniques in the same way as are public behaviors. Perhaps, in Louise's case, both public complaints about pain and private pain behavior were decreased as a function of the extinction procedure.

3. One of the greatest hazards faced by an extinction program is reinforcement from a well-intentioned person who does not understand the program or its rationale. This obstacle was encountered in one of the earliest reports on the application of extinction to a child's temper tantrums. C. D. Williams (1959) reported the case of a 21-month-old infant who screamed and cried if his parents left the bedroom after putting him to bed at night. A program was initiated in which the parent left the room after bedtime pleasantries and did not reenter it, no matter how much the infant screamed and raged. The first time the child was put to bed under this extinction procedure, he screamed for 45 minutes. By the tenth night, however, he no longer cried, but rather smiled, as the parent left the room. But about a week later, when the parents were enjoying a much needed evening out, he screamed and fussed after his aunt, the babysitter, had put him to bed. The aunt reinforced the behavior by returning to the bedroom and remaining there until he went to sleep. It was then necessary to extinguish the behavior a second time, which took almost as long as the first time.

Ayllon and Michael (1959) observed the bad effect of unwanted reinforcement in extinction, which they called "bootleg reinforcement." A patient in a psychiatric hospital engaged in such annoying psychotic talk (of the type referred to as delusional) that other patients had on several occasions beaten her in an effort to keep her quiet. To decrease her psychotic talk, the doctors instructed the nurses to ignore it and to pay attention only to sensible talk. As a result, the proportion of her speech that was psychotic decreased from 0.91 to 0.25. But later it increased to a high level, probably because of bootleg reinforcement from a social worker. This reinforcement came to light when the patient remarked to one of the nurses, "Well, you're not listening to me. I'll have to go and see Miss—[the social worker] again, 'cause she told me that if she listens to my past she could help me."

4. Kazdin and Polster (1973) demonstrated the extreme persistence of intermittently reinforced behavior in an applied setting. During daily breaks in a sheltered workshop, two developmentally disabled men who engaged in few social interactions received tokens for talking to peers. At first, every interaction was reinforced, and the daily average number of interactions generally increased. Then extinction was applied, and the behavior rapidly decreased. Next, reinforcement was reinstated. One man again received tokens for every interaction, but the other man was placed on an intermittent schedule, which was thinned gradually until, after 3 weeks, he received reinforcement at only one of the three daily breaks. Then, extinction was again carried out for both men. The man who had been on continuous reinforcement again showed a rapid decrease in social interactions. But the man who had been on an intermittent-reinforcement schedule maintained a high rate of interaction over a 5-week period. (Tokens as reinforcers are described in Chapters 10 and 23.)

The Kazdin and Polster study is one of the few applied studies to demonstrate the tendency of intermittent reinforcement to result in more responding during extinction. Examining the extinction of self-injurious behavior (such as handbiting) after it had been reinforced either intermittently or continuously and using a different measure of extinction, Lerman, Iwata, Shore, and Kahng (1996) came to a different conclusion. Nevin (1988) had pointed out that rate of responding under intermittent schedules is often much higher than rate of responding under continuous reinforcement, and surmised that this difference in response rates would carry over into extinction. He argued, therefore, that rather than simply counting the number of responses that occur during extinction, responses during extinction should be expressed as a proportion of the response rate during pre-extinction sessions. Using this measure of resistance to extinction, Lerman et al. found that problem behaviors were not more difficult to treat with extinction if they had been maintained on intermittent reinforcement rather than continuous reinforcement schedules. (It should be noted that the foregoing applies only if the behavior can occur freely in what is called a free-operant procedure. If a discrete-trials procedure is used, intermittent reinforcement results in greater resistance to extinction regardless of whether responding during extinction is measured as absolute number of responses or number of responses relative to baseline.)

Study Questions on Notes

1. How are extinction and forgetting similar, and how are they different?
2. Discuss whether the extinction program with Louise extinguished her "feelings" of pain.
3. What is bootleg reinforcement? Give an example.
4. How did Kazdin and Polster demonstrate that behavior is more persistent after intermittent reinforcement than after continuous reinforcement?
5. How did the measure of resistance to extinction used by Lerman et al. differ from that used by Kazdin & Polster? How did their results differ? Explain why this difference in measurement procedures would produce different results.

5

Getting a New Behavior to Occur: An Application of Shaping

"Frank, did you do your jogging?"

IMPROVING FRANK'S EXERCISING

After taking an early retirement at the age of 55, Frank decided to make some changes in his life. But he wasn't sure where to start. Knowing that he needed to change some of his long-standing habits, he enrolled in a behavior modification course at the local community college. Next, on the advice of his doctor, he resolved to begin a regular exercise program. Frank had been a "couch potato" all his life. He typically came home from work, grabbed a can of beer, and parked himself in front of the television set. Frank launched his exercise program with a pledge to his wife that he would jog a quarter of a mile each day. But after a couple of attempts, he returned to his couch-potato routine. He had expected too much too soon. He then decided to try a procedure called shaping *that he had studied in his behavior modification course. The following three stages summarize that procedure.[1]*

1. Specifying the final desired behavior. *Frank's goal was to jog a quarter of a mile each day. But for a chronic nonexerciser, this was more than could be expected. To reach this goal, it was necessary to reinforce some other behavior first.*
2. Identifying a response that could be used as a starting point in working toward the final desired behavior. *Frank decided that, at the very least, he would put on his sneakers and walk around the outside of the house once*

---

[1]This case is based upon one described by Watson & Tharp (1997).

(approximately 30 yards). Although this was a long way from a quarter of a mile, it was at least a start.

3. Reinforcing the starting response; then requiring closer and closer approximations until eventually the desired response occurs. *Frank decided to use the opportunity to drink a beer as a reinforcer. He explained his program to his wife and asked her to remind him that he had to complete his exercise before he could have a beer. After the first approximation had occurred on several successive afternoons, Frank increased the requirement to walking around the house twice (approximately 60 yards). A few days later, the distance was increased to walking around the house four times (approximately 120 yards), then six times (180 yards), then farther and farther until the distance was approximately a quarter of a mile, and then finally to jogging that distance. By reinforcing successive approximations to his goal, Frank reached the point where he jogged a quarter of a mile regularly. (The application of behavior modification techniques to improve self-control is discussed further in Chapter 24.)*

SHAPING

Shaping is a procedure used to establish a behavior that is not presently performed by an individual. Since the behavior has a zero level of occurrence, it is not possible to increase its frequency simply by waiting until it occurs and then reinforcing it. Therefore, the teacher begins by reinforcing a response that occurs with a greater than zero frequency and at least remotely resembles the final desired response. (Frank, for example, was first reinforced for walking once around his house because this behavior occurred occasionally and because it remotely approximated the behavior of jogging a quarter of a mile.) When this initial response is occurring at a high frequency, the teacher stops reinforcing it and begins reinforcing a slightly closer approximation of the final desired response. Thus, the final desired response is eventually established by reinforcing successive approximations to it. For this reason, shaping is sometimes referred to as "the method of successive approximations." **Shaping** can be defined as the development of a new behavior by the successive reinforcement of closer approximations and the extinguishing of preceding approximations of the behavior.

The new behaviors that an individual acquires during a lifetime develop from a variety of sources and influences. Sometimes a new behavior develops when an individual emits some initial behavior and the environment (either the physical environment or other people) then reinforces slight variations in that behavior across a number of trials. Eventually that initial behavior may be shaped so that the final form no longer resembles it. For example, most parents use the shaping procedure in teaching their children to talk. When an infant first begins to babble, some of the sounds made remotely approximate words in the parents' native language. When this happens the parents usually reinforce the behavior with hugs, caresses, kisses, and smiles. The sounds "mmm" and "daa" typically receive exceptionally large doses of reinforcement from English-speaking parents. Eventually "ma-ma" and "da-da" occur and are strongly reinforced, and the more primitive "mmm" and "daa" are subjected to extinction. At a later stage, reinforcement is given after the child says "mommy" and "daddy," and "ma-ma" and "da-da" are extinguished.

The same process occurs with other words. First, the child passes through a stage in which very remote approximations of words in the parents' native language are reinforced. Then the child enters a stage in which "baby talk" (i.e., closer approximations of actual words) is reinforced. Finally, the child is required by the parents and others to pronounce words in accordance with the practices of the verbal community before reinforcement is given. For example, if a child says "wa-wa" at an early stage, she is given a glass of water, and if she is thirsty, that reinforces the response. At a later stage, "watah" rather than "wa-wa" is reinforced with water. Finally the child is required to say "water" before water reinforcement will be given.

Of course, this description greatly oversimplifies the way in which a child learns to talk. But it serves to illustrate the importance of shaping in the process by which normal children gradually progress from babbling to baby talk and finally to speaking in accordance with prevailing social conventions. (Another reinforcement process, called automatic reinforcement, as described in Chapter 10, and a more complex process, called stimulus equivalence, as described in Chapter 12, play important roles in speech development.)

There are at least four aspects or dimensions of behavior that can be shaped: topography, amount, latency, and intensity (or force). *Topography* refers to the spatial configuration or form of a particular response (i.e., the specific movements involved). Printing a word and writing the same word are examples of the same response made with two different topographies. Topography shaping occurs, for example, when teaching a child to switch from a printing response to a writing response, shaping a child to say, "Mommy" instead of "Mama," learning to ice skate with longer and longer strides rather than short choppy steps, and shaping the proper finger movements for eating with chopsticks. An example of an early study involving topography shaping involved teaching a child to wear his glasses by reinforcing successive approximations of touching them, picking them up, putting the glasses up to his face, and finally wearing them (Wolf, Risley, & Mees, 1964).

The *amount* of a particular behavior refers to either its frequency or its duration. The *frequency* of a behavior is the number of instances that occur in a given period of time. Examples of frequency shaping include increasing the number of steps (the distance) that Frank walked in his exercise program, or gradually increasing the number of repetitions that a golfer practices a particular golf shot. The frequency of a response may also be reduced by shaping, as in a behavior modification program in which a patient with multiple sclerosis learned through shaping to gradually increase the time between (and hence decrease the frequency of) bathroom visits (O'Neill & Gardner, 1983). The *duration* of a response is the length of time that a response lasts. Examples of duration shaping include gradually lengthening the time spent studying before taking a break, or gradually adjusting the duration of stirring of pancake batter until it achieves just the right consistency.

Latency refers to the time between the occurrence of a stimulus and the beginning of a response. A common term for latency is *reaction time*. On the popular TV quiz show, *Jeopardy!*, the time from the presentation of an answer until a contestant presses a button is, presumably, the contestant's latency of thinking of the question. In a race, the time between the firing of the starter's pistol and the runner leaving the block is the latency. Latency shaping might enable the runner to react more and more quickly to the sound of the gun.

The *intensity* or force of a response refers quite literally to the physical effect the response has (or potentially has) on the environment. For an example of shaping force, consider a young farm boy whose job it is to pump water out of a well with an old hand pump. When the pump was first installed, it was freshly oiled, the boy applied a certain amount of force to the handle; it moved up and down very easily; and water was produced. Let us suppose, however, that with rain and lack of regular oiling, the pump has gradually acquired a little rust. Each day, the boy probably applies the approximate amount of force he applied the previous day. When that force is no longer reinforced by the production of water, because of the addition of the small amount of rust that has made the pump handle more difficult to move, the boy would likely apply a little more force and find that it pays off. Over several months, the boy's behavior is gradually shaped so that he presses very hard on the first trial, a terminal behavior quite different from the initial behavior of moving the pump handle very easily. Other examples of intensity shaping include learning to shake hands with increasing grip pressure and learning to apply the right amount of force when scratching, in order to relieve the itch without damaging one's skin. An example of intensity shaping in a behavior modification program involved teaching a socially withdrawn girl whose speech was barely audible to speak louder and louder until she was speaking at normal voice volume (Jackson & Wallace, 1974).

Shaping is so common in everyday life that most people aren't even aware of it. Becoming a better dancer, learning to hit a tennis ball more accurately, changing gears smoothly when driving a car with a stick shift—all involve shaping. Sometimes the shaping procedure is applied systematically (as in Frank's case), sometimes nonsystematically (such as when parents shape correct pronunciation of words spoken by their children), and sometimes shaping occurs from consequences in the natural environment (you gradually perfect your method for flipping pancakes).

FACTORS INFLUENCING THE EFFECTIVENESS OF SHAPING

1. Specifying the Final Desired Behavior

The first stage in shaping is to identify clearly the final desired behavior, which is often referred to as the *terminal behavior*. In Frank's case, the final desired behavior was jogging a quarter of a mile each day. With a definition as specific as this, there was very little possibility that Frank or his wife would develop different expectations regarding Frank's performance. If different people working with the individual expect different things, or if one person is not consistent from one training session or situation to the next, then progress is likely to be retarded. A precise statement of the final desired behavior increases the chances for consistent reinforcement of successive approximations of that behavior. The final desired be-   **Note 1** havior should be stated in such a way that all the relevant characteristics of the behavior (its topography, amount, latency, and intensity) are identified. In addition, the conditions under which the behavior is or is not to occur should be stated, and any other guidelines that appear to be necessary for consistency should be provided.

2. Choosing a Starting Behavior

Because the final desired or terminal behavior does not occur initially, and because it is necessary to reinforce some behavior that approximates it, you must identify a starting point. This should be a behavior that occurs often enough to be reinforced within the session time allowed, and it should approximate the final desired behavior. For example, Frank's behavior of walking around the house once (approximately 30 yards) is something that he did periodically. This was the closest approximation that he regularly made with respect to the final goal of jogging a quarter of a mile.

In a shaping program it is crucial to know not only where you are going (the terminal behavior) but also the level at which the individual is performing at the present time. The purpose of the shaping program is to get from one to the other by reinforcing successive approximations from the starting point to the final desired behavior, even though the former might be completely dissimilar to the latter. For example, in a classic study, Isaacs, Thomas, and Goldiamond (1960) applied shaping to redevelop verbal behavior in a catatonic schizophrenic man who had been mute for nineteen years prior to training. Using chewing gum as a reinforcer, the experimenter shaped the patient through the behaviors of eye movement toward the gum, facial movement, mouth movements, lip movements, vocalizations, word utterance, and, finally, understandable speech.

3. Choosing the Shaping Steps

Before initiating the shaping program, it is helpful to outline the successive approximations through which the person will be moved in the attempt to approximate the final desired behavior. For example, suppose that the final desired behavior in a shaping program for a child is saying "daddy." It has been determined that the child says "daa," and this response is set as the starting behavior. Let us suppose that we decide to go from the initial behavior of "daa" through the following steps: "da-da," "dad," "dad-ee," and "daddy." To begin with, reinforcement is given on a number of occasions for emitting the initial behavior ("daa"). When this behavior is occurring repetitiously, the trainer moves on to step 2 ("da-da") and reinforces that approximation for several trials. This step-by-step procedure continues until the child finally says "daddy."

We are sure that some critical questions have already occurred to you. What is a reasonable step size? How many trials at each step should one reinforce before proceeding to the next step? Unfortunately there are no specific guidelines for identifying the ideal step size. In attempting to specify the behavioral steps from the initial behavior to the terminal behavior, the teacher might imagine what steps she herself would go through. Also, it is sometimes helpful to observe students who can already emit the terminal behavior and to ask them to emit the initial and subsequent approximations. Whatever guidelines or guesses are used, it is important to try to stick to them and yet be flexible if the trainee does not proceed quickly enough or is learning more quickly than had been expected. Some guidelines for moving through the behavioral program are offered in the following section.

4. Moving Along at the Correct Pace

There are several rules of thumb to follow in reinforcing successive approximations of a final desired response:

a. Do not move too soon (that is, after too few trials) from one approximation to the next. Trying to go to a new step before the previous approximation has been well established can result in losing the previous approximation through extinction without achieving the new approximation.

b. Proceed in sufficiently small steps. Otherwise, the previous approximation will be lost through extinction before the present approximation has been achieved. However, do not make the steps unnecessarily small.

c. If you lose a behavior because you are moving too fast or taking too large a step, return to an earlier approximation where you can pick up the behavior again.

d. Items *a* and *b* caution against going too fast, and item *c* states how to correct for the negative effects of going too fast. It is also important not to progress too slowly. If one approximation is reinforced for so long that it becomes extremely strong, new approximations are less likely to appear.

These guidelines may not seem very helpful. On the one hand, it is advisable not to move too fast from one approximation to another; on the other hand, it is advisable not to move too slowly. If we could accompany these guidelines with a mathematical formula for calculating the exact size of the steps that should be taken in any situation and exactly how many reinforcements should be given at each step, the guidelines would be much more useful. Unfortunately, the experiments necessary for providing this information have not yet been carried out. The teacher must observe the behavior carefully and be prepared to make changes in the procedure—changing the size of, slowing down, speeding up, or retracing steps—whenever the behavior does not seem to be developing properly. Shaping requires a good deal of practice and skill if it is to be performed with maximum effectiveness.

Note 2

PITFALLS OF SHAPING

As with other behavior principles and procedures, shaping can be misused by people who are not knowledgeable about it. An example of this can be seen in Figure 5–1: a harmful behavior that might never have occurred without shaping is gradually developed as a result of it.

Note 3

Another example of the misuse of shaping, one that is sometimes observed in developmentally disabled children, leads to self-destructive behavior. Suppose that because of an unusual and unfortunate family situation, a small child receives very little social attention when he emits appropriate behavior. Perhaps one day the child accidentally falls and strikes his head lightly against a hard floor. Even if the child is not injured seriously, an overly solicitous parent may come running quickly and make a big fuss over the incident. Because of this rein-

Figure 5–1 A misapplication of shaping.

forcement, and because anything else the child does that is appropriate seldom evokes attention, he is likely to repeat the response of striking his head lightly against the floor. The first few times this occurs, the parent may continue to reinforce the response. Eventually, however, seeing that the child is not really hurting himself, the parent may stop reinforcing it. Since the behavior has now been placed on extinction, the *intensity* of the behavior may increase (see Chapter 4). That is, the child may begin to hit his head more forcefully, and the slightly louder thud will cause the parent to come running again. If this shaping process continues, the child will eventually hit his head with sufficient force to cause physical injury. It is extremely difficult, if not impossible, to use extinction to eliminate such violently self-destructive behavior. It would have been best never to have let the behavior develop to the point where the child's parents were forced to continue reinforcing it and increasing its strength.

Many undesirable behaviors commonly seen in special needs children—for example, violent temper tantrums, constant fidgeting, injuring other children, voluntary vomiting—are often products of shaping. It is quite possible that these behaviors can be eliminated by a combination of extinction of the undesirable behavior and positive reinforcement for desirable behavior. Unfortunately, this is often difficult to do, because (a) the behavior is sometimes so harmful that it cannot be allowed to occur even once during the period in which extinction is to take place, and (b) adults who are ignorant of behavior principles sometimes unknowingly foil the efforts of those who are conscientiously attempting to apply these principles.

In Chapter 20 we describe how to diagnose and treat problem behaviors that may have been developed inadvertently through shaping. As in medicine, however, the best "cure" is prevention. Ideally, all persons responsible for the care of other persons will be so thoroughly versed in behavior principles that they will refrain from shaping undesirable behavior.

Another kind of pitfall is the unknowing failure of a person to apply shaping when it should be applied. Some parents, for example, are simply not very responsive to their child's babbling behavior. Perhaps they expect too much from the child right from the beginning and are not inclined to reinforce extremely remote approximations of normal speech. (Some parents, for example, seem to expect their tiny new genius to say "Father!" right off the bat and are not at all impressed when the child says "da-da.") Or perhaps their personal problems interfere with their devoting the necessary attention to the child. The opposite type of problem also exists. Instead of not giving enough reinforcement for the right behavior, some parents give their children plenty of reinforcement noncontingently. Perhaps they are so overly concerned about the child's well-being that they provide the child with all kinds of reinforcement without the child ever having to say or do anything for it. In other words, although shaping is a process that most parents apply more or less appropriately (probably without even being fully aware that they are doing so, in most instances), there are some parents for whom this is not true. Thus, many variables can prevent a physically normal child from receiving the shaping that is necessary to establish normal behaviors. If a child has not learned to talk by a certain age, he or she may be labeled as developmentally disabled or autistic. It is quite possible that there are developmentally deficient individuals whose deficiency exists not because of any genetic or physical defect, but simply because they were never exposed to effective shaping procedures.

GUIDELINES FOR THE EFFECTIVE APPLICATION OF SHAPING

1. *Select the terminal behavior.*
   a. Choose a specific behavior (such as working quietly at a desk for 10 minutes) rather than a general category of behavior (for example, "good" classroom behavior). Shaping is appropriate for changing amount, latency, and intensity of behavior, as well as for developing new behavior of a different topography (form).
   b. If possible, select a behavior that will come under the control of natural reinforcers after it has been shaped.
2. *Select an appropriate reinforcer.* See Figure 3–3 and the "Guidelines for the Effective Application of Positive Reinforcement," p. 41.
3. *The initial plan.*
   a. List successive approximations of the terminal behavior, beginning with the initial behavior. To choose the initial behavior, find a behavior already in the student's repertoire that resembles the terminal behavior most closely and that occurs at least once during an observation period. If your terminal behavior is a complex sequence of activities (such as making a bed) that you have broken down into sequential steps, and if your program amounts to linking the steps together in a particular order, then your program is not best described as shaping, nor is it best developed through a shaping program. Rather, it should be developed by chaining (see Chapter 11).
   b. Your initial steps or successive approximations are usually "educated guesses." During your program, you can modify these according to the student's performance.
4. *Implementing the plan.*
   a. Tell the student about the plan before starting.
   b. Begin reinforcing immediately following each occurrence of the starting behavior.
   c. Never move to a new approximation until the student has mastered the previous one.
   d. If you are not sure when to move the student to a new approximation, utilize the following rule: move to the next step when the student performs the current step correctly in six out of ten trials (usually with one or two trials less perfect than desired and one or two trials in which the behavior is better than the current step).
   e. Do not reinforce too many times at any one step, and avoid underreinforcement at any one step.
   f. If the student stops working: you may have moved up the steps too quickly; the steps may not be the right size; or the reinforcer may be ineffective.
      (1) First, check the effectiveness of your reinforcer.
      (2) If the student becomes inattentive or shows signs of boredom, the steps may be too small.
      (3) Inattention or boredom may also mean you have progressed too rapidly. If so, return to the previous step for a few more trials and then try the present step again.

(4) If the student continues to have difficulty, despite retraining at previous steps, add more steps at the point of difficulty.

STUDY QUESTIONS

1. Identify the three basic stages in any shaping procedure, as presented at the start of this chapter, and describe them with an example (either the case of Frank or an example of your own).
2. Explain how shaping involves successive applications of the principles of positive reinforcement and extinction.
3. What is another name for shaping?
4. In terms of the three stages in a shaping procedure, describe how parents might shape their child to say a particular word.
5. What one word characterizes all the variables plotted on the vertical axis of all the graphs in the book thus far?
6. List four aspects of behavior that can be shaped. Give two examples of each.
7. What do behavior modifiers mean by *terminal behavior* in a shaping program? Give an example.
8. Why bother with shaping? Why not just learn about the use of straightforward positive reinforcement to increase a behavior?
9. Define shaping.
10. How do you know you have enough successive approximations or shaping steps of the right size?
11. How do you know if you are allowing enough reinforced trials to occur at each of the approximations?
12. Give an example of how shaping might be accidentally used to develop an undesirable behavior. Describe some of the shaping steps in your example.
13. Give an example of how the failure to apply shaping might have an undesirable result.
14. Give an example from your own experience of a terminal behavior that might best be developed through a procedure other than shaping (see p. 69). Explain why shaping would probably not be effective in developing that behavior.
15. Why is it necessary to avoid reinforcing too many times at any shaping step?
16. Why is it necessary to avoid underreinforcement at any shaping step?
17. Why do we refer to positive reinforcement and extinction as principles, and to shaping as a procedure? (Hint: see Chapter 1, p. 8.)

APPLICATION EXERCISES

A. Exercise Involving Others

Think of a normal child, one between the ages of 2 and 7, with whom you have had contact (for example, a sister, brother, or neighbor). Specify a realistic behavior of that child that you might try to develop by utilizing a shaping procedure. Identify the starting point you would choose, the reinforcer, and the successive approximations you would go through.

B. Self-Modification Exercises

1. Take a close look at many of your own behaviors—for example, sporting skills, personal-interaction skills, lovemaking skills, and study skills. Identify at least three specific behaviors that were probably shaped by others, either knowingly or unknowingly. Identify at least three specific behaviors that were probably shaped by the natural environment. Put each of your examples in sentence form, approximately as follows: "I was probably shaped to hit a ping-pong ball with a good chop stroke. That is, after learning basic ping-pong skills, each time I tried a bit of a chop, the ball would fly off the table. Eventually, a slight chop was reinforced by the ball landing on the table and the other person hitting the ball into the net. As the other person learned to return my chops, I was reinforced for putting slightly increasing amounts of chop on the ball. In all cases, the reinforcement was returning the ball to the other side of the table and even greater reinforcement was returning it to the other side of the table so that the other person missed."

2. Select one of your behavioral deficits, perhaps one that you listed at the end of Chapter 2. Outline a complete shaping program that you (with a little help from your friends) might use to overcome that deficit. Make sure that your plan follows the above guidelines for the effective application of shaping.

NOTES AND EXTENDED DISCUSSION

1. Shaping appears to be useful in modifying not only external behavior but also internal behavior. For example, R. W. Scott and colleagues (1973) demonstrated that shaping could be used to modify heart rate of an individual while watching a television program. Although the sound portion of the TV program was on continuously, the video portion appeared only when the individual's heart rate changed by a few beats per minute from the initial baseline rate. When the subject's heart rate remained at a new level for three consecutive sessions, the video portion was used to reinforce a further change in heart rate. In one case involving a psychiatric patient suffering from chronic anxiety and manifesting a moderately elevated heart rate, the investigators shaped several decreases in the client's heart rate. Interestingly, when the client's heart rate had been decreased to a lower level, reports from his ward indicated that "he seemed less 'tense' and 'anxious'" and that "he made fewer requests for medication." In this study, the device monitoring the client's heart rate was hooked up to the video portion of the TV.

In other studies, information about a person's physiological processes, such as heart rate or muscle tension, is displayed on a screen or in some way made immediately available to the individual. Such techniques, which are referred to as **biofeedback,** enable individuals to gain control over the physiological processes being monitored. Clinical applications of biofeedback have successfully used it to reduce epileptic seizures by helping individuals learn to control electrical activity associated with their seizures (Goldstein, 1990), to reduce blood pressure, thereby enabling hypertensive patients to use less medication (Olson & Kroon, 1987), and to reduce chronic headaches (Sarafino, 1994).

2. How fast should you move from one step to the next? How large should step size be? One reason there are no specific answers to these questions is the difficulty of measuring specific step sizes and consistently reinforcing responses that satisfy a given step size. Human judgment is simply not fast enough or accurate enough to ensure that any given shaping procedure is being applied consistently in order to make comparisons between it and other consistently applied shaping procedures. This is particularly true when topography is the aspect of behavior that is being shaped. Computers, however, are both accurate and fast and may therefore be useful in answering fundamental questions concerning which shaping procedures are most effective (Midgley, Lea, & Kirby, 1989; Pear & Legris, 1987). For example, using two video cameras that were connected to a microcomputer which was programmed to detect the position of a pigeon's head within a test chamber, Pear and Legris (1987) demonstrated that a computer can shape where the pigeon moves its head.

In addition to providing a methodology for studying shaping, these studies suggest that computers may be able to shape at least some kinds of behavior as effectively as humans. For example, a device that shapes movements may help a person regain the use of a limb that has been paralyzed from a stroke or accident. Such a device would have the advantage over a human shaper in its precision, its ability to provide extremely rapid and systematic feedback, and its patience (i.e., computers are nonjudgmental and untiring).

3. Rasey and Iversen (1993) provided a good laboratory demonstration of a potential maladaptive effect of shaping. They reinforced rats with food for extending their noses over the edge of a platform on which they were standing. Over trials the rats were required to extend their noses farther and farther over the edge before receiving reinforcement. Eventually, each rat extended its nose so far over the edge that it actually fell off the platform. A net under the platform kept the rat from being injured; however, this experiment demonstrates that animals (and thus, probably humans as well) can be shaped to engage in behavior that is harmful to them.

Study Questions on Notes

1. Describe how Scott and colleagues used shaping to decrease the heart rate of a man suffering from chronic anxiety.
2. Describe how computer technology might be used to shape specific limb movements in a paralyzed person.
3. Describe how computer technology might be used to study shaping more accurately than can be done with the usual shaping procedures.
4. Describe an experiment demonstrating that maladaptive behavior can be shaped.

Developing Behavioral Persistence Through the Use of Intermittent Reinforcement

"Tom, let's see how many arithmetic problems you can do."

IMPROVING TOM'S WORK RATE IN MATH CLASS

Tom, a 13-year-old boy of average intelligence, was enrolled in the seventh grade at Humboldt State College Elementary School.[1] During math classes, Tom exhibited a great deal of nonattending behavior, and made frequent errors on arithmetic problems. With the support of Tom's teacher, two behavior modifiers introduced a strategy for improving Tom's work rate. One of them worked with Tom every day during math class, where Tom received a worksheet containing arithmetic problems to solve. During the first two days, whenever Tom completed two problems correctly, the behavior modifier responded with, "Good work," or "Excellent job," or some similar positive reaction. During the next two days, the number of problems to be completed before praise was given was increased to four. Two days after that, Tom had to complete eight problems correctly before receiving praise. And during the final two days, no praise was given until Tom had completed 16 problems.

The praise schedule had a positive effect on Tom's work rate. From the beginning to the end of the study, Tom's rate of correct problem solving tripled, with the highest work rate occurring when Tom was praised following each 16 problems solved. Moreover, by the end of the study, Tom was attending to the task 100 percent of the time.

---

[1]This case is based on a report by Kirby and Shields (1972).

SOME DEFINITIONS

The term **intermittent reinforcement** refers to the maintenance of a behavior by reinforcing it only occasionally (i.e., intermittently) rather than every time it occurs. Tom's work behavior was not reinforced after each work response. Instead, he was reinforced after a fixed number of responses had occurred. On this reinforcement schedule, Tom worked at a very steady rate. (Note: *response rate* and *response frequency* are synonomous terms; although we tended to use the latter in the earlier chapters of this book, we now switch to the former.)

To talk about intermittent reinforcement, we must first define schedule of reinforcement. A **schedule of reinforcement** is a rule specifying which occurrences of a given behavior, if any, will be reinforced. One of the two simplest schedules of reinforcement is **continuous reinforcement.** Had Tom received reinforcement for each problem solved, we would say that he was on a continuous reinforcement schedule. Many behaviors in everyday life are reinforced on a continuous reinforcement schedule. Each time you turn the tap, water spews forth. Each time that you insert and turn the key in the front door of your home or apartment, you're reinforced by the opportunity to enter.

The second of the two simplest schedules of reinforcement is the opposite of continuous reinforcement. It is called **extinction.** As we have seen in Chapter 4, on an extinction schedule no instance of a given behavior is reinforced. The effect is that the behavior eventually decreases to a very low level or disappears altogether.

Between these two extremes—continuous reinforcement and extinction—lies intermittent reinforcement: one may reinforce certain instances of a given behavior while allowing other instances to go unreinforced. After all, it is often not practical to reinforce each occurrence of a desired response. Many real-life activities are not reinforced this way. You do not always get good grades after studying. You have to work for an hour before you earn an hourly wage, and you probably won't get your paycheck until the end of the week. Experiments on the effects of various strategies for reinforcing behaviors have been studied under the topic of *schedules of reinforcement*. Any rule specifying a procedure for occasionally reinforcing a behavior is called an **intermittent-reinforcement schedule.** There are an unlimited number of such schedules. Because each produces its own characteristic behavior pattern, the different schedules are suitable for different types of applications. In addition, certain schedules are more practical than others to apply (e.g., some are more time-consuming or labor-intensive than others).

Note 1

Some intermittent-reinforcement schedules increase and maintain behavior, whereas others (to be discussed in the next chapter) decrease it. Intermittent schedules that increase and maintain behavior have several advantages over continuous reinforcement: (a) the reinforcer remains effective longer than with continuous reinforcement because satiation takes place more slowly; (b) behavior that has been reinforced intermittently tends to take longer to extinguish than behavior that has been continuously reinforced (see Note 4 in Chapter 4); (c) individuals work more consistently on certain intermittent schedules than on continuous reinforcement; and (d) behavior that has been reinforced intermittently persists more readily when transferred to reinforcers in the natural environment.

In this chapter we discuss four types of schedules for increasing and maintaining behavior: ratio, simple interval, interval with limited hold, and duration. Each of these is subdivided into fixed and variable, giving eight basic schedules.

RATIO SCHEDULES

The payment schedule for Tom (in the case at the beginning of this chapter) was a *fixed-ratio (FR)* schedule. In an FR schedule, reinforcement occurs each time a set number of responses of a particular type are emitted. Recall that early in his program, Tom had to complete two problems for each reinforcement. This schedule is abbreviated FR 2. Later he had to solve 4 arithmetic problems for reinforcement. This is abbreviated FR 4. Finally, he had to make 16 responses, which is abbreviated FR 16. Note that the schedule was increased in steps. If Tom's arithmetic responses had been put on FR 16 immediately (i.e., without the intervening FR values), his behavior might have deteriorated and appeared as though he were on extinction. This deterioration of responding from increasing an FR schedule too rapidly is sometimes referred to as *ratio strain*.

FR schedules, when introduced gradually, produce a high steady rate until reinforcement and a postreinforcement pause (i.e., a pause in responding following reinforcement). The length of the postreinforcement pause depends on the value of the FR—the higher the value, the longer the pause. They also produce high resistance to extinction (see Chapter 4, p. 52). **Note 2**

In a *variable-ratio (VR)* schedule, the number of responses required to produce reinforcement changes unpredictably from one reinforcement to the next. The number of responses required for each reinforcement in a VR schedule varies around some mean value, and this value is specified in the designation of that particular VR schedule. Suppose, for example, that over a period of several months, a door-to-door salesperson averages one sale for every ten houses called upon. This does not mean that the salesperson made a sale at exactly every tenth house. Sometimes a sale might have been made after calling upon five houses. Sometimes a sale might have been made at two houses in a row. And sometimes the salesperson might have called on a large number of houses before making a sale. Over several months, however, a mean of ten house calls was required to produce reinforcement. The salesperson was reinforced on a VR schedule, in this case, abbreviated VR 10. VR, like FR, produces a high steady rate of responding. However, it also produces no (or at least a very small) postreinforcement pause. The salesperson can never predict exactly when a sale will occur and is likely to continue making housecalls right after a sale. Three additional differences in the effects of VR versus FR schedules are that the VR schedule can be increased somewhat more abruptly than an FR schedule without producing ratio strain, the values of VR that can maintain responding are somewhat higher than FR, and VR schedules produce a higher resistance to extinction than FR schedules of the same value.

The natural environment contains many examples of ratio schedules. A common example of an FR schedule is paying an industrial worker for a specified number of completed parts (called piece-rate pay). Like Tom, the student who must do a specified number of problems or read a specified number of pages to complete a homework assignment is responding on an FR schedule. Asking someone for a date is an example of behavior on a VR schedule, because even the most popular people often have to ask an unpredictable number of different people to obtain an acceptance. Slot machines are programmed on VR schedules, in that the gambler has no way of predicting how many times he or she must put a coin in the slot and pull the lever to hit a payoff. Similarly, casting for fish is also reinforced on a VR schedule in that one must cast an unpredictable number of times in order to get a bite.

Ratio schedules are used when one wants to generate a high rate of responding and can monitor each response (since it is necessary to count the responses in order to know when to deliver reinforcement on a ratio schedule). The FR schedule is more commonly used than VR in behavioral programs because FR is simpler to administer. For example, ratio schedules have been used in a task designed to teach developmentally disabled children to name pictures of objects. The procedure involves presenting a carefully designed sequence of trials in which the teacher sometimes speaks the name of the picture for the child to imitate and sometimes requires that the child correctly name the picture. Correct responses are reinforced with praise (e.g., "Good!") and a treat; however, children make more correct responses and learn to name more pictures when correct responses are reinforced with a treat on a ratio schedule than when they are continuously reinforced with the treat. This is true, however, only if the ratio schedule does not require too many correct responses per reinforcement. As the response requirement increases, performance improves at first but then begins to show ratio strain (see Stephens, Pear, Wray, & Jackson, 1975). The optimal response requirement differs for different individuals and for different tasks. For example, Tom increased his response rate even when the FR was increased to 16. Other students may have shown a decrease before FR 16 was introduced. In general, the higher the ratio at which an individual is expected to perform, the more important it is to approach it gradually through exposure to lower ratios. The optimal ratio value that will maintain a high rate of response without producing ratio strain must be found by trial and error.

SIMPLE INTERVAL SCHEDULES

In a *fixed interval (FI)* schedule, the first response after a fixed period of time following the previous reinforcement is reinforced (see Figure 6–1), and a new interval begins. All that is required for reinforcement to occur is that the individual engage in the behavior after reinforcement has become available because of the passage of time. The size of the FI schedule is the amount of time that must elapse before reinforcement becomes available (e.g., if 1 minute must elapse before the behavior can be reinforced, we call the schedule an FI 1-minute schedule). Note from Figure 6–1 that although the passage of a certain amount of time is necessary for reinforcement to occur in an FI schedule, the passage of time alone is not sufficient. For reinforcement to occur, a response must occur sometime after the

TIME PERIODS

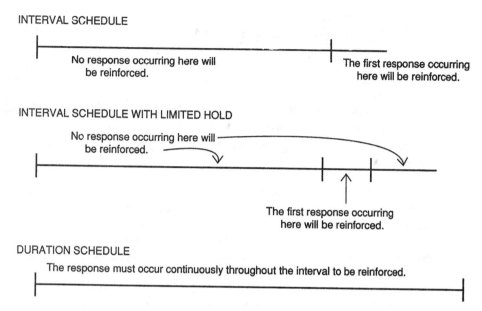

Figure 6–1   Diagrams illustrating the differences between the time-based schedules described in the text. In each diagram the horizontal line represents a period of
time.

specified time interval. Note also that there is no limit on how long after the end
of the interval a response can occur in order to be reinforced. Finally, note that a
response occurring before the specified interval is up has absolutely no effect on
the occurrence of the reinforcer.

The typical effects of an FI schedule are illustrated in the following example.
Suppose that two young children (approximately ages 4 and 5) play together each
morning. Approximately 2 hours after breakfast, a parent has a midmorning
snack prepared for them; and approximately 2 hours after that, lunch is prepared
for them. Thus, the behavior of arriving at the kitchen is reinforced on an FI
2-hour schedule. Within each 2-hour period, as the time draws to a close, the children begin making more and more frequent trips to the kitchen, each time asking,
"Is our food ready yet?" After eating, they run out and play, and there's a fairly
lengthy pause before they start once again to make trips to the kitchen. The children's behavior of going to the kitchen is characteristic of behavior reinforced on
an FI schedule. That is, provided that the individuals who are so reinforced don't
have access to clocks or others who will tell them the time, then FI schedules produce (a) a rate of responding that increases gradually throughout the interval until reinforcement and (b) a postreinforcement pause. The length of the postreinforcement pause depends on the value of the FI—the higher the value (i.e., the
more time between reinforcers), the longer the pause. Most of us, however, rely
on our clocks to tell us when to do things that are reinforced on an FI schedule.

We usually wait until the reinforcer is available, then make one response and receive it. (But note that the behavior of glancing at a clock or watch follows the typical FI pattern. Can you see why?)

In a *variable-interval (VI)* schedule, the length of the interval changes unpredictably from one reinforcement to the next. The lengths of the intervals in a VI schedule vary around some mean value, and this value is specified in the designation of that particular VI schedule. For example, if a mean of 25 minutes is required before reinforcement becomes available, the schedule is abbreviated VI 25 minutes. VI produces a moderate steady rate of responding and no (or at most a very small) postreinforcement pause. Like the intermittent schedules discussed previously, VI produces a high resistance to extinction relative to continuous reinforcement. But although steady for a long time, responding is lower during extinction after VI than it is after FR or VR.

Numerous examples of interval schedules can be found in the natural environment. A job that pays by the hour is sometimes cited as an example of an FI schedule, but this is not correct, because hourly pay assumes that the individual works during the hour. An FI schedule, however, requires only one response at the end of the interval. Going to pick up one's paycheck approximates an FI schedule in that the check is only ready after a certain period of time and going to the pay window does not make it ready any sooner. Checking one's mailbox is also an example of an FI schedule if mail is delivered at the same time each day. However, if one receives mail infrequently, checking one's mailbox approximates a VI schedule, since one cannot predict when there will be any letters in the mailbox. Checking one's answering machine for messages or one's computer for e-mail are also examples of VI schedules, since messages may be left at any time.

Simple interval schedules are not often used in behavior modification programs for several reasons: (a) FI produces postreinforcement pauses; (b) although VI does not produce postreinforcement pauses, it does generate lower response rates than ratio schedules do; and (c) simple interval schedules require continuous monitoring of behavior after the end of each interval until a response occurs.

INTERVAL SCHEDULES WITH LIMITED HOLD

When what is called a *limited hold* is added to an interval schedule, it can have a powerful effect on behavior. We'll explain how it works by describing an effective strategy for managing the behavior of kids on a family car trip. It's based on **The Timer Game.**[2] When one of the authors' two boys (2½ years apart) were children, family car trips were trying, to say the least. With Mom and Dad in the front seat and the boys in the back seat, nonstop bickering between the boys seemed to be the rule of the day ("You're on my side," "Give me that," "Don't touch me," etc.). After several unpleasant trips, Mom and Dad decided to try a variation of the timer game. First, they purchased a timer that could be set at values up to 25 min-

---

[2]This procedure was developed on the basis of a study by Wolf, Hanley, King, Lachowicz, and Giles (1970).

utes and that produced an audible "ding" when the set time ran out. Then, at the beginning of a car trip, they announced the new rules to the boys: "Here's the deal. Every time this timer goes 'ding,' if you're playing nicely, you earn an extra five minutes for watching late night TV in the motel room (a powerful reinforcer for the boys). But if you're bickering, you lose that five minutes forever. We'll play the game until we get there." Thereafter, a parent set the timer at random intervals for the duration of the trip. The results seemed miraculous. From nonstop bickering, the boys switched to mainly cooperative play. Although it only required an instant of cooperative play to earn a reinforcer, the boys never knew when that opportunity might occur. The result: continuous cooperation. The reinforcement schedule applied in this case was a VI with a limited hold.

A **limited hold** is a finite time, after a reinforcer becomes available, that a response will produce the reinforcer. A limited hold is essentially a deadline for meeting the response requirement of a schedule of reinforcement. For the boys in the timer game, following a VI, the reinforcer was available only while the timer went "ding." An interval schedule with a limited hold is the same as a simple interval schedule with the added requirement that the response must be earned during the limited time that it is available after the interval has passed. That is, once a reinforcement is "set up" its availability is "held" only for a limited period (hence the term "limited hold"). The addition of a limited hold to an interval schedule is indicated by writing the abbreviation for the schedule followed by "/LH" and the value of the limited hold. For example, if a limited hold of 2 seconds is added to an FI 1-minute schedule, the resulting schedule is abbreviated FI 1 minute/LH 2 seconds. In the above example of the boys in the back seat, the limited hold was zero seconds—because they had to be behaving appropriately at the *instant* the "ding" occurred to receive reinforcement.

Interval schedules with limited hold produce effects similar to those produced by ratio schedules (including strain if large increases in interval size are introduced abruptly)—provided that the limited hold is small. For small FIs, FI/LH produces effects similar to those produced by FR schedules. VI/LH produces effects similar to those produced by VR schedules. Thus, interval schedules with limited hold are sometimes used when a teacher wants to produce ratio-like behavior but is unable to count each instance of the behavior (e.g., when the teacher can monitor the behavior only periodically or at irregular intervals).

In the natural environment, a good approximation of an FI/LH schedule is waiting for a bus. Buses usually run on a regular schedule (e.g., one every twenty minutes). An individual may arrive at the bus stop early, just before the bus is due, or as it is arriving—it makes no difference, for that person will still catch the bus. So far, this is just like a simple FI schedule. However, the bus will wait only a limited time—perhaps one minute. If the individual is not at the bus stop within this limited period of time, the bus goes on and the person must wait for the next one. A good approximation of behavior on a VI/LH schedule is telephoning a friend whose line is busy. Note that as long as the line is busy, we will not get through to our friend no matter how many times we dial, and that we have no way of predicting how long the line will be busy. However, after finishing the call, our friend may leave or may receive another call. In each case, if we do not call during one of the limited periods in which the line is free and the friend is at home, we miss the reinforcement of talking to our friend and must wait another unpredictable period before we again have an opportunity to gain this particular reinforcement. Other examples of VI/LH in everyday life are shown in Figure 6–2.

Interval schedules with limited hold are common in behavior modification projects. For example, a teacher faced with a classful of rambunctious young students might use a variation of the timer game, such as a VI 30 mins/LH 0 seconds schedule to reinforce in-seat behavior. That is, if the children are working quietly at their seats whenever the timer rings after a variable 30-min interval, they would receive some desirable item such as points that could be accumulated toward extra free time.

DURATION SCHEDULES

In a duration schedule, reinforcement occurs after the behavior has been engaged in for a continuous period of time. In a *fixed-duration (FD)* schedule, the period that the behavior must be engaged in is fixed from reinforcement to reinforcement. The value of the FD schedule is the amount of time that the behavior must be engaged in continuously before reinforcement occurs (e.g., if it is 1 minute, we call the schedule an FD 1-minute schedule). In a *variable-duration (VD)* schedule the interval of time that the behavior must be engaged in continuously changes unpredictably from reinforcement to reinforcement. The mean interval is specified in the designation of the VD schedule. For example, if the mean is 1 minute, the schedule is abbreviated: VD 1 minute. Both FD and VD schedules produce long periods of continuous behavior. The FD schedule, however, produces a postreinforcement pause whereas the VD schedule does not (or, at most, a very

Note 3   short one).

The natural environment provides a number of examples of duration schedules. For instance, a worker who is paid by the hour might be considered to be on an FD schedule. Melting solder might also be an example of behavior on an FD schedule. To melt the solder, one must hold the tip of the soldering iron on the solder for a continuous fixed period of time. If the tip is removed, the solder cools quickly and the person has to start over again and apply heat for the same continuous period. An example of a VD schedule might be rubbing two sticks together to produce fire, since the amount of time this takes varies as a function of factors such as the size, shape, and dryness of the sticks. Another example of a VD schedule is waiting for traffic to clear before crossing a busy street.

In behavior modification programs, duration schedules are useful only when the target behavior can be measured continuously and reinforced on the basis of its duration. One should not assume that this is the case for any target behavior. Presenting reinforcement contingent on a child studying or practicing the piano for an hour *may* work. However, it may also only reinforce sitting at the desk or in front of the piano. This is particularly true of something like studying, for which it is difficult for the parent or teacher to observe whether the desired behavior is occurring (the child may be daydreaming or reading a comic book

Response: Hitchhiking (holding out thumb when a car comes along)
Reinforcer: Getting a ride

Contingency arrangement: After an unpredictable time of cars passing, the response pays off.

Response: Stacking pieces on a pegboard
Reinforcer: Getting all the pieces stacked
Contingency arrangement: After a fixed number of responses, all the pieces will be stacked.

Response: Taking clothes out of dryer
Reinforcer: Clothes are dry

Contingency arrangement: After a fixed period of time, the first response will pay off.

Response: Watching TV
Reinforcer: Viewing an enjoyable scene
Contingency arrangement: Enjoyable scene occurs unpredictably, and lasts briefly.

Figure 6–2 Examples of people responding on intermittent reinforcement schedules.

hidden in the text). Practicing the piano is easier to monitor because the parent or teacher can hear whether the child is doing the lesson.

Eye contact is a behavior that is commonly reinforced on duration schedules in training programs with developmentally disabled and autistic children. Many such children do not make eye contact with others, and any attempt by an adult to initiate this behavior causes the children to quickly avert their eyes from the adult. Eye contact is important as a prerequisite to further social development.

OVERVIEW OF EIGHT BASIC SCHEDULES FOR INCREASING AND MAINTAINING BEHAVIOR

Note 4

The eight schedules we discuss in this chapter and their characteristic effects are illustrated in Table 6–1. Note that the eight basic schedules have been classified as either ratio, simple interval, interval with limited hold, or duration schedules, and as either fixed or variable. **Ratio schedules** make reinforcement contingent on a certain number of responses being completed; **simple interval schedules** make reinforcement contingent on a response being made after a certain time period has elapsed; **interval schedules with limited hold** make reinforcement contingent on a response occurring within a limited period of time after a certain time period has elapsed; and **duration schedules** make reinforcement contingent on a response being made for a certain continuous period of time.

Thus, the schedules in each of the categories listed along the side of Table 6–1 have certain requirements based on either number of responses (i.e., ratio schedules) or time plus a response(s) (i.e., simple interval schedules, interval schedules with limited hold, and duration schedules) that must be met in order for reinforcement to occur.

CONCURRENT SCHEDULES OF REINFORCEMENT

In most situations, we have the option of performing more than just one type of behavior. At home during a particular evening, for example, a student might have the options of watching TV, surfing the Internet, doing homework, talking on the phone with a friend, and perhaps several other possibilities. Each of these different behaviors is likely to be reinforced on a different schedule. The schedules of reinforcement that are in effect for that particular student at that particular time are called **concurrent schedules of reinforcement.** Which option is the student likely to engage in? In 1961, Herrnstein proposed the *matching law,* which states that the time devoted to an activity in a concurrent situation is proportional to the rate of reinforcement of that activity relative to the rates of reinforcement on the other concurrent activities. Subsequent research has indicated that additional factors are likely to influence one's choice when several options are available. Research indicates that the response chosen in such situations depends on: (a) the types of schedules that are operating (e.g., VI might receive preference over VR, even when the latter provides a higher rate of reinforcement), (b) the im-

TABLE 6–1 CHARACTERISTIC EFFECTS AND APPLICATIONS OF BASIC REINFORCEMENT SCHEDULES FOR INCREASING AND MAINTAINING BEHAVIOR

Schedule	Fixed	Variable	Application
Ratio	High steady rate; short postreinforcement pause; high R.T.E.*	High steady rate; no postreinforcement pause; high R.T.E.	To increase and maintain rate of specific responses that can be easily counted, such as solving addition or subtraction problems correctly, or correct repetitions of a sport skill.
Simple Interval	Gradually increasing rate; long post-reinforcement pause; moderate R.T.E.	Moderate steady rate; no postreinforcement pause; high R.T.E.	Not commonly used in behavioral programs.
Interval with Limited Hold	High steady rate (with small intervals); short postreinforcement pause; moderate R.T.E.	High steady rate; no postreinforcement pause; high R.T.E.	To increase and maintain duration or steady rate of behaviors such as on-task behavior of children in a classroom, cooperative behavior of children on a family car trip, or treading water by persons at a swimming class.
Duration	Continuous behavior; moderate R.T.E.	Continuous behavior; high R.T.E.	To increase and maintain behaviors that can be monitored continuously and that should persist throughout a period of time, such as practicing piano lessons.

*R.T.E. = resistance to extinction.

mediacy of reinforcement, (c) the magnitude of reinforcement (e.g., studying for an exam worth 50 percent of the student's grade might be chosen over watching a boring TV show), and (d) the response effort involved in performing the different options (Friman & Poling, 1995; Mazur, 1991; Myerson & Hale, 1984; Neef, Mace, & Shade, 1993; Neef, Mace, Shea, & Shade, 1992; Neef, Shade, & Miller, 1994).

An understanding of research on concurrent schedules is valuable when designing a behavior modification program. Suppose, for example, that you are attempting to decrease an undesirable behavior by reinforcing a desirable alternative behavior. You should ensure that the schedule of reinforcement for the desirable alternative behavior involves more immediate reinforcers, more frequent reinforcement, more powerful reinforcement, and a response of less effort than that which occurs for the undesirable behavior.

PITFALLS OF INTERMITTENT REINFORCEMENT

The most common pitfall of intermittent reinforcement often traps not only the uninitiated but also those with some knowledge of behavior modification. It involves what may be described as inconsistent use of extinction. For example, a parent may at first attempt to ignore a child's tantrums. But the child persists, and in despair the parent finally "gives in" to the child's obnoxious demands for attention, candy, or whatever. Thus, the child obtains reinforcement on a VR or VD schedule, and this leads to further persistent tantrumming in the future. Many times, parents and staff say that they had to give in to the child's demands because "extinction was not working." However, the resulting intermittent reinforcement produces behavior that will likely occur at a higher rate and hence take longer (at least in absolute terms; see Note 4 of Chapter 3) to extinguish than behavior that has been continuously reinforced.

In our work, we have encountered cases in which children have screamed until exhausted and then, as soon as they've rested, done the same thing again. (This is called spontaneous recovery; see p. 53.) Eventually, even such severe tantrums can be eliminated by extinction, but this requires a good deal of time and patience. We suspect that such persistent undesirable behavior would not occur in the first place were it not for the inadvertent application of intermittent reinforcement.

GUIDELINES FOR THE EFFECTIVE USE
OF INTERMITTENT REINFORCEMENT

To use intermittent schedules effectively in generating and maintaining desired behaviors, it is important to observe the following rules:

1. Choose a schedule that is appropriate to the behavior you wish to strengthen and maintain.
2. Choose a schedule that is convenient to administer (but, of course, remain consistent with the first rule).

3. Use appropriate instruments and materials to determine accurately and conveniently when the behavior should be reinforced. For example, if you are using a ratio schedule, make sure that you have a counter of some sort—be it a wrist counter (as used for keeping golf scores), a string of beads, or simply pencil and paper. Similarly, if you are using an interval or duration schedule, make sure that you have an accurate timer appropriate to your schedule. If you are using a variable schedule, make sure that you have arranged to follow a sequence of random numbers that vary around the mean you have chosen.

4. The frequency of reinforcement should initially be high enough to maintain the desired behavior and should then be decreased gradually until the final desired amount of behavior per reinforcement is being maintained. (Recall that for Tom, the fixed ratio was at first very small and was then increased.) Always remain at each stage long enough to ensure that the behavior is strong. If you increase the requirement too rapidly, the behavior will deteriorate and you will have to return to an earlier stage (possibly continuous reinforcement) to recapture it. This is similar to the shaping procedure described in Chapter 5.

5. Inform the individual in language that he or she can understand of the schedule you are using. A number of studies (Pouthas, Droit, Jacquet, & Wearden, 1990; Shimoff, Matthews, & Catania, 1986; Wearden, 1988) indicate that people perform more efficiently on various schedules if they have specific rules to follow regarding the schedule in effect (see discussion of rule-governed behavior in Chapter 16).

STUDY QUESTIONS

1. Describe the praise schedules used to increase Tom's rate of solving math problems. What type of schedule of reinforcement do these praise schedules represent?
2. Define and give an example of each of the following:
   a. intermittent reinforcement
   b. schedule of reinforcement
   c. continuous reinforcement
3. Describe four advantages of intermittent over continuous reinforcement for maintaining behavior.
4. Name the schedules of reinforcement used to develop behavior persistence (i.e., the ones described in this chapter).
5. Explain what an FR schedule is. Describe the details of two examples of FR schedules in everyday life (at least one of which is not in the text). (By everyday life, we mean situations that occur commonly and that are not training programs, as defined in question 12.)
6. What are three characteristic effects of an FR schedule?
7. What is ratio strain?
8. Explain why FR would not be used to teach students to sit at their desks.
9. Explain what a VR schedule is. Describe the details of two examples of VR schedules in everyday life (at least one of which is not in the text).
10. Describe how a VR schedule is similar to an FR schedule, procedurally. Describe how it is different, procedurally.
11. What are three characteristic effects of a VR schedule?
12. Describe two examples of how FR or VR might be applied in training programs. (By training program, we refer to any situation in which someone would like to increase and maintain a behavior of someone else, such as parents wanting to influence a behavior of a child, a teacher wanting to influence a behavior of students, a coach

wanting to influence a behavior of athletes, an employer wanting to influence a behavior of employees, etc.)

13. What is an FI schedule?
14. What is a VI schedule?
15. Explain why simple FI schedules are not often applied in training programs.
16. Explain what an FI/LH schedule is, and describe the details of two examples from everyday life (at least one of which is not in the text). (*Hint*: Think of behaviors that occur at certain fixed times, such as arriving for meals, plane departures, and cooking.)
17. Describe how an FI/LH schedule is similar to a simple FI schedule, procedurally. Describe how it differs, procedurally.
18. Suppose that a professor gives an exam to students every Friday. The studying behavior of the students would likely resemble the characteristic pattern of an FI schedule in that studying would gradually increase as Friday approaches, and the students would show a break in studying (similar to a lengthy postreinforcement pause) after each exam. But this is not really an example of an FI schedule for studying. Can you explain why?
19. Explain what a VI/LH schedule is. Describe the details of two examples of VI/LH schedules that occur in everyday life (at least one of which is not in the text).
20. What are three characteristic effects of a VI/LH schedule?
21. Describe two examples of how VI/LH might be applied in training programs.
22. Explain what an FD schedule is. Describe the details of two examples of FD schedules that occur in everyday life (at least one of which is not in the text).
23. Suppose that each time that you put bread in your toaster and press the lever, it takes 30 seconds for your toast to be ready. Is this an example of an FD schedule? Why or why not? Would it be an FD schedule if (a) the catch that keeps the lever down doesn't work, or (b) the timer that releases it doesn't work? Explain in each case.
24. Explain why FD might not be a very good schedule for reinforcing study behavior.
25. Describe two examples of how FD might be applied in training programs.
26. Explain what a VD schedule is. Describe the details of two examples of VD schedules that occur in everyday life (at least one of which is not in the text).
27. If an individual has an option of engaging in two or more behaviors which are reinforced on different schedules by different reinforcers, what four factors, in combination, are likely to determine the response that will be made?
28. Describe how intermittent reinforcement works to the disadvantage of people who are ignorant of its effects. Give an example.
29. For each of the photos in Figure 6–2, identify the schedule of reinforcement that appears to be operating. In each case, justify your choice of schedule.

APPLICATION EXERCISES

A. Exercises Involving Others

Assume that the following behaviors have been established:
1. dishwashing behavior of roommate or spouse
2. dusting behavior of son or daughter
3. doing mathematics assignments by a student

You are now faced with the task of maintaining them. Following the guidelines for the effective use of intermittent reinforcement, describe in detail the best schedules to use and how you might apply them for each of the above behaviors.

B. Self-Modification Exercise

Assume that you have been assigned a 200-page book to read during the next few days. Select an appropriate reinforcer for yourself, and identify the best schedule on which to dispense the reinforcer. Describe the reasons for your selections (characteristic effects, ease of application, etc.), and outline the mechanics of how you might implement the program and complete it successfully.

NOTES AND EXTENDED DISCUSSION

1. The effects of the various schedules of reinforcement have been worked out mainly with animals. The classic authoritative work on this topic, written by Ferster and Skinner (1957), deals mostly with pigeons pecking on a response key to obtain reinforcement in the form of access to grain for a few seconds. A number of experiments have been conducted to determine whether humans show the same patterns of responding that other animals do when exposed to basic schedules of reinforcement. In one common procedure, for example, a human volunteer presses a lever to produce points that can be exchanged for money or some other reinforcing item. In many cases, however, humans responding under these conditions do not show the behavior patterns described in this chapter. In particular, humans often do not show decreased response rates and pauses in responding where animals typically do (see reviews by Baron & Galizio, 1983; Lowe, 1979). One possible reason for these differences between humans and animals has to do with the complex verbal behavior humans have typically been conditioned to emit and to respond to—that is, humans can verbalize rules (as described in Chapter 16) that may influence them to show different behavior patterns than animals show when exposed to various reinforcement schedules (Michael, 1987). Thus, humans may make statements to themselves about the schedule of reinforcement in effect and respond to those statements rather than to the actual schedule itself. For example, humans may tell themselves that the experimenter will be pleased if they respond at a high rate throughout the session—even though the schedule may be one that normally generates a low rate of responding—and this self-instruction may then produce a high rate. Evidence for this view comes from data indicating that the patterns shown by preverbal infants are similar to those shown by animals (Lowe, Beasty, & Bentall, 1983), and gradually become less similar as children become increasingly verbal (Bentall, Lowe, & Beasty, 1985). In addition, rate and patterns of responding on various schedules of reinforcement can be very much influenced by instructions (Catania, Matthews, & Shimoff, 1982; Hayes, Brownstein, Zettle, Rosenfarb, & Korn, 1986), although whether and to what extent they are may depend on the type of schedule and whether the instructions are given by the experimenter or by a computer (Torgrud & Holborn, 1990).

2.   An analysis of records kept by the novelist Irving Wallace suggests that novel writing follows a fixed-ratio pattern (Wallace & Pear, 1977). Wallace typically stopped writing immediately after completing each chapter of a book he was working on. After a brief pause of a day or so he resumed writing at a high rate, which he maintained until the next chapter was completed. In addition, longer pauses typically occurred after a draft of a manuscript was completed. Thus, one might reasonably argue that completed chapters and completed drafts of manuscripts are reinforcements for novel writing and that these reinforcements occur according to FR schedules. It should, of course, be recognized that novel writing is a complex behavior and that other factors are also involved.

3.   There is evidence that, when FR and FD both appear to be applicable, the former schedule is preferable. Semb and Semb (1975) compared two methods of scheduling workbook assignments for elementary school children. In one method, which they called "fixed-page assignment," the children were instructed to work until they finished 15 pages. In the other method, "fixed-time assignment," they were instructed to work until the teacher told them to stop. The amount of time they were required to work was equal to the average amount of time they spent working during the fixed-page condition. In both methods, each child received free time if he or she answered correctly at least 18 of 20 randomly selected workbook frames; otherwise, the child had to redo the entire assignment. On the whole, the children completed more work and made more correct responses under the fixed-page condition than under the fixed-time condition.

4.   Schedules of reinforcement can help us understand behavior that has frequently been attributed to inner motivational states. This can be illustrated by several rather familiar examples.
   a.   A college student named Jill works very hard at her studies and achieves top marks. An equally bright student named Jack hardly cracks a book, receives low marks, and eventually drops out of school. It might be said that Jill has more internal motivation than Jack does. However, the actual reason for the different scholastic performances of the two students might lie in their histories of reinforcement schedules. Perhaps in grade school Jill had teachers who reinforced her frequently for studying behavior, and then gradually less frequently as she progressed through grade school and high school. When she entered college her reinforcement frequency was decreased still further, but the transition occurred gradually enough that her studying was still maintained at a high rate. Perhaps Jack was not so fortu-

nate. Perhaps, for example, his reinforcement frequency was decreased too sharply when he entered high school. This would have caused his studying to suffer a decline (i.e., ratio strain), thus providing him with even fewer reinforcements and causing an even further weakening of the behavior. When he entered college his studying behavior was just too weak to be maintained by the very sparse reinforcement schedules that unfortunately are characteristic of many higher educational institutions. The result was that Jack's studying behavior, already weakened in high school, suffered severe ratio strain and he dropped out.

b.   Similar considerations can help us understand the behavior of the dedicated scientist, artist, business person, and others. For example, the scientist's behavior is on a high VR schedule. He or she works sometimes for months, even years, on each experiment. And many experiments are unsuccessful. When we consider that most scientific behavior has been adjusted to such schedules more or less by accident, it is little wonder that there are so few dedicated scientists. Knowledge of schedules of reinforcement may help us learn how to develop more dedicated scientists without having to wait for accidental environmental events to develop them for us.

c.   Schedules of reinforcement can also help us understand the causes of behavior that some might attribute to "inner compulsions." Consider the pathological gambler. Because this individual is obviously acting against his or her own best interests, it is sometimes said that he or she has an inner motive of masochism—a need for self-punishment. However, it seems that (at least in many cases) the pathological gambler is a victim of an accidental adjustment to a high VR schedule. Perhaps when first introduced to gambling, this individual won several large sums in a row. Over time, however, the gambler won bets less frequently until now his or her gambling is being maintained at a high rate by very infrequent reinforcements.

Study Questions on Notes

1.   Who wrote the classic authoritative work on schedules of reinforcement, and what is the title of their book?
2.   What may account for the failures to obtain the schedule effects in basic research with humans that are typically found in basic research with animals?
3.   Describe how FR schedules may be involved in novel writing.
4.   Might it be better to reinforce a child for dusting the living room furniture for a fixed period of time or for a fixed number of items dusted? Explain your answer.
5.   Briefly describe how schedules of reinforcement can help us understand behavior that has frequently been attributed to inner motivational states.

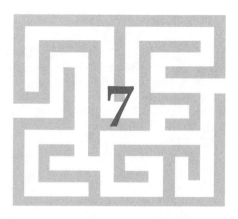

Types of Intermittent Reinforcement to Decrease Behavior

"Tommy, a little less talking out, please!"

DECREASING TOMMY'S TALKING OUT

Tommy, an 11-year-old developmentally disabled student was judged by his teacher to be the most disruptive student in his special education classroom.[1] He frequently engaged in inappropriate talking and other vocalizations during class. The behavior was troublesome not so much because of its nature, but because of the high rate at which it occurred. A program was therefore undertaken, not to eliminate it, but rather to reduce it to a less bothersome level.

The undesirable behavior, "talking out," was given the following precise behavioral definition: "talking to the teacher or classmates without the teacher's permission; talking, singing, or humming to himself; and making statements not related to the ongoing class discussion." A practice teacher located in the back of the room recorded Tommy's talk-outs during one 50-minute session per day. (A second trained observer also recorded Tommy's talk-outs, to ensure the accuracy of the observations.)

In phase 1 of the program, the behavior was recorded for 10 sessions. It was found that Tommy averaged about one talk-out every 9 minutes (or about 0.11 per minute). In phase 2, Tommy was told the definition of a talk-out and instructed that he would be allowed 5 minutes of free play time at or near the end of the day if at the end of the 50-minute session he had made three or fewer talk-outs (i.e., less than about one every 17 minutes). At the end of each session, Tommy was told by

---

[1]This case is based on Deitz and Repp (1973).

the teacher whether he had met the requirement, but during the session he was never told the number of talk-outs recorded.

This procedure was quite effective. During phase 2, which lasted 15 sessions, Tommy averaged about one talk-out every 54 minutes (0.02 per minute). Moreover, he never exceeded the upper limit of three per session.

In the third and final phase, the reinforcement schedule was removed and Tommy was told that he would no longer receive free time for low rates of talk-outs. Over the eight sessions of this phase for which data were taken, his rate of talking out increased to an average of one every 33 minutes (0.03 per minute). Although this rate was higher than the rate during the treatment procedure (phase 2), it was still a great deal lower than the rate before the procedure was introduced (phase 1). Thus, the treatment had a beneficial effect even after reinforcement was removed.

DIFFERENTIAL REINFORCEMENT OF LOW RATES

If reinforcement occurs only when responding is occurring at a low rate, responding will subsequently tend to occur at a low rate. This phenomenon is called **differential reinforcement of low rates.** Tommy's case illustrates one way in which low-rate behavior can be reinforced differentially. In that case, an interval was specified (50 minutes) and reinforcement occurred at the end of the interval if it contained fewer than a specified number of responses (three talk-outs).   **Note 1**

This method, like those discussed in Chapter 6, involves a schedule of intermittent reinforcement. However, the schedules in Chapter 6 are used to increase and maintain appropriate behavior. The schedules in this chapter are used to decrease responding that is inappropriate (see S. O'Brien & Repp, 1990). *Differential reinforcement of low rates (DRL)* constitutes one class of schedules for decreasing responding. There are two main ways in which DRL can be programmed: *limited-responding* DRL and *spaced-responding* DRL. Limited-responding DRL is the type of schedule used with Tommy. The total number of talk-outs each session was recorded, and reinforcement was given if that total was limited to not more than some specific number, which, in this case, was three.

In limited-responding DRL, the maximum allowable number of responses for reinforcement to occur can be specified for an entire session, or for separate intervals throughout a session. For example, it would have been possible to divide Tommy's 50-minute session into three intervals, each approximately 17 minutes long, and to give Tommy reinforcement at the end of each interval in which a limit of one talk-out occurred.

Limited-responding DRL is useful when two conditions hold: (a) some of the behavior is tolerable but (b) less of it is better. In Tommy's case, the teacher believed that three talk-outs per session would not be too disruptive; no doubt she would have preferred none at all, but she did not wish to impose too stringent a requirement on Tommy. Therefore, Tommy would hear that he had earned his five minutes of free time by making three, two, one, or zero talk-outs during any given session.

Spaced-responding DRL is useful when the behavior you want to reduce is actually desirable, provided that it does not occur at too high a rate. In other words, following an interval in which the behavior does not occur, an instance of the behavior is required for reinforcement. For example, a student who always calls out the correct answer deprives classmates of the chance to respond to the teacher's questions. Naturally we would not wish to eliminate this child's correct answering of questions; we would hope, however, to reduce the calling-out behavior to a more appropriate level. We might do this by placing the behavior on the following type of DRL schedule: any target response that occurs after 15 minutes of the previous target response is immediately reinforced; any target response that occurs within 15 minutes of the previous target response is *not* reinforced. Note that a target response before the interval has passed causes the timing of the interval to start over again. This procedure is called a spaced-responding DRL 1-response/15-minute schedule. This type of schedule requires that responses be emitted in order for reinforcement to occur. On the limited-responding schedule used with Tommy, the individual need not respond at all to obtain reinforcement.

Another example of the use of spaced-responding DRL is the reinforcement of slow speech in a student who speaks too rapidly. The student would be asked questions such as "How are you?" or "Where do you live?" for which standard responses are reinforced—but only if they encompass a certain minimum time period whose length is determined by what the teacher regards as a normally acceptable rate of speech. Thus, the sequence of respond-wait-respond is reinforced (provided that the wait is long enough). As another example, Lennox, Miltenberger, & Donnelly (1987) used a spaced-responding DRL to decrease the eating rate of three profoundly developmentally disabled individuals who ate their meals at such a rapid rate that it was considered unhealthy.

DIFFERENTIAL REINFORCEMENT OF ZERO RESPONDING

In Tommy's case, the teachers were willing to put up with a certain amount of talking out. But consider the case of Gerry, a 9-year-old boy of apparently normal intelligence who scratched or rubbed his skin so severely that he produced open sores all over his body. Because of this problem, he had spent most of his time in hospitals and had never attended school, even though he did not exhibit mental retardation. A DRL procedure in such a case would not be acceptable. The procedure that was used is referred to as DRO (pronounced "dee-arr-oh"), which stands for **differential reinforcement of zero responding.** Working with the nurses in the hospital, researchers (Cowdery, Iwata, & Pace, 1990) began with a schedule referred to as DRO 2 minutes. If scratching occurred during the two-minute interval, the interval started all over. However, if scratching did not occur (i.e., was at a zero rate), then Gerry was given tokens that he could later exchange for access to TV, snacks, video games, and various play materials. Over several days, the interval was increased to a DRO 4 minutes, a DRO 8 minutes, a DRO 15 minutes, and eventually to a DRO 30 minutes. Although the DRO was initially applied during relatively brief sessions, it was subsequently extended to the entire day. Eventually, after spending two years in a hospital, Gerry was discharged and his parents continued to use the procedure at home.

Technically, when Gerry was reinforced on a DRO 30 minutes, he would have received a token for doing anything *other* than scratching. For this reason, a DRO is sometimes referred to as **differential reinforcement of other responding.** Practically, however, we're sure that Gerry would not have been allowed to do *anything* other than scratching. If, for example, he began breaking windows instead of scratching, we're sure that the behavior modifiers would have intervened. DRO schedules have been successfully used to decrease a variety of target behaviors, such as inappropriate behaviors in classrooms (Repp, Dietz, & Dietz, 1976), bedtime thumbsucking in children (Knight & McKenzie, 1974), and self-injurious behavior of developmentally disabled persons (Mazaleski, Iwata, Vollmer, Zarcone, & Smith, 1993).

If an undesirable behavior occurs often and for long intervals, it would be wise to begin with a DRO of short duration. For example, DRO 5 minutes might be used to eliminate tantrum behavior. This procedure could be carried out by resetting a stopwatch to zero each time a tantrum occurred and allowing it to "tick off" seconds when the tantrum stopped. Reinforcement would occur when a continuous 5 minutes had elapsed with no tantrumming. When the nonoccurrence of the behavior is under good control of this contingency, the schedule should be increased—for example, to DRO 10 minutes. The size of DRO should continue to be increased in this fashion until (a) the behavior is occurring very rarely or not at all and (b) a minimum amount of reinforcement is being given for its nonoccurrence.

DIFFERENTIAL REINFORCEMENT OF INCOMPATIBLE RESPONDING

When applying a DRO, some behavior is occurring when the reinforcer is received. Even though Gerry wasn't scratching, for example, he was doing something when the 30-minute interval passed and he was given a token. An alternative is to specify explicitly an incompatible response that is to be reinforced in eliminating a particular target response. By an incompatible response, we mean a response that cannot be emitted at the same time as the target response. For example, sitting and standing are incompatible behaviors. If we decide to decrease a particular target response by reinforcing an incompatible response, the schedule is referred to as DRI, which stands for **differential reinforcement of incompatible responding.** Suppose, for example, that you are a grade school teacher who wants to eliminate the running-around-the-room behavior of a so-called hyperactive child in your classroom. One possibility would be to put the unwanted behavior on a DRO schedule; however, it might be replaced by an incompatible behavior that is also undesirable—such as, for example, lying on the floor. To avoid this, you might use DRI, instead of DRO, by specifying the incompatible behavior that is to be reinforced. You might, for example, reinforce sitting quietly at one's desk. An even better choice would be completing school work, since this behavior is more useful to the child. As another example, Allen and Stokes (1987) used **Note 2** a DRI to improve cooperative behavior of children during visits to the dentist.

Several children were identified who frequently cried, gagged, and moved their heads while the dentist was providing treatment. Allen and Stokes successfully applied DRI to strengthen the incompatible behavior of being still and quiet while the children were being treated in the dentist's chair.

The use of DRI to eliminate an undesirable behavior is essentially what we recommended in Chapter 4 when we stated: "Extinction is most effective when combined with positive reinforcement for some desirable alternative behavior." Technically, providing that you can withhold the reinforcer maintaining a behavior, DRI is the extinction of that behavior while at the same time reinforcing an alternative or incompatible behavior. In fact, DRI (and the other schedules discussed in this chapter) will likely be effective if you use the reinforcer that was maintaining the undesirable behavior; techniques for identifying that reinforcer are described in Chapter 20. The choice of schedule for reinforcing the incompatible behavior should be based on considerations discussed in Chapter 6.

PITFALLS OF SCHEDULES FOR DECREASING BEHAVIOR

Pitfalls of DRO and DRI are similar to the pitfalls already discussed for reinforcement (Chapter 3), extinction (Chapter 4), and schedules of intermittent reinforcement to increase behavior (Chapter 6). One interesting pitfall that is unique to DRL should be described here. Understanding it may help us to appreciate how underachievers are frequently generated in our society.

Consider what happens when a child starts performing well in school—by giving correct answers to questions, for example. At first, the teacher is quite impressed and enthusiastically reinforces the behavior. But as the rate of the behavior increases, the teacher gradually becomes less impressed. This is "obviously a bright child," and so one expects a high rate of good behavior from her. Thus, the reinforcement gradually decreases, perhaps to zero, as the rate of the behavior increases. Eventually, the child learns that she obtains more reinforcement if she performs at a low rate, because the teacher is more impressed with good behavior when it occurs infrequently than when it occurs frequently. Many kids breeze through school showing only occasional "flashes of brilliance" instead of developing to their full potential. To avoid this type of inadvertent DRL schedule, teachers should define precisely the behavior they want to maintain at a high rate. They should then make sure that they reinforce this behavior on an appropriate schedule, whether or not they happen to be impressed with it on any particular occasion.

GUIDELINES FOR THE EFFECTIVE USE OF INTERMITTENT SCHEDULES TO DECREASE BEHAVIOR

1. Decide which type of schedule should be used to reduce the target behavior. Use limited-responding DRL if some of the target behavior is tolerable, but the less the better. Use spaced-responding DRL if the behavior is desirable as long as it does not occur too rapidly or too frequently. Use DRO if the behavior should be eliminated and there is no danger that the DRO procedure might result in the reinforcement of

an undesirable alternative behavior. Use DRI if the behavior should be eliminated and there is a danger that DRO would strengthen undesirable alternative behavior.
2. Decide what reinforcer to use. In general, the procedure will be most effective if the reinforcer is the one maintaining the behavior that you want to reduce and if the reinforcer can be withheld for that behavior (see Chapter 20).
3. Having chosen which schedule to use, and a reinforcer, proceed as follows:
   a. If a limited-responding DRL schedule is to be used
      (1) record as baseline data the number of target responses per session for several sessions or more to obtain an initial value for the DRL schedule that will ensure frequent reinforcement.
      (2) gradually decrease the responses allowed on the DRL in such a way that reinforcement occurs frequently enough throughout the procedure to ensure adequate progress by the student.
      (3) gradually increase the size of the interval to decrease response rate below that obtained with (2).
   b. If a spaced-responding DRL schedule is to be used
      (1) record baseline data over several sessions or more, determine the average time between responses, and use this average as the starting value of the DRL schedule.
      (2) gradually increase the value of the DRL schedule in such a way that reinforcement occurs frequently enough throughout the procedure to ensure adequate progress by the student.
   c. If DRO is to be used
      (1) record baseline data over several sessions or more to obtain an initial interval for the DRO.
      (2) use DRO starting values that are approximately equal to the mean value between instances of the target behaviors during baseline.
      (3) gradually increase the size of the interval in such a way that reinforcement occurs frequently enough to ensure adequate progress by the student.
   d. If DRI is to be used
      (1) choose an appropriate behavior to be strengthened that is incompatible with the behavior to be eliminated.
      (2) take baseline data of the appropriate behavior over several sessions or more to determine how frequently the appropriate behavior should be reinforced to raise it to a level at which it will replace the inappropriate behavior.
      (3) select a suitable schedule of reinforcement for increasing the appropriate behavior (see Chapter 6).
      (4) while strengthening the incompatible behavior, apply the guidelines for the extinction of the problem behavior, as described in Chapter 4.
      (5) gradually increase the schedule requirement for the appropriate behavior in such a manner that it continues to replace the inappropriate behavior as the reinforcement frequency decreases.
4. If possible, inform the individual, in a manner that he or she is able to understand, of the procedure that you are using.

STUDY QUESTIONS

1. Describe briefly, point by point, how Tommy's talking out in class was reduced.
2. Explain, in general, what a DRL schedule is. Give an example of a DRL schedule that occurs in everyday life.

3. Distinguish between limited-responding DRL and spaced-responding DRL.
4. How is a spaced-responding DRL different from an FI schedule, procedurally?
5. How is a spaced-responding DRL different from an FD schedule, procedurally?
6. Describe in some detail two examples (at least one of which is not in the text) of how DRL would be useful in treating a behavioral problem.
7. Explain what a DRO schedule is. Give an example of a DRO schedule that occurs in everyday life.
8. Describe in some detail two examples (at least one of which is not in the text) of how DRO might be useful in treating a behavioral problem.
9. What does the "O" in DRO stand for? Explain your answer.
10. Explain what a DRI schedule is. Give an example.
11. What happens if the frequency of reinforcement on DRL or DRO or DRI is too low or is decreased too rapidly?
12. Describe how DRL works to the disadvantage of people who are ignorant of its effects. Give an example.
13. Explain how DRL, DRO, and DRI differ from the intermittent-reinforcement schedules discussed in Chapter 6.

APPLICATION EXERCISES

A. Exercises Involving Others

1. For each of the two types of DRL schedules cited in Study Question 3, describe a possible application in training programs with developmentally disabled children. Describe in detail how you would program and administer DRL in these situations.
2. Describe two possible applications of DRO in programs of early-childhood education. Describe in detail how you would program and administer DRO in these situations.

B. Self-Modification Exercise

Describe in some detail how you might use one of the schedules in this chapter to reduce one of your own behaviors that you would like to occur less frequently.

NOTES AND EXTENDED DISCUSSION

1. One might think that the five minutes of free play that occurred near the end of the day functioned as a reinforcer for decreasing Tommy's talk-outs much earlier in the day. Recall from Chapter 3, however, that the direct effects of reinforcement operate only over very short intervals. Therefore, Tommy's improvement cannot be attributed to the direct effect of the free play (near the end of the day) as a reinforcer for the behavior of working quietly in the classroom. Rather, when Tommy was working quietly, the immediate consequence was probably praise and attention from the teacher, who might have said: "You're doing great, Tommy; keep it up and you'll earn another five minutes of free play. Just think of how much fun you're going to have." The praise may have been a reinforcer for Tommy's improved performance. In addition, Tommy might have spent much of the day telling himself how much fun he was going to have during his extra play time. This rehearsal of a rule (as will be explained in Chapter 16) may help to bridge the time gap between the occurrence of desirable behavior during the 50-minute session and the reinforcer of extra play time that was dispensed on a much delayed basis.

2. An alternative to DRI is the *differential reinforcement of alternative behavior* (DRA), which is a procedure that involves reinforcing a behavior that is topographically dissimilar to, but not necessarily incompatible with, the problem behavior (Vollmer & Iwata, 1992). Suppose, for example, that a student in a classroom shows a high frequency of talking to other children. A program in which the student would be reinforced for completing assigned tasks would be a DRA in that the child might be able to complete the tasks and still talk with other children. A program in which the child might be reinforced for working on assigned tasks without talking would be a DRI. The success of DRA or DRI is likely to depend on such factors as the strength of the reinforcers to be earned for the alternative or incompatible behavior versus those produced by the undesirable behavior, the details of DRA or DRI schedule for the alternative or incompatible response versus the schedule of reinforcement for the problem behavior, and the extent to which the extinction of the problem behavior can be successfully applied along with the reinforcement for the alternative or incompatible response (Vollmer & Iwata, 1992).

Study Questions on Notes

1. What might account for the effectiveness of the delayed reinforcement contingency applied to Tommy's talk-outs? (There are at least two points.)
2. Distinguish between DRI and DRA.
3. Describe three factors that might affect the success of a DRI program.

8

Doing the Right Thing at the Right Time and Place Is a Matter for Stimulus Discrimination Learning

"Now, children, please work at your desks."

LEARNING TO FOLLOW TEACHER'S INSTRUCTIONS

The teacher in a regular third-grade class in an Auckland suburban elementary school had a problem.[1] When she was giving instructions to the class, she wanted the children to listen attentively from their seats. At other times, she wanted them to work quietly on their own. But 9 of the 34 children posed special problems of inattention and poor in-seat behavior. These youngsters frequently argued, shouted, hit and kicked other youngsters, banged furniture, and left the classroom without permission. They did listen attentively and work quietly occasionally, but not often and usually not when the teacher wanted them to. This was clearly a situation in which the desired behavior (listening attentively or working quietly) was in the children's repertoire (i.e., they could do it) but did not occur at the desired times.

A procedure for getting the desired behavior to occur at the desired time was introduced during an oral and written language lesson from 9:30 to 10:20 every morning. During several mornings, observers recorded the *on-task* behavior of the nine problem children *during teacher instruction,* when they were to remain silently in their seats and attend to the teacher, and *during work periods,* when they were to write a story, draw a picture, or perform other activities prescribed by the teacher. The problem children were typically on-task less than 50 percent of the time. The teacher then introduced an interesting system to the children. She made a large chart, on one side of which was printed with red letters:

---

[1]This example is based on a study by Glynn and Thomas (1974).

*LOOK AT THE TEACHER
STAY IN YOUR SEAT
BE QUIET*

On the other side, in green letters, was

*WORK AT YOUR PLACE
WRITE IN YOUR BOOKS
READ INSTRUCTIONS ON THE BLACKBOARD*

The children were each given a 10-by-12-inch card with several rows of squares on it, one row for each day of the week, and the definitions of on-task behaviors during teacher instruction and during work periods were explained to them. The children were told that a "beep" would be heard several times throughout the lesson, and they were to mark themselves on-task by placing a checkmark in one of the squares if they were "doing what the chart says" when a beep occurred. The beeps occurred an average of once every two minutes. The children were also told that, at the end of the lesson, they would be able to cash in each checkmark for one minute of free play time in a nearby room that contained a variety of games and toys. The program was introduced for all of the children in the class, although data were taken only on the nine problem children. In very short order, the sign telling them what to do exerted strong control over their behavior, influencing them to perform the desired behavior at the desired times. The program increased the on-task behavior of the nine problem children to approximately 91 percent.

STIMULUS DISCRIMINATION LEARNING AND STIMULUS CONTROL

As we have seen in previous chapters, behavior is strongly affected by its consequences. Behavior that is reinforced increases. Behavior that is not reinforced decreases. However, any behavior is valuable only if it occurs at the right times and in appropriate situations. For instance, at an intersection it is desirable to stop the car when the light is red, not when the light is green. Executing a perfect double back flip will earn you valuable points in a gymnastics routine, but it probably won't have the same effect in your first corporate-level job interview. As we acquire new behaviors, we also learn to produce those behaviors at the right time and place. How do we learn to do this successfully?

To understand the process, we must first recognize that there are always other people, places, or things that are around when behavior is reinforced or extinguished. For example, when little Johnny is playing in the street with his friends, swearing is likely to be reinforced by laughter and attention. When little Johnny is sitting at the dinner table at Grandpa and Grandma's on Sunday, his swearing is not likely to be reinforced, and may even be punished. After several such experiences, the people and things that were around during reinforcement and extinction come to cue the behavior—swearing by Johnny becomes highly probable in the presence of the kids on the street, and very improbable in his grandparents' house.

Any situation in which behavior occurs can be analyzed in terms of three sets of events: (a) the stimuli that exist just prior to the occurrence of the behavior, called antecedent stimuli (such as the street scene or the dinner table at Grandma and Grandpa's house just before Johnny swore), (b) the behavior itself (Johnny's swearing), and (c) the consequences of the behavior (either approval from Johnny's friends, or disapproval from Grandma and Grandpa). Recall from Chapter 1 that **stimuli** (plural of **stimulus**) are the people, objects, and events currently present in one's immediate surroundings that can be detected by one's sense receptors, and that can affect behavior. Chairs, books, lights, pens, people, trees, and shoes are all potential stimuli, as are all types of sounds, smells, tastes, and physical contacts with the body. Any stimulus can be an antecedent or a consequence of a behavior. Identifying the antecedents and consequences of a behavior is sometimes referred to as an *ABC assessment: Antecedents, Behavior, and Consequences.*

When a behavior is reinforced in the presence of a particular stimulus and not others, that stimulus begins to exert control over the occurrence of that behavior. For example, in the program at the Auckland elementary school, when the children saw the sign in big red letters saying LOOK AT THE TEACHER (etc.), they listened carefully to what the teacher had to say, because doing so was reinforced in the presence of that stimulus. We say that the stimulus exerted control over the behavior. When a particular behavior is more likely to occur in the presence of a particular stimulus and not others, we say that the behavior is under the control of that stimulus.

We use the term **stimulus control** to refer to the control of a stimulus over a behavior as a result of that behavior having been reinforced in the presence of that stimulus. **Good (or effective) stimulus control** refers to a strong correlation between the occurrence of a particular stimulus and the occurrence of a particular response; that is, when the stimulus occurs, the response is likely to follow. For example, suppose that you have just put money into a vending machine and you are looking for your favorite candy bar. You see the name of that bar beside a particular button, and you press that button. The sign exerted good stimulus control over your button-pressing behavior. Similarly, in the lead example for this chapter, the sign LOOK AT THE TEACHER (etc.) exerted good stimulus control over the children's behavior of paying attention.

While some stimuli are consistent predictors that a particular behavior will be reinforced, other stimuli are consistent predictors that a particular behavior will not be reinforced. An OUT OF ORDER sign on a vending machine is a cue that the behavior of inserting money into the machine will not be reinforced. The appearance of an empty cup is a cue that raising the cup to your lips will not result in a drink. Through experience, we learn to refrain from emitting certain behaviors in the presence of certain stimuli because we have learned that those behaviors will go unreinforced. Thus, good stimulus control also exists when a particular stimulus controls the absence of a particular behavior as a result of that behavior having gone unreinforced in the presence of that stimulus.

The procedure by which we learn to emit a specific behavior in the presence of some stimuli, and not in the presence of other stimuli, is called *stimulus discrimination learning*. This procedure involves reinforcement of a behavior in the presence of a specific stimulus, and extinction of that behavior in the presence of a different stimulus. Such stimuli are referred to as discriminative stimuli.

DISCRIMINATIVE STIMULI: S^Ds AND S^Δs

Two types of discriminative stimuli are abbreviated as S^Ds (pronounced "ess-dees") and S^Δs (pronounced "ess-deltas"; the symbol Δ, pronounced "delta", is the Greek letter D). If a response has been reinforced only in the presence of a particular stimulus, then that stimulus is an S^D. Loosely speaking, an S^D is a signal that a particular response will pay off. If a response has been extinguished only in the presence of a particular stimulus, then that stimulus is an S^Δ. Thus an S^Δ is a signal that a particular response will not pay off. We may think of an S^Δ as a stimulus that, in the fashion of the characters in the movie *Wayne's World*, says "not" to reinforcement, as in, "Let's reinforce Tanya's tantrums—**NOT!!!**" **Note 1**

Through stimulus discrimination learning, individuals come to emit responses in the presence of S^Ds and learn not to emit them in the presence of S^Δs. In our example of Johnny's swearing, the stimulus of the kids in the street is an S^D for the response of swearing because that response has been reinforced by their laughter and attention. The stimulus of Grandpa and Grandma is an S^Δ for the response of swearing because swearing was not reinforced in their presence. This can be diagrammed as follows:

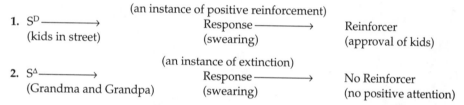

```
                        (an instance of positive reinforcement)
1. S^D ─────────→            Response ─────────→        Reinforcer
   (kids in street)          (swearing)                 (approval of kids)

                        (an instance of extinction)
2. S^Δ ─────────→            Response ─────────→        No Reinforcer
   (Grandma and Grandpa)     (swearing)                 (no positive attention)
```

A stimulus can simultaneously be an S^D for one response and an S^Δ for another; that is, in the presence of a particular stimulus, one response will be reinforced while another will not be reinforced (e.g., see Figure 8–1). For example, if you are eating dinner with friends and someone asks you, "Please pass the pepper," that statement is an S^D for your response of passing the pepper, and it is an S^Δ for you to pass the salt. As another example, when the teacher in the Auckland classroom presented the sign LOOK AT THE TEACHER (etc.), that stimulus was an S^D for the children's on-task behavior (staying in their seats and attending to the teacher), and it was an S^Δ for their off-task behavior (writing in their books, running around the room, etc.). This may be diagrammed as follows:

```
                        (an instance of positive reinforcement)
S^D ─────────→               Response ─────────→        Reinforcer
(The chart:                  (on-task behavior:         (checkmarks on
LOOK AT THE TEACHER          staying in seat and        squares: could
STAY IN YOUR SEAT            attending to teacher)      be exchanged
BE QUIET)                                               later for time in toy room)

                        (an instance of extinction)
S^Δ ─────────→               Response ─────────→        No Reinforcer
(The chart:                  (off-task behavior)        (no checkmarks
LOOK AT THE TEACHER                                     or toy room)
STAY IN YOUR SEAT
BE QUIET)
```

The sign is an S^Δ for inserting money, and an S^D to seek out a different machine (one that is not out of order)

The sign is an S^D for a female to enter and "go" to the bathroom, and an S^Δ for a male to enter

The sign is an S^D for driving in the direction of the arrow, and an S^Δ for driving in a direction against that signified by the arrow.

Figure 8–1 Many stimuli are simultaneously an S^D for one response and an S^Δ for a different response, although such stimuli do not always control the appropriate responses.

A phrase that is frequently used in connection with the type of diagrams on page 101 is *contingency of reinforcement*. According to Skinner (1969, p. 7), an "adequate formulation of the interaction between an [individual] and [his or her] environment must always specify three things: (1) the occasion upon which a response occurs, (2) the response itself, and (3) the reinforcing consequences. The interrelationships among them are the 'contingencies of reinforcement.'" Thus, all the reinforcement schedules (including extinction) discussed earlier in combination with the contexts in which they occur are contingencies of reinforcement, as is any arrangement among stimulus, response, and consequences. Earlier in this chapter we described ABC (antecedent, behavior, consequence) assessment. We can now see that performing an ABC assessment is the same as identifying the contingencies of reinforcement controlling a behavior.

Stimulus discrimination training refers to the *procedure* of reinforcing a response in the presence of an S^D and extinguishing that response in the presence of an S^Δ. After sufficient training, the *effect* is stimulus control—the response occurs to the S^D and not to the S^Δ. Sometimes our culture and physical environment will set up stimuli as S^Ds and S^Δs for our behavior, but we are not always "appropriately" controlled by those S^Ds and S^Δs. Suppose that a child finishes the main course at mealtime and demands of his mother, "Gimme dessert!" instead of asking, "Please may I have my dessert?" Let us suppose, further, that the parents decide that when the child has finished his main course, only a polite request for dessert ("Please may I have my dessert?") will be reinforced. In other words, the empty plate in that situation is an S^D by definition in that it is a stimulus signaling that a particular response (such as asking "Please may I have my dessert?") will be reinforced. Although the parents have set up that stimulus as an S^D it may take **Note 2** several trials (and perhaps some instruction by the parents) before the child finally emits the appropriate behavior. Thus, stimuli may be set up as S^Ds by one's parents (or peer group), but they do not necessarily control one's behavior. In many situations, a person standing beside a door with an armful of groceries is an S^D for someone to open the door, and that behavior is likely to be reinforced with social approval. The sight of a famous singer is an S^D for a fan to ask for an autograph, which may be reinforced by the singer giving one.

Examples of this sort could be cited at length. Although many of the stimuli in these examples are S^Ds by definition, in that appropriate responses emitted in their presence would be followed by reinforcement, these stimuli frequently do not actually control the behavior of the individuals of concern (for additional examples of ineffective stimulus control, see Figure 8–1). The failure of one individual to respond to the discriminative stimuli provided by another can be a major source of difficulty in a variety of interpersonal situations. For example, even though a spouse may not be "in the mood" for lovemaking, the partner may not respond to the subtle cues provided. Individuals often are preoccupied with other matters, tired, depressed, excited, and so forth. Sometimes these private behaviors are signaled very obviously, and sometimes the signals are not so obvious. When other individuals do not respond to the S^Ds and S^Δs provided, unpleasant interactions frequently follow. A comment, a glance, a touch, or a smile may mean far more or less than was intended. Misinterpretations occur between lovers, parents and children, friends, and employers and employees. It is often extremely helpful to analyze these situations as problems of stimulus control, for at least one of the individuals in such situations has not learned to provide appropriate S^Ds and S^Δs or to respond appropriately to the S^Ds and S^Δs provided. Some of the reasons for inappropriate responses to S^Ds and S^Δs are discussed later in this chapter. **Note 3**

Stimulus-control problems such as the above might be described as instances of *failure to discriminate*. Other difficulties arise from *failure to generalize*. These difficulties will be discussed in Chapter 12.

FACTORS DETERMINING THE EFFECTIVENESS
OF STIMULUS DISCRIMINATION TRAINING

1. Choosing Distinct Signals

If it is important to develop stimulus control of a particular behavior, it is desirable to identify controlling S^Ds that are very distinctive. For example, in the case of the parents who wanted to teach their child to ask, "Please may I have my dessert?" when the child had eaten all of his or her dinner, it might be advisable for the parents to make the child's empty plate distinctive. For instance, one of the parents might wipe the plate clean, and say "Wow, your plate is really clean!" Would you like your dessert now?" If, on the other hand, the parents sometimes provide the dessert when part of the main course is left on the plate, then the stimulus that they wish to function as an S^D for the response of asking for dessert is much more difficult to discriminate from other stimuli (namely, having slightly more food on the plate), and the discrimination training is likely to go more slowly. Similarly, some of the misunderstandings among lovers, friends, and others might be averted if the stimuli that were meant as S^Ds were made much more distinctive and described to the other person. (Techniques that help people present clearer discriminative stimuli to indicate their needs and feelings to others are collectively called *assertiveness training* [e.g., see Martin & Osborne, 1993].)

When considering a stimulus to be set up as an S^D for the behavior of another person, you might ask yourself the following questions:

Note 4

1. Is the stimulus different from other stimuli along more than one dimension? That is, is it different in location, size, color, and sensory modality (vision, hearing, touch, and so on)?
2. Is the stimulus one that can be presented only (or at least mainly) on occasions when the desired response should occur, so that confusion with the occurrence of the stimulus on other occasions is avoided?
3. Is the stimulus such that there is a high probability of the person attending to it when it is presented?
4. Are there any undesirable responses that might be controlled by the chosen stimulus? If some undesirable response follows the stimulus, it will interfere with the development of new stimulus control with the desired response.

Careful attention to these questions will increase the chances that your stimulus discrimination training will be effective.

2. Minimizing the Opportunities for Error

Consider the example of a child learning to pick up a phone when it rings, but not when it doesn't ring. The response of picking up the phone if the phone has not been ringing is a response to an S^Δ. This type of response is typically referred to as an *error*. Stimulus control can be developed much more effectively when the teacher attempts to minimize the possibility of errors on the part of the student. For example, if a parent is trying to teach a child to answer the phone appropriately, the parent might move the phone out of reach if the phone is not ringing and add verbal prompts of this sort: "Now remember, we don't pick up telephones when they are not ringing. We only answer them just after they've begun to ring." Then, as soon as the phone rings (perhaps a phone call from a friend, made specifically for training purposes), the parent can immediately place the phone in front of the child and say, "The phone is ringing. Now you should answer it."

At this point you might be thinking, "But often we want to teach people to respond to subtle cues. Why should we then maximize distinctive signals?" Let us simply reply that choosing distinctive cues and minimizing errors will lead to more effective stimulus control than might otherwise occur. In Chapter 9, we discuss techniques for gradually introducing discriminations involving very subtle cues. For the moment, it is important to keep in mind that efforts to choose distinctive signals and to minimize errors will lead to the development of effective stimulus control more quickly and with much less frustration for the student (and the teacher too) than attempts to develop discriminations that involve very subtle cues.

3. Maximizing the Number of Trials

As we mentioned in Chapters 3 and 4, a number of instances of positive reinforcement or extinction are usually necessary before any really obvious behavior change is noticeable to a casual observer. Likewise, effective stimulus control is often developed after a person is reinforced for emitting the desired behavior in the presence of S^Ds on a number of trials, and alternately experiences extinction of that behavior in the presence of S^Δs on a number of trials. In general, it is well accepted that a number of reinforced trials are necessary for the development of consistent behaviors in developmentally disabled and other behaviorally deficient individuals. What many people forget is that this is often true for all of us when we are acquiring new discriminations. In the example of a husband and wife, one of whom is "not in the mood," it is important for that partner to realize that the other partner may not learn to respond to subtle cues, or even obvious cues, with just one or two trials. After a number of instances of reinforcement for correct responding to the S^Ds, those S^Ds will likely control the response on subsequent trials.

4. Make Use of Rules: Describe the Contingencies

The development of stimulus control often involves trial and error—several trials of positive reinforcement for a behavior in the presence of an S^D, and several trials of that behavior going unreinforced in the presence of an S^Δ. In the case of Johnny's swearing, for example, his swearing behavior came under the control of the kids in the street as S^Ds (and came not to occur in the presence of Grandma and Grandpa as S^Δs) through trial and error. But the children in the classroom example at the start of this chapter did not take a few trials to show evidence of stimulus control. During the very first session after the teacher explained the new set of classroom rules, the children showed an immediate increase in on-task behavior in the presence of the appropriate signs (LOOK AT THE TEACHER, etc.), and they immediately earned reinforcement for doing so.

Johnny's swearing likely illustrates what is called *contingency-shaped behavior*. This is behavior that is developed by the direct-acting effects of reinforcement in the absence of statements to or by the individual specifying the contingency. In contrast, the behavior of the children in the classroom in the example at the beginning of this chapter illustrates what is called *rule-governed behavior*. A rule describes a contingency of reinforcement—stimuli, behavior, and consequences. Rule-governed behavior is behavior that is controlled by the statement of a rule. When you wish to develop good stimulus control over a particular behavior, you should always provide the individual with a rule or set of rules stating what behaviors in what situations will lead to what consequences. Because of our complex conditioning histories for following instructions, the addition of a set of rules to a stimulus discrimination program may lead to instantaneous stimulus control.

One way to look at the difference between contingency-shaped behavior and rule-governed behavior is to ask yourself if an animal could do it. Johnny's dog, for example, would probably not snarl at Grandma and Grandpa's house if its snarling was never reinforced there. But Johnny's dog could not verbalize, either overtly or covertly, "I'd better not snarl at Johnny's grandparents' house because they don't reward me for that behavior there." In our example of Johnny's swearing, we are assuming that he doesn't verbalize the contingency operating on his swearing any more than his dog verbalizes the contingency operating on his snarling. In the classroom example, in contrast, the children verbalized the rules they were given which, in turn, exerted immediate control over their behavior; hence, their behavior was rule-governed. Use of rules is discussed further in Chapter 16.

PITFALLS OF STIMULUS DISCRIMINATION TRAINING

Any effective method can be misapplied, and stimulus discrimination training is no exception. One of the authors observed an example of this with a 7-year-old developmentally disabled boy who banged his head against hard surfaces unless an adult was holding his hand. As soon as the adult dropped the child's hand and moved away, the child would immediately dive to the floor and begin banging his head hard enough to cause considerable bleeding. This behavior occurred only when the child was standing on a hard floor or on concrete. It did not occur when he was standing on a rug or on grass. The reason for this is easy to see. No one would come running to give him attention if he banged his head on a soft carpet or on grass, since he did not injure himself when he did that. Of course, the staff had no choice but to give him attention when he banged his head on hard surfaces. Otherwise, he would have injured himself seriously. The staff had thus inadvertently taught the boy the following discrimination:

1. S^D ⟶   Response ⟶   Reinforcer
   (hard surface)   (banging head)   (attention from staff)
2. S^Δ ⟶   Response ⟶   No Reinforcer
   (soft surface)   (banging head)   (no attention from staff)

There are numerous examples of situations in which people inadvertently teach others to respond inappropriately to particular cues. If they were aware of what they were doing, they would not teach those discriminations. Behavioral episodes of the following sort are common in many households with young children: Terry, a 3-year-old boy, is playing with the remote control for the TV set. Mother says quietly, "Terry, please leave that alone." Terry continues to fiddle with the remote control. A few minutes later, Mother hollers a little louder and a little less politely, "Terry, put that down." Terry continues to fiddle with the remote, rapidly changing channels, which was a natural reinforcer for Terry. A minute or two later, Mother says, this time loudly and with a threatening look, "Terry, for the last time leave the remote alone and get away from the TV set before I get really mad!" Terry finally moves away from the TV set and Mother says, "Now, that's better, Terry. Mommy likes it when you do what I tell you; why didn't you do that in the first place?" It is probably obvious to you that Mother has just reinforced Terry for responding to her third-level threats. The discrimination Terry is learning is that of waiting until Mother is really angry and threatening before attending to her requests.

If you feel that you have to tell an individual something many times before he or she responds, or that nobody listens to you, or that others are not doing the right thing at the right time and place, you should closely examine your interactions with these individuals for instances of misapplication of stimulus discrimination training.

GUIDELINES FOR EFFECTIVE STIMULUS DISCRIMINATION TRAINING

1. *Choose distinct signals.* Specify the S^Ds and at least one S^Δ. (In other words, specify conditions under which the behavior should and should not occur.)
2. *Select an appropriate reinforcer.* See Figure 3–3.
3. *Develop the discrimination.*
   a. Arrange for the student to receive several reinforced trials in the presence of the S^D.
      (1) Specify clearly in a rule the S^D-desirable response-reinforcer sequence. Help identify the cues that indicate that the behavior will be reinforced versus the cues that indicate that the behavior will not be reinforced, and use instructions when appropriate to teach the student to act in a particular way under one set of circumstances but not under another.
      (2) Keep verbal cues constant initially.
      (3) Post the rules in a conspicuous place, and review them regularly.
      (4) Recognize that stimulus control over the student's behavior will not develop if the student is not attending to the cues; therefore, use dramatic gestures to emphasize the cues.
      (5) To teach the student to act at a specific time, present additional cues for correct performance just before the action is to occur rather than after he or she has performed incorrectly.
   b. When the S^Δ is presented, make the change from the S^D very obvious and follow the rules for extinction for the behavior of concern. Stimuli that can acquire control over behavior include such things as geographical location of training place; physical characteristics and location of furniture, equipment, and people in the

training room; time of day of training; and sequence of events that precede and
accompany training. A change in any of these may disrupt stimulus control.
4. *Weaning the person from the program* (discussed in more detail in Chapter 12).
    a. If the behavior occurs in the right place at the right time at a desirable rate during
       a dozen or so of the opportunities for the behavior, and if it is not occurring in S^A
       situations, it might be possible to gradually eliminate contrived reinforcers and
       maintain the behavior with social approval.
    b. Look for other natural reinforcers in the environment that might maintain the be-
       havior once it is occurring in the presence of S^Ds and not in the presence of S^As.
    c. Plan periodic assessments of the behavior after the program is terminated in or-
       der to ensure that it is occasionally being reinforced, and that the desired fre-
       quency of the behavior in the presence of S^Ds is being maintained.

STUDY QUESTIONS

1. What is a stimulus?
2. What is meant by good stimulus control? Describe an example.
3. Define and give an example of an S^D. Identify the response in the example.
4. Define and give an example of an S^A. Identify the response in the example.
5. What is the difference between a stimulus and a discriminative stimulus?
6. Distinguish between stimulus control and stimulus discrimination training.
7. Shaping and stimulus discrimination training are similar in that they both involve
   successive applications of reinforcement and extinction. In what two ways are they
   dissimilar?
8. Describe an example (not from the text) of a stimulus that is an S^D for one behavior
   and an S^A for a different behavior.
9. For any two stimuli that have been set up as an S^D and an S^A but whose relationship
   to the behavior is described best as ineffective stimulus control, what would be the
   behavior in the presence of these stimuli?
10. What is an ABC assessment?
11. Identify examples of S^Ds and S^As as follows: two S^Ds from Table 3–1, two S^Ds from
    Table 3–3, two S^As from Table 4–1, and two S^As from Table 4–2.
12. When you are considering the selection of a stimulus to be set up as an S^D for the be-
    havior of another person, what questions might you ask yourself about that stimu-
    lus? (see p. 104)
13. For each of the questions that you asked yourself in the preceding question, provide
    an example from your own experience.
14. What do we mean by an error in discrimination training?
15. Consider the task of teaching a child to discriminate the proper placement of a knife,
    fork, and spoon at a table setting. Describe several different ways that one might re-
    arrange the training environment to present distinct signals and to minimize the
    likelihood of errors.
16. What are "contingencies of reinforcement"? Explain.
17. With examples, distinguish between rule-governed and contingency-shaped behav-
    ior.
18. Was the children's high on-task behavior to the posted rule in the Auckland class-
    room likely rule-governed or contingency-shaped? Justify your choice.
19. Describe an example of how ignorance of stimulus discrimination training may lead
    parents or other caregivers to develop an undesirable behavior in a child or adult in
    their care.

APPLICATION EXERCISES

Exercises Involving Others

1. Identify five situations in which you presented an S^D that controlled the behavior of some other person. Clearly identify the general situation, the controlling S^D, the behavior controlled, and the reinforcers.
2. Describe five situations in which you presented an S^Δ to some other person. Clearly identify the general situation, the S^Δ, the behavior for which your stimulus was an S^Δ, and the consequences. Indicate whether or not the S^Δ controlled the behavior appropriately.
3. Briefly describe a situation in which someone close to you has not been doing the things that you would like him or her to do, and you suspect the problem is that you are not presenting clear-cut S^Ds and S^Δs. Describe how you might present clearer S^Ds and S^Δs to develop better stimulus control over the desired behavior in that person.

Self-Modification Exercises

1. Identify five S^Ds that controlled your behavior during the past day or two. Clearly identify the general situation, the controlling S^D, the behavior controlled, and the reinforcers.
2. Choose an excessive behavior of yours that you might like to decrease. For that behavior, carefully monitor those situations in which the behavior occurs and does not occur over a two- or three-day period. Clearly identify the controlling S^Ds, and, if possible, some controlling S^Δs for the behavior. Such information will prove to be extremely helpful if you decide to set up a self-control program after completing this book.
3. On the basis of the material you have read thus far in this book, describe in detail how you might set up specific control of your study behavior so as to improve your learning of the discriminations that are necessary in mastering the remainder of the material in this book. (*Hint:* Consider stimulus control, reinforcement, extinction, incompatible behaviors, and schedules of reinforcement.)

NOTES AND EXTENDED DISCUSSION

1. It is important to note that we are speaking loosely here to help make the terminology more understandable. In general, one should be very careful to use well-defined behavioral terminology when speaking of an S^D. As Michael (1982) has pointed out, saying that a stimulus is "an S^D for reinforcement," "a cue for reinforcement," or "a stimulus for reinforcement" is sloppy use of the terminology because it omits reference to the *response* controlled by the S^D. Instead, one should say that a stimulus is an S^D for a response because the stimulus has been correlated with the availability of a particular reinforcer for that response.

Likewise, Michael suggests that it is inappropriate to say that an S^D is a stimulus that *signals* reinforcement or *predicts* reinforcement. These expressions are borrowed from cognitive psychology, which is to be distinguished from behavioral psychology by the former's focus on hypothetical intervening processes. In saying that a stimulus signals reinforcement, for example, one is implying that the individual is taking in some sort of information and processing it. According to Michael, "What action occurs as a result of this information and how this action is controlled by the information is generally left for future study, or, in flirtation with a nondeterministic position, 'left to the organism'" (1982, p. 48). (In Chapter 26 we discuss attempts to integrate cognitive psychology and behavior modification.) It should be noted, however, that our use of the word *signal* on p. 101 does specify the response and is therefore not as objectionable as the examples Michael cites. Besides, as we indicated, we were speaking loosely to help make the behavioral terminology clear to the reader.

2.   Consider the following scenario: A young man has been talking to a delightful young woman whom he has just met. Just before leaving, she says to him, "If you give me your phone number, I'll call you tonight." She has presented a stimulus in the presence of which rummaging through his pockets for a pen to write down his number will be reinforced. But is her statement an S^D? No, it does not fit the definition of an S^D—that is, it is not a stimulus that has been correlated with the availability of the pen as a reinforcer for his behavior of searching for the pen. In everyday language, she did *not* influence his behavior of searching for the pen by telling him how to get it. Rather, she changed his behavior by making him "want" the pen—i.e., by making the pen ***reinforcing*** for him at that moment. In such situations, Michael (1993) suggests that it is useful to use the term **conditioned establishing operation (CEO),** which is an object or event that (a) momentarily increases the effectiveness of another object or event as a conditioned reinforcer and (b) evokes behavior that in the past has been followed by that object or event. (Conditioned reinforcers, discussed further in Chapter 10, are previously neutral stimuli that acquire reinforcer value through appropriate pairings with other reinforcers.) As contrasted with unconditioned EOs (UEOs), discussed in Chapter 3, CEOs affect behavior because of prior learning. Thus, the example of the woman asking the man to write his telephone number was an EO in that it momentarily increased the effectiveness of a pen as a reinforcer and evoked behavior (searching his pockets) that in the past had produced a pen. The example was a *conditioned* EO because of the man's prior learning experiences with pens. Like UEOs, CEOs might be thought of as **motivational variables** in that they influence the direction and likelihood of behavior.
    In summary, here's how a CEO is similar to and different from an S^D: While both S^Ds and CEOs exert control over behavior (by altering the momentary frequency of behavior), only CEOs alter the momentary effectiveness of consequences as reinforcers. In everyday language, an S^D is a cue that tells you what to do to get what you already want; a CEO is a motivator that momentarily changes what you want and at the same time increases the likelihood of behavior that has enabled you to get it in the past.

3.   In an experiment by Redd and Birnbrauwer (1969), one adult provided candy, ice cream, or sips of soft drinks along with much praise when a group of developmentally disabled children played cooperatively with each other. At other times, a second adult provided the same reinforcers at regular time intervals, whether or not the children were cooperative or uncooperative. After a number of trials with the two different adults, the children began to show a great deal of cooperative play whenever the first adult appeared, but cooperated at a much lower level in the presence of the second adult. Thus, if a child is delightful in the presence of others but a "monster" in your presence, check the reinforcement contingencies that you are applying.

4. Some forms of stimulus control are more complex than a single stimulus (such as a green light or a sign in a window) controlling a single response (such as crossing a street or going into a shop to buy something). One complex type of stimulus control, called *contextual control*, is that in which the general setting or context may alter the manner in which an individual responds to particular stimuli (Baer, Wolf, & Risley, 1987; Michael, 1982). For example, when you drive in Great Britain, the highway dividing line is an S^D to steer to the left of it, whereas when you drive in Canada, it is an S^D to steer to the right of it. In this example, the country in which you are driving is the context that determines how a particular stimulus controls your behavior. Knowledge of contextual control can be important in designing effective behavioral treatments. For example, Haring and Kennedy (1990) found that a procedure that was effective in reducing an autistic girl's self-stimulatory behavior when she was performing classroom tasks was not effective in reducing it when she was doing leisure activities; and, conversely, a procedure that was effective in reducing her self-stimulatory behavior when she was doing leisure activities was not effective in reducing it when she was performing classroom tasks.

Study Questions on Notes

1. Give examples of a precise use and imprecise uses of the term S^D. What specifically is wrong with the imprecise uses?
2. What is a CEO? How does it differ from an S^D? Give an example to illustrate the distinction.
3. How might you explain the behavior of a child who is usually a "perfect angel" with one parent and a "holy terror" with the other? Outline an experiment supporting your explanation.
4. What is meant by the term *contextual control*? Illustrate with an example.
5. Just before starting to cross a street, a pedestrian visiting Canada from England observed that the street was clear to his right, stepped into the street, and was struck by a car. Explain how lack of contextual control was involved in this accident.

Developing Appropriate Behavior with Fading

"Peter, what's your name?"

TEACHING PETER HIS NAME

Peter possessed an extensive mimicking repertoire (he could repeat many of the words other people said) but had little other verbal behavior.[1] He would mimic many words, even when it was not appropriate. For example, when asked "What's your name?," he would reply "Name." Sometimes he would repeat the entire question, "What's your name?" This was a problem of stimulus control in which questions (stimuli) evoked mimicking responses rather than appropriate answers.

Using the following procedure, a university student, Veronica, taught Peter to respond appropriately to the question "What's your name?" First, Veronica identified an effective reinforcer. Since Peter had been taught to work for plastic chips that could be exchanged for treats such as candy and popcorn, Veronica decided to use the chips as reinforcers.

Peter sat at a small table in a quiet room, and Veronica sat across from him. In a very soft whisper, Veronica asked, "What's your name?" then, very loudly and quickly and before Peter could respond, she shouted, "PETER!" Of course, Peter mimicked the word "Peter," and Veronica reinforced this with "Good boy!" and a chip. You may wonder how this could represent any progress, since the boy was still only mimicking the student. However, over several trials Veronica began asking the question "What's your name?" more loudly and began supplying the answer "Peter" more quietly. In each case, she continued to reinforce the correct response—"Peter." Eventually, Veronica asked loudly, "What's your name?" and simply mouthed the word "Peter." Nevertheless, the boy responded with the correct answer, "Peter." Over several trials, Veronica ceased even mouthing the correct answer, but Peter still responded correctly to the question "What's your name?"

---

[1]This case is taken from Martin, England, Kaprowy, Kilgour, and Pilek (1968).

FADING

Fading is the gradual change, on successive trials, of a stimulus that controls a response, so that the response eventually occurs to a partially changed or completely new stimulus (Deitz & Malone, 1985). In the case described, Peter would at first say his name only when it was said to him. Through a fading process, the stimulus control over the response "Peter" was gradually transferred from the stimulus "Peter" to the stimulus "What's your name?" (At this point one might ask whether Peter knew that he was saying his own name. But this is a vague question, so let's try to phrase it more behaviorally. Would Peter have consistantly responded correctly when asked other questions involving his name; e.g., would he have consistently answered "Peter" when shown his reflection in the mirror and asked "Who's that?" Probably he would not have. Teaching him to answer "What's your name?" was an appropriate and important start to teaching him to answer questions involving his name and to his knowing that he was saying his name.)

Fading is involved in many everyday situations in which one person teaches a behavior to another person. Parents are likely to fade out their help and support when teaching a child to walk or ride a bicycle. A dance instructor might use less and less hand pressure to guide a student through new dance steps. And as a teenager progresses in drivers' ed, the driving instructor is likely to provide fewer and fewer verbal hints to attend to various traffic regulations.

In any situation in which a stimulus exerts strong control over a response, fading can be a very useful procedure for changing the stimulus control. The discovery and development of fading techniques have led to some changes in educators' views regarding the learning process. At one time, it was believed that people had to make mistakes while learning to know what not to do. However, errorless transfer of a discrimination can occur, and it has at least three advantages over procedures involving trial and error. First, errors consume valuable time. Second, if an error occurs once, it tends to occur many times, even though it is being extinguished. (Remember from Chapter 4 that during extinction, "things may get worse before they get better.") Third, the nonreinforcement that occurs when errors are being extinguished often produces emotional side effects such as tantrums, aggressive behavior, and attempts to escape from the situation.

We have used fading procedures in many learning situations in our programs with developmentally disabled and autistic individuals and very young children. In teaching students to name an item of clothing—a shirt, for example—teachers might proceed according to the following instructions:

1. Point to your shirt and say "shirt." Keep doing this until the student consistently mimics "shirt" a number of times, and immediately reinforce each correct response. (This assumes that you have a student who is able to mimic this particular word. It also assumes that the student has been trained to look at any item you point to.)
2. When the student consistently mimics "shirt," present the stimulus that you want to control the response, and at the same time gradually fade out saying "shirt." That is, you might say, "What's this? Shirt" while pointing to the shirt. In response, the student usually mimics "shirt." Over several trials, gradually decrease the intensity of

saying "shirt" to zero, so that the student eventually responds with the answer "shirt" to the stimulus of someone pointing at a shirt and asking "What's this?" Again, each appropriate response is to be reinforced.

Fading can also be used to teach tracing, copying, and drawing circles, lines, squares, triangles, numerals, and letters of the alphabet. To teach a student to trace a circle, the teacher might begin with a large number of sheets with a heavily dotted circle on each of them. The teacher places a pencil in the student's hand, says "Trace the circle," and then guides his hand so that the pencil traces the circle by connecting the dots. Immediately after this, of course, the student receives a reinforcer. After several such trials, the teacher fades out the pressure of her hand as a cue controlling the student's tracing, by

1. lightly holding the student's hand for several trials;
2. touching her fingertips to the back of the student's hand for several trials;
3. pointing to the item to be traced;
4. finally, simply giving the instruction, "Trace the circle." (Steps 1, 2, and 3 are always accompanied by this instruction.)

Once the teacher has taught the student to trace, she can teach the student to draw or copy by fading out the dotted cues that guide the tracing. For example, the teacher might use a sheet on which there are several dotted circles. The circles progress from a heavily dotted circle on the left to a circle with very few dots on the right. The teacher points to the most heavily dotted circle and instructs the student, "Trace the circle here." The desired response is reinforced, and the procedure is repeated for each of the more lightly dotted circles. On subsequent steps, the dots can be faded out completely so that the student will draw a circle in the absence of dots. It is then a simple matter to fade in the instruction "Draw a circle" to this newly acquired response. The instruction "Copy a circle," said while the teacher points to a circle, can also be faded in and come to control the response. Teaching the student to copy many different figures in this fashion will eventually enable him to copy adequately figures that he has had little experience copying.

Thus, fading occurs along *dimensions* of stimuli, such as the loudness of the question that Veronica presented to Peter, or the pressure of a teacher's hand that guides a student's printing, or the clarity of dots that a student might be expected to trace. In general, a dimension is any characteristic that can be measured on some continuum. Thus far, we have talked of fading across very specific stimulus dimensions, but fading can also occur across changes in a general situation or setting. For example, in one of the authors' programs with autistic children, we wanted to have a group of autistic boys respond appropriately in a classroom setting (Martin et al., 1968). But these boys were very disruptive, especially in a group situation. Therefore, we could not at first place them in a classroom setting. We decided first to obtain the desired behavior from each child in an individual situation and then fade in the classroom setting.

Our initial training sessions were conducted in a small room in which there were several chairs and tablet-arm desks. Two or three teachers (university students) worked individually with two or three students on a one-to-one ratio. The procedures involved eliminating tantrums through extinction and reinforcing sitting attentively, appropriate verbal behavior, drawing, copying, and other desirable behaviors. Each child's desk was placed against the wall in such a fashion as to make it difficult for him to leave the situation.

Within one week, the children learned to sit quietly, attend to the teacher, and mimic words in verbal training. Stimulus control was established between the general training situation and the children's attentiveness. But our goal at that time was to teach the children to function appropriately in a regular classroom situation with one teacher at the front of the class. If we had switched immediately to this situation after the first week, however, much inattentiveness and disruptive behavior would no doubt have occurred. Therefore, over a period of four weeks, we gradually changed from one small room with three students and three teachers to a standard-sized classroom with seven students and one teacher. This fading occurred along two stimulus dimensions.

One dimension was the physical structure of the room. We moved the children from the small room to the regular large classroom. However, we did so by first placing the three tablet-arm desks against the wall of the regular classroom, just as we had done in the small room. The three chairs that the teachers sat in were also moved to the regular classroom. The rest of the classroom was empty. Over several days, the tablet-arm desks were gradually moved away from the wall and toward the center of the room until, finally, the three desks were side by side. Additional desks and furnishings were added one at a time until the children were finally sitting in desks in a normally furnished classroom.

The second dimension was the number of children per teacher. Fading along this dimension was carried out at the same time that fading along the first dimension took place. At first, one teacher worked with one student for several sessions. The teacher then worked with two students, alternating questions between them for several sessions. In this fashion, the student-teacher ratio was increased gradually until only one teacher worked with as many as seven children in a classroom situation.

Care should be taken to avoid confusing fading with shaping. Both are procedures of gradual change. However, as described in Chapter 5, shaping involves reinforcement of slight changes in a behavior so that it gradually comes to resemble the target behavior. The stimulus situation generally stays about the same, and the behavior changes from an initial behavior (not necessarily resembling the target) to the final target behavior. Fading, on the other hand, involves reinforcement of a specific response in the presence of slight changes in a stimulus so that the stimulus gradually comes to resemble the stimulus that you wish to control that particular response. Thus, *shaping involves the gradual change of a response while the stimulus stays about the same; fading involves the gradual change of a stimulus while the response stays about the same.*

USING FADING PROCEDURES TO TEACH VERBAL SKILLS

The lead case to this chapter showed how fading was used to teach an autistic child to respond appropriately to the question "What's your name?" Fading can be used in a similar manner to teach a wide variety of appropriate responses to questions. If a child can imitate a given object's name, for example, fading can be used to teach the child to identify that object vocally when asked what it is. Sometimes, of course, an individual cannot even imitate a particular verbal response—in that case, shaping is generally used to establish the imitative behavior prior to establishing the naming behavior.

Fading can also be used to teach fairly complex verbal skills. Consider the following use of fading to teach an eight-year-old autistic boy to count objects.[2] Danny had participated in a reinforcement program in which he earned poker chips that could be exchanged for food, candy, and other goodies. His attention span had been increased and he had learned to identify and recite the numerals 1 through 10. To teach Danny to count up to 10 objects, the teachers developed a detailed training procedure that utilized fading. Danny was required to complete 10 consecutive correct trials at each of six steps before progressing to the next step. After Danny had progressed successfully through all six steps for a given numeral, he was returned to step 1 for the next numeral. The steps were as follows:

Step 1

Danny received a sheet of white paper with a numeral printed on the upper right-hand corner and a corresponding number of circles drawn on the paper (see Figure 9–1A). A trial began with the teacher pointing to the numeral, such as 5, in the upper

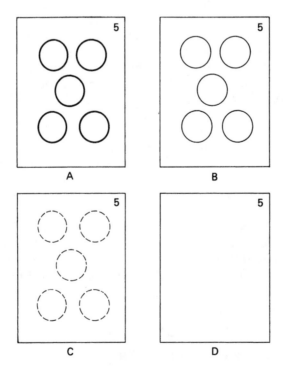

Figure 9–1 The stimulus sheets used in Danny's fading program.

---

[2]This case is taken from Murrell, Hardy, and Martin (1974) and is paraphrased by permission of the publisher.

right-hand corner of the page and asking, "Danny, what number is this?" Danny consistently identified the numeral 5 correctly, to which the teacher responded, "Good boy Danny. Put five circles on the paper." Danny then filled the outlined circles with circles cut from orange felt and received approval and a poker chip. If Danny responded incorrectly, the teacher said "no" and demonstrated the correct response. After 10 consecutive correct trials, Danny was moved to step 2 of the training procedure for that particular numeral.

Step 2

The procedure remained the same as in step 1, except that the outlines of the circles were finer (see Figure 9–1B).

Step 3

The procedure was the same as in step 1, except that the outlines of the circles were now broken lines (see Figure 9–1C).

Step 4

The procedure was the same as in step 1, except that the paper on Danny's desk was now blank, with only the numeral printed in the top right-hand corner (see Figure 9–1D).

Step 5

The procedure was the same as in step 1, except that the sheet of paper was not placed on Danny's desk. Instead, at the start of the trial Danny was shown the appropriate numeral cut from the felt material and asked, "Danny, what number is this?" When Danny correctly identified the numeral, such as 5, the teacher said, "Good boy, Danny. Now place five circles on your desk." After doing this correctly, he received reinforcement. As in all previous steps, Danny had to complete 10 consecutive trials correctly before moving on to the next step.

Step 6

The procedure was the same as in step 5, except that Danny was required to place the appropriate number of orange circles in the teacher's hand rather than on the desk. Following Danny's correct identification of the numeral, such as 5, the teacher held out her hand and said, "Good boy, Danny. Now give me five circles." On the first trial of step 6, the teacher held her hand on the desk. During the second through the fifth trials, the teacher gradually raised her hand off the desk and held it in midair directly in front of Danny. During the last few trials, Danny was taking the correct number of circles from a pile and placing them in the teacher's hand.

After Danny completed 10 consecutive trials on step 6, the numeral was considered learned. He was then taught to count the next numeral, proceeding through the same six steps. In this way, Danny learned to count objects for all of the numerals 1 through 10. Danny made only six errors in the entire training program. You can see how fading was utilized in several different ways in this program.   **Note 1**

FACTORS INFLUENCING THE EFFECTIVENESS OF FADING

1. Choosing the Final Desired Stimulus

The *final desired stimulus* (i.e., the stimulus we want to evoke or produce the behavior at the end of the fading procedure) should be chosen carefully. It is important to select the final desired stimulus so that the occurrence of the response to that particular stimulus is likely to be maintained in the natural environment. Some fading programs make the error of stopping with a stimulus that does *not* include some aspect of the situation that the student will frequently encounter in the natural environment. Consider Danny's case. It would have been easy for the teachers to stop training after step 5, for Danny was clearly counting out the correct number of circles and placing them on his desk when asked to do so. However, classroom observation indicates that a natural occurrence is for a teacher to approach a student, hold out her hand, and ask the student to give her a specific number of objects. The training program was therefore carried on through step 6. Moreover, the teachers conducted further training with Danny: following step 6, he was asked to count out other items (such as bingo chips; wooden blocks; and puzzle pieces of varying sizes, shapes, and colors) under the training procedure utilized in step 6.

2. Choosing the Starting Stimulus

At the beginning of a fading program, it is important to select a *starting stimulus* that reliably evokes the desired behavior. In Danny's training program, the teacher knew that Danny would place a felt circle on the heavy outline of a circle if there was such an outline on the piece of paper in front of him. Therefore, the heavy outline of a circle was the starting stimulus selected to teach Danny to count. In the task of teaching Peter his name, Veronica knew that Peter would mimic the last word of a question when that word was spoken loudly. Therefore, the starting stimulus with Peter was the question "What's your name?" said very softly and followed quickly by the shouted answer, "Peter!"

Supplemental stimuli that control the desired behavior but that are not a part of the final desired stimulus are sometimes referred to as **prompts** (Touchette & Howard, 1984). It is helpful to distinguish among *verbal prompts*, which are verbal hints or cues; *gestural prompts*, which are certain motions that the teacher makes, such as pointing to the correct cue without touching the student; *modeling prompts*, in which the teacher demonstrates the correct behavior (modeling is discussed further in Chapter 17); *physical prompts* (also called *physical guidance*), in which the teacher touches the student to guide him/her; and *environmental prompts*, in which the environment is altered in a manner that will evoke the desired behavior.

Environmental prompts are further subdivided into extra-stimulus prompts and within-stimulus prompts. An *extra-stimulus prompt* is something that is added to the environment to make a correct response more likely. Suppose, for example, that a parent wanted to teach a child to place a knife, fork, and spoon appropriately when setting up a table for dinner. The parent might draw a knife, fork, and a spoon in their appropriate location on a placemat, and require the child to place the utensils appropriately. Of course, correct responses would be reinforced. Over time, the extra-stimulus prompts of the line drawings could gradually be erased or faded. A *within-stimulus prompt* is an alteration in the characteristics of the S^D or the S^Δ to make them more noticeable, and therefore easier to discriminate. In the table-setting example, training might be initiated with a normal fork and knife continuously remaining in their normal position, and with a large wooden spoon as the training item. The initial focus would be on teaching the child to place the spoon in the correct position. Over trials, the size of the spoon could be faded back to normal. This process could then be repeated with the knife and the fork, until the child can set the table correctly. Several studies have indicated that within-stimulus prompt fading is more effective than extra-stimulus prompt fading with developmentally disabled and autistic children (Schreibman, 1975; Wolfe & Cuvo, 1978; Witt & Wacker, 1981).

The teacher may provide any or all of these types of prompts to ensure the correct response. For example, suppose that the teacher wishes to develop appropriate stimulus control of the instruction "Touch your head" over the response of the student touching her head. The teacher might initiate training by saying, "Touch your head. Raise your hand and put it on your head like this," while touching his own head. In this example, "Raise your hand and put it on your head like this" is a verbal prompt, the teacher's action of putting his hand on his head is a modeling prompt. Selecting several kinds of prompts that, together, reliably produce the desired response will minimize errors and maximize the success of the fading program.

3. Choosing the Fading Steps

When the desired response is occurring reliably to the prompts given at the onset of the training program, the prompts can then be gradually removed over trials. The steps through which the prompts are to be eliminated should be carefully chosen. **Note 2** Unfortunately, effective use of fading is, like effective use of shaping, still somewhat of an art. It is very important to monitor the student's performance closely to determine the speed at which fading should be carried out. If the student begins to make errors, the prompts may have been faded too quickly or through too few fading steps. It is then necessary to backtrack until the behavior is again well established before continuing with fading. On the other hand, if too many steps are introduced or too many prompts are provided over a number of trials, the student might become overly dependent on the prompts. Consider the example of teaching a child to touch her head when asked to do so. If the teacher spends a great many trials providing the prompt of touching his own head, the child may become dependent on it and attend much less to the instruction "Touch your head."

PITFALLS OF FADING

Just as other behavior principles and procedures can be applied unknowingly by those who are not familiar with them, so can fading be misused. However, it appears to be more difficult to misuse fading inadvertently because the necessary gradual change in cues rarely occurs by chance.

The case of the child who banged his head on hard surfaces (described in Chapter 8) might be an example of the effects of the misuse of fading. In Chapter 5 we pointed out that shaping might produce such behavior. It is also possible that fading is responsible for it. Suppose that the child began attracting attention initially by hitting his head on soft surfaces, such as grass. At first, this behavior may have caused adults to come running to see if the child had injured himself. When they eventually learned that no injury resulted from this behavior, they ceased providing it with attention. The child may then have progressed to hitting his head with the same force but on slightly harder surfaces, such as carpeted floors. For awhile, this perhaps increased the amount of attention elicited from adults, but this amount of attention may eventually have decreased when the adults learned that the child did not injure himself in this way. Only when the child graduated to hitting his head on surfaces such as hard floors and even concrete, which caused real and serious self-injury, did the adults give him continued attention. Note that throughout this example there was a gradual change in the stimulus (the type of floor surface) evoking the undesired behavior; eventually, the behavior was evoked by the most undesirable stimulus possible. Thus, this example fits the technical definition of fading.

GUIDELINES FOR THE EFFECTIVE APPLICATION OF FADING

1. *Choosing the final desired stimulus.* Specify very clearly the stimuli in the presence of which the target behavior should eventually occur.
2. *Selecting an appropriate reinforcer* (See Chapter 3).
3. *Choosing the starting stimulus and fading steps.*
   a. Specify clearly the conditions under which the desired behavior now occurs—that is, what people, words, physical guidance, and so forth, are necessary, at present, to evoke the desired behavior.
   b. Specify clearly the dimensions (such as color, people, and room size) that you will fade to reach the desired stimulus control.
   c. Outline the specific fading steps to be followed and the rules for moving from one step to the next.
4. *Putting the plan into effect.*
   a. Present the starting stimulus and reinforce the correct behavior.
   b. Across trials, the fading of cues should be so gradual that there are as few errors as possible. However, if an error occurs, move back to the previous step for several trials and provide additional prompts.
   c. When the desired stimulus control is obtained, review the guidelines in previous chapters for weaning the student from the program (a topic that is discussed in more detail in Chapter 12).

STUDY QUESTIONS

1. Define fading and give an example of it.
2. Why is it advantageous to establish stimulus control without errors?

3. Identify three stimulus dimensions along which fading occurred in the examples cited in the first two sections of this chapter.
4. Describe an example from this chapter in which the training situation remained constant but a specific stimulus dimension was faded.
5. Describe an example from this chapter in which the general training situation was faded.
6. Describe how you might use fading to teach your pet to perform a trick. Describe how you might use shaping to teach your pet to perform another trick. Drawing from your examples, distinguish clearly between fading and shaping.
7. Assume that you have an 18-month-old child who will imitate the word "chip." Describe in detail how you might use fading to teach your child to correctly identify a chip (i.e., a potato chip) when you point to it and ask "What's that?"
8. Describe two stimulus dimensions that were faded in the program through which Danny learned to count.
9. What do we mean by *final desired stimulus*? Give an example.
10. What do we mean by *starting stimulus*? Give an example.
11. Define prompt. Describe an example that is not from the text.
12. Define the five major categories of prompts. Give an example of each from this chapter.
13. Define within-stimulus prompt, and describe an example that is not from the text.
14. Define extra-stimulus prompt, and describe an example that is not from the text.
15. How many reinforced trials should occur at any given fading step before the stimuli of that particular step are changed? (*Hint*: What suggestions were made in the examples in this chapter?)

APPLICATION EXERCISES

A. Exercises Involving Others

1. Suppose that a two- or three-year-old child has reached the stage at which he is beginning to wander away from his front yard. The child has already learned some speech, and you wish to teach him to answer the question "Where do you live?" Outline a fading program with which you could teach the answer to this question; indicate what you would use as a reinforcer, the number of trials you would have at each fading step, and so forth.
2. Assume that you must teach a severely developmentally disabled child, or a very young normal child, to eat with a spoon. Outline a program in which you would use all five of the major categories of prompts. Describe how each of the prompts would be faded.
3. Suppose that the official temperature scale has been switched recently from degrees Fahrenheit to degrees Celsius (or centigrade). The government has assigned you the job of designing an effective program for teaching citizens to respond knowledgeably to the Celsius scale (without covertly translating a specific Celsius temperature back into Fahrenheit when they hear the Celsius rating). You have been given complete freedom to work with the radio and/or television weather announcers. Describe a plan that would accomplish this task. Include a precise statement of your target stimulus control, your starting stimulus control, and the fading steps you would use.

B. Self-Modification Exercise

Suppose that you detest certain vegetables from the cabbage family—like broccoli—but research studies have convinced you that you can reduce your chances of heart disease and cancer by eating more of these vegetables. Outline a fading program that you could use to increase the amount of broccoli (and other such vegetables) that you eat. (*Hint:* Your program should not—at least in the long run—increase your fat intake, as that would defeat its purpose.)

NOTES AND EXTENDED DISCUSSION

1.   As Marx (1992) has pointed out, the type of procedure used in teaching Danny to count objects is superior to the common procedure of simply teaching children to recite numerals because such recitation does not teach the child the "concept of number." The procedure used by Murrell et al. (1974) taught Danny that a given numeral (e.g., 5) corresponds to sets of a specific number of objects (e.g., five outlines of circles on paper being one set and five orange felt circles being another set corresponding to the numeral 5). Marx developed a similar counting program that involves teaching children to pick out a number of spoons to place in a corresponding number of empty cups. In Marx's program, correspondences between sets of the same size (e.g., five empty cups and five spoons) are taught prior to teaching the numerals. Research has not yet determined whether teaching the number concept prior to numerals is more effective than teaching numerals at the same time as the concept of number, as in the Murrell et al. study.

2.   There are at least four different methods of removing prompts gradually: (a) decreasing assistance; (b) increasing assistance; (c) graduated guidance; and (d) time delay. *Decreasing assistance*, in which a starting stimulus that evokes the response is gradually removed or changed until the response is evoked by the final desired stimulus, is the method that is illustrated by all the examples of this chapter. *Increasing assistance* takes the opposite approach: The teacher begins with the final desired stimulus, and introduces prompts only if the student fails to respond appropriately to the final desired stimulus. The level of the prompts is gradually increased during a trial in which the student failed to respond at the preceding level until eventually the student responds to the prompt. *Graduated guidance* is similar to the method of decreasing assistance, except that the teacher's physical guidance is gradually adjusted from moment to moment within a trial as needed, and then faded across trials. For example, the teacher may grasp the student's hand firmly at the beginning of the trial and gradually reduce the force on the student's hand as the trial progresses. With *time delay*, the final desired stimulus and the starting stimulus are presented together at first; then, rather than changing the starting stimulus, the time interval between the final desired stimulus and the starting stimulus is gradually increased until eventually the individual is responding only to the final desired stimulus. Many studies have indicated little or no difference in the effectiveness of these different prompt-removal methods (for a review, see Dem-chak, 1990).

Study Questions on Notes

1. Describe how fading might be used with Marx's procedure for teaching the number concept.
2. Which of the prompt-removal procedures fit the definition of fading given at the beginning of this chapter, and which do not? Explain.

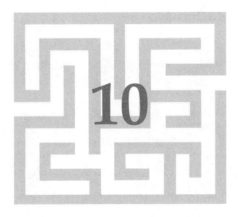

Developing and Maintaining Behavior with Conditioned Reinforcement

"OK, team! Here's how you can earn an Eagle Effort Award."

COACH DAWSON'S POINT PROGRAM[1]

"Let's see a little concentration out there. You should hardly ever miss lay-ups in drills!" shouted Jim Dawson at basketball practice. Jim was coach of the Clinton Junior High basketball team in Columbus, Ohio. He was concerned about the players' performance during a series of drills that he used to open each practice. There was also an attitude problem. *"Some of them just aren't team players,"* he thought to himself. *"Some of them really have a bad attitude."*

With the help of Dr. Daryl Siedentop of Ohio State University, he worked out a motivational system in which players could earn points for performance in lay-up drills, jump-shooting drills, and free-throw drills at daily practice. In addition, they could earn points by being a team player and encouraging their teammates by making supportive comments. Points were deducted if Coach Dawson saw a lack of hustle or a bad attitude. The points were recorded by student volunteers who served as managers for the team. All of this was explained to the players in detail. At the end of a practice, the coach praised players who earned a lot of points, as well as players who earned more points than in the previous practice. In addition to reviewing their records of points earned at each practice, players who earned a sufficient number of points had their names posted in a conspicuous place on the "Eagle Effort" board in the hall leading to the gymnasium and were rewarded with an "Eagle Effort" award at a postseason banquet. Overall, the system was highly

---

[1]This example is based on a report by Siedentop (1978).

effective. Performance in lay-up drills improved from an average of 68% before the system to an average of 80%. Jump-shooting performance improved from 37% to 51%. Free-throw shooting at practices improved from 59% to 67%. However, the most dramatic improvement was in the team player category: The number of supportive comments increased rapidly to such an extent that the managers could not monitor them all. In addition, while at first most of the comments were "pretty phony," over sessions they became increasingly sincere. By the end of the season the players were exhibiting positive attitude behaviors to a remarkable extent and, in Coach Dawson's words, "We were more together than I ever could have imagined."

UNCONDITIONED AND CONDITIONED REINFORCERS

We have inherited the capacity to be reinforced by some stimuli without prior learning. Such stimuli or events are called **unconditioned reinforcers** (that is, stimuli that are reinforcing without being conditioned). (They are sometimes also called *primary* or *unlearned* reinforcers.) Examples include food for a hungry person, water for a thirsty person, warmth for someone who is cold, and sexual contact for someone who has been deprived of such contact. Other stimuli become reinforcers because of particular experiences. Specifically, stimuli that are not originally reinforcing can become reinforcers by being paired or associated with other reinforcers. Stimuli that become reinforcers in this way are called **conditioned reinforcers.** (They are sometimes also called *secondary* or *learned* reinforcers.) Examples of conditioned reinforcers include praise, a picture of a loved one, books that we like to read, our favorite television programs, and clothes that make us look good. When a   **Note 1** stimulus becomes a reinforcer through association with other reinforcers, the other reinforcers are sometimes called **back-up reinforcers.** Back-up reinforcers can be either conditioned or unconditioned reinforcers.

The points that Coach Dawson used at basketball practices were not primary reinforcers for the players. We doubt that the players would have worked very hard, if at all, to get points for their own sake. The players worked hard because the points were paired with back-up reinforcers, including praise from Coach Dawson, the "Eagle Effort" award at the postseason banquet, and the posting of the players' names on the "Eagle Effort" board in the hall leading to the gymnasium.   **Note 2**

Some conditioned reinforcers, called **tokens,** can be accumulated and exchanged for back-up reinforcers. A behavior modification program in which individuals can earn tokens for specific behaviors and can cash in their tokens for back-up reinforcers, is called a **token system** (examples of token systems have been seen in earlier chapters—recall Peter and Danny in Chapter 9—and token reinforcement programs, are discussed further in Chapter 23). Just about anything that can be accumulated can be used as the medium of exchange in a token system. In some token systems individuals earn plastic discs (such as poker chips), which they can retain until they are ready to cash them in for backup reinforcers. In other token systems, they are paid with "paper money," on which is written the amount earned, the individual's name, the name of the employee who paid him, the date, and the task the individual performed to earn the token. In still others, as in Coach Dawson's program, individuals receive points, which are recorded on a chart beside their names or in notebooks they keep with them.

Tokens constitute one type of conditioned reinforcer, but stimuli that cannot be accumulated can also be conditioned reinforcers. A common example, already mentioned, is praise. A mother who expresses pleasure at her child's good behavior is simultaneously disposed to smile at the child, hug him, play with him, and give him a treat or a toy. Praise is normally established as a conditioned reinforcer during childhood, but it continues to be maintained as one for adults: When people praise us, they are generally more likely to favor us in various ways than when they do not praise us.

Although it is normal for praise to become a conditioned reinforcer, it is not always so for some developmentally delayed people. Perhaps for them, there were few occasions on which praise was paired with effective backup reinforcers. Indeed, this may be one reason for their behavioral handicaps. Praise is used so commonly as a reinforcer in our society that any individual for whom it is not reinforcing cannot be expected to acquire many socially desirable behaviors. It would seem that such an individual would almost necessarily become behaviorally handicapped—no matter what his or her innate potential for intellectual and other social development might be. Of course, if one's innate potential is not very great to begin with, one may emit socially desirable behavior so rarely that people in the natural environment seldom or never praise the behavior. Thus, lack of contact with praise precludes it from becoming a conditioned reinforcer, which makes it even more difficult to develop socially desirable behaviors. It follows that those working with others should ensure that praise becomes and remains a conditioned reinforcer for them. In training programs, this is typically done by praising desirable behavior just prior to presenting other types of reinforcement.

Before closing this section we might mention briefly the principle of *conditioned punishment*, which is very similar to that of conditioned reinforcement. Just as a stimulus that is paired with reinforcement becomes reinforcing itself, so a stimulus that is paired with punishment becomes punishing itself. "No!" and "Stop that!" are examples of stimuli that become conditioned punishers, because they are often followed by punishment if the individual continues to engage in the behavior that provoked them. Moreover, punishing tokens as well as reinforcing ones are possible. The demerit system used in the military is an example of a punishing-token system. There are, however, problems associated with the use of punishment (see Chapter 13).

FACTORS INFLUENCING THE EFFECTIVENESS OF CONDITIONED REINFORCEMENT

1. The Strength of the Backup Reinforcers

The reinforcing power of a conditioned reinforcer depends in part upon the reinforcing power of the backup reinforcer(s) on which it is based. For example, suppose that Coach Dawson had used only praise as a backup reinforcer for those players who earned points. In that case, the points would have been effective reinforcers only for the players for whom the coach's praise was an effective reinforcer.

2. The Variety of Backup Reinforcers

A stimulus can become a conditioned reinforcer because of pairings with a single backup reinforcer. This is illustrated by the example of an ice cream vendor who rings a bell when entering each neighborhood. After a few pairings, the sound of the ice cream vendor's bell will be a conditioned reinforcer for the children in the neighborhood. In contrast, a stimulus that is paired with many different kinds of backup reinforcers is referred to as a **generalized reinforcer.** Early in life, for example, parents feed their infants, wash them, play with them, and meet their needs in many other ways. Because it is thus paired with many kinds of reinforcers, adult attention becomes a powerful generalized reinforcer. Similarly, money is a powerful generalized reinforcer for us because of its pairings with food, clothing, shelter, transportation, entertainment, and other reinforcers. (see Figure 10–1).

The reinforcing power of a conditioned reinforcer depends in part on the number of different backup reinforcers available for it. This factor is related to the preceding one in that, if there are many different backup reinforcers available, then at any given time at least one of them will probably be strong enough to maintain tokens at a high reinforcing strength for any individual in the program.

Figure 10–1   Why is money a generalized conditional reinforcer?

3. The Schedule of Pairing with the Backup Reinforcer

In Chapter 6, we saw that behavior is more persistent if reinforcement does not follow every occurrence of the target behavior. Likewise, conditioned reinforcement is more effective if backup reinforcement does not follow each occurrence of the conditioned reinforcer. For example, the players in Coach Dawson's program had to earn a certain number of points before they were given backup reinforcement.

4. Extinction of the Conditioned Reinforcer

For a conditioned reinforcer to remain effective, it must continue to be associated with a suitable backup reinforcer. Had Coach Dawson discontinued the backup reinforcers for his praise and the "Eagle Effort" program, the players may eventually have stopped working for the points. Ceasing to provide backup reinforcement for a conditioned reinforcer is called *extinction of a conditioned reinforcer* and is similar to the procedure described in Chapter 4 for extinguishing a response.

PITFALLS OF CONDITIONED REINFORCEMENT

People who are unfamiliar with the principle of conditioned reinforcement may unknowingly misapply it in various ways. One very common misapplication occurs when an adult scolds a child for behaving inappropriately, but (a) does not provide any type of "backup punishment" (see Chapter 13) along with the scolding, and (b) does not reinforce desirable alternative behavior. The scolding, no doubt, is given in the expectation that it will be punishing, but often this is not the case. Indeed, the attention that accompanies such negative verbal stimuli may even be highly reinforcing, especially for developmentally handicapped individuals, who often do not receive much attention from adults. In this way, scoldings and other negative verbal stimuli (such as "No!") can become conditioned reinforcers, and the individual will behave inappropriately to obtain them.

Indeed, even stimuli that are normally punishing can become conditioned reinforcers through association with powerful primary reinforcers. The classic example is the parent who spanks a child for misbehavior and then, "feeling guilty" from the ensuing piteous crying, immediately hugs the child and gives her ice cream or some other treat. The possible outcome of this unthinking procedure is that the child will develop a "liking for lickings"; that is, the spanking could become a conditioned reinforcer that would maintain, not eliminate, the misbehavior it follows.

Extinction of a conditioned reinforcer can be unknowingly applied with unfortunate results by those who are unfamiliar with this aspect of conditioned reinforcement. An example of this is a teacher who awards stars for good behavior but fails to use effective backup reinforcers. The result is that the stars eventually lose whatever reinforcing power they may have had when they were first introduced. Failure to use effective backup reinforcers can account for the lack of motivation students sometimes show on certain token systems.

Note 3

GUIDELINES FOR THE EFFECTIVE USE
OF CONDITIONED REINFORCEMENT

The following guidelines should be observed in applying conditioned reinforcement:

1. A conditioned reinforcer should be a stimulus that can be managed and administered easily in the situation in which you plan to use it. For example, points were ideally suited for the players in Coach Dawson's program.
2. As much as possible, use the same conditioned reinforcers that the individual will encounter in the natural environment. For example, it is desirable in training programs to transfer control from artificial-token systems to the monetary-token system used in the natural environment, or to naturally given praise and attention from others.
3. In the early stages of establishing a conditioned reinforcer, backup reinforcement should be presented as quickly as possible after the presentation of the conditioned reinforcer. Later, the delay between conditioned reinforcement and the backup reinforcement can be increased gradually, if desired.
4. Use generalized conditioned reinforcers wherever possible; that is, use many different types of backup reinforcers, not just one. This way, at least one of the backup reinforcers will probably be strong enough at any given time to maintain the power of the conditioned reinforcer.
5. When the program involves more than one individual (as was the case in Coach Dawson's program), avoid destructive competition for conditioned and backup reinforcers. If one person receives reinforcement to the detriment of another, that may evoke aggressive behavior in the second individual and/or his desirable behavior may extinguish. This rule implies in particular that one should avoid making an issue out of the fact that one individual is earning more conditioned and backup reinforcement than another. Of course, people differ in their abilities, but the bad effects of these differences can be minimized by designing programs so that each individual earns a good deal of reinforcement for performing at his or her own level.
6. In addition to these rules, one should follow the same rules for conditioned reinforcers that apply to any positive reinforcer (see Chapter 3). Additional details for establishing token economies are described in Chapter 23.

STUDY QUESTIONS

1. Explain what an unconditioned reinforcer is. Give two examples.
2. Explain what a conditioned reinforcer is. Give and explain two examples.
3. Explain what a backup reinforcer is. Describe and explain two examples.
4. What were the backup reinforcers in Coach Dawson's program?
5. If Coach Dawson had not paired praise and the "Eagle Effort" program with the points, the players may have continued to work because of a variety of natural reinforcers that may have been paired with the points during the players' experience growing up in Western society. What might these natural reinforcers have been?
6. Which of the five categories of reinforcers in Figure 3–3 include primarily unconditioned reinforcers and which include primarily conditioned reinforcers? Defend your answer.
7. What are tokens? Explain in two or three sentences what a token system is.

8. Give two examples of stimuli that are conditioned reinforcers but not tokens. Explain why they are conditioned reinforcers.

9. Why is it important for those working with developmentally disabled individuals to ensure that praise becomes a conditioned reinforcer for them?

10. Explain what a conditioned punisher is. Give and explain two examples.

11. Explain what a generalized reinforcer is. Explain why a conditioned reinforcer that is a generalized reinforcer is more effective than one that is not.

12. Is praise a generalized reinforcer? Defend your answer.

13. Were the points in Coach Dawson's program a generalized reinforcer? Defend your answer.

14. Explain what extinction of a conditioned reinforcer is.

15. How does the schedule of pairing a conditioned and backup reinforcer affect the strength of the conditioned reinforcer?

APPLICATION EXERCISES

A. Exercise Involving Others

What are the probable reinforcers involved in each of the following situations? Are these reinforcers unconditioned or conditioned? Justify your choice.

1. An individual walks through a park in the autumn and admires the beautifully colored leaves on the trees.

2. A person finishes jogging 3 miles and experiences the runner's "high" (caused by the release of endorphins in the brain).

3. A teenager finishes mowing the lawn and is allowed to use the family car.

4. A thirsty child holds a glass of milk to her lips and drinks several swallows.

B. Self-Modification Exercise

Identify a behavioral deficiency of yours that you would like to overcome. Next, describe the details of a plausible token system that might be applied by a friend or a relative to help you overcome your behavioral deficiency.

NOTES AND EXTENDED DISCUSSION

1. Why is it that babies babble a great deal, even when no adults are around? How is it that infants appear to learn new words when those words are not immediately followed by any observable form of reinforcement? A part of the answer lies with automatic conditioned reinforcement—a strengthening effect following a response that occurs even though another person does not deliberately reinforce that response (Skinner, 1957). Suppose, for example, that a parent says "goo goo goo" to an infant while providing reinforcement (tickling, touching, clapping, etc.). After several such trials, the sounds "goo goo" will become conditioned reinforcers.

Later, when the infant is in the crib alone, the infant may begin saying "goo goo" because of the automatic conditioned reinforcement received from reproducing the same sound. More generally, vocal responses of infants may increase in frequency because the sounds that those vocal responses produce have become conditioned reinforcers, and they automatically strengthen the production of those vocal responses. Recent studies have clearly confirmed this role of automatic conditioned reinforcement in early language acquisition (Smith, Michael, & Sunberg, 1996; Sunberg, Michael, Partington, & Sunberg, 1996). Automatic reinforcement appears to be important not only in language acquisition, but also in the strengthening of a variety of practical and artistic behaviors (Skinner, 1957; Vaughan & Michael, 1982).

2. Recall from Chapter 3 that positive reinforcers have a direct-acting effect on behaviors that immediately precede them. However, the points in Coach Dawson's program were not awarded until the end of practice. Why then did the players show improvement in performance?

Perhaps they noticed managers recording points just after a correct behavior was performed, which may have served as a conditioned reinforcer. As positive peer comments increased, these likely served as conditioned reinforcers for improved performance. Perhaps the players verbally rehearsed rules such as, "If I make more jump shots I'll earn more points," and such statements may have exerted rule-governed control over the improved performance (see Chapter 16). Thus, even though the overall improvement might be attributed to the point program and the points were conditioned positive reinforcers, the improved performance of the players in practice may not have been due to the direct-acting effect of those points as conditioned reinforcers.

3. We discussed earlier how knowledge of schedules of reinforcement can help us to understand behavior that has often been attributed to inner motivational states (see Chapter 6, Note 4). Knowledge of conditioned reinforcement can also help us to understand such behavior. For an industrious college student, for example, good grades are likely powerful conditioned reinforcers. In this person's childhood, a good report was probably followed by words of endearment, hugs, and special treats. Now that he or she is a young adult, the backup reinforcers that maintain grades may be more difficult to identify, but the good grades likely still occur and they are probably conditioned reinforcers (and may be combined with the schedule effects discussed in Chapter 6).

Study Questions on Notes

1. How is conditioned reinforcement involved in influencing babies to babble sounds in their native language, even when no adults are around to reinforce this behavior?

2. Can we attribute the improved performance of Coach Dawson's basketball players entirely to the direct-acting effects of points as conditioned reinforcers? Why or why not?

3. Describe how knowledge of conditioned reinforcement can help us to understand behavior that is often attributed to inner motivational states.

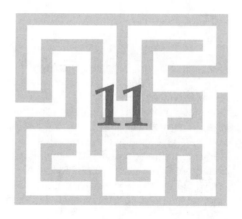

Getting a New Behavior to Occur with Behavioral Chaining

"Agnes, please make a coffee pack for me."

TEACHING AGNES TO ASSEMBLE A COFFEE PACK

Agnes was a developmentally disabled woman with an IQ of 22 who lived in a group home with several other severely handicapped women.[1] The group home staff was told that if Agnes could learn to perform vocational tasks, she might be able to attend a work training program that had a contract with an airline company to assemble coffee packs. This task involved appropriately stuffing a plastic bag with a folded paper napkin, coffee whitener, a sugar pack, and a plastic stir stick. The airline company distributed these packs with coffee on their domestic flights. Angela Pallotta-Cornick, a graduate student, decided to try to teach Agnes to perform this task, partly because Agnes would follow simple instructions.

Before beginning training, Angela conducted a test to see what Agnes could do without any training at all. She placed some samples of each of the components of the task in front of Agnes. She then showed Agnes a completed coffee pack and asked her to make one just like it. Agnes promptly stuffed the plastic bag with plastic stir sticks. It seemed clear that Agnes could not assemble the coffee pack appropriately, at least under the test conditions.

Assembling a coffee pack consists of a sequence of responses that must be followed, one response at a time, in the proper order. To facilitate teaching the task to Agnes, the entire process of assembling a coffee pack was divided into the following 15 sequential units or steps:

---

[1]This example is taken from Pallotta-Cornick (1978).

1. *Pick up one napkin.*
2. *Fold napkin in half (making it narrower).*
3. *Sharpen crease with forefinger.*
4. *Fold napkin in half (making it shorter).*
5. *Pick up one plastic bag.*
6. *Open plastic bag.*
7. *Pick up folded napkin.*
8. *Put napkin into plastic bag with folded end first.*
9. *Pick up one coffee whitener.*
10. *Put coffee whitener into plastic bag.*
11. *Pick up one sugar pack.*
12. *Put sugar pack into bag over napkin, with logo on sugar pack clearly visible.*
13. *Pick up one stir stick.*
14. *Put stir stick into the bag.*
15. *Lift plastic bag so that contents all go to the bottom.*

The training procedure carried out by Angela involved a series of trials, on each of which Agnes was required to perform all 15 steps in the appropriate sequence. At each step, Angela verbally prompted Agnes to perform the step. If Agnes performed the step appropriately, she was praised and then prompted to perform the next step. If Agnes performed the step inappropriately, Angela used verbal instructions and physical guidance to help Agnes perform the correct response, and then Agnes was required to go on to the next step. Incorrect performance of a step was not followed by praise. Following successful completion of step 15, Agnes received more praise and also an edible of her choice. In this way, Agnes practiced assembling coffee packs over a number of trials, performing each of the steps in the appropriate order on each trial. As Agnes became increasingly proficient at performing the steps, Angela provided less and less verbal help. Eventually, all Angela had to say was "Do all you can" and Agnes would perform all 15 steps correctly. Even though Agnes was severely developmentally disabled, she learned to assemble the coffee packs appropriately after approximately six 20-minute sessions.

STIMULUS-RESPONSE CHAINING

A stimulus-response chain is a sequence of discriminative stimuli (S^Ds) and responses (Rs) in which each response except the last produces the S^D for the next response, and the last response is typically followed by a reinforcer. What Agnes had acquired in learning to assemble a coffee pack was such a sequence of stimuli and responses. The first stimulus (S^D1) for the entire sequence was the instruction, "Please assemble the coffee pack"; this was the instruction that was given in the presence of a completely unassembled coffee pack. The response (R_1) to that stimulus was "picking up one napkin." The napkin in hand was the stimulus for the response "folding the napkin in half." The napkin in half was the stimulus for the response "sharpening the crease with the forefinger," and so on until the entire coffee pack was assembled. At that point Agnes received edible reinforcers and extra praise. The reason for calling this procedure a stimulus-response chain can be seen by writing it out as follows:

$$S^D_1 \rightarrow R_1 \rightarrow S^D_2 \rightarrow R_2 \rightarrow S^D_3 \rightarrow R_3 \ldots S^D_{15} \rightarrow R_{15} \rightarrow S^+$$

The stimulus-response connections are the "links" that hold the chain together. As the saying goes, "a chain is only as strong as its weakest link." Similarly, if any response is so weak that it fails to be evoked by the S^D preceding it, the next S^D will not be produced and the rest of the chain will not occur. The chain will be broken at the point of its weakest link. The only way in which to repair the chain is to strengthen the weak stimulus-response connection by means of an effective training procedure.

The symbol S^+ at the far right of the diagram symbolizes the positive reinforcer that follows the last response in the chain. It designates the "oil" that one must apply regularly to keep the chain rust free and strong.

Many behavioral sequences that you perform in everyday life are behavioral chains. Playing a particular song on a musical instrument, brushing your teeth in the morning, lacing and tying your shoes, and making a sandwich are all behavioral chains. But not all behavioral sequences are behavioral chains. Studying for an exam, writing an exam, and attending the next class to get your grade represent a general sequence of behavior that you experience in each of your courses. But this general sequence consists of a variety of activities (reading, memorizing, writing, etc.), with many breaks in the action (studying, then sleeping, then going to class, etc.). It is not made up of a consistent series of stimuli and responses in which each stimulus (except the last) is a conditioned reinforcer for the previous response and serves as an S^D for the next response.

METHODS FOR TEACHING A BEHAVIOR CHAIN

There are three major methods of teaching a stimulus-response chain. One method is called **total task presentation.** With this method, the student or client attempts all the steps from the beginning to the end of the chain on each trial and continues with total task trials until all steps are mastered. This was the strategy used to teach Agnes to assemble coffee packs.

A second major method of teaching a stimulus-response chain is called **backward chaining.** This method gradually constructs the chain in a reverse order from that in which the chain is performed. That is, the last step is established first, then the next-to-last step is taught and linked to the last step, then the third-from-last step is taught and linked to the last two steps, and so on, progressing backward toward the beginning of the chain. Backward chaining has been used in numerous programs, including teaching various dressing, grooming, and verbal behaviors to developmentally disabled individuals. To teach a developmentally disabled boy to put on a pair of slacks, for example, we break down the task into the following seven steps:

1. Taking the slacks from the dresser drawer.
2. Holding the slacks upright with the front facing away from the individual.
3. Putting one leg in the slacks.
4. Putting the other leg in the slacks.
5. Pulling the slacks all the way up.
6. Doing up the button or snap.
7. Doing up the zipper.

When we use backward chaining to teach an individual this chain, we start with the last step. The trainer helps the individual to put on the slacks so that all the steps are completed except for step 7. The individual is then taught to finish by doing up the zipper. When this has been taught, the trainer then starts the individual from step 6 and teaches him to finish from there. That is, the individual is taught to do up the button (step 6), which is the S^D for doing up the zipper, and to finish. When he consistently makes both responses in sequence, the slacks are pulled down to his ankles. He is then taught to pull them all the way up (step 5), which is the S^D for the response of step 6. On each trial, the individual completes all the steps learned previously. The training proceeds in this backward fashion, with one step being added at a time, until the individual can perform all seven steps.

Students often find backward chaining strange, apparently because they think that it teaches an individual to perform the chain backward, as the name suggests. Naturally, this is not true. There is a very good theoretical rationale for using backward chaining. Consider the example of teaching a developmentally disabled boy to put on a pair of slacks. By starting with step 7, the response of "doing up the zipper" was reinforced in the presence of the snap done up. Therefore, the sight of the snap done up became an S^D for step 7, doing up the zipper. On the basis of the principle of conditioned reinforcement, the sight of the snap done up also became a conditioned reinforcer for whatever preceded it. After several trials at step 7, the trainer went on to step 6. The behavior of doing up the snap produced the stimulus, sight of the snap done up. The sight of the snap done up had become a conditioned reinforcer, and it immediately followed performing step 6. Thus, when one uses backward chaining, the reinforcement of the last step in the presence of the appropriate stimulus, over trials, establishes that stimulus as a discriminative stimulus for the last step and as a conditioned reinforcer for the next-to-the-last step. When the step before the last is added, the S^D in that step also becomes a conditioned reinforcer, and so on. Thus, the power of the positive reinforcer that is presented at the end of the chain is transferred down the line to each S^D as it is added to the chain. In this way, backward chaining has a theoretical advantage of always having a built-in conditioned reinforcer to strengthen each new response that is added to the sequence.

The third major method of teaching a stimulus-response chain is called **forward chaining.** With this method, the initial step of the sequence is taught first, then the first and second steps are taught and linked together, then the first three steps, and so on until the entire chain is acquired. At least partly because backward chaining resembles a reversal of the natural order of things, forward chaining and total task presentation are used more often in everyday situations outside the behavior modification setting. Among the many examples that can be cited to illustrate forward chaining, consider the way in which a child might be taught to pronounce a word, such as "milk." He might be first taught to say "mm," then "mi," then "mil," and finally "milk."   **Note 1**

The three major chaining formats are diagrammed in Figure 11–1. Which is most effective? Bellamy, Horner, and Inman (1979) concluded that total task presentation has several practical advantages over the other chaining formats for teaching developmentally disabled persons. Total task presentation requires the

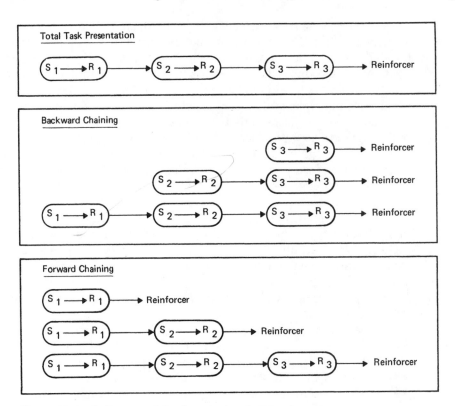

Figure 11–1   A diagram of the three major chaining formats.

trainer to spend less time in partial assembly or disassembly to prepare the task for training; it appears to focus on teaching response topography and response sequence simultaneously and, therefore, should produce results more quickly; and it appears to maximize the learner's independence early in training, especially if some steps are already familiar to the learner. Moreover, several studies have demonstrated that total task presentation is at least as good as, or better than, backward chaining or forward chaining for teaching various tasks to developmentally disabled persons (Martin, Koop, Turner, & Hanel, 1981; Spooner, 1984; Yu, Martin, Suthons, Koop, & Pallotta-Cornick, 1980). In general, total task presentation is probably also the method of choice for individuals who are not developmentally disabled. But there are some clear exceptions. For example, when giving driving instructions it is highly advisable to teach the use of the brake prior to the use of the accelerator (for obvious reasons!).

CHAINING COMPARED WITH FADING AND SHAPING

Chaining, fading, and shaping are sometimes called the *gradual change procedures* because they each involve progressing gradually through a series of steps to produce a new behavior or new stimulus control over a behavior. It is important to keep clear the distinctions among the three gradual change procedures.

In shaping, the steps consist of reinforcing closer and closer approximations to the final desired response (see Chapter 5). In fading, the steps consist of reinforcing the final desired response in the presence of closer and closer approximations to the final desired stimulus for that response (see Chapter 9). In chaining, the steps usually consist of reinforcing more and more of the specific stimulus-response links that comprise the chain. An exception to this is the method of total task presentation; in this case all the links are taught right from the beginning of training, and shaping or fading may be used to develop the responses or to bring them under the control of their appropriate stimuli. Because shaping or fading is used, the procedure is still a gradual change procedure. Table 11–1 summarizes some of the similarities and differences of the three procedures as they are typically applied.

FACTORS INFLUENCING THE EFFECTIVENESS OF CHAINING

1. Do a Task Analysis: Identify the Components of the Final Sequence

The behavioral sequence you wish to develop must be broken down into individual components, and the proper order of the sequence must be kept. The process of breaking a task down into smaller steps or component responses to facilitate training is referred to as **task analysis.** Examples of task analyses for teaching complex skills include apartment-upkeep skills (Williams & Cuvo, 1986), menstrual care skills (Richman, Reiss, Bauman, & Bailey, 1984), tennis skills (Buzas & Ayllon, 1981), play execution of the offensive backfield on a youth football team (Komaki & Barnett, 1977), leisure skills (Schleien, Wehman, & Kiernan, 1981), and pedestrian skills for walking safely through traffic (Page, Iwata, & Neef, 1976).

As with the selection of shaping steps (discussed in Chapter 5), the selection of chaining steps or components is somewhat subjective. The components should be simple enough to be learned without great difficulty. If you wanted to teach a severely developmentally disabled child to brush her teeth, it would be a mistake to consider the task in terms of the three gross steps of putting toothpaste on the brush, brushing, and rinsing. For the child to master the chain, each of these steps would have to be subdivided into even smaller steps. The components should also be selected so that there is a clear-cut stimulus or set of stimuli signaling the completion of each component. This will facilitate the development of those stimuli as conditioned reinforcers for preceding responses and as S^Ds for subsequent responses throughout the chain. For example, in utilizing chaining to teach a child appropriate hand-washing behavior, you might select putting water in the sink as one of the components. It would be important to specify a particular level of water, and perhaps even make a mark (at least temporarily) approximately halfway up the sink, to provide a very clear stimulus that terminates the end of this particular component (which you might define as "holding the water taps on until the water level reaches the halfway mark").

TABLE 11–1   SIMILARITIES AND DIFFERENCES AMONG SHAPING, FADING, AND CHAINING

	Shaping	Fading	Chaining
Terminal behavior	1. New behavior along some physical dimension such as topography, amount, or intensity.	1. New stimulus control of a particular behavior.	1. New sequence of responses, with a "clear-cut" stimulus signaling the end of each response and the start of the next.
	2. The final behavior consists of only the last shaping step.	2. The final stimulus control consists of only the last fading step.	2. The final behavior consists of all the chaining steps.
General training procedures	1. Often involves an unstructured environment in which the student has the opportunity to emit a variety of behaviors.	1. Typically involves a structured environment since the stimuli present must be controlled precisely.	1. Typically involves a semistructured or structured teaching environment.
	2. Proceeds in a forward fashion in terms of the "natural order" of behavior.	2. Proceeds in a forward fashion in terms of the "natural order" of behavior.	2. May proceed in a forward or backward fashion in terms of the "natural order" of behavior.
Other procedural considerations	1. Often involves instructional control; may involve some physical prompting at successive steps, but usually minimally. May also involve some fading at successive steps but this is unusual.	1. May involve some shaping, although this is unusual.	1. Frequently involves verbal and physical prompts, physical guidance, fading, and perhaps shaping at successive steps.
	2. Involves successive application of reinforcement and extinction.	2. Involves successive application of reinforcement; if extinction has to be used, fading has not proceeded optimally.	2. Typically involves fewer extinction trials than in shaping, because of the strong stimulus control established by prompting and fading at successive steps.

After completing your task analysis, review each of the controlling stimuli for each of the responses in the sequence. Ideally, each controlling stimulus should be clearly distinctive from the other controlling stimuli. If similar stimuli control different responses, there is a greater chance for error and confusion by the client. If, in your task analysis, two of the controlling stimuli are quite similar and there appears to be nothing you can do about it, then consider artificially coding one of the stimuli in some way to make acquisition of the chain easier.

2. Consider Strategies for Independent Use of Prompts by Students

Many clients may be able to use prompts independently to guide the mastery of a chain of behaviors. If the students are able to read, a *written task analysis* might effectively prompt clients to appropriately complete behavior chains (e.g., see Cuvo, Davis, O'Reilly, Mooney, & Crowley, 1992). If they are unable to read, a series of picture prompts might guide clients through behavior chains. For example, Thierman and Martin (1989) prepared a picture prompt album to guide severely developmentally disabled adults to complete behavior chains that improved the quality of their household cleaning. The clients were taught to look at the picture of an appropriate step, perform that step, and then transfer a self-monitoring adhesive dot to indicate that the step had been completed. The strategy proved to be quite effective. Another strategy that involves independent use of prompts to guide completion of behavioral chains involves reciting *self-instructions*. Developmentally disabled individuals, for example, have been taught to recite self-instructions in order to prompt correct completion of vocational tasks (Salend, Ellis, & Reynolds, 1989), completion of math problems correctly (Albion & Salzburg, 1982), and correctly sorting letters into boxes (Whitman, Spence, & Maxwell, 1987).

3. Conduct a Preliminary Modeling Trial

Before requiring your client to perform a sequence of responses, model the entire sequence while verbally describing the performance of each step. (Guidelines for modeling are described in Chapter 17.) If only one sample of the training task is available, the task must be disassembled after the modeling trial and components rearranged for the client to perform the task. Otherwise, the client can be trained using alternative samples of the task.

4. Begin Training the Behavioral Chain

Give the client an initial request to begin work and to complete the steps of the task.[2] For example, "Okay, Agnes, please assemble the coffee pack." If at any step the client stops responding or appears distracted, you should first provide a pac-

---

[2]The step or steps to begin with will depend on whether you use total task presentation, backward chaining, or forward chaining.

ing prompt such as "What's next?" or "Carry on." If the client performs a response incorrectly or fails to begin responding at any step within a reasonable period of time, you should proceed with error correction. Provide the necessary instructional and/or physical guidance to help the client perform that step correctly. After an error is corrected, go on to the next step.

5. Use Ample Social and Other Reinforcers

During each trial, the correct completion of each step should be praised immediately (Koop, Martin, Yu, & Suthons, 1980). In addition, the client should receive an additional reinforcer (such as an edible) contingent upon successful completion of the last step in the chain. As the client becomes more skillful in performing the steps, the praise can be eliminated gradually so that performance of the chain is eventually maintained by the single reinforcer at the end of the chain.

6. Decrease Extra Assistance at Individual Steps as Quickly as Possible

Depending on the details of the task analysis, it will likely be necessary to provide some additional instruction or physical assistance in correcting errors with clients. Across successive trials, this extra assistance should be faded as quickly as possible. It is important not to provide assistance to the point where you create a dependency in your client. That is, be careful not to reinforce the client for making errors or for waiting for your help at particular steps.

PITFALLS OF CHAINING

Just as relatively simple undesirable responses are often established inadvertently through the thoughtless administration of positive reinforcement, so also are undesirable chains. Probably the most common kind of undesirable chaining occurs when an inappropriate response precedes an appropriate response that is reinforced; both responses are thereby strengthened. An example of this type of chaining is the distracting habit exhibited by some speakers of prefacing each remark with "uh." A similar though somewhat more serious example is the making of bizarre facial expressions prior to each utterance.

Some seemingly sound behavior modification procedures can promote undesirable chaining if the behavior modifier is not careful. This was illustrated in a project by Olenick and Pear (1980) to teach names of pictures to developmentally disabled children. The children were given a question trial in which they were shown a picture to be named and were asked, "What's this?" Correct responses were reinforced. If the children made an error, they were then given an imitation trial in which the teacher presented the question and then immediately modeled the answer (e.g., "What's this? Cat"). Olenick and Pear (1980) observed that some children made a large number of errors even when it appeared that they could name the pictures appropriately. The researchers suggested that for these youngsters, a chain had developed in which errors on question trials were reinforced by imitation trials because an easier response (imitation) was reinforced on these trials. Olenick and Pear solved this problem by lowering the reinforcement rate for correct responses on imitation trials, while maintaining a high reinforcement rate for correct responses on question trials.

Self-control problems that plague many people provide several other examples of undesirable behavioral chains. Consider the problem of overeating. Although there are undoubtedly a variety of possible reasons for overeating, one of the more frequent causes may be the inadvertent development of undesirable behavioral chains. For example, it has been observed that some overweight people eat very rapidly. An examination of the behavioral sequence involved suggests the following chain: loading food onto the utensil, placing food in the mouth, reloading utensil while chewing the food, simultaneously swallowing the food while raising the next load of food to the mouth, and so forth. This behavioral chain can be broken successfully by extending the chain and introducing delays. A more desirable chain might be the following: loading food onto the utensil, placing food in the mouth, putting down the utensil, chewing the food, swallowing, waiting three seconds, reloading the utensil, and so on. In other words, in the undesirable chain the person gets ready to consume the next mouthful before even finishing the present one. A more desirable chain separates these components and introduces brief delays.

Another undesirable behavioral chain that is manifested by some overweight people consists of watching TV until a commercial comes on, going to the kitchen during the commercial, getting a snack, and returning to the TV program (which reinforces getting the snack). There are a variety of procedures for solving such self-control problems, and these are discussed more fully in Chapter 24. The point to remember here is that undesirable behaviors are frequently components of unintentionally developed behavioral chains.

Note 2

GUIDELINES FOR THE EFFECTIVE USE OF CHAINING

One should observe the following rules when developing stimulus-response chains:

1. Do a task analysis. Identify the units of the chain that are simple enough to be learned without great difficulty by the individual to whom you are teaching the chain.
2. The units must be taught in the proper sequence. Otherwise, poor stimulus control will develop in that when one step is completed it will not necessarily be a discriminative stimulus for the next step, but rather may control some other step (as when a young child learns to count incorrectly, for example, 1, 2, 4, 3).
3. To expedite learning, use a fading procedure to decrease extra help that may be needed by a client to perform some of the steps.
4. If you are using backward or forward chaining, make sure that on each trial the student performs the entire set of components learned up to that point.

5. Early in training, use ample reinforcement for correct performance of individual steps. Gradually decrease this reinforcement as the client becomes more skillful.
6. Make sure that the reinforcement provided at the end of the chain conforms to the guidelines for the effective application of positive reinforcement given in Chapter 3. The more effective this terminal reinforcement, the more stable the chain of responses. This does not mean, however, that once a chain is developed it must be reinforced each time it occurs in order to be maintained. After Agnes had been taught to assemble a coffee pack, coffee pack assembly could be viewed as a single response, which could, if desired, be put on any intermittent reinforcement schedule.

STUDY QUESTIONS

1. Why was the coffee pack assembly program for Agnes divided into 15 steps (as opposed to, say, 4 or 40 steps)?
2. Briefly describe the chaining procedure used to teach Agnes to assemble coffee packs.
3. Describe or define a stimulus-response chain, and give an example other than the examples in this chapter.
4. Why do you suppose a behavioral chain is called a chain?
5. In a chain, a given stimulus is both an S^D and a conditioned reinforcer. How can this be? Explain with an example.
6. Using examples, distinguish between a behavioral sequence that is a chain and one that is not a chain.
7. In the behavioral chain of driving a car, accelerating, and changing gears (assume that you have a four-speed transmission), how is the chain of the driver who has a tachometer (and uses it) different from the chain of the driver who does not have a tachometer?
8. Name and describe briefly three major chaining methods.
9. Describe how each of the three major chaining methods might be used to teach bed making.
10. Which of the major chaining methods do the authors recommend, and why?
11. Distinguish among the types of terminal behavior typically established by shaping, fading, and chaining.
12. What is meant by the term *task analysis*? Describe a plausible task analysis appropriate for teaching a three-year-old child the behavior of tying a knot in a shoelace.
13. Briefly describe three strategies to help individuals use prompts independently to guide the mastery of a chain of behaviors.
14. Give an example of a pitfall of chaining. Explain how this pitfall can be avoided.

APPLICATION EXERCISES

A. Exercises Involving Others

1. Describe how you might use chaining to teach a child to lace his or her shoes.
2. Describe how you might use chaining to teach a child to tie a knot.
3. Describe how you might use chaining to teach a child to tie a bow.
4. Try out your chaining programs in application exercises 1–3 and see how they work.

B. Self-Modification Exercise

Identify a behavioral deficit of yours that might be amenable to a chaining procedure. Describe in detail how you might use the guidelines for the effective use of chaining to overcome this deficit.

NOTES AND EXTENDED DISCUSSION

1. In a variation on forward chaining referred to as the *pure part* method, different parts of a chain are taught separately and then all are combined to form a whole. Suppose that you wished to teach someone to swim using a front crawl stroke. With appropriate guidance and flotation devices, the student might first be taught the proper arm stroke, then the proper kick, and then proper head turning and breathing. Finally, all three parts would be put together into one entire or whole sequence. Weld and Evans (1990) found little difference between pure part learning and total task presentation on teaching severely and moderately developmentally disabled adolescents to prepare a bag of lunch and to make a greeting card.

2. Chains that contain a response member that is not necessary for reinforcement are called *adventitious chains,* and the process that produces them is called *adventitious chaining.* Special care often needs to be taken to avoid undesirable adventitious chaining.

Study Questions on Note

1. Describe the pure part method of chaining. How does it differ from standard forward chaining?
2. Describe an example of an adventitious chain that is not from this chapter.

Transferring Behavior to New Settings and Making It Last: Generality of Behavioral Change

"Hi, there. I have a nice surprise for you in my car."

TEACHING STAN TO PROTECT HIMSELF

During recess time, four-year-old Stan was playing with a toy near the edge of his preschool playground, unaware that a stranger was observing him intently from a distance. No teacher was in sight. Gradually, the stranger approached until he was standing beside Stan.

"Hi, there," said the stranger, "What's your name?"

"Stan," the boy replied.

"Nice day, isn't it, Stan?"

The stranger engaged Stan in small talk for a few minutes. Then, casting his eyes around the school yard, the stranger casually asked, "Stan, how would you like to go for a walk with me?"

The stranger seemed friendly and Stan was used to taking directions from adults. He stood up and approached the stranger. Just then, a teacher appeared and the stranger quickly moved away.

An attempted child abduction? Not exactly. The stranger was actually an assistant in an experiment designed to study a method of teaching self-protection to young children, and Stan was being tested to determine his suitability for the experiment.[1] He and two other children (Patti and John), who also appeared susceptible to lures often used by child molestors, were included in the experiment. The children were tested several times to verify that they would go with a stranger

---

[1]This case is based on an experiment by Poche, Brouwer, and Swearingen (1981).

who approached them using any of several kinds of lures (e.g., "Your teacher said it was all right for you to come with me" and "I have a nice surprise in my car. Would you like to come and see it?"). Then training was begun. Two adult trainers acted out a scene in which one trainer approached the other and used one of the lures. The other trainer responded with, "No, I have to go ask my teacher," and ran toward the school building. The child was then instructed to respond in the same way as the second trainer to the lure of the first trainer and was provided with social reinforcement (e.g., praise) that was occasionally followed with material and activity reinforcement (e.g., stickers, playing on the swings) when he or she did so.

Responses were trained to one lure per day. When a child consistently responded correctly to the first lure, responding was trained to a second lure, and then to a third lure. In addition to the lures being varied in this manner, the exact location of each session on the school grounds was also varied by approximately 75 feet. After training was completed, each child was tested in a community setting to determine if the response established during training would be performed in a novel setting. All three children responded correctly to the lures in that setting. After 12 weeks, Stan and Patti were tested again in the community setting. Stan continued to respond perfectly, whereas Patti made the correct verbal response but stayed in the vicinity of the stranger.

GENERALITY

We say that training produces *generality* when the trained behavior transfers from the training situation to the natural environment, when training leads to the development of new behavior that has *not* been specifically trained, or when the trained behavior is maintained in the natural environment over time. But before examining strategies for programming for generality of behavior change over these three areas, it is helpful to know about stimulus generalization and response generalization.

Stimulus Generalization

Stimulus generalization occurs when behavior becomes more probable in the presence of one stimulus or situation as a result of having been reinforced in the presence of another stimulus or situation. Thus, stimulus generalization is the opposite of stimulus discrimination. There are several reasons for the occurrence of stimulus generalization.

Stimulus Generalization Due to Physical Similarity The more physically similar two stimuli are, the more stimulus generalization will occur between them. This is an inherited (i.e., unlearned) characteristic. There are many examples of such stimulus generalization in everyday life. Consider a case that is familiar to many parents: an infant learns to say "doggy" to a large, hairy, four-legged creature with floppy ears and a friendly bark. Later, the infant sees a different kind of large dog and says "doggy." This is an instance of stimulus generalization, because a previously reinforced response ("doggy") was emitted in the presence of a new stimulus (a new kind of dog) that was physically similar to the first stimulus. Still later, the infant sees a small pony, and again says "doggy." This is likely another instance of stimulus generalization, even though the response in this case is incorrect, which proves that not all instances of stimulus generalization are favorable, and illustrates why it is necessary to teach discriminations, as described in Chapter 8.

Stimulus Generalization Due to Conceptual Learning   Consider a red pencil and a red automobile. As adults, we can easily recognize them as being similar (defined in terms of a particular wavelength of light) in the sense that both are red. But to a child these stimuli are very different, and a child may not show stimulus generalization from the pencil to the car. And although a child may show stimulus generalization from one type of large dog to another type of large dog, the child might not show generalization from a large German shepherd to a tiny Chihuahua. Stimulus generalization is not likely to occur in the latter case until the child has learned the stimulus class "dog." A *stimulus class* is a set of stimuli, all of which have some physical characteristic in common. For example, look around the room you are in and list the objects you see that are red. These objects constitute the stimulus class that we might label "red objects." Although these objects are different in many respects, they all have the color red in common. Another word for stimulus class is *concept*. To teach a child the concept red, you might reinforce the response "red" to many different red-colored objects, and extinguish that response to objects that are not red. To teach the concept of wetness, you would reinforce the response "wet" to many different wet objects, and extinguish that response (and reinforce the response "dry") to dry objects.

When an individual emits an appropriate response to all the members of a stimulus class and does not emit that response to stimuli that do not belong to the class, we say that the individual generalizes to all members within a stimulus class (or concept) and discriminates between stimulus classes (e.g., between red objects and blue objects). When an individual responds in this manner, such as to the concept "red," we say that the individual is showing conceptual behavior (Keller & Schoenfeld, 1950, p. 155). In Stan's case, Stan demonstrated appropriate conceptual behavior to the concept "stranger," and responded correctly to a stranger's lures in the community setting, even though he had been trained to do so to different strangers in a different setting. A follow-up study (Poche, Yoder, & Miltenberger, 1988) has shown that the training stimulus in such programs need not be a real person; many children will appropriately reject a stranger's lures when the training is by videotape.

It is important to note that verbal behavior is not necessarily involved in conceptual behavior. Pigeons, although completely nonverbal, can readily learn a surprising range of concepts. By presenting slides to them and reinforcing pecks at slides that are exemplars of a particular concept while withholding reinforcement for pecks at slides that are not exemplars of that concept, researchers have taught pigeons concepts such as "person," "a specific person" (i.e., the same person dressed differently, in many different poses and situations), "human-made objects," "tree," "fish," and some number concepts such as "16 versus 20" (Herrnstein & deVilliers, 1980; Herrnstein & Loveland, 1964; Herrnstein, Loveland, & Cable, 1976; Vaughan & Herrnstein, 1987; Honig & Stewart, 1988; Lubow, 1974). The proof that the pigeons have learned a concept is that they generalize to new instances of it; that is, they respond correctly to new exemplars that they have not experienced. Presumably the pigeons are responding to some physical similarity between instances of a given concept, although what it is in most cases has thus far defied analysis.

Stimulus Generalization Due to Equivalence Classes   With stimulus generalization due to physical similarity, an individual will respond to a new stimulus because that new stimulus is physically quite similar to an S^D that was present in stimulus discrimination training. With stimulus generalization due to conceptual learning, an individual responds to a new stimulus because the individual has learned that the new stimulus has a characteristic in common with the original S^D, even though the new stimulus and the original S^D have many differing characteristics. But often we generalize from one stimulus to another when the stimuli are completely dissimiliar and have no common feature. If you are told, for example, to drop off a term paper at a door marked with a "3," you could do so whether the door was marked "three" or "3" or "III" or " ∴". Although these four stimuli are very different, they are *functionally equivalent* in the sense that they would all control the same behavior. Procedures to establish functional equivalence of physically different stimuli are referred to generally as **stimulus equivalence training** (Sidman & Tailby, 1982).

Studies of stimulus equivalence have commonly used a matching-to-sample training format. Suppose that a three-year-old child is shown one of the training panels in Figure 12–1. When Panel 1 is presented, the number 3 appears in the top box and the child is encouraged to press one of the three bottom boxes. If the child presses the correct box (the one showing the three dots), the child is reinforced with an edible. Across trials, either the first, second, or third training panel is randomly presented. Within each training panel, the position of the correct response in the bottom three positions is randomly changed across trials. When the child correctly and consistently matches the 3 to ∴, and ∴ to III, and III to three, then the test panel is presented (see Figure 12–1). When presented with "three" as the display, will the child correctly match it to ∴? If the answer is "yes," then three and ∴ have become members of a stimulus equivalence class. Thus, if the **Note 1** child who had completed the above experiment then learns the Spanish word for three, that Spanish word is also likely to occur under appropriate circumstances to all of the other members of the equivalence class for three shown in Figure 12–1.

As we grow up, we acquire many equivalence classes where all members of a class control the same response, but where the members of the class are physically very different. And when a new behavior occurs to one member of an equivalence class, that behavior is likely to be controlled by other members of the class without explicit training. In everyday speech, we would say that the members of **Note 2** stimulus equivalence classes "mean" the same thing.

Stimulus equivalence is readily demonstrated in verbally competent individuals, but unlike conceptual learning (see previous paragraphs), it has not been demonstrated conclusively with severely language-disabled individuals or with animals (Devany, Hayes, & Nelson, 1986; Hayes, 1989). There are two possible reasons for this. One is that only individuals who can learn language can learn stimulus equivalence classes, because the brain structures required to learn language are the same ones required to learn stimulus equivalence classes. The other

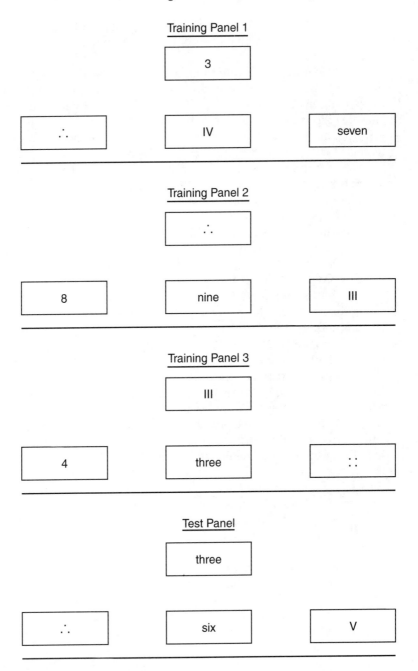

Figure 12–1   Visual displays in a stimulus equivalence experiment.

possibility is that the ability to learn stimulus equivalence classes develops from being trained on many different stimulus equivalence relations, and this kind of training is necessarily involved when we learn language (as when we learn the different representations of the number "three," the different words for "drinking utensil," that tomatoes and mushrooms are both "vegetables," and so on).

Response Generalization

Not to be confused with stimulus generalization is a phenomenon called *response generalization*. This occurs when a behavior becomes more probable in the presence of a stimulus or situation as a result of another behavior having been strengthened in the presence of that stimulus or situation. Like stimulus generalization, response generalization occurs for several reasons.

Response Generalization Due to Physical Similarity   The more physically similar two responses are, the more response generalization will occur between them. If, for example, you learn a forehand shot in racquetball, chances are that you would be able to perform a forehand shot in squash or tennis. The responses involved are very similar. Similarly, you will probably find roller blading relatively easy to learn if you have first learned to ice skate, because the responses involved in the two activities are similar.

Response Generalization Due to Response Conceptual Learning   Just as there are large classes of stimuli that share a common characteristic while differing in many other characteristics, there are also widely different responses that share a common characteristic. We call learning to show response generalization within classes of responses with a common characteristic **response conceptual learning** (to distinguish it from stimulus conceptual learning, as discussed previously). Perhaps the clearest examples of response conceptual classes consist of verbal responses, such as English plural nouns which usually share the common characteristic of ending in "s."

A child who has learned to add "s" to the ends of words pertaining to more than one object or event may show response generalization even when it is grammatically incorrect (e.g., saying "foots" instead of "feet" while looking at a picture of two feet). In Stan's case, if a stranger tried to lure Stan and he said, "No, I have to ask my mother [instead of my teacher]," this would be an example of response conceptual generalization because the two sentences are different but have a common grammatical structure and share some of the same words.

Response Generalization Due to Equivalence Classes   Just as stimuli can be members of equivalence classes, so can responses. If you are asked to start a fire, for example, you might obtain and strike a match, flip a cigarette lighter, place a stick in an existing fire and use it to start a new fire, or perhaps even rub two sticks together. As another example, a child who learns to "be honest" might tell the truth, return valued articles left or dropped by others, and refrain from copying another student's answers. All of these responses are functionally equivalent in the sense that they are likely to bring praise from various members of the child's community.

An important application of response equivalence classes in applied settings is termed **behavioral momentum.** As a result of some members of a response equivalence class being emitted and reinforced, the probability of other members occurring momentarily increases. For example, there are certain instructions that a child is likely to follow but others that he or she is unlikely to follow. Following instructions in general is a response equivalence class. Thus, to increase the probability that the child will follow instructions he or she normally does not follow, it is often effective to first give the child instructions that he or she is likely to follow and reinforce compliance with those instructions. If the instructions that the child is less likely to follow are then given soon after this, the chances are greatly increased that he or she will follow them (Mace & Belfiore, 1990; Mace et al., 1988; Singer, Singer, & Horner, 1987).

Note 3

The Importance of Generality

To be effective, a therapeutic behavioral change must show *stimulus generalization* from the training situation to the natural environment, and it should also sometimes show *response generalization* to new behaviors. Therapeutic behavioral change must also be *maintained* in the natural environment. **Programming for generality** of behavioral change is concerned with these three areas. In an important article, Stokes and Baer (1977) described a number of strategies for programming for generality. We will describe these strategies under the categories of programming for stimulus generalization, response generalization, and behavior maintenance.

FACTORS INFLUENCING THE EFFECTIVENESS
OF PROGRAMMING GENERALITY
OF BEHAVIORAL CHANGE

1. Programming Stimulus Generalization

In discussing generality, we distinguish two situations: (a) the *training* situation and (b) the *target* situation—a situation in which we want generality to occur. The target situation is usually, but not necessarily, the natural environment. The initial occurrence of stimulus generalization depends critically on the physical similarity between the training and target situations. The more similar they are, the more stimulus generalization (and hence the less discrimination) there will be between

Note 4　them.

a. Train in the Target Situation　Thus, the first effort of the behavior modifier attempting to program stimulus generalization should be to make the final stages of the training situation similar to the target situation in as many ways as possible. Other things being equal, the best way in which to do this is to train in the target situation itself.

b. Vary the Training Conditions　This might be done by conducting training sessions with relatively little control over the stimuli presented in the presence of which correct responses are reinforced. If behaviors are brought under the control of a greater variety of stimuli during training, then there is an increased probability of some of those stimuli being present in the target situation. Thus, in the lead case for this chapter, no attempt was made to control background stimuli, such as playground and traffic noise, as might be done in more basic research.

c. Program Common Stimuli   A third tactic is to program common stimuli deliberately by developing the behavior to specific stimuli that are present in both the training and target settings. For example, H. M. Walker and Buckley (1972) described a program in which social and academic classroom behaviors were taught to children in a remedial classroom. Stimulus generalization to the regular academic classroom was assured by using the same academic materials (i.e., common stimuli) in both classrooms.

A useful strategy for programming common stimuli is to bring the desired behavior under the control of instructions or rules that the student can rehearse in novel situations (Guevremont, Osnes, & Stokes, 1986; Stokes & Osnes, 1986). Stan might have been taught the rule, "If someone approaches me whom I don't know, I should tell them that I have to go to my teacher and then run to the school building." Rehearsal of an appropriate rule in novel settings might lead to desired behavior, even though the stimuli in the novel settings are physically dissimilar to the stimuli that were present during training. (Rule control over behavior is discussed further in Chapter 16.)

d. Train Sufficient Stimulus Exemplars   A fourth tactic, one that Stokes and Baer (1977) considered to be one of the most valuable areas for programming generality, is called *training sufficient stimulus exemplars*. With this technique, "generalization to untrained stimulus conditions . . . is programmed by the training of sufficient exemplars (rather than all) of these stimulus conditions." Thus, in the lead case for this chapter, training occurred in several different places in the schoolyard and with several different lures.

2. Programming Response Generalization

It appears that there has been less concern in the literature for tactics for programming response generalization than there has been for programming stimulus generalization. This may be because there is a great emphasis in our educational system on teaching students the "correct" answers to questions. Variations on correct answers (that may show response generalization) are either not accepted or are followed by reinforcers of an inferior quality (such as a *B* instead of an *A* as a grade on a mathematics exam). Nevertheless, there are some strategies for programming response generalization, two of which are described now.

a. Train Sufficient Response Exemplars   A strategy for programming response generalization is similar to that for training sufficient stimulus exemplars. This is referred to as *training sufficient response exemplars* (Stokes & Baer, 1977). Guess, Sailor, Rutherford, and Baer (1968) taught a developmentally disabled girl to use plural nouns correctly in speech with this technique. With appropriate prompting and reinforcement, they first taught the girl to name objects correctly in the singular and the plural when presented with one object (e.g., cup) and two objects (e.g., cups). They continued in this way until, after a number of exemplars of the correct singular and plural labels had been taught, the girl appropriately named new objects in the plural even though only the singular labels for these objects had been taught. Thus, the girl showed response generalization.

Note 5

b. **Vary the Acceptable Responses During Training**   Another strategy is to vary deliberately the responses that are acceptable during training. For example, in developing creativity, Goetz and Baer (1973) deliberately reinforced children during block building in a nursery school setting for any response that was different from prior block building responses. This tactic led to an increase in the creative block building demonstrated by the children.

3. Programming Behavior Maintenance

It is one thing to program stimulus generalization to a new setting, or response generalization to new behaviors. It's another thing for a therapeutic behavioral change to last (in those new settings or with those new behaviors). Maintenance depends critically on whether the behavior will continue to be reinforced. Stimulus generalization occurs each time you program generality to a new setting. But making it last in that new setting is a problem of maintenance. There are four general approaches to the problem of achieving lasting generality or maintenance in target situations.

a. **Behavioral Trapping: Allow Natural Contingencies of Reinforcement to Take Effect**   In a **behavioral trap,** reinforcers in the natural environment maintain a behavior that was initially developed by programmed reinforcers (Baer & Wolf, 1970; Kohler & Greenwood, 1986). Making use of a behavioral trap can be a very effective way to program generality. This approach requires the behavior modifier to realistically identify contingencies in the natural environment and then to tailor the target behavior so that it will be trapped (i.e., maintained) by those contingencies. Talking is an obvious example of behavior that is heavily reinforced in most environments. After speech has been established in a training situation, it may continue unabated in the natural environment because of the natural contingencies of reinforcement for it there. Indeed, it often seems necessary only to establish vocal imitation and a few object-naming responses for the natural contingencies of reinforcement to take over and develop functional speech behavior. As another example, behavioral trapping might be involved in overcoming a child's shyness. Playing with other children is a behavior that might gradually be shaped in a shy child. Once this behavior is strongly established, however, the behavior modifier probably will not have to worry about reinforcing it further. The other children will take care of that themselves in the course of their play, for, indeed, that is what social play is all about. Another example of behavioral trapping is shown in Figure 12–2.

b. **Change the Behavior of People in the Natural Environment**   A second approach to the problem of achieving lasting generality is usually more difficult than the first. It involves actually changing the contingencies in the target situation so that they will maintain the behavior that has generalized from the training

Figure 12–2 An example of behavioral trapping.

situation. In following this approach, it is necessary to work with people in the target situation—ward staff, parents, teachers, neighbors, and others who have contact with the target behavior. The behavior modifier must teach these individuals how to reinforce the behavior (if it is desirable) or how to extinguish it (if it is undesirable) appropriately. The behavior modifier must also occasionally reinforce the appropriate behavior of these individuals—at least until it comes into contact with the improved target behavior, which will then, ideally, reinforce their continued application of the appropriate procedures.

As an example of this second approach, consider the case of a child living at home who has shown a very high frequency of tantrumming. Possibly this is her sole means of gaining attention and other reinforcers from her parents. There is little doubt that more desirable behaviors could be established in a training situation, but such behaviors would not be maintained in the home situation unless the contingencies operating there were changed. A behavior modifier called in on this case might therefore adopt the following plan. In a training situation designed to teach the child to play with toys rather than to tantrum, the behavior modifier would first adjust the desired behavior to an appropriate schedule—for instance, VI/LH with infrequent reinforcement (because it will not be practical for the parents to give frequent reinforcement in the home environment). Having accomplished this, the behavior modifier would begin generalization training in the home environment. The behavior modifier would show the mother how to keep accurate records of the child's desirable and undesirable behavior. At first, the mother, with the help and prompting of the behavior modifier, would frequently reinforce the child for playing with her toys in the living room. Gradually, she would decrease the frequency of reinforcement to have more time for activities that did not involve the child. She would use a kitchen timer, or similar device, to remind herself to reinforce the child. Throughout this procedure, the behavior modifier would frequently reinforce the mother for appropriately managing and recording the child's behavior. Then the behavior modifier would fade out of the situation by visiting less and less frequently to check the mother's records. But if the program deteriorated, he or she would temporarily stop the fading process and spend enough time in the training situation to correct matters. Ideally, the mother's behavior of appropriately reinforcing the target behavior would eventually be maintained by the child's good play behavior and her decreased whining, crying, and tantrumming.

c. Use Intermittent Schedules of Reinforcement in the Target Situation   After a behavior has generalized to a target situation, it may be desirable to reinforce the behavior deliberately in the target situation on an intermittent schedule for at least a few reinforced trials. The intermittent schedule should make that behavior more persistent in the target situation and thereby increase the probability of the behavior lasting until it can come under the control of natural reinforcers.

d. Give the Control to the Individual   A subarea within behavior modification has been concerned with helping individuals to apply behavior modification to themselves. This area, which has been referred to as *self-management, self-modification*, and behavioral *self-control*, has produced many books containing easy-to-follow "how-to-do-it" procedures that help individuals to manage their own behavior. This area is discussed more fully in Chapter 24. Concerning the problem of maintaining behavior in target situations, giving the control to the individual might occur in one of two major ways. First, it might be possible to teach an individual to assess and record instances of his or her own generalized behavior and apply a specific procedure to that behavior as suggested in Chapter 24. Second, as suggested by Stokes and Baer (1977), it might be possible to teach an individual a means of *recruiting a natural community of reinforcement* to maintain generalized responding. For example, in a study by Hildebrand, Martin, Furer, and Hazen (1990), some of the developmentally disabled workers in a sheltered workshop usually showed very low productivity. On the few occasions when they worked at a high rate, they received little feedback from staff. Hildebrand and colleagues taught the workers to meet a productivity goal, and then to call staff members' attention to their good work. This led to increased feedback for the workers from the staff, and helped to maintain a higher level of productivity by the workers.

PITFALLS OF GENERALITY

All the components of generality have potential pitfalls as well as positive aspects. Consider stimulus generalization. Without stimulus generalization, learning would be of very limited value. No matter how perfectly a person learned something, he or she would have to learn it all over again every time the situation changed even slightly. (Just imagine how annoying it would be to learn to dance to a piece of music only to discover that you had to learn to dance all over again when a new song was played.) But stimulus generalization has its disadvantages too, in that a behavior learned in a situation in which it is appropriate may then emerge inconveniently in a situation in which it is inappropriate.

A conspicuous example of the stimulus generalization of a desirable behavior to an inappropriate situation that can often be seen among developmentally disabled individuals involves greetings and displays of affection. Of course, it is highly desirable for these behaviors to occur under appropriate circumstances; but when an individual walks up to and hugs a total stranger, the results can be less than favorable for a number of obvious reasons. The solution to this problem is to teach the individual to discriminate between situations in which different forms of greetings and expressions of affection are appropriate and situations in which they are inappropriate.

Another example of inappropriate stimulus generalization of a desirable behavior may be the destructive competitiveness demonstrated frequently by some individuals and occasionally by all of us. Such behavior may stem in part from the strong reinforcement given in our culture for winning in sports and for achieving high grades in our educational system. As a wise person once remarked, "It may be true that wars have been won on the playing fields of Eton, but they have also been started there."

The opposite type of problem is the stimulus generalization of an undesirable behavior from the situation in which it developed to a new situation for which it is also undesirable. Suppose that an overly protective grandparent, while supervising a grandchild who is learning how to walk, provides a great deal of attention each time the child falls (presumably out of a concern that the child might be injured). As a result, falling increases in frequency. When the child is returned to the parents, the excessive falling might generalize to their presence as well.

A different pitfall is a lack of desirable stimulus generalization. This can be seen in the typical study habits of students. Frequently, students cram for exams the night before the examination. They memorize certain verbal chains in response to certain prompts and questions. What they frequently fail to consider is the importance of bringing their knowledge of the material under broader stimulus control than just one or two questions; that is, they do not program for generalization. A great many people have had the same experience with learning a second language. One of the authors was among the many who took a second language during four years of high school. At the end of that time, he was clearly incapable of speaking the language. He had a certain repertoire for answering questions on French exams, translating English articles into French, and translating French articles into English, but this repertoire had not been brought under the stimulus control of a typical conversational setting.

Another example of lack of desirable stimulus generalization occurs in the interaction between parents and their children. In various social situations, such as restaurants, parents frequently do not present the same stimuli to their children, or provide the same contingencies of reinforcement, that they present at mealtimes in the home situation. Consequently, the children frequently do not generalize their table manners and good behaviors that occur at home to the restaurant or other social settings. It is not uncommon to hear a parent lament, "I thought I taught you how to be a good child, and now look at you." We hope that after reading this book and performing the study questions and study exercises, the same parents will do a much better job of programming stimulus generalization. (If not, you will probably hear us lament, "I thought I taught you how to be a good behavior modifier, and now look at you.")

The pitfalls just listed indicate how stimulus generalization can work to the disadvantage of those who are ignorant of it. There are also many pitfalls for programming maintenance of behavior change. These were described at the end of Chapters 6 and 7 concerning schedules of reinforcement.

GUIDELINES FOR PROGRAMMING GENERALITY OF BEHAVIORAL CHANGE

To ensure stimulus and response generalization from the training situation to the natural environment, and to ensure behavior maintenance, the behavior modifier should observe the following rules as closely as possible:

1. Choose target behaviors that are clearly useful to the individual, as these are the behaviors that are most likely to be reinforced in the natural environment.
2. Teach the target behavior in a situation that is as similar as possible to the environment in which you want the behavior to occur.
3. Vary the training conditions so as to maximally sample relevant stimulus dimensions for transfer to other situations and to reinforce various forms of the desirable behavior.
4. Establish the target behavior successively in as many situations as is feasible, starting with the easiest and progressing to the most difficult.
5. Program common stimuli (such as rules) that might faciliate transfer to novel environments.
6. Vary the acceptable responses in the training settings.
7. Gradually reduce the frequency of reinforcement in the training situation until it is less than that occurring in the natural environment.

8. When changing to a new situation, increase the frequency of reinforcement in that situation to offset the tendency of the individual to discriminate the new situation from the previous training situation.
9. Make sure that sufficient reinforcement for maintaining the target behavior occurs in the natural environment. This rule requires especially close attention in the early stages of transferring the target behavior from the training situation to the natural environment. Add reinforcement as necessary, including reinforcement to those people (such as parents and teachers) who are responsible for maintaining the target behavior in the natural environment, and then decrease this reinforcement slowly enough to prevent the target behavior from deteriorating.

STUDY QUESTIONS

1. Define stimulus generalization and give an example.
2. What do we mean by stimulus class? By conceptual behavior? Describe an example of each.
3. Describe how you might teach the concept "honest" to a child. Would your program teach a child to be honest? Why or why not?
4. What is a primary distinction between stimulus generalization involving concepts and stimulus generalization involving equivalence classes?
5. Define or describe response generalization due to physical similarity, and give an example.
6. Define or describe response generalization due to response conceptual learning, and give an example.
7. Define or describe response generalization due to response equivalence classes, and give an example.
8. Which of the strategies for programming stimulus generalization appear to capitalize on stimulus generalization due to physical similarity? Justify your choices.
9. List the three aspects of programming for behavioral generality. Describe an example of each aspect.
10. Briefly describe how behavioral generality was demonstrated in the experiment to teach self-protection skills to children.
11. Explain the difference between stimulus generalization and stimulus discrimination. Describe examples illustrating the difference.
12. Briefly describe four tactics for programming stimulus generalization. Give an example of each.
13. How might the teaching of a rule facilitate stimulus generalization? State the general factor for programming for generalization that seems to be operating, and illustrate with an example.
14. Briefly describe two tactics for programming response generalization. Give an example of each.
15. Briefly describe four tactics for programming behavior maintenance in a target situation. Give an example of each.
16. What do we mean by behavioral trapping? Give an example.
17. Give two examples of a pitfall of stimulus generalization, one of which involves generalization of a desirable behavior to an inappropriate situation and the other of which involves generalization of an undesirable behavior.
18. Give an example of a pitfall of response generalization.
19. Give an example of a pitfall of behavior maintenance.

APPLICATION EXERCISES

A. Exercise Involving Others

1. Choose one of the cases described in the previous chapters in which there was no effort to program generality. Outline a specific plausible program for producing generality in that case.

B. Self-Modification Exercises

1. Describe a recent situation in which you generalized in a desirable way. Clearly identify the behavior, the training situation, and the test situation.
2. Describe a recent situation in which you generalized in an undesirable way (in other words, the outcome was undesirable). Again, identify the behavior, training situation, and test situation.
3. Consider the behavior deficit for which you outlined a shaping program at the end of Chapter 5. Assuming that your shaping program will be successful, discuss what you might do to program generality. (See the factors influencing the effectiveness of generality that were discussed earlier in this chapter.)

NOTES AND EXTENDED DISCUSSION

1. Technically, stimulus equivalence requires the demonstration of three relationships, reflexivity, symmetry, and transitivity. Consider the top panel in Figure 12–1. Suppose, after training, that the child learns to correctly press the panel "∴" when shown "3" as the sample. After training, we then place "∴" in the top panel and "3" is then randomly placed with the other two choices. If the child, when now shown ∴, correctly identifies "3", the child has demonstrated symmetry. Reflexivity is a simpler relationship and simply involves recognizing instances of a stimulus. In other words, a child is able to match 3 to 3, ∴ to ∴, and III to III. Transitivity is the type of relationship successfully demonstrated when the child passes the test in the fourth panel shown in Figure 12–1. In other words, as a result of learning to match A to B and B to C, an individual now matches A to C without specific training to do so. For a description of a behavioral framework within which to view stimulus equivalence, see Hayes (1991) and Barnes (1994).

2. Since Skinner (1957) published a behavioral account of language, psycholinguists have argued that operant conditioning is inadequate to explain a child's acquisition of his or her native language (Brown, 1973; Chomsky, 1959; Pinker, 1994). Their argument is based largely on the view that children learn more about language than is directly trained or directly reinforced. However, through automatic conditioned reinforcement (described in Note 2 of Chapter 10), infants are able to emit vocal behaviors that have not been directly reinforced. And through stimulus equivalence training, children can learn that physically different sounds can "mean" the same thing as other sounds, provided that they are members of the same equivalence class, and even though some of those sounds have not been directly paired with each other. Such factors can explain the acquisition of syntax and grammar, and provide empirical support for Skinner's behavioral view of language development (Stromer, Mackay, & Remington, 1996).

3. The term **behavioral momentum** also refers to the fact that adding reinforcements in the presence of an S^D for a response increases that response's resistance to change even if the added reinforcements are not contingent on that response (Nevin, 1992). For example, providing extra reinforcement to developmentally disabled individuals receiving reinforcement (in the form of popcorn and coffee) for sorting dinnerware decreased the disruptive effect that a video music/dance program played at the same time had on their sorting behavior, even though the extra reinforcement was not contingent on the sorting behavior (Mace, McCurdy, & Quigley, 1990). Although the two uses of the term "behavioral momentum" pinpoint two sets of real phenomena, it is not clear that using this term to describe both sets is theoretically justified (Plaud & Gaither, 1996). (Thus, we might say that theoreticians have perhaps responded inappropriately by putting these two sets of phenomena into the same stimulus equivalence class.)

4. An example of this occurred in a study by S. J. Welch and Pear (1980) in which objects, pictures of objects, and photographs of the objects were compared as training stimuli for naming responses in four severely developmentally disabled children in a special training room. It was found that three of the four children displayed considerably more generalization to the objects in their natural environment when they were trained with the objects rather than the pictures or photographs of the objects. The fourth child, who was also the most proficient linguistically, displayed substantial generalization regardless of the type of training stimulus used. A follow-up study by Salmon, Pear, and Kuhn (1986) indicates that training with objects also produces more generalization to untrained objects in the same stimulus class than does training with pictures. The results therefore suggest that parents and teachers of severely developmentally disabled children should use objects as training stimuli as much as possible whenever generalization to these stimuli is desired.

5. This instance of response generalization (as is true with the examples given on page 149) is somewhat more complex than our straightforward definition given at the beginning of this chapter. It does appear, in this example, that the reinforcement of a specific response has increased the probability of similar responses. The new form of the response (the plural for a new object), however, is also occurring to a new stimulus (the new object itself). Thus, stimulus generalization is also involved.

Study Questions on Notes

1. Using examples, explain what is meant by reflexivity, symmetry, and transitivity.
2. How have studies of stimulus equivalence provided support for a behavioral view of language development?

3. What rule for programming stimulus generalization is exemplified by the study in which object and picture names were taught to developmentally disabled children? Explain.

4. Describe the two ways in which the term "behavioral momentum" has been used in the behavioral literature.

Eliminating Inappropriate Behavior Through Punishment

"Ben, don't be so aggressive."

ELIMINATING BEN'S AGGRESSIVENESS

Ben was a 7-year-old boy enrolled in a public school program for severely disturbed children.[1] He had been diagnosed as developmentally delayed, and the staff in the school had noticed an increase in the frequency with which Ben aggressively hit other children and/or the staff. In fact, during baseline observations over approximately three weeks, the frequency of Ben's hits averaged about 30 per day. Something had to be done.

Although painful consequences have been demonstrated to reduce undesirable behaviors when presented as punishers, such consequences have been found to be unacceptable in a number of situations, including many public school classrooms. Therefore, the staff decided to examine whether contingent exercise might decrease Ben's hitting behavior.

A number of precautions were taken to ensure that the contingent exercise would in no way be detrimental to Ben's health. The procedures were explained thoroughly to the parents, and parental consent was obtained for Ben's participation in the program. The procedures were also reviewed and approved by the ethical review board of the school district in which the program was carried out. The program was conducted at Ben's school throughout the school day. On the day that the contingent exercise was introduced, Ben's first hit was followed by the nearest adult saying, "Ben, no hitting. Stand up and sit down ten times." The adult

---

[1]This example is based on an article by Luce, Delquadri, and Hall (1980).

then held Ben's hand and lifted it over his head to prompt standing up and then pulled his upper body forward to prompt sitting down, at the same time saying "Stand up, sit down" for the ten exercises. Although Ben showed some verbal resistance to the exercise on a few occasions, the staff reported that physical prompting was necessary only on the first few training trials. On subsequent days, only verbal reminders were necessary to prompt the exercise task. From an average of approximately 30 hits per day during baseline, Ben's hits dropped to a frequency of 11 on the first day of the exercise program, 10 on the second day, 1 on the third day, and either 0 or 1 thereafter.

After two weeks of the procedure, the staff stopped applying the contingent exercise program to see what would happen to Ben's hits. The frequency of hits remained low for four days, but then they began to increase over the next four days. The staff reinstituted the contingent exercise program and observed an immediate drop in the frequency of hitting to near zero. The program continued formally for another two months, and the staff recorded one hit on each of three days during that entire time. Ben could run about and interact with other children and no longer showed the distressful aggressiveness characteristic of his past behavior.

THE PRINCIPLE OF PUNISHMENT

A **punisher** is an event that, when presented immediately following a behavior, causes the behavior to decrease in frequency. Once an event has been determined to function as a punisher for a particular behavior of an individual in a particular situation, that event can be used to decrease other behaviors of that individual in other situations. Associated with the concept of a punisher is the **principle of punishment:** *If, in a given situation, somebody does something that is immediately followed by a punisher, then that person is less likely to do the same thing again when he or she next encounters a similar situation.* In Ben's case, contingent exercise was a punisher for his aggressive hitting behavior.

Note that the meaning of punishment for behavior modifiers is quite specific, and differs from the meaning of the word "punishment" for most laypersons in our general culture. Consider, for example, sending a person to jail as "punishment" for committing a crime. First, going to jail is not likely to be an immediate consequence of committing the crime. Second, many individuals believe that "punishment" should involve retribution (as in saying that the "punishment" must fit the crime, and that more serious crimes deserve more severe sentences). Third, in the general culture, "punishment" is applied, in part, as a deterrent to potential "wrong-doers." For behavior modifiers, however, "punishment" is simply a technical term referring to the application of a consequence that has the effect of decreasing the likelihood of future instances of any behavior that it immediately follows. When we use the word punishment in this chapter and elsewhere in this book, therefore, please think of it in that sense.

Like positive reinforcement, punishment affects our learning throughout life. The immediate consequences of touching a hot stove teach us not to do that again. As infants, the bruises from a few falls helped to teach us better balance while learning to walk. A light swat on your behind from concerned parents may have taught you not to run into the street during heavy traffic. And we've all had our behavior affected by revoked privileges or reprimands from teachers. But it is important to recognize that there is some controversy within the field of behavior modification regarding the *deliberate* use of punishment, some of which is perhaps due to the layperson's view of punishment discussed above. Some people have gone so far as to suggest, or at least strongly imply, that punishment should never be used deliberately. We return to this issue later in this chapter, after discussing the different types of punishment and the factors that influence the effects of punishment in suppressing behavior.

TYPES OF PUNISHERS

Many kinds of events, when delivered as consequences for behavior, fit our definition of punisher given above. Most of these events can be classified into the following categories (see Van Houten, 1983): (a) physical punishment, (b) reprimands, (c) timeout, and (d) response cost. Although there is some overlap among these categories, they provide a convenient way in which to organize punishment procedures. We now consider each category in turn.

Physical (Aversive) Punishment

Physical punishment includes all punishers that activate pain receptors or other sense receptors that typically evoke feelings of discomfort. Physical punishers are also referred to as *aversive stimuli, aversive punishers,* or simply—*aversives.* Some examples of aversive punishers are spankings, pinches, electric shock, ammonia vapor, cool baths, loud or harsh sounds, prolonged tickling, and hair tugging. Such stimuli or events are called **unconditioned punishers** (that is, stimuli that are punishing without any prior training or conditioning).

Aversive punishment is not pleasant for the client or the therapist; nevertheless, there are cases in which clients have benefitted greatly from the procedure. A dramatic example is what may have been the lifesaving treatment of a 6-month-old baby (Sajwaj, Libet, & Agras, 1974). Sandra was admitted to a hospital because of a failure to gain weight that was associated with the constant bringing up of food (ruminating). She was underweight and undernourished, and death was a distinct possibility. Preliminary observations indicated that a few minutes after being given milk, Sandra would begin ruminating and would continue for about 20 to 40 minutes until she had apparently lost all the milk she had consumed. Sajwaj and colleagues decided to administer lemon juice as a punisher. During treatment, Sandra's mouth was filled with lemon juice immediately after staff members detected the vigorous tongue movements that reliably preceded her rumination. After 16 feedings with lemon juice punishment, the rumination had decreased to a very low level. To ensure that the improvement was due to the treatment program, Sajwaj and co-workers suspended the use of lemon juice for two feedings. The result was a dramatic increase in rumination. Following additional treatment, Sandra was discharged to foster parents, who maintained the treatment until it was no longer necessary.

Reprimands

Reprimands are strong negative verbal stimuli (e.g., "No! That was bad!") contingent on inappropriate behavior. They also usually include a fixed stare and, sometimes, a firm grasp. In Chapter 10 we noted that a stimulus paired with punishment becomes itself a punisher. Such a stimulus is called a **conditioned punisher.** It is likely that the verbal component and the fixed stare of a reprimand are conditioned punishers, in part because of their being paired with the other component (the firm grasp), which may be a form of physical punishment. In some cases, the effectiveness of reprimands has been increased by pairing them with other forms of punishment. For example, Dorsey, Iwata, Ong, and McSween (1980) paired reprimands with a water mist spray to suppress self-injurious behavior in developmentally disabled individuals. This caused the reprimands to become effective not only in the original setting but also in a setting where the mist had not been used.

Timeout

Timeout involves transferring an individual from a more reinforcing to a less reinforcing situation following a particular behavior (Van Houten, 1983, p. 28). There are two types of timeouts: exclusionary and nonexclusionary. **Exclusionary timeout** consists of removing the individual from the situation in which reinforcement is occurring for a short time (e.g., 5 minutes). Often a special room, called a *timeout room*, is used for this purpose. The timeout room is bare of anything that might serve as a reinforcer and may be padded to prevent self-injury. The period of detention in the timeout room should not be very long; about 5 minutes is usually quite effective. A **nonexclusionary timeout** consists of introducing into the situation a stimulus associated with less reinforcement. An example of this is the *timeout ribbon* introduced by Foxx and Shapiro (1978). Children in a classroom wore a ribbon that was removed for a short time when a child was disruptive. When not wearing the ribbon, the child was not allowed to participate in classroom activities and was ignored by the teacher.

Note 1

Response Cost

Response cost involves the removal of a specified amount of reinforcer following a particular behavior (Reynolds & Kelly, 1997). Examples of response cost in everyday life are library fines, traffic tickets, and charges for overdrawn checking accounts. Response cost is sometimes used in behavior modification programs in which clients earn tokens as reinforcers (Kazdin, 1977a). Working in a classroom setting, for example, Sullivan & O'Leary (1990) showed that loss of tokens (each of which could be exchanged for one minute of recess) for off-task behavior successfully decreased off-task behavior. Note that response cost differs from time-out in that there is no change in the prevailing reinforcement contingencies when it is administered. Response cost is also not to be confused with extinction. In an extinction procedure, a reinforcer is withheld following a previously reinforced response. In response cost, a reinforcer that is in the client's possession is taken away following an undesirable response.

FACTORS INFLUENCING THE EFFECTIVENESS OF PUNISHMENT

1. Maximizing the Conditions for a Desirable Alternative Response

To decrease an undesirable response, it is maximally effective to concurrently increase some desirable alternative response. This means that you should identify some desirable response that will compete with the undesirable behavior to be eliminated. You should also attempt to identify powerful S^Ds that control the desirable behavior and present these to increase the likelihood that the behavior will occur. To maintain the desirable behavior, you should also have effective positive reinforcers that can be presented on an effective schedule. Because the staff members in Ben's case were concerned with examining contingent exercise as a punisher by itself, they did not incorporate a specific positive reinforcement contingency for a desirable alternative to Ben's hitting. They might easily have done so, however.   **Note 2**

When consulted by individuals who are thinking about using a punishment procedure to decrease an undesirable behavior, we always recommend that they first design effective positive reinforcement and stimulus control programs for desirable alternative behaviors (Figure 13–1). Thus, if you are considering developing and using a punishment program to decrease undesirable behavior, we

Figure 13–1   An example of the reinforcement of a desirable alternative behavior.

strongly urge you first to review and apply the information in the earlier chapters concerning positive reinforcement and stimulus control. You should also familiarize yourself with the arguments against the use of punishment, which are summarized later in this chapter.

2. Minimizing the Cause of the Response to Be Punished

To maximize the opportunity for the desirable alternative behavior to occur, anyone attempting a punishment program should first minimize the causes of the punished behavior. This implies two things. First, one should try to identify the current stimulus control of the punished behavior. Second, one should try to identify existing reinforcers for the undesirable behavior. If the behavior is occurring, it is likely that occasional reinforcers are maintaining it. Identifying the antecedents and consequences for a behavior is referred to as a functional assessment, and is discussed in more detail in Chapter 20. In Ben's case, the teachers were unable to identify S^Ds that consistently evoked hitting, nor could they identify maintaining reinforcement contingencies.

It is important to emphasize that punishment may often not be necessary. Minimizing the causes of the undesirable behavior while maximizing the conditions for a desirable alternative behavior may cause the latter to compete so strongly with the former that it is greatly reduced or completely suppressed without the use of punishment.

3. Selecting a Punisher

It is important to be sure that the punisher is effective. Some stimuli may seem to be punishing when in fact they are not. For example, a parent may say "No! Naughty boy! Stop that!" to a child who is engaging in an undesirable behavior. The child may immediately cease the undesirable behavior and emit some other, desired behavior that will continue to receive the attention of the adult. The adult might then conclude that the reprimand was an effective punisher. However, if the adult were to keep track of the frequency of that undesirable behavior in the future, he or she might find that the verbal reprimand was not a punisher, but in fact a reinforcer. The child may have stopped temporarily because, having obtained the attention of the adult, he can emit other behavior that will maintain the adult's attention, at least for a short time. In other words, the verbal reprimand may function as an S^D for subsequent desirable behaviors of the child, regardless of the effects of the verbal reprimand as a punisher or a reinforcer on the preceding undesirable behavior. Several studies indicate that verbal reprimands often function as positive reinforcers and that the long-term frequency of the undesirable behavior that evoked the reprimand is therefore likely to increase. This is not to say that verbal reprimands or threats are never punishing. Situations in which they are effective, however, seem to be those in which they are consistently backed up by a strong punisher.

Note 3

To be effective, the punishing stimulus should be fairly intense. Frequently, individuals start with a weak punisher in the belief that they can increase its strength if it is not effective. The following process will be familiar to many parents: A child emits some undesirable behavior, which is followed by a mild reprimand by the parent. The behavior reoccurs, and the parent provides a stronger reprimand, perhaps coupled with a frown. The behavior is repeated, and the parent severely scolds the child. The behavior is repeated, and the child receives a scolding and a mild shaking. The behavior is repeated until finally the parent delivers a spanking. There are two problems here. One is that the undesirable behavior may be very harmful or dangerous: If that behavior consists of running out in the street and playing in the traffic, then the long-term consequences of allowing it to occur many times are potentially disastrous. The second problem is that the severe punisher, the spanking, may have lost a good deal of its effectiveness by the time it is applied. Gradually increasing the intensity of a punisher is not nearly as effective as introducing the punisher in its final form on the first occasion (Azrin & Holz, 1966).

The punisher selected should be one that can be presented immediately following the undesirable behavior. The punisher should also be one that can be presented in a manner such that it is in no way paired with positive reinforcement. This requirement often presents difficulties in situations in which the punisher is delivered by an adult and the individual being punished receives very little adult attention. If a child has received a lot of loving attention from an adult during a period of time prior to the occurrence of the undesired behavior, and the adult immediately presents a strong verbal reprimand following the undesirable behavior, then the verbal reprimand might be punishing. On the other hand, if that reprimand is the only adult attention that has been received by the child for an extended period of time, then that reprimand is a form of adult attention and may in fact be reinforcing.

Contingent exercise turned out to be a very suitable punisher for Ben. It was highly effective, could be presented immediately following the undesirable behavior, and could be presented in a manner such that it was in no way paired with positive reinforcement. The care and attention that the staff gave to choosing the actual exercise task obviously paid off. The staff chose the task because it could be prompted by a voice command from a staff member, Ben frequently performed the behavior in various play situations; it could be carried out in a variety of settings; and it appeared to tire Ben quickly without causing any unnecessary strain.

Rather than selecting just one punisher, it may be more effective to select several that are varied over successive instances of the undesirable behavior. For example, Charlop, Burgio, Iwata, and Ivancic (1988) applied either a reprimand, physical restriction, a timeout, or a loud noise as a punisher following aggression and self-stimulation by developmentally disabled children. In some sessions, only one of the punishers was applied. In other sessions, the four punishers were varied. The children showed less aggression and self-stimulation during sessions when the teacher varied the punishers.

4. Delivering the Punisher

Punishment is most effective when the punisher is presented immediately following the undesirable behavior. If the punisher is delayed, some more desirable behavior may occur prior to the punisher and this desirable behavior may be affected by the punisher to a much greater extent than the prior undesirable
behavior. The classic example of this is the mother who asks her husband after he
returns home from work to punish their son, who has misbehaved earlier in the
day. This request is doubly disastrous: Not only does the child receive punishment, even though he may now be engaging in good behavior, but the father is
punished for coming home from work. We do not mean to imply that delayed
punishment is completely ineffective. As we point out in our discussion of rule-
governed behavior in Chapter 16, most humans are adept at bridging rather large
time gaps between their behavior and its consequences. Even so, immediate punishment is much more effective than delayed punishment.

The punisher should be delivered after *every* instance of the undesirable behavior (see, for example, Kircher, Pear, & Martin, 1971). Occasional punishment is
not nearly as effective as punishment that follows every instance of the undesirable behavior. This implies that, if the teacher is unable to detect most instances of
the behavior to be punished, he or she should have serious doubts about the
value of implementing a punishment procedure.

The delivery of the punishment should in no way be paired with positive
reinforcement. As already mentioned, such a pairing weakens the punisher. In
addition, the person administering the punishment should remain calm when doing so. Anger and frustration on the part of the punisher may reinforce the undesirable behavior or inappropriately alter the consistency or intensity of the punishment. A calm, matter-of-fact approach ensures that a punishment program will
be followed as it has been designed, and that the person administering the punishment will be less likely to apply a punisher at inappropriate times (i.e., when
angry or annoyed) rather than immediately following an occasion of undesirable
behavior.

5. Using Rules

As we described for positive reinforcement and extinction, it is not necessary that
the individual be able to talk about or understand why his or her behavior was
punished. Nevertheless, appropriate use of rules will probably help to decrease
the undesirable behavior and increase the desirable alternative behavior more
quickly (e.g., see Bierman, Miller, & Stabb, 1987). The person for whom the program is implemented should be initially told something like: "In such-and-such
situations, each time that [the problem behavior] occurs, [the punisher] will occur. On the other hand, each time that [the desirable alternative behavior] occurs
instead, [the reinforcing item] will be presented." It is very important that emphasis be placed on the behavior, not the behaver. It is the behavior that is undesirable, not the individual. Appropriate use of rules is discussed further in
Chapter 16.

SHOULD PUNISHMENT BE USED?

The use of punishment has always been highly controversial, even before the advent of behavior modification, but the controversy appears to have intensified in recent years (Repp & Singh, 1990). A number of organizations concerned with helping people have formulated, or appear to be in the process of formulating, official statements against at least some uses of punishment. For example, the Practice Directorate of the American Psychological Association and the National Association of School Psychologists have provided testimony to the United States Congress in support of an amendment banning the use of corporal (that is, physical) punishment for emotionally disturbed children ("PD Supports Ban on Corporal Punishment," 1990). In 1990, the American Association on Mental Retardation adopted a policy statement condemning "aversive procedures which cause physical damage, pain, or illness" and "procedures which are dehumanizing—social degradation, verbal abuse and excessive reactions" (AAMR Revises Policy, 1990).

There are some who argue that nonaversive methods for eliminating unacceptable behavior are always at least as effective as aversive methods and that, therefore, there is never any justification for using aversive forms of punishment (see Guess, Helmstetter, Turnbull, & Knowlton, 1986; Guess, Turnbull, & Helmstetter, 1990). No humane person would think it is ethical to use aversive methods if nonaversive methods that are equally effective are available. It appears, however, that there are some extremely harmful behaviors that, in some cases, can be suppressed only with aversive punishment. For example, there are some developmentally disabled and autistic individuals who repeatedly engage in severe self-injurious behavior—damaging their vision by gouging their eyes, damaging their hearing by clapping their hands against their ears, causing tissue damage and bleeding by banging their heads on hard objects or tearing at their flesh, becoming malnourished by inducing vomiting after eating—that places them in great danger of either disabling or killing themselves. A number of studies in the literature demonstrate that these behaviors can be suppressed by aversive punishment (see Favell et al., 1982; Linscheid, Iwata, Ricketts, & Griffen, 1990). Once the self-injurious behavior is suppressed, positive reinforcement is then used to maintain desirable alternative behavior, but this cannot be done until the self-injurious behavior has been controlled. The only alternative to using **Note 4** aversive punishment, in many cases, appears to be restraint—for example, tying heavily padded mittens to the individual's hands, or even tying the individual to a wheelchair or bed—but this effectively prevents the person from learning desirable behavior to replace the undesirable behavior.

Several authors have described methods that they claim can effectively replace all forms of aversive control (see McGee et al., 1987; Meyer & Evans, 1989). For the most part, the methods described are based on the behavior principles discussed in Chapters 3 to 12 of this text. Although these authors provide many good examples of alternatives that should be tried before resorting to aversive methods, it is not clear that the methods they propose can effectively replace aversive methods in all cases. What is clear is that the decision to use or not use aversive methods in a particular case requires considerable professional training and expertise and should not be made by unqualified individuals. Treatment of severe behavior problems, which are the only type for which aversive punishment should be considered, is therefore best left to professionals who have advanced degrees in psychology or other helping professions from accredited universities and who are members of accredited professional organizations (Griffith & Spreat, 1989).

Although much intense controversy centers on aversive punishment, other forms of punishment are also under attack. Few people would argue that all forms of punishment can be eliminated. It is extremely difficult, however, to specify the exact degree of punishment that is appropriate in a given situation. Regarding timeout, Meyer and Evans (1989, p. 102) state: "The time-out area need not be incredibly comfortable and desirable, but also should not be extremely unpleasant." Clearly, this recommendation leaves a great deal of room for subjectivity in selecting a timeout area. Meyer and Evans also oppose the use of exercise as a punisher—such as that used with Ben—although they regard exercise as beneficial if used to "calm" an individual following inappropriate behavior (p. 137). Unfortunately, it is very difficult—perhaps even impossible—to distinguish between these two functions of exercise, because requiring someone to exercise for the purpose of "calming" may also *punish* behavior that it follows (according to the technical definition of punishment given at the beginning of this chapter). It appears that what Meyer and Evans are actually concerned with is that if punishment has to be used, it must never be used in a humiliating or degrading manner. We certainly concur in this. Regardless of the nature of a person's disability, or the inappropriateness of his or her behavior, that person should always be treated in a manner that shows respect for him or her as a human being.

Even though the use of punishment is highly controversial, it is clear that punishment can have a number of potentially harmful effects. These may be summarized as follows:

1. Punishment tends to elicit aggressive behavior. Experiments with animals show that painful stimuli cause them to attack other animals—even though these other animals had nothing to do with inflicting the painful stimuli (Azrin, 1967). Some research (Berkowitz, 1988, 1989) suggests that this finding also applies to humans. Thus we should not be surprised to observe individuals who have just been punished attacking other individuals. Clearly, such behavior is an undesirable side effect of punishment.

2. Punishment can produce other undesirable emotional side effects, such as crying and general fearfulness. Not only are these side effects unpleasant for all concerned, they frequently interfere with desirable behavior—especially if it is of a complex nature.

3. Punishment may cause the situation and people associated with the aversive stimulus to become conditioned punishers. For example, if you are trying to teach a child to read, and if you punish the child whenever he or she makes a mistake, anything associated with this situation—such as printed words, books, the person who delivers the punishment, the type of room in which the punishment occurs—will tend to become punishing. The child may attempt to escape or avoid these stimuli (see Chapter 14). Thus, instead of helping the individual to learn, punishment may drive him or her away from people, objects, and events associated with the learning situation.

The punisher need not be particularly strong to have the undesirable effects mentioned in points 1 to 3. For example, a teacher we know of used a timeout chair as a punisher for students in her first-grade class. For some unknown reason—perhaps it had something to do with the fact that the chair was black and the teacher told rowdy children to go sit in the "black chair"—the chair became frightening to the students. Years later, former students who come back to visit her still mention how fearful they had been of the "black chair," even though nothing bad ever happened to them when they sat there. When the teacher discovered the problem with the chair she changed her procedure. It is no longer black and she now calls it the "calming down chair," and she periodically demonstrates its benign qualities to her students by sitting in it herself when she feels the need to calm down!

4. Punishment does not establish any new behavior; it only suppresses old behavior. In other words, punishment does not teach an individual what to do; at best, it only teaches what not to do. For example, the main defining characteristic of developmentally disabled persons is that they lack behavior that the majority of people have. The primary emphasis for these individuals, then, should be on establishing new behavior rather than on merely eliminating old behavior. Reinforcement is required to accomplish this task.

5. Children often model or imitate adults. If adults apply punishment to children, the children are apt to do the same to others. Thus, in punishing children we may inadvertently be providing a model for them to follow in presenting aversive stimuli toward others (Bandura, 1965, 1969). For example, children who were taught a game in which they were fined for incorrect behavior fined other children to whom they taught the game (Gelfand et al., 1974).

6. Because punishment results in quick suppression of undesirable behavior, it can tempt the user to rely heavily on it and neglect the use of positive reinforcement for desirable behavior. However, the undesirable behavior may return after only a temporary suppression, or some other undesirable behavior could occur. The person administering punishment may then resort to progressively heavier doses, thereby creating a vicious circle with disastrous side effects.

Some behavior modifiers maintain that all the problems can be eliminated or greatly reduced with the proper use of punishment (e.g., Johnston, 1985; Repp & Singh, 1990; Van Houten, 1983), and considerable data support this contention (Axelrod & Apsche, 1983). However, because punishment is so easy to abuse, we recommend that it be used only as a last resort, and then only by appropriately trained individuals (also see Chapter 29).

PITFALLS OF PUNISHMENT

We have discussed extensively the many potentially harmful side effects lying in wait for those who try to use punishment without being familiar with its properties. At least as serious are the many instances in which punishment is applied by people who are not aware that they are doing so. A common example is criticizing or ridiculing a person for inadequate behavior. Criticism and ridicule are generally punishing, and they will likely suppress future instances of that behavior and tend to drive the individual away from the person administering them. Yet the inadequate behavior that is criticized and ridiculed may be an approximation of more adequate behavior. Suppressing it could destroy the individual's opportunity to obtain the adequate behavior through the use of shaping. In everyday language, the individual becomes discouraged and gives up in his or her attempt to develop adequate behavior. In addition, because he or she will attempt to escape from and avoid the person administering the criticism and ridicule (see Chapter 14), that person will have lost a great deal of potential reinforcing effectiveness.

Another example of someone's applying punishment without being aware of it is the person who says "That was good, but..." Suppose that a teenager helps a parent with the dishes and the parent replies, "Thanks for helping, but next time don't be so slow." We are sure that, based on the foregoing discussion, you can describe a much more effective and pleasant way for the parent to react.

In our view, punishment should be applied only in conjunction with positive reinforcement for a desirable behavior, and only for the purpose of eliminating undesirable behaviors that cannot be reduced in other ways.

GUIDELINES FOR THE EFFECTIVE APPLICATION OF PUNISHMENT PROCEDURES

The rules for the effective use of punishment are probably violated more than those for other principles. Therefore, if you propose a punishment procedure (even one involving a mild punisher), you owe it to yourself and the person whose behavior is to be punished to do an effective job.

1. *Selecting a response.* Punishment is most effective with a specific behavior (such as jumping on the arm of the chair) rather than a general category of behavior (such as wrecking furniture).
2. *Maximize the conditions for a desirable (nonpunished) alternative response.*
   a. Select a desirable alternative behavior that competes with the behavior to be punished such that the alternative behavior can be reinforced. If possible, select a behavior that will be maintained by the natural environment after the termination of your reinforcement program.
   b. Provide strong prompts to increase the likelihood that the desirable alternative behavior will occur.
   c. Reinforce the desirable behavior with a powerful reinforcer on an appropriate schedule.
3. *Minimize the causes of the response to be punished.*
   a. Try to identify and eliminate many or all of the S^Ds for the undesirable behavior, at least early in the training program.
   b. Try to eliminate any possible reinforcement for the undesirable behavior.

4. *Select an effective punisher.*
   a. Choose an effective punisher that can be presented immediately following the undesirable behavior.
   b. The punisher should be one that will in no way be paired with positive reinforcement following the undesirable behavior.
   c. Select a punisher that can be presented following every instance of the undesirable behavior.
5. *Apply punishment.*
   a. Tell the individual about the plan before starting.
   b. Present the punisher *immediately* following *every* instance of the response to be decreased.
   c. Administer the punisher in a calm and matter-of-fact manner.
   d. Take care not to pair punishment of the undesirable behavior with reinforcement for that behavior.
6. In all programs involving punishment, careful data should be taken on the effects of the program. The conditions under which the program should be applied must be stated clearly, written down, and followed.

STUDY QUESTIONS

1. Describe how Ben's aggressive behavior was eliminated.
2. How was stimulus control an important part of the punishment contingency for Ben?
3. What is a punisher? State the principle of punishment.
4. How is the meaning of the term "punishment" for behavior modifiers different from the meaning of that term for most laypersons?
5. Describe four different types of punishers and illustrate each with an example.
6. Under which of the four categories of punishment would you put the type of punishment used with Ben? Justify your choice.
7. Define conditioned punisher and illustrate with an example.
8. Distinguish between exclusionary and nonexclusionary timeout.
9. If you do a good job of attending to the first two factors influencing the effectiveness of punishment, you may not have to apply punishment. Discuss.
10. What are the problems with gradually increasing the intensity of the punishing stimulus over successive applications of that stimulus?
11. What steps might you follow to experimentally determine if a verbal reprimand was a punisher for a particular child?
12. What is a common example of the response-contingent withdrawal of positive reinforcement that is applied as punishment by parents to their children?
13. Procedurally, describe the differences between extinction, response cost, and exclusionary timeout.
14. In the subsection "Delivering the Punisher," we suggested that if the teacher is unable to detect most instances of a behavior to be punished, then the teacher should have serious doubts about the value of implementing a punishment procedure.
   a. From the information in this chapter, what reasons can you cite to support this suggestion?
   b. What alternative means of managing the situation are available to the teacher?
15. What are four concerns of the teacher in regard to applying punishment (see Guidelines section)?
16. In view of the controversy regarding the use of punishment, do you agree with the way punishment was used with Ben? Defend your answer.

17. Cite six potentially harmful side effects of the application of punishment.
18. Describe an example illustrating how punishment is applied by people who are not aware that they are doing so.

APPLICATION EXERCISES

A. Exercises Involving Others

1. Consider the behavior of speeding (driving a car in excess of the speed limit) in our culture.
   a. Briefly outline the current contingencies with respect to speeding.
   b. Compare the current contingencies for speeding with the guidelines for the effective application of punishment procedures. Identify those guidelines that were either ignored or flagrantly violated by the lawmakers and law enforcers.
2. Consider the behavior of littering the highways in your area. Answer the questions that you answered for speeding in Exercise 1.

B. Self-Modification Exercise

Choose a behavior of yours that you would like to decrease. With the help of a friend, describe in detail a punishment program that would likely decrease that behavior. (Make the program as realistic as possible, but do not apply it.) Your punishment program should be consistent with all the guidelines for the effective application of punishment.

NOTES AND EXTENDED DISCUSSION

1. After reviewing studies that examined various durations of timeouts in punishment programs from a wide spectrum of populations and behavior problems, Brantner and Doherty (1983) concluded that relatively short durations of timeout have generally been effective. Also, as indicated by White et al. (1972), ethical considerations (such as avoiding timeout durations in excess of what is necessary) and practical considerations (such as avoiding lengthy timeouts that take the individual away from a learning environment) must also be considered in selecting a particular timeout duration.

2. C. R. Johnson, Hunt, and Siebert (1994) combined reinforcement with punishment to treat *pica*, which is the ingestion of inedible objects or non-nutritive substances. Commonly seen among severely and profoundly developmentally disabled individuals, this serious disorder has been associated with lead poisoning, intestinal blockage, intestinal perforation, and intestinal parasites. Items commonly ingested include cigarettes and cigarette butts, plastic objects, hair, paint chips, dirt and sand, and bits of paper. The client, a profoundly developmentally disabled

15-year-old, was taught to eat only those items that were placed on a bright yellow plastic placemat. In addition to the natural reinforcement from eating the items on the placemat, the client was praised by the staff for selecting and ingesting those items. Items that were not on the placemat that were ingested were followed by a consequence that was punishing for the client (his face was washed with a cool damp cloth for 15 seconds).

3. The potential reinforcing value of reprimands was demonstrated in a study by Madsen, Becker, Thomas, Koser, and Plager (1970). A teacher was instructed to increase her use of the reprimand "Sit down!" when the children were out of their seats. As a consequence of the teacher saying "Sit down!" more often, the children's out-of-seat behavior increased.

4. A highly controversial device called the *Self-Injurious Behavior Inhibiting System (SIBIS)* has appeared on the market. The device, which is strapped to the head, is designed to detect self-injurious blows to the head and deliver an aversive electric shock to the arm or leg, contingent on such blows. Despite the controversy concerning the SIBIS, a group of researchers (Linscheid, Iwata, Ricketts, Williams, & Griffin, 1990) tested it with five individuals whose severely self-injurious head beating had not been responsive to nonaversive treatments. The data indicated that the device was effective in completely eliminating the self-injurious behavior and produced no detrimental side effects. Linscheid, Pejeau, Cohen, and Footo-Lenz (1994) reported that application of SIBIS not only led to a decrease in self-injurious behavior, but that this improvement was also associated with positive side effects.

Study Questions on Notes

1. What is pica? What factors influencing the effectiveness of punishment did Johnson et al. (1994) incorporate into their treatment program for pica?
2. How did Madsen and colleagues (1970) demonstrate that reprimands can actually be reinforcing?
3. What is the Self-Injurious Behavior Inhibiting System? In view of the controversy regarding the use of punishment, do you believe that testing and using this device is appropriate? Defend your answer.

14

Establishing a Desirable Behavior by Using Escape and Avoidance Conditioning

"Jason, that's bad for your health!"

CURING JASON'S SLOUCHING

Jason was a model employee. An attendant at the Anna State Hospital, he was hardworking, punctual, and well liked by the patients.[1] Unfortunately, Jason constantly slouched while he worked. At first glance, slouching might not seem like a serious problem. But slouching by staff presented an inappropriate role model for the psychiatric patients at the hospital. Poor posture by such individuals frequently discourages social acceptability when they return to the community. Moreover, many medical authorities believe that there is a causative relationship between good posture and good health.

Fortunately for Jason, some psychologists at the hospital were conducting research on behavioral engineering—the use of apparatus to manage contingencies to change behavior. Jason agreed to wear a specially designed shoulder harness which held an elastic cord across his back. The elastic cord was wired to a small tone generator and a clicker. When Jason wore a shirt and sweater over the harness, it was completely concealed from view.

Here's how the apparatus worked: When Jason slouched, the elastic cord stretched and caused a click sound. Three seconds later, a loud aversive tone sounded and remained on until Jason stopped slouching. Thus, when Jason exhibited good posture, he could escape the sound of the tone. And if he continued to display good posture, he could avoid the loud tone altogether. The

---

[1]This case is based on Azrin, Ruben, O'Brien, Ayllon, & Roll (1968).

results were dramatic. Before Jason wore the apparatus, he slouched almost 60 percent of the time. But when he wore the apparatus, he slouched only 1 percent of the time. When Jason removed the apparatus, his slouching did recover somewhat (to approximately 11 percent). But the clear demonstration of the effects of the apparatus gave him hope that he could cure his slouching habit.

ESCAPE CONDITIONING

Three behavioral principles were used in Jason's case: escape conditioning, avoidance conditioning, and punishment. The principle of **escape conditioning** states that there are certain stimuli whose removal immediately after the occurrence of a response will increase the likelihood of that response. In the escape procedure used with Jason, the removal of the loud tone following the response of showing good posture increased the probability that Jason would show good posture each time the tone was presented.

Note that escape conditioning is similar to aversive punishment in that both involve the use of an aversive stimulus (or punisher). Procedurally, however, escape conditioning and punishment differ in terms of both the antecedents and the consequences of behavior. With regard to antecedents, in escape conditioning, the aversive stimulus must be present prior to a response, whereas the aversive stimulus is not present prior to a response that is punished. With regard to consequences, in escape conditioning the aversive event is removed immediately following a response, whereas in punishment the aversive stimulus (or punisher) is presented immediately following a response. In terms of results, with the punishment procedure the likelihood of future behavior is *decreased*, whereas in the escape conditioning procedure, the likelihood of behavior is *increased*.

Another name for escape conditioning is *negative reinforcement* (Skinner, 1953). The term "reinforcement" indicates that it is analogous to positive reinforcement, in that both strengthen responses that they follow. The term "negative" indicates that the strengthening effect occurs because the response leads to the removal (i.e., the taking away or subtraction) of an "aversive" event.

Escape conditioning is common in everyday living. In the presence of a bright light, we have learned to escape the intensity of the light by closing our eyes or squinting. When a room is too cold, we escape the chill by putting on an extra sweater (see Figure 14–1). When it's too hot, we escape the heat by turning on the fan or air conditioner. If a street crew is repairing the street outside our room, you might close the window to escape the noise. Other examples of escape conditioning are presented in Table 14–1.

AVOIDANCE CONDITIONING

Escape conditioning has the disadvantage that the aversive stimulus must be present for the desired response to occur. In the escape procedure used with Jason, the loud tone was on before Jason showed good posture. Therefore, escape

Figure 14–1   Many of our behaviors are strengthened by escape conditioning.

conditioning is generally not a final contingency for maintaining behavior but rather is preparatory training for avoidance conditioning. Thus, Jason was influenced by avoidance conditioning after he had demonstrated escape behavior.

The principle of **avoidance conditioning** states that a behavior will increase in frequency if it prevents an aversive stimulus from occurring. During the avoidance procedure used with Jason, good posture prevented the tone from occurring. Note that both escape conditioning and avoidance conditioning involve the use of an aversive stimulus. And with both, the likelihood of a behavior is increased. But an escape response removes an aversive stimulus that has already been presented, while an avoidance response prevents an aversive stimulus from occurring at all.

The click of the apparatus when Jason slouched was a *warning stimulus*—it signalled the occurrence of the tone 3 seconds later. Other names for a warning stimulus are *conditioning aversive stimulus* and *conditioned punisher*. Jason quickly learned to show good posture at the sound of the click in order to avoid the forthcoming back-up punisher, the aversive tone. This type of avoidance conditioning, which includes a warning signal that enables the individual to discriminate a forthcoming punisher, is called *discriminated avoidance conditioning*.

Note 1

Because the sound of the click became a conditioned punisher (through pairings with the back-up punisher), the procedure used with Jason also included a punishment component. If Jason showed poor posture, then the sound of a click, a conditioned punisher, would occur. Thus, when Jason began wearing the apparatus, good posture was strengthened through escape conditioning; good posture

TABLE 14-1 EXAMPLES OF ESCAPE CONDITIONING

Aversive situation	Escape responses by individual	Removal of aversive situation	Long-term effects
1. A child sees an adult with a bag of candies. The child begins to scream "candy, candy, candy."	To terminate the screaming, the adult gives the screaming child a candy.	The child stops screaming.	In the future, the adult is more likely "to give in to" the screaming child because of escape conditioning (and the child is more likely to scream when she sees a candy bag, because of the positive reinforcement she gains for doing so).
2. A woman is playing golf and it starts to rain.	The golfer puts on a rainsuit.	The golfer escapes the feeling of rain beginning to wet her clothes.	The golfer is more likely to put on a rainsuit when it rains.
3. A nonverbal child has had shoes put on her that are too tight and are pinching her toes.	The child makes loud noises in the presence of an adult and points to her toes.	The adult removes the shoes (and perhaps puts on larger shoes).	The child is more likely to make loud noises and point to her sore feet (or to other areas of pain) more quickly in similar situations in the future.
4. A jogger experiences a sensation of sore lips while jogging on a windy day.	The jogger puts chapstick on his lips.	The sensation of soreness ceases.	The jogger is more likely to use chapstick to sooth sore lips.
5. A staff member in a zoo encounters a pile of smelly dung on the floor of the monkey cage.	The staff member walks away without cleaning it up.	The staff member escapes the aversive smell (and avoids having to clean up the dung).	In the future, the staff member will likely walk away from dung on the floor of the monkey cage.

was maintained through avoidance conditioning, and poor posture was immediately punished. It's no wonder that the results were so dramatic.

  Avoidance conditioning is also common in everyday living. In too many classrooms, unfortunately, children learn to give the right answers primarily to avoid the teacher's ridicule and to avoid poor grades. Our legal system is based largely on avoidance conditioning. We pay our taxes to avoid going to jail. We put money in parking meters to avoid getting a ticket. We pay our parking fines in order to avoid a court summons. Other examples of avoidance conditioning are presented in Table 14–2.

  Behavioral theoreticians have debated among themselves the theoretical explanation for avoidance responding. The increase in positively reinforced responses and escape responses, and the decrease in punished responses, are all explained by their immediate consequences. But in successful avoidance conditioning, the immediate consequence appears to be that *there is no immediate consequence.* Since theoreticians tend to dislike paradoxes such as this, behavioral theo-

TABLE 14–2 EXAMPLES OF AVOIDANCE CONDITIONING

Situation	Warning stimulus	Avoidance response	Immediate consequences	Aversive consequences avoided
1. You enter a restaurant.	A Little League baseball team is just being seated at one end of the restaurant.	You sit at the other end of the restaurant.	You escape the immediate vicinity of the children.	You avoid the noise they will make.
2. You are walking down the aisle of a shopping mall.	You notice a person whom you dislike coming out of a store some distance away.	You immediately enter the nearest store.	You no longer see the person whom you dislike.	You avoid an unpleasant confrontation.
3. A child playing in her front yard feels anxious when she sees the neighbor's dog (the dog had previously knocked the child down and scared her by barking loudly).	The dog starts running toward the child.	The child goes into her house.	The sight of the dog is removed, and the child feels less anxious.	The child avoids being knocked down by the dog again.
4. One of the authors is about to leave his office to go home.	He remembers that his son is practicing his drumming at home.	He phones home to ask his son to stop practicing.		He avoids experiencing extremely loud drumming when he enters his house.

reticians have asked themselves the following question: Are there immediate consequences that perhaps are easily overlooked by the casual observer but that might nevertheless maintain avoidance responses?

There appear to be several possibilities. One possibility in discriminated avoidance conditioning is that the avoidance response is strengthened because it terminates the warning stimulus. For example, in Jason's case, the loud tone was the back-up punisher. Because the clicking sound was paired with the tone, the click became an aversive stimulus. When Jason showed good posture in the presence of the click, the immediate result was that the clicking noise ceased. Although Jason's good posture was an avoidance response with respect to the tone, we might view it as an escape response with respect to the click. This type of explanation might enable us to account for the first three examples of avoidance conditioning in Table 14–2.

A second possible explanation of avoidance conditioning in some cases is illustrated by aspects of the third example in Table 14–2. In the presence of the warning stimulus, the child felt anxious. Immediately following the avoidance response, she felt less anxious. The possibility that avoidance responses occur because they enable us to escape from anxiety is discussed further in the next chapter.

But how do we explain the avoidance response in the fourth example in Table 14–2? Perhaps thoughts of experiencing his son's loud drumming were aversive, and these thoughts ceased following the phone call. Or perhaps the explanation may involve rule-governed control over behavior (discussed further in Chapter 16). While such explanations are plausible, they are clearly speculative. You can see why behavior modifiers are puzzled about how to explain avoidance responding in terms of the identification of immediate consequences.

PITFALLS OF ESCAPE AND AVOIDANCE

People often unknowingly apply escape and avoidance conditioning with the result that undesirable behaviors are strengthened. For example, observations of family interactions by Snyder, Schrepferman, and St. Peter (1997) indicated that parents of children labeled as antisocial frequently strengthened aggressive behavior in their children by "backing off" or "giving in" when the aggressive behavior occurred. As another example, parents may inadvertently establish inappropriate verbal behavior with a child who desperately promises, "I'll be good; I won't do it again" to escape or avoid punishment for some infraction of parental authority. When such pleas are successful, the pleading behavior is strengthened and thus increased in frequency under similar circumstances, but the undesirable behavior the parent meant to decrease may have been affected very little or not at all. Verbal behavior having little relation to reality may be increased while the undesirable target response may persist in strength.

Another example of this pitfall can be seen if prisoners learn to make the "right" verbal statements to obtain early parole, but sometimes it is merely their verbal behavior that has been modified, not their antisocial behaviors (e.g., assaults, property destruction). Apologies, confessions, and the "guilty look" characteristic of transgressors in all walks of life can be traced to similar contingencies. Lying or misrepresenting the facts is a way of avoiding punishment, if one can get away with it. (Other examples of undesirable behavior maintained by escape conditioning are presented in Chapter 20.)

A second pitfall of escape and avoidance is the inadvertent establishment of conditioned aversive stimuli, to which an individual then responds in such a way as to escape or avoid them. For example, if a coach hollers at, criticizes, and ridicules athletes, the athletes may show improved skills primarily to avoid or escape the wrath of the coach, but they're also likely to avoid the coach, who has become a conditioned aversive stimulus, off the athletic field. And if the coaching tactics become too aversive, some team members might quit the sport entirely. As another example, some teachers, by their excessive use of punishment, transform themselves, their classrooms, and the learning materials they use into conditioned aversive stimuli. All too frequently, this situation produces individuals who avoid teachers, school, and books and who therefore fail to advance academically. Clearly, this is a most unfortunate consequence of escape and avoidance conditioning.

A final pitfall of escape conditioning is that in many situations it maintains undesirable behaviors of the teacher and other caregivers. This can easily be seen in the first example in Table 14–1.

GUIDELINES FOR THE EFFECTIVE APPLICATION OF ESCAPE AND AVOIDANCE

The following rules should be observed by any person who applies escape and avoidance:

1. Given a choice between maintaining behavior on an escape or an avoidance procedure, the latter is to be preferred. There are two reasons for this. First, in escape conditioning the back-up punisher must be present prior to the target response, whereas in avoidance conditioning the back-up punisher occurs only when the target response fails to occur. Second, in escape conditioning the target response does not occur when the back-up punisher is not present, whereas in avoidance conditioning responding decreases very slowly when the back-up punisher may no longer be forthcoming.
2. The target behavior should be established by escape conditioning before it is put on an avoidance procedure. Avoidance behavior is usually easier to establish if escape behavior is established first. Thus, in the example at the beginning of this chapter, Jason learned how to escape the loud noise prior to learning how to avoid it.
3. During avoidance conditioning, a warning stimulus should signal the impending punisher. This enhances conditioning by providing a warning that failure to respond will result in aversive stimulation. An example from the natural environment is the printed word VIOLATION on a parking meter, which indicates that the motorist may receive a parking ticket if he or she does not put a coin in the meter. The clicker served a similar function for Jason, indicating that the tone would occur 3 seconds later unless he showed good posture. And if Jason showed good posture during the 3 seconds, he could avoid the loud tone. (Similarly, putting a coin in a parking meter removes the VIOLATION sign and prevents a ticket.)
4. Escape and avoidance conditioning, like punishment, should be used cautiously. Because these procedures involve aversive stimuli, they can result in harmful side ef-

fects, such as aggression, fearfulness, and a tendency to avoid or escape any person or thing associated with the procedure.

5. Positive reinforcement for the target response should be used in conjunction with escape and avoidance conditioning. Not only will it help to strengthen the desired behavior, but it will also tend to counteract the undesirable side effects mentioned. The procedure used with Jason would probably have worked even better if positive reinforcement for good posture had been added to it. (This was not done because the experimenters were interested in the escape and avoidance procedure by itself.)

6. As with all the procedures described in this text, the individual concerned should be told—to the best of his or her understanding—about the contingencies in effect. Again, as with all these procedures, however, instructions are not necessary for escape and avoidance conditioning to work.

STUDY QUESTIONS

1. Define escape conditioning, and describe an example that is not in the text.
2. How is escape conditioning similar to punishment? How do they differ, procedurally? How do their effects differ?
3. Procedurally, in what two ways is escape conditioning different from positive reinforcement? How are their effects similar?
4. Procedurally, what are two differences between escape conditioning and avoidance conditioning?
5. How are conditioned positive reinforcers and conditioned punishers similar, and how are they different?
6. Give two other names for *conditioned punisher*.
7. Describe two examples of escape conditioning in everyday life.
8. Describe two examples of avoidance conditioning in everyday life.
9. How is a conditioned aversive stimulus like an S^D? How are they different?
10. From your knowledge of strategies for programming generality (from Chapter 12), what recommendations would you make to Jason to bring about a total, long-term cure for his slouching?
11. Explain in behavioral terms, with an example of your own, why individuals frequently reinforce the undesirable behavior of other individuals. (*Hint:* See the first example in Table 14–1.) Clearly identify the behavior principles involved.
12. Explain how escape conditioning might maintain an adult's behavior of responding inappropriately to a child's extreme social withdrawal.
13. Describe three types of immediate consequences that might maintain avoidance responses.
14. Briefly describe three pitfalls of escape and avoidance. Give an example of each. (If possible, use examples other than those in the text.)

APPLICATION EXERCISES

A. Exercise Involving Others

Successful avoidance behavior means that an individual has been conditioned to respond (probably to a warning signal) in such a way as to avoid the occurrence of a back-up punisher. This means that the avoidance behavior might persist even if (for whatever reasons) the environment has changed such that the back-up punisher will no longer be presented regardless of the individual's behavior. Why is this so? Describe an example that illustrates this effect.

B. Self-Modification Exercise

Construct a chart similar to Table 14–1 in which you present five examples of escape conditioning that have influenced your behavior. Present each example in terms of the categories of aversive situation, escape responses, removal of aversive stimulus, and probable long-term effects on the escape response.

NOTE AND EXTENDED DISCUSSION

1. A less common type of avoidance conditioning does not involve a warning signal. This type of avoidance is known as Sidman avoidance (after Murray Sidman, who studied this type of avoidance extensively with lower organisms; e.g., Sidman, 1953). In a typical Sidman avoidance conditioning experiment with a laboratory rat, a brief electric shock punisher is presented every 30 seconds without a preceding warning stimulus. If the rat makes a designated response, the shock will be postponed for 30 seconds. Under these conditions, the rat will learn to make the appropriate avoidance response on a regular basis and will be relatively shock free. This type of avoidance conditioning is also referred to as nondiscriminated, noncued, or free operant avoidance conditioning. Sidman avoidance has been demonstrated with humans (Hefferline, Keenan, & Harford, 1959) and appears to underlie some everyday examples of preventive behaviors. Consider, for example, that when the roads are muddy, drivers use lots of windshield washer fluid. To avoid running out of fluid, many of them regularly refill the container, even though there is no warning stimulus that the container (hidden under the hood) is near empty. (However, in Chapter 16, you'll see that this type of example might also be explained as rule-governed behavior.)

Study Question on Note

1. What is Sidman avoidance conditioning? Give an example from everyday life.

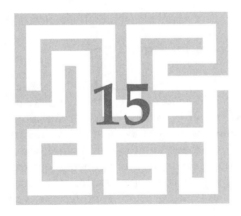

Procedures Based on Principles of Respondent Conditioning

"I hate that word!"

MAKING WORDS "UNPLEASANT"

Sue was a student in first-year psychology at Arizona State University.[1] As a participant in an experiment, she had been asked to memorize a list of words that were presented to her, one word at a time. Sitting as comfortably as one can be with electrical wires attached to one ankle, and wearing headphones, Sue read the words as they were presented: chair; smile; small; large (ZAP! CLANG!—Sue was startled by the feeling of a mild electric shock to her ankle, and the sound of a loud "clang" through the headphones). Sue continued to memorize the words on the list. The word large *appeared several times, and each time it was paired with the mild shock and the loud sound. During the experiment, the shock and the sound caused Sue to feel anxious (as measured by her galvanic skin response [GSR], an increase in the electrical conductivity of the skin that occurs during a sweat gland reaction). As a result of pairing the word* large *with the mild shock and the loud sound, hearing the word* large *by itself now caused Sue to feel anxious. Afterward, when Sue was asked to rate the pleasantness of the meaning of the words, Sue rated* large *as much more unpleasant than the other words.*

(Note: During a debriefing session, Sue learned the purposes of the experiment. She also discovered that saying the word large *many times without pairing it with the mild shock and the loud tone caused that word to gradually lose its unpleasantness.)*

---

[1]This example is based on an experiment by Staats, Staats, & Crawford, 1962.

OPERANT VERSUS RESPONDENT BEHAVIOR

The principles and procedures described in the previous pages of this book are mainly those of *operant conditioning,* a term initially used by Skinner (1938) in a very special sense, namely to refer to the observation that behavior could be modified by its consequences. As we have seen, consequences that cause a behavior to increase are called *reinforcers,* and those that cause it to decrease are called *punishers.* Behaviors that operate on the environment to generate consequences, and are in turn controlled by those consequences, are called *operant behaviors.* Examples include putting gas in your car, asking for directions, writing an exam, turning on a TV set, and making breakfast.

Although operant principles have widespread applicability, some behavior does not seem to fit the model of operant conditioning. Some of our behaviors, like Sue's anxious feelings to the mild shock, seem to be reflexive (i.e., elicited by prior stimuli quite apart from the consequences of the behaviors). Examples include feeling frightened when watching a scary movie, blushing when told that your fly or blouse is undone, and becoming sexually aroused when watching x-rated movies. These are called *respondent behaviors,* and a different set of principles seems to apply to them. In this chapter we briefly describe these principles and how they differ from those of operant conditioning. In addition, we highlight some of the applications of these principles.

PRINCIPLE OF RESPONDENT CONDITIONING

The respondent-conditioning principle is based on the fact that certain stimuli automatically elicit certain responses apart from any prior learning or conditioning experience. These "automatic" stimulus-response relationships are called *unconditioned reflexes.* Examples of such reflexes are shown in Figure 15–1.

The reflexes in Figure 15–1 are unconditioned because the stimuli elicit the responses without prior conditioning (in other words, they are inborn). A stimulus that elicits a response without prior learning or conditioning is called an *unconditioned stimulus* (US). A response elicited by such a stimulus is called an *unconditioned response* (UR). In the experiment with Sue, the mild shock and loud sound were USs, and Sue's GSR response was a UR.

Respondent Conditioning[2]   For each of the responses in Figure 15–1, there are stimuli that do not elicit them. In that sense, such stimuli are considered *neutral.* For example, assume that a particular stimulus (such as the sound of classical music) is neutral in the sense that it does not elicit a particular response (salivation) in a particular individual. The principle of *respondent conditioning* states that if that stimulus (the sound of classical music) is followed closely in time by a US (food in the mouth), which elicits a UR (salivation), then the previously neutral stimulus (sound of classical music) will also tend to elicit the response of salivation in the future. Of course, it may take more than just one pairing of classical

---

[2]Respondent conditioning is also commonly referred to as *classical conditioning* or *Pavlovian conditioning.*

UNCONDITIONED REFLEX

Unconditioned Stimulus ·······························>	Unconditioned Response
Digestive system	
Food ··>	salivation
Bad food ···>	sickness, nausea
Object in esophagus ·····························>	vomiting
Reproductive system	
Genital stimulation ·······························>	vaginal lubrication, penile erection, orgasm
Nipple stimulation ·······························>	milk release (in lactating women)
Circulatory system	
High temperature ································>	sweating, flushing
Sudden loud noise ·······························>	blanching, pounding heart
Respiratory system	
Irritation in nose··································>	sneeze
Throat clogged·····································>	cough
Allergens ··>	asthma attack
Muscular system	
Low temperature ································>	shivering
Blows or burns ·································>	withdrawal
Tap on patellar tendon·························>	knee jerk
Light to eye ·······································>	pupil constriction
Novel stimulation ·······························>	reflexive orienting
Infant reflexes	
Stroking the cheek ······························>	head turning
Object touches lips ·····························>	sucking
Food in mouth ···································>	swallowing
Object in the hand ·······························>	grasping
Held vertically, feet touching ground ·············>	stepping

Figure 15–1 A partial list of unconditioned reflexes. John D. Baldwin and Janice I. Baldwin, *Behavior Principles in Everyday Life*, 2nd ed. 1986, p. 44. Reprinted by permission of Prentice-Hall, Inc., Englewood Cliffs, N.J.

music with food before the sound of classical music would elicit any noticeable amount of salivation. Figure 15–2 illustrates respondent conditioning.

If a salivation response was in fact conditioned to the sound of classical music, the stimulus-response relationship would be referred to as a ***conditioned reflex***. The stimulus in a conditioned reflex is called a ***conditioned stimulus*** (CS; e.g., the sound of the classical music), and the response in a conditioned reflex is referred to as a ***conditioned response*** (CR; e.g., salivation to the classical music). In the experiment with Sue, the word *large* became a CS eliciting a GSR response as a CR. You can see how respondent conditioning might explain your reactions to certain words (like *cancer*) or even to a single letter (like "F" on an exam). As indicated by Sue's rating of the word *large* as unpleasant, such pairings contribute to the meaning of words on a personal level (Staats, 1996; Tyron & Cicero, 1989).

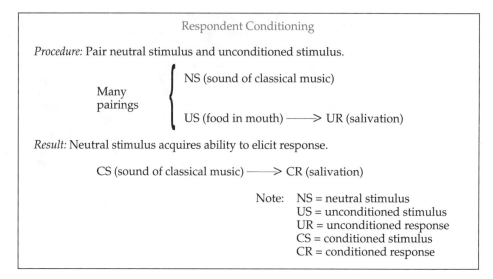

Figure 15–2   Model for respondent conditioning.

CSs and S^Ds   Note that CSs are like S^Ds in that both produce responses that have been conditioned to them. The conditioning procedures that established them differ, however. In addition, the ways in which CSs and S^Ds produce their responses seem to differ. Responses produced by CSs frequently seem to be more automatic or consistent. To capture this difference, standard behavioral terminology refers to CSs as *eliciting* the responses conditioned to them, whereas S^Ds are said to *evoke* the responses conditioned to them. In addition, operant behavior is sometimes said to be *emitted* by an individual, whereas respondent behavior is *elicited* by a stimulus. Throughout this text, we have been consistent in the use of the terms *elicit, evoke,* and *emit.*

Factors Influencing Respondent Conditioning   There are several variables that influence the development of a conditioned reflex. First, *the greater the number of pairings of a CS with a US, the greater is the ability of the CS to elicit the CR,* until a maximum strength of the conditioned reflex has been reached. If a child is scared several times by the loud barking of a dog, the sight of the dog will elicit a stronger fear than if the child had only been scared by the dog just once.

Second, *stronger conditioning occurs if the CS precedes the US by half a second, rather than by a longer time or rather than following the US.* Conditioning in the latter case is difficult to attain. If a child sees a dog, and then is immediately frightened by the dog's loud barking, sight of the dog is likely to become a CS with fear as a CR. On the other hand, if the child hears loud barking of a dog hidden from view, and a few seconds later sees a dog trot around the corner of a building, the fear caused by the loud barking is not likely to be transferred to the sight of the dog.

Third, *a CS acquires greater ability to elicit a CR if the CS is always paired with a given US than if it is only occasionally paired with the US.* If a couple, for example, consistently lights a candle in the bedroom just before having sex, and not at other times, then the candlelight is likely to become a CS eliciting sexual arousal. On the other hand, if they light a candle in the bedroom every night but have sex there only one or two nights each week, then the candlelight will be a weaker CS for sexual arousal.

Fourth, *when several neutral stimuli precede a US, the stimulus that is most consistently associated with the US is the one most likely to become a strong CS.* A child may experience thunderstorms in which dark clouds and lightning are usually followed by loud claps of thunder, which cause fear. On other occasions, the child sees dark clouds, but there is no lightning or thunder. The child will acquire a stronger fear of lightning than of the dark clouds because lightning is more consistently paired with thunder.

Fifth, *respondent conditioning will develop more quickly and strongly when the CS or US or both are intense rather than weak* (Lutz, 1994; Polenchar, Romano, Steinmetz, & Patterson, 1984). A child will acquire a stronger fear of lightning if the lightning is exceptionally bright and the thunder is exceptionally loud, than if either or both are relatively weak.   **Note 1**

RESPONDENT EXTINCTION

Once respondent conditioning occurs, does it stay with us forever? Not necessarily. It may be reversed through the principle of ***respondent extinction,*** which involves presenting a CS while withholding the US. After a number of such presentations, the CS gradually loses its capability of eliciting the CR. Let's suppose that a child reaches out to touch a large dog just as the dog barks very loudly, scaring the child. As a function of the pairing of the loud bark with the sight of the big dog, the sight of the big dog alone now elicits crying and trembling, a Pavlovian conditioned response that we label fear. Now let's suppose that the parent takes the child to a dog show. Although there are lots of large dogs around, they have been trained to walk and sit quietly while on display. Repeated contact with these dogs will help the child overcome fear of the sight of dogs. Sight of dogs loses its capability of functioning as a CS to elicit the fear reaction as a CR. Many of the fears that we acquire during childhood—fears of the dentist, the dark, thunder and lightning, and so on—undergo respondent extinction as we grow older, as a function of repeated exposure to these things in the absence of dire consequences. Figure 15–3 illustrates respondent extinction. And luckily for Sue, after encoun-

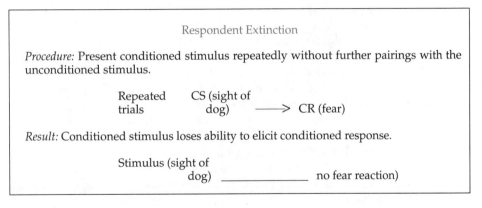

Figure 15–3 Model for respondent extinction.

tering the word *large* several times without further pairings with the shock and tone, it gradually lost its ability to elicit anxiety.

COUNTERCONDITIONING

Recall from Chapter 4 that operant extinction proceeds more quickly and effectively if an alternative response is reinforced. A similar rule holds for respondent extinction: A conditioned response may be eliminated more effectively if a new response is conditioned to the conditioned stimulus at the same time that the former conditioned response is being extinguished. This process is called *counterconditioning*. Stated technically, a CS will lose its ability to elicit a CR if that CS is paired with a stimulus that elicits a response that is incompatible with the CR. To illustrate this process, suppose that instead of simply exposing the child in the above example to dogs, we encouraged the child to play with another child who has a friendly dog. As the child plays with his or her friend and the friend's dog, some of the positive emotions elicited by the friend will become conditioned to the friend's dog. These positive conditioned emotional responses will help counteract the negative conditioned emotional responses previously elicited by dogs and thus more quickly and more effectively eliminate those responses.

RESPONDENT AND OPERANT CONDITIONING COMPARED

Respondent and operant conditioning procedures appear to influence two different kinds of behaviors. Nevertheless, there are a number of parallels between the procedures. Some of the differences and parallels between respondent and operant conditioning are presented in Figure 15–4.

Any behavioral sequence is likely to include both respondent and operant conditioning. In some situations, we might select certain stimuli and responses from a sequence to study respondent conditioning. Or we might examine that same sequence somewhat differently and study operant conditioning. Consider the behavioral sequence shown in Figure 15–5. As you can see, the sound of the bell in Figure 15–5 appears to be involved in both respondent and operant conditioning.

Here is another example of a behavioral sequence that involves both respondent and operant conditioning. A small child runs to pet a large dog. Never having had any reason to fear dogs, the child shows no fear now. Suppose, however, that the dog playfully jumps at the child and knocks him down. Quite naturally, the child will begin crying because of the pain and surprise of this rough treatment. Now what will happen the next time the child sees the dog or one that resembles it? Of course, the child will probably start crying and showing other types of fear behavior. Thus, a stimulus (sight of dog) that previously did not elicit a particular response (crying and other types of fear behavior) has come to do so because it was paired with a stimulus (suddenly being knocked down) that did elicit that response.

	OPERANT	RESPONDENT
Type of Behavior	Behavior that is emitted by the individual; sometimes referred to as voluntary; usually involves skeletal muscles.	Behavior that is reflexive; said to be elicited by prior stimuli; referred to as involuntary; usually involves smooth muscles and glands that control our gastrointestinal tract and blood vessels.
Reinforcement	*Procedure:* Presentation of a positive reinforcer following a response (or the removal of an aversive stimulus following a response). *Result:* **Behavior increases in frequency.**	*Procedure:* Pairing of previously neutral stimulus with an unconditioned stimulus. *Result:* **Neutral stimulus acquires capability of eliciting a conditioned response, and the stimulus is then called a conditioned stimulus.**
Extinction	*Procedure:* Reinforcer is withheld following a previously reinforced response. *Result:* **Response decreases in frequency.**	*Procedure:* Conditioned stimulus is presented without further pairings with the unconditioned stimulus. *Result:* **Conditioned stimulus loses capability of eliciting conditioned response.**
Spontaneous Recovery	*Procedure:* A "rest" period is introduced following an extinction session in which a behavior had completely decreased. *Result:* **Following the rest, the previously extinguished response will again occur, although to a lesser extent than during the extinction session.**	*Procedure:* A rest period is introduced following an extinction session in which trials occurred until a conditioned stimulus no longer elicited a conditioned response. *Result:* **Following the rest, the conditioned stimulus once again elicits a conditioned response, although to a lesser extent than during the extinction session.**

Figure 15–4   Operant and respondent conditioning compared.

It is important to note that in this example, the child's experience with the dog will have two important effects on the youngster's behavior. First, as we mentioned, the child will have a fear reaction (consisting of trembling, crying, the secretion of adrenalin into the blood, and an increased heart rate, among other

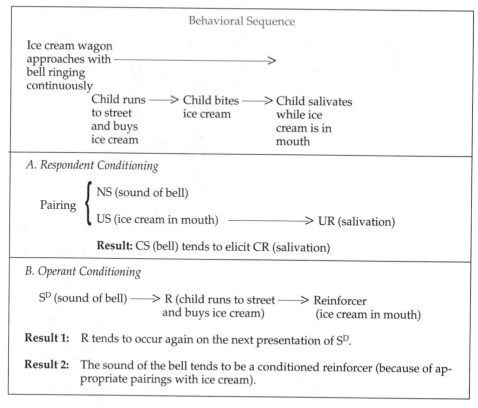

Figure 15–5 A behavioral sequence that includes both operant and respondent conditioning, and that leads to the development of a stimulus as a conditioned reinforcer.

things) whenever he sees a dog that resembles the one that knocked him down. This fear reaction to dogs is, as we mentioned, a response that has been respondently conditioned. Second, any behavior (such as looking over a backyard fence) that leads to the sight of a dog resembling the one that knocked him down will likely decrease in frequency. Moreover, the child will tend to avoid or get away from such dogs. In other words, those dogs will have become conditioned punishers for the child. In Chapter 13, we stated that a stimulus that is not punishing can become punishing if it is paired with a stimulus that is punishing. Some psychologists would theorize that the sight of the dog has become a conditioned punisher because it elicits fear as a result of respondent conditioning and that the fear so elicited is aversive.

It is evident that the same procedure that will cause a stimulus to elicit fear will also cause that stimulus to be a conditioned punisher. This is illustrated in Figure 15–6.

Thus, it is not always possible to discuss a behavioral sequence just in terms of operant conditioning. It might be said that the child in the preceding example had been punished for approaching dogs by having been knocked down by a dog. Although this might explain why the child no longer approaches dogs, it

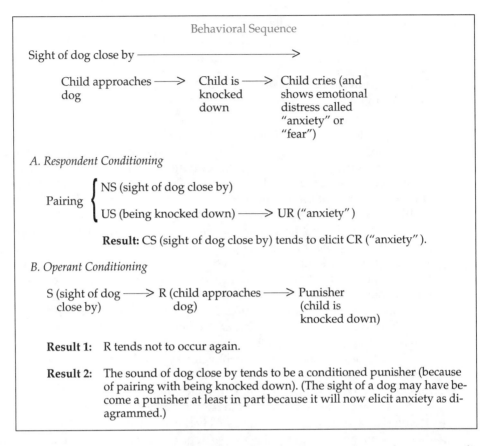

Figure 15–6   A behavioral sequence that involves both respondent and operant conditioning, and that leads to the development of a stimulus as a conditioned punisher.

does not explain why he experiences fear (which can be measured in terms of internal bodily reactions) when he sees a dog. It therefore appears that it is necessary to add the principle of respondent conditioning to our list of basic behavioral principles (see Pear & Eldridge, 1984).

RESPONDENT AND OPERANT COMPONENTS OF EMOTIONS

Emotions play an important role in our daily lives. To fully understand this important topic, we examine the role of respondent and operant conditioning in four areas: (a) the reaction that one feels during the experience of an emotion (such as the "queasiness" in the pit of one's stomach just before an important job interview); (b) the way that one learns to outwardly express or disguise an emotion (such as clasping one's hands tightly to hide nervousness); (c) how one becomes aware of and describes one's emotions (for example, "I'm a little nervous" as opposed to "I'm really angry"); and (d) some causes of emotions.

The Respondent Component of Emotions: Our Feelings

The respondent component of emotions involves that part of our nervous system referred to as the *autonomic nervous system*, which is involved in internal responses such as heart beat, breathing, digestion, and glandular functioning. These physiological activities are part of what is called "emotional behavior." What happens inside you, for example, in a moment of great fear? Your body is physically aroused—mobilized for action. Your adrenal glands secrete adrenalin into your bloodstream for extra energy. Your heart rate increases dramatically. At the same time, you breathe much more rapidly, providing an increased supply of oxygen to the blood. This oxygen surges through your body with the increased heart rate, supplying more oxygen to your muscles. You may begin to sweat, which acts as a cooling mechanism in preparation for increased energy output of the body. At the same time that these changes are occurring, you may get a "queasy" feeling in your stomach. Blood vessels to the stomach and intestines constrict and the process of digestion is interrupted, diverting blood from your internal organs to your muscles. Your mouth becomes dry as the action of the salivary glands is impeded. You might even temporarily lose bowel or bladder control (a reaction that for our primative ancestors lightened their bodies in preparation for flight and tended to deter their pursuers). These internal reactions of the body mobilize one's resources for fighting or fleeing. These reactions clearly had survival value in our evolutionary history, but they may not always be useful in modern society (e.g., when called upon to make a speech or to answer a question in class).

Autonomic responses occur as unconditioned reactions to stimuli, and such responses can be visible as blushing, trembling, and crying. In studies of newborn infants, sudden loss of support, loud sounds, and a sudden push elicit the unconditioned responses of a sudden catching of breath, a clutching or grasping response, puckering of lips, and crying that we label as *fear*. Hampering an infant's movements, on the other hand, elicits crying, screaming, and body stiffening that we label as *anger*. And tickling, gentle rocking, and patting appear to be unconditioned stimuli for the responses of smiling, gurgling, and cooing, labeled as *joy*. Cross-cultural evidence suggests that these reflexive reactions may be universal (Ekman, 1972). We learn to describe these physiological components of our emotions as our *feelings*.

Although the exact number of inherited emotional reflexes must await further research, there is no doubt about the importance of respondent conditioning for attaching physiological components of emotions to new stimuli. Nearly every organ and gland controlled by the autonomic nervous system is susceptible to respondent conditioning (Airapetyantz & Bykov, 1966). When experimenters have demonstrated respondent conditioning of emotions with humans, they have often relied on the visible signs of the physiological changes to demonstrate that learning has occurred. Consider a classic experiment by John B. Watson and

Rosalie Rayner (1920). They were interested in demonstrating that fears could be learned through Pavlovian procedures. They conducted their experiment with "Little Albert," an 11-month-old infant. During preliminary observations, it was demonstrated that Albert was not afraid of a variety of items that were placed near him when he was happily playing on a rug on the floor. Watson then introduced a white rat (of which Albert had previously shown no fear) and while Albert was watching the rat closely, Watson banged a steel bar with a hammer just behind Albert's head. The loud noise caused startle, crying, and other fearful behavior in Albert. After a total of seven pairings of the loud noises within the sight of the rat over two separate sessions approximately 1 week apart, Albert showed a very strong fear reaction to the rat. Whenever the rat appeared, Albert cried, trembled, and showed the facial expression for fear. When other items were introduced, for which Albert had previously shown no fear, Albert's fear had spread to these items as well. In particular, this fear was transferred to a rabbit, a dog, a seal skin coat, and a piece of cotton. Unfortunately, Albert's parents moved away before Watson and Rayner had a chance to decondition the fear. However, Mary Cover Jones (1924) followed up some of Watson's suggestions and demonstrated that fear reactions in infants could be eliminated with respondent extinction. It would be considered unethical today to subject infants to aversive stimuli for experimental purposes. Procedural questions about the Watson and Rayner study have also been raised (B. Harris, 1979). Nevertheless, the finding that fears are influenced by reflexive learning is well established.

The feelings associated with other emotions are also influenced by respondent conditioning. At a family reunion, for example, family members experience many happy moments. A few weeks later, when viewing the photos taken at the reunion, the pictures will likely be conditioned stimuli eliciting "happy" feelings. But there is more to emotions than the autonomic responses that we feel. Let's see how operant conditioning is also involved.

An Operant Component of Emotions: Our Actions

When you experience an emotion-causing event, your body responds with an immediate physiological reaction and accompanying facial expression. But then what happens? That depends on your operant learning experiences. In a situation that causes anger, for example, one person might shout and swear. Another person in that same situation might clench their fists and walk away (see Figure 15–7). Little Albert initially showed the respondent components of fear of crying and trembling. But he also showed operant fear responses: When the white rat was presented, Albert crawled away as fast as he could. Because the operant component of emotions depends on each individual's prior learning history, these secondary displays of emotion vary from person to person and culture to culture. Fans at a sporting event in North America, for example, are likely to show their displeasure towards unsportsmanlike play by booing, while fans in Europe express their displeasure by whistling. We learn to display our emotions in ways that have been operantly reinforced in the past. Operant conditioning is also involved when we're taught to be aware of our emotions.

Figure 15–7   Withholding reinforcers following a previously reinforced response can cause anger.
What are some operant and respondent components of anger?

Another Operant Component of Emotions:
Our Awareness

As we grow up, people around us teach us to label our emotions. Depending
upon our behavior, moms and dads ask things such as, "Why are you so angry?"
or "Aren't you having fun?" or "How are you feeling?" From such experiences,
we learn about "being angry," "feeling happy," and "feeling sad." By age 9, most
children have learned to recognize a large number of emotional expressions in
themselves and others (Izard, 1991). Nevertheless, many emotions are not easily
described or defined. We can account for this difficulty to some extent by considering the multiple sources of control over the naming of behavior that we describe as emotional. Suppose you see a girl's brother grab the girl's toy train and
run away, and the girl runs after her brother and screams at him. You might suggest that the girl is angry. The next day, when coming out of your house, you see
the same girl screaming and running after her brother. You might again conclude
that she is angry. But in the second instance, the children are simply enjoying a
game of tag. Thus, when labeling emotions, we don't always have access to the
emotion-causing events, the inside feelings, and the observable operant behaviors. This contributes to inconsistencies in the way that we talk about emotions.

Some Causes of Emotions

Presentation and withdrawal of reinforcers and presentation and withdrawal of punishers constitute four major causes of emotions. Presentation of reinforcers causes the emotion called *happiness*. Getting an "A" on an exam, receiving a compliment, cashing your paycheck, watching a funny movie, all involve the presentation of positive reinforcers. Withholding or withdrawal of reinforcers causes the emotion called *anger*. All of us have experienced such anger-causing events as a vending machine that takes your money but fails to produce the goods, being kept waiting in the doctor's office, a pen that stops writing in the middle of a quiz, and having a ticket line close just before we get to the window to buy a ticket. The presentation of punishers or aversive stimuli cause the emotion called *anxiety*. Approaching scary-looking strangers in a dark alley, seeing a car drive directly toward you at a high speed, or hearing a dog bark right behind you are all likely to cause you to feel anxious. Finally, withdrawal of aversive or punishing events causes an emotion that is called *relief*. For example, when a female receives the results from a test of a lump on her breast, or a male learns about the results of an assessment of an enlarged prostate, and the individual learns that the problem is not cancer, the individual is likely to feel relief. Each of these causes of emotions is likely to occur on a continuum from very mild to very strong. Presentation of rewards, for example, can cause emotions ranging from mild pleasure to happiness to ecstasy. Withdrawal of rewards can cause emotions ranging from mild annoyance to anger to rage. Presentation of aversive events can cause mild apprehension, anxiety, or stark terror. And the effects of withdrawal of aversive events might range from mild relief to an emotional collapse. Other emotions might represent a mixture of some of these basic emotions (e.g., see Martin & Osborne, 1993).

   To summarize, many of our emotions are caused by either the presentation or withdrawal of reinforcers or punishers. Our emotions have three important characteristics: (a) the autonomic reaction that you feel inside during the experience of an emotion (typically accompanied by visible signs, such as frowns or smiles), which is influenced by respondent conditioning; (b) the way that you learn to express an emotion overtly (such as shouting, jumping up and down), which is influenced by operant conditioning; and (c) the way that you become aware of and describe your emotions, which is also influenced by operant conditioning. (For a more detailed discussion of operant and respondent components of emotions, see G. L. Martin & Osborne, 1993.) In Chapters 25 and 26 we'll discuss examples of how respondent and operant conditioning have been used to change troublesome emotions.

APPLICATIONS OF RESPONDENT CONDITIONING PRINCIPLES

Applications of respondent conditioning and extinction have involved controlling allergies, immune system function, reactions to drugs, sexual arousal, nausea, blood pressure, thoughts, fears, and emotions. In Chapter 25, we discuss ap-   **Note 2** plications of respondent principles to treat phobias. In this section, we illustrate its application to several other types of problems.

Aversion Therapy

Certain kinds of positive reinforcers can be very troublesome. People who find pastries and other sweets overly reinforcing tend to eat too many fattening foods and become overweight. Similarly, people who find cigarettes, alcohol, and other harmful commodities overly reinforcing tend to overindulge in these reinforcers to the detriment of their health and well-being. People who obtain sexual rein- forcement in socially unacceptable ways—for instance, by seducing children— tend to endanger others, by exposing them to potentially harmful experiences, and themselves, by risking imprisonment and other social sanctions.

Aversion therapy was developed largely as an attempt to counteract the power of undesirable reinforcers (those that tend to be overindulged in or that harm others). Before describing some of the methods of aversion therapy, we should caution the reader that their safe and effective use requires special exper- tise. These procedures, as the label *aversion therapy* implies, involve the use of aversive stimulation. As we have seen in Chapter 13, there are serious dangers in the use of aversive stimulation. It should therefore be used only by qualified ex- perts who know when and how it is most likely to be effective, and how to guard against potentially harmful side effects.

Basically, aversion therapy involves the repeated pairing (i.e., over a num- ber of trials) of an undesirable reinforcer with an aversive event. The rationale of aversion therapy is counterconditioning; that is, it is assumed that the undesir- able reinforcer should then become less reinforcing, because it will come to elicit a response similar to that elicited by the aversive stimulus.

For example, in the treatment of alcoholism, a person may be given a drug that will make him/her nauseous. Just before the drug takes effect, he/she is given a sip of an alcoholic beverage. Thus, the sight, smell, and taste of the drink is followed immediately by nausea. This pairing of alcohol with nausea is re- peated over a number of sessions. Eventually, alcohol itself should tend to elicit nausea, which may cause the individual to avoid alcohol. How well the therapy works in any given case depends, at least in part, on other treatment factors— such as whether the client continues taking the drug after leaving the hospital, and on operant processes operating in the natural environment—such as whether the client receives social reinforcement for his/her subsequent choosing of nonal- coholic over alcoholic beverages at parties, restaurants, and bars.

In a study in which alcoholics experienced the pairing of alcohol drinking with disulfiram (Antabuse) medication, less than 1 percent of the clients contin- ued to take the drug after release from a hospital (Lubetkin, Rivers, & Rosenberg, 1971). In another study, only 7 percent of the patients continued to take disulfi- ram after 1 year (Ludwig, Levine, & Stark, 1970). An aversion-conditioning com- ponent involving disulfiram, however, proved to be a valuable addition to a pro- gram for treating alcoholics that included a multiple-component behavior therapy program with procedures directed toward job finding, marital counseling, social and recreational programming, and a buddy system (Azrin, 1976; Azrin, Sisson, Meyers, & Godley, 1982). Similar results have also been obtained for cigarette smoking. The aversion-conditioning procedure in this case involved requiring subjects to smoke one cigarette after another rapidly until nausea occurred. In this way, the smell and flavor of cigarettes was paired with an aversive stimulus (nausea). This procedure, called *rapid smoking aversion therapy*, caused short-term cessation of smoking but did not show successful long-term effects (Danaher, 1977). When the rapid smoking aversion procedure was added to a multiple-component behavioral counseling program for quitting smoking, however, both short-term and long-term results were better than with the behavior counseling program alone (Tiffany, Martin, & Baker, 1986).

Symbolic representations (such as pictures, slides, and filmstrips) of the undesirable reinforcers, rather than the actual reinforcers themselves, are commonly used in aversion therapy. This is largely a matter of convenience. Slides, videotapes, or computer disks containing pictures of a wide variety of troublesome reinforcers can easily be stored in the therapist's office. Moreover, it is relatively easy to make new stimuli appropriate to individual cases. These stimuli can then be presented at specified intervals and for specified durations and can be associated with the onset or termination of the aversive stimulus in a precisely controlled manner. In addition, their use precludes various problems that would arise if the actual undesirable reinforcers were used during therapy. To give an extreme example, one obviously would not use real children in treating a child molester. It is generally acceptable, however, to use pictures of children in various poses, but therapists should consult the laws of the country in which they are working before using this type of procedure.

Although aversion therapy appears to be a valuable addition to multiple-component programs for treating various problems, such as alcohol drinking and cigarette smoking, it is not widely used. As indicated by Wilson (1991), its limited use stems from ethical concerns about the use of aversive stimulation in treatment, the increased expense typically associated with conducting aversion therapy under the continual supervision of a therapist or in a hospital, and the fact that there's a fairly high dropout rate from treatment by clients who experience aversion therapy.

Treatment for Chronic Constipation

An example of respondent conditioning of a desirable response is the treatment for chronic constipation developed by Quarti and Renaud (1964). Defecation, the desired response in cases of constipation, can be elicited by administering a laxative. However, reliance on such drugs to achieve regularity is not the healthiest solution because of the undesirable side effects that often result. Quarti and Renaud had their clients administer to themselves a distinctive electrical stimulus—a mild, nonpainful electric current—immediately prior to defecating. Defecation was initially elicited by a laxative, and then the amount of the drug was gradually decreased until defecation was elicited by the electrical stimulus alone. Then, by applying the electrical stimulus at the same time each day, several of the clients were eventually able to get rid of the electrical stimulus, because the natural environment stimuli characteristically present at that time each day acquired control over the behavior of defecating. Thus, these clients achieved regularity without the continued use of artificial stimulation (also see Rovetto, 1979).

Treatment of Nocturnal Enuresis (Bed-wetting)

Another example of respondent conditioning of a desirable response is the bell-pad treatment for nocturnal enuresis (M. A. Scott, Barclay, & Houts, 1992). One possible explanation for nocturnal enuresis, a problem that is rather common in young children, is that pressure on the child's bladder when he is asleep and has to urinate does not provide sufficient stimulation to awaken him. A device that seems to be effective for many enuretic children consists of a bell connected to a special pad under the bottom sheet on the child's bed. The apparatus is wired so that the bell sounds and awakens the child as soon as the first drop of urine makes contact with the pad. Eventually, in many cases, the child will awaken before he urinates—apparently because the response of waking up has been conditioned to the stimulus of pressure on the bladder. Naturally, the procedure should be supplemented with reinforcement to the child when he goes to the toilet at night so that this behavior will occur instead of bed-wetting.

Note 3

A CAUTIONARY NOTE

Chapters 3 through 13 described basic principles and procedures of operant conditioning, along with guidelines for their application. Chapter 14 presented information on escape and avoidance conditioning, and this chapter presented information on respondent conditioning. Chapters 16 through 26 describe additional information for designing and executing behavioral programs. We believe that mastery of the material in Chapters 3 through 13 and 16 through 26 will enable the reader to design, implement, and maintain a variety of behavior modification programs effectively. We do not make such a claim for the material in Chapters 14 and 15. Additional information and guidance are necessary before the reader attempts to carry out programs involving escape or avoidance conditioning and respondent conditioning.

STUDY QUESTIONS

1. What is the basic tenet of operant conditioning?
2. Give five examples of unconditioned reflexes (two of which are not in the text). Describe both the stimulus and the response.
3. State the principle of respondent conditioning. Clearly describe and diagram two examples of respondent conditioning (one of which is not in the text).

4. Define and give an example of the following: unconditioned stimulus, unconditioned response, conditioned stimulus, and conditioned response.
5. In a sentence each, briefly describe five variables that influence the development of a conditioned reflex.
6. State the principle and describe an example of respondent extinction.
7. Describe the process of counterconditioning. Describe an example of counterconditioning that is not in the text.
8. Compare respondent and operant conditioning in terms of behavior, reinforcement, extinction, and spontaneous recovery.
9. Explain how respondent conditioning and operant conditioning can interact to cause an individual to escape or avoid a particular stimulus. Use diagrams and examples to clarify your explanation.
10. Describe several physiological activities that we experience in a moment of great fear.
11. Describe unconditioned reflexes that appear to characterize the emotions of fear, anger, and joy.
12. In the experiment with Little Albert, what was the US? the UR? the CS? the CR?
13. Cross-cultural studies of emotions suggest that emotions are both universal and culture-specific. How can we explain this apparent contradiction?
14. In a sentence each, summarize three important characteristics that make up our emotions.
15. For what general type of problem is aversion therapy used? Give three examples of such problems (one of which is not in the text).
16. Describe four causes of emotions, give an example of each, and name the usual labels for these emotions.
17. Why should aversion therapy be used only by competent professional practitioners?
18. Describe the basic procedure and rationale of aversion therapy. Give an example of aversion therapy.
19. Briefly describe a respondent-conditioning procedure for treating constipation. Identify the US, UR, CS, and CR.
20. Describe a respondent-conditioning procedure for treating nocturnal enuresis. Identify the US, UR, CS, and CR.

APPLICATION EXERCISES

A. Exercise Involving Others

Pick an emotion (e.g., anger), and observe the operant displays of that emotion in two people you know. Are their operant components of that emotion similar or different?

B. Self-Modification Exercise

Consider an emotion that you frequently experience. Describe how the experiencing of that emotion includes both respondent and operant responses.

NOTES AND EXTENDED DISCUSSION

1. Another factor influencing respondent conditioning is that organisms are biologically predisposed to be more readily conditioned to some neutral stimuli as CSs than to others. Humans, for example, will more quickly learn fears to stimuli that may have posed a threat to survival, such as snakes and insects, than to stimuli that were likely nonthreatening in our ancestors' history, such as pictures of flowers (Ohman, Dimberg, & Ost, 1984).

2. Pavlovian conditioning procedures may affect the functioning of our immune system. Ader and Cohen (1982) found with rats that pairing of saccharine with an immune-suppressive drug established saccharine as a conditioned stimulus that elicits immune suppression. Other studies have also demonstrated classical conditioning of various aspects of immune responses in other species (Ader & Cohen, 1993; Maier, Watkins, & Fleshner, 1994; Turkkan, 1989). This exciting new area of research on the effects of conditioning processes on the functioning of the body's immune system is called *psychoimmunology* or *psychoneuroimmunology*. There is already the promise of clinical applications of research from this area. For example, consider the problem that chemotherapy for cancer involves chemical agents that are immunosuppressive. When repeated chemotherapy was done in the same room in the same hospital setting for women suffering from ovarian cancer, the women eventually displayed immunosuppression after simply being brought to that room of the hospital prior to chemotherapy (Bovjberg et al., 1990). A simple solution to such a problem would be to give chemotherapy in different environmental contexts, rather than always in the same room.

3. In a case study with a 15-year-old female resident of Boys' Town, Friman and Vollmer (1995) demonstrated that a urine alarm may also be used effectively with diurnal enuresis (daytime wetting). The moisture-sensitive part of the alarm system was attached to the girl's underwear and the alarm was attached unobtrusively to her outer clothing. Although the procedure was successful almost immediately, it appears that its success was based on escape and avoidance rather than respondent conditioning. This was indicated in part by the fact that whenever the alarm sounded, the child seemed embarrassed and quickly left for the bathroom. Thus, her reduced wetting may have been under the control of aversive social stimuli that occured when the alarm sounded.

Study Questions on Notes

1. Describe the field of psychoimmunology. What is its potential applied importance?
2. Discuss how different behavior principles may be responsible for the success of a urine alarm with nocturnal and diurnal enuresis.
3. Discuss whether all stimuli are equally capable of becoming CSs.

16

Capitalizing on Existing Stimulus Control: Rules and Goals

Suppose that a sport psychologist is talking to a young figure skater a few minutes before she will skate her program in an important competition. Showing signs of extreme nervousness, the skater expresses her concerns: "I hope I don't fall on my double axel. I hope I don't come in last. What if I don't skate well?" How can the sport psychologist help the skater? Given the assumption that her negative self-talk is what is causing the skater to feel anxious and that this anxiety might interfere with good skating, it would seem desirable to design a program to develop more confident self-talk. But there's no time to go through a number of shaping steps to do this. Respondent extinction might be used to decrease feelings of excessive nervousness, but that, too, requires more time than is available in the few minutes before she is to perform. An alternative solution is for the psychologist to present stimuli that, because of the skater's conditioning history, already control the desired behavior. For example, the psychologist might ask the skater to repeat self-talk that is likely to elicit feelings of confidence, such as "I've landed all of my jumps in practice and I can land them all here. I'll focus on the things that I do when I'm skating well, and I'll take it one step at a time. I'll smile, have fun, and play to the judges," and so on. The psychologist might also encourage the skater to practice a relaxation technique called *deep center breathing* in which she breathes low down in her abdomen, and quietly says, "r-e-l-a-x" each time she exhales. In other words, because of our various learning experiences over many years and because we have been reinforced for responding to certain stimuli, those stimuli (people, places, words, smells, sounds, etc.) are likely to exert control over our behavior when they are introduced. Before designing a behavior modification program, it's important to ask, "Can I capitalize on existing forms of stimulus control?" Treatment packages that do so fall into the categories of rules, goals, modeling, physical guidance, and situational inducement. We'll discuss the first two categories in this chapter and the others in the next chapter.

RULES

As described in Chapter 8, a **rule** is a description (verbal or written) of a three-term contingency of reinforcement (antecedents-behavior-consequences). Speaking loosely, it is a statement that a specific behavior will pay off in a particular situation. When we were infants, rules were meaningless to us. But as we grew older, we learned that following rules often led to rewards (e.g., "If you eat all your vegetables, you can have dessert"), or enabled us to avoid punishers (e.g., "If you don't be quiet, I'll send you to your room"). Thus, a rule functions as an S^D, a cue that emitting the behavior specified by the rule will lead to the reinforcer identified in the rule, or a cue that not following the rule will lead to a punisher (Brownstein & Shull, 1985; Skinner, 1969; Vaughan, 1989).

Note 1

Sometimes rules clearly identify reinforcers or punishers associated with following the rules, as illustrated in the above examples. In other cases, consequences are implied. When a parent says to a child in an excited voice, "Wow! Would you look at that!," looking in the indicated direction will likely enable the child to see something interesting. Reinforcers are also implied for rules stated in the form of *advice*. For example, the advice "You should get a good education" typically implies that doing so will lead to a well-paying job. On the other hand, rules given in the form of a *command* or a *threat* imply that noncompliance will be punished. For example, the command "Don't touch that vase" implies that touching it will lead to unpleasantness (such as a reprimand).

Rules that do not identify all three aspects of a contingency of reinforcement might be referred to as *partial rules*. The examples of the partial rules in the preceding paragraph focused on the behavior. Other partial rules identify the antecedent (e.g., "school zone"), while the behavior ("drive slowly") and the consequences ("to avoid a speeding ticket") are implied. In other instances, partial rules identify the consequences (e.g., "98 percent payout"), while the antecedents ("at our casino") and the behavior ("put money in our slot machines") are implied. Because of our various learning experiences, partial rules also control our behavior.

Contingency-Shaped Versus Rule-Governed Behavior

Suppose that little Bobby whispers something funny to his sister while attending church with their parents. Bobby's sister ignores him (and his mom gives his hand a firm squeeze), and Bobby is less likely to whisper funny comments in church. Now suppose that little Bobby whispers funny comments to his teammates on the pee-wee hockey team while his coach is trying to explain how to execute a play. Bobby's teammates laugh, and his whispering is strengthened in that setting. In these examples, we would refer to Bobby's whispering as *contingency-shaped behavior*—behavior that has been strengthened (or weakened) in settings by the direct-acting effects of consequences in those settings. Now let's suppose that Bobby's coach, wanting to decrease Bobby's disruptive whispering, says to Bobby at the start of a practice, "If you listen carefully and don't whisper when I'm talking to the team, we'll have an extra five minutes of scrimmage at the end of practice." During the practice, Bobby frequently repeats the rule, makes it through the practice without whispering, and he and the team earn the reinforcer. In this example, listening attentively to the coach without whispering would be referred to as *rule-governed behavior*—behavior that is controlled by the statement of a rule.

Contingency-shaped behavior involves immediate consequences, and the behavior is typically strengthened gradually through trial and error. In the case of Bobby's whispering, for example, his whispering initially came under the control of his teammates at hockey practice as S^Ds through several trials involving immediate reinforcement for whispering. His whispering gradually decreased in the presence of his sister and parents at church as S^Δs as a result of several trials of extinction. Rule-governed behavior, on the other hand, often involves delayed consequences, and frequently leads to immediate behavior change. When Bobby's coach gave him a rule concerning whispering at practices, Bobby's behavior improved immediately. It did not take a few trials to show evidence of stimulus control, even though the reinforcer for following the rule was delayed until the end of practice.

Knowledge of rule-governed behavior enables us to more fully explain some applications we presented earlier that involved indirect-acting effects of reinforcers. You may recall the case of Fernando in Chapter 3. When Fernando was told that he would be given a slip of paper that could be exchanged for 2 pesos immediately contingent upon arriving to work on time, he was never again late for work through the duration of the study. This was not an example of the direct-acting effects of reinforcement, because the reinforcer of 2 pesos occurred well after the behavior of leaving earlier for work. Instead, it was likely Fernando's rehearsal of a rule (e.g., "If I leave earlier, I will arrive on time and I can earn two extra pesos") that served as an S^D for the rule-following behavior of leaving a half-hour earlier in the morning. You might also remember the example in Chapter 10, of Coach Dawson's point program at basketball practices. Because they were not awarded to the players until the end of a practice, points were delayed considerably following various behaviors (such as improved shooting percentages) that had occurred earlier in that practice. Thus, the improved performance was not due to the direct-acting effects of the points as conditioned reinforcers. The players likely verbally rehearsed rules during practices, such as "If I make more jump shots, I'll earn more points," and such self-statements may have exerted rule-governed control over the improved performance.

Often, behavior that might seem to be strengthened by the direct-acting effects of reinforcement may result, at least partly, from the existence of rule-governed behavior. For example, the child who has just cleaned her room and is told, "Good girl for cleaning your room," may tend to engage in this behavior more frequently. The stimulus "good girl for cleaning your room" seems to be acting as a reinforcer in this instance. But the child has also been given a rule—namely, "If I clean my room, I'll be a good girl" (and Mom and Dad will be nicer to me, etc.)—which tends to exert rule-governed control over the room-cleaning behavior in the future, quite apart from the reinforcing effect of praise. (This is one reason why we would not use "good girl for cleaning your room" as a reinforcer for the child doing her homework!)

When Are Rules Especially Helpful?

We have argued in Chapter 3 that behavior modification programs should *always* include instruction in the form of rules, even with individuals with limited verbal skills. And in Chapter 29, we discuss ethical reasons why behavior modification programs should be clearly explained to all clients. But there are some specific situations with verbal people where including rules in a behavior modification program is especially effective (Baldwin & Baldwin, 1986; Skinner, 1969, 1974).

When Rapid Behavior Change Is Desirable   Correct use of rules can produce behavior change much more rapidly than shaping or chaining or trial-and-error experiences with reinforcement and extinction. In the example of the sport psychologist attempting to help the figure skater, the skater was essentially being given a rule (i.e., "If I focus on the things that I think about when I'm skating well at a practice, then I'll land all the elements in my program, just like I do at practice."). Rehearsing the rule might help the skater to focus on the cues that normally enable her to land her jumps, rather than worrying about falling. The rule might also function as a conditioned stimulus to elicit the relaxed feelings that were typically experienced at practices (and which may be a part of the contextual stimuli that control good skating).

When Consequences That You Might Provide for a Behavior Are Too Delayed to Directly Reinforce That Behavior   Suppose that a parent wants to encourage a child to study for an hour or so each evening during the week. A suitable reinforcer might be allowing the child to stay up late on the weekend to watch a movie—something that the child really likes to do. But movie watching on Friday night is long delayed from studying for an hour on Monday. By adding a rule, "If you study for an hour each night this week, you can watch the late movie on Friday night," the parent has increased the chances of the delayed reinforcer having an indirect-acting effect on the desired behavior.

When You Would Like to Maintain a Behavior for Which Natural Reinforcers Are Immediate, but Highly Intermittent   Suppose that the sales people in a department store are working on a commission. During the post-Christmas season in recessionary times, sales are very slow. The salespeople are immediately reinforced when they make a sale (by the fact that the sale gives them more money), but they must approach a great many customers before a sale is made. In other words, the schedule of reinforcement is very lean, so that ratio strain may occur. The store manager might increase the persistence of the salespeople by encouraging them to rehearse the rule, "Be persistent! The very next customer might mean a sale."

When a Specific Behavior Will Lead to Immediate and Severe Punishment   Rules can help people learn appropriate behavior when learning "the hard way" can be extremely costly. For example, surprising though it may seem, some students are genuinely unaware that copying parts of a textbook word-for-word on a term paper without acknowledging the source is unacceptable. All students should be taught, long before they ever reach college, the rule "Copying from a source without giving credit is plagiarism and can lead to serious academic penalty."

Why Do Rules Control Our Behavior?

It's easy to understand why people would learn to follow rules that describe direct-acting consequences. Following the rule "Try this new flavor of ice cream, you'll love it" will be reinforced immediately by the taste of the ice cream. Failure to follow the rule "Move back from the campfire or you'll burn yourself" will likely lead to a fairly immediate punisher. *But why do we follow rules that identify very delayed consequences?* There are several possibilities. First, although the reinforcer identified in a rule might be delayed for an individual, other people might provide immediate consequences if the individual follows (or does not follow) the rule. In the example of the parent who provides the rule for her child, "If you study for an hour each night this week, you can watch the late movie on Friday night," the parent might also say, after an instance of studying on Monday night, "Good for you. Keep it up and you'll be able to stay up late on Friday."

Second, an individual might follow a rule and then immediately make reinforcing statements to himself or herself. In the case of Fernando, after complying with the rule that served as an S^D for leaving a half-hour earlier for work in the morning, he might have speculated about what he might buy with the extra pesos that he would earn. (Self-reinforcement is discussed further in Chapter 24.) Alternatively, failure to comply with a rule might lead to self-punishment.

A third possibility is that our operant-respondent interactions (see Chapter 15) give us a reinforcement history such that following rules is automatically strengthened and failure to follow rules is automatically punished. Suppose you give yourself the rule "I better start studying my behavior modification text now or I'll fail the exam tomorrow." Perhaps because of your history of being punished for failing to meet deadlines, such a statement may increase the aversiveness of stimuli associated with not studying for the exam, which would elicit some anxiety. When you comply with the rule, those stimuli decrease and your rule following is maintained by escape conditioning. Technically, we would say that the statement of a rule functions as an establishing operation to increase the reinforcement strength or effectiveness of the consequences of appropriate rule following (Malott, 1989, also see Note 1). In everyday language, rehearsal of the deadline causes you to feel anxious, and responding to the rule to make the deadline then makes you feel a lot better. Of course, whether or not such automatic consequences will continue to influence your rule following will depend on the extent to which you continue to experience punishment for noncompliance with rules and failure to meet deadlines.

Although we have given many examples illustrating how rules generally enhance the development and maintenance of behavior, it is important to realize that there are exceptions to this generalization. Rules introduce extra stimuli and responses that, in some circumstances, can have the net effect of interfering with contingency-shaped behavior. A person trying to verbalize and follow rules may, in these circumstances, become somewhat like the proverbial centipede that got itself all tied in knots trying to think about how it walked!

Effective and Ineffective Rules

We've said that a rule is an S^D—a cue that performing the behavior as specified in the rule will lead to a reinforcer or escape from or avoidance of a punisher. But all rules aren't created equal. Many people, for example, might follow the rule "Try this new flavor of ice cream; it's delicious." But fewer, unfortunately, are likely to follow the rule "Always wear a helmet when rollerblading in order to avoid brain damage from an accident." Let's look at four conditions that affect the likelihood of rule-following behavior.

Specific Versus Vague Descriptions of Behavior   Provided that a rule describes adequate reinforcement for rule following, a rule that describes behavior specifically is more likely to be followed than a rule that describes a behavior vaguely. Telling young figure skaters, for example, that they will become better skaters if they work hard at practices is less effective than telling them, "If you try to complete at least 60 jumps and spins during each 45-minute practice, you will become a better skater than if you complete fewer than that number."

Probable Versus Improbable Consequences   Rules are likely to be followed if they identify behavior for which the consequences are highly probable, even though the consequences may be delayed. If a parent tells her teenage child, "If you mow the lawn on Monday, I'll give you $10.00 on Saturday," and assuming that that parent always follows up on such rules, then it is highly likely that the teenager will mow the lawn on Monday. If the teenager does so, receiving the $10.00 the following Saturday is a certainty. On the other hand, rules are likely to be ineffective if they describe low probability outcomes for behavior, even though those outcomes would be immediate if they occurred (Malott, 1989, 1992). To illustrate this point, consider that most people know that wearing a lifejacket when canoeing could save their lives. And most people know that wearing a helmet when rollerblading could prevent brain damage from a serious accident. So why do many people go canoeing without a lifejacket, or rollerblading without a helmet? One reason (that does not necessarily involve rules) may be that desirable safety behavior in such instances leads to fairly immediate punishers (e.g., the lifejacket and the helmet are hot and uncomfortable). Another reason is that such rules (i.e., to wear a lifejacket while canoeing and a helmet while rollerblading) involve low probability consequences. Many people have gone canoeing without ever upsetting the canoe. And the rollerblader knows that a rollerblading accident sufficient to cause brain damage is unlikely. We are not suggesting that rules should not be used in such situations. The rollerblader might be encouraged to rehearse, before rollerblading, "If I wear my helmet, I can avoid the possibility of serious brain damage." But for a rule to be effective when it describes improbable consequences, it may need to be supplemented by other behavior management strategies, such as modeling (see Chapter 17), self-monitoring (see Chapter 24), or behavioral contracting (see Chapter 24).

Sizeable Consequences Versus Small but Cumulatively Significant Consequences   Rules that describe sizeable consequences are likely to be effective. In the example cited above involving $10.00 for mowing the lawn, $10.00 was a sizeable consequence for that teenager. However, a rule is less likely to be effective if the consequence is quite small following each instance of rule following, even though such consequences may be cumulatively significant. Suppose, for example, that an individual resolves that, "I'm going to stop eating desserts," and "I'm going to exercise three times a week." Why are such rules often ineffective? One reason (that does not necessarily involve rules) is that there are direct-acting consequences that support behavior that is incompatible with following the rule. Eating a dessert is immediately reinforced by the delicious taste. And exercising often involves fairly immediate punishers (getting hot, sweaty, and tired). The second reason that such rules are ineffective is that the supportive consequences of a single instance of following such a rule are too small to be noticeable, and are only cumulatively significant (Malott, 1989, 1992). (Other possibilities are discussed in Chapter 24.) That is, it's not the excess weight from the single extra dessert that's a problem; it's the increased weight that occurs when you have the extra dessert on many occasions (see Figure 16–1). Likewise, a single instance of exercising won't produce observable benefits. It's the accumulation of the benefits of exercising on many occasions that is eventually noticeable. Rules that describe immediate small consequences that are harmful or beneficial only after they have accumulated (and therefore only after a long delay) are likely to be ineffective unless complemented by some of the self-management strategies described in Chapter 24.

Deadlines Versus No Deadlines   Suppose that a preschool teacher says to a child, "If you put all the toys away, I'll bring you a treat next week." Is the child likely to put the books away for such a delayed reinforcer? What if the teacher

Figure 16–1   Why are some rules (such as "resisting extra dessert") so difficult to follow?

says to the child, "If you put all the toys away *right now*, I'll bring you a treat next week." Would specifying "right now" make a difference? Surprisingly, it would. Braam and Malott (1990) found that with 4-year-old children, rules to perform behavior with no deadline and a 1-week delay of the reinforcer were relatively ineffective, while rules to perform behavior *with a deadline* and a 1-week delay of a reinforcer were quite effective. Very early in life, we learn that meeting deadlines is likely to be reinforced and failing to meet deadlines leads to unpleasantness.

To summarize, *rules that describe **deadlines** for **specific behavior** that will lead to **sizeable** and **probable outcomes** are often effective, even when the outcomes are delayed.* On the other hand, *rules that describe behavior vaguely, that do not identify a deadline for the behavior, and that lead to small or improbable consequences for the behavior are often ineffective.*

Guidelines for Using Rules Effectively

Here are some general guidelines for the effective use of rules:

1. The rules should be within the understanding of the individual to whom they are applied.
2. Rules should clearly identify:
   (a) the circumstances in which the behavior should occur;
   (b) the specific behavior in which the individual is to engage;
   (c) a deadline for performing the behavior;
   (d) the specific consequences involved in complying with the rule; and/or
   (e) the specific consequences for not complying with the rule.
3. Rules should describe probable and sizeable outcomes, rather than improbable and small outcomes. (Rules that describe improbable and/or small consequences may need to be supplemented by some of the procedures described in Chapter 24.)
4. Complex rules should be broken into easy-to-follow steps.
5. Rules should be delivered in a pleasant, courteous manner.
6. Fading should be used as necessary to fade out rules if you want other stimuli that are present to take control of the behavior.

GOALS

In industrial and organizational settings over the past 20 years, goal-setting programs have led to improved performance in such areas as truck loading, safety behavior, keypunching, customer service, and typing (Locke & Latham, 1990). In sports, goal-setting programs have led to improvements in such areas as laps completed in running, foul shots in basketball, serves in tennis, and accuracy in archery (Locke & Latham, 1985). In general, a **goal** describes a level of performance toward which an individual or group should work.

In everyday language, goals are considered to be motivational. They are seen as committing one to the effort and dedication that is necessary to achieve success; they give one a sense of purpose and help to keep one on target. From a behavioral perspective, however, a goal might be considered as a rule. For example, if a basketball player says, "I'll practice shooting foul shots until I can make 10 in a row," that player has identified the circumstances (practicing foul shots), the behavior (making 10 in a row), and although the reinforcer is not stated, it is certainly implied (then I'll be a better basketball player and will likely score a higher percentage of foul shots in games). And like the use of rules, goal setting is often applied to influence individuals to improve performance where reinforcers are delayed (a bonus in a work setting is received well after the work has been completed) or are immediate but highly intermittent (the basketball player might initially make only one out of every 30 foul shots).

Although goal setting might be viewed as use of rules, the circumstances where one might apply goal setting are often somewhat different than those described at the beginning of this chapter. We previously suggested that it is possible to capitalize on stimulus control by using rules to bring about instant behavior change. The sport psychologist, for example, was concerned with helping the figure skater "on the spot." Goal setting, on the other hand, is often used to influence individuals to work towards some objective over a period of time or during a number of practice opportunities. We wouldn't expect the basketball player to immediately meet the goal of making 10 foul shots in a row. Nevertheless, setting a practice goal in that type of situation is likely to lead to faster performance improvement than if the player just practiced shooting foul shots without a particular goal in mind.

Effective and Ineffective Goal Setting

The efficacy of goal setting as a performance improvement strategy is well established, provided that a number of conditions are met (Locke & Latham, 1990).

Specific Goals Are More Effective Than Vague Goals Rather than a goal of "having a better relationship," a couple might agree to spend a half-hour of quality time together (such as going for a walk), telling each other on a daily basis at least three things that they appreciate about their relationship, and sharing equally the responsibility of how to spend their money. It would be more effective for an individual considering dieting to say that he wants to lose 10 lbs (or 5 kgs), rather than saying that he wants to "lose some weight." As another example, saying that you want to save a specific percentage of your take-home pay might be more effective than the goal of "wanting to save some money."

Goals with Respect to Learning of Specific Skills Should Include Mastery Criteria A mastery criterion is a specific guideline for performing a skill such that if the guideline is met, the skill is likely to be mastered. This means that if an individual has met a mastery criterion for a skill, he or she has learned the skill well enough so that, if asked to do it sometime later, the skill would likely be performed correctly. Examples of mastery criteria for learning athletic skills might include making six 4-foot putts in a row in golf, hitting ten backhands in a row down the line in tennis, making ten foul shots in a row in basketball, or hitting five curveballs in a row out of the infield in baseball. In other words, goals should identify a particular quantity, level, or standard of performance.

Goals Should Identify the Circumstances Under which the Desirable Behavior Should Occur A goal for a wrestler to "practice take-downs" is somewhat vague. A goal to "practice arm-drag take-downs until three in a row occur" adds a quantity dimension but still does not indicate the circumstances under which the behavior should occur. A goal to "practice arm-drag take-downs until three in a row occur on an opponent offering moderate resistance" identifies the circumstances surrounding the performance.

Realistic, Challenging Goals Are More Effective Than "Do Your Best" Goals The phrase "just do your best" is often spoken by coaches to young athletes just before a competition, by parents to their children who are about to compete or perform in some way, by teachers to students before tests are presented, and by employers to employees in certain jobs. A number of studies, however, have demonstrated that "do your best" goals are not nearly as effective as are specific goals for improving performance. Perhaps "do your best" goals are ineffective because they are vague. Or perhaps individuals who are instructed to simply "do their best" set relatively easy goals, and as suggested by Locke and Latham (1990), difficult or challenging goals may produce better performance than moderate or easy goals. From a behavioral perspective, we might assume that those who identify a specific goal for an individual are more likely to consistently provide back-up reinforcers for meeting the goal than when the goal is simply to "do your best." The person providing the backup reinforcers may not reinforce your behavior when you have done your best. (The converse may also apply: the person providing reinforcers to you may reinforce something less than your best performance.)

The judgment of whether or not a goal is easy or difficult is somewhat subjective, given that our information about someone's physiological and behavioral capabilities is always incomplete. The accuracy of that judgement might be maximized, however, by considering the individual's current level of performance and the range of performance on similar tasks by others of similar ability.

Public Goals Are More Effective Than Private Goals   Consider the following experiment with three groups of students who were all given the same booklet of material to study. The first group of students participated in a public goal-setting program. Each student set a goal concerning the amount he or she would study and the score that the student hoped to receive on a test (to be given at the end of the program) of the material studied. These students announced their goals to other members of their group. The second group of students practiced private goal setting. They were treated the same as the first group except that they kept their goals to themselves and didn't tell anyone about them. The third group of students was not asked to set any goals. They were a control group who were simply given the material to study for the same amount of time as the first group, with the knowledge that they would receive a test at the end of the experiment. The results: The public goal-setting group scored an average of 17 percentage points higher on the test than either of the other two groups, who performed about the same (Hayes et al., 1985). Similar results on the effects of public goals versus private goals were found by Seijts, Meertens, and Kok (1997). Hayes and colleagues theorized that setting a public goal results in a public standard against which performance can be evaluated, and that it implies social consequences for achieving or not achieving the goal(s).

Although goals that someone else knows about may be more likely to be met than private goals that nobody knows about, the public component must be practiced with some caution. Suppose that you recommend goal setting as a part of a behavior modification program to help someone exercise consistently. If you recommend that the exerciser share the goals with another person, that person should be someone who is likely to prompt the exerciser with gentle reminders when goals are not met, and who will offer encouragement when progress is satisfactory. That person should *not* be someone who will send the exerciser on a heavy-duty guilt trip for not meeting the goals. This issue is discussed further in Chapter 29.

Goal Setting Is More Effective If Deadlines Are Included   We all have a history of being reinforced for meeting various deadlines, and for encountering aversiveness when deadlines are not met. Capitalizing on this history increases the effectiveness of goal setting. Suppose that you set a goal for yourself during the coming year of writing more letters to friends and relatives. You are more likely to meet that goal if you resolve that, by February 1st, you'll have written to specific individuals, by March 1st you'll have written to so many more, and so on.

Goal Setting Plus Feedback Is More Effective Than Goal Setting Alone   Goals are more likely to be met if feedback indicates degree of progress toward the goal. One way of providing feedback is to chart the progress being made. As discussed in Chapter 18, individuals who chart their progress toward a goal are likely to find improvements in the chart to be reinforcing. Another way of providing feedback is to break long-term goals into a number of shorter term goals. Suppose that a couple decides to repaint their entire house, inside and out. Shorter-term goals might include painting the bedroom by the end of February, then the living room by a certain date, and then the kitchen, and so on.

Goal Setting Is Most Effective When Individuals Are Committed to the Goals Goals are likely to be effective only if there is a continuing commitment to them by the individuals involved. By commitment, we mean a statement by the client that the goal is important, that they will work toward it, and that they recognize the benefits of doing so. One way of gaining commitment is to have the client participate in the goal-setting process. Research indicates that self-selected goals are at least as effective as those that are externally imposed (Fellner & Sulzer-Azaroff, 1984).

Guidelines for Goal Setting

Many individuals in everyday life attempt to capitalize on goal setting with their annual New Year's resolutions. But there are clearly some ways of setting goals that are more effective than others for influencing behavior. If, for example, goals are quite vague or a "do your best" resolution, with no deadlines or timelines for meeting them, and without a feedback mechanism for monitoring progress, then they are not likely to influence behavior. If, on the other hand, you practice goal setting according to the following guidelines, then your goals are likely to be a useful short-cut tactic to behavior modification:

1. Set goals that are specific, realistic, and challenging.
2. Be clear about the specific consequences that might occur for meeting the goal or not meeting the goal.
3. Break longer-term goals into several shorter-term goals.
4. If the goal is complex, devise an action plan for meeting it.
5. Set deadlines for goal attainment.
6. Ensure that individuals involved are committed to the goals.
7. Encourage the client to share the goals with a friendly supporter.
8. Design a system for monitoring progress toward goals.
9. Provide positive feedback as progress toward goals is achieved.

STUDY QUESTIONS

1. What basic procedures discussed in Chapters 3–15 of this text might be used to
   (a) increase an infrequent behavior?
   (b) decrease an excessive behavior?
   (c) develop a behavior that never occurs?
   (d) get a desired behavior to occur in the presence of appropriate stimuli?
2. Define a *rule* and give an example.
3. A teacher of a second-grade class complains to you, "When I tell the children to stay at their desks and work, they never listen to me." Describe the contingencies that are likely operating with respect to that rule given by the teacher to the kids in the class.
4. Illustrate, with an example, how a rule might function as an S^D.
5. Describe the difference between, and illustrate with examples, rule-governed versus contingency-shaped behavior.
6. Give two examples of direct-acting and two examples of indirect-acting reinforcers on your behavior.
7. Using examples, briefly describe four situations in which the addition of rules to a behavior modification program might be especially helpful.
8. Describe, using examples, three explanations why we might follow rules that identify very delayed consequences.
9. Explain (in terms of contextual stimulus control, as described in Note 4 of Chapter 8) why the tone of voice of someone giving you instructions might determine whether or not you will follow the instructions appropriately.
10. How might we explain the behavior of someone who fails to wear a helmet when riding a bicycle even though that person knows that wearing a helmet could prevent brain damage from a serious accident?
11. How might we account for the relative ineffectiveness of such rules as "I need to go on a diet" or "I'll floss my teeth after every meal"?
12. In a couple of sentences, distinguish between rules that are often effective versus rules that are often ineffective in controlling behavior.
13. In general, what do we mean by a goal? Describe an example.
14. Is goal setting different from using rules? Discuss.
15. Briefly list six guidelines that summarize effective versus ineffective goal setting as a behavior modification strategy.
16. From a behavioral perspective, why might realistic, challenging goals be more effective than "do your best" goals?
17. From a behavioral perspective, why might public goals be more effective than private goals?

APPLICATION EXERCISES

A. Exercises Involving Others

1. Choose a behavior that a parent might want to change in a child, such that there is no obvious immediate, natural reinforcer for that behavior. Describe how the parent, following the guidelines for using rules effectively, might capitalize on rule-governed behavior to bring about a desired outcome.

2. Consider a practice setting for a youth sport with which you are familiar. Describe how a coach might use goal setting to influence desirable practice behavior of a young athlete in that setting. Indicate how the coach has followed the guidelines for goal setting.

B. Self-Modification Exercise

1. Consider the guidelines for using rules effectively. Now consider a behavior of yours that you have not emitted but that you would like to perform, or a behavior of yours that someone else would like you to emit, but that has not been occuring. Describe how rules might be used effectively to influence you to emit that behavior. (Identify a rule with respect to that behavior, and structure the contingencies according to the guidelines for using rules effectively.)

2. Identify some behavior of yours that was probably contingency-shaped. It might be something like riding a bicycle, balancing on one foot, eating with a knife and fork or chopsticks, whistling a short tune, or flipping flapjacks. Devise a measure (e.g., number of errors) of how well you perform the behavior, and using the measure, record your performance of the behavior on several trials. Next write out a set of rules for performing the behavior, and again perform and record the behavior on several occasions, carefully following the rules. According to your measure, how did the addition of rules affect your performance? Interpret your finding.

NOTE AND EXTENDED DISCUSSION

1. Suppose that a family is camping on a cold fall evening. A parent might say to a child, "Move your sleeping bag closer to the campfire and you'll feel warmer." You may recall from Note 2 in Chapter 8 that in everyday language, an S^D is a cue that tells you what to do to get what you already want, which characterizes the above example. But in other instances, a rule might more accurately be described as a conditioned establishing operation (CEO) (Blakeley & Schlinger, 1987; Malott, 1989; Michael, 1993; Schlinger & Blakeley, 1987). In everyday language, recall that a CEO is a motivator that momentarily makes something reinforcing for you and at the same time increases the likelihood of behavior that has enabled you to get it in the past (see Note 2 in Chapter 8). Suppose a parent says to his teenage daughter, "Each time that you mow the lawn, you can earn 3 points, and each time that you trim the hedges you can earn 2 points. When you accumulate 20 points, you can have the car for a weekend." In this example, you can see that the rule would more accurately be described as a CEO than as an S^D. It made points reinforcing for the daughter, and it told her how to get them.

Study Questions on Note

1. What is a CEO? Using an example, illustrate how a rule might function as a CEO. (*Hint:* We do not mean "chief executive officer.")
2. Are goals S^Ds, CEOs, or both? Justify your choice.

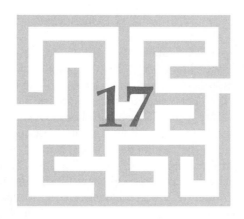

Capitalizing on Existing Stimulus Control: Modeling, Guidance, and Situational Inducement

As we indicated in the previous chapter, behavior modification programs should include instruction in the form of rules that can be followed easily. But sometimes it's better to *model* the desired behavior in addition to telling a person what is expected. And if "show-and-tell" is not enough, you may need to *physically guide* a client through the desired actions on a few trials, and/or *rearrange the environment* to make a desired behavior more likely to occur. This chapter describes these additional strategies for capitalizing on existing forms of stimulus control.

MODELING

Modeling is a procedure whereby a sample of a given behavior is presented to an individual to induce that individual to engage in a similar behavior. As is true for rules, modeling can be quite powerful. You may convince yourself of this by performing the following simple experiments:

1. For an entire day, speak only in a whisper, and note how often people around you also whisper (this is a good experiment to try when you have laryngitis).
2. Yawn conspicuously in the presence of other people, and note their frequency of yawning.
3. Stand looking at a window of an empty department store for an hour, and note how many people stop and also look in the window.

In each case, compare the data obtained with data obtained under comparable circumstances when the behavior is not being modeled.

As with rules, modeling is in such common use by the general public that few people (other than behavior modifiers) think of it as a behavior modification procedure. Parents, for example, use it rather unsystematically, but quite effectively in many cases, to teach politeness, caring, language, and other behaviors to their children. When a dog walks by a parent and a 2-year-old child, the parent might say, "Look at the doggie. Can you say 'doggie'?" Or when teaching a child how to make a sandwich, a parent might say, "Do it this way" while modeling the desired behavior. Modeling affects the behavior of individuals of all ages, not just young children. When teenagers first enter high school they see how the older kids dress and talk, and the younger students are soon dressing the same way and using the same expressions. Neither of the authors can ever remember the day for garbage pickup with the rotating schedule in their neighborhood. We simply imitate the behavior of our neighbors who always have their garbage placed at the curb at the appropriate time on the scheduled day. All of us in our daily lives have frequent opportunities to observe the actions of others, and we frequently imitate their behaviors.

Note 1
What determines whether or not we will imitate the behavior of a model? Although there are several possible explanations, clearly our history of being reinforced (or punished) for imitating others is an important factor. And because we've each had different experiences, we would expect that the specific factors that determine which modeled behaviors might serve as S^Ds for imitation vary somewhat from person to person. Nevertheless, there are several factors common to the experience of most persons that are likely to influence the effectiveness of modeling as a behavior modification technique (Bandura, 1986).

Arrange for Peers to be Models   People are more likely to imitate someone who is similar to them in various ways (age, socioeconomic status, physical appearance, etc.) than someone who is quite different from them. Friends and peers are more likely to be imitated than are strangers or individuals outside one's peer group. This is especially true for children. Thus, whenever possible, use peers as models in your behavior modification programs. Consider the case of an extremely withdrawn nursery school child who almost never interacts with other children. This behavior problem could be treated with shaping. A method that can perhaps produce faster results, however, is to have the child observe several instances of another child joining in the activities of a group of children. The group should be responding to the model in a reinforcing manner (e.g., by offering her play material, talking to her, and smiling). To ensure that the modeling occurs under opportune circumstances and in a suitable fashion, it may be necessary to instruct certain children to perform as models and to instruct the children in the group to behave in a conspicuously reinforcing manner to the models. It is sometimes convenient and effective to film or videotape a number of such episodes for viewing by socially withdrawn children (see O'Connor, 1969). The presentation of modeling scenes through film, videotape, and other media is called **symbolic modeling.** Studies show that this type of modeling can sometimes be as effective as the real thing.

Show the Behavior and Its Effects   Suppose that you want to improve your debating skills. Are you more likely to imitate the discussion strategies of friends who consistently get their points across or friends who consistently lose arguments? Clearly, the perceived competence of the model in obtaining desired consequences is a factor that determines the effectiveness of modeling as a behavior modification technique. Even with children, peers who are more proficient at obtaining consequences for various behaviors are more likely to be imitated than are children who are less proficient at doing so (Schunk, 1987). To capitalize on this factor when using modeling in your behavior modification program, arrange for the client to observe the model emit the desired behavior and receive a reinforcer.

Studies in social psychology have indicated that high-status and highly prestigious persons are more likely to be imitated than individuals of lower status or prestige. This might be interpreted as a subcategory of the competence factor. A popular teenager is likely to be imitated by peers because he or she is frequently observed receiving positive consequences for various behaviors.

Use Multiple Models   Sarah, a 35-year-old real estate salesperson and part-time student, drank beer regularly with six other women at a small local tavern on Friday afternoons. All of them were taking a course on behavior modification, but Sarah was unaware that her own drinking behavior was being studied. During several sessions of baseline, she invariably approximated 72 ounces of beer in an hour. During the first experimental phase, one of the other women modeled a drinking rate of half that of Sarah. Sarah's drinking was not affected. Similarly, her drinking was unaffected when two of the other women modeled drinking rates exactly half of hers. However, when four other women modeled drinking rates that were half of Sarah's, her drinking rate was also cut in half (DeRicco & Niemann, 1980). Clearly, the number of persons modeling a particular behavior is a factor in determining whether or not that behavior might be imitated.

Combine Modeling With Rules   With verbal people, modeling is likely to be most effective when combined with rules and other behavioral strategies.

The following excerpt from a therapy session illustrates this (J. C. Masters, Burrish, Hollon, & Rimm, 1987, pp. 100–101). The client being treated was a male college student who had difficulty asking for dates over the telephone. In the excerpt, the client is rehearsing asking for a date. Note how the therapist combines instruction and shaping with modeling.

Client: By the way (pause) I don't suppose you want to go out Saturday night?

Therapist: Up to actually asking for the date you were very good. However, if I were the woman, I think I might have been a bit offended when you said "By the way." It's like your asking her out is pretty casual. Also, the way you phrased the question, you are kind of suggesting to her that she doesn't want to go out with you. Pretend for the moment I'm you. Now, how does this sound: "There's a movie at the Varsity Theater this Saturday that I want to see. If you don't have other plans, I'd very much like to take you."

Client: That sounded good. Like you were sure of yourself and liked the woman too.

Therapist: Why don't you try it?

Client: You know that movie at the Varsity? Well, I'd like to go, and I'd like to take you Saturday, if you don't have anything better to do.

Therapist: Well, that certainly was better. Your tone of voice was especially good. But the last line, "if you don't have anything better to do," sounded like you don't think you have much to offer. Why not run through it one more time?

Client: I'd like to see the show at the Varsity, Saturday, and, if you haven't made other plans, I'd like to take you.

Therapist: Much better. Excellent, in fact. You were confident, forceful, and sincere.

This example also illustrates a technique referred to as **behavioral rehearsal** or **role rehearsal,** in which a client practices particular behaviors (i.e., plays a role) in a practice setting to increase the likelihood that those behaviors will occur appropriately in the real world. In the above example, the client rehearsed asking for a date. A combination of instructions, modeling, behavioral rehearsal, and consequence management has been used to enhance performance in a variety of areas, such as social skills training (Huang & Cuvo, 1997), assertion training (Schroeder & Black, 1985), and anger management training (Larkin & Zayfert, 1996).

Guidelines for Using Modeling

Here are some general guidelines for the effective use of modeling:

1. If possible, select models who are friends or peers of the client and who are seen as competent individuals with status or prestige.
2. If possible, use more than one model.
3. The complexity of the modeled behavior should be suitable for the behavioral level of the client.
4. Combine rules with modeling.
5. Have the client watch the model perform the behavior and be reinforced (preferably by natural reinforcers).
6. If possible, design the training so that correct imitation of the modeled behavior will lead to a natural reinforcer for the client. If this is not possible, arrange for reinforcement for correct imitation of the modeled behavior.
7. If the behavior is quite complex, then the modeling episode should be sequenced from very easy to more difficult approximations for the individual being treated.
8. To enhance stimulus generalization, the modeling scenes should be as realistic as possible.
9. Use fading as necessary so that stimuli other than the model can take control over the desired behavior.

PHYSICAL GUIDANCE

Physical guidance is the application of physical contact to induce an individual to go through the motions of the desired behavior. Some familiar examples of guidance are a dance instructor leading a pupil through a new dance step, a golf instructor grasping the novice's arms and moving them through the proper swing and follow-through, and a parent holding a child's hand while teaching her to cross the street safely. Guidance is always only one component of a teaching procedure. Both the dance instructor and the golf instructor will also use instruction (they will tell the student what to do and give pointers), modeling (they will demonstrate the appropriate physical postures and motions), and reinforcement for correct responses or approximations to them (such as "Excellent!" or "Much better!"). Likewise, the parent teaching her child to cross the street safely will use rules (e.g., by saying, "Look both ways") and modeling (e.g., by looking both ways in an exaggerated manner).

Some uses of guidance in behavior modification programs were given in Chapter 9—for example, using guidance and fading to teach a child to touch his head upon request. Guidance is generally used as an aide in teaching individuals to follow instructions or imitate a modeled behavior, so that instruction and/or modeling can then be used (without guidance) to establish other behaviors. For example, in one procedure for teaching instruction following, a child is placed in a chair opposite the teacher. At the beginning of a trial the teacher says, "Johnny, stand up" and then lifts the child onto his feet. Reinforcement is then presented immediately, as though the child himself had performed the response. Next, the teacher says, "Johnny, sit down," and grasping the child's shoulders the teacher gently but firmly presses him down on the chair. Again, immediate reinforcement is presented. The process is repeated over numerous trials while guidance is faded out (see Kazdin & Erickson, 1975.) After this set of instructions is learned, the behavior modifier teaches another set (such as "Come here" and "Go there"), using a similar procedure. Less and less guidance may be required to teach successive instruction-following until eventually even fairly complex instruction-following behavior can be taught with little or no guidance.

As in teaching instruction following, the teacher who uses guidance to teach model imitation to a child starts with a few simple imitations (such as touching one's head, clapping one's hands, tapping the table, standing up, and sitting down) and adds new imitations as the previous ones are learned. Each time, the teacher says "Do this" while modeling the response and guiding the child to perform the response. Correct responses are reinforced and guidance is faded out over trials. This facilitates the development of **generalized imitation,** whereby an individual, after learning to imitate a number of behaviors (perhaps with some shaping, fading, guidance, and reinforcement), learns to imitate a new response on the first trial without reinforcement (Baer, Peterson & Sherman, 1967).

Another common application of guidance is in helping individuals to overcome fears. Helping a person who is terrified of water might involve gradually leading her by the hand into the shallow end of a swimming pool and supporting her while she floats. The least fear-provoking aspects of a situation should be introduced first, and the more fear-provoking aspects later in a very gradual manner. One should never try to force an individual to do more than she feels comfortable doing. The more fearful the person is, the more gradual the process should be. In the case of a very fearful individual one may have to spend many sessions simply sitting with her on the edge of the pool. (Use of modeling and other procedures to help a client overcome extreme fears is discussed further in Chapters 25 and 27.)

Guidelines for Using Physical Guidance

Some general guidelines for the effective use of guidance are as follow:

1. Make sure that the client is comfortable and relaxed while being touched and guided. Some initial relaxation training may be necessary to accomplish this (relaxation training is discussed further in Chapter 25).
2. Determine the stimuli that you want to control the behavior so that they can be conspicuously present during guidance.
3. Consider using rules or cue words during guidance so that they may eventually control the behavior. When teaching a novice right-handed golfer the proper shoulder turn during a golf swing, for example, the instructor might say the cue words, "Left shoulder to chin, right shoulder to chin" while guiding the novice through the backswing and the downswing.
4. Reinforcement should be given immediately after the successful completion of the guided response.
5. Guidance should be sequenced gradually from very easy to more difficult behavior for the individual being treated.
6. Use fading as necessary so that other stimuli can take control over the behavior.

SITUATIONAL INDUCEMENT

Largely because of our similar histories of reinforcement and punishment, there are numerous situations and occasions in our society that control similar behavior in many of us. The interiors of certain public buildings, such as churches, museums, and libraries, tend to suppress loud talking. Parties tend to evoke socializing and jovial, carefree behavior. Catchy melodies prompt humming and singing, and strident march music tends to incite participation in a foot-stamping parade. The assorted stimuli associated with Christmas induce cheerfulness, friendliness, and gift buying.

The term *situational inducement* refers to influencing a behavior by using situations and occasions that already exert control over the behavior. Such techniques, like others we have discussed, no doubt predate recorded history. Ceremonious gatherings involving singing and dancing probably served to strengthen a sense of community in ancient tribes, just as they do today in almost all cultures. Monasteries and convents have been used for centuries to promote asexual religious behavior by providing an environment conducive to reading religious texts and meditating and by restricting opportunities for the sexes to interact.

Supermarkets and department stores use many situational features to induce buying. Among these are the attention-evoking manner in which the products are displayed, and pictures showing the products in an attractive way. Fine restaurants provide a relaxing atmosphere to induce leisurely enjoyment of a full-course meal. If the restaurant becomes crowded and people are waiting for tables, fast music may be played to induce rapid eating.

Examples of situational inducement can also be found in the home. Many people prominently display items such as interesting objets d'art, a fancy computer or stereo equipment, and even unusual pets, that they have acquired partly to stimulate conversation when guests arrive. If a guest seems about to mishandle one of these conversation pieces, the host may use situational inducement by handing the potential offender a drink.

Situational inducement has been used in a number of imaginative and effective ways in behavior modification programs to help increase or decrease target behaviors, or to bring them under appropriate stimulus control. Examples can be discussed conveniently under four somewhat overlapping categories: (a) rearranging the existing surroundings, (b) moving the activity to a new location, (c) relocating people, and (d) changing the time of the activity.

Rearranging the Existing Surroundings

An interesting example in the first category occurred in a case reported by the well-known behaviorist Israel Goldiamond (1965). Goldiamond was consulted by a married couple who were having a problem in their relationship.[1] When the couple were together in the house, the husband could not refrain from screaming at his wife over her once having gone to bed with his best friend. One of the goals that was decided upon, therefore, was to replace screaming with civilized conversational behavior. Goldiamond reasoned that the husband's screaming had probably come under the control of the S^Ds in the home environment and that one way in which to weaken the behavior in that situation would be to change those S^Ds. He therefore instructed the couple to rearrange the rooms and furniture in the house to make it appear considerably different. The wife went one step further and bought herself a new outfit. Goldiamond then provided for the reinforcement of civilized conversation in the presence of these new S^Ds that were not associated so strongly with screaming (how he did this is explained more fully in the next section). It was important to do this as quickly as possible, because if screaming occurred too often in the presence of the new S^Ds, it would become conditioned to them just as it had been conditioned to the old S^Ds.

---

[1] It should not be thought that this simplified example from the early days of behavior modification is representative of contemporary application of behavior modification to marital counseling. Detailed discussion of this topic is given in Chapter 26, and in Bornstein and Bornstein (1986).

Another example of rearranging the existing surroundings is altering the furniture and other items in one's room to promote better and more persistent studying behavior. One might, for example, improve the lighting, clear one's desk of irrelevant material, move the bed as far as possible from the desk, and have the desk facing away from the bed. Better yet, if possible, one should not even have the bed in the same room as the desk because the bed is an S^D for sleeping. To prevent nonstudy behaviors from being conditioned to the new stimuli, one should engage only in studying behavior in the rearranged environment (see Goldiamond, 1965).

Letter writing is a behavior that is difficult to maintain because it involves a long delay of reinforcement (it takes at least several days to get a return letter). One way in which to strengthen your tendency to write, however, is to place before you a picture of the person to whom you are writing. This is another example of rearranging stimuli to control behavior.

Moving the Activity to a New Location

The second category of situational inducement is illustrated by another part of the procedure Goldiamond used in the case of the husband who screamed at his wife. The spouses were instructed that, immediately after rearranging the furniture at their home, they were to go to a place that would induce civilized conversation. It was hoped that this behavior would continue until they returned home, and would then come under the control of the new S^Ds in the home.

To quote from Goldiamond's report (1965, p. 856),

> Since it was impossible for [the husband] to converse in a civilized manner with his wife, we discussed a program of going to one evening spot on Monday, another on Tuesday, and another on Wednesday.
>
> "Oh," he said, "you want us to be together. We'll go bowling on Thursday."
>
> "On the contrary," I said, "I am interested in your subjecting yourself to an environment where civilized chit-chat is maintained. Such is not the case at a bowling alley."
>
> I also asked if there was any topic of conversation which once started would maintain itself. He commented on his mother-in-law's crazy ideas about farming. He was then given an index card and instructed to write "farm" on it and to attach a $20 bill to that card. The $20 was to be used to pay the waitress on Thursday, at which point he was to start the "farm" discussion which hopefully would continue into the taxi and home.

Changing the location of the activity is one approach to problems relating to studying (see Figure 17–1). The student using this approach should select a special place that is conducive to studying and that has distinctive stimuli that are not associated with any behavior other than studying. A reserved carrel in a university library is ideal for this purpose, although any other well-lit, quiet area with adequate working space would be suitable. Depending on the extent of appropriate study behavior in the student's repertoire, it may be necessary to combine relocating the activity with some of the basic procedures discussed in Part II

Figure 17–1   An example of situational inducement.

of this text. For severe deficiencies, behavior incorporating good study skills should first be shaped and then placed on either a low-duration or a low-ratio schedule in the special studying area. The value of the schedule should then be increased gradually so that the behavior will eventually be maintained at the desired level. Appropriate reinforcement (such as coffee with a friend) should be arranged to occur immediately after the schedule requirement has been met. Should one experience a tendency to daydream or to engage in other nonstudy behavior while in the studying area, one should do a little more productive studying and then leave immediately so that daydreaming does not become conditioned to the stimuli in the studying area. Similarly, the husband in the case reported by Goldiamond was instructed to go to the garage and sit on a specially designated "sulking" stool whenever he was in the house and felt a tendency to sulk—this being a behavior that was threatening the recently strengthened conversational behavior after screaming had been eliminated.

Relocating People

The third category of situational inducement, relocating people, was not illustrated in Goldiamond's case study. The procedures used in that case were effective; therefore, a separation of the spouses was not necessary. Although relocating the participants is generally a measure of last resort when dealing with individuals who wish to maintain their respective relationships, it is sometimes the most practical tactic in other circumstances. If you just cannot get along with Sam Jones, and there is no particular reason for you to associate with him anyway, then why try to change his behavior and/or yours to make the two of you more compatible? Both of you will probably be happier respecting each other from a distance. Relocating people can also be used to bring about the opposite effect, that is, to bring people together. For example, getting dates is a problem for many college students. To deal with this problem, therapists often recommend that clients increase their contact with the opposite sex.

Teachers of small children often change seating arrangements to relocate pupils whose close proximity leads to various types of disruptions. This is usually much easier than designing and carrying out reinforcement and/or punishment programs to eliminate undesirable interactions, and the end result may be just as effective, or more so.

Changing the Time of the Activity

The final category of situational inducement involves taking advantage of the fact that certain stimuli and behavioral tendencies change predictably with the passage of time. For example, two sexual partners may find that sexual activity is better for them in the morning than at night when one of them is "too tired." Changing the time of an activity has been used effectively in weight-control programs. People who cook for their families sometimes put on excess weight by "nibbling" while preparing meals and then sitting down for a full-course dinner. Rather than foregoing dinner with one's family, a partial solution to this problem is to do the preparation, except for the actual cooking, shortly after having eaten the previous meal, while the tendency to eat is still relatively weak (see LeBow, 1981, 1989).

Guidelines for Using Situational Inducement

Situational inducement covers a broad set of procedures. Its use, therefore, is considerably less straightforward than is that of the other methods discussed in this chapter. In short, a good deal of imagination is typically required if it is to be used effectively. We suggest the following guidelines:

1. Clearly identify the desired behavior to be strengthened, and, if appropriate, the undesirable behavior to be decreased.
2. Next, brainstorm all possible environmental arrangements in the presence of which the desired behavior has occurred in the past or is likely to occur. Remember, situations and controlling stimuli can be anything—people, places, times, days, events, objects, and so on.
3. From the list of stimuli that have controlled the target behavior in the past, identify those that could be easily introduced to control the desirable behavior and/or the undesirable behavior.
4. Arrange for the client of concern to be exposed to the stimuli that control the target behavior in the desired way and to avoid locations and arrangements that do not have this control.
5. Make sure that undesirable behavior never occurs in the presence of situations introduced to strengthen desirable behavior.
6. When the desirable behavior occurs in the presence of the new arrangement, be sure that it is reinforced.

STUDY QUESTIONS

1. List four strategies that you might follow to influence the effectiveness of modeling as a behavior modification technique.
2. Describe two recent situations in which you were influenced by modeling to emit a behavior. For each instance, describe whether or not the four factors that influence the effectiveness of modeling were present.
3. What is meant by symbolic modeling? Describe how this might explain how a city-dwelling child might learn to fear snakes.
4. Describe the results of the study of modeling of alcohol drinking by DeRicco and Niemann.
5. Describe the specific steps you might go through in using modeling to overcome the extreme withdrawal behavior of a nursery school child who never interacts with other children. Identify the basic principles and procedures being applied in your program.
6. In the dialogue between the client and the therapist concerning the client's difficulty in asking for dates, briefly describe
   a. how modeling was involved.
   b. how instructions were involved.
   c. how shaping was involved.
7. Define or describe behavior rehearsal, and give an example.
8. What is meant by physical guidance? How does it differ from gestural prompting (see p. 118).
9. What is generalized imitation? Describe an example.
10. Identify a behavior that you were influenced to perform as a result of physical guidance. Describe how guidance was involved.
11. What do we mean by the term *situational inducement*? Which term given previously in this book has essentially the same meaning? (see p. 118)
12. Describe each of the four proposed categories of situational inducement.
13. Give an example from your own experience of each of the four categories of situational inducement.
14. For each of the following examples, identify the category of situational inducement in which it might best be placed and indicate why.

a. On Saturday afternoon, an exercise buff can't seem to "get up the energy" to lift weights. To increase the likelihood of weight lifting, she places the weights in the center of the den (where she usually exercises), turns on the TV to the Saturday afternoon wrestling matches, and opens her *Muscle Beach* magazine to the centerfold showing her favorite body builder.

b. It is said that Victor Hugo, the famous writer, controlled his work habits in his study by having his servant take his clothes away and not bring them back until the end of the day (Wallace, 1971, pp. 68–69).

c. To stop drinking, an alcoholic surrounds himself with members of Alcoholics Anonymous and stops seeing his old drinking buddies.

d. Another exercise buff has decided to jog a mile every night before going to bed. Alas, "the road to hell [or perhaps to heart attack] is paved with good intentions." Late nights, good TV, wine with dinner, and other delights take their toll. Three months later, our "exercise buff" is still overweight and out of shape because of many missed jogging nights. He therefore changes the routine and begins jogging each day immediately upon arriving home and before eating dinner.

e. After many interruptions while working on this book at the university, the authors began working at one of their homes.

15. According to the proposed guidelines for the use of rules, modeling, and physical guidance,

a. What behavior principle is used with all three procedures?

b. What two other behavioral procedures are likely to be used with all three procedures?

APPLICATION EXERCISES

A. Exercise Involving Others

Outline a program that a parent might follow to teach a 2-year-old child to respond consistently to the instruction "Please bring me your shoes." Indicate how your program might use rules, modeling, and guidance, and how it follows the guidelines for the effective application of each.

B. Self-Modification Exercise

Select two of your behaviors from the following list:

1. doing the dishes immediately after a meal
2. getting up when the alarm rings
3. feeling happy
4. cleaning up your bedroom twice per week
5. doing some exercises daily
6. increasing your studying

Describe how you might influence each behavior by combining at least four of the following tactics: rules, modeling, guidance, rearranging the existing surroundings, moving the activity to a new location, relocating people, and changing the time of the activity. Make your suggestions highly plausible in regard to the situation.

NOTE AND EXTENDED DISCUSSION

1. Historically, learning by imitation has been given an important place in a number of different psychological theories, not just behavioristic ones. In Freudian (psychoanalytic) theory, a male child typically develops certain "male" behavior patterns through identification with his father, whereas a female child develops female behavior patterns through identification with her mother. Thus, the absence of a strong male figure with whom to identify could (in Freudian theory) lead to feminine traits—even homosexuality—in a boy who identifies excessively with the mother. Gestalt psychologists considered imitative learning to be innate in higher species and attempted to show, for example, that chimpanzees could learn to solve problems by watching other chimpanzees solve them. Bandura (1977) defined *observational learning* (also called *vicarious learning*) as the increase or decrease of an observer's behavior that is similar to that of a model, as a result of watching the model's behavior be reinforced or punished. Bandura believes that this type of learning can occur without external reinforcement for the observer, although he agrees that external reinforcement may be necessary to influence the observer to perform the behavior. If so, then it seems that we would have to add observational learning as a basic type of learning. Many behavioral psychologists, however, believe that the behavioral learning principles described in Chapters 3 to 15 of this book can account for behavior acquired through observation.

There are several processes by which observational or imitative behavior might be learned. First, an individual is frequently reinforced when he or she performs the same actions that another individual performs; hence, other people's actions tend to become S^Ds for engaging in similar actions. (For example, a child who watches someone open a door to go outside receives the reinforcement of going outside when he or she performs the same action.) Second, to the extent that other people are reinforcing to us, their actions acquire conditioned reinforcing properties; hence, we receive conditioned reinforcement when we perform the same actions. A third possibility is that once we have learned to imitate simple responses, we can then imitate more complex behaviors, provided that these are composed of the simpler responses. (For example, once an individual has learned to imitate "al," "li," "ga," and "tor" as single syllables, or as units of various words, she can then imitate the word "alligator" the first time she hears it (Skinner, 1957). A fourth possibility is that imitative behavior is not just a set of separate stimulus-response relationships but is itself an operant class of responses. In other words, it is possible that, once a person is reinforced for imitating some behaviors, he or she will then tend to imitate other behaviors, even if they contain no elements in common with the imitative behaviors that were reinforced. As indicated earlier in this chapter, this is referred to as generalized imitation. (For a more detailed interpretation of vicarious learning from a contemporary behavioral approach, see Masia and Chase, 1997).

Study Questions on Note

1. How did Bandura define observational learning? What is another name for observational learning?
2. Describe four processes by which imitative behavior might be learned, and give an example of each.

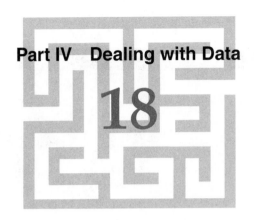

18

Behavioral Assessment: Initial Considerations

Throughout this book, numerous examples illustrate the effectiveness of behavior modification procedures. Many of these examples are accompanied by graphs showing the changes (increases or decreases) that occurred in behavior when particular procedures were applied. Some of the graphs also include follow-up observations indicating that the improvements were maintained after the programs had terminated. The graphs were presented not just to make it easier for you to understand the material. Precise records of behavior are an inseparable part of behavior modification procedures. Indeed, some people have gone so far as to say that the major contribution of behavior modification has been the insistence on accurately recording specific behaviors and making decisions on the basis of recorded data rather than merely on the basis of subjective impressions. As with Linus and his blanket in the popular *Peanuts* cartoons, the behavior modifier and the data sheet are inseparable.

The behaviors to be improved in a behavior modification program are frequently called **target behaviors. Behavioral assessment** involves the collection and analysis of information and data in order to identify and describe target behavior, identify possible causes of the behavior, select appropriate treatment strategies to modify the behavior, and evaluate treatment outcome.

MINIMAL PHASES OF A PROGRAM

A successful behavior modification program typically involves four phases during which the target behavior is identified, defined, and recorded: (a) a screening phase, for clarifying the problem and determining who should treat it; (b) a baseline, or preprogram assessment phase; (c) a treatment phase; and (d) a follow-up phase. In this section, we will give you a brief overview of these phases. In subsequent sections and chapters, we will discuss them in greater detail.

Screening and General Disposition Phase

As expressed by R. P. Hawkins (1979), a question commonly asked when a client first appears at the door of a clinic or educational institution is, "Does this case belong here?" One function of the screening phase is to determine whether a particular agency or behavior modifier is the appropriate one to deal with a potential client's behavior. If not, the results of this phase should indicate which agency or individual should deal with the client. A second function of the general disposition phase is to provide information as to which behavior(s) should be baselined. For example, a behaviorally oriented center for children with learning difficulties might screen a child to determine whether his or her academic skills are unusual enough to require some sort of program that is not ordinarily provided by the school. To achieve this initial assessment, the agency might use a number of different preliminary indicators, ranging from teachers' reports to the child's IQ score (although these indicators would, of course, be interpreted simply as crude measures of behavior, rather than as measures of underlying traits). As indicated, behavior modifiers may make use of traditional tests, such as intelligence tests, in their screening and general disposition assessments—although they typically don't interpret them in the traditional manner. Behavior modifiers also use other assessment devices to aid in pinpointing specific behaviors of interest, as described later in this and the next chapter.

Baseline Phase

During the baseline phase, the behavior modifier assesses the target behavior to determine its level prior to the introduction of the program or treatment, and analyzes the individual's current environment to identify possible controlling variables of the behavior to be changed. Assessment of possible controlling variables of the target behavior is referred to as a functional assessment, and is discussed further in Chapter 20.

A baseline phase follows from the importance that behavior modifiers place on directly measuring the behavior of concern, and from using changes in the measure as the best indicator that the problem is being helped (see Chapter 1). If a child is having difficulty in school, for example, the behavior modifier would be considerably more interested in a baseline of specific behavioral excesses or deficits that constitute the problem (e.g., reading deficiency, inattentive behavior, excessive fighting with other children) than in the child's score on an intelligence test (although the behavior modifier would probably not be disinterested in the latter information).

Treatment Phase

Ideally, after making a precise baseline assessment, a behavior modifier will design an effective treatment program to bring about the desired behavior change. In educational settings, such a program is typically referred to as a training or teaching program. In community and clinical settings, the program is referred to more often as an intervention strategy or a therapy program.

Behavior modification programs typically provide for frequent observation and monitoring of the behavior of interest during training or treatment. In some cases, the difference between behavior modification and other approaches on this point is primarily a matter of degree. Traditional educational practices typically involve periodic assessment during the teaching program for the purpose of monitoring the performance of the students. Certain clinical treatment programs involve assessment of the clients at various intervals. Moreover, some programs that have been labeled behavior modification have consisted primarily of before-and-after measures and have lacked precise, ongoing recording during treatment. Nevertheless, many behavior modifiers have emphasized and practiced, to a degree rarely found in other approaches, frequent monitoring of the behavior throughout the application of the specific treatment or intervention strategies.

Follow-up Phase

Finally, the follow-up phase is carried out to determine whether the improvements achieved during treatment are maintained after the termination of the program. This phase reflects the strong emphasis that behavior modifiers give to assessment *after* the termination of the treatment or intervention phase whenever possible, because a problem has not really been solved if the improvement is not permanent. Thus, behavior modification experts agree that programs should include a follow-up phase in which the persistence of the desirable behavior change is evaluated following termination of the program.

In many cases, such as behavioral programs involving one or two behaviors and a small number of individuals, it is both possible and desirable to gather reliable follow-up information. In some cases, this might consist of precise observation or assessment under natural circumstances in which the behavior is expected to occur. In other projects, however, precise follow-up observations simply are not possible. Consider a behavior modification program set up for an entire classroom and conducted for many months. At the end of the program, the children may go on to another class, graduate to another program, leave the school, or in some other way become unavailable for follow-up observation. Under these circumstances, it would be impossible to do anything other than conduct pre- and post-tests that would sample a few of the behaviors developed by the behavior modification program.

SOURCES OF INFORMATION FOR BASELINE ASSESSMENT

Defining target behaviors clearly, completely, and in measurable terms is an important prerequisite to the design and implementation of a behavior modification program. Behavioral assessment procedures for collecting information to define and monitor target behaviors fall into three categories; indirect assessment procedures, direct assessment procedures, and experimental assessment procedures.

Indirect Assessment Procedures

In many situations in which a behavior modification program might be applied, the behavior modifier (e.g., a nurse, a teacher, a parent, a coach) can directly observe the behavior of interest. But suppose that you are a behavior therapist who, like other professional therapists, sees clients in your office at regularly scheduled appointment times. It would be impractical for you to observe your clients regularly in the situations in which the target behaviors occur. Moreover, what if some   **Note 1** of your clients wanted to change some of their thoughts and feelings that others couldn't observe? (As discussed in Chapter 26, thoughts and feelings are regarded by behavior modifiers as private behaviors.) In such situations, behavior therapists have made considerable use of indirect assessment procedures. The more common among these are interviews with the client and significant others, questionnaires, role playing, obtaining information from consulting professionals, and client self-monitoring. Indirect assessment procedures have the advantages of being convenient, not requiring a substantial amount of time, and potentially providing information about covert behaviors. However, they suffer from the disadvantages that those providing information may not remember relevant observations accurately, or they might have particular biases that would influence them to provide inaccurate data.

Interviews with the Client and Significant Others   Observation of an initial interview across a random sample of behavior therapists and therapists of other orientations is likely to show numerous commonalities. Because many clients are anxious when first meeting a therapist, the therapist typically does much of the initial talking. The therapist might begin by describing briefly the types of problems with which he or she typically works. The therapist might then ask a number of simple questions concerning the background of the client, or the therapist might ask the client to complete a simple demographic referral form. The therapist might next invite the client to describe, in general terms, what the problem is. During initial interviews, behavior therapists and traditional therapists are likely to use similar techniques to help the client feel at ease and to gain information about the problem, such as being a good listener, asking open-ended questions, requesting clarification, and expressing concern for and acknowledging the validity of the client's feelings and problems.

In interviewing the client and significant others (the client's spouse, parents, or anyone else directly concerned with the client's welfare), behavior therapists attempt to establish and maintain *rapport* (i.e., a relationship of mutual trust) with the client and any significant others included, just as do traditionally oriented therapists. This relationship can be facilitated by the therapist's being especially attentive to the client's description of the problem while refraining from expressing personal values that may unduly influence the client, showing empathy by communicating some understanding of the client's feelings to the client, and emphasizing the confidentiality of the client-therapist relationship (Morganstern, 1988).

Some behavior therapists deliberately keep the discussion during the initial interview at a general level. Others lead the discussion more directly to the presenting problem. Although there are individual differences among behavior therapists in this respect, it is probably accurate to say that behavior therapists are likely to focus discussion on the specific behaviors that characterize the problem or problems of a client relatively soon in the therapeutic relationship. This can be done by asking a number of questions about a problem and its controlling variables. At some point in the interviewing process, the behavior therapist will help the client to identify major problem areas; select one or two problem areas for initial treatment focus; translate the problem areas into specific behavioral deficits or excesses; attempt to identify controlling variables of the problem behavior; and identify some specific behavioral objectives for treatment. Specific behavioral questionnaires and role playing are often used to facilitate this process.

Questionnaires A well-designed questionnaire can provide information that may be useful in assessing a client's problem and developing the behavioral program for the client. Several types of questionnaires are popular with behavior therapists.

Life history questionnaires provide demographic data such as marital status, vocational status, and religious affiliation, and background data such as sexual, health, and educational histories. Two notable examples of such questionnaires are Cautela's Behavioral Analysis History Questionnaire (1977) and Wolpe's Life History Questionnaire (see Wolpe, 1982).

Note 2

Problem checklists have the client indicate which problem(s) applies to him or her from a detailed list of problems. Such questionnaires are particularly useful in helping the therapist completely specify the problem or problems for which the client is seeking therapy (Jensen & Haynes, 1986). An example of such a questionnaire is the Behavior Self-Rating Checklist (Upper, Cautela, & Brook, 1975).

Survey schedules provide the therapist with information needed to conduct a particular therapeutic technique with the client. The questionnaire shown in Figure 3–3 provides information useful in applying positive reinforcement procedures. Other types of survey schedules are designed to provide information preparatory to using other behavioral procedures. Different types of survey schedules can be found in Cautela (1977, 1981).

Third-party rating scales permit significant others and professionals involved with the client to assess subjectively the frequency and/or quality of certain behaviors. An example of such a checklist for use with developmentally disabled individuals is the OBA (Objective Behavioral Assessment of the Severely and Moderately Mentally Handicapped) (Hardy, Martin, Yu, Leader, & Quinn, 1981). The OBA enables third-party informants who are familiar with the behavior of the client being evaluated to rate whether or not the client can perform a variety of tasks such as putting on a shirt or tying shoelaces. Incidentally, the OBA can also be used as a direct observation instrument.

Role Playing If it is not feasible for the therapist to observe the client in the actual situation in which the problem occurs, an alternative is to recreate that situation (or at least certain crucial aspects of it) in the therapist's office. That, essentially, is the rationale behind role playing in which the client and therapist enact interpersonal interactions related to the client's problem. For example, the client may enact himself or herself being interviewed for a job with the therapist playing the role of the interviewer. Not only is role playing frequently used in conjunction with behavioral interviews in assessing a problem, but it is also used in treating it (for example, see pp. 219–20).

Information from Consulting Professionals If other professionals (e.g., physicians, physiotherapists, teachers, nurses, social workers) have been dealing with the client in any way related to the problem, relevant information should be obtained from them. A client's problem might be related to some medical factor about which his or her physician could provide extremely important information for dealing with the problem. Before such steps are taken, however, appropriate permission should always be obtained from the client.

Client Self-monitoring Self-monitoring, the direct observation by the client of his or her own behavior, may be the next best thing to direct observaton by the therapist. We mention it under indirect assessment procedures, however, because the therapist does not observe the behavior directly. Thus, as with the other indirect assessment procedures, the therapist cannot have as much confidence in the observations as would be the case if she or some other trained observer had made them.

The characteristics of behavior that might be self-monitored are the same as those that would be observed directly by a trained observer and are described in Chapter 19. Self-monitoring might also aid the discovery of the causes of the problem behavior, as discussed in Chapter 20. Additional examples of self-monitoring are provided in Chapter 24.

Direct Assessment Procedures

As illustrated by each of the case histories at the beginning of Chapters 3 through 14, specific behaviors of a client were precisely defined and directly observed by other individuals. This characteristic defines a direct assessment procedure. The main advantage of direct assessment procedures over indirect assessment procedures is that the former are likely to be more accurate. Disadvantages of direct assessment procedures are that they tend to be time-consuming, they require that observers be appropriately trained, and they cannot be used to monitor covert behaviors. Chapter 19 is devoted to discussion of direct assessment procedures.

Experimental Assessment Procedures

Experimental assessment procedures are used to clearly demonstrate the antecedent events that exert control over a problem behavior, and/or the consequences responsible for maintaining that problem behavior. Such procedures are referred to as experimental functional analyses (or more simply as functional analyses) in that they attempt to demonstrate that the occurrence of a behavior is a function of certain controlling variables. Such procedures are discussed in detail in Chapter 20.

DATA! DATA! DATA! WHY BOTHER?

There are a number of reasons for recording accurate data during the baseline and throughout a program. First, *an accurate behavioral assessment provides a description of the problem that will help the behavior modifier to decide whether or not he or she is the appropriate one to design a treatment program.* Considerations relevant to this are described in more detail in Chapter 22.

Sometimes an accurate baseline will indicate that what someone thought to be a problem is actually not a problem. For example, a teacher may say, "I don't know what to do with Johnny; he's always hitting the other kids." But after taking a baseline, the teacher may discover that the behavior actually occurs so rarely that it does not merit a special program. Both of the authors have experienced this phenomenon more than once. Others have too, as illustrated by the following example from Greenspoon (1976, p. 177).

> The reliance on casual observation led a woman to complain to a psychologist that her husband rarely talked to her during mealtime. She said that his failure to talk to her was becoming an increasing source of annoyance to her and she wanted to do something about it. The psychologist suggested that she prepare a chart and record on the chart the number of times that he initiated a conversation or responded to the verbal behavior that she emitted. She agreed to the suggestions. At the end of a week, she called back to inform the psychologist that she was surprised and pleased to report that she had been in error. It turned out that her husband both initiated conversation and responded to her verbal emissions at a very high rate.

A second reason for assessing and recording behavior carefully is that *the initial assessment process often helps the behavior modifier to identify the best treatment strategy.* Discovering potential reinforcers for an individual during the baseline phase, for example, is clearly useful for increasing a behavioral deficit. Determining whether a behavioral excess of an individual is reinforced by the attention of others, or whether it enables the individual to escape from the demands of an unpleasant task, or is controlled by some other variable, can be helpful for designing an effective intervention program. As indicated previously, using information from a baseline to analyze the causes of behavior is referred to as a *functional assessment* and is discussed further in Chapter 20.

A third reason for recording accurate data during the baseline and throughout a program is that *accurate baseline data provide a means for clearly determining whether the program has produced, or is producing, the desired change in behavior.* Sometimes people claim that they do not need to record data to know whether a desirable change in behavior has occurred. No doubt this is often true. A mother obviously needs no data sheet or graphs to tell her that her child is completely toilet-trained: There is ample evidence (or, it is hoped, lack of it) in the child's pants.

But not all cases are so clear-cut—at least not immediately. Suppose that a child is acquiring toileting behavior very slowly. The parent may think that the program is not working and abandon it prematurely. With accurate data, this type of mistake can be avoided. This point is well illustrated by the following case.[1]

Dr. Lynn Caldwell was consulted by a woman whose 6-year-old son was, in her words, "driving me up a wall with his constant slamming of the kitchen door

---

[1]This case was described by Lynn Caldwell at the first Manitoba Behavior Change Conference, Portage la Prairie, Manitoba, 1971.

everytime he goes out of the kitchen." Dr. Caldwell asked the mother to obtain a baseline of the target behavior by tallying each instance of it on a sheet of paper attached to the refrigerator. Over a 3-day period, the total number of door slams was 123. Dr. Caldwell then instructed the mother to provide approval each time the boy went through the door without slamming it. But she was to administer a brief timeout whenever he slammed the door (he was to go back and remain for 3 minutes in whichever room he had just left, and the mother was to ignore him during that time) and then require him to proceed through the door without slamming it. After applying this procedure for 3 days, the mother brought the tally sheet to Dr. Caldwell. "This behavior modification stuff doesn't work," she complained, pointing to the large number of tally marks on the data sheet. "He's just as bad as he ever was." But when the tally marks were counted, there were only 87 of them over the 3 days of treatment, compared with the 123 that were entered over the 3 days of baseline. Encouraged by this observation, the mother continued the program, and the behavior quickly dropped to an acceptable level of about 5 per day (after which the satisfied mother did not make further contact with Dr. Caldwell).

Without accurate data, one might also make the opposite type of error. One might conclude that a procedure is working and continue it when in fact it is ineffective and should be abandoned or modified. For example, F. R. Harris et al., (1964) described the case of a boy in a laboratory preschool who had the annoying habit of pinching adults. His teachers decided to use a behavior modification procedure to encourage him to pat rather than pinch. After the procedure had been in effect for some time, the teachers agreed that they had succeeded in reducing pinching by substituting patting. When they looked at the data recorded by an outside observer, however, they saw clearly that, although patting was considerably above the level it had been during the baseline recordings, pinching had not decreased from its baseline level. Perhaps concentrating on the procedure and/or the patting so diverted the teachers that they had failed to notice the pinching as much as they had before introducing the procedure. In any case, had it not been for the recorded data, the teachers probably would have wasted a great deal more time and effort than they did on an ineffective procedure.

A fourth reason for accurately recording and graphing behavior is that *publicly posted results can be both prompts and reinforcers for the behavior modifier for carrying out a program*. Staff in training centers for the developmentally disabled, for example, often become more conscientious in applying procedures when up-to-date charts or graphs clearly showing the effects of the procedures are posted conspicuously. Parents and teachers alike may find that their efforts to modify children's behavior are strengthened by graphic representation of the improved behavior.

A fifth reason for recording and graphing behavior is that the *displayed data may lead to improvements apart from any further treatment program*, a process referred to as **reactivity** (Foster, Bell Dolan, & Burge, 1988). Students who graph their own study behavior (e.g., by recording the daily number of paragraphs or pages studied, or the amount of time spent studying) may find increases in the graph to be reinforcing (see Figure 18–1). Data that are presented appropriately can be reinforcing even to young children. For example, an occupational therapist at a

Figure 18–1 Monitoring and charting performance can serve at least five functions. Can you name them?

school for handicapped children once consulted one of the authors concerning a 7-year-old girl who each morning took an excessive amount of time taking off her outside garments and hanging them up. It appeared that the teachers could not be persuaded to stop attending to the child when she was in the cloakroom. The author suggested that the therapist somehow attempt to influence the child with a graph of the amount of time she spent in the cloakroom each morning. The procedure that the therapist devised proved to be as effective as it was ingenious.[2]

A large chart was hung on the wall. The chart was colored green so as to represent grass, and a carrot patch was depicted near the bottom of it. Days were indicated along the bottom of the chart and the amount of time in the cloakroom was indicated along the side. Each day, a circle was marked on the chart to indicate the amount of time spent in the cloakroom in the morning, and a small paper rabbit was attached to the most recent circle. Using simple language, the therapist explained the procedure to the child and concluded by saying, "Now let's see if you can get the bunny down to eat the carrots." When the rabbit was down to the level of the carrots, the child was encouraged to keep him there: "Remember, the longer the bunny stays in the carrot patch, the more he can eat." A follow-up showed that the improved behavior persisted over a period of 1 year.

---

[2]We are grateful to Nancy Staisey for providing us with the details of this procedure.

Behavior modifiers were not the first to discover the usefulness of recording one's behavior to help modify that behavior. As with many other supposedly "new" psychological discoveries, the real credit should perhaps go to the writers of great literature. For example, novelist Ernest Hemingway used self-recording to help maintain his literary output. One of his interviewers reported (Plimpton, 1965, p. 219):

> He keeps track of his daily progress—"so as not to kid myself"—on a large chart made out of the side of a cardboard packing case and set up against the wall under the nose of a mounted gazelle head. The numbers on the chart showing the daily output of words differ from 450, 575, 462, 1250, back to 512, the higher figures on days Hemingway puts in extra work so he won't feel guilty spending the following day fishing on the gulf stream.

The well-known author Irving Wallace used self-recording even before he was aware that others had done the same. In a book touching on his writing methods (Wallace, 1971, pp. 65–66), he commented:

> I kept a work chart when I wrote my first book—which remains unpublished—at the age of nineteen. I maintained work charts while writing my first four published books. These charts showed the date I started each chapter, the date I finished it, and number of pages written in that period. With my fifth book, I started keeping a more detailed chart which also showed how many pages I had written by the end of every working day. I am not sure why I started keeping such records. I suspect that it was because, as a free-lance writer, entirely on my own, without employer or deadline, I wanted to create disciplines for myself, ones that were guilt-making when ignored. A chart on the wall served as such a discipline, its figures scolding me or encouraging me.

STUDY QUESTIONS

1. What is meant by the term *target behavior?* Illustrate with an example from an earlier chapter.
2. Define behavioral assessment.
3. Briefly describe the minimal phases of a behavior modification program.
4. What is a prebaseline phase often called, and what functions does it serve?
5. What is the difference between a training program, a therapy program, and an intervention strategy?
6. What is an important prerequisite to the design and implementation of a behavior modification program?
7. Briefly distinguish between direct and indirect assessment procedures.
8. Describe two circumstances that might lead one to use indirect assessment procedures.
9. Briefly describe the advantages and disadvantages of indirect assessment procedures.
10. Briefly describe the advantages and disadvantages of direct assessment procedures.
11. List and describe briefly the five main types of indirect assessment procedures.
12. List and describe briefly four types of questionnaires used in behavioral assessments.

13. Give five reasons for collecting accurate data during a baseline and throughout a program.
14. What error is exemplified by the case of Dr. Caldwell and the doorslammer's mother? Explain how accurately recorded data counteracted this error.
15. What error is exemplified by the case of the boy who went around pinching adults? Explain how accurately recorded data counteracted this error.
16. Briefly describe the details of the clever graphing system devised for the child who got the rabbit to the carrot patch.
17. What is meant by reactivity in behavioral assessment? Illustrate with an example.
18. Briefly describe how self-recording was used by Ernest Hemingway and Irving Wallace to help them maintain their writing behavior.

NOTES AND EXTENDED DISCUSSION

1. A major purpose of traditional psychodiagnostic assessment is to identify the type of mental disorder assumed to underlie abnormal behavior. To help therapists diagnose clients with different types of presumed mental illness, the American Psychiatric Association developed the *Diagnostic and Statistical Manual of Mental Disorders* (DSM 1, 1952). The manual was later revised as the DSM II in 1968, the DSM III in 1980, the DSM III-R (R is for "revised") in 1987, and the DSM IV in 1994. Behavior modifiers made little use of the first two DSMs. They rejected the psychiatric scheme for diagnosis because they did not agree with the medical model of abnormal behavior on which the DSMs were based, and because there was little evidence that diagnoses based on that model were reliable or valid (Hersen, 1976). However, the DSM III, DSM III-R, and DSM IV are improvements on the first two manuals in several respects. First, they are more atheoretical and more empirically based, rather than being grounded in psychodiagnostic theorizing. Second, they provide a comprehensive statistical description of individual disorders that can be quite useful, including such information as essential and correlated features, average age of onset, average course of the disorder, degree of impairment, complications, predisposing factors, prevalence, sex ratio, familial patterns, and requirements for differential diagnosis. Third, they use a multidimensional recording system that provides extra information for planning treatment, managing the case, and predicting outcomes. The first two dimensions include descriptions of the various disorders. The third dimension requires identification of physical disorders and conditions as well. The fourth dimension requires identification of "psychosocial stressors" that may contribute to the problem. The fifth dimension requires a rating of the individual's highest level of adaptive functioning. With the improvements in the DSMs, behavior therapists in psychiatric settings are increasingly likely to classify their patients according to the DSM IV, in addition to conducting detailed behavioral assessments (Wixted, Morrison, & Rinaldi, 1993).

2. Martin, Toogood, and Tkachuk (1997) described problem checklists for sport psychology consulting. For example, the sport psychology questionnaire for basketball players asks such questions as: "Would you say that, just before or during a game, you need to improve at tuning out negative thoughts, staying relaxed and not getting too nervous?" and "Do you need to improve at identifying and reacting to your opponents' weaknesses and making adjustments as the game progresses?" Their manual includes problem checklists for 21 sports. Each checklist contains 20 items to identify areas in which an athlete may need to improve before or during competitions, 5 items to identify areas in which an athlete may need to improve concerning postcompetition evaluations, and 17 items to identify areas in which an athlete may need to improve at practices. While formal research on the forms has been limited, those checklists that have been formally researched have shown high test-retest reliability and high face validity (Lines, Tkachuk, & Martin, 1997; Schwartzman, Toogood, & Martin, 1997). Feedback from athletes and sport psychology consultants who have used the various forms has been uniformly positive concerning their value in obtaining useful assessment information.

Study Questions on Notes

1. Why did behavior therapists reject traditional psychodiagnostic assessments as exemplified by the DSM I and DSM II?

2. How do DSM III, DSM III-R, and DSM IV differ from the first two DSMs?

Direct Behavioral Assessment: What to Record and How

Let us suppose that you have chosen a particular behavior to be modified. How do you directly measure, assess, or evaluate that behavior?

As we mentioned in Chapter 18, behavior modifiers generally prefer direct to indirect measurement of a behavior whenever direct measurement is feasible. In measuring behavior directly, there are six general characteristics to consider: topography, amount, intensity, stimulus control, latency, and quality.

CHARACTERISTICS OF BEHAVIOR TO BE RECORDED

Topography

As indicated in Chapter 4, topography refers to the form of a particular response (i.e., a description of the specific movements involved). Suppose that a teacher wanted to shape a developmentally disabled child to raise her arm as a means of obtaining attention in a classroom. The teacher might identify the levels of arm raising described in Table 19–1 and proceed with a shaping program from step 1 through step 6.

Picture prompts are sometimes useful for helping observers to identify variations in the topography of a response. One of the authors developed detailed checklists with picture prompts for evaluating swimming strokes of young competitive swimmers. Figure 19–1 shows the checklist for the backstroke.

TABLE 19–1   LEVELS OF ARM RAISING FROM POOR QUALITY
TO GOOD QUALITY

1. While sitting at a table and resting both arms on the table,	the student raises an arm so that the hand and forearm are 2 inches off the table.
2. While sitting at a table and resting both arms on the table,	the student raises an arm so that it is approximately at the student's chin level.
3. While sitting at a table and resting both arms on the table,	the student raises an arm so that it is approximately at the student's eye level.
4. While sitting at a table and resting both arms on the table,	the student raises an arm so that his hand is slightly above his head.
5. While sitting at a table and resting both arms on the table,	the student raises an arm so that it is pointing upward with his hand six inches above his head, but the elbow is still bent.
6. While sitting at a table and resting both arms on the table,	the student raises an arm so that it is pointing straight above his head.

Amount

Two common measures of the overall amount of a given behavior are its frequency and its duration. **Frequency** refers to the number of instances of the behavior that occur in a given period of time. (The word *rate* is often used interchangeably with frequency.) If you are interested in teaching self-feeding to a developmentally disabled girl, for example, you might examine the frequency of slopping and the frequency of eating with the hands during mealtime. The first step would be to attempt to define slopping and eating with hands in such a way that you or anyone else could observe the child and decide when either of these responses occurred. Let us suppose that you define the responses in the following way:

1. *Slopping food.* An instance of slopping is to be recorded whenever food drops and lands anywhere except in the mouth or back on the plate, as a result of
   a. the child moving a utensil from her plate to her mouth, or vice versa;
   b. the child loading her utensil with food or attempting to cut through it;
   c. the child moving her plate around;
   d. the child dropping food from her mouth.
      Each of these occurrences is to be counted as one instance of slopping, regardless of the actual amount of food that may be dropped on any one occasion.
2. *Eating with the hands.* An instance of eating with the hands will be recorded each time the child touches food with her hand(s) while putting the food in her mouth. If the student slops while using her hands, then we record an instance of slopping as well as an instance of eating with the hands.

Now you know what behaviors to look for. Your next step is to take a baseline of how many slops and how many instances of eating with hands occur dur-

Hands: Fingers together
Arms: Roll shoulder into your ear
(Recovery) Arm comes over straight
Arm comes over close to ear
Little finger enters water first

Arms: Lower arm bends to almost 90 degrees under shoulder
(Pull) As arm straightens underwater, snap wrist at thigh and down

Legs: Leg action begins at the hips
Knees move up and down very little
Knees don't break the surface
Toes point down at bottom of kick
Toes just break surface at top of kick

Body: Hips kept high in the water
Hips kept as flat as possible
Head: Tilted up slightly, ears in water
Head kept stationary, don't rock

Figure 19–1   Checklist for the backstroke.

ing several meals. If you have a helper to observe your student during the meal,

Note 1   he or she might use a data sheet such as that shown in Figure 19–2.

In many situations, an individual doesn't have a helper or the time to take data with paper and pencil. Fortunately, there are other ways of measuring quantity that require minimal time. One such method is to use a counter, such as the

			Observation	
	Instances	Total	Time	Additional Comments
Slops:	ЖН ЖН //	12	20 min	Evening meal, three other students at the table. Meal: soup, mashed potatoes, hamburger, veg., jello, milk.
Eating With Hands	///	3	20 min	Evening meal, three other students at the table. Meal: same as above.

Date: *January 1*   Observer: *John H.*
Student: *Corrine*

Figure 19–2   A sample data sheet for recording slopping and eating with the hands at mealtimes.

relatively inexpensive wristwatch type used by golfers to record their score. With these counters you can count up to 99 simply by pressing a button for each instance of the behavior. Another easy recording technique is to transfer an item, such as a bead, from one pocket to another. At the end of the session, or at the end of the day, depending on the particular behavior being recorded, the number of beads in the second pocket is counted and recorded. You could also use an electronic calculator. Press "+1" each time an instance of the behavior occurs and the calculator keeps track of the total. Hand-held computers have been used to record more than one behavior or the behavior of more than one individual, along with the times at which each instance of behavior occurs (Paggeot, Kvale, Mace, & Sharkey, 1988; Repp, Karsh, Felce, & Ludewig, 1989). Adequate ways of measuring behavior that require little of the observer's time can almost always be found.

After the daily data have been tallied, they are transformed to a graph. Let us suppose that, over 10 meals, our observer recorded the following number of slops: 21, 27, 19, 18, 20, 24, 26, 16, 17, 23. Let us assume, further, that during the next 10 meals the student was presented with a brief timeout (in which she and her chair were pulled back from the table and held there for 10 seconds) following each slopping response. (In this example, we assume that the child could eat properly, so that no shaping was necessary—see Chapter 5.) During this program of timeout, the slops per meal were as follows: 10, 8, 5, 3, 1, 3, 2, 5, 6, 4. As shown in Figure 19–3, these data might be graphed in either of two ways. Figure 19–3A is called a *cumulative* record because each of the responses cumulate, or is added to the previous response. For example, consider meal 1. During meal 1, 21 slops occurred; therefore, a dot is made up the side at 21 and across the bottom at meal 1 (see point *A*). At meal 2, 27 slops occurred. These 27 slops cumulate (i.e., are added) to the 21 slops at meal 1, making a total of 48 slops. Therefore, our second dot is placed so that it corresponds to 48 at the side and to meal 2 across the bottom (see point *B*). During meal 3, 19 slops occurred, and these 19 are added to the

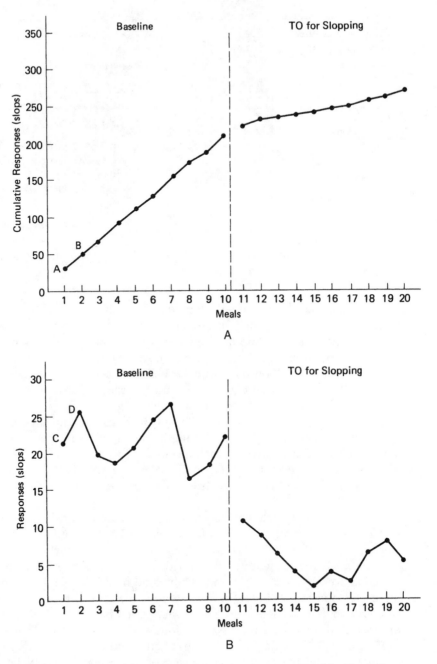

Figure 19–3   A cumulative graph (A) and a frequency graph (B) of the same
data.

cumulative total, 48, from the previous two meals. Thus, our third dot is placed at a spot corresponding to 67 on the vertical line and meal 3 on the horizontal line. In this way, the performance during any one meal is added to the total performance during previous meals, and then graphed on the cumulative record.

The first 10 points of the graph describe the child's performance during evening meals when no attempt was made to influence slopping. An inspection of the performance on the first ten meals of the cumulative record shows a medium slope (not too steep and not too low) of the graph line. The slope of the line gives us an idea of how many responses occurred over a given period of time. In other words, it provides an indication of the rate of response. The rate of response is directly related to the slope of the graph line: a steep slope indicates a very high rate of response and a low slope indicates a low rate of response. In Figure 19–3A, the medium slope during our initial observations indicated a medium rate of responding. One feature of the cumulative record should be noted: the line can never decrease. If the child is not performing at all, in which case there is no response cumulating with what is already there, then the line would be flat.

The next 10 points of the graph describe the child's performance during the treatment program. During meals 11–20, each time the child slopped, her chair was pulled back from the table and held there for 10 seconds. If the child was quiet at the end of 10 seconds, she was allowed to move up to the table again and resume her meal. This brief timeout clearly decreased the slopping behavior (e.g., see Martin, McDonald, & Omichinski, 1971). This is represented on the cumulative record by a very low slope.

A second type of graph is shown in Figure 19–3B. We call it a *frequency graph*. The features of this graph will become obvious if we consider how each of the points is plotted. Since 21 slops occurred during meal 1, a point is made corresponding to 21 on the vertical line and meal 1 on the horizontal line (see point C). Since 27 slops occurred during the second meal, a point is made corresponding to 27 on the vertical axis and meal 2 on the horizontal axis. Thus, the line can decrease, increase, or stay flat, depending on the number of instances of the response during successive meals. The differences and similarities between a cumulative record and frequency graph can be seen by comparing Figure 19–3A to Figure 19–3B.

It is sometimes possible to design a recording sheet that both records the raw data and serves as a final graph. Let us consider the fictitious case of a child, Jackie, who engaged in frequent biting attacks on the teacher and teacher's aids in the classroom. Let us suppose that a bite was defined as any instance of Jackie touching his teeth to the skin or clothes of a member of staff, and that staff members were requested to watch Jackie as closely as possible during the day. Each time they observed an instance of biting, they were to quickly move away from Jackie, and go to the chart on the front desk and place an X in the appropriate place. The chart is shown in Figure 19–4.

As you can see from Figure 19–4, the instances of biting were recorded up the side of the graph and the days of the program were recorded across the bottom of the graph. Each time an instance of biting occurred, the staff would simply add an X for the appropriate day to the number of Xs that were already on the

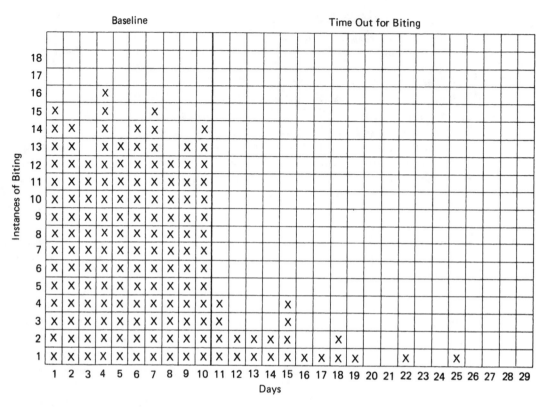

Figure 19–4 Jackie's biting behavior. Each X represents one bite.

chart for that particular day. The graph shows clearly that the hypothetical treatment program of placing Jackie in a timeout chair (located at the side of the room) for 3 minutes following each instance of biting worked quite well to decrease the biting attacks to zero. This type of graph is especially useful for those who do not have the time to rechart their behavior tallies from their data sheet to a graph.

Each instance of a behavior that is recorded in terms of frequency, such as slopping or biting as defined, is a separate, individually distinct behavior that is easy to tally in a given period of time. Behavior modifiers have recorded the frequency of such behaviors as saying a particular word, swearing, throwing objects, completing arithmetic problems, chewing mouthfuls of food, taking puffs on a cigarette, and exhibiting nervous twitches. Each of these behaviors has characteristics such that successive occurrences of the given behavior are relatively brief and the amount of time that it takes to perform the behavior is relatively similar from one occasion to the next.

While frequency is a common measure of the amount of behavior, the duration of a behavior is also sometimes important in measuring amount. The **duration** of behavior is the length of time that it lasts. In dealing with a behavior such as temper tantrumming, you may be more concerned with its duration than with its frequency. In fact, frequency can be quite ambiguous when trying to apply it to something like temper tantrums. What should we count as a separate response?

Each cry, scream, or kick on the floor? Or should we count each episode of tantrumming as a separate response? It's usually difficult to answer these questions. We can generally avoid these types of questions, however, by focusing on the duration of tantrumming. Other examples of behaviors for which duration of responding may be more appropriate than frequency of responding are listening attentively, sitting in one's seat in a classroom, watching television, talking on the telephone, and taking coffee breaks.

If you are concerned simply with keeping track of the duration of some activity over successive sessions, or days, then you might easily tabulate and present these data for effective visual display on a combined data sheet/graph. For example, an individual concerned with monitoring his or her TV watching might prepare a chart showing cumulative minutes of TV watching up the side and days across the bottom. Stopwatches or clocks are usually used to record time.

Intensity

Sometimes we are concerned with measuring the **intensity** or force of a response. Assessments of intensity often utilize instrumentation. For example, when voice loudness is the behavior of concern, decibel level can be measured by a device called a voice meter. To measure the strength of grip pressure (such as during a handshake), a device called a dynamometer can be used. Measures of force are common in the skills involved in various sports. Machines are now available the assess how hard a pitcher can throw a baseball or a hockey player can hit a hockey puck. With these types of devices, the speed of an object is used to infer the force with which it was propelled.

Stimulus Control

We often wish to assess a behavior in terms of the conditions under which it might be observed to occur. As we pointed out in Chapter 8, the term *stimulus control* is used to indicate that a certain behavior occurs in the presence of certain stimuli (and not others). Hardy and others (1981) designed a detailed system called the *Objective Behavioral Assessment of the Severely and Moderately Mentally Handicapped* (OBA). The OBA assesses the stimulus control of basic self-care skills, social and advanced self-care skills, sheltered domestic skills, prevocational motor dexterity skills, and sheltered work performance of severely and moderately developmentally disabled persons. In this test, the student is instructed to perform a particular behavior—for example, "Please put on your socks." The student's behavior is then scored as shown in Table 19–2.

Hardy et al. (1981) identified specific behaviors that appear to be taught in many training programs with severely and moderately developmentally disabled persons. Those target behaviors were then specified in the behavior test; instructions were prepared for the tester; and definitions of the different types of prompts were standardized so that the behaviors could all be assessed on the basis of the rating system just described. This testing system for identifying the con-

TABLE 19–2   SCORING STUDENT BEHAVIOR FROM THE OBA

Test item	Score
The test item was performed appropriately in all respects without further prompting or guidance of any kind after a specific instruction was presented.	3
The test item was performed appropriately only after the instruction and a verbal prompt were provided by the tester.	2
The test item was performed appropriately only after the instruction and a prescriptive verbal prompt (similar to the verbal prompt except that it provides much more detail) were given concurrently with modeling of the desired behavior.	1
The test item was not performed appropriately to the preceding level of prompting.	0

ditions under which the behavior will occur is very useful for placement and evaluation of students in individualized training programs.

In many cases, behavior modification programs concerned with the development of preverbal and verbal skills are typically preceded by behavior assessments of the stimulus control of the student's verbal behavior. Tests are available that determine the conditions under which the students will emit appropriate imitative behavior, echoic behavior, or object identification (e.g., Kaprowy, 1975). For that matter, any test in which a student is given instructions, some paper, and a pencil and is asked to answer the questions is a test of the stimulus control of behavior—are the correct answers under the control of the questions? In many training programs, the critical measure of behavior is whether or not the student identifies some pictorial or printed stimulus correctly. In such cases, the student's identification response is said to be controlled by the stimulus that the student is identifying.

Latency

Another characteristic of behavior with which we are sometimes concerned is its LATENCY—the time between the occurrence of a stimulus and the beginning of a response. For example, a child in a classroom might work effectively once she gets started. The problem is that she shows a very long latency; that is, after the teacher asks her to do something, she fools around "forever" before starting. Like duration, latency is usually assessed with stopwatches or clocks.

Quality

Concern about the quality of a behavior is frequently encountered in everyday life. Teachers might describe the quality of a child's handwriting as "good," "average," or "poor." In judgmental sports like diving, gymnastics, and figure skating, the athletes receive points based on the quality of their performances. And in our own lives, we regularly make resolutions to do various activities "better." But quality is not an additional characteristic to those mentioned previously. Rather it is a refinement of one or more of them. Sometimes, differences in judgements of quality are based on topography, such as when a figure skating jump that is landed on one foot is considered better than one that lands on two feet. With respect to frequency, many general evaluations of whether or not a person is good or poor at some task relate to how many times they tend to emit some behavior in a given period of time. For example, the person who is a good student is most likely someone who shows a high frequency of studying and answering test questions correctly. One who is said to be a "cooperative child" shows a high frequency of doing what he or she is told. In terms of latency, a runner who leaves the block very quickly after the firing of the starter's pistol might be considered to have a "good" start, while a runner who shows a longer latency had a "poor" start. Thus, quality of response is essentially an arbitrary designation of one or more of the previous characteristics of behavior that is identified as having some functional value.

CONTINUOUS RECORDING, INTERVAL RECORDING, AND TIME-SAMPLING RECORDING

For any given behavior, one could attempt to record that behavior whenever the individual has an opportunity to emit it. In most cases, this method is far too ambitious for our time and resources. One alternative is to designate a specific segment of time, such as a 1-hour training session, an afternoon, a mealtime, or a recess time, and attempt to record every instance of the specified behavior throughout that interval. Recording every instance of a behavior during a specified time segment is called *continuous recording*.

An alternative strategy is *interval recording*. Here, a specific block of time is selected (such as a 30-minute observation period). This time is then divided into equal intervals of relatively short duration (frequently, intervals of 10 seconds). A specified behavior is then recorded a maximum of once per interval throughout the observation period, regardless of how many times the behavior might occur during each interval and regardless of the duration of the behavior. An observer might use a tape recorder that plays a prerecorded beep (or some such signal) every 10 seconds. Let us suppose that the behavior of concern is an appropriately defined social-interaction response. If the response occurs once during a 10-second interval, a tally is made on the data sheet (for a sample data sheet, see Figure 19–5). If several responses or continuous social interaction occurs during the 10-second interval, the observer still makes only one tally. As soon as the beep is heard, indicating the start of the next 10-second interval, the behavior is again recorded either 1 or 0 depending on its occurrence. Behavior recorded in this way is typically graphed in terms of the percentage of observation intervals in which it is observed.

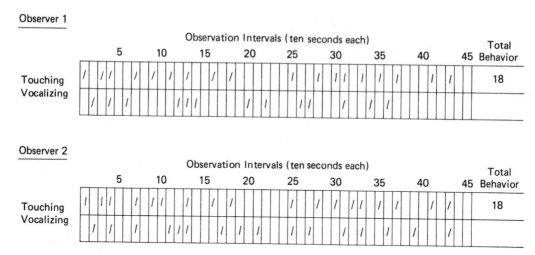

Figure 19–5   Sample data sheet for interval recording.

Another behavior observation technique frequently used is *time sampling* (e.g., see Powell, Martindale, & Kulp, 1975). In time-sampling recording, a behavior is scored as occurring or not occurring during very brief observation intervals, each of which is separated from the others by a much longer period of time. For example, a parent of a preschool child might be concerned about the frequency of the child's sitting and rocking back and forth (a self-stimulation behavior). It might be useful to have records of this behavior whenever it occurs and for as long as it occurs throughout the child's waking hours, but in general this is not realistic. An alternative is for the parent to seek out the child once every hour and make a note of whether or not the child shows any sitting and rocking behavior during a 15-second observation interval: Each observation interval is separated from the next by approximately 1 hour. This type of observational technique enables one observer to observe one or more behaviors of one or more students, even though the observer has many other commitments during the day. An example of a data sheet for time sampling appears in Figure 19–6.

Often, a recording procedure between interval recording and time-sampling recording is used. An observer might watch the student for a specified interval (say, 10 seconds) and then record the behavior during the next 10 seconds. This strategy of *observe* (for 10 seconds) and *record* (for 10 seconds) would continue over a given period of time (for instance, a half-hour). In this way, one observer may record the behavior of several students. In such a case, the observer might watch one student for 10 seconds and then record a behavior as occurring or not occurring, watch another student for 10 seconds and record a behavior as occurring or not occurring, and so forth, until all the students have been observed once. All of the students would then be observed a second time, a third time, and so forth, throughout the observation period. Strictly speaking, such an observation system could also be described as time sampling with a very brief time between observation intervals.

DATE _____

	Behavior			Location			Comments
Time	Sitting	Standing	Rocking	Kitchen	Living Room	Bedroom	
8:00 AM							
9:00							
10:00							
11:00							
12:00 PM							
1:00							
2:00							
3:00							
4:00							
5:00							
6:00							
7:00							
8:00							
9:00 PM							

Figure 19–6 A time-sampling data sheet for recording behavior of a child who frequently sits and rocks.

ASSESSING THE ACCURACY OF OBSERVATIONS

R. P. Hawkins and Dotson (1975) identified three sources of error that can affect the accuracy of observations. First, the *response definition* might be vague, subjective, or incomplete, so that the observer has problems in taking accurate observations. Second, the *observational situation* might be such that it is difficult for an observer to detect the behavior because of distractions or other obstructions to the observing process, or because the behavior is too subtle or complex to be observed accurately in that situation. Third, the *observer* might be poorly trained, unmotivated, biased, or generally incompetent. We might add two other possible sources of error: poorly designed *data sheets* and cumbersome *recording procedures*. Because any one of these sources of error, or a combination of them, might be present in any behavior modification project, behavior modifiers frequently conduct **interobserver reliability (IOR)** estimates. Two independent observers might record observations of the same behavior of the same individual during a given session. They are careful not to influence or signal each other while they are recording or to peek at each other's observations. The question is, given their best efforts while using the available behavior definitions and recording procedures, and considering their own training, how closely will their scores compare? There are several ways of evaluating their scores, but two IOR procedures are more common than the others.

One IOR procedure can be illustrated as follows. Let us return to our example of the observer who is recording the number of slops, as defined earlier in this chapter. On day 1 our observer recorded 21 slops. Let us suppose that on day 2 we bring in a second observer, who stands on the other side of the table and watches our student. The second observer is familiar with the definition of slopping and uses a copy of the data recording sheet used by our first observer. At the end of the meal, our first observer recorded 27 slops. Let us suppose that our second observer scored 29 slops. This can be converted to an estimate of our IOR by dividing the smaller number by the larger number and multiplying by 100%: IOR equals 27 divided by 29 times 100% equals 93%. Now it is important to ask what this IOR score means. It means that the two observers agreed quite closely (almost 100%) on the total *number* of slops. It does not mean that they agreed on 27 specific responses, with the second observer counting 2 extra to make 29. It is quite possible that one observer recorded a slop and that the second observer missed it. The second observer could then have counted a slop that the first observer missed. This could have gone on throughout the meal, in which case the two observers would have disagreed completely on specific individual responses. Nevertheless, their agreement on the total gives us more confidence in the actual total number of slops that were tallied, in spite of the possible disagreement on individual cases. This approach of counting two totals and then dividing the smaller by the larger and multiplying by 100% is quite common when the two observers are counting the frequency of a particular response over a period of time.

The second IOR procedure is used with interval recording. Recall that in interval-recording procedures, one and only one response can be recorded during each brief period of time (usually 5 or 10 seconds) over an extended observation period. If we have two independent observers recording the same behavior, and each is using an interval-recording procedure, then the question is: How do their successive intervals compare in terms of those that contain a response versus those that do not? Let us suppose that two observers are recording two types of social interaction for one child. The behaviors are defined as touching another child and vocalizing in the direction of the other child. Their interval scores are shown in Figure 19–5.

As you can see, the first observer counted 18 instances of touching, as did the second observer. However, the two observers agreed on only 16 of these 18 instances. Each counted 2 instances that the other missed, yielding a total of four disagreements. Our IOR is obtained by dividing the number of intervals on which they agree that the behavior occurred by the total number of intervals on which either recorded a behavior (agreements divided by agreements plus disagreements on the occurrence of a behavior), and multiplying by 100%:

Note 2

$$IOR = \frac{16}{16+4} \times 100\% = \frac{16}{20} \times 100\% = 80\%$$

What is considered to be an acceptable IOR score in behavior modification studies? It has been suggested that by convention an IOR score should be between 80% and 100% (Kazdin, 1994, p. 71). Potential variation in computational procedures, however, renders the final IOR value potentially misleading when considered by itself. We would suggest that readers of behavior modification literature consider the response definitions, observer-training procedures, recording system, method of calculating IOR, and the final IOR value as a total package when judging the reliability of reported data. Defects in any of these might make the results suspect.

STUDY QUESTIONS

1. What is meant by the topography of a response? Describe an example.
2. What are two measures of the amount of behavior? Define and give an example of each.
3. Describe three ways of keeping track of the number of times a certain response occurs during a day.
4. Prepare a cumulative graph of the following instances of a behavior that was observed during successive sessions: 3, 7, 19, 0, 0, 0, 27, 12, 12, 6.
5. Describe at least four ways in which a cumulative graph of a set of data differs from a frequency graph of the same data.
6. On a cumulative graph, what can you infer from the following?
   a. a steep slope
   b. a low slope
   c. a flat line
7. What two characteristics do behaviors recorded in terms of frequency usually show?
8. What is another word for the intensity of a response?
9. What do we mean by the latency of a response? Give an example.
10. What behavioral characteristic does the OBA assess? Explain your answer.
11. What behavioral characteristics do we use to assess the quality of a response? Discuss using examples.
12. Describe with an example the continuous-recording system.
13. Describe with an example the interval-recording system.
14. Describe with an example the time-sampling recording system.
15. When would one likely select an interval-recording system over a continuous-recording system?
16. Describe five sources of error in recording observations.
17. In a sentence or two, what do we mean by interobserver-reliability? (Describe it in words, and don't give the procedures for calculating IORs.)
18. Using the procedure described in the text for computing IORs with interval data, compute an IOR for the data of vocalizing, as recorded by observers 1 and 2 (Figure 19–5). Show all your computations.
19. According to convention, what is an acceptable IOR in a research program? What does "by convention" mean?

APPLICATION EXERCISES

A. Exercise Involving Others

Select a behavioral deficit or excess that was modified successfully (e.g., Peter's tantrums), as described in one of the other chapters. For that behavior:

1. Design a plausible data sheet.
2. Prepare a summary of some representative data (real or hypothesized), including a column for sessions and a column for the instances of behavior per session.
3. Graph your data in a frequency graph.
4. Graph your data in a cumulative graph.

B. Self-Modification Exercise

Select one of your own behavioral excesses or deficits. For that behavior, answer questions 1 to 4 in the previous exercise.

NOTES AND EXTENDED DISCUSSION

1. When the observational method affects the behaviors being observed, we say that the observation is **obtrusive.** To record observations **unobtrusively** means that the observations should not cause those being observed to deviate from their typical behavior. In other words, we don't want our observations to influence the behavior we are observing. There are several ways to ensure that your observations are unobtrusive. One possibility is to observe the behavior from behind a one-way window, as illustrated in the case of Darren in Chapter 3. Another possibility is to inconspicuously observe individuals from a distance. This strategy was used to study the drinking habits of patrons in bars in a midsized American city (Sommer, 1977). Another method is to have a confederate make observations while working side-by-side with a client in a normal work setting (S. Rae, Martin, & Smyk, 1990). Other alternatives include videotaping with a hidden camera and evaluating products of the behavior of the client (such as items littered in a public campground; Osborne & Powers, 1980). However, such tactics raise another problem. Is it ethical to observe individuals without their consent? The American Psychological Association (APA) (1992) has developed a set of ethical guidelines governing all types of experiments of psychological researchers. Among the factors these guidelines stipulate for making observations for experimental purposes are whether there is formal consent from the person being observed or from his or her guardian, whether the observations will aid in carrying out a therapeutic program for the person being observed, whether the confidentiality of the observations will be maintained, and whether specific individuals or groups can be identified from any reports stemming from the observations.

2. The procedure that we have suggested for computing IOR during interval recording is that of dividing the number of intervals on which observers agree that a behavior occurred by the total number of intervals on which either recorded a behavior (agreements plus disagreements on a behavior) and multiplying by 100%. Some researchers, however, include in their measure of agreements those agreements between two observers that no behavior occurred—in other words, agreements on blank intervals. When very few behaviors have been recorded, however, this can greatly inflate a reliability score. For example, consider the 45 observation intervals given in Figure 19–5. Let us suppose that observer 1 recorded an instance of touching during interval 5 and that observer 2 recorded an instance of touching during interval 6. No other instances of touching were recorded. In such a case, the two observers would disagree completely on the occurrence of the behavior; the IOR would be zero if IOR is computed as suggested in the text. However, if agreements on blank intervals are included, the IOR equals 43 agreements divided by 43 agreements plus 2 disagreement times 100%, which equals 95.6%. Because of this distortion, many researchers follow the proposal that we have suggested in the text for computing IOR and do *not* count agreements on blank intervals. In other words, intervals in which neither observer scores a behavior are ignored. An acceptable exception to this would be when one is concerned with decreasing a behavior and having agreement that the behavior did not occur. These points and other comments on the complexity of computing IOR are discussed in more detail in Barlow, Hayes, and Nelson (1984), Barlow and Hersen (1984), and Poling, Methot, & LeSage (1995).

Study Questions on Notes

1. What is the difference between obtrusive versus unobtrusive observations?
2. When is it especially misleading to include agreement on blank intervals in computing the IOR? Give an example.
3. When might it be acceptable to include agreement on blank intervals in your computation of an IOR? Why would this be acceptable?

Functional Assessment
of the Causes
# of Problem Behavior

Throughout Part II of this book, especially in the "pitfalls" sections, we have repeatedly pointed out how misapplication of behavior principles by those who are unaware of them can cause problem behavior. Increasingly, behavior analysts are utilizing an understanding of the causes of problem behaviors in order to treat them more effectively.

A functional assessment of the causes of problem behaviors involves asking (a) what are the antecedents (i.e., the S^Ds, see Chapter 8, or the eliciting stimuli, see Chapter 15) for the behavior, and (b) what are the immediate consequences (i.e., the positive or negative reinforcers) for the behavior? More specifically, we ask if the behavior is being controlled or elicited by particular stimuli. Is it being reinforced? Does the behavior lead to escape from aversive events? From the client's point of view, what function does the behavior serve? The answers to such questions have important implications for planning effective treatment.

APPROACHES TO FUNCTIONAL ASSESSMENT

Let us now consider procedures for identifying variables that are controlling specific problem behaviors, and examples of how such knowledge can help in designing a treatment program. In general, you will see that the information presented here follows quite logically from the basic principles and procedures discussed in the earlier chapters of this book.

Questionnaire Assessment

One way to discover antecedents and consequences that control problem behavior is to do a questionnaire analysis in which people familiar with the client are asked a series of relevant questions. For example, Durand and Crimmins (1988) devised a questionnaire called the Motivational Assessment Scale to help staff determine whether problem behavior of developmentally disabled persons was maintained by sensory feedback, escape from aversive conditions, attention from others, or tangible reinforcers. Kearney and Silverman (1990) developed a similar questionnaire called the School Refusal Assessment Scale to assess variables responsible for children refusing to attend school. Rolider and Van Houten (1993) described a stimulus control checklist in which parents or other mediators were asked questions to identify precursors of problem behaviors of developmentally disabled persons. Sobell, Toneatto, and Sobell (1994) reviewed questionnaires for identifying antecedents and consequences of excessive alcohol drinking. As with other indirect assessment procedures (see Chapter 19), such questionnaire measures to functionally assess maladaptive behaviors may not always be reliable (Sturmey, 1994; Zarcone, Rodgers, Iwata, Rourke, & Dorsey, 1991).

Observational Assessment

Another way to discover controlling variables is to do an observational or a descriptive analysis in which one carefully observes and describes the antecedents and immediate consequences of the problem behavior in its natural settings. (For examples, see Table 3–3 in Chapter 3.) From these descriptions, one forms hypotheses about the S^Ds and S^Δs of the problem behavior, and about its controlling consequences. Then one devises and implements a treatment plan based on these hypotheses. If the treatment is successful, the descriptive analysis is validated.

Experimental Functional Analysis

A third way to discover controlling variables is to directly assess their effects on the problem behavior of an individual, which is referred to as an experimental functional analysis. Consider the case of Susie, a 5-year-old developmentally disabled child who had been referred for therapy because of a high frequency of self-injurious behavior, including banging her head and slapping her face. Was this a way for Susie to get attention (positive reinforcement, see Chapter 3) from well-meaning adults who, following an instance of self-abuse, would run to Susie saying, "Don't do that! You'll hurt yourself"? Was it a way for Susie to escape from having to perform various tasks (negative reinforcement, see Chapter 14) in nursery school (i.e., when Susie was abusive, the teachers likely backed off from asking her to do those tasks)? Or were the injurious behaviors self-reinforcing (perhaps the tingling sensation in her skin felt good afterwards)? To directly assess these possibilities, Iwata, Pace, Kalsher, Cowdery, and Cataldo (1990) studied Susie's self-abusive behavior over several sessions in a therapy room. In an "attention" condition, the therapist approached Susie and voiced concern following instances of self-abuse (e.g., "Oh Susie, what's wrong?"). In a "demand" condition, the therapist presented various educational tasks to Susie at a rate of 1 every 30 seconds. In other sessions, Susie was either left alone in an empty therapy room or was observed when the therapy room contained a number of toys and games. These conditions were compared in what is called an *alternating-treatment* or *multi-element* research design (see Chapter 21). Across several sessions, the results were clear. Susie was frequently self-abusive in the demand condition but was rarely self-abusive in any of the other conditions.

Armed with this functional analysis, the therapist designed a treatment program in which the self-injurious escape behavior was extinguished by continuing the demand when Susie engaged in self-abuse. Instead of backing off following instances of self-abuse, Susie was physically guided to complete the various educational activities as they were presented. By the fifth session, self-abuse had decreased to near zero; and Susie was more compliant in performing the various tasks.

Because the treatment was successful, we may infer that the therapist had correctly identified the cause of the behavior through the experimental functional analysis. In other words, the success of the treatment validated the results of the experimental functional analysis. (For additional discussion and examples of functional analyses, see the special issue on it in Vol. 27 [1994] of the *Journal of Applied Behavior Analysis*.)

There has been some confusion in the literature concerning the terms functional assessment and functional analysis. Some writers have used the terms interchangeably. Others (e.g., Cone, 1997; Horner, 1994) have distinguished between the terms as we have in this book. That is, a functional assessment refers to a variety of approaches for attempting to identify antecedents and consequences for behavior, while a functional analysis refers to the systematic manipulation of environmental events to experimentally test their role as antecedents that control specific behaviors, or as consequences in maintaining specific behaviors. To help you remember that functional analysis refers to the *experimental testing* of hypotheses concerning the causes of behavior, we will continue to refer to such activities as experimental functional analyses. The great majority of published examples of experimental functional analyses to date have focused on problem behaviors of persons with developmental disabilities. Examples of experimental functional analyses with other problems include attention deficit/hyperactive disorder (Dupaul & Ervin, 1996), and the emotional problems of an 11-year-old boy in the 5th grade (Kern, Childs, Dunlap, Clarke, & Falk, 1994).

Although experimental functional analyses can provide convincing demonstrations of the controlling variables of problem behaviors, they do have some limitations (Sturmey, 1995). First, although an experimental functional analysis can often be conducted with a high-frequency behavior, such as in the case of Susie's self-abuse described above, many behavior problems that occur in community settings occur at frequencies of less than one per day (Whitaker, 1993). Experimental functional analyses for the latter behaviors require a great deal of time before sufficient data can be obtained to draw valid conclusions. Second, they cannot be applied to extremely dangerous behaviors, such as suicide threats (Sturmey, 1995). Third, because they require scheduling of a number of observational sessions, the expense and manpower requirements may be prohibitive. These and other potential problems limit the feasibility of experimental functional assessments in some circumstances (Cone, 1997; Sturmey, 1995).

We now take a detailed look at some major categories of causes of problem behaviors and examples of the general type of treatment that may be indicated in each category.

MAJOR CAUSES OF PROBLEM BEHAVIORS

Problem Behaviors Maintained by Attention from Others (Social Positive Reinforcement)

As we have seen in the "pitfalls" sections of earlier chapters, behavioral excesses often are developed and maintained by the social attention they evoke. Indicators that the behavior is maintained by attention include (a) whether attention reliably follows the behavior; (b) whether the individual looks at or approaches a caregiver just before engaging in the behavior; and (c) whether the individual smiles just before engaging in the behavior. All three of these occurring together are a strong indication that the behavior is maintained by attention.

If a causal analysis indicates that the behavior is maintained by attention, treatment involving social reinforcement would be recommended. For example, one might devise a treatment using attention when the individual is not engaging in the problem behavior (DRO, see Chapter 7) or is engaging in some behavior that is incompatible with it (DRI, see Chapter 7). The goal of such a program would be to eliminate the undesirable behavior. Another alternative is to get the behavior to occur when it is more appropriate (i.e., bring it under appropriate stimulus control, see Chapter 8) and then to decrease it to the point that it is acceptable. This strategy is illustrated by the following case.

A Case of Pestering   Lori was an attractive, severely developmentally disabled little girl with an angelic face.[1] She was small for her age and had an irresistible appeal. Perhaps in part because of these characteristics, she had gradually been shaped to be extremely persistent in her approach to the staff, so much so that she had become a chronic pest. The following sequence was typical. While Bonnie, the nurse in charge of the ward, sat working in her office, Lori peeked in and said, "Hi." "Hi, Lori, I'm busy now but I'll talk to you later," said Bonnie. "You busy now?" said Lori. There was no response from Bonnie who was trying to work and to ignore Lori's pestering. "You work hard?" asked Lori. (No response from Bonnie.) "Hi," said Lori. (No response from Bonnie.) "You don't love me?" said Lori with a sad look. "Of course I love you, Lori," said Bonnie, unable to resist any longer.

Although the staff attempted to ignore Lori's excessive pestering, it was almost impossible to do so consistently unless one were exceptionally hard-hearted toward cute little girls. An observational analysis indicated that the antecedent

---

[1]This example is based on an unpublished case report at Cedar Cottage, The Manitoba Developmental Centre, Portage la Prairie, MB, 1971.

for Lori's pestering consisted of a staff member in Lori's vicinity (within approximately 15–20 feet), and that the behavior was being maintained by a schedule of intermittent positive social reinforcement.

Since total elimination of the behavior would have been extremely difficult, and probably not even desirable, the staff designed a procedure for eliminating the behavior only partially—that is, eliminating it only when it was most disruptive. Because pestering appeared to be a function of social attention from staff, they decided to use this reinforcer in the program. Each staff member received a 2 × 4-inch card to be pinned to his or her shirt or dress. The card was red on one side and green on the other. On the first morning of the procedure, a staff member walked quickly toward Lori, before she had a chance to begin pestering, and said quickly and firmly, "Hi, Lori. See my card [while pointing to the card]? I can't talk to you because I'm busy and the card is red. I'll see you later." The staff member then quickly turned and walked away, leaving Lori standing in a state of stunned silence. Within a few seconds, the staff member returned with the green side of the card showing. Smiling pleasantly, she said, "Hi, Lori. See my card? It's on the green side and I'm not busy, so now I can talk to you." The staff member then proceeded to engage Lori in a brief conversation. When there was a pause in the conversation, the staff member suddenly assumed a business-like attitude, turned the card to the red side, and said, "I can't talk to you now, Lori. My card will be red for awhile. I'll see you later." The staff member then quickly walked away before Lori had a chance to respond.

During the first few days of the procedure, the green side was usually showing, and Lori's pestering was reinforced. At times when the staff had their cards turned to the red side, they consistently ignored Lori's pestering. Over several days, the staff introduced the red side for longer and longer periods of time. Lori quickly learned to discriminate whether or not a nearby staff member was available for conversation, and she responded appropriately. After 2 weeks, the staff managed their red and green cards individually. Moreover, over time, Lori appeared to learn more subtle discriminations, such as distinguishing between staff behaviors when they were busy versus when they were relaxing or socializing. And if the staff were busy, she would refrain from pestering.

Problem Behaviors Maintained by Self-Stimulation (Internal Sensory Positive Reinforcement)

Behaviors are often reinforced by some form of sensory stimulation from our bodies. For example, massaging one's scalp produces an enjoyable tingling sensation. Unfortunately, with autistic and developmentally disabled persons, this type of consequence might also maintain self-stimulatory behaviors such as body rocking, hand flipping, and gazing at lights; and self-injurious behaviors such as slapping or scratching one's face. Reinforcers for such behaviors might consist of sensory or perceptual feedback including vestibular sensations, visual patterns, repetitive sounds, and tactile or kinesthetic sensations (Guess & Carr, 1991; Lovaas, Newsom, & Hickman, 1987). An indicator that the behavior is being maintained by the internal reinforcing effect of self-stimulation would be that the behavior continues unabated at a steady rate although it has no apparent effect on other individuals or the external environment. If it appears that stereotypic or self-injurious behavior is maintained by sensory reinforcement, then an important component of treatment might be the enrichment of the individual's environment so as to reduce his or her deprivation of sensory stimulation. Alternatively, extinction of a self-stimulatory behavior by altering the sensory consequences that the behavior produces might be effective, as illustrated by the following case.

A Case of Face-Scratching   This case, described by Rincover and Devaney (1982), illustrates an experimental functional analysis and treatment of a problem behavior maintained by sensory stimulation. Sarah was a 4½-year-old developmentally disabled child who severely scratched her face with her nails. Although her nails were cut so short that it was impossible for them to tear her skin, her scratching still resulted in worsening skin irritations and abrasions. Observations during daily 5-hour classes in a treatment center for developmentally disabled persons indicated that the scratching occurred frequently during the day. She scratched when smiling, when upset, when interacting with others, when alone, and whether or not demands were placed on her. Clearly, the behavior appeared to be motivated by sensory rather than social reinforcement. The treatment therefore consisted of sensory extinction. Each day, her hands were covered with thin rubber (dishwashing) gloves that did not prevent her from scratching, but did eliminate the sensory stimulation (and prevented her from damaging her skin). The result was an immediate and substantial decrease in the rate of scratching. Within 4 days, scratching was eliminated. During follow-up sessions, the gloves were removed, first for just 10 minutes a day, then for longer and longer intervals until finally they were no longer needed.

Problem Behaviors Maintained
by Environmental Consequences
(External Sensory Positive Reinforcement)

Some problem behavior might be maintained by reinforcing sights and sounds from the nonsocial external environment. A child who throws toys, for example, might enjoy the loud noise when they land. Flushing items down the toilet repeatedly or letting taps run to overflow a sink might be maintained by the sights produced. For an indicator that a particular problem behavior is being reinforced by nonsocial external sensory stimulation, note whether the individual continues the behavior undiminished even though it appears to have no social consequences over numerous occasions. If a functional assessment indicates that the behavior is maintained by external sensory reinforcement, then a component of the treatment program might involve sensory reinforcement of a desirable alternative behavior, as illustrated in the following case.

A Case of Flushing Jewelry Down the Toilet   This case, described to one of the authors by a mother of a developmentally disabled child who was living at home, illustrates a problem behavior that may have been maintained by social attention, by sensory stimulation from the nonsocial external environment, or by both. Frequently during the day, and always just when the mother was busy in the kitchen, the child would go to the mother's bedroom, take a piece of jewelry out of the jewelry box, carry it to the bathroom, and flush it down the toilet. She would then come and tell her mother what she had done. (For the purposes of assessment and treatment, the mother had replaced her jewelry with "junk" jewelry.) An observational assessment suggested two possible explanations of the problem behavior. First, the appearance of the jewelry swirling around the toilet bowl before disappearing might have functioned as a sensory reinforcer. Second, the entire sequence of activities may have been a behavioral chain that was reinforced by mother's attention when the child told her what she had done. The treatment procedure that was used accounted for both possibilities. Specifically, the girl was given several prompted trials during which, when mother and daughter were both in the kitchen, the mother took the daughter by the hand, went into the bedroom, prompted the daughter to take a piece of jewelry out of the box, and guided the daughter to bring the jewelry into the kitchen and drop it in a jar on the kitchen table, which produced an audible tinkling sound. Thus, the sound of the jewelry as it dropped into the jar may have served as a sensory reinforcer to replace the sight of the jewelry disappearing down the toilet. In addition, the new sequence (or behavioral chain) was highly reinforced with praise and a treat from mom. Just in case mother's attention was the variable maintaining the original sequence, her attention was now contingent upon a new sequence.

After several guided trials, the mother was able to initiate the sequence of behaviors by instructing the child while they were both in the kitchen. The child was not given an opportunity to go into the bedroom on her own. On the start of the third day, the child was instructed that any time she wanted to, when mom was in the kitchen, she could get some jewelry, place it in the jar in the kitchen and receive a treat from mom. To enhance the likelihood of this new sequence, the mother took a photograph of the daughter putting the jewelry into the jar on the kitchen table and placed the picture beside the jewelry box in the bedroom. During the next 3 weeks, the daughter continued periodically to bring jewelry to the kitchen and to receive treats for doing so. Not once did she flush jewelry down the toilet. Eventually, the girl stopped playing with mother's jewelry altogether.

Problem Behaviors Maintained by Escape from Demands (Social Negative Reinforcement)

Many of our behaviors are maintained by escape from aversive stimuli (see Chapter 14), such as squinting in the presence of bright light, or covering your ears to escape a loud sound. Escape from aversive stimuli (escape conditioning or negative reinforcement) can also cause problem behaviors. For some individuals, for example, requests by others may be aversive. The problem behavior may be a way of escaping from the demands being placed on that individual. When requested to answer difficult questions, some children may engage in tantrums that are strengthened by the withdrawal of the request. A strong indicator that a problem behavior is in this category is that the individual engages in the behavior

Note 1

only when certain types of requests are made of him or her. If your functional assessment supports this type of interpretation, it might be possible for the behavior modifier to persist with requests (demands) until compliance (rather than the problematic escape behavior) occurs. As illustrated in the case of Susie's self-abusive behavior earlier in this chapter, removing the escape function of a behavioral excess will cause that behavior to decrease. Alternatively, with nonverbal persons, you might teach the individual some other way of communicating (such as by finger tapping or hand raising) that the task is aversive. In this way, the behavioral excess can be replaced by an adaptive response that produces the same or similar function as that which was produced by the problem behavior (Mace, Lalli, Lalli, & Shey, 1993). In other situations, you might design a treatment program in which the level of difficulty of the requested behavior starts low, and is gradually increased, as illustrated by the following case.

A Case of Unwanted Tarzan Noises   Edward was an 8-year-old mildly developmentally disabled child who was in a special education class.[2] His teacher, Ms. Millan reported to one of the authors that Edward consistently (three or four times a day) made loud "Tarzan" noises in class. A questionnaire assessment indicated that Edward made the Tarzan noises whenever he was asked questions for which he did not know the answer. Rather than giving wrong answers, Edward would burst out with his Tarzan imitation. Needless to say, the Tarzan noises disrupted the class. (Ms. Millan reported that one of the other boys climbed on a desk and jumped up and down while scratching himself underneath the armpits and making noises like Cheetah the Chimp.) It appeared that Edward's outbursts enabled him to escape from questions that he found difficult. Therefore, the program Ms. Millan implemented at first eliminated such questions. Each day, she spent some time with Edward individually regarding the work to be done for the next day. During these sessions, she quizzed Edward on his knowledge of the subject matter. Although he would occasionally make mistakes, he did not make Tarzan noises. Because only he and Ms. Millan were present during those sessions, the behavior was apparently under the stimulus control of the presence of the other class members.

During class, over the next 2 weeks, Ms. Millan asked Edward questions to which he knew the answers and gave him a great deal of approval for correct answers. Then, over the next 2 weeks, she began asking slightly more difficult questions, each of which was prefaced with a strong prompt such as "Now, Edward, here's a question that's a little difficult. But I'm sure you can answer it, and if you can't we'll figure out the answer together, won't we class?" Thus, if Edward did give a wrong answer, he was immediately engaged with the teacher and the rest of the class in an attempt to figure out the answer. This gave Edward the opportunity to receive the attention of the class for desirable behavior, rather than for the undesirable Tarzan noises. The entire project required approximately a month of careful attention from Ms. Millan. Thereafter, Edward required no special atten-

---

[2]The details of this case were provided by a student in a behavior modification course for resource teachers taught by G. Martin at the Winnipeg School Division #1, Winnipeg, MB, January–March, 1973.

tion. To maintain his good behavior, Ms. Millan made sure that she periodically asked Edward questions to which he knew the answers.

Elicited Problem Behaviors (Respondents)

Some problem behavior appears to be elicited (i.e., respondent) rather than controlled by its consequences (i.e., operant). For example, aggression can be elicited by aversive stimuli (Chapter 13) or by the withholding of a reinforcer following a previously reinforced response (i.e., extinction, see Chapter 4). And emotions have elicited components (see Chapter 15). If a previously neutral stimulus has occurred in close association with an aversive event, for example, that stimulus might come to elicit troublesome anxiety. Several behavioral checklists have been published for conducting questionnaire assessments of the CSs that elicit the respondent components of emotions. Examples include the Fear Survey Schedule (Cautela, Kastenbaum, & Wincze, 1972) and the Fear Survey for Children (Morris & Kratochwill, 1983). Descriptive or experimental functional analyses could also be conducted to determine the specific stimuli, circumstances, or thoughts that might elicit respondent components of emotions (Emmelkamp, Bouman, & Scholing, 1992). The two main indicators that a problem behavior is elicited are that it consistently occurs in a certain situation or in the presence of certain stimuli and that it is never followed by any clearly identifiable reinforcing consequence. Another indicator, as suggested by the term *elicited*, is that the behavior seems to be involuntary (i.e., the person seems unable to inhibit it). If a problem behavior appears to be elicited, the treatment might include establishing one or more responses that compete with it so that their occurrence precludes the occurrence of the undesirable response (i.e., counterconditioning, see Chapter 15), as illustrated in the following example.

A Respondent Conditioning Approach to Reducing Anger Responses   Joel was a 26-year-old mildly developmentally disabled individual who had recently been dismissed from a dishwashing position due to angry outbursts towards coworkers and supervisors. A questionnaire assessment with the client's mother and staff members of the Association for Retarded Citizens (with whom the client was associated), and observational assessments with the client himself, led to the identification of three categories of CSs for respondent components of emotions. The CSs included "jokes" (humorous anecdotes told to the client), "criticism" (especially about deficiencies in the client's conduct or appearance), and "heterosexual talk" (discussions of dating, marriage, etc.). Within each category, a hierarchy of provoking events was established, ranging from those that caused least anger to those that caused the most anger. The respondent components of emotions included rapid breathing, facial expression associated with anger, and trembling. Operant components of emotion were also monitored, including talking loudly and avoiding eye contact with the speaker. Treatment focused primarily on counterconditioning. Joel was first taught how to relax using a process called progressive muscle relaxation (described further in Chapter 25). Then, while in a state of relaxation, a CS for anger from one of the categories was presented. For example, a "joke-related" situation was described to Joel and he was asked to imagine it while remaining relaxed. Across several sessions, more and more of the CSs for anger were introduced, gradually proceeding up each of the hierarchies from situations that caused least anger to those that caused most anger. (As described in Chapter 25, this procedure is referred to as systematic desensitization.) In addition to the clinic-based procedures, Joel was requested, while at home, to listen to a tape recording that induced the muscle relaxation, and to practice the relaxation exercises when CSs for anger were encountered in everyday life. Overall, the program was very successful. Anger-related responses decreased to a very low level during training sessions, and generalized to natural settings for each of the categories (Schloss, Smith, Santora, & Bryant, 1989).

MEDICAL CAUSES OF PROBLEM BEHAVIORS

Often, the controlling variables with which behavior modifiers are concerned lie in the individual's external environment. But sometimes a behavior that appears problematic may have a medical cause. For example, a nonverbal individual may bang his or her head against hard objects to reduce pain from an internal source, such as an ear infection (negative reinforcement). A medical cause may be indicated if the problem emerges suddenly and does not seem to be related to any changes in the individual's environment.

In order to encourage behavior modifiers to gather all possible information about the causes of problem behaviors, Jon Bailey and David Pyles have developed the concept of *behavioral diagnostics* (Bailey & Pyles, 1989; Pyles & Bailey, 1990). Behavioral diagnostics is an approach to behavioral assessment that examines antecedents, consequences, and medical and nutritional variables as potential causes of problem behaviors. Examples of data collected might include health/medical variables (such as menstrual cycles or constipation), nutrition variables (such as caloric intake or food allergies), medications, and of course, the kinds of antecedents and consequences of behavior illustrated in this chapter. The concept of behavioral diagnostics is broader than that of a functional assessment, and may have the effect of making behavioral procedures more acceptable to medical personnel (who have a long history of emphasizing diagnosis prior to treatment). Consistent with this broader view, variables that influence problem behavior of many individuals are listed in Table 20–1. Variables that commonly act as antecedents or consequences for problem behavior with developmentally disabled persons are listed in Demchak and Bossert (1996).

If there is any chance that a behavior problem has a medical cause, a physician should be consulted prior to treating the problem. This is not to say that behavioral techniques cannot be effective if the problem has a medical cause; on the contrary, often they can. For example, hyperactivity is often treated by a combination of behavioral and medical procedures (Barkley, 1990). Such treatment, however, should be carried out in consultation with a physician (see Chapter 2 for a discussion of behavioral approaches to medical problems).

TABLE 20–1   FACTORS TO CONSIDER IN ASSESSING CAUSES
OF PROBLEM BEHAVIOR

General Setting
  Low overall level of reinforcement
  Conditions that cause discomfort (e.g., hot, noisy, crowded)
  Presence or absence of particular people
Organismic Variables
  State of health (e.g., flu, headache, allergies)
  Motivational state (e.g., hungry, thirsty)
  Emotional state (e.g., angry, jealous)
  Temporary, repeatable states (e.g., fatigue, menstrual cramps)
Task Variables
  Too difficult
  Improper pace (too fast, too slow)
  Lack of variety
  Lack of choice
  Lack of perceived importance
Specific Antecedents
  Sudden change in immediate surroundings
  Introduction of new tasks
  Excessive demands
  Unclear instructions
  Removal of reinforcers
  Witholding of reinforcers following previously-reinforced responses
  Presentation of aversive stimuli
  Being told to wait
  Seeing someone else be reinforced
Specific Consequences: Problem behavior leads to
  Escape from demands
  Attention from others
  Sympathy
  Getting one's way
  Tangible reinforcers
  Internal sensory feedback
  External sensory feedback

GUIDELINES FOR CONDUCTING
A FUNCTIONAL ASSESSMENT

1. Define the problem behavior in behavioral terms.
2. Identify antecedent events that consistently precede the problem behavior.
3. Identify consequences that immediately (although possibly intermittently) follow the problem behavior.
4. As suggested by behavioral diagnostics, consider health/medical/personal variables that might contribute to the problem.
5. Based on guidelines 2, 3, and 4, form hypotheses about the consequent events that maintain the problem behavior, the antecedent events that elicit it or evoke it, and/or the health/medical/personal variables that exacerbate it.
6. Take data on the behavior, its antecedents and consequences in its natural setting, and health/medical/personal variables to determine which of the hypotheses in guideline 5 are likely to be correct.

7. If possible, do an experimental functional analysis by directly testing the hypotheses developed in guideline 5.
8. Incorporating the principles discussed in Part II of this text, and following the guidelines for designing treatment programs in Chapter 22, develop and carry out a treatment program based on the hypothesis that is most likely to be correct, as determined by guidelines 6 and 7.
9. If the treatment is successful, accept the causal analysis as confirmed. If it is not successful, redo the functional assessment, or attempt a solution still based on the principles in Part II of the book, and follow the guidelines in Chapter 22.

STUDY QUESTIONS

1. Briefly describe three ways of discovering controlling variables of problem behavior.
2. What is the difference between a functional assessment and an experimental functional analysis of a problem behavior?
3. Briefly describe how an experimental functional analysis indicated that Susie's self-abusiveness was likely maintained because it enabled her to escape from demanding adults. How did the treatment condition confirm the functional analysis?
4. Describe three limitations of experimental functional analysis.
5. In a sentence or two each, outline six possible causes of problem behaviors.
6. What are three indicators that a problem behavior is probably maintained by the social attention that follows it?
7. What is sensory extinction? Explain with reference to an example.
8. What is an indicator that a problem behavior is being reinforced by nonsocial external sensory stimulation? Give an example illustrating this indicator.
9. What were two plausible explanations of the behavior of the developmentally disabled child of flushing jewelry down the toilet? How did the treatment procedure account for both possibilities?
10. What is a strong indicator that a problem behavior is being maintained as a way of escaping from demands placed on that individual? Give an example illustrating this indicator.
11. Suppose that a nonverbal child screams loudly as a way of escaping from demands placed on the child by adults in various training settings. Describe two alternative strategies that the adults might follow to deal with the problem behavior.
12. What are the two main indicators that a problem behavior is elicited by prior stimuli (vs. being maintained by reinforcing consequences)? Give an example illustrating this indicator.
13. Describe the main components in the treatment of Joel's anger.
14. According to Bailey and Pyles, what is behavioral diagnostics? In what sense is this term broader than functional assessment?

APPLICATION EXERCISES

A. Exercise Involving Others

Identify a behavioral excess of someone you know well (but do not identify that person). Try to identify the stimulus control and maintaining consequences for that behavior. Based upon your functional assessment, what do you think would be the best treatment procedure?

B. Self-Modification Exercise

Identify one of your own behavioral excesses. Try to identify the stimulus control and maintaining consequences for that behavior. Based upon your functional assessment, what do you think would be the best treatment procedure to decrease or eliminate that excess?

NOTE AND EXTENDED DISCUSSION

1. It is also plausible to suppose that some problem behaviors might be maintained by nonsocial negative reinforcement (i.e., they enable the individual to escape from aversive nonsocial external sensory stimulation). A nonverbal child might repeatedly remove her shoes because they squeeze her toes too tightly. Or an individual who wore loose fitting t-shirts all through high school and college might find himself in the position of having a job that requires a buttoned-up collar and a tie. Such an individual might frequently loosen the top button and the tie (knowingly or unknowingly). Of course, it is debatable as to whether or not such behaviors are undesirable. For the nonverbal child, removing her shoes may be a way of communicating that they are too tight. And some might argue that buttoned-up collars and ties are unnecessary in any environment.

Study Questions on Note

1. Describe an example not in the text of how nonsocial negative reinforcement could produce undesirable behavior.

Doing Research
in Behavior Modification

A minimal behavior modification program has four phases: a *screening phase*, for clarifying the problem and determining who should treat it; a *baseline phase*, for determining the initial level of the behavior prior to the program; a *treatment phase*, in which the intervention strategy is initiated; and a *follow-up phase*, for evaluating the persistence of the desirable behavioral changes following termination of the program. Many behavior modification projects go beyond these minimal phases, however, and demonstrate convincingly that it was indeed the treatment that caused a particular change in behavior. The value of such demonstrations might be illustrated best with a hypothetical example.

Our example involves a second-grade student's frequency of successfully completing addition and subtraction problems in daily half-hour math classes. The student, Billie, was performing at a much lower level than were any of the other students and was showing a great deal of disruptive behavior during the class. The teacher, Ms. Johnson, reasoned that an increase in Billie's performance at solving the assigned math problems might make it more pleasurable for Billie to work at the problems and might thereby decrease his disruptive interactions with those around him. During a 1-week baseline, Ms. Johnson assigned a certain number of problems to the class and recorded the number that Billie completed successfully during each half-hour period. Billie averaged successful completion of 7 math problems per half-hour, less than half the class average of 16 problems per half-hour. Ms. Johnson next introduced a reinforcement program. She told Billie that for each math problem he completed successfully he could add one extra minute of time to his physical education class on Friday afternoon, an activity that appeared to be highly pleasurable for him. Billie's performance improved during the first week of the program. During the second week, he averaged 19 correct math problems per half-hour class.

Can the teacher attribute the improvement in Billie's performance to the treatment? Our initial tendency might be to say "yes," in that performance is much better now than it was during the original baseline. Consider, however, that the improvement may have been the result of other factors. For example, a bad cold could have depressed Billie's baseline performance, and the recovery from his cold have been the cause of his improved mathematical performance after the program was introduced. Or a new student who set a good example for Billie to model may have been seated near him during the treatment phase but not during the baseline. Or perhaps the problems assigned during the treatment phase were easier than those assigned during baseline. Or perhaps something that the teacher could not possibly have been aware of was responsible for his improved performance.

In any program in which a treatment phase is introduced for the purpose of modifying some behavior, it is quite possible for an uncontrolled or interfering variable or condition to occur concurrently with the treatment, such that the change in the behavior is due to the uncontrolled variable rather than the treatment itself. A behavior modification research project attempts to demonstrate convincingly that it was the treatment, rather than some uncontrolled variable, that was responsible for the change in the behavior in question.

THE REVERSAL-REPLICATION (ABAB) RESEARCH DESIGN

Let us suppose that Ms. Johnson, being scientifically inclined, is aware of the possibilities noted earlier and would like to demonstrate convincingly that it was indeed her program that was responsible for Billie's improvement. (Besides satisfying her curiosity, there are several practical reasons why she might have wanted such a demonstration. It would indicate if she should try a similar procedure with another problem Billie might have, if she should recommend similar procedures to Billie's other teachers, and if she should try similar procedures with other students in her class.) Therefore, at the end of the second week of the reinforcement program, she eliminated the reinforcement and returned to the baseline condition. Let us suppose that the hypothetical results of this manipulation by the teacher are those shown in Figure 21–1.

By the end of the second week of return to the baseline conditions (which is called a *reversal*), Billie was performing at a level approximately that of his original baseline. Ms. Johnson then reintroduced the treatment phase, just as it had been before, and, as can be seen in Figure 21–1, Billie again improved his performance. Ms. Johnson had replicated both the original baseline and the original treatment effects. If some uncontrolled variable was operating, one must hypothesize that it was occurring mysteriously at exactly the same time the treatment program was operative and was not occurring when the treatment program was removed. This becomes much less plausible with each successful replication of

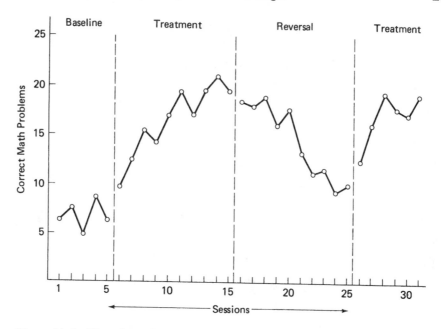

Figure 21–1 Hypothetical data showing a reversal-replication (ABAB) design for Billie.

the effect. We now have much more confidence that it was indeed the teacher's procedure that produced the desired behavioral change. Ms. Johnson demonstrated a cause-effect relationship between a particular behavior, sometimes referred to as *a dependent variable*, and her treatment program, sometimes referred to as the *independent variable*.

Note 1

The type of experimental strategy that Ms. Johnson employed is called a **reversal-replication** design. It is so named because it includes a reversal to baseline conditions followed by a replication of the treatment phase (and, it is hoped, of the effect). The baseline condition is often abbreviated "A," and the treatment condition "B." Hence, this design is also called an **ABAB** design. ABAB designs have also been called *withdrawal* designs for the reason that, during the B phases, the treatment is withdrawn (Poling, Methot, & LeSage, 1995). For a recent application of this design, see Ivancic, Barrett, Siminow, and Kimberly (1997).

Although the reversal-replication design appears simple at first glance, beginning students doing behavior modification research quickly encounter several questions that are not easy to answer. Assuming that problems of response definition, observer accuracy, and data recording (discussed in Chapter 19) have been solved, the first question is this: How long should the baseline phase last? The difficulties of answering this question might be appreciated best by viewing Figure 21–2. Which of the baselines in Figure 21–2 do you consider to be the most adequate? If you selected baselines 4 and 5, we agree. Baseline 4 is acceptable because the pattern of behavior appears stable and predictable. Baseline 5 is acceptable because the trend observed is in a direction opposite to the effect predicted for the independent variable. Ideally then, a baseline phase should con-

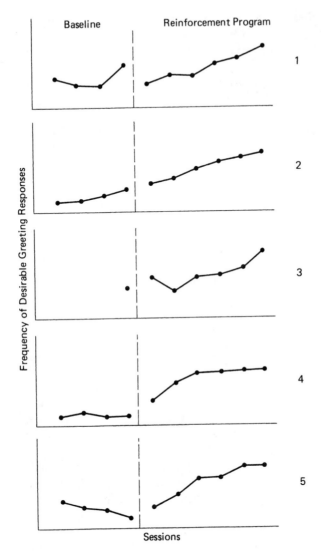

Figure 21–2 Hypothetical data for five children.

tinue until the pattern of performance is stable or until it shows a trend in the direction opposite to that predicted when the independent variable is introduced.

Other considerations, however, may lead one to shorten or lengthen a baseline in an applied research project. First, there are scientific considerations related to the newness of the behavior and the independent variables being studied. One might be more comfortable conducting a shorter baseline in a new study of behavior that has already been well researched than in a study of a less explored area. Second, practical considerations might limit the length of baseline observations. The available time of the experimenter, the availability of observers, restrictions on students for completing projects on time, and any of a number of other factors might lead one to limit or extend the baseline for nonscientific reasons. Finally, ethical considerations often affect baseline length. For example, if one is attempting to manage the self-abusive behavior of a developmentally disabled child, then an extended baseline phase is ethically unacceptable.

Another question that a beginning student in behavior modification research will encounter is this: How many reversals and replications are necessary? Again, there is no easy answer to this question. If one observes a very large effect when the independent variable is introduced, and if the area is one that has been explored before, then one replication may be sufficient. Other combinations of factors might lead the student to conduct several replications in order to convincingly demonstrate a cause-effect relationship.

Although a reversal-replication design is a common behavior modification research strategy, it does have limitations that make it inappropriate in certain situations. First, it may be undesirable to reverse to baseline conditions following a treatment phase. When treating a developmentally disabled child's self-abusiveness, for example, it would be ethically unacceptable to reverse to baseline immediately following a successful treatment.

Second, it may be impossible to obtain a reversal. For example, behavioral trapping may prevent a reversal. In Chapter 12, we described how a shy child might be taught to interact with his peers; once the teacher's reinforcement produces the desirable interaction, the child's behavior might be "trapped" by his peers who maintain it after the withdrawal of the teacher's attention. Other behaviors might be trapped by the individual's physical rather than social environment. Once a golf pro has taught a novice golfer to hit a golf ball over 200 yards, it is unlikely that the golfer will deliberately return to his original, unorthodox swing, which produced a 150-yard drive.

MULTIPLE-BASELINE DESIGNS

As we noted, a major purpose of behavior modification research is to demonstrate the control imposed on behavior by a particular treatment. Multiple-baseline designs are used to accomplish this without reversing to baseline conditions.

A Multiple Baseline Across Behaviors

Let us suppose that Ms. Johnson was concerned with demonstrating the effects of her reinforcement procedure on Billie's academic performance, but she did not want to do a reversal and risk losing the improvement shown by Billie. She might have accomplished her demonstration of treatment control over improved performance by constructing a **multiple-baseline design across behaviors.** Her first step would have been to baseline two or more behaviors concurrently. Specifically, she might have recorded Billie's performance in solving math problems during math class, his performance in spelling correctly during English class, and his sentence writing during creative writing class. These baselines might have been those shown in Figure 21–3. The multiple-baseline design across behaviors calls for the introduction of the treatment sequentially across two or more behaviors. The extra minute of physical education class per correct problem might have

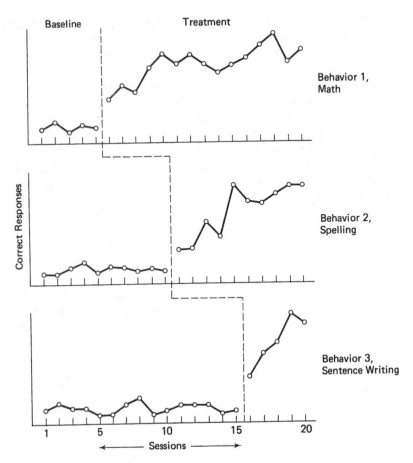

Figure 21–3 Hypothetical data illustrating a multiple-baseline design across behaviors for Billie.

been introduced in the math class while the baseline condition was continued during spelling and writing classes. If the results were those shown in Figure 21–3, the teacher might next have introduced the treatment for the second behavior—correct spelling.

Finally, the teacher might have introduced the treatment for the third behavior—sentence writing. If performance was as indicated in Figure 21–3, then it clearly indicated that the behavior changed only when the treatment was introduced. This example provides a good demonstration of the control of the treatment over several behaviors. For another example of application of this design, see Gena, Krantz, McClannahan, and Poulson (1996).

The application of this design assumes that the behaviors are relatively independent. If Ms. Johnson had applied the treatment program to one behavior while the other two behaviors were kept at baseline conditions, and if an improvement had been observed in all three behaviors concurrently, then she could not have confidently attributed the improvement to the treatment itself. An example of such response generalization was reported by Nordquist (1971). Other limitations are that it may not be possible to find two or more suitable behaviors or sufficient observers to gather the necessary data on several behaviors.

A Multiple Baseline Across Situations

Another variety of multiple-baseline design studies the effects of a treatment on a single behavior that occurs in several situations. For example, Allen (1973) was concerned with decreasing bizarre verbalizations of Mike, an 8-year-old boy diagnosed as being "minimally brain damaged." While attending a sleep-in summer camp, Mike fantasized for hours about his pet penguins whom he called "Tug Tug" and "Junior Polka Dot." These verbalizations interfered with Mike's interactions with both his peers and the camp counsellors. During an initial baseline phase, data were collected on the verbalizations in four situations: during trail walks in the evening, in the dining hall, in Mike's cabin, and during education classes. The treatment, an extinction program in which verbalizations were ignored, was then introduced in the first situation (trail walking), while the remaining three situations continued on baseline. Following the successful reduction of the verbalizations during trail walking, treatment was introduced to the second situation, the dining hall, and the remaining two situations continued on baseline. Eventually, the treatment was introduced sequentially across the remaining two situations. The daily number of bizarre verbalizations decreased to near zero in each situation following the introduction of treatment to that situation.

A potential problem with a **multiple-baseline design across situations** is that, when the treatment is applied to the behavior in the first situation, it may cause subsequent improvement in all situations (i.e., stimulus generalization across situations). When this happens, the experimenter is not able to conclude that the improvement was necessarily the result of the treatment. Other potential limitations are that the behavior may occur in only one situation, or there may not be sufficient observers to gather the necessary data.

A Multiple Baseline Across People

Yet another multiple-baseline design demonstrates the effectiveness of a treatment by applying it sequentially to individuals. For example, Fawcett and Miller (1975) used a **multiple-baseline-across-people** design to demonstrate the effectiveness of a combination of procedures (called a *treatment package*) designed to improve public-speaking behaviors. Public-speaking skills of three individuals were recorded during initial public-speaking sessions. The first individual was then given the package while the others continued on baseline. Exposure to the treatment improved the public speaking behaviors of the first individual. The package was introduced sequentially to the second person, and then to the third person, and each time it led to an improvement in public-speaking behaviors. This demonstration of improvement in individuals who receive treatment sequentially across time is also a convincing demonstration of the effectiveness of a treatment program. For a recent application of this design, see Fau, Davis, and Peck (1996).

A potential problem with the multiple-baseline-across-people design is that the first individual might explain the treatment or model the desirable behavior to the other individuals, causing them to improve in the absence of treatment, (e.g., see Kazdin, 1973). Also, it is not always possible to find two or more individuals who can be multiply baselined, nor the additional observers to gather the necessary data.

ALTERNATING-TREATMENTS (OR MULTI-ELEMENT) DESIGNS

The preceding research designs are ideally suited for demonstrating that a particular treatment was indeed responsible for a specific behavioral change. But what if one wanted to compare the effects of different treatments for a single behavior of a single individual? Multiple-baseline designs are not well suited for this purpose. An alternative design for such a concern is the **alternating-treatments design** (Barlow & Hersen, 1984). As the name suggests, this design involves alternating two or more treatment conditions considerably more rapidly than would be done in a reversal-replication design. For example, Wrighton (1978) was concerned with comparing several treatments for decreasing self-stimulatory behavior of a developmentally disabled teenager during classroom periods for posture training. Two of the treatments that were compared consisted of demerit points (exchanged for a 3-minute timeout on a variable-ratio schedule) delivered by a teacher contingent on self-stimulatory behavior, and extinction (no particular consequences were given for the self-stimulation). These two conditions were programmed in randomly alternating sessions. To minimize the possibility of generalization of the results of treatment in one session to the alternative treatment in another session, Wrighton provided distinctive stimuli associated with the different sessions: She wore a poncho and a black wig under the extinction condition and a yellow ski suit (with her normal red hair) during the demerit point condition. In this way, it was possible for her to compare the relative effects of the two treatments by having each in effect in randomly alternating sessions. The results can be seen in the top panel of Figure 21–4. For a recent example of the alternating-treatments design, see Daly, Martens, Kilmer, and Massie (1996).

A potential problem with this design is that differential effects of the two treatments observed might be due, in part, to control exerted by the different stimuli associated with the treatments (such as Wrighton's poncho vs. her ski suit). Another problem is that the two conditions may interact; that is, one of the treatments may produce an effect either because of the contrast to the other treatment in alternating sessions or because of stimulus generalization across conditions. And in many studies using an alternating-treatment design, interactions have occurred (Hains & Baer, 1989). In other words, if just one of the treatments had been applied, the effects observed may have been very different. Anticipating these potential problems, Wrighton conducted two additional phases, one of

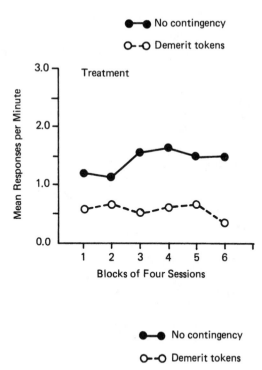

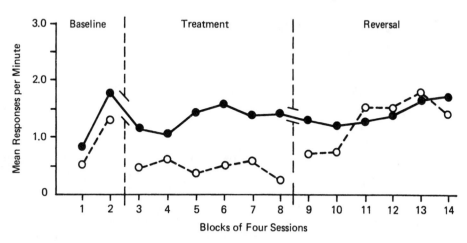

Figure 21–4 Self-stimulatory behavior of a developmentally disabled teenager during posture-training sessions. The top panel shows data from an alternating-treatment design comparing two treatments. These data were the middle phase of an experiment combining an ABA reversal design with an alternating-treatment design, as shown in the bottom panel. *Note:* Adapted from "Comparative Effects of Demerit Tokens, Response Cost and Timeout to Decrease Self-Stimulatory Behavior During Posture Training with Severely and Profoundly Retarded Women," by P. A. Wrighton, 1978, Unpublished doctoral dissertation, University of Manitoba.

which preceded the data shown in the top panel of Figure 21–4. A baseline and a reversal phase were conducted in which she wore the appropriate clothes but did not apply the demerit point contingency. During the baseline and reversal phase, extinction of the self-stimulatory behavior occurred in all sessions. The results can be seen in the bottom panel of Figure 21–4. These results demonstrate that the separation of the curves in the treatment phase was not due to differential effects of the associated stimulus conditions and that the extinction sessions were not affected by the contrast to the demerit sessions.

As suggested by Sidman (1960, p. 326), it is possible to use the alternating-treatments design to study topographically different forms of behavior. An example of such an application was described briefly in Note 3 of Chapter 8. Other examples were described by Koop et al. (1980); Martin et al. (1981); Stephens et al. (1975); and Yu et al. (1980).

Another name for the alternating-treatments design is **multi-element design.** This term is particularly appropriate when the conditions being compared are not actually theraputic treatments. Consider the functional analysis performed on Susie's self-injuring behavior, as described in Chapter 20. In this example, you will recall, several conditions were alternated—an attention condition, a demand condition, an alone condition with toys and games, and an alone condition in an empty room. These conditions were not being compared in order to determine which one was an effective treatment, but rather to help determine the cause of the behavior in order to design an effective treatment.

DATA ANALYSIS AND INTERPRETATION

Note 2

Researchers who employ the behavior modification research designs described earlier typically analyze their data without using control groups and statistical techniques that are more common in other areas of psychology. The evaluation of the effect of a particular treatment is typically made on the basis of two major sets of criteria: scientific and practical. Scientific criteria are the guidelines used by a researcher to evaluate whether or not there has been a convincing demonstration that the treatment was responsible for producing a reliable effect on the dependent variable. This judgment is commonly made by visually inspecting the graph of the results. Problems in deciding whether or not a treatment produced a reliable effect on a dependent variable might best be appreciated by examining Figure 21–5. Most observers of the five graphs would probably agree that there is a clear, large effect in graph 1, a reliable though small effect in graph 2, and questionable effects in the remaining graphs.

There are seven commonly used guidelines for inspecting data to judge whether or not the treatment had an effect on the dependent variable. There is greater confidence that an effect has been observed the greater the number of times that it is replicated, the fewer the overlapping points between baseline and treatment phases, the sooner the effect is observed following the introduction of the treatment, the larger the effect in comparison to baseline, the more precisely the treatment procedures are specified, the more reliable the response measures,

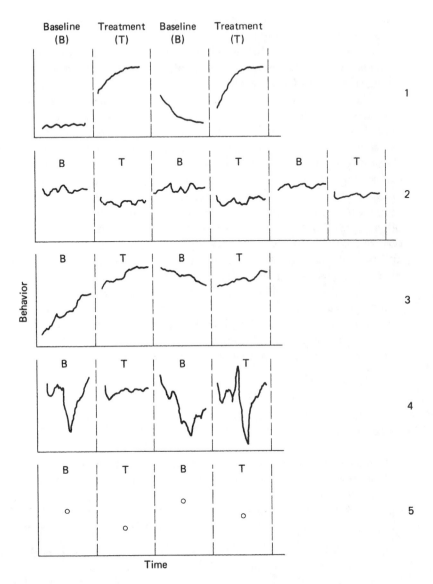

Figure 21–5   Some hypothetical data.

and the more consistent the findings with existing data and accepted behavioral theory.

Judging whether or not a significant effect has occurred from a scientific point of view is one thing; evaluating the practical importance of behavior change to the client, other significant individuals in the client's life, and society in general is something else again. In evaluating the practical impact—sometimes referred to as *clinical effectiveness*—of the treatment, we must consider more than the scientific guidelines for judging the treatment's effect on behavior. That is, if graph 2 in Figure 21–5 were a graph of self-abusive behavior, the reliable cause-effect relationship demonstrated therein might be of little clinical significance. If the individual is still extremely self-abusive, as indicated by the performance during treatment phases, then the people responsible for caring for that child would not be satisfied. Judgments about the clinical or applied importance of behavioral change are referred to as judgments of *social validity*.

Wolf (1978) has suggested that behavior modifiers need to socially validate their work on at least three levels: (a) They must examine the extent to which target behaviors identified for treatment programs are really the most important for the client and society; (b) they must be concerned with the acceptability to the client of the particular procedures used, especially when alternative procedures can accomplish approximately the same results; and (c) they must ensure that the consumers (the clients and/or their caregivers) are satisfied with the results. One social validation procedure involves subjective evaluation in which clients or other significant individuals are asked about their satisfaction with the goals, procedures, and results. Another procedure is to conduct preference tests with clients and to determine which of two or more alternatives they prefer. In a third procedure, the goals as well as the results of treatment are validated socially by comparing results with clients to the average performance of some comparison group, such as nondeviant peers. These strategies are discussed in more detail by Kazdin (1977b) and Wolf (1978). Social validation helps to ensure that behavior modifiers do the best job that they can in helping individuals function fully in society. Other strategies to ensure accountability of treatment specialists are discussed in Chapter 29.

STUDY QUESTIONS

1. Briefly describe the minimal components of a behavior modification program.
2. In two or three sentences, distinguish between a minimal behavior modification program and behavior modification research.
3. In two or three sentences, explain why we cannot necessarily claim that a change in behavior during a minimal behavior modification program was due to the treatment.
4. Describe briefly, with reference to an example, the four components of the reversal-replication design. What is another name for this design?
5. Ideally, how long should the baseline phase of the reversal-replication design continue?
6. In a sentence or two each, describe why baselines 1, 2, and 3 from Figure 21–2 are inadequate.
7. What scientific, practical, and ethical considerations might lead one to lengthen or shorten a baseline?
8. How many reversals and replications are necessary in a reversal-replication design?
9. Identify two limitations of the reversal-replication design, and give an example of each.
10. State an advantage of a multiple-baseline design over a reversal design.
11. Describe briefly, with reference to an example, a multiple-baseline design across behaviors.
12. When is a multiple-baseline design across behaviors inappropriate?

13. Describe briefly, with reference to an example, a multiple-baseline design across situations.
14. When is a multiple-baseline design across situations design inappropriate?
15. Describe briefly, with reference to an example, a multiple-baseline design across people.
16. When is a multiple-baseline design across people inappropriate?
17. Describe briefly, with reference to an example, an alternating-treatments design. What is another name for this design? Explain why that name might sometimes be preferred.
18. Briefly describe two potential problems with the alternating-treatments design.
19. In a sentence or two each, what are the scientific and practical criteria for evaluating the effects of a particular treatment?
20. For graphs 3, 4, and 5 in Figure 21–5, describe why it is difficult to draw conclusions about the effects of the treatments.
21. What seven criteria would give you maximum confidence that the treatment in an ABAB design had produced a significant effect on the dependent variable?
22. What are the three levels of social validation and why are they important?

APPLICATION EXERCISES

A. Exercise Involving Others

Suppose that you are teaching some students about doing research that utilizes reversal and multiple-baseline designs. Your students must do a research project in which they select a dependent variable and then evaluate the effects of some treatment upon that dependent variable. Your task as teacher is to analyze the material in this chapter to prepare a guide that will help the students to select the appropriate research design. Your guide should take the form of a series of questions that they might ask, the answers to which would lead to a particular design. For example, if (a) and (b), then choose a reversal design; but if (c), (d), and (e), then choose a multiple-baseline design; and so forth.

B. Self-Modification Exercise

As described in Chapter 18, self-recording without any additional behavioral procedures sometimes causes **reactivity**—the self-recording alone leads to behavioral change. Let us suppose you have decided to describe a self-recording procedure and then to investigate that as a treatment in a self-modification program. Describe a plausible multiple-baseline design that would enable you to assess self-recording as an effective self-control treatment.

NOTES AND EXTENDED DISCUSSION

1. Two considerations in evaluating a possible cause-effect relationship are *internal validity* and *external validity*. A finding is internally valid if the independent variable did, in fact, cause observed changes in the dependent variable. A finding is externally valid to the extent that it can be generalized to other behaviors, individuals, settings, or treatments.

2. The research designs described in this chapter are referred to as single-case or within-subject research designs. In most of these designs, an individual serves as his or her own control in the sense that performance of that individual in the absence of treatment is compared to that individual's performance during treatment. More common designs in many areas of psychology are control-group or between-subjects research designs. A control-group design typically involves at least two groups, one that receives the treatment and one that does not. The average performance of the two groups is then compared according to appropriate statistical procedures. Single-case designs are more popular than control-group designs among behavior modifiers for a number of reasons (Hrycaiko & Martin, 1996). First, they focus on repeated measurement of an individual's performance across a number of sessions, and therefore provide potentially valuable information on individual variation in performance. Group designs, with their emphasis on the average performance of groups, typically gather data at a single point in time, and do not focus on continuous monitoring of individual clients over time. Second, because experiments using single-case designs typically include three to five individuals, a researcher needs to locate only a few individuals with the same performance problem in order to evaluate an intervention. With group designs, it is often difficult to locate enough individuals with the same performance problem to form the different groups. Third, because all individuals in a single-case design receive the intervention at one time or another, an applied researcher is not faced with resistance from clients (or their significant others) to participate in a no-treatment control group. Fourth, because single-case designs rely on a replication logic rather than the sampling logic of the group design (Smith, 1988), they are not hampered by some of the assumptions required of group designs. Group designs, for example, assume that the dependent variable is distributed in the population in some fashion (usually normally) and that the samples are randomly selected from that population. Often, however, these assumptions are either not assessed or not met. For these and other reasons, behavior modifiers favor single-case designs. For a discussion of some common misunderstandings about single-case designs, see Hrycaiko and Martin (1996). For a discussion of reasons for using between-subjects designs, see Poling et al. (1995).

Study Questions on Notes

1. What do we mean by *internal validity? external validity?*
2. List four reasons why many behavior modifiers prefer single-case designs to group designs.

Planning, Applying, and Evaluating a Treatment Program

This chapter provides *general* guidelines that should be followed when designing a behavioral program. The client might be a developmentally disabled person, a psychiatric patient, a normal child or teenager at home, a normal child or teenager in a classroom or community setting, or perhaps a normal adult. The situation is one in which you, the behavior modifier, or a mediator (parent, teacher, or some other person) would be largely responsible for carrying out the program.

A PROBLEM HAS BEEN REFERRED: SHOULD YOU DESIGN A PROGRAM?

Behavioral problems have a variety of causes, exist in a variety of different forms, and differ widely in degree of complexity and severity. The fact that a problem has been referred is not always sufficient reason for proceeding with program design and implementation. To decide where to begin or, indeed, if to begin at all, it is helpful to try to answer the following questions. It is usually possible to obtain answers to these questions during the screening and general disposition phase of behavioral assessment described in Chapter 18.

1. *Was the problem referred primarily for the benefit of the client?* If the problem was referred by others, then you must determine if the accomplishment of the goal will be for the benefit of the client. If its accomplishment is for the benefit of others, it should *at least* be neutral for the client. One must be careful about one's ethics, and some referrals might simply stop here.

2. *Can the problem and the goal be specified such that you are dealing with a specific behavior or set of behaviors that can be counted, timed, or measured in some way?* Many referrals are very vague, subjective, and general, such as, "Johnny is hyperactive"; "My child is driving me up a wall"; "I'm really an unorganized person"; "I don't want Teddy to be so darn stubborn." If the problem is initially vague (e.g., if it is merely labeled "aggression"), you must specify a component behavior(s) (e.g., kicking furniture) that can be measured or assessed behaviorally. In such cases, however, it is extremely important then to ask whether dealing with the component(s) will solve the general problem in the eyes of the referring agent or agencies. If it is impossible to agree with the agent on the component behaviors that define the problem, then you should probably stop here. If you do achieve agreement, it should be specified in writing, because people are sometimes forgetful and may later believe that you did not deal with the problem that they referred to you.

3. *Is the problem important to the client or to others?* There are several questions that one might ask to evaluate the importance of the problem. If the problem is an undesirable behavior, does it usually lead to much immediate aversiveness for the client or others? Will solving the problem lead to much more positive reinforcement for the client or others? Will solving the problem be likely to stimulate other desirable behaviors, directly or indirectly? If the answers to these questions are yes, then it is likely that the problem is important. If the answer is no to some of these questions, then you might reconsider your involvement with that particular problem.

Note 1

4. *Have you eliminated the possibility that there are complications involved in this problem that would necessitate referring the problem to another specialist? (In other words, are you the appropriate person to deal with this problem?)* It should be obvious that if there is any chance that the problem has serious medical complications (e.g., excessive weight gain or loss) or serious psychological complications (e.g., the danger of suicide), the appropriate type of specialist should be consulted. You should then proceed to treat the problem, if at all, only in a manner that is consistent with the recommendation of that specialist.

5. *Is the problem one that would appear to be easily manageable?* To answer this question, you might consider the following: If the problem is to decrease an undesirable behavior, has the behavior been occurring for a short time, under narrow stimulus control, and with few instances of intermittent reinforcement? A problem with these characteristics is likely to be much easier to solve than an undesirable behavior that has been occurring for a long time, under the control of many stimulus situations and with a history of intermittent reinforcement. Moreover, you should be able to identify desirable behaviors that can replace the undesirable behavior. If the problem is to teach a new behavior, you should assess whether or not the client has the prerequisite skills.

6. *If the goal is reached, might it be easily generalized and maintained?* To answer this question, you should consider the following: Can the problem and the improved behavior be managed in the natural environment? If not, can a special training setting be developed that can easily be faded into the natural environment? You should also consider if there are natural contingencies that will likely maintain the behavioral objective after it has been achieved, if you can change the people in the natural environment so that they help maintain the desired behavior, or if it is possible for the client to learn a self-control program (discussed in Chapter 24) so that the improved behavior will persist.

7. *Can you identify significant individuals (such as relatives, friends, and teachers) in the client's natural environment who might help to record observations and manage controlling stimuli and reinforcers?* When designing programs for children, for example, parents can often successfully implement and maintain the program. On the other hand, it makes little sense to accept a referral concerned with the development of a language-training program that will require approximately two hours of concentrated effort per day if you have only about one hour each week to spend on the project, if it is a single-parent family, and if the parent works full-time during the day and has four other children who occupy his/her attention in the evening.   **Note 2**

8. *If there are individuals who might hinder the program, can you identify ways of minimizing their potential interference?* It makes little sense for you to design a program if people are going to be sabotaging it all the time.

9. *On the basis of your tentative answers to these eight questions, do your training qualifications, daily schedule, and available time seem adequate for you to participate in the program?* You should only accept those referrals for which you have appropriate training and adequate time to carry out an effective program.

When a behavior modifier first enters a group home for developmentally disabled persons, the home of a family with a problem child, the classroom of a second-grade teacher, or other settings where interventions are requested, the behavioral problems and the number and complexity of potentially disruptive influences are often staggering. For obvious reasons, it is better to start simply so as to succeed in a small way rather than to attempt too much and risk failing gloriously. A careful evaluation of the initial referral in terms of these questions and considerations can often contribute greatly to the initial success of the behavioral program.

SELECTING AND IMPLEMENTING AN ASSESSMENT PROCEDURE

Let us suppose that you have decided to proceed with designing and implementing a behavioral program for a person with a behavioral handicap who has been referred to you. You might then proceed through the following steps:

1. Define the behavioral handicap in precise behavioral terms, for reliable baselining.
2. Select an appropriate baseline procedure that will enable you to
   a. monitor the problem behavior
   b. identify its current stimulus control

      c. identify the maintaining consequences of the problem behavior

      d. monitor relevant medical/health/personal variables

      e. identify an alternative desirable behavior (see Chapters 18, 19, and 20).

3. Design recording procedures that will enable you to log the amount of time devoted to the project by the professionals working on it (such as teachers and behavior modifiers). This will help you to do a cost-effective analysis.

4. Ensure that the observers have received appropriate training in identifying critical aspects of the behavior, applying the recording procedures, and graphing data.

5. If the baseline is likely to be prolonged, select a procedure for increasing and maintaining the strength of the record-keeping behavior of the data recorders.

6. Select a procedure for ensuring the reliability of the baseline observations (see Chapter 19).

7. After beginning to collect baseline data, analyze those data carefully to select an appropriate intervention strategy and decide when to terminate the baseline phase and begin the intervention phase.

We reviewed the guidelines for behavioral assessment in Chapters 18, 19, and 20, and we will not repeat them here. There are some additional considerations that a behavior modifier should review before and during assessment procedures, however.

What daily times can the mediator(s) schedule for this project? If, for example, a teacher has about 10 minutes each day just before lunchtime to devote to the project, it is senseless to design time-sampling data sheets that require her to assess behavior throughout the day. It is also senseless to gather data on a wide variety of behaviors that the teacher will never have time to examine.

Will others in the situation help or hinder your data collection? There is no sense in designing a baseline procedure to record the duration of a child's tantrumming in a home situation if a grandparent, an aunt, a brother, or other relatives are going to give the child a candy to stop tantrums because "they can't stand seeing the poor little boy upset." On the other hand, friends and relatives can often be extremely helpful, either by recording data directly or by reminding others to do so. If the help of others is to be utilized, posting data sheets and a summary of the recording procedures where everyone involved in the project can see them (such as in a conspicuous place in the kitchen) may be a desirable practice.

Will the surroundings help or hinder your assessment? Let us suppose that you wish to take a baseline on the frequency and timing of a child's urinating and defecating throughout the day. If the house has many rooms and the child wanders through them, it may be difficult to immediately detect instances of the "dirty deed." Or suppose that someone wishes to take a baseline of smoking behavior but during the baseline spends some time in the house of a friend who doesn't smoke and doesn't have ashtrays around. Obviously this is not ideal for assessment procedures. If you wish to assess the basic self-dressing skills of a severely developmentally disabled individual by presenting clothing items with appropriate instructions, and the child's favorite TV program is blaring in the background, then your assessment is not likely to be accurate.

What is the nature of the existing behavior? Is it a behavior that occurs frequently throughout the day in many situations, such as thumb sucking, fingernail biting, whining, or pestering? Or is it one that occurs once every two or three weeks, such as occasional but severe tantrums, stealing, or running away from home? Is the behavior one that requires a quality assessment, such as dusting furniture or washing and drying dishes? In some cases, your answers to these questions might influence you to withdraw from the project. A problem behavior that occurs very rarely can be extremely difficult to treat if you have very limited time available for the project. Certainly the nature of the behavior will dictate the type of recording procedure to be selected, as described in Chapter 19.

How rapidly should the behavior change? Does the behavior require immediate attention because of its inherent danger (as, for example, in the case of self-abuse)? Or is the behavior one whose immediate change would be extremely convenient for those concerned (for instance, parents who want to toilet-train their child just before going on vacation)? If the behavior is one that has been occurring for many months, and if another few days or weeks more or less can be tolerated, then you might be more diligent in the design of a detailed data-recording system to reliably assess baseline levels of performance. Examples of this latter type of behavior might include smoking, excessive TV watching, and inadequate house-cleaning.

STRATEGIES OF PROGRAM DESIGN AND IMPLEMENTATION

Some behavior modifiers appear to be extremely skillful at designing effective programs "off the top of their heads"—that is, identifying the program details critical to their success and designing programs that show quick, desirable results. There is probably no set of guidelines for you to follow that will immediately turn you into that kind of behavior modifier. Nor are there any rigid sets of guidelines to which you should adhere for every program you design. Many behaviors can be managed successfully with a very minor rearrangement of existing contingencies; others require much creativity. The following guidelines will help you to design an effective program in most instances:

1. Define the goal, and identify the target behaviors and their desired amount and stimulus control. Then answer these questions:
   a. Is the description precise?
   b. On what grounds was the goal chosen, and how is that in the client's best interest?
   c. Has the client been given all possible information about the goal?
   d. What are potential side effects of accomplishing the goal, for both the client and others?
   e. Do the answers to these questions suggest that you should proceed? If so, then continue.
2. Identify individuals (friends, relatives, teachers, and others) who might help to manage controlling stimuli and reinforcers. Also, identify individuals who might hinder the program.
3. Examine the possibility of capitalizing on existing stimulus control. Can you use:
   a. rules?

   b. goal setting?

   c. modeling?

   d. physical guidance?

   e. situational inducement (rearrange the surroundings, move the activity to a new location, relocate people and/or change the time of the activity)?

4. If you are developing a new behavior, will you use shaping, fading, or chaining?

5. If you are changing the stimulus control of an existing behavior, can you select the controlling S^Ds such that they:

   a. are different from other stimuli on more than one dimension?

   b. are encountered mainly in situations in which the desired stimulus control should occur?

   c. evoke attending behavior?

   d. do not evoke undesirable behavior?

6. If you are decreasing a behavioral excess:

   a. Can you use DRL, DRO, or DRI?

   b. Should punishment be used? Remember that punishment is only acceptable (if at all) as a last resort and under appropriate professional supervision with appropriate ethical approval.

7. Specify the details of the reinforcement system by answering these questions:

   a. How will reinforcers be selected? (See Chapter 3.)

   b. What reinforcers will be used? Can you use the same reinforcers currently maintaining a problem behavior? (See Chapter 20.)

   c. How will reinforcer effectiveness be continually monitored, and by whom?

   d. How will reinforcers be stored and dispensed, and by whom?

   e. If a token system is used, what are the details of its implementation (see Chapter 23)?

8. Specify the training setting. What environmental rearrangement will be necessary to maximize the desired behavior, minimize errors and competing behavior, and maximize proper recording and stimulus management by the mediators (those directly carrying out the program)?

9. Describe how you will program generality of behavior change (Chapter 12):

   a. Program stimulus generalization. Can you

       i) train in the test situation?

       ii) vary the training conditions?

       iii) program common stimuli?

       iv) train sufficient stimulus exemplars?

       v) establish a stimulus equivalence class?

   b. Program response generalization. Can you

       i) train sufficient response exemplars?

       ii) vary the acceptable responses during training?

       iii) use behavioral momentum to increase low probability responses within a response class?

   c. Program behavior maintenance (generality over time). Can you:

       i) use natural contingencies of reinforcement?

       ii) train the people in the natural environment?

       iii) use schedules of reinforcement in the training environment?

       iv) give the control to the individual?

10. Specify the details of the daily recording and graphing procedures.

11. Collect the necessary materials (such as reinforcers, data sheets, graphs, and curriculum materials).

12. Make checklists of rules and responsibilities for all participants in the program (staff, teachers, parents, peers, students, the client, and others)(see Figure 22–1).

Figure 22–1 Behavior modification places high value on accountability for everyone involved in behavior modification programs.

13. Specify the dates for data and program reviews and identify those who will attend.
14. Identify some contingencies that will reinforce the behavior modifiers and mediators (in addition to feedback related to the data and program reviews).
15. Review the potential cost of the program as designed (cost of materials, teacher time, professional consulting time, etc.), and judge its merit against its cost. Reprogram as necessary or desired on the basis of this review.
16. Sign a behavioral contract.
17. Implement the program.

If you have followed all these guidelines, the program is ready to go. However, step 16, signing a behavioral contract, requires some additional discussion. Behavioral contracting was described initially as a strategy for scheduling the exchange of reinforcers between two or more individuals, such as between a teacher and students (Homme, Csanyi, Gonzales, & Rechs, 1969) or between parents and children (Dardig & Heward, 1976; DeRisi & Butz, 1975; Miller & Kelley, 1994). Such contracts typically provide a clear statement of what behaviors of what individuals will produce what reinforcers and who will deliver those reinforcers. Treatment contracts between therapists and clients are also recommended, however, as a strategy for ensuring that the therapist is responsible or accountable to the client (Sulzer-Azaroff and Reese, 1982). In general, a **treatment contract** is a written agreement between the client and the behavior modifier that indicates, in some detail, how the behavior modifier will help the client overcome a behavioral problem. Richard Stuart (1975) developed a client-therapist treatment contract that clearly outlines the objectives and methods of treatment, the framework of the service to be provided, and contingencies for remuneration that may be forthcoming to the therapist. When the agreement is signed, both the client and the therapist have secured basic protections of their rights. We recommend that behavior modifiers prepare such a written agreement with the appropriate individual(s) prior to implementing a program.

The implementation of your program also requires a great deal of consideration. This might be done in two parts. First, you must be certain that those responsible for carrying out the program, the mediators, understand and agree with their roles and responsibilities. This might involve a detailed discussion and review session with the mediators. It may also involve some modeling and demonstration on your part, perhaps some role playing on the part of the mediators (depending on the complexity of the programs), and finally some monitoring and on-the-spot feedback when the program is actually implemented, so that parents, teachers, or others are encouraged to follow the program and are reinforced for doing so (e.g., see Hrydowy & Martin, 1994). The second aspect of program implementation is introducing it to the client. It is obviously very important that the initial contact of the client with the program be highly reinforcing, so that the probability of further contacts is increased. Questions to consider include: Does the client fully understand and agree with the goals of the program? Is the client aware of how the program will benefit him or her? Has the mediator spent sufficient time with the client and interacted in such a way to gain his or her trust and confidence (see Chapter 18)? Has the program been designed so that the client is likely to experience some success quickly? Will the client come in contact with reinforcers early in the program? A positive answer to such questions greatly increases the chances that the program will be successful.

PROGRAM MAINTENANCE AND EVALUATION

Is your program having a satisfactory effect? This is not always an easy question to answer. It is also not always easy to decide, by some criterion or other, what to do if the program is not having a satisfactory effect. We suggest reviewing the following guidelines to assess a program that has been implemented:

1. Monitor your data to determine whether the recorded behaviors are changing in the desired direction.
2. Consult the people who must deal with the behavioral handicap, and determine if they are satisfied with the progress.
3. Consult the behavioral journals, professional behavior modifiers, or others with experience in using similar procedures on similar problems to determine if your results are reasonable in terms of the amount of behavior change during the period the program has been in effect.
4. If on the basis of guidelines 1, 2, and 3 the results are satisfactory, proceed directly to guideline 8.
5. If on the basis of guidelines 1, 2, or 3 your results are unsatisfactory, answer the following questions and make the appropriate adjustment for any yes answer:
   a. Have the reinforcers that are being used lost their appeal?
   b. Are the procedures being applied incorrectly?
   c. Is there outside interference that is disrupting the program?

    d. Are there any subjective variables—staff or client attitudes, teacher or client enthusiasm, and so forth—that might be affecting the program?

6. If none of the answers to these four questions is yes, check to see if additional programming steps need to be added or removed. The data may show excessive error rates, which would suggest the need for additional programming steps. Or they may show very high rates of correct responses, which might indicate that the program is too easy and that a certain amount of boredom is occurring. Add, remove, or modify steps as necessary.

7. If the results are now satisfactory, proceed to guideline 8; otherwise consult with a colleague, or consider redesigning a major aspect of the program, or redoing a functional analysis to identify the antecedents and consequences controlling the target behavior.

8. Decide how you will provide appropriate program maintenance until the behavioral objective is reached (see pages 152–155).

9. Following attainment of the behavioral goal, outline an appropriate arrangement for assessing performance during follow-up observations, and assess social validity (see Chapter 21).

10. After successful follow-up observations have been obtained, determine the costs for the behavior changes that occurred (called a *cost-effective analysis*).

11. Where possible and appropriate, analyze your data and communicate your procedures and results to other behavior modifiers and interested professionals (be sure to conceal the client's identity to maintain confidentiality.)

STUDY QUESTIONS

1. What is the purpose of this chapter, and how does it relate to the other chapters in the book?

2. Assume that you are a professional behavior modifier. List at least four possible conditions under which you would *not* treat a behavioral problem that has been referred to you.

3. What does a behavior modifier do when given a vague problem (such as "aggression") to work on? Illustrate with an example.

4. How does a behavior modifier evaluate the importance of a problem?

5. How does a behavior modifier evaluate the ease with which a problem might be solved?

6. How does a behavior modifier evaluate the ease with which the desired behavioral change might be generalized to, and maintained in, the natural environment?

7. What are some considerations that a behavior modifier should review before and during assessment procedures?

8. You are about to design a treatment program. After defining the target behavior and identifying its desired level of occurrence and stimulus control, what four questions should you answer before proceeding to the design?

9. If you are thinking of capitalizing on existing stimulus control, what five categories should you consider?

10. What questions should you ask to specify the details of a reinforcement system?

11. What factors should you consider in programming for generality?

12. What strategy is recommended to ensure accountability of the therapist?

13. How can you increase the likelihood that a client's initial contact with a program will be favorable?

14. After a program has been implemented, what three things should be done to determine whether it is producing satisfactory results? (See Guidelines 1, 2, and 3.)
15. If a program is producing satisfactory results, what two things should be done prior to successfully terminating the program? (See Guidelines 8 and 9.)
16. Describe in detail the steps that should be followed if a program is not producing satisfactory results (Guidelines 5, 6, and 7).

APPLICATION EXERCISE

A. Exercise Involving Others

Suppose that you are a behavior modifier. The mother of a "normal" four-year-old child asks for your help in designing a program to overcome the child's extreme disobedience. Construct realistic but hypothetical details of the behavior problem and take it through *all* steps in each of the following stages of programming:
1. Deciding whether you should design a program to treat the problem.
2. Selecting and implementing an assessment procedure.
3. Developing strategies of program design and implementation.
4. Establishing program maintenance and evaluation. (*Note:* The problem will have to be fairly complex for you to take it through *all* the steps in each of these stages.)

NOTES AND EXTENDED DISCUSSION

1. The answer to this question may be influenced, in part, by whether or not you live in an urban or a rural setting. Rodrigue, Banko, Sears, and Evans (1996) identified a number of difficulties associated with providing behavior therapy services in rural America. While rural regions have a disproportionate number of at-risk populations that are costly to serve (e.g., elderly, children, minorities, poor persons) they typically do not offer the full array of needed mental health services and are characterized by lower availability of and accessibility to specialized services. In other words, while you may not be the ideal person to treat the problem, you may be the best person available. Before accepting the responsibility of designing a program in such a case, however, you should carefully review the ethical issues for human services discussed in Chapter 29.

2. Even if significant others are not necessary to implement a program, their availability can be extremely valuable for programming generality. Consider the problem of developing effective behavioral weight-loss programs for children (see LeBow, 1984, 1991). Israel, Stolmaker, and Adrian (1985) introduced two groups of overweight children (from 8 to 12 years of age) to an 8-week intensive multicomponent, behavioral weight-reduction program. The parents of the second group were also presented with a short course on behavioral child management skills. At the end of the 8-week treatment program, both groups of children had lost approximately the same amount of weight. After a 1-year follow-up, however, maintenance of improved weight status was superior for the children whose parents had been introduced to the behavioral child management procedures.

Study Questions on Notes

1. What impact might the setting (urban vs. rural) have on your decision, as a behavior modifier, to accept a referral?
2. How did Israel and colleagues demonstrate that utilizing significant others in a program can enhance generality?

Token Economies

Recall from chapter 10 that a conditioned reinforcer is a stimulus that was not originally reinforcing but acquires reinforcing power from being paired appropriately with other reinforcers. Some conditioned reinforcers, such as praise, are quite brief. The stimulus is gone almost as soon as it is presented. Other conditioned reinforcers, such as money, endure and can be accumulated until they are exchanged for backup reinforcers, such as food. Conditioned reinforcers of the latter type are called *tokens*. A program in which a group of individuals can earn tokens for a variety of desirable behaviors, and can exchange tokens earned for backup reinforcers, is called a **token economy.**

There are two major advantages to using token reinforcers. First, they can be given immediately after a desirable behavior occurs and cashed in at a later time for a backup reinforcer. Thus they can be used to "bridge" long delays between the target response and the backup reinforcer, which is especially important when it is impractical or impossible to deliver the backup reinforcer immediately after the behavior. Second, tokens make it easier to administer consistent and effective reinforcers when dealing with a group of individuals.

Token economies have been used on psychiatric wards, in institutions and classrooms for developmentally disabled persons, in classrooms for children and teenagers with attention-deficit hyperactivity disorder (ADHD), in normal classroom settings ranging from preschool to college and university classes, in homes for predelinquents (i.e., juveniles who have engaged in antisocial behaviors), in prisons, in the military, on wards for the treatment of drug addicts and alcoholics, in nursing homes, in convalescent centers, in normal family homes to control children's behavior and to treat marital discord, and in various work settings to increase safety behavior, decrease absenteeism and to enhance on-the-job performance (Kazdin, 1977a, 1985). Although developed primarily in institutional settings, the techniques used in token economies have been extended to various community settings to decrease littering, increase recycling of wastes, increase energy conservation, increase use of mass transportation, decrease noise pollution, increase racial integration, increase behaviors involved in gaining employment, and increase self-help behaviors in people who are disadvantaged by the present economic system. Another example is the University of Kansas Experimental Living Project, a behaviorally managed experimental community of 30 college students (S. P. Johnson, Welch, Miller, & Altus, 1991; Thomas & Miller, 1980).

In this chapter we cannot do justice to the extremely wide range of behaviors and situations to which the techniques of token economies apply. What we intend to do, however, is to give a general introduction to the use of token economies in various settings. For more specific details on establishing a token economy in a particular setting, the reader is referred to any of the excellent handbooks that are available for that purpose in several areas of application. **Note 1**

INITIAL STEPS IN SETTING UP A TOKEN ECONOMY

Deciding On the Target Behaviors

The target behaviors will be determined largely by the type of individuals with whom you are working, by the short-range and long-range objectives you wish to accomplish with those individuals, and by specific behavioral problems you are encountering that interfere with the realization of those objectives. For example, if you are the classroom teacher of a group of rambunctious first graders, your objectives will likely include teaching reading, printing, counting, addition, subtraction, and constructive social interaction. Your target behaviors would include those that are involved in these skills or are prerequisite to them. Thus, at least one of your target behaviors might be "sitting quietly when the teacher gives out instructions." A more advanced target behavior might be "correctly completing problems in a workbook."

The more homogeneous the group with which you are dealing, the easier it is to standardize the rules concerning which specific responses will be reinforced with what specific number of tokens. From this perspective, at least, it is fortunate that many groups for whom token economies are appropriate are composed of individuals who are at roughly the same behavioral level (e.g., severely developmentally disabled individuals, or college students enrolled in a PSI course— see p. 13). Even with very homogeneous groups, however, it will probably be necessary to have some specific reinforcement rules for certain individuals, according to their respective behavioral needs. This necessity for individualizing programs adds to the complexity of administering a token economy, but the resulting difficulties are not serious if a staff member is not required to handle too many radically different individual programs at once. Assigning special cases to special treatment groups may be one efficient way in which to solve the problem of individualization in certain types of settings.

Taking Baselines

Just as is done before initiating other procedures, baseline data on the specific target behaviors should be obtained before initiating a token economy. It may be that your clients are already performing at a satisfactory level and that the potential benefits to be gained from setting up a token economy do not justify the time, effort, and cost involved in doing so. After the program has been started, comparing the data with the baseline data will enable you to determine the effectiveness of the program.

Selecting Backup Reinforcers

The methods for selecting backup reinforcers are essentially the same as the methods for selecting reinforcers (described in Chapter 3). Keep in mind, however, that a token system will generally increase the variety of practical reinforcers that you can use, because they need not be limited to those that can be delivered immediately following a desired response.

In considering reinforcers that are normally available, take extreme caution to avoid the serious ethical problems that can arise. Several states have passed legislation affirming the rights of mentally ill patients to have access to meals, comfortable beds, TV, and so on. Furthermore, a number of court decisions have upheld these civil rights of patients. Therefore, never plan a program that might involve depriving individuals of something that legally and morally belongs to them.

After establishing what your backup reinforcers are going to be and how you are going to obtain them, you should next consider the general method of dispensing them. A store or commissary is an essential feature of most token economies. In a small token economy, such as a classroom, the store can be quite simple, say, a box located on the teacher's desk or another table in the room. In a larger token economy, such as a prison, the store would typically be much larger, perhaps occupying one or more rooms. Regardless of the size of the store, a definite method of keeping records of purchases must be devised so that an adequate inventory (especially of items in high demand) can be maintained at all times, within the limit of your budget.

Selecting the Type of Tokens to Use

Tokens can take on any of the forms that money has assumed. Poker chips are often used, but personal "checks," entries in a "bankbook," marks on a chart on the wall or in notebooks carried by clients, stars or stamps to be pasted in booklets—all these and numerous other possibilities may suit the needs of your particular token economy, depending mainly on the type of client involved.

In general, tokens should be attractive, lightweight, portable, durable, easy to handle, and, of course, not easily counterfeited (Figure 23–1). If automatic dispensers of backup reinforcement are used, you should ensure that your tokens will operate those devices. You should also ensure that you have an adequate number of tokens for your clients. For example, Stainback, Payne, Stainback, and Payne (1973) suggest that you should have on hand about 100 tokens per child when starting a token economy in a classroom.

You should also acquire the necessary accessories for handling and storing tokens. For example, school children may need boxes, bags, or purses in which to store the tokens they have earned.

Identifying Available Help

Help from other individuals may not be essential in a small token economy, such as a classroom, but is certainly to be desired especially in the initial stages of the program. In a large token economy, such as a psychiatric facility, such help is essential.

Figure 23–1 Tokens should not be easily counterfeited.

There are a number of sources from which help may be obtained: (a) people already assigned to work with the clients (e.g., teachers' aides, nurses' aides, teaching assistants); (b) volunteers (e.g., homemakers, retired couples, senior citizens, members of civic organizations and community action groups); (c) behaviorally advanced individuals within the institution (e.g., conscientious fifth graders assigned to help manage a token economy for first graders); and (d) members of the token economy itself. In some cases, clients have been taught to deliver tokens to themselves contingent on appropriate behavior.

Note 2

After the token economy begins to function smoothly, more and more of its members will gradually become able to assume more and more responsibility in helping to achieve its goals. For example, at Achievement Place, a group home for predelinquent boys (see Fixsen & Blase, 1993), some of the youths supervised others in carrying out routine household tasks. The supervisor, or "manager," as he was called, had the authority to both administer and remove tokens for his peers' performances. Of the several methods that were studied for selecting managers, democratic elections proved to be best in terms of the performances of the youths and their effectiveness in accomplishing their tasks (Phillips, Phillips, Wolf, & Fixsen, 1973; Wolf, Braukmann, & Ramp, 1987). In another experiment at Achievement Place, some youths served with remarkable effectiveness (and earned tokens for doing so), despite their having very little adult supervision and no specific training, as therapists for others who had speech problems (Bailey, Timbers, Phillips, & Wolf, 1971). In some courses that use PSI, students who are among the first to master an assignment have served to evaluate the performance of other students on that assignment and to give them immediate feedback concerning their performance. Another method used in college and university classes is to give the students a test near the beginning of the term on the first several sections of the course material. Those students who demonstrate on this test that they can readily master the course material are each put in charge of a small group of students, whom they help to tutor and supervise throughout the remainder of the course (K. R. Johnson & Ruskin, 1977).

In deciding how you are going to obtain workers who will help to manage your token economy, you will need to consider how their helping behavior is to be reinforced. Your approval is, of course, a potential reinforcer that should be used generously. Permission to continue working in the token economy and to work at desired jobs are additional reinforcers at your disposal.

Choosing the Locations

No special locations are essential for a token economy, which is nice since the designer of a token economy often has little or no choice in its location. Some locations are better than others, however, depending on the type of token economy under consideration. For example, college instructors using token economies (i.e., PSI courses) often arrange to have their courses scheduled in lecture halls or very large classrooms designed originally for at least twice as many students as the number anticipated to attend class at any given time. Movable desks are generally preferred over stationary ones because they enable students to work easily in small groups. Classrooms with token economies are often very noisy places and give the initial impression of mass confusion to a casual observer. Surprising as it may seem, however, almost all students soon adjust quite well to the noise, so that it does not prevent them from working with great efficiency.

SPECIFIC IMPLEMENTATION PROCEDURES

Before and during the implementation of a token economy there are, as with any other new program, a number of specific procedures to be decided on and implemented. These can be categorized as follows.

Keeping Data   Here we are concerned with what sort of data sheets should be used, who is to record the data, and when the data are to be recorded.

The Reinforcing Agent   It is important to decide who is going to administer reinforcement, and for what behaviors. For example, Ayllon and Azrin (1968) recommended that, when several managers dispense tokens to several clients (such as on a hospital ward), only one person should be assigned to reinforce a particular response at a particular time. Otherwise, "no one individual can be held responsible for failure to administer the reinforcement procedures properly, since any deviation, omission, or modification is easily attributed to the behavior of some other employee" (Ayllon & Azrin, 1968, p. 136).

In addition, care should be taken to ensure that tokens are always delivered in a positive and conspicuous manner immediately following a desired response. Friendly, smiling approval should be administered along with the token, and the client should be told (at least in the initial stages) why she or he is receiving the token.

Number or Frequency of Tokens to Pay   There are several important considerations concerning the amount of tokens to give for a particular behavior. One consideration is the stage of the economy, that is, how accustomed the clients are to receiving tokens. Stainback and others (1973) recommended that 25 to 75 tokens per child is not excessive on the first day of a token economy in a classroom. They recommended further that the number be decreased gradually to 15 to 30 each day. Other considerations are the therapeutic value of the behavior being reinforced and the likelihood that the client will engage in it without tokens. As an example of the latter consideration, the number of tokens that college students could earn for doing chores in their residence was related to the amount of time required to perform the chore (S. P. Johnson et al., 1991).

Managing the Backup Reinforcers   Here we have to consider how frequently backup reinforcers will be available to be purchased (that is, how frequently "store time" should be scheduled). In the beginning, the frequency should probably be quite high, then decreased gradually. For school children, Stainback and others (1973) recommended that store time be held once or twice per day for the first 3 or 4 days and then decreased gradually in frequency until it is held only once each week (Friday afternoon) by the third week of the token economy.

It is also necessary to decide how many tokens each backup reinforcer will cost. In addition to the monetary cost, which is the most obvious consideration in assigning token values to backup reinforcers, two other factors should be considered. One is supply and demand. That is, charge more for items whose demand exceeds the supply and less for items whose supply exceeds the demand. This will help to maintain an adequate supply of effective reinforcers and promote optimal utilization of the reinforcing power of each backup reinforcer. The other factor to consider is the therapeutic value of the backup reinforcer. A client should be charged very little for a backup reinforcer that is beneficial to him or her. This will help to induce the client to partake of the reinforcer. For example, a client whose social skills need improving may be charged only a few tokens for admission to a party because of the valuable behavior that participating in this event may help to develop.

Possible Punishment Contingencies   The use of tokens provides the possibility of using fines as punishment for inappropriate behavior. This type of punishment may be preferable, from an ethical point of view, to physical punishment and timeout. As with all forms of punishment, it should be used sparingly and only for clearly defined behaviors (see Chapter 13).

If fines are used in a token economy, it may be necessary to add training contingencies that teach clients how to accept fines in a relatively nonemotional, nonaggressive manner. Such contingencies were described by Phillips, Phillips, Fixsen, and Wolf (1973) for their token economy with predelinquent youths. In that economy, the contingencies related to fines probably helped to teach youths an important social skill: how to accept reprimands from law enforcers in society.

Supervision of Staff   The managers of a token economy, no less than the clients, are subject to the laws of behavior. They must receive frequent reinforcement for appropriate behavior, and their inappropriate behavior must be corrected if the token economy is to function effectively. Their duties must therefore be specified clearly, and they must be supervised in the performance of those duties.

Continuous supervision is generally impractical. Therefore, time sampling should be used. The director of the economy should start with frequent supervision and then gradually reduce its frequency. A desirable schedule of staff supervision and reinforcement might be a VI/LH to maintain a high, steady rate of appropriate staff performance (see Ayllon & Azrin, 1968, p. 151).

Handling Potential Problems   In the design of a token economy, as with any complex procedure, it is wise to plan for potential problems. Some of the problems that are likely to arise in a token economy are (a) confusion, especially during the first few days after the initiation of the economy; (b) staff shortages; (c) attempts by clients to get tokens they have not earned or backup reinforcers for which they do not have enough tokens; (d) clients playing with tokens and manipulating them in distracting ways; and (e) failure to purchase backup reinforcers. All these and other problems that may arise can almost always be managed by careful planning beforehand.

PREPARING A MANUAL

The final stage to complete before implementing the token economy is to prepare a manual or written set of rules describing exactly how the economy is to run. This manual should explain in detail what behaviors are to be reinforced, how they are to be reinforced with tokens and backup reinforcers, the times at which reinforcement is to be available, what data are to be recorded, how and when they are to be recorded, and the responsibilities and duties of every staff member. Each rule should be reasonable and acceptable to clients and staff. Every staff member should receive a copy of the manual or a clear and accurate version of those portions of it pertaining to his or her specific duties and responsibilities. If feasible, each client should be given a clear and accurate version of those portions of the manual pertaining to him or her. If the client is not able to read fluently but can understand the spoken language, a clear explanation of the relevant portions of the manual should be provided.

The manual should include definite procedures for evaluating whether or not the rules are being followed adequately and procedures for ensuring that they are. Methods for arbitrating disputes concerning the rules should be included in the manual, and the participation of clients in the arbitration procedures should be provided to the greatest extent that is practical and consistent with the goals of the token economy. Effecting such client participation is a step toward developing the behaviors involved in individual initiative, self-government, and other skills that are so highly prized in the natural environment. Toward this end, it is desirable at some stage in the token economy to have the clients themselves participate in constructively revising old rules and designing new ones for running the economy. The rules should also be capable of modification when there is evidence that a change is desirable. Sudden and drastic changes, however, can generate undesirable emotional behavior in clients. Moreover, clients may become disinclined to follow the rules when they are changed frequently or arbitrarily. So that rule modifications may occur in the smoothest manner possible, it seems advisable to have the manual itself specify the basis on which it will be revised. Advance notification of impending rule changes should be given to all concerned, and revisions and additions to the manual should be explained, discussed, justified, put in writing, and disseminated prior to being put into effect.

PROGRAMMING GENERALITY TO THE NATURAL ENVIRONMENT

Token economies are sometimes regarded as ways in which to manage problem behavior in institutional settings. They do serve this function, but this observation should not let us neglect their more important function of helping clients to adjust to the natural environment beyond the institution. Kazdin (1985) has summarized a large amount of data indicating that token economies are effective with diverse populations, and that the gains achieved with token economies are often maintained for at least several years following the termination of the program. However, because social reinforcement, not tokens, prevails in the natural environment, a token economy should be designed so that social reinforcement gradually replaces token reinforcement.

There are two general ways of weaning a client from tokens. One is to eliminate them gradually. The second is to decrease their value gradually. The first alternative can be accomplished by gradually making the schedule of token delivery more and more intermittent, by gradually decreasing the number of behaviors that earn tokens, or by gradually increasing the delay between the target behavior and token delivery. The second alternative can be accomplished by gradually decreasing the amount of backup reinforcement that a given number of tokens can purchase or by gradually increasing the delay between token acquisition and the purchase of backup reinforcers. At present, we cannot say which method or combination of methods produces the best results. In addition, all the considerations involved in programming generality (discussed in Chapter 12) should be reviewed.

Gradually transferring control to the clients themselves so that they plan and administer their own reinforcements is another step in preparing clients for the natural environment. An individual who can evaluate his or her own behavior, decide rationally what changes need to be made in it, and program effectively for these changes is clearly in a good position to cope with almost any environment. Methods for establishing these skills are discussed in Chapter 24.

ETHICAL CONSIDERATIONS

Token economies involve the systematic application of behavior modification techniques on a relatively large scale. The possibilities of abusing the techniques, even unintentionally, are thereby magnified. Precautions should be taken to avoid such abuse. One such precaution is to make the system completely open to public scrutiny, provided that such openness is subject to the approval of clients or their advocates. Ethical considerations involving all behavior modification programs are discussed extensively in Chapter 29.

A SUMMARY OF CONSIDERATIONS IN DESIGNING A TOKEN ECONOMY

1. Review some appropriate literature.
2. Identify your target behaviors.
   a. List some short-range and long-range objectives.
   b. Arrange your objectives in order of priority.
   c. Select those objectives that are most important for the clients and that are prerequisites for later objectives.
   d. Identify several of the priority objectives on which to start, emphasizing those that can be accomplished quickly.
   e. Pinpoint a number of target behaviors for each of the starting objectives.
3. Take a baseline of your target behaviors.
4. Select your backup reinforcers.
   a. Use reinforcers that are usually effective with the population of interest.
   b. Use the Premack Principle (see Chapter 3).
   c. Collect verbal information from the clients concerning their reinforcers.
   d. Give the clients catalogs that will help them to identify reinforcers.

e. Ask clients what they like to do when they have free time away from work or other demands.
f. Identify natural reinforcers that might be programmed.
g. Consider the ethics and legalities regarding the reinforcers on your list.
h. Design an appropriate store to keep, display, and dispense your backup reinforcers.

5. Select the most appropriate type of token for your client. (They should be attractive, lightweight, portable, durable, easy to handle, and not easy to counterfeit.)
6. Identify those who are available to help manage the program.
   a. Existing staff
   b. Volunteers
   c. University students
   d. Residents of the institution
   e. Members of the token economy themselves
7. Obtain an appropriate location and necessary equipment.
   a. Accept the location with the greater space.
   b. Equipment and furnishings should be easily movable.
   c. Rearrange the setting so that behaviors of the clients can be detected most easily and reinforced immediately.
8. Decide on specific implementation procedures.
   a. Design appropriate data sheets and determine who will take data and how and when it will be recorded.
   b. Decide who is going to administer reinforcement, how it will be administered, and for what behaviors.
   c. Decide on the number of tokens that can be earned per behavior per client per day.
   d. Establish "store" procedures and determine the token value of backup reinforcers.
   e. Be wary of punishment contingencies. Use them sparingly, only for clearly defined behaviors, and only when it is ethically justifiable to do so.
   f. Ensure that staff duties are clearly defined and that a desirable schedule of staff supervision and reinforcement is implemented.
   g. Plan for potential problems.
9. Prepare a token economy manual for the clients and the staff.
10. Institute your token economy.
11. Plan strategies for obtaining generality to the natural environment.
12. Monitor and practice relevant ethical guidelines at each step.

STUDY QUESTIONS

1. What is a token economy?
2. What are two major advantages to using token reinforcers?
3. List a number of settings in which token economies have been used (at least five).
4. List a number of behaviors that token economies have been designed to develop (at least five).
5. List and briefly describe six initial steps in setting up a token economy.
6. What is the store of a token economy? Give examples.
7. What six characteristics should a token have?
8. Identify three sources of potential volunteer help in managing a token economy.

9. What do you think are some advantages in having the members of the token economy themselves function as the main source of help?
10. Before and during implementation of a token economy, what eight specific procedures must be decided on and implemented?
11. What are some of the advantages and disadvantages of assigning only one person to reinforce a particular response at a particular time in a token economy on an institutional ward?
12. How should tokens be delivered?
13. How many tokens should you have for each student in the group?
14. According to Stainback and others, how often should store time be held during the first few days of a token economy?
15. For a token economy program involving a number of staff, describe a plausible VI/LH schedule of staff supervision (think of a variation of the timer game from chapter 6).
16. Why would a VI/LH schedule be preferred to an FI/LH schedule for staff supervision?
17. Describe two general methods of weaning clients from tokens when transferring behavior to the natural environment.
18. If one decides to effect a gradual decrease in the number of behaviors that earn tokens, what general guidelines might be followed in deciding which behaviors no longer require token reinforcement? That is, where do you start and on which behaviors do you start?
19. What is one precaution to help ensure high ethical standards for a token economy?

APPLICATION EXERCISES

A. Exercises Involving Others

1. For a group of individuals of your choosing (for instance, in an elementary school classroom, a university class, or training program for developmentally disabled persons), identify five plausible goals for a token economy.
2. Define precisely the target behaviors related to each of the five goals listed in exercise 1.
3. Describe a number of things you might do to identify backup reinforcers for the group of individuals you choose in exercise 1.

NOTES AND EXTENDED DISCUSSION

1. Much of the material in this chapter is covered in greater detail in the following major works on token economies: Ayllon and Azrin (1968), which deals with token economies in mental hospitals; Stainback et al. (1973), which deals with token economies in elementary school classrooms; M. W. Welch and Gist (1974), which deals primarily with token economies in sheltered workshops; Ayllon and others

(1979), which describes token programs in prisons; and Kazdin (1977a), which presents a comprehensive review of token-economy research. For more information on token systems for children and teens with ADHD, see Barkley (1996). For more information on the use of token-economy procedures in college and high school courses, in which systems incorporating these procedures are sometimes called Personalized System of Instruction (PSI), see Keller and Sherman (1982); Sherman et al., Ruskin and Semb (1982); and p. 13 of this book.

2. For example, S. Rae et al. (1990) designed a program to pay tokens to developmentally disabled clients in a sheltered workshop for showing improved on-task performance. The tokens could be redeemed for items in the workshop cafeteria. But the workshop had insufficient staff to reliably keep track of those clients who were on-task and those who were not. A solution was to teach the workers to self-monitor their own on-task performance. A pencil and a sheet with squares on it were placed in front of each worker. The workers were taught that when a buzzer sounded, they should mark an *X* on one of the squares if they were on-task. The buzzer was set to go off at six random times during a half-day. When a worker earned six *X*s, he or she could exchange them for a token. The total program proved to be effective for increasing the on-task behavior of the workers on a variety of workshop tasks.

3. Lippman and Motta (1993) compared the effect of token removal with token reinforcement on chronic psychiatric patients living in community residences. One group of patients received tokens for engaging in appropriate behaviors such as eating nutritious meals and wearing clean clothes daily. Another group received free tokens and had them removed if they did not engage in appropriate behavior. Both groups showed improved performance on the targeted behaviors in comparison to a control group that did not receive any special treatment. In addition, the "punishment" group performed at least as well as the reinforcement group and did not show any negative emotional effects as measured by a test of mood states. In a similar study with hyperactive and aggressive children, Sullivan and O'Leary (1990) reported that removing tokens for off-task behavior was as effective as presenting tokens for on-task behavior.

Study Questions on Notes

1. Describe a token program in which clients in a sheltered workshop administered tokens to themselves.
2. Describe a study indicating that token removal can be as effective as presenting tokens in a token economy. Explain which of the following basic principles were being compared in this study: positive reinforcement, negative reinforcement, and/or punishment.

Helping an Individual
to Develop Self-Control[1]

Al and Mary just finished having donuts and coffee in the campus cafeteria. "I think I'll have another doughnut," said Al. "They look so delicious! I just don't have the willpower to resist. Besides," he added, while patting his protruding midsection, "one more won't make any difference."

Many problems of self-control involve self-restraint—learning to decrease excessive behaviors that have immediate gratification—such as excessive smoking, eating, drinking, and TV watching. Other problems of self-control require behavioral change in the opposite direction—responses that need to be increased—such as studying, exercising, being assertive, and performing household chores. Many people speak as though there is some magical force within us—called *willpower*—that is responsible for overcoming such problems. People probably believe this, in part, because others are always saying things like, "If you had more willpower you could get rid of that bad habit" or "If you had more willpower you could improve yourself and get some better habits." Most of us have heard such advice many times. Unfortunately, it's usually not very helpful advice because the person offering it almost always neglects to tell us how we can get more of this so-called willpower. It is more useful to look at how problems of self-control stem from differences between effective versus ineffective consequences of a behavior. From such a starting point, we proceed to a model for self-control.

[1]Material in this chapter was described by Martin and Osborne (1993) and is paraphrased with permission.

Finally, we describe how most successful self-control programs proceed through five basic steps.

CAUSES OF SELF-CONTROL PROBLEMS

"I just *can't* resist having an extra dessert."

"I *really* should get into an exercise program. I wish I weren't so lazy."

"My term paper is due; I have a big midterm; and I *have* to finish writing up that lab assignment. What am I doing here at this bar? Why aren't I home studying?"

Do any of these sound familiar? If you're like most people, you've probably heard yourself say such things many times. These are the sorts of times when we are tempted to talk about not having enough "willpower."

Let's see how such situations can be explained by examining how immediately significant, delayed, cumulatively significant, and improbable consequences affect (or fail to affect) behavior.

Problems of Behavioral Excesses

One type of self-control problem consists of behavioral excesses—doing too much of something. Examples are overeating, excessive TV watching, drinking too much coffee, and so on. All such behavioral excesses lead to immediate reinforcers (good taste of food, enjoyable scenes on TV, etc.). And even though they might also lead to negative consequences, the latter are often ineffective. Let's see why.

Immediate Reinforcers versus Delayed Punishers for a Behavior   Suppose that a teenager wants to go out with friends. But there is still homework to be done. When the parents ask about the homework, the teenager lies and is allowed to leave with his friends. Lying is immediately reinforced. The lie is not discovered until later, and the consequent punishment (e.g., being grounded, failing the assignment) is long delayed from the instance of lying. If a behavior leads to immediate reinforcers but delayed punishers, the immediate reinforcers often win out. Many problems of self-control stem from this fact (Brigham, 1989b). The immediate backslapping and laughter of friends after someone "chugs" a pitcher of beer may override the delayed punishing consequences of a hangover. The immediate reinforcing consequences from sexual behavior with a best friend's spouse or partner may override the delayed hurt and emotional anguish when the friend finds out and is no longer a friend.

Immediate Reinforcers versus Cumulatively Significant Punishers for a Behavior
Consider the problem of eating too many sweets. Eating an extra dessert is immediately reinforced by the good taste. And although the negative effects (excess cholesterol, etc.) of the extra dessert are immediate, they are too small to be noticed. Rather, it is the accumulation of extra desserts on many occasions that causes a health problem. As another example, consider the problem of smoking.

The immediate consequences of smoking (nicotine effects, etc.) are positive for smokers. And although there are immediate negative effects (additional tar deposited on the smoker's lungs), the harmful outcomes from a single cigarette are too small to counteract the enjoyment of smoking. Rather, it is the accumulation of the effects of hundreds of cigarettes that results in shortness of breath, sore throat, coughing, and possible lung cancer. Thus, for many self-control problems, the immediate reinforcement for consumption of harmful substances (nicotine, cholesterol, etc.) wins out over the unnoticeable immediate negative effects that are only cumulatively significant (Malott, 1989).

Immediate Reinforcers (for Problem Behavior) versus Delayed Reinforcers (for Alternative Desirable Behaviors)   Let's suppose it's a Thursday evening in the middle of your term. Your roommate just rented a movie that you would like to watch. But you also have an exam the next day. Do you watch the movie (and all those enjoyable scenes) or do you study for three hours (and receive a higher grade a week or two later)? Unfortunately, many students choose the movie. Consider the case of a worker who receives a large Christmas bonus from the company. Will the worker blow the Christmas bonus on a highly pleasurable ski trip, or invest it in a tax-free retirement fund? Which would you choose if you were the worker? For self-control problems involving a choice between two alternative behaviors, both of which result in positive outcomes, the one that produces the immediate reinforcer frequently wins out (Brigham, 1989b).

Problems of Behavioral Deficiencies

Another type of self-control problem consists of responses that need to be increased—such as flossing your teeth, taking good lecture notes, and exercising regularly. Such behaviors usually lead to small, immediate punishers. And even though there may be positive outcomes if the behaviors occur, or major negative outcomes if the behaviors don't occur, both of these outcomes are often ineffective. Let's see why.

Immediate Small Punishers for a Behavior versus Reinforcers That are Cumulatively Significant   For nonexercisers, an initial exercising session can be quite unpleasant (time consuming, tiring, stressful, etc.). And even though an instance of exercising may have immediate benefits (increased blood circulation, better removal of waste products, etc.), such outcomes are too small to be noticed. Rather, it is the accumulation of the benefits of exercising on many occasions that is eventually noticeable. Many people fail to follow desirable health practices (exercising, taking prescribed medications, etc.) because doing so leads to immediate small punishers, whereas the positive effects, though immediate, are too small to be effective until they have accumulated over many trials (Malott, 1989).

Immediate Small Punisher for a Behavior versus Immediate but Highly Improbable Major Punisher if the Behavior Does Not Occur   Most people know that wearing eye protection when playing racquetball can prevent serious eye damage and that wearing a helmet when riding a bicycle could prevent brain damage from a serious accident. Why, then, are there many people who do not wear goggles when playing racquetball or helmets when riding bicycles? First, such behaviors usually lead to immediate mild punishers (the goggles and the helmet may be hot and uncomfortable). Second, although the major punishers for not performing the behavior would be immediate, they are highly improbable.

Immediate Small Punisher for a Behavior versus a Delayed Major Punisher if the Behavior Does Not Occur Why do many people fail to floss their teeth or put off going for a dental checkup or fail to take good lecture notes? In this type of self-control problem, there are immediate weak punishers contingent upon performing. The dental floss hurts your gums or your fingers. The sound of the dentist's drill is unpleasant. Your fingers get tired while taking good lecture notes. And while the delayed consequences (such as a major toothache or a poor grade) can be much more aversive, they occur long after many missed flossing opportunities or cancelled dental appointments or missed lecture notes. Unfortunately in such situations, the immediate consequences often win out.

A MODEL FOR SELF-CONTROL

An effective model of self-control must deal satisfactorily with the causes of self-control problems described in the preceding section. The model that we describe here has two parts. The first part requires clear specification of the problem as a behavior to be controlled. The second part requires that you apply behavioral techniques (i.e., emit controlling behavior) to manage the problem. In that sense, this model of self-control consists of doing one thing (apply techniques of behavioral change or behavior modification) to increase the chances of doing some other thing (i.e., behaving in a way that solves the problem). An individual must behave in some way that arranges the environment to manage his or her own subsequent behavior. This means emitting a *controlling behavior* to effect a change in a *behavior to be controlled* (Skinner, 1953).

This raises the problem of *controlling the controlling behavior*. That is, because self-control implies that some components of a person's behavior control other components of his or her behavior, the question arises as to what is to control this controlling behavior. If we answer that the individual is to control his or her own controlling behavior, then what we are saying is that the controlling behavior is itself to be controlled by a controlling behavior. But then the question is: what is to control *that* controlling behavior. Thus, in matters of self-control, the problem of controlling the controlling behavior is always present and must be taken into account.

Note 1

Controlling behaviors include all the ways of managing antecedents and consequences discussed previously in this text. When individuals attempt to manage consequences for their own behaviors, however, they encounter a difficulty not encountered when people manage consequences for others. This difficulty is that of *short-circuiting of contingencies*. The process can be easily seen in the following two simple examples:

1. Suppose that you want to study more efficiently because this behavior will eventually lead to many positive outcomes—such as getting the kind of job you want, being able to talk intelligently with other people, and understanding events in the world around you. But these outcomes are far in the future. It is therefore very difficult for them to compete with the weaker but more immediate reinforcement of even a moderately entertaining TV program. It might seem logical to use your TV watching to reinforce your studying behavior. On the other hand, studying does not turn on the TV; flicking the power switch on the TV set or remote control does. There is a good chance, therefore, that the reinforcement contingency will be short-circuited, in the sense that the reinforcer will be consumed without the desired behavior having occurred, as illustrated in Figure 24–1.

2. Suppose that you want to decrease your food intake because you know that overeating can cause health problems and make you less attractive physically to other people. But these punishers are only cumulatively significant (i.e., overeating only once or a few times will not give you a heart attack or cancer, or make you overweight). Therefore, they have a hard time competing with the reinforcement residing in that piece of pie sitting in front of you. You might decide to bring a stronger, more immediate punishment to bear on the problem by pinching yourself each time you take a bite of pie. But the pain that you feel punishes

Figure 24–1   An example of short-circuiting.

the skin squeezing (pinching) as much as it punishes pie eating. There is a good chance, therefore, that the punishment contingency will be short-circuited in the sense that the undesirable behavior will occur and the punisher will not follow it. The pinching disappears while you, feeling perhaps a little guilty, continue to enjoy the pie.

Despite this difficulty, however, self-control can be achieved and is well worth the effort involved.

STEPS IN A SELF-CONTROL PROGRAM

Unlike most of the cases considered previously in this book, the candidate for a self-control program realizes that he or she has a problem and has probably attempted to solve it alone. Failing in that effort, many individuals will go to a therapist. The role of the therapist is to help the person develop and strengthen controlling behavior.

Clinical behavior therapy is discussed in Chapter 27. In this chapter, let us assume that you are using behavior modification to treat one of your self-control problems. As you probably have noticed from the numerous self-help books available, there is no lack of material for you to read on how to manage your per- **Note 2** sonal problems. We describe how to do so through the following steps: (a) specify the problem and set goals, (b) make a commitment to change, (c) take data and assess the causes of the problem, (d) design and implement a treatment plan, and (e) prevent relapse.

1. Specify the Problem and Set Goals

What is it that you would like to change? How will you know if you have succeeded? To answer these questions, you need to try to specify the problem and set some goals in quantitative terms. For Al (in the example beginning this chapter), this was relatively easy—his goal was to lose 30 pounds. Stated more precisely, he wanted to use about 1,000 calories more each day than he consumed to give a weight loss of about 2 pounds each week. Many problems of self-control can be easily specified in quantitative terms. It's relatively easy, for example, to set specific goals in the areas of weight control and exercise. In contrast, other self-improvement goals are more difficult to measure. These would include "having a more positive attitude towards school," "becoming less tense," or "improving a relationship." Mager (1972) refers to such vague abstractions as "fuzzies." A fuzzy is an acceptable starting point for identifying a self-control goal, however, you must then "unfuzzify" the abstraction by identifying the performance(s) that would cause you to agree that your goal has been achieved. Mager outlined a number of useful steps for this process:

    a. Write out the goal.
    b. Make a list of the things that you should say or do that clearly indicate that you've met the goal. That is, what would you take as evidence that your goal has been achieved?

c. Given a number of people with the same goal, how would you decide who had met the goal and who had not?

d. If your goal is an outcome (rather than something that you do) such as achieving a certain weight, accumulating a certain amount of money, or having a clean room, then make a list of specific behaviors that will help you to achieve that outcome.

2. Make a Commitment to Change

Note 3

Commitment to change refers to a rule that you state to yourself (and perhaps to others) that it is important to change your behavior, that you will work toward doing so, and that you recognize the benefits of doing so. Perri and Richards (1977) demonstrated that *both* a commitment to change *and* knowledge of change techniques were important for successful accomplishment of self-modification projects by undergraduate psychology students. In problem areas such as eating, smoking, studying, or dating, successful self-managers had both a stronger commitment to change and used more behavior change techniques than did unsuccessful self-managers (Perri & Richards, 1977).

A high probability of success in changing your behavior requires actions to keep your commitment strong. First, make a list of all of the benefits for changing your behavior. Write them out and post them in a conspicuous place. Second, make your commitment to change public (Hayes et al., 1985; Seijts et al., 1997). Increasing the number of people who can remind you to stick to your program increases your chances of success (Passman, 1977). Third, rearrange your environment to provide frequent reminders of your commitment and your goal (Graziano, 1975). You could write your goals on 3 × 5" cards and leave them in conspicuous places, such as taped to the door of your fridge or on the dashboard of your car. Or you might creatively use photographs to remind you of your goal. Also, make sure those reminders are associated with the positive benefits of reaching your goal. Fourth, invest considerable time and energy in planning your project initially (Watson & Tharp, 1997). Prepare a list of statements related to your investment in your project so that you can use those statements to help strengthen and maintain your commitment (e.g., "I've put so much into it, it would be a shame to quit now"). Fifth, because you will undoubtedly encounter temptations to quit your project, plan ahead for various ways to deal with any temptations (Watson & Tharp, 1997).

3. Take Data and Analyze Causes

The next step is to take data on the occurrence of the problem behavior — when, where, and how often it occurs. This is especially important when the goal is to decrease excessive behaviors. As indicated in Chapter 18, there are a number of reasons for keeping track of the problem behavior, not the least of which is to provide a reference point for evaluating progress. For many self-control projects, a 3 × 5" card and a pencil can be used to tally instances of the problem as they occur throughout the day.

There are a number of techniques for increasing the strength of record keeping. If the problem behavior is smoking, you should record each cigarette before it is smoked, so that the behavior will reinforce recording it. You might set up external reinforcers that are controlled by other people. You might give control of your spending money to someone who can monitor your behavior continuously for extended periods of time and who could return your money contingent upon consistent data taking. You might also get other people to reinforce your recording behavior by (a) telling friends about your self-modification project, (b) keeping your recording chart or graph in an obvious place to increase the likelihood of feedback from friends, and (c) keeping your friends informed on how the project and results are progressing. Contingencies mediated by other people are an important safeguard against the short-circuiting processes described at the beginning of this chapter.

In some cases (as pointed out in Chapter 18), recording and graphing the behavior may be all that's needed to bring about improvement. A convincing demonstration of this effect was made by Maletsky (1974). Three of the five cases that he studied were completed successfully, even though Maletsky was careful not to introduce any treatment other than the counting and graphing of unwanted behaviors. The first case concerned repetitive scratching that resulted in unsightly lesions on the arms and legs of a 52-year-old woman. The woman had been suffering with this problem for 30 years. The second case concerned a 9-year-old boy's repetitive hand raising in class. (Often he didn't know the answers to the teacher's questions.) The third case involved the out-of-seat behavior in school of a hyperactive 11-year-old girl. In all three cases, the behavior decreased over a 6-week period as a result of the daily counting and graphing. In some cases, it might even be possible to count each thought, desire, or urge to emit a behavior before the behavior occurs. McFall (1970) reported a study in which recording each urge to have a cigarette was sufficient to decrease not only the likelihood of subsequently taking a cigarette, but also the number of urges.

When recording the frequency of the problem during these initial observations, you should take a close look at the antecedents that might be S^Ds or S^Δs for the problem behavior, and at the immediate consequences that might be maintaining the problem. From this exercise often comes suggestions for successful programming strategies.

Recall Al at the beginning of the chapter. When he began examining the circumstances in which he typically snacked, Al made a surprising finding: The great majority of instances of eating were followed immediately by some other reinforcing event.

> A bite of a doughnut—then a sip of coffee;
> Another potato chip while watching TV—his favorite basketball player just scores another basket;
> Another candy to munch on while in his car—the stop light turns green and Al drives away;
> And so on.

Al ate while drinking coffee, while drinking beer, while talking to friends, while talking on the phone, while riding in a car . . . in other words, while coming into contact with a wide variety of reinforcing events in the natural environment. As we indicated in earlier chapters, the effects of reinforcers are automatic and do not depend on an individual's awareness. Moreover, aspects of the different settings became S^{D}s for Al's excessive eating. No wonder Al had trouble dieting.

Thus, during preliminary observations, it's important to analyze antecedents for the undesired behavior, immediate consequences that might maintain the undesired behavior to be eliminated, and the immediate consequences (or lack of them) of the behavior that you wish to develop. This information can be very useful in the next step of your program.

4. Design and Implement a Program

Throughout your life, in certain *situations* certain *behaviors* have had certain *consequences*. Each of these three variables provides a fertile area for selecting self-control techniques.

Manage the Situation   When we defined stimulus control in Chapter 8, we said that certain responses occur in the presence of some stimuli and not others. Because this is so, it is possible for you to capitalize on the stimuli that control your responses when planning self-control programs. As indicated in Chapters 16 and 17, it is helpful to think of major classes of stimuli that control our behavior, such as instructions, modeling, guidance, our immediate surroundings, other people, and the time of day.

Instructions.   Meichenbaum (1977) suggested that almost every self-modification program should include some self-instructions. Self-instructions have been used in formal self-management projects to increase exercise and study behavior (Cohen, DeJames, Nocera, & Ramberger, 1980), reduce fears (Arrick, Voss, & Rimm, 1981), reduce nail-biting (C. S. Harris & McReynolds, 1977), and improve a variety of other behaviors (Watson & Tharp, 1997). Before planning instructions for your self-control program, we encourage you to review the guidelines for using rules and goals in Chapter 16.

Modeling.   Modeled behavior is another class of stimulus events that is useful in self-control programs. For example, do you want to improve your skills at introducing yourself to another person at social gatherings? Find someone who's good at it, observe that person's behavior, and try to imitate it. A procedure called *participant modeling* (described more fully in the next chapter) is an especially effective method for reducing fears. With this procedure, the fearful person observes a model interact with the fear-inducing stimulus and then imitates the model.

Physical guidance.   In Chapter 17, we described how behavior modifiers use physical contact to induce an individual to go through the motions of the desired behavior. In his classic analysis of self-control, Skinner (1953) described how individuals also use physical restraint to control their own behavior. You might, for example, keep your hands in your pockets to avoid nail biting, cover your eyes to avoid looking at someone during an embarrassing moment, put your hand over your mouth to suppress a laugh on a solemn occasion, or clasp your hands to avoid striking someone in a moment of anger.

The immediate surroundings.   Do you have trouble studying at home? Try going to the library, where studying is a high-probability behavior (Brigham, 1982). Many people have a particular behavior they would like to decrease. That behavior occurs in particular situations. An alternative desirable behavior occurs in other situations. A useful strategy is to rearrange the environment to present cues for the desirable alternative behaviors (see Chapter 17).

Other people. As we said above, modeling is one way of providing strong prompts for you to engage in some behavior. Another strategy is to simply change the people around you. You've learned to behave in one way with some people and in another way with others. For example, you're likely to talk without swearing when in conversation with Grandma and Grandpa, but are more likely to swear when shooting the breeze with the gang. In some cases, your self-adjustment program will consist of minimizing contact with certain people. Marlatt and Parks (1982) have indicated that people with addictive behaviors are more likely to relapse if they hang out with others engaging in those behaviors.

The time of day. We've all learned to do certain things at certain times. Sometimes our problems are related to that fact. Sometimes it's possible to achieve successful self-control by changing the time of the activity. For example, many students are most alert in the morning. Yet they spend their free time during the mornings having coffee with friends and socializing, and leave their studying to the evening when they are less alert. Successful self-control of studying for such students might be accomplished by moving studying to mornings and socializing to evenings.

Manage the Behavior If the behavior of concern is relatively simple—such as swearing—you're likely to focus more on antecedents and consequences. If the behavior is complex, you need to spend some time focusing on the behavior itself. If your goal is to acquire some complex skills, it's helpful to consider task analysis, mastery criteria, and chaining. *Mastery criteria* are performance requirements for practicing a skill such that if the criteria are met, the behavior has been learned.

Consider, for example, learning to play golf. Simek and O'Brien (1981) task-analyzed a golf game into 22 components. They arranged these in a behavioral progression for instructional purposes and identified mastery criteria for each component (see Table 24–1). Then they taught a group of novices by starting with 10-inch putts rather than by first teaching them to swing a club, as is often done by golf pros. Why? For two reasons. First, it seemed like the simplest response—and the general rule is to start with the simple and proceed to the complex. Second, it incorporated a powerful natural reinforcer for performing the response correctly—namely, hitting the ball into the hole (note that this is similar to the argument for using backward chaining—see Chapter 11). Gradually, as mastery criteria for simple responses were met, the length of the shot was increased to longer putts, then to short chip shots, to longer chip shots, to short pitch shots, to longer pitch shots, to middle iron shots, eventually to hitting fairway woods, and finally a driver. "But how well did they score when put on a golf course?" one might ask. In a study with 12 novice golfers, six of the golfers completed the behavioral progression and mastery criteria in eight lessons. The other six golfers received eight lessons of traditional instruction from a golfer who had taught golf for several years. All 12 then played a complete, 18-hole round of golf. The behavioral progression group "whipped" the traditional group handily, beating them by an average of 17 strokes.

TABLE 24–1   A BEHAVIORAL PROGRESSION AND MASTERY CRITERIA
FOR LEARNING GOLF

	Complete golf chain and mastery criterion	
Step	Shot	Mastery criterion
1.	10-inch putt	4 putts consecutively holed
2.	16-inch putt	4 putts consecutively holed
3.	2-foot putt	4 putts consecutively holed
4.	3-foot putt	4 putts consecutively holed
5.	4-foot putt some break	2 holed, 2 out of 4 within 6 inches
6.	6-foot putt	4 consecutively within 6 inches
7.	10-foot putt	4 consecutively within 12 inches
8.	15-foot putt	4 consecutively within 15 inches
9.	20-foot putt	4 consecutively within 18 inches
10.	30-foot putt	4 consecutively within 24 inches
11.	35-foot chip, 5 feet off green, 7-iron	4 out of 6 within 6 feet
12.	35-foot chip, 15 feet off green, wedge	4 out of 6 within 6 feet
13.	65-foot chip	4 out of 6 within 6 feet
14.	25-yard pitch	4 out of 6 within 10 feet
15.	35-yard pitch	4 out of 6 within 15 feet
16.	50-yard pitch	4 out of 6 within 15 feet
17.	75-yard shot	4 out of 6 within 30 feet
18.	100-yard shot	4 out of 6 within 40 feet
19.	125-yard shot	4 out of 6 within 45 feet
20.	150-yard shot	4 out of 6 within 54 feet
21.	175-yard shot	4 out of 6 within 66 feet
22.	200-yard shot (if within your range)	4 out of 5 within 90 feet

Note: From *Total Golf: A Behavioral Approach to Lowering Your Score and Getting More Out of Your Game* (p. 2),
by T. C. Simek and R. M. O'Brien, 1981. Huntington, NY: B-Mod Associates. Copyright 1981 by T. C. Simek and
R. M. O'Brien. Reprinted with permission.

Shaping is an important strategy for self-improvement projects in which
your ultimate goal involves a large behavioral change from your starting point.
Important rules of thumb to keep in mind include start small, meet mastery criteria before moving up a step, and keep progressive steps small. Studies of dieters,
for example, have reported that those who set small, gradual shaping steps for reducing calories were more likely to develop self-control of binge eating (Gormally, Black, Daston, & Rardin, 1982; R. C. Hawkins & Clement, 1980).

Manage the Consequences   One strategy for manipulating consequent events is
to eliminate certain reinforcers that may inadvertently strengthen a particularly
undesirable behavior in a particular situation. When Al analyzed his eating problem, he noticed that in addition to the taste of food itself, other reinforcers (TV,
pleasant conversation, etc.) were usually associated with eating. A major feature
of Al's dieting control program, therefore, should be to disassociate eating from
these other activities. Recommendations by LeBow (1981) to accomplish this include (a) develop an eating place in the home that is to be used only for that pur-

pose, and eating only there when at home; (b) using the same eating utensils and placemats at each meal; (c) eating only at designated times; and (d) keep food out of every room but the kitchen.

A second way of manipulating consequences is by self-recording and self-graphing the target behavior (e.g., see Watson & Tharp, 1997). Seeing a line that shows gradual improvement can serve as a prompt to think a variety of positive thoughts. It can also serve as a prompt for extra social attention from others for sticking to a self-control program.

A third way of manipulating consequences involves arranging for specific reinforcers to be earned by you for showing improvement or even for just sticking to the program (see Watson & Tharp, 1997). This is especially important if your desired behavior will lead to small but cumulatively significant or highly improbable reinforcers, or if failure to perform your desired behavior will lead to small but cumulatively significant or highly improbable punishers. There are two main strategies for managing reinforcers in a self-control program: managing them yourself or asking others to manage them for you. As an example of self-management of reinforcers, consider a program initiated by one of the authors. During the winter, he began an exercise program that involved running 2 miles (14 laps) three times a week at the university's underground track. The author found that after 9 or 10 laps, fatigue thoughts would come to mind and he would frequently talk himself out of doing the last few laps, saying such things as, "Oh well, I've done pretty well by running 11 laps." He decided to try a self-reinforcement program to increase the frequency of antifatigue thoughts during the last few laps. Specifically, during the 10th through 14th laps, he would think some antifatigue thought and then follow it with a pleasurable thought. The particular antifatigue thought that he chose was about a TV physical fitness commercial claiming that "the average 60-year-old Swede is in the same physical condition as the average 30-year-old Canadian" (we have since learned that the claim is false, but this is not important to our illustration). Each time the author got to a particular spot on the track, he thought about the very healthy Swede jogging merrily along. At the next turn, he thought about something enjoyable, such as making love to a desirable woman. He enjoyed the pleasurable thought across the end of the track and then would simply not think the Swede thought or the reinforcing thought down the other side of the track. In this way he was able to engage in a private behavior that counteracted the fatigue thoughts and was able to strengthen that behavior. After practicing this determinedly for about 2 weeks, he was able to put the fatigue thoughts completely out of mind.

Was the effectiveness of this program really the result of self-reinforcement? Not necessarily. There are at least three other possibilities: (a) The program might have worked equally well if the author had not thought the reinforcing thoughts—perhaps thinking the antifatigue thoughts themselves would have been sufficient; (b) the reinforcing thoughts may have been effective because they increased the distinctiveness of the antifatigue thoughts that were reinforcing for other reasons (this is essentially the process discussed under the second way of manipulating consequent events); (c) the reinforcing thoughts may have increased the conditioned reinforcing properties of the antifatigue thoughts through association with them (this would be similar to having a pleasant meal on an airplane to help enhance the conditioned reinforcing aspects of flying so as to overcome a fear of flying).

Asking others to manage reinforcers for you is a common strategy in self-control programs (Watson & Tharp, 1997). For example, Mary decided to initiate a jogging program. She also decided that she would receive money immediately after jogging. Also, if she jogged every day, she could select and engage in one of several possible social activities with her husband. If she met her goals, Mary's husband dispensed the reinforcers. The program was quite successful (Kau & Fischer, 1974).

Some guidelines for incorporating reinforcers into your program include: (a) make it possible for you to earn specific reinforcers on a daily basis; (b) set up bonuses that can be earned for progress on a weekly basis; (c) vary the reinforcers from one day to the next and one week to the next so as to prevent boredom with the entire system; (d) if possible and desirable, have other individuals dispense the reinforcers to you for meeting your goals; and (e) tell others about your progress.

Recall the Premack Principle from Chapter 3. The Premack Principle states that any activity that you are more likely to perform can be used to strengthen a behavior that you are less likely to perform. This strategy can also be used in self-control programs. High-frequency behaviors used in documented cases of self-improvement have involved making telephone calls (F. J. Todd, 1972), urinating (W. G. Johnson, 1971), opening daily mail at the office (Spinelli & Packard, 1975), and sitting on a particular chair (Horan & Johnson, 1971).

5. Prevent Relapse and Make it Last

Let's suppose you've made good progress on your self-control program: you've lost those 20 pounds, or you haven't had a cigarette in 3 months, or your studying has paid off and you got an "A" on your last two exams. Now the question is: Will it last? Will you be able to maintain your gains over the long run? Unfortunately, relapses are common in self-control programs (Marlatt & Parks, 1982). By *relapse*, we mean going back to the unwanted behavior at approximately the same rate that you were at before you started your program. Just as the three variables of *situations*, *behaviors*, and *consequences* were valuable areas to consider when designing your program, they also provide a useful framework for analyzing causes of relapses and how to prevent them.

Causes of Relapse in Situations   A strategy in preventing relapses is to recognize their possible causes and to take steps to minimize them. Let's look at some examples involving situations.

Avoidable setback situations.   A common cause of relapses in self-control programs is a failure to anticipate setback situations—when one is at risk for returning to earlier unwanted behavior patterns. Some setback situations can simply be avoided until you are better able to cope with them. For example, Carla decided to quit smoking. Initially she believed that she couldn't resist the temptation to smoke while playing poker with her friends on Friday nights. Her strategy was simply to not play poker for the first month of the program. Fred decided to go on a diet, to eat more healthfully, and to consume fewer calories. But he knew that he couldn't resist the banana splits at the ice cream store beside the super-market where he usually bought groceries. His solution—he changed the place where he shopped so that he didn't have to walk by the ice cream store and resist his favorite dessert. If you can successfully avoid setback situations until after you have achieved some success with your self-control program, you might then be better able to cope with situations that provide strong cues for the problem be-havior.

Unavoidable setback situations.   Some setback situations simply can't be avoided. A strategy to prevent relapse is to anticipate unavoidable setback situations and to take steps to cope with them. Consider John's case. John had faithfully fol-lowed his exercise program for a month-and-a-half, but he was about to embark on a motorhome trip. He knew that the complete change in routine and the duties each night around the campground were not conducive to exercising. His solu-tion was to obtain his travelling companions' approval to stop travelling each night half an hour early. While the others relaxed in the motorhome, John exer-cised. They then all shared in the campground duties. The more that you can rec-ognize unavoidable setback situations before they are encountered, the better are your chances for planning coping strategies.

Overreaction to occasional setbacks.   Janice, after 2 weeks of sticking faithfully to her schedule for studying, rented five movies and watched TV for 10 hours straight. Fred, following a month of successful dieting, had a triple-topping sun-dae at the ice cream parlor three days in a row. Very few people achieve success-ful self-control without experiencing an occasional setback. But temporary set-backs are not a problem provided that you get right back into your program. If you suffer a setback, don't dwell on it. Instead, use a review of the many occa-sions when you have stuck to your program as a prompt to set new goals and to make a renewed commitment to stick with it.

Counterproductive self-talk.   When people attempt to change, they are bound to encounter stumbling blocks. In such situations, counterproductive self-talk can exacerbate the problem and may lead to a relapse. People who have difficulty di-eting may say things to themselves like, "I'm too hungry to wait until dinner. I'll have a snack to tide myself over." That type of self-talk is a cue to eat.

What kinds of self-talk in your self-control program might lead to a relapse? For each example that you can think of, identify desirable alternative self-talk that might have the opposite effect. Dieters, for example, might tell themselves things like, "I feel hungry, but I'm not starving. I'll just focus on something to take my mind off food."

Causes of Relapse in the Specification of the Response   Sometimes relapses oc-cur because individuals do not pay sufficient attention to the response compo-nent of their self-control program. Let's look at some examples.

A fuzzy target behavior.   Tracy wanted to improve her golf skills. But after a month of regular practice at the driving range, she wasn't sure if she was improving. The problem was that "wanting to improve" was too vague. She had not specified her target behavior precisely enough. If Tracy's goal had been to hit five drives in a row over 175 yards, or to hit three 7-irons in a row within 30 feet of the 100-yard marker, or to make four 3-foot putts in a row, then she would have been able to evaluate her progress more easily. As we described earlier, a fuzzy goal is an acceptable starting point, but you must then unfuzzify your target behavior by phrasing it in a way such that you and others can easily recognize it when it occurs.

A long-term target behavior.   Suppose that you set a long-term goal for yourself of obtaining an "A" in a particular course. Your goal is clear, but it's a long way away. For such projects, you should set short-term goals that provide specific progress checks along the way. With respect to your goal of obtaining an "A," you might set a short-term goal of studying the material for that course for a minimum of 1 hour every day. Another short-term goal might be to complete a certain number of study questions each day. Daily short-term goals should be precisely stated and realistic and should move you in the direction of your long-term goal.

Trying too much too soon.   Some self-control projects never get off the ground because they are too ambitious. Wanting to eat more healthfully, exercise more, floss your teeth regularly, manage your money more wisely, and get better grades are admirable goals, but trying to improve in all areas at once is a formula for failure. If you've identified several areas to improve, prioritize them in order of their personal value to you. From the top two or three priority areas, select one to work on. Starting small increases your likelihood of success.

Causes of Relapse in Consequences   Recall our model of self-control. It involves emitting a *controlling behavior* to manage a *behavior to be controlled.* Inadequate or poorly scheduled consequences for either of these behaviors can lead to a relapse. Let's look at some examples.

Failure to incorporate everyday rewards into your program.   Many people begin self-control programs with a great deal of enthusiasm. But after awhile, the extra work from recording, graphing, rearranging the environment, and so forth can become quite burdensome. One way to prevent relapse is to link your self-control program to everyday rewarding activities. One person we know linked his exercise program to his penchant for watching movies on his VCR. His goal was to exercise a minimum of four times a week. On average, he also rented movies about four nights a week. He therefore signed a contract with his wife that he would watch a movie only if he first walked to the rental store to pick up the movie—a distance of approximately 1½ miles. Examine ways that you can incorporate daily rewarding activities into the support of your self-control program.

Consequences that are only cumulatively significant.   Suppose that your dieting program has been successful. You decide that your new slim body can easily handle an extra dessert. And of course, one dessert is not a problem. Rather, it is the accumulation of extra desserts on many occasions that will put the pounds back on. As we described earlier, for many self-control problems, the immediate reinforcement for consumption of harmful substances (such as the extra dessert) is likely to win out over the negative consequences from those substances because the negative effects are noticeable only after they have accumulated over many trials. Individuals with these types of self-control problems are very likely to experience a relapse. One strategy to prevent relapse in such situations is to set specific dates for postchecks and to list specific strategies to follow if the postchecks are unfavorable. For example, if your self-control program was one of weight reduction, you might agree with a friend that you will weigh yourself in your friend's presence once a week. If your weight increases to a specified level, then (with encouragement from your friend) you will immediately return to your program.

Additional Strategies to Make It Last   Additional strategies to prevent relapse and to maintain your gains over the long term involve all three factors of situations, responses, and consequences. One strategy is to practice the self-control steps outlined in this chapter to improve additional behaviors. You are more likely to continue using self-control techniques if you practice them on more than one self-control project (Barone, 1982). Moreover, you are more likely to be able to deal with a relapse if you are skillful in the self-control techniques that brought about the improvement in the first place.

Perhaps the most effective way to make it last is to involve supportive others in your program, both in the short term and in the long term. One strategy is to set up a buddy system. When you start your project, you might find a friend or relative with a similar problem and set mutual maintenance goals. Once a month, you could get together and check each other's progress. If your progress has been maintained, you could celebrate in a previously agreed-upon way. In a study of smokers, for example, Karol and Richards (1978) found that smokers who quit with a buddy and who telephoned encouragement to each other showed greater reduction of smoking in an 8-month follow-up than did smokers who tried to quit on their own.

A particularly effective strategy is to sign a behavioral contract with supportive others. A **behavioral contract** is a clear written statement of what behaviors of what individuals will produce what rewards, and who will deliver those rewards. It usually involves two or more people, although "self-contracts" have also been used. A form that you might use for your contract is presented in Table 24–2.

A contract serves at least four important S^D functions:

1. It ensures that all parties involved agree to the goals and procedures and that they do not lose sight of them during the course of the treatment.
2. Because the goals are specified behaviorally, the contract also ensures that throughout the program all parties will agree on how close they are to reaching the goals.
3. The contract provides the client with a realistic estimate of the cost of the program to him or her in time, effort, and money.
4. The signatures on the contract help to ensure that all parties will faithfully follow the specified procedures, because in our society signing a document is a strong S^D indicating a commitment.

As we have stressed in previous chapters, behavior modification procedures should be revised in appropriate ways when the data indicate that they are not producing satisfactory results. Thus, your contract should be open to renegotiation at any time. If you find that you simply cannot meet some commitment specified in your contract, you should so inform the other signatories at your next meeting with them. The difficulty would then be discussed, and if it seemed desirable, a new contract replacing the previous one would be drafted and signed. But before doing so, you might examine the following troubleshooting guide for behavior contracts.

TABLE 24–2   A FORM FOR A BEHAVIORAL CONTRACT

My specific goals for my self-control program are:
_____
_____
_____
_____

Short-term goals for my self-control program include:
_____
_____
_____
_____

To observe, record, and graph my behavior, I will:
_____
_____
_____

To minimize the causes of the problem, I will:
_____
_____
_____
_____

The details of my treatment plan include:
1. Steps to manage the situation
_____
_____
_____
_____

2. Steps to manage consequences
_____
_____
_____
_____

3. Steps to deal with or change complex behavior
_____
_____
_____
_____

4. Rewards that I can earn for sticking to and/or completing my project include:
_____
_____

Additional steps that I will take to increase and maintain my commitment to the project and to prevent relapse include:
_____
_____

Schedule for review of progress:
_____
_____

Signatures of all involved and the date of the agreement:
_____   _____   _____
(Date)   (Your signature)   (Supporter's signature)

Troubleshooting Guide[2]

The following questions may help you to spot the problems in your contracting system:

The Contract

1. Was the target behavior specified clearly?
2. If the target behavior was complex, did the contract ask for small approximations to the desired behavior?
3. Were specific deadlines identified for the target behavior?
4. Did the contract clearly identify situations where the target behavior should occur?
5. Did the contract provide for immediate reinforcement? Are the reinforcers still important and valuable to you?
6. Could reinforcers be earned often (daily? weekly?)?
7. Did the contract call for and reward accomplishment rather than obedience?
8. Was the contract phrased in a positive way?
9. Do you consider the contract to be fair and in your best interests?

The Mediator (your co-signer)

1. Did the mediator understand the contract?
2. Did the mediator dispense the kind and amount of reinforcement specified in the contract?
3. Did the mediator meet with you on the dates specified in the contract?
4. Is a new mediator required?

Measurement

1. Are the data accurate?
2. Is your data collection system too complex or too difficult?
3. Does your data collection system clearly reflect your progress in achieving the target behavior?
4. Do you need to improve on your data collection system?

CIRCUMVENTING THE THERAPIST

So far we have considered only very simple examples of self-management. Some problems, however, require a step-by-step self-modification project that may last several months or more. Such cases may involve a therapist providing instructions, some modeling, and an opportunity for behavioral rehearsal and role playing by the client. Recall the example in Chapter 17 in which the therapist utilized instructions, modeling, shaping, and role playing to help a college student learn how to ask for a date. In other cases, a therapist might interact extensively with a client to help him or her develop self-control over self-verbalizations. Cognitive psycholo-

---

[2]Adapted from DeRisi and Butz, *Writing Behavioral Contracts: A Case Simulation Practice Manual* (1975, pp. 58–60).

gists generally describe this approach (which we discuss in more detail in Chapter 26) as helping individuals to change their behavior by changing their beliefs or thoughts. In some cases, therapists helping clients in complex self-control programs might go through all the steps in the guidelines in Chapter 22, especially those cited in the section entitled "Strategies of Program Design and Implementation." Chapter 27 discusses approaches to problems that require therapeutic help.

It should be clear from the preceding sections in this chapter, however, that many people who have mastered some behavior modification principles can use them to control their own behavior without having to see a therapist. A student who has mastered this and previous chapters should have little difficulty in handling a simple behavior problem that has been bothering him or her (although we would still recommend seeing a therapist about serious problems). Perhaps the student would like to decrease smoking, nail biting, swearing, or abusive remarks to others. Or perhaps he or she would like to enhance studying, exercising, personal tidiness, consideration of others, or public speaking. The student probably does not need a therapist to help accomplish these goals.

A person who has read this book already knows how to take data; a therapist is not needed to help do that. That person knows also how to plan a program and evaluate its effectiveness, how to apply a large number of behavior modification principles and techniques, and how to use a behavioral contract to prevent short-circuiting. In short, many people can be their own behavior therapists.

STUDY QUESTIONS

1. What do people seem to mean when they talk about *willpower*? Is willpower a useful concept? Why or why not?
2. Briefly describe three causes of self-control problems of behavioral excesses, and illustrate each with reference to an example.
3. Briefly describe three causes of self-control problems of behavioral deficiencies, and illustrate each with reference to an example.
4. What are the two types of short-circuiting? Give an example of each.
5. In two or three sentences, describe the model of self-management presented in this chapter.
6. List five steps that characterize many programs in self-adjustment.
7. List the steps that Mager recommends to "unfuzzify" a vaguely stated problem or self-control goal.
8. How does this book define *commitment*?
9. Describe four steps that you could take to strengthen and maintain your commitment to a program of self-control.
10. Illustrate how Al was inadvertently reinforced for eating numerous times throughout the day.
11. List six major classes of stimuli that you might consider when planning how to manage the situation in a self-control program.
12. Define and give an example of mastery criteria.
13. In a sentence or two each, describe three different ways of manipulating consequences in self-control programs.
14. Briefly describe four possible causes of relapse in situations, and indicate how each might be handled.

15. Briefly describe three possible causes of relapse in the specification of the response, and indicate how each might be handled.
16. Briefly describe two possible causes of relapse in consequences, and indicate how each might be handled.
17. What is a behavioral contract? Describe its essential features.
18. What important stimulus-control functions does a behavioral contract serve?
19. Describe several ways in which another person can be used to help prevent short-circuiting in a self-control program.
20. Is it plausible to suggest that many individuals can become their own behavior therapists? Justify your answer.

APPLICATION EXERCISES

A. Exercise Involving Others

Describe a self-control problem experienced by someone that you know. Is the problem best characterized as a behavioral deficiency or a behavioral excess? What seems to be the cause of the problem?

B. Self-Modification Exercises

1. Using the information in this and the preceding chapters, describe how you might go about following all five steps of a self-control program for bringing about successful self-adjustment for a behavior of yours that you would like to change.
2. Implement your program and take data for a minimum of 3 weeks. Then write a summary report of the results (approximately 5 to 10 pages, plus graphs).

NOTES AND EXTENDED DISCUSSION

1. Suggestions for controlling the controlling behavior occur throughout this chapter. Theoretically, we assume that most of the contingencies that teach us and maintain our controlling behaviors are provided by the society in which we live (see Skinner 1953, p. 240).

2. How effective are self-help manuals? Although a review by Rosen (1987) found major limitations to their usefulness, meta-analysis—a statistical procedure for combining the data analysis of many studies—suggests that somewhat more positive conclusions are in order (Gould & Clum, 1993; Scogin, Bynum, Stephens, & Calhoon, 1990). That does not mean that all self-help books in book stores have been evaluated. However, experiments that examined sophisticated, complex, self-help manuals based on behavioral principles indicated that self-administered treatments stand a good chance of success. The most successful targets for improvement involved study habits, depression, parenting skills, social skills, and overcoming anxiety and fears. Less successful self-treatment programs occurred with the control of alcohol drinking, smoking, and overeating (Gould & Clum, 1993; Seligman, 1994). Also, a number of studies have demonstrated that university students who have read various editions of the self-modification book by David Watson and Ronald Tharp were more successful at completing self-improvement projects than students who did not read the book (Watson & Tharp, 1997).

3. A commitment to do something is verbal behavior that corresponds to other behavior that one later engages in if the commitment is kept. A number of studies have been conducted on training a correspondence between stated intentions (commitments) and later behavior. For example, Ward and Stare (1990) prompted a group of kindergarten children to state that they were going to play in a certain designated area prior to playing there (correspondence training). Specifically, the children were prompted to say, "I'm going to play at the workbench today." The children received a token if they made this statement. After 4 minutes of play, children who played at the workbench received another token for playing at the workbench after saying that this is what they would do. Compared to a group of children who simply received tokens for playing in the designated area, the group that received correspondence training showed more instances of following through on stated intentions to engage in another activity (playing with toys), even though they received no tokens for following through on this commitment. The results thus showed that correspondence training on one response can generalize to a new response. This tendency to generalize correspondence training may be what makes it possible for us to keep commitments for behavior change that we have made to ourselves. Correspondence training is also one way that humans learn self-awareness or self-knowledge (Dymond & Barnes, 1997).

4. Catania (1975, 1976) and Goldiamond (1976), have argued that it is inappropriate to use the label *self-reinforcement* to refer to a procedure in which an individual emits some behavior and then presents a reinforcing consequence immediately after, such as in the case of the author thinking of the Swede and then thinking about a pleasurable event. Certainly it is possible for an individual to consume a reinforcer following some behavior. A professor grading papers might decide to grade five papers and then to eat a handful of peanuts. If paper grading increases in frequency, however, it is inappropriate to attribute the increase to self-reinforcement. The problem is that this implies that the increase is due to positive reinforcement as conceptualized in basic and applied research where short-circuiting is not a problem because reinforcers are dispensed by the behavior modifier. We must remember, however, with self-reinforcement, that short-circuiting can occur at any time; and in fact—from the definition of reinforcement—seems inevitable (also, see Skinner, 1953, p. 238). From a review of the experimental literature on this point, Brigham (1989b) noted that "To date, unequivocal empirical evidence to support the notion of self-reinforcement as an effective applied procedure is non-existent and certainly does not justify the major role that the concept has been given in many treatments of self-management" (p. 27).

Study Questions on Notes

1. In this chapter, self-control refers to an individual behaving in some way that arranges the environment to control his or her own subsequent behavior. What provides the ultimate control over this controlling behavior? Discuss.

2. With which behavior problems are self-help manuals most effective and least effective?

3. What is correspondence training? Briefly describe how generalized correspondence was demonstrated in kindergarten children.

4. Given the problem of short-circuiting, is self-reinforcement possible? Defend your answer.

Systematic Self-Desensitization

Barb, a normal, healthy young woman, had one quirk: She was terrified of airplanes. The mere thought of getting into a plane was enough to make her panic. Even calling a ticket agent to make a reservation caused her heart to pound wildly. Her fear of flying was so strong that she cancelled her reservation to visit a friend in another city, even though her friend offered to pay for the ticket.

Many people have fears that are so intense that they are virtually incapacitated by them. A person might have such an intense fear of heights that he cannot walk up a single flight of stairs or look out of a second-story window without experiencing acute anxiety. Another person might be so terrified of crowds that she cannot bear to go into public places. Surprising as it may seem, trying to convince these people that their fears are irrational often has no beneficial effect. They usually know that their fears have no rational basis and would like to control them, but they cannot because the fears are automatically elicited by specific stimuli. Such intense, irrational, incapacitating fears are called *phobias*.

What about Barb? Was she stuck with her phobia for life? Not at all. Barb decided that it was time to take a stand—no more trip cancellations. Because she had another opportunity to fly for a visit with her friend, she started a program to overcome her fear. A little over 2 weeks later, Barb took her first plane trip, and enjoyed it immensely. She has successfully enjoyed flying many times since. How did she overcome her anxiety? By using a procedure called systematic self-desensitization. But before telling you about the details of Barb's program, we briefly describe several behavioral treatments for simple phobias.

BEHAVIORAL TREATMENTS OF SIMPLE PHOBIAS

People like Barb, who experience a phobia, suffer from an anxiety disorder. According to the DSM IV,[1] these disorders are characterized by (a) fear/anxiety that results in physiological changes such as sweaty hands, dizziness, or heart palpitations; (b) the escape and/or avoidance of situations in which the fear is likely to occur; and (c) interference by the behaviors with the individual's life. The DSM IV identifies several types of anxiety disorders. A *simple phobia* is a persistent, irrational fear of a circumscribed stimulus. Barb suffered from a simple phobia. A *social phobia* is an extreme, irrational fear of more general social situations in which one might be humiliated or embarrassed by one's own public actions or by the judgment of others. Another type of anxiety disorder is one in which people suffer from *panic attacks* during which they experience chest pain, choking, shortness of breath, sweating, dizziness, and other sensations that occur suddenly and usually last for several minutes. Victims complain of feeling out of control, and usually attempt to escape the situation in which they occur. According to behavior therapist David Barlow, panic disorder has gone from being virtually unrecognized by the mental health community approximately 20 years ago, to being the most common form of anxiety diagnosed (Seppa, 1996). The DSM IV also describes other types of anxiety disorders. In this chapter, we focus on the treatment of simple phobias. (Treatment of anxiety disorders is discussed further in Chapter 27.)

Recall from Chapter 15 that respondent extinction involves the presentation of a conditioned stimulus without the unconditioned stimulus for a number of times until the conditioned stimulus no longer elicits the conditioned response. It should not come as a surprise, then, to learn that the way to eliminate the respondent component of a fear is to expose the client repeatedly to the object or event that has become a conditioned stimulus for that fear (Borden, 1992). Exposure to feared objects can be done through imagery, by asking the individual to imagine various experiences with the feared object, or through actual presentation of the objects to the client in real life (referred to as *in vivo*).

Flooding   With this approach, the therapist tries to get the client in the presence of the feared stimulus very early during therapy, to maintain exposure for long periods of time (such as an hour or more per session), and to prevent an avoidance or escape response. The goal is to elicit intense levels of anxiety by the conditioned stimulus so that respondent extinction will occur. In some cases, if the distress experienced by the client is overwhelming, flooding may involve graded levels of exposure to the feared stimulus. A fear of heights, for example, might be treated with flooding by having the client look out the window on the first floor, then the third floor, then the seventh floor, and finally from the top of a 10-story building. The feared stimulus may be presented in imagination or *in vivo*. Whereas *in vivo* is generally preferred because it increases the intensity of the anx-

---

[1]DSM IV, which you will recall from Chapter 18, is the latest (1994) version of the *Diagnostic and Statistical Manual of Mental Disorders* of the American Psychiatric Association (1994).

iety levels that are elicited, there is no evidence that *in vivo* exposure is more effective than imagery exposure with simple phobias (Borden, 1992).

Participant Modeling   With this approach, the therapist models for the client approaches to the feared stimulus. This is typically done in a graded fashion. If a client had a fear of birds, for example, the therapist might observe a budgie in a cage from about 10 feet away while the client watched. The client would then be encouraged to model this behavior, and would be praised for doing so. After several trials, the process might be repeated from a distance of 5 feet from the bird, then 2 feet from the bird, then right beside the cage, then with the cage door open, and so forth. Watching someone else behave fearlessly with respect to a feared object, and then imitating that person, appears to be an effective strategy for helping a client overcome that fear.

Systematic Desensitization   Unlike the preceding strategies, which are conceptualized as simple respondent extinction, systematic desensitization is based on the process of counterconditioning. Joseph Wolpe (1958), its developer, hypothesized that a reasonable treatment for phobias was to identify responses that were opposite to fear and to teach the client to engage in those responses in situations that normally produced fear. A fear antagonistic behavior that Wolpe found to be suitable for this purpose was relaxation.

With this approach, the therapist first helps the client to construct a fear hierarchy—a list of approximately 15 to 20 items that cause fear, with those that elicit the least amount of fear at the bottom, and those that elicit the most amount of fear at the top. Next, the client learns a deep muscle relaxation procedure that requires him/her to tense and then relax a set of muscles so that they are more deeply relaxed following the tensing than before. This tension-relaxation strategy is applied to muscles of all major areas of the body (such as arms, neck, face, and shoulders) and, after several sessions, enables an individual to relax deeply in a matter of minutes. Finally, actual therapy begins. While relaxing, a client is instructed to clearly imagine the first scene in the hierarchy. After a few seconds, the client is instructed to relax for about 15 to 30 seconds and then to reimagine the scene. In this way, the therapist proceeds up the hierarchy with the client imagining each scene twice and typically working up through three to five scenes per session. If anxiety is felt at any point, it is signalled by the client raising a finger and is followed by one of several steps which usually enable the client to proceed without experiencing any further anxiety. When the client finishes the last scene in the hierarchy, he/she can generally encounter the actual feared objects without undue distress. No doubt the positive reinforcement that the client receives then helps to maintain continued interactions with the stimuli that previously elicited intense, debilitating fear. Although systematic desensitization is normally carried out with imagery, it can also be done *in vivo*.

Comparison studies of treatment of simple phobias have demonstrated no meaningful differences among these different treatments (Borden, 1992). Therefore, because only systematic desensitization has been adapted to a self-management program, we'll tell you how to apply it—using Barb's case as an illustration—in the next section.

SYSTEMATIC SELF-DESENSITIZATION

Systematic *self*-desensitization is essentially the same procedure as systematic desensitization, except that the client progresses through the various desensitization stages by him- or herself. The steps outlined below are suitable for problematic simple phobias that are not too intense or debilitating (for severe phobias or other

Figure 25–1 An example of a failure to identify all anxiety-eliciting simuli prior to desensitization.

types of anxiety disorders, we recommend that professional help be obtained). Based on Barb's method of dealing with her fear of flying, your systematic self-desensitization program will take you through the following phases: (a) constructing a fear hierarchy, (b) learning deep muscle relaxation, and (c) carrying out the actual therapy steps of the self-desensitization process.

Constructing the Fear Hierarchy

To construct a fear hierarchy, first list from 10 to 30 fear-producing situations related to your undesirable fear. Then arrange these situations in order, starting with the situation that causes the least fear and ending with the situation that causes the most fear. To accomplish this task, get a stack of 3 × 5" index cards and proceed as follows.

1. Take one of the index cards, and on the front write a brief phrase about the fear-eliciting situation that makes you only slightly nervous. For example, if your fear is that of flying, the phrase might be "sitting at home and phoning the airline to make a reservation." Now turn the index card over, and on the back list several stimuli that will help prompt you to realistically imagine yourself actually experiencing the phone call. The prompts might include such things as the color of your phone and the sound of a voice saying, "Airline reservations desk—may I help you?" A sample index card is shown in Figure 25–2.

2. Take another index card, and list a situation that elicits a slightly larger amount of fear. Again, on the back of that card provide yourself with some verbal prompts that will help you clearly imagine experiencing that situation. Continue in this manner until all the fear-producing situations are listed on note cards arranged so that each situation produces a little more anxiety than the preceding one. You now have a fear hierarchy. An example of Barb's fear hierarchy for her fear of flying is shown in Table 25–1.

Note that each item in Table 25–1 refers to a specific, concrete situation that can be imagined in vivid detail, rather than a vague general idea. For example, item 10 is to be preferred to "waiting for the plane," for it is more likely to prompt specific images of sitting in the lounge, listening to the announcements of flight numbers, and so forth.

3. Your next step is to validate your fear hierarchy by making sure that your cards have been arranged in the proper order (they should start with the situation that produces the least anxiety and end with the situation that generates the most anxiety) and that the steps between them are sufficiently small (no "jump" in anxiety level from one item to the next should be too large). This should be done as follows:

    a. Rate each item in your hierarchy on a scale from 0 to 100; 100 means that the situation elicits the maximum conceivable amount of anxiety (extreme panic and absolute terror) when encountered in the natural environment, and 0 means that the situation produces absolutely no emotion when encountered in real life. This value is referred to as the number of *subjective units of discomfort* (suds) elicited by the situation.

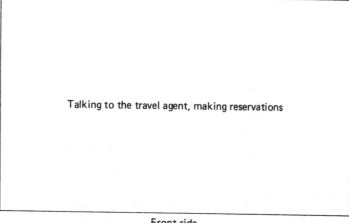

Figure 25–2 A sample index card for a fear-producing situation.

b. Check whether your original order of items in the hierarchy and your suds ratings are consistent (each item in the hierarchy should have a higher suds ranking than the item below it and a lower ranking than the item above it). If they are not consistent, redo both the hierarchy and the suds ratings until they are completely consistent.

c. Use your suds ratings to ensure that the distances between items in the hierarchy are sufficiently small and approximately equal (rule of thumb: distances between items should be no greater than 5 to 10 suds). Construct new items and insert **Note 1** them between any items that are greater than 10 suds apart.

d. Number each of the cards in order, starting with the card causing the least anxiety as number 1.

e. If you cannot make suds ratings without apparent inconsistencies between the ratings and your hierarchy, or within the ratings themselves, cease your attempt at self-desensitization and seek professional clinical desensitization (it would ap-

TABLE 25–1   EXAMPLE OF A FEAR-OF-FLYING HIERARCHY

1. The plane has landed and stopped at the terminal. I get off the plane and enter the terminal, where I am met by friends.

2. A trip has been planned, and I have examined the possible methods of travel and decided "out loud" to travel by plane.

3. I have called the travel agent and told him of my plans. He gives me the times and flight numbers.

4. It is the day before the trip, and I pack my suitcase, close it, and lock it.

5. It is 10 days before the trip, and I receive the tickets in the mail. I note the return address, open the envelope, and check the tickets for the correct dates, times, and flight numbers.

6. It is the day of the flight, I am leaving home. I lock the house, put the bags in the car, and make sure that I have the tickets and money.

7. I am driving to the airport for my flight. I am aware of every plane I see. As I get close to the airport, I see several planes—some taking off, some landing, and some just sitting on the ground by the terminal.

8. I am entering the terminal. I am carrying my bags and tickets.

9. I proceed to the airline desk, wait in line, and have the agent check my tickets and then weigh and check my bags.

10. I am in the lounge with many other people, some with bags also waiting for flights. I hear the announcements over the intercom and listen for my flight number to be called.

11. I hear my flight number announced, and I proceed to the security checkpoint with my hand luggage.

12. I approach the airline desk beyond the security checkpoint, and the agent asks me to choose a seat from the "map" of the plane.

13. I walk down the ramp leading to the plane and enter the door of the plane.

14. I am now inside the plane. I look at the interior of the plane and walk down the aisle, looking for my seat number. I then move in from the aisle and sit down in my assigned seat.

15. The plane is in flight, and I decide to leave my seat and walk to the washroom at the back of the plane.

16. I notice the seat-belt signs light up, so I fasten my seat belt and I notice the sound of the motors starting.

17. Everyone is seated with their seat belts fastened, and the plane slowly moves away from the terminal.

18. I notice the seat-belt signs are again lighted, and the pilot announces that we are preparing to land.

19. I am looking out the window and suddenly the plane enters clouds and I cannot see out the window.

20. The plane has stopped at the end of the runway and is sitting, waiting for instructions to take off.

21. The plane is descending to the runway for a landing. I feel the speed and see the ground getting closer.

22. The plane has taken off from the airport and banks as it changes direction. I am aware of the "tilt."

23. The plane starts down the runway, and the motors get louder as the plane increases speed and suddenly lifts off.

Note: This example is based on a case described by Roscoe, Martin, & Pear (1980).

pear that several major anxieties are present and interacting—a condition that may be too complex to be dealt with by the nonprofessional).

If strong anxiety has occurred while you are constructing the hierarchy or developing your suds ratings, you might adopt one of two strategies: Either discontinue your program and seek professional clinical help or continue your program but eliminate the five most anxiety-producing situations. After completing your desensitization program minus the five most anxiety-producing situations, you should then be able to develop a program for those items, because they will likely cause much less anxiety if you have successfully completed the earlier items.

Learning Deep Muscle Relaxation

After you have constructed your hierarchy, you should next learn to relax all your muscles completely and to recognize when they are relaxed. Do this by alter- **Note 2** nately tensing and relaxing your muscles while attending closely to the internal activities and sensations you are feeling at the time. Instructions for achieving deep muscle relaxation are presented in Table 25–2.

It would be most effective if a friend with a low, even, soothing voice could record these relaxation instructions on tape. That way, you can listen to them rather than having to read them. While your friend is reading the instructions, he or she should pause 5 seconds for each "(p)" that appears in them.

Let us assume that the instructions have been recorded on tape. You should now find a quiet, dimly lit, private setting with as few distracting stimuli as possible; a comfortable couch, bed, or reclining chair; and a time when you will not be interrupted for 20 to 30 minutes. Lie or sit on the couch, bed, or chair, which should support you with minimal use of your own muscles. Now turn on the tape recorder and follow the instructions.

After you have practiced the relaxation method on several different occasions, you will find that you are able to skip some of the steps and achieve the same deeply relaxed state in a shorter period of time. Eventually, you should be able to go directly to step 20 and achieve a completely relaxed state within a matter of minutes. We recommend that you gradually eliminate steps according to the following pattern:

1. Practice the entire 20 steps in Table 25–2 on at least three occasions spread over a minimum of 2 days.
2. Make a new tape recording consisting of steps 1, 8, 15, and 20. Use this new tape on at least three occasions spread over a minimum of 2 days.
3. Make a new tape consisting of steps 1 and 20. Use this new tape on at least two occasions spread over a minimum of 1 day.

After completing this program, which takes approximately 1 week, you should be able to relax totally in a matter of minutes. When you accomplish that goal, you are ready to begin the next phase of your self-desensitization program. You should *not* attempt to apply relaxation procedures in the actual fear-

TABLE 25–2 INSTRUCTIONS TO BE RECORDED ON TAPE AND PLAYED TO ACHIEVE DEEP MUSCLE RELAXATION

1. Listen closely to these instructions. They will help you to increase your ability to relax. Each time I pause, continue doing what you were doing before the pause. Now, close your eyes and take three deep breaths. (p) (p)[a]

2. Make a tight fist with either hand. Squeeze it tightly. Note how it feels. (p) Now relax. (p)

3. Once again, squeeze your hand tightly and study the tension that you feel. (p) And once again, just relax and think of the tension disappearing from your fingers. (p) (p)

4. Make a tight fist with your other hand. Squeeze it as tightly as you can and note the tension in your fingers and your hand, and your forearm. (p) Now relax. (p)

5. Once again, squeeze your fist tightly. (p) And again, just relax. (p) (p)

6. Make a tight fist with one hand and bend your arm to make your biceps hard. Hold it tense. (p) Now relax totally. Feel the warmth escape down your biceps, through your forearm, and out of your fingers. (p) (p)

7. Now make a tight fist with the other hand and raise your hand to make your biceps hard. Hold it tightly, and feel the tension. (p) Now relax. Concentrate on the feelings flowing through your arm. (p) (p)

8. Now, squeeze both fists at once and bend both arms to make them totally tense throughout. Hold it, and think about the tension you feel. (p) Now relax, and feel the total warmth and relaxation flowing through your muscles. All the tension is flowing out of your fingertips. (p) (p)

9. Now, wrinkle your forehead and squint your eyes very tight and hard.[b] Squeeze them tight and hard. Feel the tension across your forehead and through your eyes. Now relax. Note the sensations running through your eyes. Just relax. (p) (p)

10. Okay, squeeze your jaws tight together and raise your chin to make your neck muscles hard. Hold it, bite down hard, tense your neck, and squeeze your lips really tight. (p) Now relax. (p) (p)

11. Now, all together, wrinkle up your forehead and squeeze your eyes tight, bite down hard with your jaws, raise your chin and tighten up your neck, and make your lips tight. Hold them all and feel the tension throughout your forehead, and eyes, and jaw, and neck, and lips. Hold it. Now relax. Just totally relax and enjoy the tingling sensations. (p) (p) (p)

12. Now, squeeze both your shoulders forward as hard as you can until you feel your muscles pulling tightly right across your back, especially in the area between your shoulder blades. Squeeze them. Hold them tight. Now relax. (p) (p)

13. Now squeeze your shoulders forward again and, at the same time, suck your stomach in as far as you can and tense your stomach muscles. Feel the tension throughout your stomach. Hold it. (p) Now relax. (p) (p)

14. Once more, squeeze your shoulder blades forward again, suck in your stomach as far as you can, tense your stomach muscles, and feel the tension throughout your upper body. Now relax. (p) (p)

15. Now, we are going to review all of the muscle systems that we have covered so far. First, take three deep breaths. (p) (p) Ready? Tighten up both fists and bend both of your arms to squeeze your biceps tight. Wrinkle your forehead and squeeze your eyes tight. Bite down hard with your jaws, raise your chin, and hold your lips tight. Squeeze your shoulders forward and suck in your stomach and

(continued)

TABLE 25–2 *(CONTINUED)*

push your stomach muscles against it. Hold them all. Feel the tremendous tension throughout. Now relax. Take a deep breath. Just feel the tension disappearing. Think about the total relaxation throughout all of your muscles—in your arms, in your head, in your shoulders, in your stomach. Just relax. (p) (p)

16. Now, let's go to your legs. Bring one heel in tight toward your chair, push it down hard, and raise your toes so that your calf and your thigh are extremely tense. Squeeze your toes up and push your heel down hard. Now relax. (p) (p)

17. One more time, bring your left heel in tight toward your chair, push it down hard, and raise your toes so that your calf and your thigh are extremely tense. Push down on the heel and raise your toes. Now relax. (p) (p)

18. Now, bring your other heel in tight toward your chair and push it down and raise your toes so that your calf and your thigh are extremely tense. Push your heel down, squeeze your toes up, and squeeze your leg in tight. Now relax. (p) (p)

19. Now, let's do both legs together. Squeeze your heels in tight toward your chair, push down on your heels, and raise your toes as high and as tight as you can. Hold it. (p) Now relax. (p) (p)

20. Now, take three deep breaths. (p) Now, tense all the muscles as they are named, exactly as you have practiced: fists and biceps, forehead, eyes, jaw, neck, lips, shoulders, stomach, legs. Hold it. (p) Now relax. (p) (p) Breathe in deeply three times. Notice how relaxed all of your muscles feel. Now one more time, tense everything! Hold it! (p). And relax. Let all the tension disappear. Breathe normally and enjoy the completely tension-free state of your body and muscles. (p) (p) (p) (p) (p) (p) Now turn the tape off.

aEach "(p)" represents a pause of five seconds. (The numerals should not be read out loud.)

bIndividuals who wear contact lenses might want to remove them before doing this exericse.

producing settings until you have completed the training. Even then, it would be best to wait until your self-desensitization program is progressing smoothly before making any unnecessary contacts with the actual fear-producing stimuli.

Implementing the Self-Desensitization Program

Now that you have constructed your fear hierarchy and are able to relax completely within minutes, you are ready to start your program. This is done according to the following steps:

1. Find a quiet, private place that is free from distractions (preferably, the same place in which your relaxation practice sessions were conducted).
2. Place your stack of cards containing the fear items within easy reach. The cards should be in order, with the least fear-producing card on top and the most fear-producing card on the bottom.
3. Take several minutes and relax completely, as you have been practicing prior to this session.
4. When you are in a state of complete relaxation, take the card on top of the deck and look at the brief phrase that characterizes the situation that would normally cause some slight anxiety. Now turn the card over and look at the prompts that are to help you to visualize the first situation clearly and vividly. After looking at the prompts, close your eyes and try to imagine that you are actually in that situation, as

TABLE 25-3 DATA RECORDED BY THE CLIENT WHOSE FEAR-OF-FLYING HIERARCHY APPEARS IN TABLE 24–1[a]

Session (and date)	Task	Suds ranking of items			
		Original suds ranking[b]	Immediately after desensitization	When encountered in the natural environment	
				Contact 1 (Outbound flight: Aug. 26)	Contact 2 (Return flight: Sept. 6)
1 (Aug. 11)	Prepare hierarchy and do suds ranking on all items				
2 (Aug. 13)	Prepare cards				
3 (Aug. 14)					
4 (Aug. 15)	Learn deep muscle relaxation				
5 (Aug. 16)					
6 (Aug. 17)					

Session	Items:				
7 (Aug. 18)	1	0	0	0	0
	2	5	0	5[c]	—[d]
	3	6	0	6[c]	—[d]
	4	10	0	0	0
	5	13	0	0	—[d]
8 (Aug. 19)	6	17	0	0	0
	7	23	0	1	0
	8	27	0	0	0
	9	29	0	0	0
	10	30	0	0	0
	11	35	0	1	0
9 (Aug. 20)	12	38	0	0	0
	13	43	0	0	0
	14	46	0	0	0
10 (Aug. 21)	15	50	0	0	0
	16	60	0	0	0
	17	70	0	0	0
11 (Aug. 22)	18	75	0	0	0
	19	80	0	—[d]	—[d]
	20	90	0	1	0
12 (Aug. 23)	21	97	3	3	3
	22	99	9	9	9
	23	100	6	(25)5[e]	0

aFor descriptions of the items, see the corresponding item numbers in Table 25–1.

bThe original suds ranking was done during session 1.

cThese items were encountered in the natural environment prior to desensitization training.

dThese items were not encountered in the natural environment.

eWhen the plane suddenly moved from the end of the runway after having been stopped, the client was unprepared and a suds ranking of 25 resulted. However, she was able to recover her composure during the actual situation and reduce her anxiety to a suds ranking of 5.

prompted by your card. After about 10 seconds, place the card in a separate pile and relax totally. Relax for about 30 seconds, and during this time completely forget about the scene that you have just imagined. Think only of your muscles and how completely relaxed you feel while breathing deeply.

5. Now pick up the same card again, and then close your eyes and imagine that situation for at least 10 seconds. Put the card down in a separate place, and relax completely for another 30 seconds. During this time do not think of the scene that you were just imagining while in a relaxed state. After the 30 seconds are up, consider the amount of anxiety you felt while imagining this scene the second time. If you were able to imagine the scene with approximately five or fewer suds, then you are ready to proceed to card 2. If you felt more than five suds of anxiety, you should repeat the same routine once or twice more. If you felt less than five suds of anxiety, then relax for two minutes and repeat the procedure with the second card.

6. If you have great difficulty in imagining a scene, or in relaxing while imagining it, or if you feel more than 10 suds of anxiety, immediately stop imagining and induce deep muscle relaxation for a minute or two. Then repeat the item for only 3 to 5 seconds rather than a full 10 seconds.

7. If step 6 doesn't work, go back to the previous item and imagine that item for 20 seconds on two successive presentations of the item. Then, again try the item that caused the difficulty.

8. If you still have problems with a particular item, try to construct three new items with smaller steps between them to correct the difficulty encountered with that item. Proceed through the new items exactly as described.

9. In general, you should be able to proceed through one to four items per session; however, it is all right to go as slowly as one item per session, if necessary. On the other hand, if you do not feel anxiety, you should not hesitate to go through as many as four items per session, or perhaps more.

10. Each session should begin with an item that was completed successfully in the previous session.

11. Sessions should not last more than about 20 minutes. They might be conducted as frequently as twice per day and no less frequently than once per week.

12. If you experience difficulties that do not yield to the corrective procedures in steps 6 to 8, cease self-desensitization attempts and seek professional clinical help.

It is important to keep track of your progress. Thus, at the end of each session, you should record on a separate sheet of paper the name and number of the particular items you imagined successfully, the number of exposures to each item successfully imagined, the suds ratings of the items completed in that session, and the date of the session. We also recommend that you graph your data in a way that is meaningful to you. To understand your progress better, you should also indicate the suds rating of the item when you first prepared your anxiety hierarchy and the final suds rating, which, ideally, will be less than five. In addition, if in real life you experience the actual situation represented by a successfully completed item, assess your suds rating in the real situation and compare it with your rating when imagining the situation. This will give you some indication of the success of your generalization to the natural environment (see Figure 25–1). Table 25–3 shows the progress record and self-desensitization data taken by Barb, who prepared the fear-of-flying hierarchy shown in Table 25–1.

WHEN TO SEEK PROFESSIONAL ASSISTANCE

D. L. Watson and Tharp (1972, p. 189) suggested seeking professional assistance if any of the following conditions are present:

1. Uncomfortable anxiety during the creation of the hierarchy.
2. Overlapping hierarchies, indicated by contradictory or paradoxical suds ratings of the items.
3. Inability to produce vivid imagery.
4. Inability to control the beginning or ending of an image.
5. Inability to desensitize high enough on the hierarchy to meet your goals.

Provided that these conditions are not present, evidence supports the general recommendations of this chapter (Wenrich, General, and Dawley, 1976). It appears that individuals can often learn to overcome their own simple phobias by following the specific procedures of self-desensitization.

STUDY QUESTIONS

1. Briefly describe the three characteristics of an anxiety disorder.
2. Briefly describe three different types of anxiety disorders
3. In two or three sentences, describe flooding.
4. In two or three sentences, describe participant modeling.
5. In several sentences each, describe the three main phases of systematic desensitization.
6. Briefly explain the difference between systematic desensitization and systematic self-desensitization.
7. What is a fear hierarchy (in two or three sentences)?
8. What is a suds rating? How are suds ratings used?
9. At the beginning of the section entitled "Learning Deep Muscle Relaxation," there are several suggestions that amount to using situational inducement. Briefly describe three such suggestions.
10. When carrying out a self-desensitization program, what should an individual do if the anxiety felt while imagining a particular scene is greater than 10 suds?
11. How fast should one go through the hierarchy in a self-desensitization program?
12. What are the conditions under which self-desensitization should be discontinued and professional advice sought?

APPLICATION EXERCISE

Self-Modification Exercise

Choose a particular undesirable fear or phobia that you have and attempt a self-desensitization program by following the procedures described in this chapter. Prepare a written report of your procedures and results.

NOTES AND EXTENDED DISCUSSION

1. Although others have also recommended that the distance between items be approximately 5 to 10 suds (e.g., Wenrich et al., 1976, p. 28), this figure seems to be based on informal clinical observations rather than on rigorous empirical data.

2. Ever since Jacobson (1938) first described his relaxation method, a number of individuals have described different variations of it. Cautela and Groden (1978), Davis, Eschelman, and McKay (1980), and Smith (1990) published comprehensive relaxation manuals. According to these authors, therapists, parents, and teachers, without prior training, can follow the illustrations and simple verbal descriptions of the procedures so that they can learn relaxation themselves and teach it to others.

Study Questions on Notes

1. How firm is the evidence that the starting distance between self-desensitization items should be 5 to 10 suds?
2. What is the advantage of Jacobson's procedure, and its variations, over just telling people to relax?

Cognitive Behavior Modification

Although behavior modifiers have often tended to reject other psychological approaches (such as Freudian psychoanalysis), some blending has taken place between behavior modification and certain types of treatment collectively called *cognitive therapy*. The word **cognition** means *belief, thought, expectancy, attitude,* or *perception*. Accordingly, cognitive therapists regard their approach to be primarily that of helping a client overcome his or her difficulties by getting rid of unproductive, debilitating thoughts or beliefs and adopting more constructive ones. Many behavior modifiers have noted certain similarities between the goals and procedures of cognitive therapists and their own. Cognitive therapists, in turn, have adopted some behavior modification methods. Out of this mutual appreciation has grown an area that has come to be known as *cognitive behavior modification* (Meichenbaum, 1986) or *cognitive behavior therapy* (Ingram & Scott, 1990). Although cognitively oriented and behaviorally oriented therapists disagree on some issues, they have learned from each other (e.g., see Dougher, 1997; Hawkins & Forsyth, 1997; Wilson, Hayes, & Gifford, 1997). In addition, both approaches are firmly committed to the view that the criterion for judging the effectiveness of any treatment is the amount of measurable improvement that occurs in the client's behavior. The purpose of this chapter is to describe briefly some of the procedures referred to as cognitive behavior modification.

"THINKING," "FEELING," AND PRIVATE BEHAVIOR

As we indicated in Chapter 15, there appear to be two important categories of behaviors: operant and respondent. Much of what we call "thinking" and "feeling" in everyday life can be described in terms of these two fundamental behavioral categories.

Try the following exercise: Close your eyes and imagine that you're sitting on a lawn chair in your backyard on a warm summer day. You look up and see the clear blue sky. Imagine a few white fluffy clouds drifting slowly along. Chances are that you will be able to form a clear image of the blue sky and the white fluffy clouds—so clear that you can almost see the colors. Thus, one type of thinking appears to consist of imagining in response to words—imagining so vividly that it can sometimes seem almost like the real thing. This probably comes about through respondent or Pavlovian conditioning (see Chapter 15). If you actually look at a clear blue sky, the color elicits activity in the visual system much as food elicited salivation in Pavlov's dogs. As you grew up, you experienced many trials in which the words *blue sky* were paired with actually looking at and seeing a blue sky. As a consequence, when you close your eyes and imagine that you are looking at a blue sky (with white fluffy clouds), the words likely elicit activity in your visual system so that you experience the behavior of "seeing" the actual scene. This has been referred to as *conditioned seeing* (Skinner, 1953). In a broader sense, we might think of *conditioned sensing*. That is, just as we acquire conditioned seeing through experience, we also acquire conditioned hearing, conditioned smelling, and conditioned feeling. Consider the example described by Martin and Osborne (1993) in which an individual experienced numerous passionate sexual encounters with a partner who consistently used a very distinctive perfume. Then one day someone walked past that individual in a department store wearing that same perfume. The individual immediately imagined seeing the partner (conditioned seeing), felt "tingly" all over (conditioned feeling), and even imagined that he heard the partner's voice (conditioned hearing). This sort of thing is also a part of what goes on during fantasy. To experience a fantasy or to read or listen to a story is, in some sense, to be there. It's as though you can see what the people in the story see, feel what they feel, and hear what they hear. We're able to do this because of many instances of conditioned sensing. Our long histories of associating words with actual sights, sounds, smells, and feelings enable us to experience the scenes that an author's words describe. The internal actions that occur when we're thinking are real—we're really seeing, or feeling, or hearing when we respond to the words (Malott & Whaley, 1983).

Note 1   Imaging (conditioned seeing) and other types of conditioned sensing constitute one type of thinking. Another type of thinking is simply self-directed verbal behavior, or *self-talk*. As we indicated in earlier chapters, our verbal behavior is taught to us by others through operant conditioning. We learn to speak because of effective consequences for doing so. As children, we learn to ask for such things as our favorite foods and the opportunity to watch our favorite cartoons, and we learn to say things that please Mom and Dad, aunts and uncles, and others. Much of our thinking is verbal behavior. We learn to think out loud as children because it helps us to perform tasks more efficiently (R. N. Roberts, 1979). When children first start attending school, they often say rules out loud to themselves to adjust to difficult tasks (R. N. Roberts & Tharp, 1980). When they are about 5 or 6 years old, however, they also begin to engage in subvocal speech in the sense that their self-talk begins to occur below the spoken level (Vygotski, 1978).

We learn to talk silently to ourselves at a very early age largely because we encounter punishers when we think out loud (Skinner, 1957). For example, teachers in school require children to think to themselves because thinking out loud disturbs the other students. As another example, naturally distressed reactions from others teach us to keep certain thoughts to ourselves. When you go to a party and are being introduced to the hostess, your first reaction might be, "Wow, is that an ugly dress!" But you probably won't say it out loud; instead you will just "say it to yourself" or "think" it. Because much of our thinking goes on at a level that is not observable by others, we refer to it as *covert*, or *private*. It may include private respondent behavior (conditioned sensing), private operant behavior (self-talk), or both. Although private behavior is more difficult to "get at," we assume that in other respects it is the same as public behavior; that is, the principles and procedures applicable to private behavior are fundamentally the same as those that apply to public behavior. In short, we assume that the principles and procedures of operant and respondent conditioning apply to thinking.

Often, an instance of what we would refer to as thinking includes both respondent and operant components. To illustrate, consider the following example (described by Martin & Osborne, 1993). One of the authors grew up on a farm just outside of a small town. He attended school in the town and it was very important to him to be accepted by the town children. One of the town kids, Wilf, frequently teased him about being a "farmer." "Hey, gang," Wilf would say, "here comes Garry the farmer. Hey, Garry, do you have cow dung on your boots?" Now imagine that it's Saturday afternoon and Garry and his family are getting ready to go to town. Garry will be going to the Saturday afternoon matinee at the Roxy Theatre with the rest of the gang (a big deal because they didn't yet have TV on the farm). Garry says to himself, "I wonder if Wilf will be there" (operant thinking). Garry can picture Wilf clearly (conditioned seeing) and can imagine Wilf teasing him about being a farmer (both operant thinking and conditioned hearing). Thoughts of the aversive experience elicit unpleasant feelings (a reflexively learned response). Garry reacts by paying special attention to his appearance in the hope that appearing citified will give Wilf nothing to say.

Thinking (primarily self-talk and imagining) constitutes one type of private behavior. Another important category of private behavior is our *feelings*. As we indicated in Chapter 15, our feelings—made up of activity of the autonomic nervous system, such as breathing, heart rate, and glandular secretions—are the respondent components of emotional behavior. As illustrated by the work of Joseph Cautela and his colleagues, thinking and feeling as private behaviors are a proper subject matter for behavior modifiers and can readily be dealt with in terms of operant and respondent conditioning principles (Cautela and Kearney, 1986, 1990).

You can see that, contrary to the impression given by many introductory psychology texts (Jensen & Burgess, 1977), behavior modifiers do not ignore what goes on inside the person. Although it is true that the great majority of studies in behavior modification have been concerned with observable behavior, more and more behavior modifiers have taken an interest in dealing with private behavior. In doing so, they have also tended to avoid certain words, such as *cognition* and *belief*, that are used quite freely by other social scientists. There are usually more precise ways of talking about behavior and behavioral procedures. (For a discussion of situations in which cognitive language is more suitable than behavioral language, and vice versa, see Pear, 1983.) As we have just illustrated, the word *thinking* might refer to public behavior, private behavior, operant behavior, respondent behavior, or some mixture of these. It is more precise to refer to the actual behavior of interest (whether it is private or public, respondent or operant). Moreover, to use special words such as *cognition* and *belief* to refer to private behavior implies that the principles and procedures applicable to private behavior are fundamentally different from those that apply to public behavior.

However, as indicated earlier, we assume that the principles and procedures of operant and respondent conditioning apply to private as well as to public behavior. In Chapter 24 we described how one of the authors, in a self-control jogging program, increased his antifatigue thoughts by following them with thoughts of a highly reinforcing activity. Although the effect was probably not as strong as it would have been had his jogging been immediately reinforced with the actual experiences that he merely imagined, no new principles had to be introduced to account for the effect. In Chapter 25 we described how a client self-desensitized her fear of flying by imagining the fear-producing situations while in a relaxed state. Presumably, the private "seeing behavior" (imagining) was so similar to actually seeing the fear-producing situations that the relaxation response generalized to those situations.

In each of these cases, as well as in a number of other examples presented in this book, private behavior was modified to bring about desired changes in public behavior. In no case, however, was it necessary to assume that private behavior is fundamentally different from public behavior. On the contrary, the treatments used were based on the assumption that the same general principles and procedures are applicable to both public and private behavior.

From this point of view of public and private behavior, we will describe some details of an actual case. We then describe some methods that others have called *cognitive* procedures.

CAROL'S CASE[1]

"I'm a failure. I feel ugly and useless. I keep thinking about not being able to stay in a relationship, not being able to have a husband. I get really down and I don't want to do anything. And then I start crying," Carol explained to the psychologist. "Sometimes at work, when I'm thinking of how Fred left me, I go to the bathroom and cry. Sometimes I can't stop crying for a whole hour."

Carol and Fred had been engaged for three years. Three months before she began her sessions with the psychologist, Fred had left Carol for another woman. Since then, Carol had suffered obsessive thoughts about Fred and about herself. These occurred on a daily basis, were extremely distressing to Carol, and had a negative effect on her job performance.

At the end of her first session with the psychologist, Carol agreed that each time she thought about Fred for more than a couple of minutes, she would record

---

[1]This case is based on a report by Martin (1982).

her thoughts on an index card. Carol also agreed to collect some specific photographs and to bring them to the next session. One week later, Carol and the psychologist carefully examined the observations that she had collected on the index cards. They agreed on a rating scale to evaluate each of her days with respect to her thoughts about her former boyfriend. A score of 5 was considered a very bad day and a score of 0 was considered a very good day. If Carol reported feeling very unhappy, that she couldn't stop thinking of Fred for a long period of time, and she cried for a total of 1 hour or more, then she assigned that day a score of 5. If, on the other hand, she experienced only fleeting thoughts of Fred during the day, and such thoughts were not particularly disturbing, then the day was assigned a score of 0. Specific guidelines were also agreed upon for scores of 1, 2, 3, and 4. These latter scores were assigned as the unhappy thoughts and duration of crying during the day increased from the guidelines for scoring 0 to the guidelines for scoring 5. Her ratings for that first week of assessment averaged 4.2—a very unhappy week for Carol.

Carol agreed to implement the following procedure: Each time she experienced a thought characteristic of those that caused her to cry, she would stop what she was doing, clasp her hands, close her eyes, and "silently" yell "Stop!" to **Note 2** herself. Then she would open her eyes and take five photographs from her purse. The photographs were arranged in a particular order and encircled by a rubber band. With the psychologist's guidance, she had written specific statements on the back of each of them. With the photographs facing down, she looked at the back of the first one and read, "I'm my own boss. My life is ahead of me. I can do what I want to do." She turned the photo over and looked at her picture taken at the airport the previous year, before departure on a trip alone on which she had had a great time. For the next 5 to 10 seconds, she thought about how much she would like to travel again, and about the fun that she had had on her previous trip. Carol continued in this way with the four remaining photographs, which were prepared similarly to the one just described. Following this entire procedure, which required approximately 1 to 2 minutes to complete, Carol recorded the problem thoughts on her index card and returned to her previous activities. She was also instructed to vary the positive thoughts when viewing the photographs at different times.

The results of the program are shown in Figure 26–1. At the beginning of treatment, Carol still had some unhappy days, but her decreasing scores showed that she was improving. After seven treatment sessions, Carol decided that she no longer needed help.

This case is characteristic of cognitive behavior modification for two reasons. First, the focus was primarily on changing Carol's disturbing thoughts. Second, it relied on self-recording of private behaviors to demonstrate effectiveness. Nevertheless, this case can be interpreted in terms of operant and respondent conditioning. Like the strategies described in Chapters 16 and 17, the treatment attempted to capitalize on existing stimulus control. Silently yelling "Stop!" to herself was conceptualized as a stimulus change designed to disrupt the undesirable thoughts in whatever setting they occurred. In those same settings, the photographs and instructions controlled both respondent images and operant self-talk. The photographs elicited a variety of images that were considered

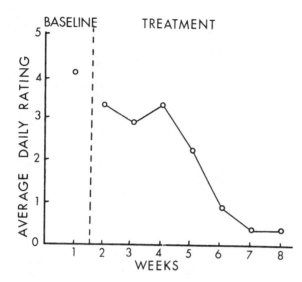

Figure 26–1   Average daily rating
of the occurrence of obsessive
thoughts by Carol. Each data point
represents the average of the daily
ratings assigned to obsessive
thoughts by Carol, averaged across
7 days of the week. A high rating
indicates that obsessive thoughts
were highly prevalent during the
day. A low rating indicates the absence of obsessive thoughts. *Note:*
From "Thought Stopping and Stimulus Control to Decrease Persistent
Disturbing Thoughts," by G. L.
Martin, 1982, *Journal of Behavior
Therapy and Experimental Psychiatry,*
13(3), p. 217. Copyright 1982, with
kind permission from Elsevier Science Ltd, The Boulevard, Langford
Lane, Kidlington 0X5 1Gb, UK.

incompatible with the unhappy thoughts. The instructions prompted coping self-
statements to compete with the undesirable self-talk about Fred, her former
boyfriend. One immediate consequence of thinking desirable alternative
thoughts was a self-recording response on an index card. Whether or not the self-
recording functioned as a conditioned reinforcer, it was assumed that the content
of the desirable thoughts would be reinforcing in and of themselves. Moreover, it
was assumed that as Carol continued behaving in her natural environment, she
would encounter a variety of natural reinforcers following the desirable alternative private behaviors. Finally, the statements likely exerted rule-governed control over some of Carol's actions.

 As in Carol's case, most cognitive behavior modification procedures appear
to involve therapeutic manipulations that emphasize stimulus control. Let's look
at some of these procedures.

SOME COGNITIVE BEHAVIORAL PROCEDURES

 A major theoretical assumption of cognitive therapy is that individuals interpret
and react to events in terms of their perceived significance; that is, our beliefs, expectations, and attitudes affect our behavior. A second theoretical assumption is
that cognitive deficiencies can cause emotional disorders. It follows from these assumptions that the primary focus of therapy is to fundamentally change a client's
cognitions. Stated simply, cognitive therapists believe that faulty thinking is the
cause of emotional and behavioral problems, and the primary focus of cognitive
therapy is to change faulty thinking. Techniques for doing so can be described in

three general classes: cognitive restructuring methods, self-instructional coping methods, and problem-solving strategies (Ingram & Scott, 1990). Although these techniques are sometimes simply called cognitive therapy, we refer to them here as cognitive behavior modification or cognitive behavior therapy for two reasons. First, these approaches deal mainly with the client's private verbal behavior relating to him- or herself and the surrounding world. Second, therapists who use these techniques generally also include behavior modification components in their treatments.

Cognitive Restructuring Methods

Do you ever find yourself saying such things as "I always make a mess of things," "I'm such a klutz," "I never do things right"? Cognitive psychologists consider such self-statements to be irrational (after all, you do *some* things right). They believe that such irrational thoughts can cause anxiety, sadness, anger, or other troublesome emotions. Their approach to therapy is to help people identify such irrational ideas or beliefs, and to replace them with realistic statements about the world. Approaches that focus on substituting rational thoughts and appraisal of information for irrational or dysfunctional thinking are referred to as *cognitive restructing* methods.

Ellis's Rational-Emotive (Behavior) Therapy   Cognitive behavior modification has received strong impetus from the well-known cognitive therapist Albert Ellis (e.g., see Ellis, 1984; Ellis & Dryden, 1997; Ellis & Bernard, 1985). The original name for his approach, **rational-emotive therapy (RET),** was based on the premise that most everyday emotional problems (and related behaviors) stem from irrational statements that people make to themselves when events in their lives are not the way they would like them to be. People tend to "catastrophize": they tell themselves that things are so horrible they can't possibly "stand it." Jimmy, for example, had slept through his alarm and was going to be late for class. Rushing to get ready, he cut himself while shaving and thought, "I'm a walking disaster! I always screw things up." Later, he got caught in a traffic jam. Thinking, "why does the worst always happen to me?" he felt angry and frustrated. Ellis considers such self-statements ("I'm a walking disaster," "worst always happens to me") to be at the root of emotional problems (Jimmy's anger and frustration). Basically, Ellis's approach is to teach his clients to counteract such "irrational" self-statements with more positive and realistic statements. To do this, Ellis directly challenges irrational ideas of a client and models rational reinterpretations of disturbing events. Jimmy might be taught to tell himself that there are far worse things than being caught in a traffic jam, and that even though things could be better, they could certainly be a lot worse. Whereas his situation may be annoying or inconvenient, it is not catastrophic, and, moreover, there are usually things that he can do to improve it. (For example, see Figure 26–2.)

Ellis (1993) later added the word *behavior* to the name of his therapy, now calling it *rational-emotive behavior therapy* (REBT). He did so because, despite being considered a cognitive therapist, he frequently uses *in vivo* behavioral "homework" assignments. Jimmy, for example, might be told to write down each time

Figure 26–2 An exaggerated example of rational-emotive therapy.

he performs a complex action, such as working at his computer or changing the oil in his car, to prove to himself that he is not a walking disaster. The homework assignments are usually designed to help the client to challenge irrational beliefs and to confront troublesome emotions head on.

Based on clinical experience, Ellis & Bernard (1985) claim that REBT has been used successfully with a wide variety of problems, such as depression resulting from a broken love affair (the client may be telling himself that he simply cannot live without the love of a particular person); extreme fears, such as speech anxiety (the client may be telling herself that it would be absolutely horrible if some members of the audience thought poorly of her speaking skills); and lack of self-confidence (the client may be telling himself that he will inevitably fail at whatever he attempts, and that such failure will only prove once again what a rotten person he is). For a practical guide to REBT, see Dryden and DiGiuseppe (1990), and Yankurn & Dryden (1997).

Beck's Cognitive Therapy Aaron T. Beck (1976), independently of Ellis, developed a cognitive therapy procedure that is similar to REBT. His cognitive therapy was originally developed for the treatment of depression. He has also applied his approach to a wide variety of problems, however, including manic states, anxiety disorders, hysteria, obsessional disorders, psychosomatic disorders, and phobias (see Beck, Emery, & Greenberg, 1985). In addition, Beck has written a self-help book for couples that shows how they can use cognitive therapy to improve their relationships (Beck, 1988). Kingdon and Turkington (1984) have extended the approach to cases of schizophrenia.

According to Beck (1976), people with emotional disorders engage excessively in aberrant, fallacious, or dysfunctional thinking, and this is what causes (or exacerbates) their problems. Among the various types of dysfunctional thinking are the following:

1. *Dichotomous thinking*, which is thinking in absolute terms; for example, assuming that one is a failure if one gets any grade less than an "A."
2. *Arbitrary inference*, which is drawing a conclusion on the basis of inadequate evidence; for example, misinterpreting a frown on the face of a passerby to mean that the passerby disapproves of him or her.
3. *Overgeneralization*, which is reaching a general conclusion on the basis of too few instances; for example, assuming that a single failure means that one cannot succeed at anything.
4. *Magnification*, which is exaggerating the meaning or significance of a particular event; for example, believing that it is terrible or catastrophic not to obtain something that one wants very badly.

The first step in Beck's procedure is to have the client identify the dysfunctional thoughts and maladaptive assumptions that may be causing unpleasant emotions. A client might be encouraged, for example, to recall or imagine situations that elicited such emotions and to focus on the thoughts experienced in those situations. Next, once the debilitating thought or dysfunctional assumption has been identified, there are several methods that are used in counteracting it. One such method used by Beck is *reality checking* or *hypothesis testing*. After the client has identified the debilitating belief or thought and has learned to distinguish it as a hypothesis rather than as a reality, he or she is then in a position to test it experimentally. If a client believes that everyone he meets turns away from him in disgust, the therapist might help him devise a system for judging other people's facial expressions and body language so that the client can determine objectively if the thoughts behind his problem are indeed accurate. Third, like Ellis, Beck frequently uses homework assignments that contain liberal doses of behavior modification procedures. Depressed individuals, for example, frequently neglect various routine tasks such as showering or bathing, bedmaking, and housecleaning. Homework assignments might be directed toward reestablishing these behaviors. As another example, clients might be encouraged to participate in role rehearsal sessions. A client who believed that store clerks thought she was inept changed this negative view of herself when she played the role of a salesclerk waiting on her.

Comparison of the Approaches of Ellis and Beck   There are some obvious similarities between Beck's approach and Ellis's REBT. Both approaches assume that the client's difficulty is caused by some type of inappropriate thought pattern, such as a tendency to exaggerate or catastrophize unpleasant events. Both focus on changing a client's irrational thinking. And both use various behavioral homework assignments. A difference seems to be that Beck does not emphasize the tendency of clients to catastrophize or "awfulize" nearly as much as Ellis. Also, transcripts of sessions with clients conducted by Beck and Ellis suggest that Beck takes a gentler, less confrontational approach than does Ellis to changing clients' irrational beliefs.

Self-Instructional Coping Methods

Methods like those of Ellis and Beck attempt to directly change the faulty thinking that is thought to cause emotional problems. Other approaches focus more on helping clients to develop *coping skills* for dealing with stressful situations that are largely out of their control. One such approach is that of Donald Meichenbaum (1977, 1986). Like Ellis and Beck, Meichenbaum focuses on substituting positive thoughts for negative ones. But he also emphasizes the role of self-instruction (i.e., telling oneself what to do in various situations) in bringing about desired behavior changes. Often, the emphasis in his approach is more on teaching the client to cope with the negative emotions than on completely eliminating them. For example, following treatment, one phobic client said,

> It [self-instructing] makes me able to be in the situation, not to be comfortable, but to tolerate it. I don't talk myself out of being afraid, just out of appearing afraid . . . you immediately react to the things you're afraid of and then start to reason with yourself. I talk myself out of panic. (Meichenbaum, 1986, p. 372).

The first step in Meichenbaum's approach is to help the client identify certain internal stimuli produced by the stressful situation and by negative statements the client makes to him- or herself (e.g., "I can't deal with this," "I'm no good"). The client learns to use these internal stimuli as S^Ds for engaging in appropriate self-instruction. Next, through modeling and behavioral rehearsal, the client learns self-talk to counteract negative self-statements in the presence of the stressful situation. A client who is nervous about public speaking might be taught to say, "The fact that I'm anxious just before giving a speech doesn't mean I'm going to blow it—my anxiety is just a way of preparing me to be alert and do a good job." Third, the client is taught to self-instruct the steps for taking appropriate action (e.g., "I'll take three deep breaths, smile, then follow my notes and give my speech") while imagining the performance of those actions. Finally, the client is instructed to make self-reinforcing statements immediately after he or she has successfully coped with the stressful situation (e.g., "I did it! Wait 'til I tell my therapist about this!"). To further help the client develop coping skills for dealing with stressful situations in the natural environment, the therapist may give **stress inoculations** (Meichenbaum, 1985). These are stressful stimuli, such as putting one's arm in freezing water, watching a gruesome film, or recalling a stressful visit to the dentist, to which the client is exposed in the therapy setting. Just prior to and during exposure to such stressful situations, the client practices appropriate coping skills. Research indicates that stress inoculations can be particularly helpful for clients with anxiety or stress problems (Meichenbaum, & Deffenbacher, 1988).

Like Ellis and Beck, Meichenbaum also uses behavior modification techniques such as relaxation training (described in Chapter 25) and various homework assignments. Besides working with adults, Meichenbaum has also used self-instructional methods in helping hyperactive and withdrawn children to manage their behavior (see Meichenbaum, 1986).

Problem-Solving Methods

Cognitive restructuring and self-instructional methods focus on counteracting dysfunctional thinking and negative self-talk. Problem-solving methods focus on correcting faulty reasoning by teaching people how to proceed through logical reasoning to satisfactory solutions to personal problems. D'Zurilla and Goldfried (1971) outlined the following five general steps in personal rational problem solving:

1. *General orientation.* The client is encouraged to recognize problems and to realize that it is possible to deal with them by acting systematically rather than impulsively. When faced with a problem, for example, the client might be taught to make such statements as "I know I can work this out if I just proceed step-by-step." "Let me see how I can rephrase this as a problem to be solved."
2. *Problem definition.* When asked to specify the problem, most clients reply in very vague terms—for example, "I've been very upset lately." By specifying the history of the problem and the variables that seem to be controlling it, it is generally possible to define the problem more precisely. For example, a close analysis might indicate that what is upsetting the client is that she shares the apartment with a very untidy roommate and she can't stand the "mess" she feels forced to live in.
3. *Generation of alternatives.* After defining the problem precisely, the client is instructed to brainstorm possible solutions—that is, to "let her mind run free" and to think of as many solutions as she can, no matter how far-fetched. For example, possible solutions might be to (a) move; (b) self-desensitize to messiness; (c) speak assertively to her roommate about keeping the place neat; (d) try to shape neat behavior in her roommate; (e) negotiate a behavioral contract with her roommate; (f) throw her roommate's things out of the window; and (g) throw her roommate out the window.
4. *Decision making.* The next step is to examine the alternatives carefully, eliminating those that are obviously unacceptable, such as (f) and (g). She should then consider the likely short-term and long-term consequences of the remaining alternatives. Writing out the positives and negatives of various alternatives has been demonstrated to improve satisfaction with decision making, to increase the likelihood of sticking to decisions, and to lead to more productive choices and fewer regrets (Janis and Mann, 1977; Janis & Wheeler, 1978). On the basis of these considerations, she should select the alternative that seems most likely to provide the optimum solution, and (with the help of the therapist) devise a plan for carrying it out.
5. *Verification.* When the plan is put into effect, the client is encouraged to keep track of progress to ensure that it solves the problem. If it doesn't, the problem-solving sequence must be restarted and another solution attempted.

Foxx and Faw (1990) described a program for teaching problem-solving skills to psychiatric patients and discussed how generalization of these skills might be enhanced. In addition, D'Zurilla (1986) and Nezu and Nezu (1989) described how the problem-solving approach might be applied to a variety of clinical problems.

EVALUATION OF "COGNITIVE" TECHNIQUES

How effective are cognitive techniques in reducing maladjustment? And what should be included in an evaluation of their effectiveness? To the extent that Ellis's approach is successful, is it because the therapist vigorously disputes the clients irrational beliefs (a "cognitive" component)? Or is it because of the homework assignments (behavioral components)? After all, the homework assignments are likely to influence the client to confront anxiety-evoking situations in real life, and we know that exposure-based methods are very effective for helping individuals to overcome anxiety disorders (see Chapter 25). Or is the improvement the result of a combination of both the correction of faulty thinking *and* the homework assignments?

Before examining research on these questions, let's clarify the nature of the *"cognitive"* components versus the *"behavioral"* components of treatments (as described by cognitive therapists). (As described earlier, and as discussed later in this chapter, we believe that *all* of these treatment components can be interpreted behaviorally.) So-called *cognitive components* of treatment are designed to correct the faulty thinking that is hypothesized to cause problems. They include identification of maladaptive thoughts, changing negative self-statements to positive self-statements, challenging of dysfunctional beliefs, verbal corrections of distorted views or processes, Socratic-method questioning of faulty assumptions, and self-instructing while imagining the performance of appropriate behavior. So-called *behavioral components* of treatment are based explicitly on respondent and operant conditioning and are applied to directly change specific behaviors (either public or private). Behavioral components would include relaxation training, behavioral rehearsal of the target behaviors, *in vivo* exposure to anxiety-producing stimuli, systematic desensitization, flooding, self-monitoring, participant modeling, token economies, and application of all of the behavioral principles and techniques described in Chapters 2 through 15. And now *the question we alluded to earlier*: Is it worthwhile to include cognitive components in treatment packages to help people deal with emotional and behavioral problems? *The answer* appears to be—sometimes.

Ellis's RET: Does Changing Faulty Thinking Reduce Maladjustment?

Gossette and O'Brien (1989, 1992) carefully examined 107 studies of RET that (1) focused on therapists' attempts to change clients' irrational beliefs and that (2) were not accompanied by other behavioral strategies (such as behavioral rehearsal, reinforced practice). They surveyed all known reports (both published studies and unpublished dissertations) in which RET was compared with no treatment (i.e., clients were simply on a waiting list or given a placebo—a procedure that is believed to have no effect), or other types of therapy. Measures included assessments of irrational thoughts, assessments of emotional distress, and assessments of other behavioral improvements (such as approaching feared objects). Ellis's approach was more effective than the various other comparison conditions in decreasing client's irrational self-talk in only 46% of the cases. This seems like a surprisingly low number considering that the main focus in RET is to change a client's irrational self-talk. An even greater concern is that RET was more effective than the comparison conditions in reducing emotional distress in only 27% of the cases. Finally, RET had *virtually no effect on other behavioral measures* (such as the extent to which clients actually approached feared objects). The results of Gossette and O'Brien's scholarly review suggest that whatever success therapists practicing RET have obtained may be due to the various homework assignments they gave rather than to their disputation of irrational beliefs.

Does the Addition of Cognitive Restructuring to Behavioral Treatment Improve Results with Clinical Populations?

Andrew Sweet and his colleagues carefully examined 29 studies that compared purely behavioral methods to those same methods with cognitive components added. They did not differentiate between the different models of cognitive therapy. Rather, "the essential identifying factor was that putative cognitions, cognitive processes, core beliefs, self-statements, attitudes, attributions, schemata, etc., were being therapeutically addressed in a verbal fashion" (Sweet & Loizeaux, 1991, p. 161.). They reported that 83% of the studies showed that *no* more beneficial outcome was achieved by adding therapy components that specifically focused on cognitive restructuring (Latimer & Sweet, 1984; Sweet & Loizeaux, 1991). Only in cases of persons with social-anxiety problems did the addition of a cognitive component appear to be helpful. In a more recent meta-analysis examining studies comparing exposure *in vivo* to exposure plus cognitive restructuring in the treatment of social phobia, however, both were found to be equally effective (Feske & Chambless, 1995). Meta-analysis is a statistical procedure for combining the data analyses of many different studies to yield the result that one large study containing all the data of the smaller studies would have produced. All in all, therefore, the data cited above indicate that the success of cognitive treatments is frequently the result of the behavioral components, and that cognitive components rarely provide added effectiveness.

Is Beck's Cognitive Therapy Valuable for the Treatment of Depression?

Although Beck and his colleagues have applied their approach to a variety of disorders, they consider it to be especially effective for depressed individuals (Beck et al., 1985). And Dobson (1989) concluded from his meta-analysis that Beck's cognitive therapy was the treatment of choice for unipolar depression. In 1989, however, the National Institute of Mental Health (NIMH) Treatment of Depression Collaborative Study came to a different conclusion. This study was one of the most sophisticated clinical trials of psychotherapy ever conducted (Elkin et al., 1989). With trained therapists at a number of sites across the United States, several approaches were compared for the treatment of persons suffering from depression. The result: Beck's cognitive therapy was no more effective than a placebo control condition. In defence of Beck's therapy, it should be pointed out that the NIMH study indicated that Beck's cognitive therapy was as effective as imipramine (a drug used in the treatment of depression) at some of the sites (Jacobson & Hollon, 1996). Also, Elkin (1994) suggested that the reason no differences between the placebo and Beck's therapy occurred may have been, in part, because the placebo (which was actually a clinical management condition) was surprisingly effective. Nevertheless, in accordance with the NIMH findings, a published set of guidelines for treating severe depression stated that cognitive behavior therapy may be no more effective than a placebo (American Psychiatric Association, 1993). Although proponents of Beck's approach have since made suggestions for improving the effectiveness of cognitive behavior therapy (e.g., Thase, 1994), research has not yet demonstrated the benefits of such modifications.

In another evaluation of cognitive treatment of depression, results were mixed. In December of 1989, the Agency for Health Care Policy and Research (AHCPR) of the U.S. Public Health Service was established by Federal Public Law 101–239 and mandated to develop clinical practice guidelines for use by primary care practitioners and other health providers (Clinton, McCormick, & Besteman, 1994). Depression was the first psychiatric disorder identified by AHCPR for guideline development. Before developing treatment guidelines, the Depression Guideline Panel conducted a meta-analysis of published, randomized controlled trials for treatment of mildly to moderately depressed outpatients (Depression Guideline Panel, 1993). Overall efficacy was found to be:

- 55.3% for behavior therapy that included activity scheduling, self-control therapy, social skills training, and problem solving;
- 52.3% for interpersonal psychotherapy that focused on resolving interpersonal difficulties thought to cause the depression;
- 46.6% for cognitive therapy that aimed at symptom removal by changing patients' distorted, negative thinking and/or correcting faulty assumptions; and
- 34.8% for brief dynamic psychotherapy that focused on core conflicts based on personality and situational variables.

Thus, cognitive therapy was approximately 12% more effective than brief dynamic psychotherapy, but approximately 9% less effective than behavior therapy. What are we to make of such mixed results?

A BEHAVIORAL INTERPRETATION OF COGNITIVE BEHAVIOR MODIFICATION

More than two decades have passed since cognitive behavior modification was heralded as a significant advance over traditional behavior modification (Mahoney & Thoreson, 1974). In response to early criticisms of cognitive behavior modification (see Greenspoon & Lamal, 1978; Ledwidge, 1978; Rachlin, 1977; Skinner, 1977; Wolpe, 1976), Mahoney and Kazdin (1979) suggested that such criticisms were premature and that critics should await the results of clinical research. Many of the results are now in. In many studies, as indicated earlier, the addition of cognitive techniques to standard behavioral treatments did little to improve overall treatment results. But in some instances, cognitive components have been of benefit. How do we deal with this discrepancy? We believe that cognitive techniques can be worthwhile, but that they can be used most effectively when they are analyzed from a consistent behavioral point of view. A behavioral interpretation suggests: (a) cognitive techniques rely largely on rule-governed behavior; (b) rules control behavior when they link the behavior to effective environmental consequences; therefore, (c) cognitive techniques will effectively change behavior if and only if there are sufficient links to the external environment. Let's examine this interpretation in more detail.

Cognitive Techniques Rely on Rule-Governed Behavior

You will recall from Chapter 16 that a rule is a description of a situation where a certain response will produce certain consequences. The statement of a rule (e.g., "If I study for 3 hours tonight, I'll get an 'A' on my behavior modification exam tomorrow") can exert control over behavior (it can influence you to study for 3 hours). From a behavioral perspective, cognitive techniques deal largely with rule-governed behavior (Poppen, 1989; Zettle & Hayes, 1982). Suppose that a client who happens to be coming down with a flu says to an RET therapist: "Everything I do is wrong. If I don't go to work tomorrow, I'll be fired. But if I don't get some rest, I'll get pneumonia." And suppose the therapist counters with, "Nonsense! If you call in and explain your poor health, your employer likely won't fire you." In this instance, the client has been given a rule, namely, "If I call in tomorrow and explain my situation, I'll be able to stay home and recuperate and still keep my job." By complying with such a rule, the client encounters positive consequences in the natural environment (assuming that he can stay home and rest and not get fired), and the irrational self-statements ("Everything I do is wrong," "I'll be fired!") are less likely to occur because they are not supported by the outcomes of the risk-taking behavior.

As illustrated by this example, cognitive therapists capitalize on rule-governed behavior to help their clients. As indicated in Chapter 16, however, there are guidelines for using rules effectively. In particular, rules are most likely to be effective when they describe specific behavior that leads to sizable and probable environmental consequences and when they contain deadlines for the desired behavior. Are these guidelines always practiced by cognitive therapists when they give rules to clients to correct faulty thinking? Let's analyze some examples.

Effective and Ineffective Applications of Cognitive Restructuring

*Some cases of cognitive restructuring may be **effective** because the therapist teaches the client to rehearse rules that identify specific behaviors that are likely to be maintained in the natural environment.* Reconsider the example of Jimmy, the student who overslept, cut himself while shaving, and later got stuck in traffic. Jimmy's irrational self-talk might be thought of as faulty rules. His statement, "I always screw things up," implies the rule: "If I attempt this task I will encounter failure." Such a rule might cause him to avoid a variety of tasks that he is capable of performing. The resulting failure to meet various deadlines for such tasks might elicit some anxiety. A cognitive therapist might dispute such irrational self-statements, challenge Jimmy to replace them with rational self-statements, and give him homework assignments that will support rational thinking. Jimmy might be taught to rehearse rules that would help him accomplish various tasks that he has problems completing successfully. For example, he might rehearse such rules as: "I do some things quite well. I'll follow the computer assignment instructions carefully so that I can complete the assignment by the deadline," or "If I take my time, I can change the oil in my car without making a mess." Such rules would counteract Jimmy's irrational self-talk ("I always screw things up") and would likely lead to behavior that will be reinforced. After all, Jimmy has successfully completed such tasks on previous occasions. The therapist has helped him to replace inaccurate rules with more accurate ones, and behavior appropriate to the more accurate rules is likely to be maintained by the natural environment. In such cases, cognitive restructuring can be helpful. In general, if an individual's irrational self-talk largely involves rules that are inaccurate generalizations about his or her performance ("I never do things right"), or inaccurate generalizations about the reactions of others ("I'm always treated unfairly"), then the substitution of more accurate rules ("I often do things right," "I'm often treated fairly by people") can easily be tested. The more accurate rules are then likely to be maintained by the natural environment.

But now consider other types of irrational thinking. According to Ellis and Grieger (1977), irrational thinking also includes categories referred to as "awfulizing" (e.g., "It's absolutely awful that I lost my job") and "musterbation" (e.g., "I must get a job or I'm a rotten person"). When a client expresses such thoughts, an RET therapist might challenge the client ("Why is it awful?" or "Just because you don't have a job doesn't make you a rotten person"). And even though a client may learn (in order to avoid or escape aggressive questioning by the therapist) to express that being without work is not awful or that he is not a rotten person, the client is still out of work. In such cases, cognitive restructuring is less likely to be helpful. The client has not been given a set of rules (e.g., "I'll check the want ads," "I'll go to the employment agency") that are likely to lead to effective action that will be maintained by the natural environment. And even if the client had been given clear rules for effective behavior, he or she may be deficient in the necessary behaviors (time management, assertiveness, persistence, etc.) needed to find a job. *Thus, in some cases of cognitive restructuring, the rules may be* **ineffective** *because they don't identify specific behaviors that lead to supportive environmental consequences, or because the client is deficient in the behaviors specified by the rules.* As expressed by Poppen (1989, p. 346), "It almost seems that Ellis tries to teach folks that it does not matter what happens to them as long as they think rationally about it" (see Figure 26–2).

Self-Instruction and Problem-Solving Methods Use Effective Rules

Both self-instruction and problem-solving training have been used to help individuals in a variety of settings (e.g., see D'Zurilla, 1988; Meichenbaum, 1986). Although there have been some negative findings by practitioners attempting to apply these methods (e.g., Billings & Wasik, 1985; Bryant & Budd, 1982; Gesten et al., 1982; Nelson & Carson, 1988), negative results have not been reported with these cognitive behavioral strategies to the degree described above for cognitive restructuring methods. Why? Perhaps the explanation lies in the greater degree to which self-instruction and problem-solving methods incorporate environmental consequences for overt behaviors that are influenced by the client's self-talk. In other words, *these approaches tend to teach rule-governed behavior that leads to effective consequences.* Teaching a student who is nervous about giving a speech in class to recognize the fact that she is nervous, to then emit some coping self-statements, and to then self-instruct the steps for taking appropriate action is essentially giving the student a set of rules to follow. If the rules successfully govern the behavior (the student does in fact give the speech and receive some positive feedback), then the use of those rules will have been strengthened. Because there is a focus on performing the behavior successfully *in addition to* self-instructions to do so, there is a greater chance of successful behavior change than if the focus had just been on the self-instructions alone. Similarly, in problem solving, whereas the first three steps (general orientation, problem definition, and generation of alternatives) involve self-talk, the fourth and fifth steps (decision making and verification) require that the individual take action and solve the problem. Once again, self-talk is appropriately linked to overt behaviors and supportive environmental consequences.

CONCLUDING COMMENTS

Although the behavioral applications we have described briefly in this chapter are usually called *cognitive,* and although they are often said to be directed toward modifying thoughts, beliefs, and attitudes, their distinguishing characteristic seems to be that they deal with private verbal behavior as well as with public behavior. They do not appear to involve any behavior principles besides those discussed in the previous chapters of this book. All behavior practitioners should be open to innovative procedures for helping people change their behavior. At the same time, as the chapter has pointed out, there are practical as well as theoretical advantages to looking at such procedures from a consistent behavioral viewpoint. In addition, it is especially important that, whenever possible, practitioners use procedures that have been validated in the research literature and avoid procedures that have not been validated.

STUDY QUESTIONS

1. Cognitive behavior modification is a blend of what two types of treatment?
2. What does the word *cognition* mean?
3. Describe an example of *respondent thinking.*
4. Describe an example of *operant thinking.*
5. In what way did Carol's case involve stimulus control procedures?
6. Why have behavior modifiers tended to avoid certain words such as *cognitions* and *beliefs*?

7. Discuss whether reputable behavior modifiers deny the existence and importance of thoughts and feelings.

8. Describe several examples cited in this chapter (or Chapters 24 and 25) in which individuals' private behaviors influenced their public behaviors.

9. What basic assumption do the authors of this text make about public and private behavior?

10. When behavior modifiers speak of private behavior, to what are they referring?

11. What are two major assumptions of cognitive therapy?

12. According to the authors of this text, with what do cognitive therapists and cognitive behavior modifiers mainly deal?

13. In what two ways is Carol's case cognitive behavior modification?

14. In a sentence or two, what are cognitive restructuring methods?

15. In a sentence or two, what is rational-emotive therapy? Who developed it?

16. Why did Ellis change the name of his therapy from RET to REBT?

17. According to Beck, what causes problems for neurotic individuals? Describe three examples.

18. Describe the basic steps in Beck's cognitive therapy.

19. Describe three similarities and two differences between the approaches of Beck and Ellis.

20. In two or three sentences, how does the focus of Meichenbaum's self-instructional coping approach differ from Ellis' REBT?

21. Briefly describe the four main steps of Meichenbaum's self-instructional approach.

22. What are *stress inoculations*?

23. In two or three sentences each, outline the five steps of problem solving described by D'Zurilla and Goldfried.

24. Distinguish between the cognitive components and the behavioral components of cognitive behavioral treatments.

25. Describe the basic comparisons that were examined and the overall results obtained in the studies on RET reviewed by Gossette and O'Brien.

26. Briefly describe the overall comparisons that were made and the findings obtained by the studies on cognitive restructuring reviewed by Sweet and his colleagues.

27. Briefly describe the study and the conclusion of the NIMH Treatment of Depression Collaborative Study concerning Beck's cognitive therapy.

28. Regarding behavior therapy versus cognitive therapy for treating mildly to moderately depressed clients, what were the conclusions of the AHCPR Depression Guideline Panel from their meta-analysis of published, randomized controlled trials?

29. Define a rule. Give an example that illustrates how a rule can function as an S^D.

30. Describe an example that illustrates how cognitive therapists capitalize on rule-governed behavior to help their clients.

31. From a rule-governed behavior interpretation of cognitive therapy, how might we explain effective versus ineffective applications of cognitive restructuring?

32. From a rule-governed behavior interpretation of cognitive therapy, how might we account for effective applications of self-instruction training or problem-solving methods? Illustrate with an example.

APPLICATION EXERCISE

Self-Modification Exercise

Consider a situation in which you sometimes experience negative thinking. It could be negative thinking about your future, about a social relationship, about work, about your performance in a university course, and so on. In a sentence, describe the general theme around which negative thinking occurs. Then write out ten different types of thoughts (these could be self-statements, images, or a mixture of the two) that you experience when thinking negatively on that particular topic or theme. Next, for each negative thought, describe an alternative positive thought or coping self-statement that you might practice to counteract the negative thought. Your coping thoughts should be *realistic*, *positive*, and *specific*, and should relate to specific positive *outcomes*.

NOTES AND EXTENDED DISCUSSION

1. A number of behavioral techniques rely on imagery. In Chapter 25, we described how Wolpe used imagery in systematic desensitization. Another procedure involving imagery is called *covert sensitization* (Cautella, 1966), which is essentially a form of aversion therapy (see Chapter 15) in which an undesirable reinforcer is paired repeatedly with an aversive event. You will recall that aversion therapy is based on counterconditioning—it is assumed that the undesirable reinforcer will become less reinforcing because it will come to elicit a response similar to that elicited by the aversive stimulus. In covert sensitization, the client imagines both the undesirable reinforcer and the aversive stimulus. This procedure is so named because the pairing of the stimuli occurs only in the client's imagination (in other words, it is *covert*) and the anticipated result of this covert pairing process is that the undesirable reinforcer becomes aversive (i.e., the client becomes sensitized to it). The procedure has been used with clients who wish to give up smoking (as described by Irey, 1972). During a particular trial, the client might be instructed to vividly imagine lighting a cigarette after dinner in a restaurant, inhaling, and then suddenly becoming so violently ill that he vomits all over his hands, his clothes, the tablecloth, and the other people at the table. He continues to vomit and then, when his stomach is empty, to gag while the other people in the restaurant stare at him in disgust. In short, the scene is made extremely realistic and aversive. When the maximum degree of aversiveness is felt, the client is instructed to imagine turning away from his cigarette and immediately beginning to feel better. The scene concludes with the client washing up in the bathroom, without his cigarettes, and feeling tremendous relief. Research on covert sensitization can be found in Cautela and Kearney (1986).

2. Carol was practicing a procedure referred to as *thought stopping* (Wolpe, 1958), which is used in cases in which a person engages in persistent, obsessive private verbal behavior that he or she cannot seem to control. The procedure involves, first, instructing the client to think the obsessive thought (such as Carol's thoughts about Fred). The therapist then suddenly yells "Stop!" Immediately, according to anecdotal clinical reports, the undesirable private verbal behavior ceases. After a few such trials to demonstrate the effectiveness of the procedure, the client is instructed to yell "Stop!" while engaging in the undesirable private behavior. Again, the behavior ceases. Over trials, the self-instruction "Stop!" is faded to the private level so that eventually the client can turn off the undesirable private behavior simply by "yelling" "Stop!" silently to him- or herself. Thought stopping is most effective if it is followed immediately by desirable alternative thoughts (Wolpe, 1990), as illustrated in Carol's case. Although there have been a number of reports of successful applications of thought stopping, most of these have involved only a few clients and the use of other procedures that may actually have been responsible for the improvement. Thus, the evidence for the effectiveness of thought stopping is, at present, weak (J. C. Masters et al., 1987).

Study Questions on Notes

1. What is the rationale of covert sensitization?
2. Describe in some detail a plausible example of covert sensitization.
3. Describe the steps that a therapist might follow in teaching a client to practice thought stopping.

Areas of Clinical
Behavior Therapy

As indicated in Chapter 2, behavior modification is being used increasingly in the treatment of clinical disorders. In this chapter we give a brief overview of ways in which the principles and techniques described in the preceding chapters are being applied to treat some of the most frequently encountered adult psychological disorders. Our intention here is not to teach you how to actually treat these disorders yourself, nor to provide an exhaustive review of behavioral treatments of them. Rather, our intention is to give you a brief introduction to the major areas in the field of clinical behavior modification and to indicate how some principles and techniques are being applied in these areas. When warranted by the data, we identify the treatment of choice for each disorder.

The disorders to be discussed here receive more detailed coverage in several excellent books (e.g., Bellack et al., 1990, Last & Hersen, 1993; Turner et al., 1992; Van Hasseldt & Hersen, 1996), and the reader interested in more specific information concerning these disorders and their treatment is referred to those texts.

ANXIETY DISORDERS: FOCUS ON AGORAPHOBIA

The DSM IV (1994) lists 13 different types of anxiety disorders. In Chapter 25 we briefly described the characteristics of three such disorders—specific phobias, social phobias, and panic disorders. One of the most debilitating anxiety disorders is **agoraphobia.**

The DSM IV (American Psychiatric Association, 1994) distinguishes between agoraphobia in connection with panic disorder and agoraphobia without a history of panic attacks. Agoraphobia connected with panic disorder is characterized by an intense fear of being in public places from which escape might be difficult or help unavailable if the person suddenly experiences a panic attack. In agoraphobia without panic disorder, there is a fear of suddenly behaving in a way that causes embarrassment or requires help, such as fear of becoming dizzy and losing balance, becoming ill and vomiting, or losing bladder or bowel control in public. In both types of agoraphobia, the individual's fears prevent him or her from going out for any purpose, at least if not accompanied by someone whom he or she trusts. This leads to increasing constriction of the individual's normal activities, thus preventing the performance of daily routines that most of us consider necessary—going to work, grocery shopping, and so forth.

Treatment

The treatment of choice for agoraphobia is *in vivo* exposure to the feared stimuli (Bouman & Emmelkamp, 1996; Craske, 1993). Sessions with prolonged exposure (2 to 4 hours) to the feared stimuli are generally more effective than sessions with brief exposure (half-hour sessions). Most studies that compared *in vivo* exposure to imaginal (as in systematic desensitization) exposure found the *in vivo* procedure to be superior. Exceptions to this were studies in which the imaginal procedure also involved *in vivo* exposure homework assignments. Studies have also found that group exposure is about equally effective as individually conducted exposure programs, and that positive results have been obtained when treatment was guided by a self-help book or a computer (with minimal therapist contact).

   Several studies have examined cognitive restructuring techniques (see Chapter 26) in the treatment of agoraphobia. In general, cognitive restructuring by itself is not an effective treatment for agoraphobia, and the addition of cognitive restructuring strategies to *in vivo* exposure does not appear to improve the results obtained with *in vivo* exposure alone (Bouman & Emmelkamp, 1996; Craske, 1993).

OBSESSIVE-COMPULSIVE DISORDERS

According to the DSM IV (American Psychiatric Association, 1994), an **obsessive-compulsive** disorder is one in which the client experiences either repetitive thoughts, images, or impulses (called *obsessions*) or repetitive overt actions (called *compulsions*) that are severe enough to be time consuming (i.e., they take more than 1 hour a day) or cause marked distress or significant impairment. Some behavior modifiers distinguish between obsessions and compulsions on the basis of their functions, with *obsessions* defined as thoughts, images, or impulses that generate anxiety or distress, and *compulsions* defined as behaviors performed to alleviate the distress brought on by the obsessions (Kozak & Foa, 1996).

Treatment

The most common treatment for obsessive-compulsive disorders is *in vivo* exposure and response prevention (Steketee, 1993). Studies have found a 65% to 75% success rate when clients receive repeated, prolonged (45 minutes to 2 hours) confrontation with stimuli that elicit the obsessive behavior (followed by anxiety), while being instructed not to engage in compulsive rituals, despite strong urges to do so (Kozak & Foa, 1996). Suppose that a client experiences obsessive thoughts about germs when touching unwashed objects, which causes considerable anxiety. Suppose further that engaging in a variety of compulsive washing rituals appears to be maintained by anxiety reduction. An exposure and response prevention treatment would involve requesting the client to touch particular "contaminated" objects while refraining from performing the washing ritual. Presumably this would eventually lead to extinction of the contaminated objects and thoughts of germs as conditional stimuli for anxiety.

As is the case with agoraphobia, *in vivo* exposure to the anxiety-evoking situations has been found to be superior to imaginal exposure. If the obsessive thoughts concern catastrophes (e.g., death, fire) that cannot be presented *in vivo*, however, those thoughts can be confronted through imagined exposure (Kozak & Foa, 1996). A meta-analysis suggests further that: (a) the combination of *in vivo* and imaginal exposure is superior to *in vivo* exposure alone; and (b) exposure directed by a therapist is more effective than leaving exposure totally under the control of the client (Abramowitz, 1996).

Regarding cognitive restructuring treatments for obsessive-compulsive behaviors, the addition of cognitive components to exposure and response prevention does not improve results obtained with exposure and response prevention alone (Kozak & Foa, 1996; Steketee, 1993). Also, although different studies have found different results, the combination of drugs and behavior therapy has shown little advantage over behavior therapy alone (Kozak & Foa, 1996).

FAILURE TO COPE WITH STRESS

All of us experience many stressful events throughout the course of a day, a week, or a month. For example, taking an exam, interviewing for a job, or simply driving to work are at least somewhat stressful for most of us. Some circumstances are more stressful than others, including being involved in military combat or a natural catastrophe such as an earthquake. Most people cope with ordinary and even large amounts of stress in an effective manner; however, some individuals are quite debilitated by stress, either because the stressful events in their lives are too intense or numerous, or because they are unable to cope with more ordinary types of stressful events. It appears that such individuals can benefit from behavioral treatments for managing stress; and, indeed, even individuals who cope adequately with stressful events can probably benefit from training in stress management (Martin & Osborne, 1993).

Treatment

Rosenthal and Rosenthal (1985) have developed a comprehensive approach to treating stress that incorporates many principles and procedures of behavior modification. For example, they teach their clients to relax when encountering stressful situations. The relaxation methods they teach include yoga and transcendental meditation, as well as Jacobson's (1938) progressive muscle relaxation described in Chapter 25. They also encourage their clients to establish a daily physical exercise regimen, because a healthy, well-developed body enables one to resist more effectively the physical effects of stressful situations. They provide assertion training to help their clients manage maladaptive anger. In addition, they use cognitive behavior modification to alter client verbalizations that often produce or exacerbate stressful situations.

DEPRESSION

Everyone has probably experienced depression at some point in his or her life. Typically, it occurs as a result of the loss of an important source of reinforcement in one's life; for example, a job, a love affair, or a loved one. The depression usually lifts after a while, as other sources of reinforcement become available. Some individuals remain depressed most of the time, however, often for no apparent external reason. Because this causes suffering and can be quite debilitating, such individuals require treatment.

Treatment

During the 1970s and 1980s, cognitive therapy was increasingly used as a treatment for depression. Some researchers went so far as to conclude that Beck's cognitive therapy was the treatment of choice for depression (e.g., Dobson, 1989). As indicated in Chapter 26, however, in 1989 the NIMH Treatment of Depression Collaborative Study came to a different conclusion. That research indicated that Beck's cognitive therapy was no more effective than a placebo control condition in the treatment of severe depression. In 1993, the Depression Guideline Panel of the U.S. Public Health Service Agency for Health Care Policy and Research published its findings on outpatient treatment of persons suffering from mild to moderate depression. On the basis of meta-analyses of published randomized control trials, overall efficacy was found to be 46.6 percent for cognitive restructuring versus 55.3 percent for behavior therapy that included activity scheduling, self-control therapy, social skills training, and problem-solving training.

The occurrence of additive effects when cognitive behavioral therapy is combined with drugs is also being questioned. Research conducted in the 1980s led behavior therapist Stewart Agras (1987, p. 209) to conclude that, "In the case of depression, the preferred treatment would be a combination of cognitive behavior therapy and an anti-depressant" drug. Subsequently, however, Bellack and Hersen (1993b) concluded that studies have not consistently supported the supposed superiority of combined drug treatment and cognitive behavior therapy over either alone.

Showing more promise in the treatment of depression is the role of exercise. Summarizing 13 studies on this topic, Tkachuk and Martin (1997) concluded that as little as six weeks of thrice-weekly supervised exercise sessions of aerobic (walk/run) or nonaerobic exercise activity of low to moderate intensity lasting from 30 to 60 minutes, can bring about significant improvements in clinically depressed individuals. The studies found exercise to be more effective than placebo control conditions and no-treatment conditions, and to compare favorably with individual psychotherapy, group psychotherapy, and cognitive therapy. In addition, follow-up assessments have indicated that treatment gains can be maintained for up to one year, particularly if some level of regular activity is continued. Most notably, exercise therapy has proven to be four to five times more cost-effective than traditional treatments for depression.

Until research convincingly demonstrates the effectiveness and ineffectiveness of various treatments for depression, many practitioners treating this disorder are likely to include most of the following cognitive and behavioral techniques.

Evoking and Testing Automatic Thoughts   The therapist and client jointly try to determine the thoughts that precede such emotions as anger, sadness, and anxiety by attempting to elicit these emotions or having the client recall or imagine situations that elicited them. The client is then encouraged to operationally define and test the validity of the automatic thoughts through a process called *reality checking* or *hypothesis testing*. For example, a client who has the automatic thought "I'm a failure in math" may define failure as "being unable to obtain a grade of 'C' after studying as long and hard as the average student." Thus, if the client does the indicated amount of study and receives a "C" or better, the automatic thought is proved wrong.

Identifying and Testing Maladaptive Assumptions   A maladaptive assumption is more general than an automatic thought and is usually not verbalized. Some examples are "In order to be happy, I must have a wife" and "I'm nobody if I don't have a job." Maladaptive assumptions can be tested by having the client examine their logic or gather evidence against the assumption, among various other ways.

Scheduling of Activities   The client is provided with homework assignments to increase his or her mastery of various activities and to engage in a daily and weekly schedule of rewarding activities. If necessary, the therapist subdivides the activity into graduated segments that the client can readily perform. As we have seen, research indicates that it would probably be effective to help the client schedule in an exercise program along with his or her other activities.

Cognitive Rehearsal   The client pictures or imagines each step involved in the completion of a particular task.

Self-Reliance and Problem-Solving Training   Depressed individuals frequently neglect even such routine tasks as showering or bathing, bedmaking, housecleaning, cooking, and shopping. In such cases, homework assignments are directed toward reestablishing these behaviors.

Skills Training   The client receives social skills training when there are social skills deficits, job-seeking training when there is unemployment-related depression, and study skills training when there is academic difficulty.

Role Playing and Role Reversal   By acting out their roles (role playing) in various situations, clients learn appropriate overt behavior, automatic thoughts, and emotional behavior in those situations. By acting out the role of others responding to them (role reversal), clients can test out their automatic thoughts concerning how others see them, which can cause clients to make less severe judgments about themselves. For example, a client who believed that store clerks thought she was inept, changed this negative view of herself when she played the role of a salesclerk waiting on her.

Diversion Techniques   Clients are taught to engage in various behaviors, such as physical, social, play, and work activities, that compete with negative self-thoughts.

ALCOHOL PROBLEMS

Excessive alcohol drinking is a major health problem in America, one that costs the economy billions of dollars each year in poor job performance and absenteeism (Feist & Brannon, 1988). Although there is considerable disagreement in the alcohol treatment field concerning definitional questions, most agencies identify three groups: nonproblem drinkers, problem drinkers, and alcoholics (e.g., see National Institute on Alcohol Abuse and Alcoholism, 1990). Definitions are further complicated by the DSM-IV, which distinguishes between substance abuse and substance dependence. Problem drinkers would likely be diagnosed as showing substance abuse—recurrent use of a substance within a 12-month period that contributes to a social, occupational, or physical problem. Alcoholics would likely be diagnosed as showing substance dependence—substance abuse combined with increased tolerance for the substance (more of it is needed to produce the usual effect) and the occurrence of withdrawal symptoms when use of the substance is stopped or delayed. Behavioral treatment procedures have been quite useful for helping problem drinkers but have shown only modest success with alcoholics.

Treatment

Behavioral treatment procedures have been quite successful in helping problem drinkers to learn to drink in moderation (Sobell, & Sobell, 1993). A program developed by Sobell and Sobell (1993) teaches problem drinkers to use goal setting to drink in moderation, to control "triggers" (S^Ds) for drinking, to learn problem-solving skills to avoid high-risk situations, to engage in self-monitoring to detect controlling cues and maintaining consequences of drinking behaviors, and to practice all of these techniques with various homework assignments.

Even though behavioral treatment programs for alcoholics have achieved only modest success, the most effective programs have utilized a number of components, including: (a) strategies (such as aversive conditioning described in Chapter 15) to decrease the reinforcing properties of alcohol; (b) programs to teach alcoholics new skills to take the place of alcohol abuse, such as social skills to deal with social situations (as opposed to getting drunk to "have a good time"); (c) strategies to prevent relapses (see Chapter 24); and (d) contingency management to provide reinforcers for work, social, and recreational activities that do not involve alcohol. Even with such multiple-component programs, success rates across studies vary tremendously. They are influenced by an individual's socioeconomic status, the availability of a regular job, the presence or absence of an intact family, and the circle of friends of the alcoholic. Those whose environments contained considerable additional support showed recovery rates as high as 68%, whereas those without such support showed success rates of approximately 18% or less (Feist & Brannon, 1988; Meyers & Smith, 1995; Sobell et al., 1990).

OBESITY

Approximately a quarter of American adults are at least 20% above desirable weight (Kuczmarski, 1992). It is considered a problem not merely because it detracts from one's physical appearance according to the standards of our culture, but also because the obese individual is at increased risk for serious health problems. The causes of obesity are complex and not well understood. Although many behaviorists once believed that obesity was the result of reinforcement for overeating, it now appears that physiological factors are involved in many cases of obesity (Keesey & Powley, 1986; Zeman, 1991).

    Regardless of the causes of obesity, it appears that in many cases it can be treated effectively with behavioral methods.   **Note 1**

Treatment

Contemporary behavioral treatment strategies for obesity do not endorse crash diets and rapid weight loss. Instead, they focus on helping obese individuals to adopt long-term lifestyle changes in eating habits and exercise, and in their attitudes toward both (Friedman & Brownell, 1996). Clients are encouraged to gradually switch to low calorie, low fat diets that meet daily nutritional requirements, and to adopt regular and sensible exercise programs. There is also a focus on long-term strategies to prevent relapse (such as those discussed in Chapter 24). Behavioral components in such programs include the following (Brownell & Fairburn, 1995; LeBow, 1991).

Self-Monitoring Clients keep daily records of the foods they eat and their caloric contents. They keep charts of their daily caloric intake and their body weight. The charts are posted in a conspicuous place in the home (see Chapter 18), and the client brings his or her records and data to therapy sessions for discussion with the therapist.

Stimulus Control Clients restrict their at-home eating to a specific location, so that only the stimuli present in that location (e.g., the kitchen table) control eating behavior (see Chapter 8).

Changing Eating Behavior Eating rate is reduced by having clients lay down utensils between bites, drink water during the meal, or take short breaks between courses (see Chapter 7).

Behavioral Contracts Clients sign a contract in which they agree to lose a certain amount of weight in a specified period of time (e.g., 1 to 2 pounds each week), in return for which they receive money or some other desired item that they have given up for this purpose (see Chapter 24).

MARITAL DISTRESS

Simply put, marital distress can be said to be present when couples in relationships have a low ratio of positive to negative interactions. The goal of behavioral marital therapy, therefore, is to increase the rate of positive interactions and decrease the rate of negative interactions (see Figure 27–1).

Treatment

Behavioral marital therapy typically proceeds according to the following stages (Sayers, Baucom, & Rankin, 1993; L. F. Wood & Jacobson, 1985).

Instigation of Positive Exchanges Each individual is asked to increase behaviors that are pleasing to the other partner, especially those classes of behavior (such as displaying affection, showing respect, expressing appreciation, etc.) that correlate highly with measures of marital satisfaction (Weiss & Halford, 1996).

Communication Training Each individual is taught to express thoughts and feelings concerning what is liked and appreciated about the other, to help the other express his or her feelings, and to be an effective listener. Beck (1988) has described how automatic thoughts and maladaptive assumptions can be involved in many types of communication problems in relationships and has recommended treating these problems with cognitive therapy (see Chapter 26).

Problem-Solving Training Clients learn to use their communication skills to systematically identify and solve problems and conflicts in their relationship. They are taught to clearly define and agree upon the problem to be solved, generate solutions, select a preferred solution that they both agree upon, and to evaluate the solution during a trial period.

Figure 27–1 What behavioral strategies might be used to help couples increase their rate of positive interactions and decrease their rate of negative interactions with each other?

Generality   There are three main components to obtaining generality of the effects of treatment: (a) Clients learn to monitor their relationship for specific critical signs of a relapse; (b) clients are encouraged to continue using the problem-solving and conflict resolution techniques that they learned in therapy; and (c) input from the therapist is decreased gradually rather than terminated abruptly.

SEXUAL DYSFUNCTION: FOCUS ON LOW SEXUAL DESIRE

Behavioral treatment of sexual dysfunctions began in the late 1950s (Semans, 1956; Wolpe, 1958). Lack of excitement and failure to obtain orgasm are two types of sexual dysfunctions that have been treated successfully with behavioral methods. After ascertaining that the problem does not have a physical cause, the therapist typically conceptualizes it as being due to conditioned anxiety responses to the sexual situation. Most of these cases respond extremely well to graduated *in vivo* exposure (W. H. Masters & Johnson, 1970). Therapists are now beginning to encounter problems that are more difficult to treat, however, and that require a combination of techniques (McConaghy, 1996). A notable example is that of low or inhibited sexual desire, which is increasingly being reported in men as well as women (LoPiccolo, 1990).

Treatment

LoPiccollo and Friedman (1988) described a model for treating inhibited sexual desire that integrates four therapeutic components.

Experiential/Sensory Awareness Exercises   These are exercises that are used to help clients verbalize unacknowledged feelings about sex (e.g., anxiety, anger, or disgust).

Insight   The client is helped to identify correctly, or at least to not misidentify, the variables responsible for his or her problem.

Cognitive Behavior Modification   The client is taught to alter irrational thoughts that inhibit his or her sexual desire.

Behavioral Assignments   As the effects of the above variables are decreased, the client receives behavioral assignments that involve mainly *in vivo* exposure.

HABIT DISORDERS: NERVOUS HABITS, MUSCLE TICS, AND STUTTERING

Many people experience a type of nervous habit, such as nail biting, knuckle cracking, lip biting, hair twirling, etc.). In many cases, these would not be considered a disorder. However, if the frequency or intensity of the habit becomes so extreme that the individual seeks treatment for it, then the behavior would be referred to as a habit disorder (Hansen, Tishelman, Hawkins, & Doepke, 1990). Note that the definition of a habit disorder is similar to the definition of compulsive behavior (described previously). A major difference is that habit disorders do not appear to be linked to various obsessive thoughts.

Woods, Miltenberger, and Flach (1996) determined that most nervous habits were likely to occur when the individual experienced heightened nervous tension. They hypothesized that the habits may have served to diminish the nervous tension experienced by the individual, and therefore be maintained by escape conditioning.

Another type of nervous habit that may become a disorder is referred to as a tic. These can include muscle tics (repetitive, jerking movements of parts of the face, neck, or other muscle groups) or vocal tics (such as excessive throat clearing). Tics are also believed to be associated with tension, and may serve to relieve the tension (Evers & Van De Wetering, 1994). Excessive stuttering is also considered to be a habit disorder.

Azrin and Nunn (1973) developed a method called *habit reversal* to treat habit disorders, and research has indicated that habit reversal is an effective treatment for nervous habits, tics, and stuttering (Woods & Miltenberger, 1995, 1996). Habit reversal includes a number of components which fall into one of three main categories (Woods & Miltenberger, 1995). The first category is *awareness training*, in which the client learns to describe the specific characteristics of the problem behavior, deliberately performs and describes the behavior in front of a mirror, and identifies the specific situations in which the behavior occurs. The second category is *competing response training*, which involves practicing a response that competes with (i.e., is incompatible with) the nervous habit, or tic, or stuttering behavior. For example, to correct "shoulder jerking," a client would be instructed to contract his or her shoulders by depressing the shoulders down as far as they will go while keeping the arms close to the body; to correct "wrist tic," a client would be instructed to "push hands on arms of chairs, desk, leg, and so on, and contract the muscles so that hands are pushing opposite the tic movement (i.e., contract hands down if the wrist jerks upward)" (Azrin, Nunn, & Frantz, 1980, p. 174). The competing reactions are practiced daily in front of a mirror at home, and also performed immediately after the occurrence of the tic movement, or just before it is likely to occur. The third category is a *motivational strategy*, which includes reviewing the inconvenience caused by the habit disorder, having a family member present for social support during treatment, and recording and graphing the daily number of episodes of the habit behavior.

STUDY QUESTIONS

1. List nine frequently encountered adult psychological disorders.
2. Define *agoraphobia*.
3. What is the treatment of choice for agoraphobia? What variations of treatment for agoraphobia are effective?
4. What are *obsessive-compulsive disorders*? What is the distinction between *obsessive* and *compulsive*, and how might they be related?
5. What is the most common treatment for obsessive- compulsive disorders? What may account for the effectiveness of this treatment?

6. Briefly describe Rosenthal and Rosenthal's approach to treating stress.
7. Is exercise an effective treatment for depression? Justify your answer.
8. Briefly describe eight cognitive and behavioral components that are likely to be included in the treatment of depression.
9. Distinguish between *problem drinkers* and *alchoholics*.
10. What are the components of Sobell & Sobell's program to help problem drinkers?
11. What are the components of successful programs for alchoholics? How sucessful are they?
12. List and briefly describe the major behavioral components of contemporary strategies for treating obesity.
13. List and briefly describe the stages according to which behavioral maritial therapy typically proceeds.
14. List and briefly describe the four therapeutic components of LoPiccollo and Friedman's model for treating inhibited sexual desire.
15. What is a habit disorder? Describe several examples.
16. Describe the three main categories of treatment components for treating habit disorder.

NOTE AND EXTENDED DISCUSSION

1. Agras, Taylor, Feldman, Losch, and Burnett (1990) studied the use of a hand-held computer in the treatment of obesity. The computer contained a number of functions. In addition to prompting the client to set daily caloric intake and exercise goals and providing feedback on his or her success in achieving the goal each day, the computer contained a function for planning meals; a trainer to promote slow eating; a message function for providing motivating and reinforcing statements at appropriate times; and a graphic function that plotted daily caloric intake, amount of exercise, and weight over a 2-week "moving-window" period. The experimenters found that a group that used the computer without additional therapy or group support lost as much weight as did a group that used the computer with group support and a group that did not use the computer and received therapy. Although the weight loss in all three groups was modest, the results suggest that computer therapy holds promise for the future, given the development of more sophisticated computers and more effective computer therapy programs.

Study Questions on Notes

1. Describe the functioning of a hand-held computer used for the treatment of obesity. How effective has this computer been shown to be?

Part VI A Historical Perspective and Ethical Issues

Giving It All
Some Perspective:
A Brief History

This chapter traces some of the highlights of the remarkable early growth of the field of behavior modification. It should be read with the following qualifications in mind:

1. Although we describe behavior modification as developing primarily through two major and separate lines of influence, there are obvious cross influences, blends, and offshoots, and it might be possible to make a case for somewhat different histories.
2. We identify what we consider to be major highlights of the development of behavior modification during its formative years: the 1950s, 1960s, and 1970s; we do not attempt a complete historical account.
3. We describe mainly historical highlights in North America.

In this history, we first consider two major orientations or traditions: one that emphasized operant conditioning and one that emphasized respondent conditioning. Then we discuss mixtures of these with other orientations.

THE OPERANT-CONDITIONING ORIENTATION:
APPLIED BEHAVIOR ANALYSIS

In 1938, B. F. Skinner published *The Behavior of Organisms*, in which he described the results of experiments on the lever-pressing behavior of rats for food or water reinforcement and, on the basis of his findings, outlined the basic principles of

Note 1
Note 2

Note 3

operant conditioning, which he clearly distinguished from respondent conditioning. This pioneering work gradually influenced other experimental psychologists to begin studying the effects of contingencies of reinforcement on the behavior of rats and other animals.

In 1950, Keller and Schoenfeld wrote an introductory psychology text titled *Principles of Psychology*. It was unlike any other text of its kind in that it discussed traditional topics in psychology primarily in terms of operant conditioning (and to a lesser extent, respondent conditioning) principles. Keller and Skinner had been graduate students together at Harvard University, and the Keller and Schoenfeld text was inspired largely by the work and writings of Skinner. *Principles of Psychology* contributed significantly to the development of the field of behavior analysis. Although less well known outside Skinnerian and operant circles, this introductory text had an important impact within the operant tradition.   **Note 4**

In 1953 Skinner published *Science and Human Behavior*. In this book he offered his interpretation of how the basic behavior principles (which had been researched on lower organisms and are described in Part II of this text) influence the behavior of people in all kinds of everyday situations. Although little supporting data existed for Skinner's generalizations to humans, his interpretations influenced others to begin examining the effects of reinforcement variables on human behavior in a number of experimental and applied settings. The results of these efforts led to much of what has been described in this text as behavior modification. The highlights of this development prior to the 1980s are presented in the top panel of Table 28–1. (See Chapters 2 and 27 for a discussion of developments in behavior modification since 1980.)

Many of the reports in the 1950s were demonstrations that positive reinforcement and extinction affect human behavior in predictable ways and/or case demonstrations that an application of a behavioral program could effect a desired behavior change. For example, Fuller (1949) reported that an institutional, bedridden, profoundly retarded adult could be taught to raise his right arm to a vertical position when arm movements were appropriately shaped and a warm sugar-milk solution was used as the reinforcer. Greenspoon (1955) demonstrated that a simple social consequence (saying "mmm-hmm") could influence college students to say certain types of words (see Note 3 in Chapter 3). Azrin and Lindsley (1956), two of Skinner's graduate students, demonstrated that jellybean reinforcement could influence pairs of young children to cooperate in playing a simple game. Each of these experiments demonstrated that consequences influence human behavior in predictable ways. None of these experiments, however, was primarily practically oriented. One of the first published reports of the 1950s that concerned practical, applied problems was that of Ayllon and Michael (1959). With Michael as his Ph.D. dissertation advisor, Ayllon conducted a number of behavioral demonstrations at the Saskatchewan Hospital, a psychiatric institution in Weyburn, Saskatchewan. These demonstrations showed how staff could use procedures such as reinforcement, extinction, and escape and avoidance conditioning to modify patient behaviors such as delusional talk, refusals to eat, and various disruptive behaviors.

Following Ayllon and Michael's article and several subsequent papers published by Ayllon and his colleagues from their work at Weyburn, similar demon-

TABLE 28–1   SOME HISTORICAL HIGHLIGHTS OF BEHAVIOR
MODIFICATION AND BEHAVIOR THERAPY PRIOR TO 1980

	Pre-1950s	1950s	Early and middle 1960s
OPERANT-CONDITIONING (SKINNERIAN) ORIENTATION	Some basic research and theory (Skinner, 1938)	Two major texts (Keller & Schoenfeld, 1950; Skinner, 1953) Some human studies and applications: profoundly retarded (Fuller, 1949), schizophrenics (Lindsley, 1956), psychotics (Ayllon & Michael, 1959), verbal conditioning (Greenspoon, 1955), stuttering (B. Flanagan, Goldiamond, & Azrin, 1958) A basic operant research journal, with some applications (*Journal of the Experimental Analysis of Behavior*, 1958–)	Some major university training centers Several books of readings (e.g., Ulrich, Stachnik, & Mabry, 1966) More applications, many to "resistant" populations: e.g., retardation (Birnbrauer, Bijou, Wolf, & Kidder, 1965; Girardeau & Spradin, 1964), autism (Ferster & DeMyer, 1962; Lovaas, 1966; Wolf, Risley, & Mees, 1964), hyperactivity (Patterson, 1965), delinquency (Schwitzgebel, 1964), psychotics (Isaacs, Thomas, & Goldiamond, 1960; Haughton & Ayllon, 1965) Child development (Bijou & Baer, 1961)
OFFSHOOTS AND MIXTURES			Premack Principle (Premack, 1965) Coverant control (Homme, 1965) Precision teaching (Lindsley, 1966) Modeling (Bandura & Walters, 1963) A major book of readings (Ullmann & Krasner, 1965), An applied journal (*Behavior Research and Therapy*, 1963–) Covert sensitization (Cautela, 1966)
RESPONDENT-CONDITIONING (AND HULLIAN AND WOLPEAN) ORIENTATION	Some basic research and theory (Pavlov, 1927; J. B. Watson & Rayner, 1920) An early application of fear desensitization (M. C. Jones, 1924) An early application of assertion training (Salter, 1949)	Two major texts (Dollard & Miller, 1950; Wolpe, 1958) Applications of systematic desensitization, assertion training, and aversion therapy to a variety of phobias and behavioral excesses Comparisons of behavior therapy and psychotherapy (Eysenck, 1959)	Some major university training centers Several books of readings (e.g., Eysenck, 1960; Franks, 1964) More applications of systematic desensitization, assertion training, and aversion therapy to a variety of classic neurotic behaviors and sexual disorders

(continued)

strations of behavioral control began to appear with some frequency in the early 1960s (see Table 28–1). This early work was characterized by two features: (a) Much of it was done with very resistant populations (such as developmentally disabled persons, autistic children, and severely regressed psychiatric patients) who had not received a great deal of successful input from traditional psychology, and (b) many of the applications took place in institutional or highly controlled settings. A notable exception to this early trend is Bijou and Baer's (1961) interpretation of child development from a strictly behavioral perspective.

TABLE 28–1   *(CONTINUED)*

Late 1960s	1970s
Additional major university training centers Isolated undergraduate and graduate courses in many universities Additional books describing applied research and procedures applicable to a variety of areas: e.g., education (Skinner, 1968), parenting (G. R. Patterson & Gullion, 1968), community work (Tharp & Wetzel, 1969), mental hospitals (Schaefer & Martin, 1969) Additional applications to a variety of areas, including self-control, delinquency, university teaching, marriage counseling, sexual behaviors, and academic skills An applied journal (*Journal of Applied Behavior Analysis,* 1968–)	Many "how-to-do-it" books in a variety of areas Behavior modification procedures described for many "traditional" areas of psychology (e.g., social, developmental, personality, abnormal, and clinical) Many other helping professions adopting behavior modification procedures (see Chapter 2) Wide variety of individual, institutional, and community applications and research
Token economies (Ayllon & Azrin, 1968b) Contingency contracting (Homme, Csanyi, Gonzales, & Rechs, 1969) Formulation of social learning theory (Bandura, 1969) Two major books (Bandura, 1969; Franks, 1969) Implosive therapy (Stampfl & Levis, 1967)	Emergence of cognitive behavior modification, social learning theory, and eclectic behavior therapy Numerous behavior modification–behavior therapy conferences and workshops Concern for behavior modification–behavior therapy as a profession, and for controls against misapplications Mixed paraprofessional and professional organizations (e.g., Association for Behavior Analysis, 1974–) Professional organizations (Association for the Advancement of Behavior Therapy, 1970–; Behavior Research and Therapy Society, 1970–; European Association of Behavior Therapy, 1971–) More journals specializing in behavior modification (see Note 2 in Chapter 2)
Several major university training centers Additional books (e.g., Wolpe, 1969) More applications to phobias, anger, asthmatic attacks, frigidity, homosexuality, insomnia, speech disorders, exhibitionism, and other behaviors	Many additional books, publications and training workshops; much additional research

In 1965, Ullmann and Krasner published their influential collection of readings, *Case Studies in Behavior Modification* (see the "offshoots and mixtures" panel in Table 28–1). This appears to be the first book with "behavior modification" in its title. In addition to collecting a number of case histories and research reports by other authors, Ullmann and Krasner compared behavior modification and the behavioral model with more traditional psychotherapeutic strategies and the medical model. Although their book is not solely in the operant tradition, because they also included many studies and discussions in the Pavlovian-Hullian tradition (to be discussed in the next section of this chapter), it undoubtedly had a significant impact on furthering behavior modification and providing, in one source, information on much of the preliminary work in this area.

In the late 1960s, the operant-conditioning orientation began to spread throughout the Western Hemisphere. Several university training centers were developed; many universities initiated at least one or two courses in behavior modification at both the graduate and undergraduate levels; and applications spread to normal school settings, to university teaching, to homes, and to other populations and locations.

By the 1970s, the operant orientation had grown considerably. This approach is frequently referred to as *applied behavior analysis*. It is somewhat surprising to find contemporary textbooks that suggest that this approach has been used primarily on client populations with "limited cognitive capacity" and where considerable environmental control is a potential characteristic of the treatment procedures. Although this was true in the 1950s and 1960s, numerous applications now occur in virtually all walks of life (see Chapters 2 and 27).

It has also been claimed that behavior analysts ignore the causes of problem behavior. In the early stages of behavior modification, there was some justification for the charge, for behavior analysts were emphasizing how managing consequences (e.g., powerful reinforcement contingencies) could alleviate problem behavior regardless of its causes. During the 1970s, however, some behavior analysts (e.g., Carr, 1977; W. L. Johnson & Baumeister, 1978; Rincover, 1978; Rincover, Cook, Peoples, & Packard, 1979) began to stress the importance of understanding the causes of—that is, the conditions producing or maintaining—problem behavior. This led to the pioneering of functional analysis methodology by Iwata, Dorsey, Slifer, Bauman, and Richman (1982), which a number of prominent behavior analysts hailed as a major new development in the field (e.g., Laties & Mace, 1993). In 1994, the *Journal of Applied Behavior Analysis* published a special issue (Vol. 27, No. 2) devoted to functional analysis approaches to behavioral assessment and treatment. It should be noted, however, that the causes functional analysis attempts to uncover are environmental causes, not the hypothetical inner causes that are often speculated about by nonbehavioral (e.g., psychoanalytic) approaches.

THE RESPONDENT-CONDITIONING (AND HULLIAN AND WOLPEAN) ORIENTATION

Late in the 19th century, the Russian physiologist I. P. Pavlov conducted experiments on digestion, which won him the Nobel Prize in Medicine in 1904. While doing this research, Pavlov discovered that stimuli paired with food will also elicit salivation, and embarked on a systematic study of what is now called *Pavlovian, classical,* or *respondent conditioning* (see Chapter 15). Results of this work were published in a classic book titled *Conditioned Reflexes* (Pavlov, 1927). In 1913, John B. Watson published an influential paper in which he argued that most human activities could be explained as learned habits. After becoming familiar with the work of Pavlov (and another Russian physiologist, I. Bechterev), J. B. Watson (1916) adopted the conditioned reflex as the unit of habit and argued that most complex activities were due to respondent conditioning (this, of course, was before Skinner distinguished between operant and respondent conditioning). At that time, some of his extreme and unsupported generalizations shook the foundations of much of traditional psychology. Watson followed his 1916 paper with a classic experiment in which he demonstrated that human emotional reactions could be conditioned in an experimental setting (J. B. Watson & Rayner, 1920; see Chapter 15 of this text).

During the next 20 years a number of somewhat isolated reports of the application of respondent-conditioning procedures to various behaviors appeared in the literature (for a list of many of these, see Yates, 1970). None of these applications, however, appears to have had any sustained impact on the development of behavior modification as we know it today.

Another influence closely related to the respondent-conditioning orientation was the work of the American learning theorist Clark Hull (1943, 1952). Hull, an early contemporary of Skinner, developed a "learning theory" that tended to capitalize on both operant conditioning as described by Skinner and respondent conditioning as described by Pavlov, meshed together in a theory that did not distinguish between the two types of conditioning. According to Hull, reinforcement was involved in Pavlovian as well as in operant conditioning. Hull did not attempt to interpret a wide variety of human behavior to the extent that Skinner did (compare Hull, 1952, with Skinner, 1953). Two other psychologists, Dollard and Miller (1950), however, translated a variety of Freudian psychodynamic concepts (which, despite their lack of empirical support, were extremely popular in those days) into the language of Hull's learning theory.

Within this Pavlovian-Hullian tradition, two significant developments occurred in the 1950s, both no doubt influenced to some extent by Dollard and Miller's book and by the learning theory of Edwin Guthrie (1935). One development occurred in South Africa, where Joseph Wolpe began some research and theorizing that drew heavily on Pavlovian conditioning, Hullian theory, and the earlier work of J. B. Watson, Mary Cover Jones, and the British physiologist, Sir Charles Sherrington. Sherrington (1947) had noted that if one group of muscles is stimulated, an antagonistic muscle group will be inhibited—and vice versa. He called this *reciprocal inhibition* and postulated it to be a general process acting throughout the nervous system. Wolpe extended the principle of reciprocal inhibition to state that if a response that is incompatible with fear or anxiety can be made to occur to a stimulus that normally produces fear or anxiety, then that stimulus will cease to elicit the fear reaction. In 1958, Wolpe published his first book on reciprocal inhibition. It was to provide a major force in the launching of the modern era of the respondent tradition of behavior therapy. Wolpe used relaxation responses, sexual responses, and assertion responses to reciprocally inhibit fear or anxiety. (When relaxation is used, the treatment procedure is typically called *systematic desensitization*; see Chapter 25.)

Also during the 1950s, Hans Eysenck in England was instrumental in criticizing traditional Freudian psychoanalytic treatment procedures and advocating learning-theory procedures as alternatives. In 1960, Eysenck published a book of readings, *Behaviour Therapy and the Neuroses*, in which he presented a number of case histories where variations of reciprocal-inhibition and respondent-conditioning procedures were used in clinical therapy. The respondent-conditioning orientation of behavior therapy has occasionally been referred to as the "Wolpe-Eysenck" school.

In the early 1960s, Wolpe moved to the United States. He began a program at Temple University in which he trained therapists in his particular version of behavior therapy. In 1963, Eysenck founded the journal *Behaviour Research and Therapy*, which publishes operant-oriented studies as well as studies with a Pavlovian flavor. As indicated in the bottom panel of Table 28–1, behavior therapy within the respondent orientation grew quite rapidly in the 1960s and 1970s and developed applications to a variety of phobic and neurotic disorders. On June 30, 1984, the behavior therapy unit at Temple University Medical Center ceased to exist. Wolpe (1985) attributed termination of the unit to misunderstanding of behavior therapy by psychodynamic psychotherapists. Nevertheless, Wolpe continued to contribute actively to the field of behavior therapy until his death in 1997.

MIXTURES AND OFFSHOOTS OF THE TWO MAJOR ORIENTATIONS

Much of behavior modification and behavior therapy clearly falls within either the operant orientation or the Pavlovian-Hullian-Wolpean orientation. Most other developments tend to be offshoots of one or the other of these traditions or fall in a gray area somewhere in between (see the "offshoots and mixtures" panel of Table 28–1).

In addition to the two major orientations, two broad theoretical models of behavior modification emerged in the 1970s: social learning theory and cognitive behavior modification.

Characteristics of *social learning theory* were outlined by Julian Rotter in 1954 in his book *Social Learning and Clinical Psychology*. The most influential of the social learning theorists, however, has been Albert Bandura (1969, 1977, 1986, 1996). This approach is "social" in the sense that it places great emphasis on the social contexts in which behavior is acquired and maintained. In addition to basic principles of respondent and operant conditioning, Bandura has strongly emphasized the importance of *observational learning*. By watching other people act and by observing what happens to them, we can then imitate their behavior. (Also, see previous discussion of modeling in Chapter 17.) Bandura also emphasizes *cognitive mediational processes* as an important influence on behavior. Based on prior experience with environmental influences as well as on current perceptions of environmental events, an individual is said to develop cognitive rules and strategies that can serve to determine future actions. An important cognitive mediational process, for example, is what Bandura calls *self-efficacy* (Bandura, 1982, 1996). This refers to a belief that one can perform adequately in a particular situation. In Bandura's words, "Given appropriate skills and adequate incentives . . . efficacy expectations are a major determinant of peoples' choices of activities, how much effort they will expend, and how long they will sustain effort in dealing with stressful situations" (1977, p. 194). (As discussed in Chapter 26, we believe that cognitions such as self-efficacy can be explained in terms of rule-governed behavior.)

A cognitive framework for therapy was contained in Bandura's (1969) book. However, *cognitive behavior modification*, as represented by individuals such as Ellis, Beck, and Meichenbaum (see Chapter 26), is an approach separate from social learning theory. Social learning theory, with its emphasis on the regulation of behavior by external stimulus events, environmental consequences, and cognitive mediational processes, provides a way of explaining behavior in a variety of contexts. Cognitive behavior modification, however, focuses mainly on explaining maladaptive behaviors in terms of dysfunctional thinking, and on treating behavior disorders through cognitive restructuring.

In addition to these four theoretical models of behavior modification, a large group of practicing behavior therapists subscribe to an eclectic approach. Lazarus (1971) has been considered as representative of this position. Referring to what he calls *multimodal* behavior therapy, Lazarus (1971, 1976) argued that the practicing clinician should not restrict himself or herself to a particular theoretical framework but should use a variety of behavior techniques along with psychoanalytic and other traditional clinical techniques, provided that they have some empirical support.

As indicated by this brief discussion of various conceptualizations of behavior modification, there is some disagreement among behavior modifiers on theoretical issues. Nevertheless, there is also considerable agreement.

THE TERMS "BEHAVIOR THERAPY," "BEHAVIOR MODIFICATION," AND "APPLIED BEHAVIOR ANALYSIS"

Some writers use the terms *behavior modification* and *behavior therapy* interchangeably. Other writers use either *applied behavior analysis* or *behavior modification* when referring to the principles discussed in the first part of this text. What is the historical use of these terms? It appears that Lindsley, Skinner, and Solomon (1953) were the first to use the term *behavior therapy*. They did so in a report describing some research in which psychotic patients in a mental hospital were reinforced with candy or cigarettes for pulling a plunger. However, those within the operant orientation subsequently made little use of the term (at least, until the 1970s). Although Lazarus (1958) next used the term *behavior therapy* when he applied it to Wolpe's reciprocal-inhibition framework, the term became popular among those within the Pavlovian-Hullian-Wolpean orientation after Eysenck (1959) used it to describe procedures published by Wolpe.

The first use of the term *behavior modification* appears to be in a chapter by R. I. Watson (1962). Since that time, many writers have distinguished between behavior modification, with its roots in operant conditioning, and behavior therapy, with its roots in Pavlovian conditioning and Hullian theory. Others, however, have not made that distinction consistently. Ullmann and Krasner (1965), for example, frequently used *behavior modification* and *behavior therapy* interchangeably. Also, critics tended to lump operant psychology with other learning theories (Chomsky, 1959) and behavior modification with Pavlovian conditioning, behavior therapy, conditioning therapy, and learning-based therapies (e.g., see Breger & McGaugh, 1965). The term *applied behavior analysis* was made popular in 1968 with the founding of the *Journal of Applied Behavior Analysis*. Some of the distinctions that have tended to characterize the uses of these different terms are presented in Table 28–2.

TABLE 28–2   A COMPARISON OF THE USES OF THE TERMS *BEHAVIOR THERAPY, BEHAVIOR MODIFICATION,* AND *APPLIED BEHAVIOR ANALYSIS*

1960s and 1970s

Behavior therapy	Behavior modification
1. The term used most often by followers of the Pavlovian-Wolpean orientation and followers of the cognitive orientation (who tended to use it interchangeably with the term *cognitive behavior modification*).	1. The term used most often by followers of the operant orientation.
2. The term tended to be used by behavioral psychologists and psychiatrists who were concerned primarily with treatment in traditional clinical settings. (For a historical time line of behavior therapy in psychiatric settings, see Malatesta, AuBuchon & Bluch, 1994.)	2. The term tended to be used by behavior specialists in schools, homes, and other settings that were not primarily the domain of the clinical psychologist and psychiatrist.
3. The term tended to be used to refer to behavioral treatments conducted in the therapist's office by means of verbal interaction ("talk therapy") between therapist and client.	3. The term tended to be used for behavioral treatments carried out in the natural environment as well as in special training settings.
4. The term was associated with an experimental foundation that was based primarily on human studies in clinical settings.	4. The term was associated with an experimental foundation in basic operant research with animals and humans, in addition to experimental studies in applied settings.

1980s and 1990s

*   The term **behavior therapy** continues to be used as described above.

*   The term **applied behavior analysis** is used increasingly by followers of the operant orientation as described in the right-hand column above.

*   The term **behavior modification** tends to have a somewhat broader meaning and includes both behavior therapy and applied behavior analysis.

    In spite of these historical distinctions, the terms are often used interchangeably. In our view, however, the term *behavior modification* has acquired a broader meaning than the other terms. And, of course, the term *behavior therapy* is clearly less appropriate than *applied behavior analysis* or *behavior modification* when dealing with nondysfunctional behavior, such as the application of PSI to normal education or organizational behavior management to the operation of a small business. To perhaps help clear up some of the confusion over the usage of the three terms, we suggest that the term *behavior modification* subsume both *behavior therapy* and *applied behavior analysis*. Behavior therapy is behavior modification carried out on dysfunctional behavior, generally in a clinical setting. Applied behavior analysis is behavior modification in which there has been an attempt to analyze or clearly demonstrate controlling variables of the behavior of concern. Behavior modification, we suggest, includes all explicit applications of behavior principles to improve specific behavior—whether or not in clinical settings and whether or not controlling variables have been explicitly demonstrated—which is how we have used the term in this book.

THE FUTURE OF BEHAVIOR MODIFICATION

Behavior modification has been applied to nearly all conceivable individual and social problems. Moreover, more and more of these applications have been concerned with prevention and social engineering in addition to amelioration of existing problems. There is no doubt that the helping professions are increasingly adopting behavior modification procedures, including such professions as social work, medicine, rehabilitation medicine, nursing, education, preventive dentistry, psychiatric nursing, psychiatry, public health, and clinical and community psychology. Applications are also occurring with increasing frequency in such areas as business, industry, sports, physical education, recreation, and the promotion of healthy lifestyles (see Chapter 2). The immediate future of behavior modification appears to be bright. Someday, a thorough knowledge of behavior techniques may become an accepted necessity in our culture and will be taught to children in elementary school along with good hygiene and physical fitness. Perhaps these children will grow up to see a world in which positive applications of behavior principles will be second nature to everyone and will result in a happy, informed, skillful, productive culture without war, poverty, prejudice, or pollution.

STUDY QUESTIONS

1. Cite seven general statements that might answer the question "What is behavior modification?" (See Chapter 1.)
2. How did Skinner's *Behavior of Organisms* and *Science and Human Behavior* influence the initial development of behavior modification?
3. Discuss Keller's contribution to the development of behavior modification (see text and Note 4).
4. Many of the early reports in the operant tradition in the 1950s were straightforward experiments that demonstrated that consequences influence human behavior. Briefly, describe two such experiments.
5. Briefly describe one of the first published reports (a very influential one) that concerned practical applications within the operant tradition.
6. What is the *Journal of the Experimental Analysis of Behavior?*
7. The publications of the early 1960s within the operant orientation seem to have been characterized by two features. What were they?
8. Was the influential book *Case Studies in Behavior Modification* strictly within the operant orientation? Why or why not?
9. What concept did J. B. Watson adopt from Pavlov? How did Watson use this concept?
10. What behavior therapy procedure do we credit to Joseph Wolpe?
11. What dual role did Hans Eysenck play in the development of behavior therapy in the 1950s?

12. What are the names of four major behavior modification/behavior therapy journals (see Table 28–1 and Note 2)?
13. Briefly, describe four current conceptual (or theoretical) models of behavior modification.
14. Describe four differences in the usage of the terms *behavior therapy* and *behavior modification* during the 1960s and 1970s. How do the terms *behavior therapy*, *behavior modification*, and *applied behavior analysis* tend to be used today?
15. If someone suggested, "Behavior modification is okay for some limited types of problems," what would you say?

NOTES AND EXTENDED DISCUSSION

1. For a discussion of the history of behavior modification from the early 1900s to the 1960s, see MacMillan (1973). More detailed discussion of the Pavlovian influences on the development of behavior therapy can be found in Franks (1969) and Yates (1970). The most complete history of behavior modification was written by Kazdin (1978).

2. In the 1950s, important historical developments in behavior modification occurred concurrently in three countries: in South Africa, where Wolpe conducted his pioneering work on systematic desensitization; in England, where Eysenck spurred on the behavior modification movement by emphasizing dissatisfaction with traditional methods of psychotherapy; and in the United States, where Skinner and his colleagues were working within the operant conditioning orientation. During the 1960s and 1970s, however, most of the major books and research papers in behavior modification and behavior therapy were based on developments in the United States. For example, three of the first four major behavior therapy journals were published in the United States and most of their articles were written in the United States (*Journal of Applied Behavior Analysis*, 1968–; *Behavior Therapy*, 1970; *Behavior Therapy and Experimental Psychiatry*, 1970–). Although the fourth journal (*Behaviour Research and Therapy*, 1963–) was edited by Eysenck in England, it too contained a large number of U.S. research reports. Since the 1970s, however, behavior modification has become a truly worldwide movement. Significant developments have occurred in Argentina (Blanck, 1983); in Australia (Brownell, 1981; King, 1996); in Brazil (Ardilla, 1982); in Canada (G. L. Martin, 1981); in Chile (Ardilla, 1982); in Columbia (Ardilla, 1982); in Costa Rica (Pal-Hegedus, 1991); in the Dominican Republic (Brownell, 1981); in England (Brownell, 1981); in France (Agathon, 1982; Cottraux, 1990); in Germany (Stark, 1980); in Ghana (Danguah, 1982); in Holland (Brownell, 1981); in Hungary (Tringer, 1991); in Italy (Meazzini & Rovetto, 1983; Scrimali & Grimaldi, 1993); in Ireland (Flanagan, 1991); in Israel (Brownell, 1981); in Japan (Sakano, 1993; Yamagami, Okuma, Morinaga, & Nakao, 1982); in Mexico (Ardilla, 1982); in New Zealand (Singh & Blampied, 1983); in Norway (Brownell, 1981); in Poland (Wandzel, Czabala, & Tyra, 1991); in Spain (Caballo & Buela-Casal, 1993); in Sri Lanka (DeSilva & Simarasinghe, 1985); in Sweden (Brownell, 1981); in Thailand (Mikulis, 1983), and in Venezuela (Ardilla, 1982).

3. Burrhus Frederick Skinner was born on March 20, 1904, in Susquehanna, Pennsylvania. At the time of his death on August 18, 1990, in Cambridge, Massachusetts, at the age of 86, Skinner was the world's best-known living psychologist and its leading behaviorist.

After receiving his bachelor of arts degree with a major in English at Hamilton College in upstate New York, Skinner was a somewhat unsuccessful writer during the next two years in New York City's Greenwich Village, and in Europe. He then entered Harvard to study psychology and received his doctorate in 1931. It was at Harvard that he formed a friendship with Fred Keller, a friendship that was to last over 60 years. After being a postdoctoral fellow at Harvard and then teaching at the University of Minnesota and at Indiana University, Skinner returned to Harvard as a professor in 1947. He remained associated with Harvard until his death.

Skinner had a remarkable career and received numerous awards, including the Distinguished Scientific Award from the American Psychological Association (1958), the President's National Medal of Science (1968), and the Humanist of the Year Award from the American Humanist Society (1972). In addition to his basic theoretical and experimental contributions, Skinner published a utopian novel, *Walden Two* (1948), worked on a project to teach pigeons to guide missiles during World War II (Skinner, 1960), and developed the concept of programmed instruction and teaching machines (Skinner, 1958). Skinner continued to be active throughout his academic career, publishing his most recent book in 1989 (*Recent Issues in the Analysis of Behavior*). He leaves a tremendous legacy: His influence on psychology is as significant as Galileo's on physics and Darwin's on biology.

4. In 1961, Keller accepted a position at the University of Sao Paulo, Brazil, where he established the first operant conditioning course in that country. With his Brazilian colleagues, Keller also developed the Personalized System of Instruction, a behavior modification approach to university teaching that has the potential to revolutionize college instruction (see Chapter 2). Keller contributed immeasurably to the development of behavior modification in Brazil. Former students of his, their students, and so on, continue to advance behavioral psychology in that country.

Study Questions on Notes

1. Name three countries that were important in the development of behavior modification in the 1950s, and the person most associated with this development in each of these countries.
2. Cite three of Skinner's contributions other than his basic research and theoretical writings.

Ethical Issues

Throughout this book we have emphasized the ethical or moral concerns that one should always bear in mind when applying behavior modification. It would be a great tragedy if this powerful scientific technology were somehow to be used in ways that harmed rather than helped humanity. Because this is a real danger, it is fitting that we devote the final chapter of this book to a more detailed discussion of ethical concerns.

The history of civilization is a continuous story of the abuse of power. Throughout the ages, various groups have used the reinforcers and punishers at their disposal to control the behavior of less powerful groups (groups who had fewer reinforcers and punishers to deliver or without the means to deliver them contingent on selected target behaviors). The effect of this tradition has generally been to increase the reinforcements occurring to the more powerful at the expense of those occurring to the less powerful. From time to time, as the proportion of total reinforcement allotted to them steadily dwindled, groups subjected to this abuse of power have successfully revolted against their oppressors and have modified existing social structures, or established new ones, to check or eliminate the possibility of future abuses. Constitutions, bills of rights, and related political documents of modern states can be viewed as formal specifications of contingencies designed to control the behavior of those who control the behavior of others. In Western democracies, for example, we have moved from the era of the divine right of monarchs to one of "government by laws, not people." Moreover, with the introduction of periodic popular elections, the people who are controlled by those who make the laws can exert a certain measure of reciprocal control: They can vote them out of office. In socialist and communist countries the revolutionary process concentrated on eliminating certain economic abuses rather than establishing democracy. In the absence of democracy other abuses developed, however, and many former communist countries are also now becoming more democratic. Nevertheless, the new social designs and practices that have emerged thus far have invariably fallen short of their objective; power continues to be abused throughout the world.

Because of this cultural history and because of people's personal experiences with others who have abused their power (i.e., used it for their own benefit and to the disadvantage of those over whom they exerted control), people have learned to react negatively to all overt attempts to manage behavior. This negative reaction is so strong that those who would control our behavior usually find that their efforts are more successful when they disguise their aims (e.g., when advertisers use the "soft sell" rather than "hard sell" or when people who want to change our opinion on an issue contrive to make it appear that we arrived at the new opinion essentially by ourselves). It should not be surprising, therefore, that in its early years, behavior modification evoked many negative reactions, ranging from suspicion to outright hostility. Behavior modification is the technology based on the science that studies the factors that control behavior. Therefore, it is no secret that behavior modification is based on two propositions: (a) Behavior can be controlled, and (b) it is desirable to do so to achieve certain objectives. Whether or not behavior is completely determined by environmental and genetic factors (everyone agrees that it is at least partially determined by these factors) makes for interesting philosophical discussions. From a practical point of view, however, it makes little difference one way or the other. The important point is that the amount of potential control over behavior is steadily increasing, as a result of new discoveries in behavioral science and refinements in behavioral technology.

Extreme wariness is a healthy reaction to any new, far-reaching advance in science or technology. Perhaps civilization would be in less danger if more precautions had been taken early in the development of, say, atomic energy. The solution to the present problems stemming from scientific and technological advances, however, does not lie in attempting to turn the clock back to a seemingly more secure, prescientific era. Science and technology are not the problem. They are merely highly sophisticated means that people have developed for solving problems. The real problem is that people frequently misuse these tools. This is, of course, a behavioral problem. It would seem, therefore, as Skinner (1953, 1971) argued, that the science of behavior is the logical key to the solution of that problem. As with other powerful sciences and technologies, however, behavior modification can be misused. It therefore is important to have ethical guidelines to ensure that it is used for the good of society. In the next section we discuss ethics from a behavioral perspective. Then, we examine some common arguments against deliberately changing behavior. Finally, we turn to the question of how safeguards can be imposed on behavior modification to ensure that it will always be used in the best interests of humanity.

A BEHAVIORAL VIEW OF ETHICS

From a behavioral point of view, the term *ethics* refers to certain standards of behavior that are developed by a culture and promote the survival of that culture (Skinner, 1953, 1971). For example, stealing is considered unethical or wrong in many cultures because of the disruptive effect it has on the culture. Many ethical guidelines, such as "stealing is wrong," likely evolved in prehistoric times. It might be that among a number of cultures that existed at a particular time before recorded history, behaving honestly in relation to material goods happened to be socially reinforced and stealing happened to be punished in some of these cultures but not in others (just as different cultures happened to reinforce different types of religious beliefs). Cultures in which honest behavior toward material possessions was not reinforced and stealing not punished, however, tended not to survive. There are a number of possible reasons for this. Perhaps the members of these cultures put so much effort into fighting each other that they were fatally vulnerable to invasions from other cultures, or they did not have enough time left over to produce an adequate amount of food for themselves. Perhaps, because of the constant fighting and bickering, these cultures were so unreinforcing to their members that the members defected in large numbers to other cultures, so that their former cultures became extinct due to lack of membership. Whatever the case, many cultures survived that reinforced nonstealing behavior and punished stealing—that is, cultures that considered nonstealing ethical or right and stealing unethical or wrong.

Thus, ethics has evolved as part of our culture in much the same way that the parts of our bodies have evolved; that is, ethics has contributed to the survival of our culture in much the same way that, for example, fingers and an opposable thumb have contributed to the survival of our species. This is not to say that people do not, at times, deliberately decide to formulate ethical rules for their culture. On the contrary, it is part of this cultural evolutionary process that at some point in the process some members of a culture begin to engage in such behavior because they have been conditioned to work toward the survival of their culture. One way in which to work toward the survival of one's culture is to formulate and enforce (through reinforcement as well as punishment) a code of ethics that strengthens that culture.

Ethical guidelines are an important source of behavioral control when immediate reinforcers influence an individual to behave in a way that leads to aversive stimuli for others. For example, whereas a thief is immediately reinforced by possession of the stolen goods, loss of those goods is aversive to the victims. To cause its members to be honest with each other, a culture might therefore develop and enforce the ethical rule, "If you steal another's possessions, you will be punished (by jail, etc.)." When members of a culture learn to follow such ethical guidelines, the guidelines exert rule-governed control over behavior (see Chapter 16). This is one way that people learn to emit behavior that is ethical and to refrain from behavior that is unethical.

With this behavioral view of ethics in mind, let's now examine whether or not behavior modifiers should attempt to deliberately change the behavior of others.

ARGUMENTS AGAINST DELIBERATELY
CONTROLLING BEHAVIOR

As we indicated earlier, because of our knowledge of the abuse of power throughout history, and because of our personal experience with others who have abused their power, we have learned to react negatively to overt attempts to change our behavior. Perhaps for these reasons, it is sometimes argued that all attempts to control behavior are unethical. A little reflection, however, shows that **Note 1** the goal of any social help profession (such as education, psychology, and psychiatry) can be achieved only to the extent that the practitioners of that profession exert control over behavior. The goal of education, for example, is to change behavior so that students will respond differently to their environment than they would had they not been educated. To teach a person to read, for example, is to change her behavior in such a way that she responds to signs, newspapers, books, and so forth in a manner that is different from the way in which she responded prior to being able to read. The goals of counseling, psychological treatment, and psychiatry likewise involve changing people's behavior so that they can function more effectively than they did prior to receiving professional help.

Perhaps because of the negative reactions of people to overt attempts to change behavior, many members of the helping professions do not like to think that they are controlling behavior. They prefer to see themselves as merely helping their clients to achieve control over their own behavior. Establishing self-control, however, is also a form of behavioral control. One simply teaches an individual to emit behavior that controls other behavior in some desired fashion. To do that, it is necessary to manage the behavior involved in self-control. In other words, it is necessary to control the behavior that controls other behavior. The helping practitioner may object that this is nevertheless not control on his or her part because the external influence over the client's behavior is withdrawn as soon as the practitioner is sure that the client is able to manage his or her own behavior. Actually, as we have emphasized repeatedly throughout this book, the practitioner has simply shifted the control to the natural environment. One may speak of this as "withdrawing control," but the control still continues, even though its form has changed. If the practitioner has been successful in achieving the behavioral objectives, the desired behavior will be maintained, and in that sense the practioner's control or influence over the behavior will persist.

Some people will grant that helping practitioners necessarily engage in the management of behavior but will nevertheless argue that it is wrong to deliberately plan to change behavior. They regard planning to be "cold" and "mechanical" and believe that it interferes with warm, loving, "spontaneous" relationships that should exist between persons. It is difficult to determine where this objection to planning comes from, because we know of no logical or empirical evidence that supports it. On the contary, many behavior modification programs that we know of are characterized by friendly, warm interactions between the individuals involved. Good behavior modifiers are genuinely interested in their clients as persons, and seem to find the time to interact with them on a personal level, just as other helping practitioners do. There is no doubt that some people show behavior that appears to be cold and mechanical. It is our impression, however, that

Note 2 such people are no more common among behavior modifiers than they are among any subgroup of those in the helping professions with other orientations.

A lack of planning, on the other hand, can be disastrous. For illustrations of this, refer to the "Pitfalls" sections in Part II, where we gave numerous examples of how behavior principles and processes can work to the disadvantage of those who are ignorant of them or who do not plan for them. If a behavior practitioner is not skillful in constructing programs for developing desirable behavior, he or she is unwittingly apt to introduce contingencies that develop undesirable behavior.

While it is often necessary to change, manage, influence, or otherwise control behavior, *it is also necessary to ensure that this is done ethically*. We have argued throughout this book that we are likely to achieve desirable behavioral change if we practice research-based principles and procedures of behavior modification. We turn now to ethical guidelines for doing so.

ETHICAL GUIDELINES

Having a set of guidelines that describe ethical applications of behavior modification is important. However, simply resolving to treat various individuals and groups in ethical ways is not a sufficient guarantee that they will be so treated. Contingencies of reinforcement must be arranged to make this happen. One way in which to arrange such contingencies is through *countercontrol*. This is "the reciprocal of control; it is the influence the controllee has on the controller by virtue of access to suitable reinforcers" (Stoltz et al., 1978, p. 19). In a democracy, for example, voters can exert a certain amount of countercontrol over elected officials: If the voters don't like the laws that are passed, they can vote the officials out of office. Similarly, a client can stop seeing a therapist as a form of countercontrol to ensure that the therapist conforms with prearranged treatment guidelines. Some individuals in treatment programs, however, such as children, psychiatric patients, geriatric patients, and severely developmentally disabled persons, are likely to lack meaningful forms of countercontrol. In such cases, other ethical safeguards may be necessary. These safeguards generally require that the behavior modifier be held accountable (i.e., responsible) to a recognized individual or group for applying acceptable procedures and producing satisfactory results.

Various groups and organizations have addressed the ethical issues involved in the application of behavior modification. Three highly reputable organizations that have done so are the Association for the Advancement of Behavior Therapy (AABT), the American Psychological Association (APA), and the Association for Behavior Analysis (ABA).

In 1977, in its journal *Behavior Therapy*, AABT published a set of basic ethical questions that one should always ask with regard to any behavior modification or behavior therapy program. These questions are reprinted in Table 29–1 and should be examined carefully. As can be seen from the table, most of these points have been made frequently throughout this book, especially in Chapter 22. If you are carrying out a behavior modification program and must answer *no* to any of these questions, it is extremely likely that the ethics of what you are doing would be considered questionable by any recognized group of behavior modifiers or be-

TABLE 29–1   ETHICAL ISSUES FOR HUMAN SERVICES

The focus of this statement is on critical issues of central importance to human services. The statement is not a list of prescriptions and proscriptions.

On each of the issues described, ideal interventions would have maximum involvement by the person whose behavior is to be changed, and the fullest possible consideration of societal pressures on that person, the therapist, and the therapist's employer. It is recognized that the practicalities of actual settings sometimes require exceptions and that there certainly are occasions when exceptions can be consistent with ethical practice.

In the list of issues, the term "client" is used to describe the person whose behavior is to be changed; "therapist" is used to describe the professional in charge of the intervention; "treatment" and "problem," although used in the singular, refer to any and all treatments and problems being formulated with this checklist. The issues are formulated so as to be relevant across as many settings and populations as possible. Thus, they need to be qualified when someone other than the person whose behavior is to be changed is paying the therapist, or when that person's competence or the voluntary nature of that person's consent is questioned. For example, if the therapist has found that the client does not understand the goals or methods being considered, the therapist should substitute the client's guardian or other responsible person for "client," when reviewing the issues listed.

A   Have the goals of treatment been adequately considered?
   1   To ensure that the goals are explicit, are they written?
   2   Has the client's understanding of the goals been assured by having the client restate them orally or in writing?
   3   Have the therapist and client agreed on the goals of therapy?
   4   Will serving the client's interests be contrary to the interests of other persons?
   5   Will serving the client's immediate interests be contrary to the client's long term interest?
B   Has the choice of treatment methods been adequately considered?
   1   Does the published literature show the procedure to be the best one available for that problem?
   2   If no literature exists regarding the treatment method, is the method consistent with generally accepted practice?
   3   Has the client been told of alternative procedures that might be preferred by the client on the basis of significant differences in discomfort, treatment time, cost, or degree of demonstrated effectiveness?
   4   If a treatment procedure is publicly, legally, or professionally controversial, has formal professional consultation been obtained, has the reaction of the affected segment of the public been adequately considered, and have the alternative treatment methods been more closely reexamined and reconsidered?
C   Is the client's participation voluntary?
   1   Have possible sources of coercion on the client's participation been considered?
   2   If treatment is legally mandated, has the available range of treatments and therapists been offered?
   3   Can the client withdraw from treatment without a penalty or financial loss that exceeds actual clinical costs?

(continued)

TABLE 29–1   *(CONTINUED)*

D   When another person or an agency is empowered to arrange for therapy, have the interests of the subordinated client been sufficiently considered?
  1   Has the subordinated client been informed of the treatment objectives and participated in the choice of treatment procedures?
  2   Where the subordinated client's competence to decide is limited, have the client as well as the guardian participated in the treatment discussions to the extent that the client's abilities permit?
  3   If the interests of the subordinated person and the superordinate persons or agency conflict, have attempts been made to reduce the conflict by dealing with both interests?

E   Has the adequacy of treatment been evaluated?
  1   Have quantitative measures of the problem and its progress been obtained?
  2   Have the measures of the problem and its progress been made available to the client during treatment?

F   Has the confidentiality of the treatment relationship been protected?
  1   Has the client been told who has access to the records?
  2   Are records available only to authorized persons?

G   Does the therapist refer the clients to other therapists when necessary?
  1   If treatment is unsuccessful, is the client referred to other therapists?
  2   Has the client been told that if dissatisfied with the treatment, referral will be made?

H   Is the therapist qualified to provide treatment?
  1   Has the therapist had training or experience in treating problems like the client's?
  2   If deficits exist in the therapist's qualifications, has the client been informed?
  3   If the therapist is not adequately qualified, is the client referred to other therapists, or has supervision by a qualified therapist been provided? Is the client informed of the supervisory relation?
  4   If the treatment is administered by mediators, have the mediators been adequately supervised by a qualified therapist?

Note: Adopted May 22, 1977, by the board of directors of the Association for Advancement of Behavior Therapy. This statement on Ethical Issues for Human Services was taken from the Membership Directory of the Association for Advancement of Behavior Therapy and is reprinted by permission of the association.

havior therapists. It should be noted, as well, that these ethical questions are relevant not only to behavior modifiers and behavior therapists, but to all providers of human services.

In 1978, a comprehensive report (Stolz & Associates, 1978) on the ethical issues involved in behavior modification was published by a commission appointed by the APA. A primary conclusion of the commission was that persons engaged in any type of psychological intervention should subscribe to and follow the ethics codes and standards of their professions. For members of the American Psychological Association and the Canadian Psychological Association, the current version of the ethics code is the American Psychological Association's Ethical Principles of Psychologists (1992), which are summarized in Table 29–2.

In 1988, in its journal, *The Behavior Analyst*, ABA published a statement of clients' rights (Van Houten et al., 1988) to direct both the ethical and appropriate application of behavioral treatment. The following discussion for the ethical application of behavior modification is based on the reports by Stolz & Associates (1978) and Van Houten et al. (1988).

TABLE 29–2   ETHICAL PRINCIPLES OF PSYCHOLOGISTS

Principle A: Competence

Psychologists recognize the boundaries of their particular competencies and the limitations of their expertise. They provide only those services and use only those techniques for which they are qualified.

Principle B: Integrity

Psychologists are honest, fair, and respectful of others. In describing or reporting their qualifications, services, products, fees, research, or teaching, they do not make statements that are false, misleading, or deceptive.

Principle C: Professional and Scientific Responsibility

Psychologists uphold professional standards of conduct and accept responsibility for their behavior. When appropriate, they consult with colleagues in order to prevent or avoid unethical conduct.

Principle D: Respect for Peoples' Rights and Dignity

Psychologists respect the fundamental rights, dignity, and worth of all people. They respect the rights of individuals to privacy, confidentiality, self-determination, and autonomy.

Principle E: Concern for Others' Welfare

Psychologists seek to contribute to the welfare of those with whom they interact professionally. When conflicts occur among psychologists' obligations or concerns, they attempt to resolve those conflicts in a reasonable fashion that avoids or minimizes harm.

Principle F: Social Responsibility

Psychologists are aware of their professional and scientific responsibilities to the community and the society in which they work and live. They apply and make public their knowledge of psychology in order to contribute to human welfare.

Note. Adapted from American Psychological Association (1992). Ethical principles of psychologists and code of conduct. *American Psychologist, 47,* 1597–1611. Copyright 1992 by the American Psychological Association. Reprinted by permission.

1. Qualifications of the Behavior Modifier

Behavior modifiers must receive appropriate academic training. They must also receive appropriate supervised practicum training to ensure competence in behavioral assessment, designing and implementing treatment programs, evaluating their results, and ensuring a thorough understanding of professional ethics. In cases in which a problem or treatment is complex or may pose risks, Van Houten et al. (1988) indicate that clients have a right to direct involvement by an appropriately trained doctoral level behavior modifier. Regardless of the level of training, the behavior modifier should always ensure that the procedures being used are consistent with the most up-to-date literature in the recognized behavior modification and behavior therapy journals.

Steps to Ensure Countercontrol and Accountability   The first step in being accountable is for the behavior modifier to describe clearly his or her credentials to the client (defined as the person whose behavior is being controlled). Some degree of accountability is also achieved by the behavior modifier meeting recognized criteria of professional status provided by membership in the local state or provincial psychological (or other appropriate professional) association. If you are not a recognized professional, and if you are carrying out a behavior modification project, then you should obtain supervision from a recognized professional in the field. Such professionals are likely to be members of ABA or AABT, or both. Thus far, only one state (Florida) has developed a behavior analysis certification program, which is one approach to protecting the consumer. Starin, Hemingway, and Hartsfield (1993) recommended that other states develop similar certification programs.

2. Definition of the Problem and Selection of Goals

Note 3

Target behaviors selected must be the most important for the client and/or society. There should be an emphasis on teaching functional, age-appropriate skills that will enable the client greater freedom to pursue preferred activities. With severely handicapped individuals especially, there should be a focus on teaching skills that promote independent functioning. Even when improved functioning requires the elimination of problem behaviors in certain situations, the goals should include desirable alternative behaviors for those situations. The goals should also be consistent with the basic rights of the client to dignity, privacy, and humane care.

Steps to Ensure Countercontrol and Accountability   Defining the problem and selecting the goals are dependent on the values of the individuals involved. For example, some people consider gay or lesbian tendencies to be a problem that should be eliminated; others do not. One form of countercontrol, therefore, is to require the behavior modifier to clearly specify his or her values relating to the client's problems. Ideally, the values on which the goals are based should be consistent with those of the client and with the long-term good of society. A second form of countercontrol is for the client to be an active participant in the selection of goals and identification of target behaviors. In situations in which this is not possible (such as cases of severe developmental disabilities), competent impartial third parties (ombudspersons, representatives of the community) who can act on behalf of a client can ensure accountability by being involved in crucial decisions concerning selection of goals.

3. Selection of Treatment

Behavior modifiers should use the most effective, empirically validated methods with the least discomfort and least negative side effects. To this end, it is generally agreed that behavior modifiers should use the least intrusive and restrictive interventions wherever possible; however, there is no clear agreement on a continuum of intrusiveness or restrictiveness. These terms appear to be used in at least three ways. First, interventions based on positive reinforcement are generally considered to be less intrusive than interventions based on aversive control. That does not mean, however, that aversive procedures should never be used. It may not be in the client's best interest for behavior modifiers to apply a slow-acting procedure if available research indicates that more aversive procedures would be more effective. As expressed by Van Houten et al. (1988, p. 114), "In some cases, a client's right to effective treatment may dictate the immediate use of quicker-acting, but temporarily more restrictive procedures."

Second, intrusive and restrictive sometimes refer to the extent to which clients are given choices and allowed freedom of movement in a therapeutic environment. In a work-training program for developmentally disabled persons, for example, the assignment of specific work tasks by staff might be considered more intrusive than allowing clients to choose among several optional work activities.

Third, intrusive and restrictive sometimes refer to the extent to which consequences are deliberately managed as opposed to naturally occurring. As we indicated in Chapter 3, natural reinforcers are unprogrammed reinforcers that occur in the normal course of everyday living. The desirability of making use of natural contingencies of reinforcement whenever possible was stressed in Chapter 12 and elsewhere in this text. If it is necessary to use contrived or deliberately programmed reinforcers early in a program, then the behavior modifier should transfer control to natural reinforcers as soon as is possible.

Steps to Ensure Countercontrol and Accountability   One way to ensure countercontrol is to stipulate that no program is to be carried out on a client who has not given informed consent to participate in that program (i.e., consent based on knowledge of the procedures to be used and their probable effects). Stated differently, the behavior modifier should explain alternative treatments that could be used, state their pros and cons, and give the client a choice. A mechanism to facilitate informed consent is the signing of a client-therapist contract that clearly outlines the objectives and methods of treatment, the framework for the service to be provided, and the contingencies for remuneration that may be forthcoming to the therapist (as described in Chapter 22). There are, however, problems with the concept of *informed consent*; namely, it involves verbal behavior that, like other behavior, is under the control of the environment. Hence, it may be manipulated in a particular fashion that may not be in the best interests of the client. The stipulation of informed consent probably provides only a partial check on the ethics of a program. In addition, there are many individuals for whom the stipulation is inapplicable (e.g., severely developmentally disabled individuals). Therefore, an additional way to help ensure that clients' rights are protected is through ethical review committees composed of professionals and members of the community who evaluate the ethics of proposed programs.

4. Record Keeping and Ongoing Evaluation

An important component of ensuring ethical treatment of clients is the maintenance of accurate data throughout a program. This includes a thorough behavioral assessment before the intervention is developed, ongoing monitoring of target behaviors as well as possible side effects, and appropriate follow-up evaluation after the treatment is concluded. Whereas behavior modifiers should always take good records, they should exercise utmost discretion in whom they permit to see those records, in order to protect the client from undue control. Confidentiality must be respected at all times.

Steps to Ensure Countercontrol and Accountability   An important form of countercontrol is to provide frequent opportunities for a client to discuss with the behavior modifier the data that assesses progress throughout the program. For this, of course, the client must have access to his or her own records. Another strategy is (with the client's permission) to expect the behavior modifier to share the client's records with those who are directly concerned with the client's progress. Feedback on the effectiveness of the program from individuals who are concerned directly with the welfare of the client is an important accountability mechanism. As we indicated in Chapter 1, the most important characteristic of behavior modification is *its strong emphasis on defining problems in terms of behavior that can be measured in some way, and using changes in the behavioral measure of the problem as the best indicator of the extent to which the problem is being helped.* Sharing these data with all concerned parties and periodic peer evaluation is the corner-stone for ensuring ethical and effective treatment programs by the behavior modifers.

CONCLUSIONS

Behavior modification has great potential to be used for the good of society and may even be used to eliminate the oppression of some humans by others that has characterized all societies from the dawn of recorded history to the present.

An important responsibility of behavior modifiers is to develop ethical safeguards for behavior modification to ensure that it is always used wisely and humanely and does not become a new tool in the oppression that has thus far characterized the human species. Of all the safeguards discussed, the most fundamental is countercontrol. Perhaps the best way for behavior modifiers to help develop effective countercontrol throughout society is to spread their skills as widely as possible, and to help educate the general public with respect to behavior modification. It should be rather difficult to use behavioral science to the disadvantage of any group whose members are well versed in the principles and tactics of behavior modification.

STUDY QUESTIONS

1. Describe in behavioral terms how the history of civilization is a story of the continuous abuse of power. From your knowledge of history or current events, give an example of this abuse.
2. From your knowledge of history or current events, give an example of what often happens when the reinforcements occurring to one group in a society fall below a certain critical level relative to the reinforcements occurring to another group in that society.

3. From a behavioral point of view, how might we account for constitutions, bills of rights, and related political documents of modern states?

4. Explain why we tend to react negatively to all overt attempts to control our behavior.

5. Why and how do people who would control our behavior disguise their aims? Give an example of this that is not in the text.

6. State two propositions on which behavior modification is based.

7. Why is extreme wariness a healthy reaction to any new, far-reaching development in science or technology? Cite and discuss an example of this.

8. What does the term *ethics* mean from a behavioral point of view?

9. Describe how ethics has evolved as a part of our culture.

10. Using an example, explain how ethical guidelines involve rule-governed control over behavior.

11. Explain why all helping professions are involved in the control of behavior, whether or not their practitioners realize it. Give an example.

12. Discuss the relative merits of planning versus not planning for behavior change.

13. Discuss countercontrol. Why is it important?

14. What was a primary conclusion of the comprehensive report by Stolz and Associates on the ethical issues involved in behavior modification?

15. In a sentence each, summarize the six ethical principles of psychologists presented by the American Psychological Association.

16. What steps can be taken to help ensure that a behavior modifier is appropriately qualified?

17. State two countercontrol measures for clients regarding the definition of problems and selection of goals.

18. What should be the characteristics of intervention methods used by behavior modifiers?

19. Discuss three possible meanings of *intrusive* and *restrictive* interventions.

20. Describe a mechanism to facilitate informed consent by the client.

21. What constitutes the cornerstone for ensuring ethical and effective treatment programs by behavior modifiers?

22. Briefly explain why it should be rather difficult to use behavior modification to the detriment of any group whose members are well versed in the principles and tactics of behavior modification.

NOTES AND EXTENDED DISCUSSION

1. Skinner (1971) argued that we can trace this attitude, at least in part, to the influence of 18th-century revolutionaries and social reformers. To counteract the aversive control utilized by tyrants, these activists developed the concept of *freedom as a rallying cry*. It was, said Skinner, a worthwhile concept in its time, for it helped to spur people to break away from aversive forms of control. Now, however, we have moved into an era in which positive reinforcement is a more predominant means of control (and will perhaps become increasingly so with the growth of behavior modification). The concept of *freedom* has therefore outlived its social usefulness. Indeed, it is harmful, in that it tends to prevent us from seeing how our behavior is controlled by positive reinforcement. Many states and provincial governments in North America, for example, have turned to public lotteries as a way to raise funds.

Most people who happily buy lottery tickets feel that they are "free" to do so, and they fail to recognize that their behavior is being controlled to the same extent as it would be if they were being "forced" to pay the same amount in taxes. But the mechanism of control is different (i.e., positive reinforcement versus avoidance conditioning). Moreover, the concept of *freedom* encourages the view that some people deserve more "dignity" than others because of their achievements, whereas in actuality one's achievements (or failures to achieve) are due to one's conditioning history and genetic predispositions. Hence, the title of Skinner's book: *Beyond Freedom and Dignity* (1971).

2. In fact, in controlled clinical trials, behavior therapists have been rated by observers as significantly more empathic and supportive than nonbehavioral clinicians (Greenwald, Kornblith, Hersen, Bellack, & Himmelhach, 1981; Sloan, Staples, Cristol, Yorkston, & Whipple, 1975). Moreover, in the absence of a warm and empathic relationship, clients will simply resist complying with the requests by behavior therapists for conducting various self-monitoring and homework assignments (Hersen, 1983; G. A. Martin & Worthington, 1982; Messer & Winokur, 1984).

3. Prilleltensky (1989, 1990) has argued that psychology as a whole, including behavior modification, has too readily accepted and promoted the status quo rather than questioning whether the status quo is really always best for human welfare. An example from the early days of behavior modification would be that of teaching children in school to sit quietly at their desks, as though there were some intrinsic merit in this behavior. Perhaps it is the rule that should be changed rather than the children. Prilleltensky argues that we should study how the status quo comes to be accepted and how we can redirect our efforts to changing it, rather than our clients, when this is more consistent with human welfare.

Study Questions on Notes

1. Discuss Skinner's view that we must go "beyond freedom and dignity" if civilization is to solve some of its most difficult problems.
2. Describe an example illustrating how governments use positive reinforcement to control behavior without citizens believing that they are being controlled.
3. Do the data support the notion that behavior modifiers are "cold and mechanical" in their treatment of clients? Explain.
4. Describe two examples in which behavior modification might be used inappropriately, in your opinion, to support the status quo. Why do you think this use of behavior modification would be inappropriate?

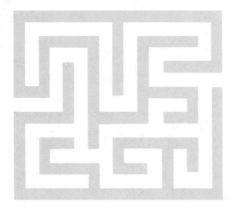

References

ABRAMOWITZ, J. S. (1996). Variance of exposure and response prevention in the treatment of obsessive compulsive disorder: A meta-analysis. *Behavior Therapy, 27,* 583–600.

ADER, R., & COHEN, N. (1982). Behaviorally conditioned immunosuppression and murine systemic lupis erythematosus, *Science, 215,* 1534–1536.

ADER, R., & COHEN, N. (1993). Psychoneuroimmunology: Conditioning and stress. *Annual Review of Psychology, 44,* 53–85.

AGATHON, M. (1982). Behavior therapy in France. 1976–1981. *Journal of Behavior Therapy and Experimental Psychiatry, 13,* 271–277.

AGRAS, W. S. (1987). Presidential address: Where do we go from here? *Behavior Therapy, 18,* 203–217.

AGRAS, W. S., TAYLOR, C. B., FELDMAN, D. E., LOSCH, M., & BURNETT, K. F. (1990). Developing computer-assisted therapy for the treatment of obesity. *Behavior Therapy, 21,* 99–109.

AIRAPETYANTZ, E., & BYKOV, D. (1966). Physiological experiments and the psychology of the subconscious. In T. Verhave (Ed.), *The experimental analysis of behavior* (pp. 140–157). New York: Appleton-Century-Crofts.

ALBERTO, P. A., & TROUTMAN, A. C. (1990). *Applied behavior analysis for teachers: Influencing student performance* (3rd ed.). Columbus, OH: Charles E. Merrill.

ALBION, F. M., & SALZBURG, C. L. (1982). The effects of self-instruction on the rate of correct addition problems with mentally retarded children. *Education and Treatment of Children, 5,* 121–131.

ALLEN, G. J. (1973). Case study: Implementation of behavior modification techniques in summer camp settings. *Behavior Therapy, 4,* 570–575.

ALLEN, K. D., & STOKES, T. F. (1987). Use of escape and reward in the management of young children during dental treatment. *Journal of Applied Behavior Analysis, 20,* 381–390.

AMERICAN ASSOCIATION ON MENTAL RETARDATION (AAMR). (1990). Revised policy on aversive procedures. *AAMR News and Notes, 3(4),* 5.

AMERICAN ASSOCIATION ON MENTAL RETARDATION (AAMR). (1992). *Mental retardation: Definition, classification, and systems of supports* (9th ed.). Washington, DC: Author.

AMERICAN PSYCHIATRIC ASSOCIATION. (1952). *Diagnostic and statistical manual of mental disorders: DSM I.* Washington, DC: Author.

AMERICAN PSYCHIATRIC ASSOCIATION. (1968). *Diagnostic and statistical manual of mental disorders: DSM II* (2nd ed.). Washington, DC: Author.

AMERICAN PSYCHIATRIC ASSOCIATION. (1980). *Diagnostic and statistical manual of mental disorders: DSM III* (3rd ed.). Washington, DC: Author.

AMERICAN PSYCHIATRIC ASSOCIATION. (1987). *Diagnostic and statistical manual of mental disorders: DSM III–R* (3rd ed.). Washington, DC: Author.

AMERICAN PSYCHIATRIC ASSOCIATION. (1993). Practice guidelines for major depressive disorder in adults. *The American Journal of Psychiatry, 150* (Suppl. 4), 1–26.

AMERICAN PSYCHIATRIC ASSOCIATION. (1994). *Diagnostic and statistical manual of mental disorders: DSM IV* (4th ed.). Washington, DC: Author.

AMERICAN PSYCHOLOGICAL ASSOCIATION (APA). (1992). *Ethical principles in the conduct of research with human participants.* Washington, DC: Author.

AMMERMAN, R. T., & HERSEN, M. (Eds.) (1995). *Handbook of child behavior therapy in the psychiatric setting.* New York: Wiley.

ARDILA, R. (1982). International developments in behavior therapy in Latin America. *Journal of Behavior Therapy and Experimental Psychiatry, 13,* 15–20.

ARRICK, C. M., VOSS, J., & RIMM, D. C. (1981). The relative efficacy of thought-stopping and covert assertion. *Behaviour Research and Therapy, 19,* 17–24.

ASSOCIATION FOR ADVANCEMENT OF BEHAVIOR THERAPY (AABT). Some findings from AABT's membership survey. *Behavior Therapist, 17,* 14.

AUBUCHON, P. G., HABER, J. D., & ADAMS, H. E. (1985). Can migraine headaches be modified by operant pain techniques? *Journal of Behavior Therapy and Experimental Psychiatry, 16,* 261–263.

AUSTIN, J. (1998). Behavioral approaches to college teaching. In J. Austin & J. E. Carr (Eds.), *Handbook of applied behavior analysis.* Reno, NV: Context Press.

AUSTIN, J. (1998). Applied behavior analysis in organizational settings. In J. Austin & J. E. Carr (Eds.), *Handbook of applied behavior analysis.* Reno, NV: Context Press.

AXELROD, S., & APSCHE, J. (Eds.) (1983). *The effects of punishment on human behavior.* New York: Academic Press.

AYLLON, T., & AZRIN, N. H. (1968). *The token economy: A motivational system for therapy and rehabilitation.* New York: Appleton-Century-Crofts.

AYLLON, T., & MICHAEL, J. (1959). The psychiatric nurse as a behavioral engineer. *Journal of the Experimental Analysis of Behavior, 2,* 323–334.

AZRIN, N. H. (1967). Pain and aggression. *Psychology Today, 1*(1), 27–33.

AZRIN, N. H. (1976). Improvements in the community-reinforcement approach to alcoholism. *Behavior Research and Therapy, 14,* 339–348.

AZRIN, N. H., & HOLZ, W. C. (1966). Punishment. In W. K. Honig (Ed.), *Operant behavior: Areas of research and application* (pp. 380–447). New York: Appleton-Century-Crofts.

AZRIN, N. H., & LINDSLEY, O. R. (1956). The reinforcement of cooperation between children. *Journal of Abnormal and Social Psychology, 52,* 100–102.

AZRIN, N. H., NUNN, R. G., (1973). Habit reversal: A method of eliminating nervous habits and tics. *Behaviour Research and Therapy, 11,* 619–628.

AZRIN, N. H., NUNN, R. G., & FRANTZ, S. E. (1980). Habit reversal vs. negative practice treatment of nervous tics. *Behavior Therapy, 11,* 169–178.

AZRIN, N., RUBEN, H., O'BRIEN, F., AYLLON, T., & ROLL, D. (1968). Behavioral engineering: Postural control by a portable operant apparatus. *Journal of Applied Behavior Analysis, 1,* 99–108.

AZRIN, N. H., SISSON, R. W., MEYERS, R., & GODLEY, N. (1982). Alcoholism treatment by disulfiram and community reinforcement therapy. *Journal of Behavior Therapy and Experimental Psychiatry, 13(2),* 105–112

BAER, D. M., PETERSON, R. F., & SHERMAN, J. A. (1967). The development of imitation by reinforcing behavioral similarity to a model. *Journal of the Experimental Analysis of Behavior, 10,* 405–416.

BAER, D. M., & WOLF, M. M. (1970). The entry into natural communities of reinforcement. In R. Ulrich, T. Stachnik, & J. Mabry (Eds.), *Control of human behavior,* (Vol. 2, pp. 319–324). Glenview, IL: Scott, Foresman.

BAER, D. M., WOLF, M. M., & RISLEY, T. R. (1968). Some current dimensions of applied behavior analysis. *Journal of Applied Behavior Analysis, 1,* 91–97.

BAER, D. M., WOLF, M. M., & RISLEY, T. R. (1987). Some still current dimensions of applied behavior analysis. *Journal of Applied Behavior Analysis, 20,* 313–329.

BAILEY, J. S., & PYLES, D. A. M. (1989). Behavioral diagnostics. *Monographs of the American Association on Mental Retardation, 12,* 85–106.

BAILEY, J. S., TIMBERS, G. D., PHILLIPS, E. I., & WOLF, M. M. (1971). Modification of articulation errors of pre-delinquents by their peers. *Journal of Applied Behaviour Analysis, 3,* 265–281.

BALDWIN, J. D., & BALDWIN, J. I. (1986). *Behavior principles in everyday life,* (2nd ed.). Englewood Cliffs, NJ: Prentice-Hall.

BANDURA, A. (1965). Influence of models' reinforcement contingencies in the acquisition of imitative responses. *Journal of Personality and Social Psychology, 1,* 589–595.

BANDURA, A. (1969). *Principles of behavior modification.* New York: Holt, Rinehart & Winston.

BANDURA, A. (1977). *Social learning theory.* Englewood Cliffs, NJ: Prentice-Hall.

BANDURA, A. (1982). Self-efficacy mechanism in human agency. *American Psychologist, 37,* 122–147.

BANDURA, A. (1986). *Social foundations of thought and action: A social-cognitive theory.* Englewood Cliffs, NJ: Prentice-Hall.

BANDURA, A. (1996). Oncological and epistemological terrains revisited. *Journal of Behavior Therapy and Experimental Psychiatry, 27,* 323–345.

BANDURA, A., & WALTERS, R. H. (1963). *Social learning and personality development.* New York: Holt, Rinehart & Winston.

BARKLEY, R. A. (1990). *Attention deficit hyperactivity disorder: A handbook for diagnosis and treatment.* New York: Guilford Press.

BARKLEY, R. A. (1996). 18 ways to make token systems more effective for ADHD children and teens. *The ADHD Report, 4,* 1–5.

BARLOW, D. H., HAYES, S. C., & NELSON, R. O. (1984). *The scientist practitioner: Research and accountability in clinical and educational settings.* New York: Pergamon.

BARLOW, D. H., & HERSEN, M. (1984). *Single-case experimental design: Strategies for studying behavior change* (2nd. ed.). New York: Pergamon.

BARNES, D. (1994). Stimulus equivalence and relational frame theory. *Psychological Record, 44,* 91–124.

BARON, A., & GALIZIO, M. (1983). Instructional control of human operant behavior. *Psychological Record, 33,* 495–520.

BARONE, D. F. (1982). Instigating additional self-modification projects after a personal adjustment course. *Teaching of Psychology, 9,* 111.

BECK, A. T. (1976). *Cognitive therapy and the emotional disorders.* New York: International Universities Press.

BECK, A. T. (1988). *Love is never enough: How couples can overcome misunderstandings, resolve conflicts, and solve relationship problems through cognitive therapy*. New York: Harper & Row.

BECK, A. T., EMERY, G., & GREENBERG, R. L. (1985). *Anxiety disorders and phobias: A cognitive perspective*. New York: Basic Books.

BECKER, W. C. (1986). *Applied psychology for teachers. A behavioral-cognitive approach*. Chicago: Science Research Associates, Inc.

BELCASTRO, F. P. (1985). Gifted students and behavior modification. *Behavior Modification, 9,* 155–164.

BELLACK, A. S. (1986). Schizophrenia: Behavior therapy's forgotten child. *Behavior Therapy, 17,* 199–214.

BELLACK, A. S., & HERSEN, M. (Eds.) (1997). *Behavioral assessment: A practical handbook* (4th ed.). New York: Pergamon.

BELLACK, A. S., HERSEN, M. (Eds.) (1993a). *Handbook of behavior therapy in the psychiatric setting*. New York: Plenum.

BELLACK, A. S., & HERSEN, M. (1993b). Clinical behavior therapy with adults. In A. S. Bellack & M. Hersen (Eds.), *Handbook of behavior therapy in the psychiatric setting* (pp. 3–18). New York: Plenum.

BELLACK, A. S., HERSEN, M., & HIMMELHOCH, J. M. (1996). Social skills training for depression: A treatment manual. In V. B. Van Hasselt & M. Hersen (Eds.), *Sourcebook of psychological treatment manuals for adult disorders* (pp. 179–200). New York: Plenum.

BELLACK, A. S., HERSEN, M., & KAZDIN, A. E. (Eds.) (1990). *International handbook of behavior modification and behavior therapy* (2nd ed.). New York: Plenum.

BELLACK, A. S., & MUSER, K. T. (1990). Schizophrenia. In A. S. Bellack, M. Hersen, & A. E. Kazdin (Eds.), *International handbook of behavior modification and behavior therapy* (2nd ed., pp. 353–376). New York: Plenum.

BELLACK, A. S., MUSER, K. T., GINGERICH, S., & AGRESTA, J. (Eds.) (1997). *Social skills training for schizophrenia*. New York: Guilford.

BELLAMY, G. T., HORNER, R. H., & INMAN, D. P. (1979). *Vocational habilitation of severely retarded adults: A direct service technology*. Baltimore: University Park Press.

BENTALL, R. P., LOWE, C. F., & BEASTY, A. (1985). The role of verbal behavior in human learning. II: Developmental differences. *Journal of the Experimental Analysis of Behavior, 47,* 165–181.

BERKOWITZ, L. (1988). Frustrations, appraisals, and aversively stimulated aggression. *Aggressive Behavior, 14,* 3–11.

BERKOWITZ, L. (1989). Frustration-aggression hypothesis: Examination and reformulation. *Psychological Bulletin, 106,* 59–73.

BIERMAN, K. L., MILLER, C. L., & STABB, S. D. (1987). Improving the social behavior and peer acceptance of rejected boys: Effects of social skill training with instructions and prohibitions. *Journal of Consulting and Clinical Psychology, 55,* 194–200.

BIJOU, S. W. (1993). *Behavior analysis of child development*. Reno, NV: Context Press.

BIJOU, S. W., & BAER, D. M. (1961). *Child development: A systematic and empirical theory* (Vol. 1). New York: Appleton-Century-Crofts.

BILLINGS, D. C., & WASIK, B. H. (1985). Self-instructional training with preschoolers: An attempt to replicate. *Journal of Applied Behavior Analysis, 18,* 61–67.

BIRNBRAUER, J. S., BIJOU, S. W., WOLF, M. M., & KIDDER, J. D. (1965). Programmed instruction in the classroom. In L. P. Ullmann & L. Krasner (Eds.), *Case studies in behavior modification* (pp. 358–363). New York: Holt, Rinehart & Winston.

BLAKELEY, E., & SCHLINGER, H. (1987). Rules: Function-altering contingency-specifying stimuli. *The Behavior Analyst, 10,* 183–187.

BLANCK, G. (1983). *Behavior therapy in Argentina*. Buenos Aires: AAPC Ediciones.

BLECHMAN, E. A., & BROWNELL K. (Eds.) (1989). *Handbook of behavioral medicine for women.* New York: Pergamon.

BLIMKE, J., GOWAN, G., PATTERSON, P., & WOOD, N. (1984). Sport and psychology: What ethics suggest about practice. *Sports Science Periodical on Research and Technology in Sport.* Ottawa, Ontario: Coaching Association of Canada.

BLUM, N., & FRIMAN, P. (1998). Behavioral pediatrics. In J. Austin & J. E. Carr (Eds.), *Handbook of applied behavior analysis.* Reno, NV: Context Press.

BORDEN, J. W. (1992). Behavioral treatment of simple phobia. In S. M. Turner, K. S. Calhoun, & H. E. Adams (Eds.), *Handbook of Clinical Behavior Therapy* (pp. 77–94). New York: John Wiley.

BORNSTEIN, P. H., & BORNSTEIN, M. T. (1986). *Marital therapy: A behavioral communications approach.* New York: Pergamon.

BOUCHARD, S., VALLIERES, A., ROY, M., & MAZIADE, M. (1996). Cognitive restructuring in the treatment of psychotic symptoms in schizophrenia: A critical analysis. *Behavior Therapy, 27,* 257–277.

BOUMAN, T. K., & EMMELKAMP, P. M. G. (1996). Panic disorder and agoraphobia. In V. B. Van Hasselt & M. Hersen (Eds.), *Sourcebook of psychological treatment manuals for adult disorders* (pp. 23–64). New York: Plenum.

BOVJBERG, D. H., REDD, W. H., MAIER, L. A., HOLLAND, J. C., LESKO, L. M., NIEDZWIECKI, D., RUBEN, S. E., & HAKES, T. B. (1990). Anticipatory immune suppression in women receiving cyclic chemotherapy for ovarian cancer. *Journal of Consulting and Clinical Psychology, 58,* 153–157.

BRAAM, C., & MALOTT, R. W. (1990). "I'll do it when the snow melts": The effects of deadlines and delayed outcomes on rule-governed behavior in preschool children. *Analysis of Verbal Behavior, 8,* 67–76.

BRANTNER, J. P., & DOHERTY, M. A. (1983). A review of time-out: A conceptual and methodological analysis. In S. Axelrod and J. Apsche (Eds.), *The effects of punishment on human behavior* (pp. 87–132). New York: Academic Press.

BRAZIER, B., & MACDONALD, L. (1981). Ethical decision-making in behavioral programming: A continuum of procedures. *Journal of Practical Approaches to Developmental Handicap, 4*(3), 11–13.

BREGER, L., & MCGAUGH, J. L. (1965). Critique and reformulation of "learning theory" approaches to psychotherapy and neurosis. *Psychological Bulletin, 63,* 338–358.

BRIGHAM, T. A. (1989a). *Managing everyday problems.* New York: Guilford Press.

BRIGHAM, T. A. (1989b). *Self-management for adolescents: A skills training program.* New York: Guilford Press.

BRISCOE, R. V., HOFFMAN, D. B., & BAILEY, J. S. (1975). Behavioral community psychology: Training a community board to problem-solve. *Journal of Applied Behavior Analysis, 8,* 157–168.

BROMFIELD, R., BROMFIELD, D., & WEISS, B. (1988). Influence of the sexually abused label on perceptions of a child's failure. *Journal of Educational Research, 82,* 96–98.

BROMFIELD, R., WEISZ, J. R., & MESSER, T. (1986). Children's judgments and attributions in response to the "mentally retarded" label: A developmental approach. *Journal of Abnormal Psychology, 95,* 81–87.

BROWN, R. (1973). *A first language: The early years.* Cambridge, MA: Harvard University Press.

BROWNELL, K.D. (1981). Report on international behavior therapy organizations. *The Behavior Therapist, 4,* 9–13.

BROWNELL, K. D., & FAIRBURN, C. G. (Eds.) (1995). *Eating disorders and obesity.* New York: Guilford.

BROWNSTEIN, A. J., & SHULL, R. L. (1985). A rule for the use of the term, "rule–governed behavior." *The Behavior Analyst, 8,* 265–267.

BRYANT, L. E., & BUDD, K. S. (1982). Self-instructional training to decrease independent work performance in preschoolers. *Journal of Applied Behavior Analysis, 15,* 259–271.

BUZAS, H. P., & AYLLON, T. (1981). Differential reinforcement in coaching skills. *Behavior Modification, 5,* 372–385.

CABALLO, V. E., BUELA-CASAL, G. (1993). Behavior therapy in Spain. *Behavior Therapist, 16,* 53–54.

CANGELOSI, J. (1997). *Classroom management strategies: Gaining and maintaining students' cooperation.* New York: Longman.

CARR, E. G. (1977). The origins of self-injurious behavior: A review of some hypotheses. *Psychological Bulletin, 84,* 800–816.

CATANIA, A. C. (1975). The myth of self-reinforcement. *Behaviorism, 3,* 192–199.

CATANIA, A. C. (1976). Self-reinforcement revisited. *Behaviorism, 4,* 157–162.

CATANIA, A. C., MATTHEWS, B. A., & SHIMOFF, F., (1982). Instructed versus shaped human verbal behavior: Interactions with nonverbal responding. *Journal of the Experimental Analysis of Behavior, 38,* 233–248.

CAUTELA, J. R. (1966). Treatment of compulsive behavior by covert desensitization. *Psychological Record, 16,* 33–41.

CAUTELA, J. R., KASTENBAUM, R., & WINCZE, J. (1972). The use of the Fear Survey Schedule and the Reinforcement Survey Schedule to survey possible reinforcing and aversive stimuli among juvenile offenders. *Journal of Genetic Psychology, 121,* 255–261.

CAUTELA, J. R. (1977). *Behavior analysis forms for clinical intervention.* Champaign, IL: Research Press.

CAUTELA, J. R. (1981). *Behavior analysis forms for clinical intervention* (Vol. 2). Champaign, IL: Research Press.

CAUTELA, J. R., & GRODEN, J. (1978). *Relaxation: A comprehensive manual for adults, children, and children with special needs.* Champaign, IL: Research Press.

CAUTELA, J. R., & KEARNEY, A. (1986). *The covert conditioning handbook.* New York: Springer.

CAUTELA, J. R., & KEARNEY, A. J. (1990). Behavior analysis, cognitive therapy, and covert conditioning. *Journal of Behavior Therapy and Experimental Psychiatry, 21,* 83–90.

CAUTELA, J. R., & UPPER, D. E. (1975). The process of individual behavior therapy. In M. Hersen, R. M. Eisler, & P. M. Miller (Eds.), *Progress in behavior modification,* (Vol. 1, pp. 276–306). New York: Academic Press.

CELIBERTI, D. A., ALESSANDRI, M., FONG, P. L., & WEISS, M. J. (1993). Current and future trends in the behavioral treatment of autism. *The Behavior Therapist, 16,* 153–160.

CHANDLER, L. K., LUBECK, R. C., & FOWLER, S. A. (1992). Generalization and maintenance of preschool children's social skills: A critical review and analysis. *Journal of Applied Behavior Analysis, 25,* 415–428.

CHARLOP, M. H., BURGIO, L. D., IWATA, B. A., & IVANCIC, M. T. (1988). Stimulus variation as a means of enhancing punishment effects. *Journal of Applied Behavior Analysis, 21,* 89–95.

CHOMSKY, N. (1959). A review of B. F. Skinner's *Verbal Behavior. Language, 35,* 26–58.

CHUNG, S. H. (1965). Effects of delayed reinforcement in a concurrent situation. *Journal of the Experimental Analysis of Behavior, 8,* 439–444.

CLARK, L. (1996). *SOS! Help for parents.* Bowling Green, KY: Parents Press.

CLINTON, J. J., MCCORMICK, K., & BESTEMAN, J. (1994). Enhancing clinical practice: The role of practice guidelines. *American Psychologist, 49*(1), 30–33.

COHEN, R., DEJAMES, P., NOCERA, B., & RAMBERGER, M. (1980). Application of a simple self-instruction procedure on adult exercise and studying: Two case reports. *Psychological Reports, 46,* 443–451.

CONE, J. D. (1997). Issues in functional analysis in behavioral assessment. *Behavior Research and Therapy, 35,* 259–275.

COTTRAUX, J. (1990). "Cogito ergo somme": Cognitive behavior therapy in France. *Behavior Therapist, 13,* 189–190.

COWDERY, G. E., IWATA, B. A., & PACE, G. M. (1990). Effects and side-effects of DRO as treatment for self-injurious behavior. *Journal of Applied Behavior Analysis, 23,* 497–506.

CRACKLEN, C., & MARTIN, G. (1983). To motivate age-group competitive swimmers at practice, "fun" should be earned. *Swimming Techniques, 20*(3), 29–32.

CRASKE, M. G. (1993). Assessment and treatment of panic disorder and agoraphobia. In A. S. Bellack & M. Hersen (Eds.), *Handbook of behavior therapy in the psychiatric setting* (pp. 229–250). New York: Plenum.

CROSBIE J., & GLENN, K. (1993). A computer based personalized system of instruction in applied behavior analysis. *Behavior Research Methods, Instruments and Computers, 25,* 366–370.

CROWELL, C. R., QUINTANAR, L. R., & GRANT, K. L. (1981). Proctor: An online student evaluation and monitoring system for use with PSI format courses. *Behavior Research Methods and Instrumentation, 13,* 121–127.

CUVO, A. J., DAVIS, P. K., O'REILLY, M. F., MOONEY, B. M., & CROWLEY, R. (1992). Promoting stimulus control with textual prompts and performance feedback for persons with mild disabilities. *Journal of Applied Behavior Analysis, 25,* 477–489.

DALY, E. J., III, MARTENS, B. K., KILMER, A., & MASSIE, D. R. (1996). The effects of instructional match and content overlap on generalized reading performance. *Journal of Applied Behavior Analysis, 29,* 507–518.

DANAHER, B. G. (1977). Research on rapid smoking: Interim summary and recommendations. *Addictive Behavior, 2,* 151–166.

DANGUAH, J. (1982). The practice of behavior therapy in West Africa: The case of Ghana. *Journal of Behavior Therapy and Experimental Psychiatry, 13,* 5–13.

DANIEL, R. F., & POLSTER, R. A. (1984). *Parent training: Foundations of research and practice.* New York: Guilford Press.

DANIELS, A. C. (1994). *Bringing out the best in people.* New York: McGraw Hill.

DARDIG, J. C., & HEWARD, W. L. (1976). *Sign here: A contracting book for children and their parents.* Kalamazoo, MI: Behaviordelia.

DAVIS, M., ESCHELMAN, E. R., & McKAY, M. (1980). *The relaxation and stress-reduction workbook.* Richmond, CA: New Harbinger Publications.

DEITZ, S. M., & MALONE, L. W. (1985). Stimulus control terminology. *The Behavior Analyst, 8,* 259–264.

DEITZ, S. M., & REPP, A. C. (1973). Decreasing classroom misbehavior through the use of DRL schedules of reinforcement. *Journal of Applied Behavior Analysis, 6,* 457–463.

DeLEON, I. G., & IWATA, B. A. (1996). Evaluation of a multiple-stimulus presentation format for assessing reinforcer preferences. *Journal of Applied Behavior Analysis, 29,* 519–533.

DEMCHAK, M. (1990). Response prompting and fading methods: A review. *American Journal on Mental Retardation, 94,* 603–615.

DEMCHAK, M. A., & BOSSERT, K. W. (1996). *Innovations: Assessing problem behaviors.* Washington, DC: American Association on Mental Retardation.

DEPRESSION GUIDELINE PANEL (1993). *Depression in primary care: Vol. 2. Treatment of major depression* (Clinical Practice Guideline, No. 5, AHCPR Pub. No. 93–0551). Rockville, MD: U.S. Department of Health and Human Services, Public Health Service, Agency for Health Care Policy and Research.

DeRICCO, D. A., & NIEMANN, J. E. (1980). In vivo effects of peer modelling on drinking rate. *Journal of Applied Behavior Analysis, 13,* 149–152.

DeRISI, W. J., & BUTZ, G. (1975). *Writing behavioral contracts: A case simulation practice manual.* Champaign, IL: Research Press.

DeSILVA, P., & SIMARASINGHE, D. (1985). Behavior therapy in Sri Lanka. *Journal of Behavior Therapy and Experimental Psychiatry, 16,* 95–100.

DEVANY, J. M., HAYES, S. C., & NELSON, R. O. (1986). Equivalence class formation in language-able and language-disabled children. *Journal of the Experimental Analysis of Behavior, 46*, 243–257.

DEVRIES, J. E., BURNETTE, M. M., & REDMON, W. K. (1991). AIDS prevention: Improving nurses' compliance with glove wearing through performance feedback. *Journal of Applied Behavior Analysis, 24*, 705–711.

DICLEMENTE, R. J., HANSEN, W. B., & PONTON, L. E. (Eds.) (1996). *Handbook of adolescent health risk behavior.* New York: Plenum.

DOBSON, K. S. (1989). Meta-analysis of the efficacy of cognitive therapy for depression. *Journal of Consulting and Clinical Psychology, 57*, 414–419.

DOLEYS, D. M., MEREDITH, R. L., & CIMINERO, A. R. (Eds.) (1982). *Behavioral psychology and medicine and rehabilitation: Assessment and treatment strategies.* New York: Plenum.

DOLLARD, J., & MILLER, N. E. (1950). *Personality and psychotherapy.* New York: McGraw-Hill.

DORSEY, M. F., IWATA, B. A., ONG, P., & MCSWEEN, T. E. (1980). Treatment of self-injurious behavior using a water mist: Initial response suppression and generalization. *Journal of Applied Behavior Analysis, 13*, 343–353.

DOUGHER, M. J. (1997). Cognitive concepts, behavior analysis, and behavior therapy. *Journal of Behavior Therapy and Experimental Psychiatry, 28*, 65–70.

DRYDEN, W., & DIGIUSEPPE, R. (1990). *A primer on rational-emotive therapy.* Champaign, IL: Research Press.

DUPAUL, G. J., & ERVIN, R. A. (1996). Functional assessment of behaviors related to attention deficit/hyperactive disorder: Linking assessment to intervention design. *Behavior Therapy, 27*, 601–622.

DURAND, V. M., & CRIMMINS, D. B. (1988). *The Motivation Assessment Scale (MAS) administration guide.* Topeka, KS: Monaco & Associates.

DYMOND, S., & BARNES, D. (1997). Behavior analytic approaches to self-awareness. *The Psychological Record, 47*, 181–200.

D'ZURILLA, T. J. (1986). *Problem-solving therapy: A social competence approach to clinical intervention.* New York: Springer.

D'ZURILLA, T. J., & GOLDFRIED, M. R. (1971). Problem solving and behavior modification. *Journal of Abnormal Psychology, 78*, 107–126.

EKMAN, P. (1993). Facial expression and emotion. *American Psychologist, 48*, 384–392.

ELKIN, I. (1994). The NIMH treatment of depression collaborative research program: Where we began and where we are. In A. E. Bergin & S. L. Garfield (Eds.), *Handbook of psychotherapy and behavior change* (4th ed., pp. 114–139).

ELKIN, I., SHEA, M. T., WATKINS, J. T., IMBER, S. D., SOTSKY, S. M., COLLINS, J. F., GLASS, D. R., PILKONIS, P. A., LEBER, W. R., DOCHERTY, J. P., FEISTER, S. J., & PARLOFF, M. B. (1989). National Institute of Mental Health Treatment of Depression Collaborate Research Program: General effectiveness treatments. *Archives of General Psychiatry, 46*, 971–982.

ELLIS, A. (1984). *Rational-emotive therapy and cognitive behavior therapy.* New York: Springer.

ELLIS, A. (1993). Changing rational-emotive therapy (RET) to rational-emotive behavior therapy (REBT). *The Behavior Therapist, 16*, 257–258.

ELLIS, A., & BERNARD, M. E. (Eds.) (1985). *Clinical applications of rational-emotive therapy.* New York: Plenum.

ELLIS, A., & DRYDEN, W. (1997). *The practice of rational-emotive behavior therapy*, 2nd ed. New York: Springer.

EMMELKAMP, P. M. G., BOUMAN, T. K., & SCHOLING, A. (1992). *Anxiety disorders: A practitioner's guide.* Chichester, UK: Wiley.

ETZEL, B., & LEBLANC, J. (1979). The simplest treatment alternative: The law of parsimony applied to choosing appropriate instructional control and errorless learning procedures for the difficult-to–teach-child. *Journal of Autism and Developmental Disabilities, 9,* 361–382.

EVANS, I. M., & MATTHEWS, A. K. (1992). A behavioral approach to the prevention of school dropouts: Conceptual and empirical strategies for children and youth placed at risk. In M. Hersen, R. M. Eisler, & P. M. Miller (Eds.), *Progress in behavior modification* (Vol. 28). Sycamore, IL: Sycamore Publishing Co.

EVERS, R. A. F., & VAN DE WETERING, B. J. M. (1994). A treatment model for motor tics based on specific tension reduction technique. *Journal of Behavior Therapy and Experimental Psychiatry, 25,* 255–260.

EYSENCK, H. J. (1959). Learning theory and behavior therapy. *Journal of Mental Science, 105,* 61–75.

EYSENCK, H. J. (Ed.) (1960). *Behaviour therapy and the neuroses.* London: Pergamon.

EYSENCK, H. J. (1994). The outcome problem in psychotherapy: What we have learned? *Behavior Research and Therapy, 32,* 477–495.

FAVELL, J. E., AZRIN, N. H., BAUMEISTER, A. A., CARR, E. G., DORSEY, M. F., FOREHAND, R., FOXX, R. M., LOVAAS, O. I., RINCOVER, A., RISLEY, T. R., ROMANCZYK, R. G., RUSSO, D. G., SCHROEDER, S. R., & SOLNICK, J. V. (1982). The treatment of self-injurious behavior. *Behavior Therapist, 13,* 529–554.

FAW, G. D., DAVIS, P. K., & PECK, C. (1996). Increasing self-determination: Teaching people with mental retardation to evaluate residential options. *Journal of Applied Behavior Analysis, 29,* 173–188.

FAWCETT, S. B., & MILLER, L. K. (1975). Training public-speaking behavior: An experimental analysis and social validation. *Journal of Applied Behavior Analysis, 8,* 125–135.

FEIST, J., & BRANNON, L. (1988). *Health psychology: An introduction to behavior and health.* Belmont, CA: Wadsworth.

FELLNER, D. J., & SULZER-AZAROFF, B. (1984). A behavioral analysis of goal setting. *Journal of Organizational Behavior Management, 6,* 33–51.

FERSTER, C. B., & DEMYER, M. K. (1962). A method for the experimental analysis of the behavior of autistic children. *The American Journal of Orthopsychiatry, 32,* 89–98.

FERSTER, C. B., & SKINNER, B. F. (1957). *Schedules of reinforcement.* New York: Appleton-Century-Crofts.

FESKE, U., & CHAMBLESS, D. L. (1995). Cognitive behavioral versus exposure-only treatment: A meta-analysis. *Behavior Therapy, 26,* 695–720.

FIXSEN, D. L., & BLASE, K. A. (1993). Creating new realities: Program development and dissemination. *Journal of Applied Behavior Analysis, 26,* 597–615.

FLANAGAN, B., GOLDIAMOND, I., & AZRIN, N. (1958). Operant stuttering: The control of stuttering behavior through response-contingent consequences. *Journal of the Experimental Analysis of Behavior, 1,* 173–177.

FLANAGAN, C. (1991). Behavior therapy and cognitive therapy in Ireland. *The Behavior Therapist, 14,* 231–232.

FORSYTH, J. P., & EIFERT, G. H. (1996). The language of feeling and the feeling of anxiety: Contributions of the behaviorisms toward understanding the function-altering effects of language. *Psychological Record, 46,* 607–649.

FOSTER, S. L., BEL–DOLAN, D. J., & BURGE, D. A. (1988). Behavioral observation. In A. S. Bellack & M. Hersen (Eds.), *Behavioral assessment: A practical handbook* (3rd ed., pp. 119–160). New York: Pergamon.

FOWLER, S. A. (1988). The effects of peer-mediated interventions on establishing, maintaining, and generalizing children's behavior changes. In R. H. Horner, G. Dunlap, & R. L. Koegel (Eds.), *Generalization and maintenance: Lifestyle changes in applied settings* (pp. 143–170). Baltimore: Paul H. Brookes.

Fox, L. (1962). Effecting the use of efficient study habits. *Journal of Mathetics, 1,* 75–86 (reprinted in R. Ulrich, T. Stachnik, & J. Mabry 1966, pp. 85–90).

Foxx, R. M., & Faw, G. D. (1990). Problem-solving skills training for psychiatric inpatients: An analysis of generalization. *Behavioral Residential Treatment, 5,* 159–176.

Foxx, R. M., & Shapiro, S. T. (1978). The timeout ribbon: A non-exclusionary timeout procedure. *Journal of Applied Behavior Analysis, 11,* 125–136.

Franks, C. M. (1964). *Conditioning techniques in clinical practice and research.* New York: Springer.

Franks, C. M. (Ed.) (1969). *Behavior therapy: Appraisal and status.* New York: McGraw-Hill.

Frederiksen, L. W., & Lovett, F. B. (1980). Inside organizational behavior management: Perspectives on an emerging field. *Journal of Organizational Behavior Management, 2,* 193–203.

Friedman, M. A., & Brownell, K. D. (1996). A comprehensive treatment manual for the management of obesity. In V. B. Van Hasselt & M. Hersen (Eds.), *Sourcebook of psychological treatment manuals for adult disorders* (pp. 375–422). New York: Plenum.

Friman, P. C., & Poling, A. (1995). Making life easier with effort: Basic findings and applied research on response effort. *Journal of Applied Behavior Analysis, 28,* 583–590.

Friman, P. C., & Vollmer, D. (1995). Succesful use of the nocturnal urine alarm for diurnal enuresis. *Journal of Applied Behavior Analysis, 28,* 89–90.

Fuller, P. R. (1949). Operant conditioning of a vegetative human organism. *American Journal of Psychology, 62,* 587–590. (Reprinted in Ullmann & Krasner 1965, pp. 337–339).

Garcia, J., Ervin, F. R., & Koelling, R. A. (1966). Learning with prolonged delay of reinforcement. *Psychonomic Science, 5,* 121–122.

Gelfand, D. M., Hartmann, D. P. Lamb, A. K., Smith, C. L., Mahan, M. A., & Paul, S. C. (1974). Effects of adult models and described alternatives on children's choice of behavior management techniques. *Child Development, 45,* 585–593.

Geller, E. S., Winett, R. A., & Everett, P. B. (1982). *Preserving the environment: New strategies for behavior change.* New York: Plenum.

Gena, A., Krantz, P. J., McClannahan, L. E., & Poulson, C. L. (1996). Training and generalization of effective behavior displayed by youth with autism. *Journal of Applied Behavior Analysis, 29,* 291–304.

Gesten, E. L., Rains, M., Rapkin, B. D., Weissberg, R. G., Flores de Apodaca, R., Cohen, E. L., & Bowan, G. (1982). Training children in social problem solving competencies: A first look and second look. *American Journal of Community Psychology, 10,* 95–115.

Ghezzi, P. (1998). Behavioral treatment of early childhood autism. In J. Austin & J. E. Carr (Eds.), *Handbook of applied behavior analysis.* Reno, NV: Context Press.

Giles, T. R. (1990). Bias against behavior therapy in outcome reviews: Who speaks for the patient? *The Behavior Therapist, 13,* 86–90.

Giles, T. R. (Ed.) (1993). *Handbook of effective psychotherapy.* New York: Plenum.

Girardeau, F. L., & Spradlin, J. E. (1964). Token rewards on a cottage program. *Mental Retardation, 2,* 345–351.

Glenwick, D. S. (1990). Commentary on the special issue: The adolescent identity development of behavioral community psychology. *The Community Psychologist, 23,* 14–16.

Glynn, E. L., & Thomas, J. D. (1974). Effect of cueing on self-control of classroom behavior. *Journal of Applied Behavior Analysis, 7,* 299–306.

Goetz, E. M., & Baer, D. M. (1973). Social control of form diversity and the emergence of new forms in childrens' block building. *Journal of Applied Behavior Analysis, 6,* 105–113.

Goldiamond, I. (1965). Self-control procedures in personal behavior problems. *Psychological Reports, 17,* 851–868 (reprinted in Ulrich, Stachnik, Mabry 1966, pp. 115–127).

Goldiamond, I. (1976). Self-reinforcement. *Journal of Applied Behavior Analysis, 9,* 509–514.

GOLDSTEIN, L. H. (1990). Behavioral and cognitive behavioral treatments for epilepsy: A progress review. *British Journal of Clinical Psychology, 29,* 257–269.

GORECZNY, A. J. (1995). *Handbook of health and rehabilitation psychology.* New York: Plenum.

GORMALLY, J., BLACK, S., DASTON, S., & RARDIN, D. (1982). The assessment of binge eating severity among obese persons. *Addictive Behaviors, 7,* 47–55.

GOSSETTE, R. L., & O'BRIEN, R. M. (1989, May). *Efficacy of rational-emotive therapy with children: Fact or artifact?* Paper presented at the meeting of the Association for Behavior Analysis, Nashville, TN.

GOSSETTE, R. L., & O'BRIEN, R. M. (1992). The efficacy of rational-emotive therapy in adults: Clinical fact or psychometric artifact? *Journal of Behavior Therapy and Experimental Psychiatry, 23,* 9–24.

GOULD, R. A., & CLUM, G. A. (1993). A meta-analysis of self-help treatment approaches. *Clinical Psychological Review, 13,* 167–189.

GRAZIANO, A. M. (1975). Futurants, coverants and operants. *Behavior Therapy, 6,* 421–422.

GREENSPOON, J. (1951). The effect of verbal and nonverbal stimuli on the frequency of members of two verbal response classes. Unpublished doctoral dissertation, Indiana University, Bloomington.

GREENSPOON, J. (1955). The reinforcing effect of two spoken words on the frequency of two responses. *American Journal of Psychology, 68,* 409–416.

GREENSPOON, J. (1976). *The sources of behavior: Abnormal and normal.* Monterey, CA: Brooks/Cole.

GREENSPOON, J., & LAMAL, P. A. (1978). Cognitive behavior modification—Who needs it? *Psychological Record, 28,* 343–351.

GREENWALD, D. P., KORNBLITH, S. J., HERSEN, M., BELLACK, A. S., & HIMMELHOCH, J. M. (1981). Differences between social skills, therapists and psychotherapists in treating depression. *Journal of Consulting and Clinical Psychology, 49,* 757–759.

GRIFFITH, R. G., & SPREAT, S. (1989). Aversive behavior modification procedures and the use of professional judgment. *Behavior Therapist, 12*(7), 143–146.

GROSS, A. M., & DRABMAN, D. S. (1990). *Handbook of clinical behavioral pediatrics.* New York: Plenum.

GUESS, D., & CARR, E. (1991). Emergence and maintenance of stereotopy and self-injury. *American Journal on Mental Retardation, 96,* 299–319.

GUESS, D., HELMSTETTER, E., TURNBULL, H. R., III, & KNOWLTON, S. (1986). *Use of aversive procedures with persons who are disabled: An historical review and critical analysis.* Seattle, WA: Association for Persons with Severe Handicaps.

GUESS, D., SAILOR, W., RUTHERFORD, G., & BAER, D. M. (1968). An experimental analysis of linguistic development: The productive use of the plural morpheme. *Journal of Applied Behavior Analysis, 1,* 297–306.

GUESS, D., TURNBULL, H. R., III, & HELMSTETTER, E. (1990). Science, paradigms, and values: A response to Mulick. *American Journal on Mental Retardation, 95,* 157–163.

GUEVREMONT, D. C., OSNES, P. G., & STOKES, T. F. (1986). Preparation for effective self-regulation: The development of generalized verbal control. *Journal of Applied Behavior Analysis, 19,* 99–104.

GUTHRIE, E. R. (1935). *The psychology of human learning.* New York: Harper & Row.

HAINS, A. H., & BAER, D. M. (1989). Interaction effects in multi-element designs: Inevitable, desirable, and ignorable. *Journal of Applied Behavior Analysis, 22,* 57–69.

HALAS, E., & EBERHARDT, M. (1987). Blocking and appetitive reinforcement. *Bulletin of the Psychonomic Society, 25,* 121–123.

HANSEN, D. J., TISHELMAN, A. C., HAWKINS, R. P., & DOEPKE, K. (1990). Habits with potential as disorders: Prevalence, severity, and other characteristics among college students. *Behavior Modification, 14,* 66–88.

HANTULA, D. A., BOYD, J. H., & CROWELL, C. I. (1989). Ten years of behavioral instruction with computers: Trials, tribulations, and reflections. *Proceedings of the Academic Microcomputer Conference* (pp. 81–92). Indianapolis: Author.

HARDY, L., MARTIN, G., YU, D., LEADER, C., & QUINN, G. (1981). *Objective behavioral assessment of the severely and moderately mentally handicapped: The OBA.* Springfield, IL; Charles C. Thomas.

HARING, T. G., & KENNEDY, C. H. (1990). Contextual control of problem behavior in students with severe disabilities. *Journal of Applied Behavior Analysis, 23,* 235–243.

HARRIS, B., (1979). What happened to little Albert? *American Psychologist, 34,* 151–160.

HARRIS, C. S., & MCREYNOLDS, W. T. (1977). Semantic cues and response contingencies in self-instructional control. *Journal of Behavior Therapy and Experimental Psychiatry, 8,* 15–17.

HARRIS, F. R., WOLF, M. M., & BAER, D. M. (1964). Effects of adult social reinforcement on child behavior. *Young Children, 20,* 8–17 (reprinted in Ulrich, Stachnik, & Mabry 1966, pp. 130–137).

HAUGHTON, E., & AYLLON, T. (1965). Production and elimination of symptomatic behavior. In L. P. Ullmann & L. Krasner (Eds.), *Case studies in behavior modification* (pp. 94–98). New York: Holt, Rinehart & Winston.

HAWKINS, R. C., & CLEMENT, P. (1980). Development and construct validation of a self-report measure of binge eating tendencies. *Addictive Behaviors, 5,* 219–226.

HAWKINS, R. P. (1979). The functions of assessment: Implications for selection and development of devices for assessing repertoires in clinical, educational, and other settings. *Journal of Applied Behavior Analysis, 12,* 501–516.

HAWKINS, R. P., & DOTSON, V. A. (1975). Reliability scores that delude: An Alice in Wonderland trip through the misleading characteristics of interobserver agreement scores in interval recording. In E. Ramp & G. Semp (Eds.), *Behavior analysis: Areas of research and application* (pp. 359–376). Englewood Cliffs, NJ: Prentice-Hall.

HAWKINS, R. P., & FORSYTH, J. P. (1997). Bridging barriers between paradigms: Making cognitive concepts relevant for behavior analysis. *Journal of Behavior Therapy and Experimental Psychiatry, 28,* 3–6.

HAYES, L. J., & ADAMS, N. (1998). Organizational behavior management in the public sector. In J. Austin & J. E. Carr (Eds.), *Handbook of applied behavior analysis.* Reno, NV: Context Press.

HAYES, S. C. (1989). *Rule-governed behavior: Cognition, contingencies, and instructional control.* New York: Plenum.

HAYES, S. C. (1991). A relational control theory of stimulus equivalence. In L. J. Hayes & P. N. Chase (Eds.), *Dialogues on verbal behavior* (pp. 19–40). Reno, Nev.: Context Press.

HAYES, S. C. (1998). Behavioral psychotherapy. In J. Austin & J. E. Carr (Eds.), *Handbook of applied behavior analysis.* Reno, Nev: Context Press.

HAYES, S. C., BROWNSTEIN, A. J., ZETTLE, R. D., ROSENFARB, I., & KORN, Z. (1986). Rule-governed behavior and sensitivity to changing consequences of responding. *Journal of the Experimental Analysis of Behavior, 45,* 237–256.

HAYES, S. C., ROSENFARB, I., WULFERT, E., MUNT, E. D., KORN, D., & ZETTLE, R. D. (1985). Self-reinforcement effects: An artifact of social standard setting? *Journal of Applied Behavior Analysis, 18,* 201–214.

HAYES, S. C., STROSAHL, K., & WILSON, K. G. (1997). *Acceptance and commitment therapy: Understanding and treating human suffering.* New York: Guilford.

HEFFERLINE, R. F., KEENAN, B., & HARFORD, R. A. (1959). Escape and avoidance conditioning in human subjects without their observation of the response. *Science, 130,* 1338–1339.

HEMBREE-KIGIN, T. L., & MCNEIL, C. B. (1995). *Parent-child interaction therapy.* New York: Plenum.

HERMANN, J. A., MONTES, A. I., DOMINGUEZ, B., MONTES, F., & HOPKINS, B. L. (1973). Effects of bonuses for punctuality on the tardiness of industrial workers. *Journal of Applied Behavior Analysis, 6,* 563–570.

HERRNSTEIN, R. J. (1961). Relative and absolute strength of response as a function of frequency of reinforcement. *Journal of the Experimental Analysis of Behavior, 4,* 267–272.

HERRNSTEIN, R. J., & DEVILLIERS, P. A. (1980). Fish as a natural category for people and pigeons. In G. H. Bower (Ed.), *The psychology of learning and motivation* (vol. 14). New York: Academic Press.

HERRNSTEIN, R. J., & LOVELAND, D. H. (1964). Complex visual concept in the pigeon. *Science, 146,* 549–551.

HERRNSTEIN, R. J., LOVELAND, D. H., & CABLE, C. (1976). Natural concepts in pigeons. *Journal of Experimental Psychology: Animal Behavior Processes, 2,* 285–302.

HERSEN, M. (1976). Historical perspectives in behavioral assessment. In M. Hersen & A. S. Bellack (Eds.), *Behavioral assessment: A practical handbook* (pp. 3–17). New York: Pergamon.

HERSEN, M. (Ed.) (1983). *Outpatient behavior therapy: A clinical guide.* New York: Grune & Stratton.

HERSEN, M. (1989). *Innovations in child behavior therapy.* New York: Springer.

HERSEN, M., & BARLOW, D. H. (1976). *Single case experimental designs: Strategies for studying behavior change.* Elmsford, NY: Pergamon.

HILDEBRAND, R. G., MARTIN, G. L., FURER, P., & HAZEN, A. (1990). A recruitment of praise package to increase productivity levels of developmentally handicapped workers. *Behavior Modification, 14,* 97–113.

HOMME, L. E. (1965). Perspectives in psychology: XXIV. Control of coverants, the operants of the mind. *Psychological Record, 15,* 501–511.

HOMME, L. E., CSANYI, A. P., GONZALES, M. A., & RECHS, J. R. (1969). *How to use contingency contracting in the classroom.* Champaign, IL: Research Press.

HONIG, W. K., & STEWART, K. (1988). Pigeons can discriminate locations presented in pictures. *Journal of the Experimental Analysis of Behavior, 50,* 541–551.

HORAN, J. J., & JOHNSON, R. G. (1971). Coverant conditioning through a self-management application of the Premack principle: Its effect on weight reduction. *Journal of Behavior Therapy and Experimental Psychiatry, 2,* 243–249.

HORNER, R. H. (1994). Functional assessment: Contributions and future directions. *Journal of Applied Behavior Analysis, 27,* 401–404.

HRYCAIKO, D., & MARTIN, G. L. (1996). Applied research studies with single-subject designs: Why so few? *Journal of Applied Sport Psychology, 8,* 183–199.

HUANG, W., & CUVO, A. J. (1997). Social skills training for adults with mental retardation in job-related settings. *Behavior Modification, 21,* 3–44.

HULL, C. L. (1943). *Principles of Behavior.* New York: Appleton-Century-Crofts.

HULL, C. L. (1952). *A behavior system.* New Haven, CT: Yale University Press.

INGRAM, R. E., & SCOTT, W. D. (1990). Cognitive behavior therapy. In A. S. Bellack, M. Hersen, & A. E. Kazdin (Eds.), *International handbook of behavior modification and therapy* (2nd ed., pp. 53–68). New York: Plenum.

IREY, P. A. (1972). Covert sensitization of cigarette smokers with high and low extraversion scores. Unpublished master's thesis, Southern Illinois University, Carbondale.

ISRAEL, A. C., STOLMAKER, L., & ADRIAN, C. A. G. (1985). The effects of training parents in general child management skills on a behavioral weight loss program for children. *Behavior Therapy, 16,* 169–180.

ISSACS, W., THOMAS, J., & GOLDIAMOND, I. (1960). Application of operant conditioning to reinstate verbal behavior in psychotics. *Journal of Speech and Hearing Disorders, 25,* 8–12 (reprinted in Ulrich, Stachnik, & Mabry, 1966, pp. 199–202).

IVANCIC, M. T., BARRETT, G. T., SIMONOW, A., & KIMBERLY, A. (1997). A replication to increase happiness indices among some people with profound developmental disabilities. *Research in Developmental Disabilities, 18,* 79–89.

IWATA, B. A., DORSEY, M. F., SLIFER, K. J., BAUMAN, K. E., & RICHMAN, G. S. (1982). Toward a functional analysis of self-injury. *Analysis and Intervention in Developmental Disabilities, 2,* 3–20.

IWATA, B. A., PACE, G. M., KALSHER, M. J., COWDERY, G. E., & CATALDO, M. F. (1990). Experimental analysis and extinction of self-injurious escape behavior. *Journal of Applied Behavior Analysis, 23,* 11–27.

414 References

Izard, C. E. (1991). *The psychology of emotions.* New York: Plenum.

Jackson, D. A., & Wallace, R. F. (1974). The modification and generalization of voice loudness in a 15-year-old retarded girl. *Journal of Applied Behavior Analysis, 7,* 461–471.

Jacobs, H. (1998). Brain injury rehabilitation. In J. Austin & J. E. Carr (Eds.), *Handbook of applied behavior analysis.* Reno, NV: Context Press.

Jacobson, E. (1938). *Progressive relaxation.* Chicago: University of Chicago Press.

Jacobson, N. S., & Hollon, S. D. (1996). Cognitive therapy versus pharmacotherapy: Now that the jury's returned its verdict, it's time to present the rest of the evidence. *Journal of Consulting and Clinical Psychology, 64,* 74–80.

Janis, I., & Mann, L. (1977). *Decision-making.* New York: Free Press.

Janis, I., & Wheeler, D. (1978). Thinking clearly about career choices. *Psychology Today, 11*(12), 66–76, 121–122.

Jensen, B. J., & Haynes, S. N. (1986). Self–report questionnaires and inventories. In A. R. Ciminero, K. S. Calhoun, & H. E. Adams (Eds.), *Handbook of behavioral assessment* (2nd ed.). New York: Wiley.

Jensen, R., & Burgess, H. (1997). Myth making: How introductory psychology texts present B. F. Skinner's analysis of cognition. *The Psychological Record, 47,* 221–232.

Johnson, C. R., Hunt, F. M., & Siebert, M. J. (1994). Discrimination training in the treatment of pica and food scavenging. *Behavior Modification, 18,* 214–229.

Johnson, K. R., & Ruskin, R. S. (1977). *Behavioral instruction: An evaluative review.* Washington, DC: American Psychological Association.

Johnson, S. P., Welch, T. M., Miller, L. K., & Altus, D. E. (1991). Participatory management: Maintaining staff performance in a university housing cooperative. *Journal of Applied Behavior Analysis, 24,* 119–127.

Johnson, W. G. (1971). Some applications of Homme's coverant control therapy: Two case reports. *Behavior Therapy, 2,* 240–248.

Johnson, W. L., & Baumeister, A. (1978). Self-injurious behavior: A review and analysis of methodological details of published studies. *Behavior Modification, 2,* 465–484.

Johnston, J. M. (1979). On the relation between generalization and generality. *The Behavior Analyst, 2,* 1–6.

Johnston, J. M. (1985). Controlling professional behavior: A review of *The effects of punishment on human behavior* by Axelrod and Apsche. *Behavior Analyst, 8,* 111–119.

Johnston, J. M., & Pennypacker, H. S. (1993). *Strategies and tactics of human behavioral research,* (2nd ed.) Hillsdale, NJ: Erlbaum.

Jones, M. C. (1924). The elimination of children's fears. *Journal of Experimental Psychology, 7,* 383–390.

Kanner, L. (1943). Autistic disturbances of affective contact. *Nervous Child, 2,* 217–250.

Kaprowy, E. A. (1975). Primary reinforcement, a token system, and attention criteria and feedback procedures with profound retardates in a verbal training classroom. Unpublished doctoral dissertation, University of Manitoba, Winnipeg, Manitoba.

Karol, R. L., & Richards, C. S. (1978, November). Making treatment effects last: An investigation of maintenance strategies for smoking reduction. Paper presented at the meeting of the Association for the Advancement of Behavior Therapy, Chicago.

Kazdin, A. E. (1973). The effect of vicarious reinforcement on attentive behavior in the classroom. *Journal of Applied Behavior Analysis, 6,* 72–78.

Kazdin, A. E. (1977a). *The token economy: A review and evaluation.* New York: Plenum.

Kazdin, A. E. (1977b). Assessing the clinical or applied importance of behavior change through social validation. *Behavior Modification, 1,* 427–451.

Kazdin, A. E. (1978). *History of behavior modification.* Baltimore: University Park Press.

KAZDIN, A. E. (1980). *Research design in clinical psychology.* New York: Harper & Row.

KAZDIN, A. E. (1982). *Single-case research designs: Methods for clinical and applied settings.* New York: Oxford University Press.

KAZDIN, A. E. (1985). The token economy. In R. M. Turner & L. M. Ascher (Eds.), *Evaluating behavior therapy outcome* (pp. 225–253). New York: Springer.

KAZDIN, A. E. (1994). *Behavior modification in applied settings* (5th ed.) Belmont, CA: Brooks/Cole Publishing Company.

KAZDIN, A. E., & ERICKSON, L. M. (1975). Developing responsiveness to instructions in severely and profoundly retarded residents. *Journal of Behavior Therapy and Experimental Psychiatry, 6,* 17–21.

KAZDIN, A. E., & POLSTER, R. (1973). Intermittent token reinforcement and response maintenance in extinction. *Behavior Therapy, 4,* 386–391.

KEARNEY, C. A., & SILVERMAN, W. K. (1990). A preliminary analysis of a functional model of assessment and treatment for school refusal behavior. *Behavior Modification, 14,* 340–366.

KEESEY, R., & POWLEY, T. (1986). The regulation of body weight. In M. R. Rosenzweig, & L. W. Porter (Eds.), *Annual review of psychology* (Vol. 37, pp. 87–105). Palo Alto, CA: Annual Reviews.

KELLER, F. S. (1968). Good-bye, teacher. . . . *Journal of Applied Behavior Analysis, 1,* 79–89.

KELLER, F. S., & SCHOENFELD, W. N. (1950). *Principles of psychology.* New York: Appleton–Century-Crofts.

KELLER, F. S., & SHERMAN, J. G. (1982). *The PSI handbook: Essays on personalized instruction.* Lawrence, KS: TRI Publications.

KERN, L., CHILDS, K. E., DUNLAP, G., CLARKE, S., & FALK, G. D. (1994). Using assessment based curricular intervention to improve the classroom behavior of a student with emotional and behavioral challenges. *Journal of Applied Behavior Analysis, 27,* 7–19.

KING, N. (1996). The Australian Association for Cognitive and Behavior Therapy. *The Behavior Therapist, 19,* 73–74.

KINSNER, W., & PEAR, J. J. (1988). Computer-aided personalized system of instruction for the virtual classroom. *Canadian Journal of Educational Communication, 17,* 21–36.

KIRBY, F. D., & SHIELDS, F. (1972). Modification of arithmetic response rate and attending behavior in a seventh grade student. *Journal of Applied Behavior Analysis, 5,* 79–84.

KIRBY, K. C., & BICKEL, W. K. (1988). Toward an explicit analysis of generalization: A stimulus control interpretation. *The Behavior Analyst, 11,* 115–129.

KIRCHER, A. S., PEAR, J. J., & MARTIN, G. (1971). Shock as punishment in a picture-naming task with retarded children. *Journal of Applied Behavior Analysis, 4,* 227–233.

KNIGHT, M. F., & McKENZIE, H. S. (1974). Elimination of bedtime thumb-sucking in home settings through contingent reading. *Journal of Applied Behavior Analysis, 7,* 33–38.

KOHLENBERG, R. J., TSAI, M., & DOUGHER, M. J. (1993). The dimensions of clinical behavior analysis. *The Behavior Analyst, 16,* 271–282.

KOHLER, F. W., & GREENWOOD, C. R. (1986). Toward technology of generalization: The identification of natural contingencies of reinforcement. *The Behavior Analyst, 9,* 19–26.

KOMAKI, J., & BARNETT, F. T. (1977). A behavioral approach to coaching football: Improving the play execution of the offensive backfield on a youth football team. *Journal of Applied Behavior Analysis, 7,* 199–206.

KONARSKI, E. A., JR., FAVELL, JAMES E., & FAVELL, JUDITH E. (Eds.) (1997). *Manual for the assessment and treatment of the behavior disorders of people with mental retardation.* Morganton, NC: Western Carolina Center Foundation.

KOOP, S., MARTIN, G., YU, D., & SUTHONS, E. (1980). Comparison of two reinforcement strategies in vocational-skill training of mentally retarded persons. *American Journal of Mental Deficiency, 84,* 616–626.

KOZAK, M. J., & FOA, E. B. (1996). Obsessive-compulsive disorder. In V. B. Van Hasselt & M. Hersen (Eds.), *Sourcebook of psychological treatment manuals for adult disorders* (pp. 65–122). New York: Plenum.

KUCZMARSKI, R. J. (1992). Prevalence of overweight and weight gain in the United States. *American Journal of Clinical Nutrition, 55*(Supp. 1), 495S–502S.

KULIK, C.-L., KULIK, J. A., & BANGERT-DROWNS, R. L. (1990). Effectiveness of mastery learning programs: A meta–analysis. *Review of Educational Research, 60,* 265–299.

LARKIN, K. T., & ZAYFERT, C. (1996). Anger management training with essential hypertensive patients. In V. B. Van Hasselt & M. Hersen (Eds.), *Sourcebook of psychological treatment manuals for adult disorders* (pp. 689–716). New York: Plenum.

LARSEN, D. W. (1983, February 14). Coach inspires more than winning. *Seattle Times* (as reported in Locke & Latham, 1985).

LAST, C. G., & HERSEN, M. (Eds.) (1993). *Adult behavior therapy case book.* New York: Plenum.

LATIES, V. G., & MACE, F. C. (1993). Taking stock: The first 25 years of the *Journal of Applied Behavior Analysis. Journal of Applied Behavior Analysis, 26,* 513–525.

LATIMER, P. R., & SWEET, A. A. (1984). Cognitive vs. behavioral procedures in cognitive behavior therapy: A critical review of the evidence. *Journal of Behavior Therapy & Experimental Psychiatry, 15,* 9–22.

LATTAL, K. A., & METZGER, B. (1994). Response acquisition by Siamese fighting fish with delayed visual reinforcement. *Journal of the Experimental Analysis of Behavior, 61,* 35–44.

LAZARUS, A. A. (1958). New methods in psychotherapy: A case study. *South African Medical Journal, 32,* 660–664.

LAZARUS, A. A. (1971). *Behavior therapy and beyond.* New York: McGraw-Hill.

LAZARUS, A. A. (1976). *Multi-model behavior therapy* New York: Springer.

LEBOW, M. D. (1991). *Overweight children: Helping your child to achieve lifetime weight control.* New York: Insight Books/Plenum.

LEDWIDGE, B. (1978). Cognitive behavior modification—A step in the wrong direction. *Psychological Bulletin, 85,* 353–375.

LEITEBERG, H. (1973). The use of single-case methodology in psychotherapy research. *Journal of Abnormal Psychology, 82,* 87–101.

LENNOX, D. B., MILTENBERGER, R. G., & DONNELLY, D. (1987). Response interruption and DRL for the reduction of rapid eating. *Journal of Applied Behavior Analysis, 20,* 279–284.

LERMAN, D. C., & IWATA, B. A. (1995). Prevalence of the extinction burst and its attenuation during treatment. *Journal of Applied Behavior Analysis, 28,* 93–94.

LERMAN, D. C., & IWATA, B. A. (1996). Developing a technology for the use of operant extinction in clinical settings: An examination of basic and applied research. *Journal of Applied Behavior Analysis, 29,* 345–382.

LERMAN, D. C., IWATA, B. A., SHORE, B. A., & KAHNG, S. (1996). Responding maintained by intermittent reinforcement: Implications for the use of extinction with problem behavior in clinical settings. *Journal of Applied Behavior Analysis, 29,* 153–171.

LEVINE, F. M., & FASNACHT, G. (1974). Token rewards may lead to token learning. *American Psychologist, 29,* 816–820.

LINDSLEY, O. R. (1956). Operant conditioning methods applied to research in chronic schizophrenia. *Psychiatric Research Reports, 5,* 118–139.

LINDSLEY, O. R. (1966). An experiment with parents handling behavior at home. *Johnstone Bulletin, 9,* 27–36.

LINDSLEY, O. R., SKINNER, B. F., & SOLOMON, H. C. (1953). *Studies in behavior therapy: Status report I.* Waltham, MA: Metropolitan State Hospital.

LINSCHEID, T. R., IWATA, B. A., RICKETTS, R. W., WILLIAMS, D. E., & GRIFFIN, J. C. (1990). Clinical evaluation of the self-injurious behavior inhibiting system (SIBIS). *Journal of Applied Behavior Analysis, 23,* 53–78.

LINSCHEID, T. R., PEJEAU, C., COHEN, S., & FOOTO-LENZ, M. (1994). Positive side-effects in the treatment of SIB using the Self-Injurious Behavior Inhibiting System (SIBIS): Implications for operant and biochemical explanations of SIB. *Research in Developmental Disabilities, 15,* 81–90.

LIPPMAN, M. R., & MOTTA, R. W. (1993). Effects of positive and negative reinforcement on daily living skills in chronic psychiatric patients in community residences. *Journal of Clinical Psychology, 49,* 654–662.

LOCKE, E. A., & LATHAM, G. P. (1985). The application of goal setting to sports. *Journal of Sport Psychology, 7,* 205–222.

LOCKE, E. A., & LATHAM, G. P. (1990). *A theory of goal setting and task performance.* Englewood Cliffs, NJ: Prentice-Hall.

LOGUE, A. W. (1995). *Self-control: Waiting until tommorow for what you want today.* Englewood Cliffs, NJ: Prentice Hall.

LOPICCOLO, J. (1990). Sexual dysfunction. In A. S. Bellack, M. Hersen, & A. E. Kazdin (Eds.), *International handbook of behavior modification and therapy* (2nd ed pp. 547–554). New York: Plenum.

LOPICCOLO, J., & FRIEDMAN, J. (1988). Broad spectrum treatment of low sexual desire: Integration of cognitive, behavioral, and systematic therapy. In S. Leiblum & R. Rosen (Eds.), *Sexual desire disorders* (pp. 107–144). New York: Guilford Press.

LOVAAS, O. I. (1966). A program for the establishment of speech in psychotic children. In J. K. Wing (Ed.), *Early childhood autism* (pp. 115–144). Elmsford, NY: Pergamon.

LOVAAS, O. I. (1977). *The autistic child: Language development through behavior modification.* New York: Irvington.

LOVAAS, O. I. (1982, August). *An overall evaluation of the young autism project.* Paper presented to the American Psychological Association, Washington, DC.

LOVAAS, O. I. (1993). The development of a treatment-research project for developmentally disabled and autistic children. *Journal of Applied Behavior Analysis, 26,* 617–630.

LOVAAS, O. I., NEWSOM, C., & HICKMAN, C. (1987). Self-stimulatory behavior and perceptual development. *Journal of Applied Behavior Analysis, 20,* 45–68.

LOVAAS, O. I., & SMITH, T. (1988). Intensive behavioral treatment with young autistic children. In B. B. Lahey & A. E. Kazdin (Eds.), *Advances in clinical child psychology* (Vol. II, pp. 285–324). New York: Plenum.

LOVAAS, O. I., & SMITH, T. (1989). A comprehensive behavioral theory of autistic children: Paradigm for research and treatment. *Journal of Behavior Therapy and Experimental Psychiatry, 20,* 17–20.

LOVE, S. R., MATSON, J. L., & WEST, D. (1990). Mothers as effective therapists for autistic children's phobias. *Journal of Applied Behavior Analysis, 23,* 379–385.

LOWE, C. F. (1979). Determinants of human operant behaviour. In M. D. Zeiller & P. Harzem (Eds.), *Advances in analysis of behaviour: Vol. I.* Reinforcement and the organization of behaviour (pp. 159–192). Chichester, England: John Wiley.

LOWE, C. F., BEASTY, A., & BENTALL, R. P. (1983). The role of verbal behavior in human learning: Infant performance on fixed interval schedules. *Journal of the Experimental Analysis of Behavior, 39,* 157–164.

LUBETKIN, B. S., RIVERS, P. C., & ROSENBERG, C. N. (1971). Difficulties of disulfiram therapy with alcoholics. *Quarterly Journal of Studies on Alcohol, 32,* 118–171.

LUBOW, R. E. (1974). High-order concept formation in pigeons. *Journal of the Experimental Analysis of Behavior, 21,* 475–483.

LUCE, S. C., DELQUADRI, J., & HALL, R. V. (1980). Contingent exercise: A mild but powerful procedure for suppressing inappropriate verbal and aggressive behavior. *Journal of Applied Behavior Analysis, 13*, 583–594.

LUDWIG, A. M., LEVINE, J. A., & STARK, L. H. (1970). *LDS and alcoholism.* Springfield, IL: Charles C. Thomas.

LUNDERVOLD, D. A., & LEWIN, L. M. (1992). *Behavior analysis and therapy in nursing homes.* Springfield, IL: Charles C. Thomas.

LUTZ, J. (1994). *Introduction to learning and memory.* Pacific Grove, CA: Brooks/Cole.

MACE, F. C., LALLI, J., LALLI, E. P., SHEY, M. C. (1993). Function analysis and treatment of aberrant behavior. In R. VanHouten and S. Axelrod (Eds.), *Behavior analysis and treatment* (pp. 75–99). New York: Plenum.

MACE, F. C., & BELFIORE, P. (1990). Behavioral momentum in the treatment of escape-motivated stereotypy. *Journal of Applied Behavior Analysis, 23*, 507–514.

MACE, F. C., HOCK, M. L., LALLI, J. S., WEST, B. J., BELFIORE, P., PINTER, E., & BROWN, D. K. (1988). Behavioral momentum in the treatment of noncompliance. *Journal of Applied Behavior Analysis, 21*, 123–141.

MACE, F. C., MCCURDY, B., & QUIGLEY, E. A. (1990). A collateral effect of reward predicted by matching theory. *Journal of Applied Behavior Analysis, 23*, 197–205.

MACMILLAN, D. L. (1973). *Behavior modification in education.* New York: Macmillan.

MADSEN, C. H., BECKER, W. C., THOMAS, D. R., KOSER, L., & PLAGER, E. (1970). An analysis of the reinforcing function of "sit down" commands. In R. K. Parker (Ed.), *Readings in educational psychology* (71–82). Boston: Allyn & Bacon.

MADSEN, C. H., JR., & MADSEN, C. R. (1974). *Teaching discipline: Behavior principles towards a positive approach.* Boston: Allyn & Bacon.

MAGER, R. F. (1972). *Goal analysis.* Belmont, CA: Fearon Publishers.

MAHONEY, M. J., & KAZDIN, A. S. (1979). Cognitive behavior modification: Misconceptions and premature evacuation. *Psychological Bulletin, 85*, 1044–1049.

MAHONEY, M. J., & THORESON, C. E. (1974). *Self-control: Power to the person.* Belmont, CA: Brooks/Cole.

MALATESTA, V. J., AUBUCHON, P. G., & BLUCH, M. (1994). A historical timeline of behavior therapy in psychiatric settings: Development of a clinical science. *Behavior Therapist, 17*, 165–168.

MALETSKY, B. M. (1974). Behavior recording as treatment: A brief note. *Behavior Therapy, 5*, 107–111.

MALOTT, R. W. (1989). The achievement of evasive goals: Control by rules describing contingencies that are not direct-acting. In S. C. Hayes (Ed.), *Rule-governed behavior: Cognition, contingencies, and instructional control.* New York: Plenum.

MALOTT, R. W. (1992). A theory of rule-governed behavior and organizational behavior management. *Journal of Organizational Behavior Management, 12*, 45–65.

MALOTT, R. W., & WHALEY, D. L. (1983). *Psychology.* Holmes Beach, FL: Learning Publications.

MARLATT, G. A., & PARKS, G. A. (1982). Self-management of addictive disorders. In P. Karoly & F. H. Kanfer (Eds.), *Self-management and behavior change: From theory to practice* (pp. 443–488). New York: Pergamon.

MARTIN, G. A., & WORTHINGTON, E. L. (1982). Behavioral homework. In M. Hersen, R. M. Isler, & P. M. Miller (Eds.), *Progress in behavior modification* (Vol. 13, pp. 197–226). New York: Academic Press.

MARTIN, G. L. (1981). Behavior modification in Canada in the 1970's. *Canadian Psychology, 22*, 7–22.

MARTIN, G. L. (1982). Thought stopping and stimulus control to decrease persistent disturbing thoughts. *Journal of Behavior Therapy and Experimental Psychiatry, 13*(3), 215–220.

MARTIN, G. L. (1992). Applied behavior analysis in sport and physical education: Past, present and future. In R. P. West, & L. A. Hammerlynk (Eds.), *Designs for excellence in education: The legacy of B. F. Skinner* (pp. 223–287). Longmont, CO: Sopris West.

MARTIN, G. L. (1997). *Sport psychology consulting: Practical guidelines from behavior analysis.* Winnipeg, Canada: Sport Science Press.

MARTIN, G. L., ENGLAND, G., KAPROWY, E., KILGOUR, K., & PILEK, V. (1968). Operant conditioning of kindergarten-class behavior in autistic children. *Behaviour Research and Therapy, 6,* 281–294.

MARTIN, G. L., KOOP, S., TURNER, C., & HANEL, F. (1981). Backward chaining versus total task presentation to teach assembly tasks to severely retarded persons. *Behavior Research of Severe Developmental Disabilities, 2,* 117–136.

MARTIN, G. L., & LUMSDEN, J. (1987). *Coaching: An effective behavioral approach.* St. Louis, MO: Times Mirror/Mosby.

MARTIN, G. L., McDONALD, S., & OMICHINSKI, M. (1971). An operant analysis of response interactions during meals with severely retarded girls. *American Journal of Mental Deficiency, 76,* 68–85.

MARTIN, G. L., & OSBORNE, J. G. (Eds.) (1980). *Helping in the community: Behavioral Applications.* New York: Plenum.

MARTIN, G. L., & OSBORNE, J. G. (1993). *Psychological adjustment to everyday living* (2nd ed.). Englewood Cliffs, NJ: Prentice-Hall.

MARTIN, G. L., & TKACHUK, G. (1998). Behavioral sport psychology. In J. Austin & J. E. Carr (Eds.), *Handbook of applied behavior analysis.* Reno, NV: Context Press.

MARTIN, G. L., TOOGOOD, S. A., & TKACHUK, G. A. (Eds.) (1997). *Behavioral assessment forms for sport psychology consulting.* Winnipeg, Canada: Sport Science Press.

MARX, M. H. (1992). Teaching mentally retarded children to count: An instrumental learning program. *The Keimyung Journal of Behavioral Sciences, 5,* 107–116.

MASIA, C. L., & CHASE, P. N. (1997). Vicarious learning revisited: A contemporary behavior analytic interpretation. *Journal of Behavior Therapy and Experimental Psychiatry, 28,* 41–51.

MASTERS, J. C., BURRISH, T. G., HOLLON, S. D., & RIMM, D. C. (1987). *Behavior therapy: Techniques and empirical findings* (3rd ed.). Orlando, FL: Harcourt Brace Jovanovich.

MASTERS, W. H., & JOHNSON, V. E. (1970). *Human sexual inadequacy.* Boston: Little, Brown.

MATSON, J. L. (1990). *Handbook of behavior modification with the mentally retarded* (2nd ed.). New York: Plenum.

MAZALESKI, J. L., IWATA, B. A., VOLLMER, T. R., ZARCONE, J. R., & SMITH, R. G. (1993). Analysis of the reinforcement and extinction components in DRO contingencies with self injury. *Journal of Applied Behavior Analysis, 26,* 143–156.

MAZUR, J. E. (1991). Choice with probabilistic reinforcement: Effects of delay and conditioned reinforcers. *Journal of the Experimental Analysis of Behavior, 55*(1), 63–77.

McCONAGHY, N. (1996). Treatment of sexual dysfunctions. In V. B. Van Hasselt & M. Hersen (Eds.), *Sourcebook of psychological treatment manuals for adult disorders* (pp. 333–374). New York: Plenum.

McEACHIN, J. J., SMITH, T., & LOVAAS, O. I. (1993). Long-term outcome for children with autism who received early intensive behavioral treatment. *American Journal on Mental Retardation, 97,* 359–372.

McFALL, R. M. (1970). The effects of self-monitoring on normal smoking behavior. *Journal of Consulting and Clinical Psychology, 35,* 135–142.

McGEE, J. J., MENOLASCINO, F. J., HOBBS, D. C., & MENOUSEK, P. E. (1987). *Gentle teaching: A nonaversive approach for helping persons with mental retardation.* New York: Human Sciences Press.

MEADOWS, S. (1996). *Parenting behavior and childrens' cognitive development.* Hillsdale, NJ: Lawrence Erlbaum Associates.

MEAZZINI, P., & ROVETTO, F. (1983). Behavior therapy: The Italian way. *Journal of Behavior Therapy and Experimental Psychiatry, 14,* 5–9.

MEICHENBAUM, D. H. (1977). *Cognitive behavior modification: An integrative approach.* New York: Plenum.

MEICHENBAUM, D. H. (1985). *Stress inoculation training.* New York: Pergamon.

MEICHENBAUM, D. H. (1986). Cognitive behavior modification. In F. H. Kanfer & A. P. Goldstein (Eds.), *Helping people change: A textbook of methods* (3rd ed., pp. 346–380). New York: Pergamon.

MEICHENBAUM, D., & DEFFENBACHER, J. L. (1988). Stress inoculation training. *Counselling Psychologist, 16,* 69–90.

MESSER, S. B., & WINOKUR, M. (1984). Ways of knowing and visions of reality in psychoanalytic therapy and behavior therapy. In H. Arkowitz & S. B. Messer (Eds.), *Psychoanalytic therapy and behavior therapy: Is integration possible?* (pp. 63–100). New York: Plenum.

MEYER, L. H., & EVANS, I. M. (1989). *Nonaversive intervention for behavior problems: A manual for home and community.* Baltimore: Paul H. Brookes.

MEYERS, R. J., & SMITH, J. E. (1995). *Clinical guide to alcohol treatment: The community reinforcement approach.* New York: Guilford.

MICHAEL, J. (1982). Distinguishing between discriminative and motivational functions of stimulus. *Journal of the Experimental Analysis of Behavior, 37,* 149–155.

MICHAEL, J. (1986). Repertoire-altering effects of remote contingencies. *Analysis of Verbal Behavior, 4,* 10–18.

MICHAEL, J. (1987). Symposium on the experimental analysis of human behavior: Comments by the discussant. *Psychological Record, 37,* 37–42.

MICHAEL, J. (1991). A behavioral perspective on college teaching. *Behavior Analyst, 14,* 229–239.

MICHAEL, J. (1993). Establishing operations. *Behavior Analyst, 16,* 191–206.

MIDGLEY, M., LEA, S. E. G., & KIRBY, R. M. (1989). Algorithmic shaping and misbehavior in the acquisition of token deposit by rats. *Journal of the Experimental Analysis of Behavior, 52,* 27–40.

MIKULIS, W. L. (1983). Thailand and behavior modification. *Journal of Behavior Therapy and Experimental Psychiatry, 14,* 93–97.

MILLER, D. L., & KELLEY, M. L. (1994). The use of goal setting and contingency contracting for improving childrens' homework. *Journal of Applied Behavior Analysis, 27,* 73–84.

MOHR, B., MULLER, V., MATTES, R., ROSIN, R., FEDERMANN, B., STREHL, U., PULVERMULLER, F., MULLER, F., LUTZENBERGER, W., & BIRBAUMER, N. (1996). Behavioral treatment of Parkinson's disease leads to improvement of motor skills and to tremor reduction. *Behavior Therapy, 27,* 235–255.

MORGANSTERN, K. P. (1988). Behavioral interviewing. In A. S. Bellack & M. Hersen (Eds.), *Behavioral assessment: A practial handbook* (3rd ed., pp. 89–107). New York: Pergamon.

MORRIS, R. J., & KRATOCHWILL, T. R. (1983). *Treating childrens' fears and phobias: A behavioral approach.* New York: Pergamon.

MUEHLENHARD, C. L., KORALEWSKI, M. A., ANDREWS, S. L., & BURDICK, C. A. (1986). Verbal and nonverbal cues that convey interest in dating: Two studies. *Behavior Therapy, 17,* 404–419.

MURRELL, M., HARDY, M. A., & MARTIN, G. L. (1974). Danny learns to match digits with the number of objects. *Special Education in Canada, 49,* 20–23.

MYERSON, J., & HALE, S. (1984). Practical implications of the matching law. *Journal of Applied Behavior Analysis, 17,* 367–380.

NATIONAL INSTITUTE ON ALCOHOL ABUSE AND ALCOHOLISM. (1990). *Seventh Special Report to the U.S. Congress on Alcohol and Heath* (USDHHS Publication No. ADM90–1656). Washington, DC: U.S. Government Printing Office.

NEEF, N. A. (1995). Research on training trainers in program implementation: An introduction and future directions. *Journal of Applied Behavior Analysis, 28,* 297–299.

NEEF, N. A., MACE, F. C., & SHADE, D. (1993). Impulsivity in students with serious emotional disturbances: The interactive effects of reinforcer rate, delay, and quality. *Journal of Applied Behavior Analysis, 26,* 37–52.

NEEF, N. A., MACE, F. C., SHEA, M. C., & SHADE, D. (1992). Effects of reinforcer rate and reinforcer quality on time allocation: Extensions of the matching theory to educational settings. *Journal of Applied Behavior Analysis, 25*, 691–699.

NEEF, N. A., SHADE, D., & MILLER, M. S. (1994). Assessing influential dimensions of reinforcers on choice in students with serious emotional disturbance. *Journal of Applied Behavior Analysis, 27*, 575–583.

NELSON, G., & CARSON, P. (1988). Evaluation of a social problem solving skills program for third- and fourth-grade students. *American Journal of Community Psychology, 16*, 79–99.

NEVIN, J. A. (1988). Behavioral momentum and the partial reinforcement effect. *Psychological Bulletin, 103*, 44–56.

NEVIN, J. A. (1992). An integrative model for the study of behavioral momentum. *Journal of the Experimental Analysis of Behavior, 57*, 301–316.

NEZU, A. M., & NEZU, C. M. (Eds.) (1989). *Clinical decision-making in behavior therapy: A problem-solving perspective*. Champaign, IL: Research Press.

NINNESS, H. A. C., GLENN, S. S., & ELLIS, J. (1993). *Assessment and treatment of emotional or behavioral disorders*. Westport, CT: Praeger.

NORDQUIST, D. M. (1971). The modification of a child's enuresis: Some response-response relationships. *Journal of Applied Behavior Analysis, 4*, 241–247.

O'BRIEN, S., & REPP, A. C. (1990). Reinforcement-based reductive procedures: A review of 20 years of their use with persons with severe or profound retardation. *Journal of the Association for Persons with Severe Handicaps, 15*, 148–159.

O'CONNOR, R. (1969). Modification of social withdrawal through symbolic modeling. *Journal of Applied Behavior Analysis, 2*, 15–22.

OHMAN, A., DIMBERG, U., & OST, L. G. (1984). Animal and social phobias. In S. Reiss, & R. Bootzin (Eds.), *Theoretical issues in behavior therapy* (pp. 210–222). New York: Academic Press.

O'LEARY, K. D. (1984). The image of behavior therapy: It is time to take a stand. *Behavior Therapy, 15*, 219–233.

OLENICK, D. L., & PEAR, J. J. (1980). Differential reinforcement of correct responses to probes and prompts in picture-naming training with severely retarded children. *Journal of Applied Behavior Analysis, 13*, 77–89.

OLSON, R. P., & KROON, J. S. (1987). Biobehavioral treatments of essential hypertension. In M. S. Schwartz (Ed.), *Biofeedback: A practitioner's guide*. New York: Guilford.

O'NEILL, G. W., & GARDNER, R. (1983). *Behavioral principles in medical rehabilitation: A practical guide*. Springfield, IL: Charles C. Thomas.

OSBORNE, J. G., & POWERS, R. B. (1980). Controlling the litter problem. In G. L. Martin & J. G. Osborne (Eds.), *Helping in the community: Behavioral applications* (pp. 103–168). New York: Plenum.

PAGE, T. J., IWATA, B. A., & NEEF, N. A. (1976). Teaching pedestrian skills to retarded persons: Generalization from the classroom to the natural environment. *Journal of Applied Behavior Analysis, 9*, 433–444.

PAGGEOT, B., KVALE, S., MACE, F. C., & SHARKEY, R. W. (1988). Some merits and limitations of hand-held computers for data collection. *Journal of Applied Behavior Analysis, 21*, 429.

PAL-HEGEDUS, C. (1991). Behavior analysis in Costa Rica. *Behavior Therapist, 14*, 103–104.

PALLOTTA-CORNICK, A. (1978). A comparison of backward and forward chaining to teach packaging and assembly tasks to severely and moderately retarded clients in a sheltered workshop. Unpublished master's thesis, University of Manitoba, Winnipeg, Manitoba.

PALMER, D. C. (1991). A behavioral interpretation of memory. In L .J. Hayes & P. N. Chase (Eds.), *Dialogues on verbal behavior*. Reno, NV: Context Press.

PASCARELLA, E. T., & TERENZINI, P. T. (1991). *How college affects students: Findings and insights from 20 years of research.* San Francisco: Jossey-Bass.

PASSMAN, R. (1977). The reduction of procrastinative behaviors in a college student despite the "contingency fulfillment problems": The use of external control in self-management techniques. *Behavior Therapy, 8*, 95–96.

PATTERSON, G. R., & GULLION, M. E. (1968). *Living with children: New methods for parents and teachers.* Champaign, IL: Research Press.

PAVLOV, I. P. (1927). *Conditioned reflexes: An investigation of the physiological activity of the cerebral cortex.* (G. V. Anrep, Trans.). London: Oxford University Press.

P.D. supports ban on corporal punishment. (1990). *Practitioner Focus, 4*(2), 5, 8.

PEAR, J. J. (1983). Relative reinforcements for cognitive and behavioral terminologies. *Psychological Record, 33*, 20–25.

PEAR, J. J., & ELDRIDGE, G. D. (1984). The operant-respondent distinction: Future directions. *Journal of the Experimental Analysis of Behavior, 42*, 453–467.

PEAR, J. J., & KINSNER, W. (1988). Computer-aided personalized system of instruction: An effective and economical method for short and long distance education. *Machine-Mediated Learning, 2*, 213–237.

PEAR, J. J., & LEGRIS, J. A. (1987). Shaping of an arbitrary operant response by automated tracking. *Journal of the Experimental Analysis of Behavior, 47*, 241–247.

PEAR, J. J., & NOVAK, M. (in press). Computer-aided personalized system of instruction: A program evaluation. *Teaching of Psychology.*

PERIN, C. T. (1943). The effect of delayed reinforcement upon the differentiation of bar responses in white rats. *Journal of Experimental Psychology, 32*, 95–109.

PERRI, M. G., & RICHARDS, C. S. (1977). An investigation of naturally occurring episodes of self-controlled behaviors. *Journal of Consulting Psychology, 24*, 178–183.

PLAUD, J. J., & GAITHER, G. A. (1996). Behavioral momentum: implications and development from reinforcement theories. *Behavior Modification, 20, 2*, 183–201.

PHILLIPS, E. L., PHILLIPS, E. A., FIXSEN, D. L., & WOLF, M. M. (1973). Behavior shaping works for delinquents. *Psychology Today, 7*(1), 75–79.

PHILLIPS, E. L., PHILLIPS, E. A., WOLF, M. M., & FIXSEN, D. L. (1973). Achievement Place: Development of the elected manager system. *Journal of Applied Behavior Analysis, 6*, 541–546.

PINKER, S. (1994). *The language instinct: How the mind creates language.* New York: William Morrow & Co.

PLIMPTON, G. (1965), Ernest Hemingway. In G. Plimpton (Ed.), *Writers at work: The Paris Review interviews* (2nd series, pp. 215–239). New York: Viking.

POCHE, C., BROUWER, R., & SWEARINGEN, M. (1981). Teaching self-protection to young children. *Journal of Applied Behavior Analysis, 14*, 169–176.

POCHE, C., YODER, P., & MILTENBERGER, R. (1988). Teaching self-protection to children using television technique. *Journal of Applied Behavior Analysis, 21*, 253–261.

POLENCHAR, B. F., ROMANO, A. G., STEINMETZ, J. E., & PATTERSON, M. M. (1984). Effects of US parameters on classical conditioning of cat hindlimb flexion. *Animal Learning and Behavior, 12*, 69–72.

POLING, A., DICKINSON, A., & AUSTIN, J. (1998). Basic and applied research in organizational behavior management. In J. Austin & J. E. Carr (Eds.), *Handbook of applied behavior analysis.* Reno, NV: Context Press.

POLING, A., & FUQUA, R. W. (1986). *Research methods in applied behavior analysis.* New York: Plenum.

POLING, A., METHOT, L. L., & LESAGE, M. G. (1995). *Fundamentals of behavior analytic research.* New York: Plenum.

POMERLEAU, O. F., & POMERLEAU, C. S. (1977). *Break the smoking habit: A behavioral program for giving up cigarettes.* Champaign, IL: Research Press.

POPPEN, R. L. (1989). Some clinical implications of rule-governed behavior. In S. C. Hayes (Ed.), *Rule-governed behavior: Cognition, contingencies, and instructional control* (pp. 325–357). New York: Plenum Press.

POTTER, B. A. (1980). *Turning around: The behavioral approach to managing people.* New York: AMACOM.

POUTHAS, V., DROIT, S., JACQUET, A. Y., & WEARDEN, J. H. (1990). Temporal differentiation of response duration in children of different ages: Developmental changes in relations between verbal and nonverbal behavior. *Journal of the Experimental Analysis of Behavior, 53,* 21–31.

POWELL, J., MARTINDALE, A., & KULP, S. (1975). An evaluation of time-sample measures of behavior. *Journal of Applied Behavior Analysis, 8,* 463–469.

PREMACK, D. (1959). Toward empirical behavioral laws. I: Positive reinforcement. *Psychological Review, 66,* 219–233.

PRILLELTENSKY, I. (1989). Psychology and the status quo. *American Psychologist, 44,* 795–802.

PRILLELTENSKY, I. (1990). Enhancing the social ethics of psychology: Toward a psychology at the service of social change. *Canadian Psychology, 31,* 310–319.

PYLES, D. A. M., & BAILEY, J. S. (1990). Diagnosing severe behavior problems. In A. C. Repp, & N. N. Singh (Eds.), *Perspectives on the use of nonaversive interventions for persons with developmental disabilities* (pp. 381–401). Sycamore, IL: Sycamore Press.

QUARTI, C., & RENAUD, J. (1964). A new treatment of constipation by conditioning: A preliminary report. In C. M. Franks (Ed.), *Conditioning techniques in clinical practice and research* (pp. 219–227). New York: Springer.

RACHLIN, H. (1977). A review of M. J. Mahoney's *Cognition and behavior modification. Journal of Applied Behavior Analysis, 10,* 369–374.

RAE, A. (1993). Self-paced learning with video for undergraduates: A multimedia Keller Plan. *British Journal of Educational Technology, 24,* 43–51.

RAE, S., MARTIN, G. L., & SMYK, B. (1990). A self-management package versus a group exercise contingency for increasing on-task behavior of developmentally handicapped workers. *Canadian Journal of Behavioral Science, 22,* 45–58.

RASEY, H. W., & IVERSEN, I. H. (1993). An experimental acquisition of maladaptive behavior by shaping. *Journal of Behavior Therapy and Experimental Psychiatry, 24,* 37–43.

REDD, W. H., & BIRNBRAUER, J. S. (1969). Adults as discriminative stimuli for different reinforcement contingencies with retarded children. *Journal of Experimental Child Psychology, 7,* 440–447.

REDMON, W. K., & DICKINSON, A. M. (Eds.) (1990). *Promoting excellence through performance management.* New York: The Haworth Press.

REID, D. (1998). Staff training and OBM in human service settings. In J. Austin & J. E. Carr (Eds.), *Handbook of applied behavior analysis.* Reno, NV: Context Press.

REPP, A. C., DEITZ, S. M., & DEITZ, D. E. (1976). Reducing inappropriate behaviors in classrooms and individual sessions through DRO schedules of reinforcement. *Mental Retardation, 14,* 11–15.

REPP, A. C., KARSH, K. G., FELCE, D., & LUDEWIG, D. (1989). Further comments on using hand-held computers for data collection. *Journal of Applied Behavior Analysis, 22,* 336–337.

REPP, A. C., & SINGH, N. (1990). *Perspectives on the use of nonaversive and aversive interventions for persons with developmental disabilities.* Sycamore, IL: Sycamore Publishing Co.

REYNOLDS, L. K., & KELLEY, M. L. (1997). The efficacy of a response-cost based treatment package for managing aggressive behavior in preschoolers. *Behavior Modification, 21,* 216–230.

RICHMAN, G. S., REISS, M. L., BAUMAN, K. E., & BAILEY, J. S. (1984). Training menstrual care to mentally retarded women: Acquisition, generalization, and maintenance. *Journal of Applied Behavior Analysis, 17,* 441–451.

RINCOVER, A. (1978). Sensory extinction: A procedure for eliminating self-stimulatory behavior in psychotic children. *Journal of Abnormal Child Psychology, 6,* 299–310.

RINCOVER, A., COOK, R., PEOPLES, A., & PACKARD, D. (1979). Sensory extinction and sensory reinforcement principles for programming multiple adaptive behavior change. *Journal of Applied Behavior Analysis, 12,* 221–233.

RINCOVER, A., & DEVANEY, J. (1982). The application of sensory extinction procedures to self-injury. *Analysis and Intervention in Developmental Disabilities, 2,* 67–81.

ROBERTS, R. N. (1979). Private speech in academic problem-solving: A naturalistic perspective. In G. Zevin (Ed.), *The development of self-regulation through private speech* (pp. 295–323). New York: Wiley.

ROBERTS, R. N., & THARP, R. G. (1980). A naturalistic study of children's self-directed speech in academic problem-solving. *Cognitive Research and Therapy, 4,* 341–353.

RODRIGUE, J. R., BANKO, C. G., SEARS, S. F., & EVANS, G. (1996). Old territory revisited: Behavior therapists in rural America and innovative models of service delivery. *The Behavior Therapist, 19,* 97–100.

ROLIDER, A., & VAN HOUTEN, R. (1993). The Interpersonal Treatment Model: Teaching appropriate social inhibitions through the development of personal stimulus control by the systematic introduction of antecedent stimuli. In R. Van Houten & S. Axelrod (Eds.), *Behavior analysis and treatment.* New York: Plenum.

ROSCOE, B., MARTIN, G. L, & PEAR, J. J. (1980). Systematic self-desensitization of fear of flying: A case study. In G. L. Martin & J. G. Osborne (Eds.), *Helping in the community: Behavioral applications* (pp. 345–352). New York: Plenum.

ROSEN, G. M. (1987). Self-help treatment books and the commercialization of psychotherapy. *American Psychologist, 42,* 46–51.

ROSENTHAL, T. L., & ROSENTHAL, R. H. (1985). Clinical stress management. In D. H. Barlow (Ed.), *Clinical handbook of psychological disorders: A step-by-step treatment manual* (pp. 145–205). New York: Guilford Press.

ROTTER, J. B. (1954). *Social learning and clinical psychology.* Englewood Cliffs, NJ: Prentice-Hall.

ROVETTO, F. (1979). Treatment of chronic constipation by classical conditioning techniques. *Journal of Behavior Therapy and Experimental Psychiatry, 10,* 143–146.

ROWAN, A. B., & ANDRASIK, F. (1996). Efficacy and cost-effectiveness of minimal therapist contact treatments of chronic headaches: A review. *Behavior Therapy, 27,* 207–234.

RUTHERFORD, R. B. (1984). *Books in behavior modification and behavior therapy.* Scottsdale, AZ: Robert B. Rutherford.

SAJWAJ, T., LIBET, J., & AGRAS, S. (1974). Lemon–juice therapy: The control of life-threatening rumination in a six-month-old infant. *Journal of Applied Behavior Analysis, 7,* 557–563.

SAKANO, Y. (1993). Behavior therapy in Japan: Beyond the cultural impediments. *Behavior Change, 10,* 19–21.

SALEND, S. J., ELLIS, L. L., & REYNOLDS, C. J. (1989). Using self-instructions to teach vocational skills to individuals who are severely retarded. *Education and Training in Mental Retardation, 24,* 248–254.

SALMON, D. J., PEAR, J. J., & KUHN, B. A. (1986). Generalization of object naming after training with picture cards and with objects. *Journal of Applied Behavior Analysis, 19,* 53–58.

SALTER, A. (1949). *Conditioned reflex therapy.* New York: Creative Age Press.

SARAFINO, E. P. (1994). *Health psychology: Biopsychosocial interactions* (2nd ed.). New York: Wiley.

SAYERS, S. L., BAUCOM, D. H., & RANKIN, L. (1993). Marital distress. In A. S. Bellack, & M. Hersen (Eds.), *Handbook of behavior therapy in the psychiatric setting* (pp. 375–394). New York: Plenum.

SCHAEFER, H. H., & MARTIN, P. L. (1969). *Behavioral Therapy.* New York: McGraw-Hill.

SCHLEIEN, S. J., WEHMAN, P., & KIERNAN, J. (1981). Teaching leisure skills to severely handicapped adults: An age-appropriate darts game. *Journal of Applied Behavior Analysis, 14,* 513–519.

SCHLINGER, H., & BLAKELEY, E. (1987). Function-altering effects of contingency-specifying stimuli. *The Behavior Analyst, 10,* 41–45.

SCHLINGER, H. D. (1995). *A behavior analytic view of child development.* New York: Plenum.

SCHLOSS, P. J., SMITH, M., SANTORA, C., & BRYANT, R. (1989). A respondent conditioning approach to reducing anger responses of a dually-diagnosed man with mild mental retardation. *Behavior Therapy, 20,* 459–464.

SCHOPLER, E., & MESIBOV, G. B. (1994). *Behavioral issues in autism.* New York: Plenum.

SCHREIBMAN, L. (1975). Effects of within-stimulus and extra-stimulus prompting on discrimination learning in autistic children. *Journal of Applied Behavior Analysis, 8,* 91–112.

SCHREIBMAN, L. (1994). Autism. In L. W. Craighead, W. E. Craighead, A. E. Kazdin, & M. J. Mahoney (Eds.), *Cognitive and behavioral interventions: An empirical approach to mental health problems.* Boston: Allyn & Bacon.

SCHROEDER, H. E., & BLACK, M. J. (1985). Unassertiveness. In M. Hersen & A. S. Bellack (Eds.), *Handbook of clinical behavior therapy with adults* (pp. 509–530). New York: Plenum.

SCHROEDER, S. R. (1972). Parametric effects of reinforcement frequency, amount of reinforcement, and required response force on sheltered workshop behavior. *Journal of Applied Behavior Analysis, 5,* 431–441.

SCHUNK, D. H. (1987). Peer models and children's behavioral change. *Review of Educational Research, 57,* 149–174.

SCHUSTERMAN, R. J., & KASTAK, D. (1993). A California sea lion (zalophus californianus) is capable of forming equivalence relations. *The Psychological Record, 43,* 823–839.

SCHWITZGEBEL, R. L. (1964). *Streetcorner research: An experimental approach to juvenile delinquency.* Cambridge, MA: Harvard University Press.

SCOGIN, F., BYNUM, J., STEPHENS, G., & CALHOON, S. (1990). Efficacy of self-administered treatment programs: Meta-analytic review. *Professional Psychology: Research and Practice, 21,* 42–47.

SCOTT, M. A., BARCLAY, B. R., & HOUTS, A. C. (1992). Childhood enuresis: Etiology, assessment, and current behavioral treatment. In M. Hersen, R. N. Eisler, & P. M. Miller (Eds.), *Progress in behavior modification* (Vol. 28). Sycamore, IL: Sycamore Publishing Co.

SCOTT, R. W., PETERS, R. D., GILLESPIE, W. J., BLANCHARD, E. B., EDMUNDSON, E. D., & YOUNG, L. D. (1973). The use of shaping and reinforcement in the operant acceleration and deceleration of heart rate. *Behaviour Research and Therapy, 11,* 179–185.

SCRIMALI, T., & GRIMALDI, L. (1993). Behavioral and cognitive psychotherapy in Italy. *The Behavior Therapist, 16,* 265–266.

SEIGTS, G. H., MEERTENS, R. M., & KOK, G. (1997). The effects of task importance and publicness on the relation between goal difficulty and performance. *Canadian Journal of Behavioural Science, 29,* 54–62.

SELIGMAN, M. E. P. (1994). *What you can change and what you can't.* New York: Knopf.

SEMANS, J. H. (1956). Premature ejaculation: A new approach. *Southern Medical Journal, 49,* 353–357.

SEMB, G., & SEMB, S. A. (1975). A comparison of fixed-page and fixed-time reading assignments in elementary school children. In E. Ramp & G. Semb (Eds.), *Behavior analysis: Areas of research and application* (pp. 233–243). Englewood Cliffs, NJ: Prentice-Hall.

SEPPA, N. (1996). Is panic disorder on the rise? *The APA Monitor, 27,* 36.

SERKETICH, W. J., & DUMAS, J. E. (1996). The effectiveness of behavioral parent training to modify antisocial behavior in children: A meta-analysis. *Behavior Therapy, 27,* 171–186.

SHERMAN, J. G., RUSKIN, R. S., & SEMB, G. B. (Eds.). (1982). *The personalized system of instruction: 48 seminal papers.* Lawrence, KS: TRI Publications.

SHERRINGTON, C. S. (1947). *The integrative action of the central nervous system.* Cambridge: Cambridge University Press.

SHIMOFF, E., MATTHEWS, B. A., & CATANIA, A. C. (1986). Human operant performance: Sensitivity and pseudosensitivity to contingencies. *Journal of the Experimental Analysis of Behavior, 46,* 149–157.

SIDMAN, M. (1953). Avoidance conditioning with brief shock and no exteroceptive warning signal. *Science, 118,* 157–158.

SIDMAN, M. (1960). *Tactics of scientific research.* New York: Basic Books.

SIDMAN, M. (1971). Reading and auditory-visual equivalence. *Journal of Speech and Hearing Research, 14,* 5–13.

SIDMAN, M., & TAILBY, W. (1982). Conditional discrimination vs. matching to sample: An expansion of the testing paradigm. *Journal of the Experimental Analysis of Behavior, 37,* 5–22.

SIEDENTOP, D. (1978). The management of practice behavior. In W. F. Straub (Ed.), *Sport psychology: An analysis of athletic behavior* (pp. 42–61). Ithaca, NY: Mouvement Publications.

SIEDENTOP, D., & TAGGART, A. (1984). Behavior analysis in physical education and sport. In W. L. Heward, T. E. Heron, D. S. Hill, & J. Trapp-Porter (Eds.), *Focus on behavior analysis in education* (pp. 104–113). Columbus, OH: Charles E. Merrill.

SIMEK, T. C., & O'BRIEN, R. M. (1981). *Total golf: A behavioral approach to lowering your score and getting more out of your game.* Huntington, NY: B-Mod Associates.

SINGER, G. H., SINGER, J. S., & HORNER, R. H., (1987). Using pretask requests to increase the probability of compliance for students with severe disabilities. *Journal of the Association for Persons with Severe Handicaps, 12,* 287–291.

SINGH, N., & BLAMPIED, N. M. (1983). Behavior modification in New Zealand. In M. Hersen, R. M. Eisler, & P. M. Miller (Eds.), *Progress in behavior modification,* (Vol. 14, pp. 173–218). New York: Academic Press.

SKINNER, B. F. (1938). *The behavior of organisms.* New York: Appleton-Century-Crofts.

SKINNER, B. F. (1948). *Walden two.* New York: Macmillan.

SKINNER, B. F. (1953). *Science and human behavior.* New York: Macmillan.

SKINNER, B. F. (1956). A case history in scientific method. *American Psychologist, 11,* 221–223.

SKINNER, B. F. (1957). *Verbal behavior.* New York: Appleton-Century-Crofts.

SKINNER, B. F. (1958). Teaching machines. *Science, 128,* 969–977.

SKINNER, B. F. (1960). Pigeons in a pelican. *American Psychologist, 15,* 28–37.

SKINNER, B. F. (1968). *The technology of teaching.* New York: Appleton-Century-Crofts.

SKINNER, B. F. (1969). *Contingencies of reinforcement: A theoretical analysis.* New York: Appleton-Century-Crofts.

SKINNER, B. F. (1971). *Beyond freedom and dignity.* New York: Knopf.

SKINNER, B. F. (1974). *About behaviorism.* New York: Knopf.

SKINNER, B. F. (1977). Why I am not a cognitive psychologist. *Behaviorism, 5,* 1–10.

SKINNER, B. F. (1989). *Recent issues in the analysis of behavior.* Columbus, OH: Charles E. Merrill.

SKINNER, B. F., & VAUGHAN, N. E. (1983). *Enjoy old age: A program of self-management.* New York: W. W. Norton.

SLOAN, R. B., STAPLES, F. R., CRISTOL, A. H., YORKSTON, N. J., & WHIPPLE, K. (1975). *Psychotherapy versus behavior therapy.* Cambridge, MA: Harvard University Press.

SMITH, J. C. (1990). *Cognitive-behavioral relaxation training: A new system of strategies for treatment and assessment.* New York: Springer.

SMITH, R., MICHAEL, J., & SUNDBERG, M. L. (1996). Automatic reinforcement and automatic punishment in infant vocal behavior. *The Analysis of Verbal Behavior, 13,* 39–48.

SMITH, R. E. (1988). The logic and design of case study research. *The Sport Psychologist, 2,* 1–12.

SNYDER, J., SCHREPFERMAN, L., ST. PETER, C. (1997). Origins of antisocial behavior: Negative reinforcement and affect disregulation of behavior as socialization mechanisms in family interaction. *Behavior Modification, 21,* 187–215.

SOBELL, M. B., & SOBELL, L. C. (1993). *Problem drinkers: Guided self-change treatment.* New York: The Guilford Press.

SOBELL, L. C., TONEATTO, T., & SOBELL, M. B. (1994). Behavioral assessment and treatment planning for alcohol, tobacco, and other drug problems: Current status with an emphasis on clinical applications. *Behavior Therapy, 25,* 533–580.

SOMMER, R. (1977, January). Toward a psychology of natural behavior. *APA Monitor,* 13–14.

SPINELLI, P. R., & PACKARD, T. (1975, February). *Behavioral self-control delivery systems.* Paper presented at the National Conference on Behavioral Self-Control, Salt Lake City, UT.

SPOONER, F. (1984). Comparisons of backward chaining and total task presentation in training severely handicapped persons. *Education and Training of the Mentally Retarded, 19,* 15–22.

STAATS, A. W. (1996). *Behavior and personality.* New York: Springer.

STAATS, A. W., STAATS, C. K., & CRAWFORD, H. L. (1962). First-order conditioning of meaning and the parallel conditioning of a GSR. *Journal of General Psychology, 67,* 159–167.

STADDON, J. E. R., & SIMMELHAG, V. L. (1971). The "superstition" experiment: A reexamination of its implications for the principles of adaptive behavior. *Psychological Review, 78,* 3–43.

STAINBACK, W. C., PAYNE, J. S., STAINBACK, S. B., & PAYNE, R. A. (1973). *Establishing a token economy in the classroom.* Columbus, OH: Charles E. Merrill.

STAMPFL, T. G., & LEVIS, D. J. (1967). Essentials of implosive therapy: A learning-theory-based psychodynamic behavioral therapy. *Journal of Abnormal Psychology, 72,* 496–503.

STARIN, S., HEMINGWAY, M., & HARTFIELD, F. (1993). Credentialing behavior analysts and the Florida behavior analysis certification program. *The Behavior Analyst, 16,* 153–166.

STARK, M. (1980). The German Association of Behavior Therapy. *Behavior Therapist, 3,* 11–12.

Statement on Facilitated Communication (Prepared by a task force of the Association of Behavior Analysis) (1995). *The ABA Newsletter, 18,* 3.

STEKETEE, G. S. (1993). *Treatment of obsessive compulsive disorder.* New York: Guilford Press.

STEPHENS, C. E., PEAR, J. J., WRAY, L. D., & JACKSON, G. C. (1975). Some effects of reinforcement schedules in teaching picture names to retarded children. *Journal of Applied Behavior Analysis, 8,* 435–447.

STOKES, T. F., & BAER, D. M. (1977). An implicit technology of generalization. *Journal of Applied Behavior Analysis, 10,* 349–367.

STOKES, T. F., & OSNES, P. G. (1986). Programming the generalization of children's social behavior. In P. S. Strain, M. J. Guralnick, & H. Walker (Eds.), *Children's social behavior: Development, assessment, and modification* (pp. 407–443). Orlando, FL: Academic Press.

STOLZ, S. B., & ASSOCIATES. (1978). *Ethical issues in behavior modification.* San Francisco: Jossey-Bass.

STROMER, R., MACKAY, H. A., & REMINGTON, B. (1996). Naming: The formation of stimulus classes, and applied behavior analysis. *Journal of Applied Behavior Analysis, 29,* 409–431.

STUART, R. B. (1971). Assessment and change of the communication patterns of juvenile delinquents and their parents. In R. D. Rubin, H. Fernsterheim, A. A. Lazarus, & C. M. Franks (Eds.), *Advances in behavior therapy* (pp. 183–196). New York: Academic Press.

STUART, R. B. (1975). *Client-therapist treatment contract.* Champaign, IL: Research Press.

STURMEY, P. (1994). Assessing the functions of aberrant behaviors: A review of psychometric instruments. *Journal of Autism and Developmental Disabilities, 24,* 293–303.

STURMEY, P. (1995). Analogue baselines: A critical review of the methodology. *Research in Developmental Disabilities, 16,* 269–284.

SULLIVAN, M. A., & O'LEARY, S. G. (1990). Maintenance following reward and cost token programs. *Behavior Therapy, 21,* 139–149.

SUNDBERG, M. L., MICHAEL, J., PARTINGTON, J. W., & SUNDBERG, C. A. (1996). The role of automatic reinforcement in early language acquisition. *The Analysis of Verbal Behavior, 13,* 21–37.

SULZER-AZAROFF, B., & REESE, E. P. (1982). *Applying behavior analysis: A program for developing professional competence.* New York: Holt, Rinehart & Winston.

SWEET, A. A., & LOIZEAUX, A. L. (1991). Behavioral and cognitive treatment methods: A critical comparative review. *Journal of Behavior Therapy and Experimental Psychiatry, 22,* 159–185.

TERENZINI, P. T., & PASCARELLA, E. T. (1994). Living with myths: Undergraduate education in America. *Change, Jan/Feb,* 28–32.

THARP, R. G., & WETZEL, R. J. (1969). *Behavior modification in the natural environment.* New York: Academic Press.

THASE, M. E. (1994). After the fall: Perspectives on cognitive behavioral treatment of depression in the "post-collaborative" era. *The Behavior Therapist, 17,* 48–52.

THIERMAN, G. J., & MARTIN, G. L. (1989). Self-management with picture prompts to improve quality of household cleaning by severely mentally handicapped persons. *International Journal of Rehabilitation Research, 12,* 27–39.

THOMAS, D. L., & MILLER, L. K. (1980). Helping college students live together. Democratic decision-making versus experimental manipulation. In G. L. Martin & J. G. Osborne (Eds.), *Helping in the community: Behavioral applications* (pp. 291–305). New York: Plenum.

TIFFANY, S. T., MARTIN, C., & BAKER, R. (1986). Treatments for cigarette smoking: An evaluation of the contributions of aversion and counselling procedures. *Behavior Research and Therapy, 24,* 437–452.

TIMBERLAKE, W., & ALLISON, J. (1974). Response deprivation: An empirical approach instrumental performance. *Psychological Review, 81,* 146–164.

TIMBERLAKE, W., & FARMER-DOUGAN, V. A. (1991). Reinforcement in applied settings: Figuring out ahead of time what will work. *Psychological Bulletin, 110,* 379–391.

TIMBERLAKE, W., & LUCAS, G. A. (1985). The basis of superstitious behavior: Chance contingency, stimulus substitution, or appetitive behavior? *Journal of the Experimental Analysis of Behavior, 44,* 279–299.

TKACHUK, G. A., & MARTIN, G. L. (1998). Critical review of research on exercise in the treatment of psychiatric disorders. Paper submitted for publication.

TODD, F. J. (1972). Coverant control of self-evaluative responses in the treatment of depression: A new use for an old principle. *Behavior Therapy, 3,* 91–94.

TODD, J. T., MORRIS, E. K., & FENZA, K. M. (1989). Temporal organization of extinction-induced responding in preschool children. *The Psychological Record, 39,* 117–130.

TORGRUD, L. J., & HOLBORN, S. W. (1990). The effects of verbal performance descriptions on nonverbal operant responding. *Journal of the Experimental Analysis of Behavior, 54,* 273–291.

TOUCHETTE, P. E., & HOWARD, J. S. (1984). Errorless learning: Reinforcement contingencies and stimulus control transfer in delayed prompting. *Journal of Applied Behavior Analysis, 17,* 175–188.

TRINGER, L. (1991). Behavior therapy in Hungary. *The Behavior Therapist, 14,* 13–14.

TROLLOPE, A. (1946). *An autobiography.* London: Williams & Norgate.

TURK, D. S., & OKIFUJI, A. (1997). Evaluating the role of physical, operant, cognitive, and affective factors in the pain behaviors of chronic pain patients. *Behavior Modification, 21,* 259–280.

TURNER, J. R., CARDON, L. R., & HEWITT, J. K. (1995). *Behavior genetic approaches in behavioral medicine.* New York: Plenum.

TURNER, S. M., CALHOUN, K. S., & ADAMS, H. E. (Eds.) (1992). *Handbook of clinical behavior therapy* (2nd ed.). New York: Wiley.

TYRON, W. W., & CICERO, S. D. (1989). Classical conditioning of meaning—I. A replication and higher order extension. *Journal of Behavior Therapy and Experimental Psychiatry, 20,* 137–142.

ULLMANN L. P., & KRASNER, L. (Eds.) (1965). *Case studies in behavior modification.* New York: Holt, Rinehart & Winston.

ULRICH, R., STACHNIK, T., & MABRY. J. (Eds.) (1966). *Control of human behavior* (Vol. 1). Glenview, IL: Scott, Foresman.

UPPER, D., CAUTELA, J. R., & BROOK, J. M. (1975). Behavioral self-rating checklist. Described in J. R. Cautela & D. Upper, The process of individual behavior therapy. In M. Hersen, R. M. Eisler, & P. M. Miller (Eds.), *Progress in behavior modification,* (Vol. 1, pp. 275–305). New York: Academic Press.

VAN HASSELT, V. B., & HERSEN, M. (Eds.) (1996). *Sourcebook of psychological treatment manuals for adult disorders.* New York: Plenum.

VAN HOUTEN, R. (1983). Punishment: From the animal laboratory to the applied setting. In S. Axelrod & J. Apsche (Eds.), *The effects of punishment on human behavior.* New York: Academic Press.

VAN HOUTEN, R., & AXELROD, S. (Eds.) (1993). *Behavior analysis and treatment.* New York: Plenum Press.

VAN HOUTEN, R., AXELROD, S., BAILEY, J. S., FAVELL, J. E., FOXX, R. M., IWATA, B. A., & LOVAAS, O. I. (1988). The right to effective behavioral treatment. *Journal of Applied Behavior Analysis, 21,* 381–384.

VAUGHAN, M. (1989). Rule-governed behavior in behavior analysis: A theoretical and experimental history. In S. C. Hayes (Ed.), *Rule-governed behavior: Cognition, contingencies, and instructional control.* (pp. 97–118) New York: Plenum Press.

VAUGHAN, M. E., & MICHAEL, J. L. (1982). Automatic reinforcement: An important but ignored concept. *Behaviorism, 10,* 217–227.

VAUGHAN, W., JR., & HERRNSTEIN, R. J. (1987). Choosing among natural stimuli. *Journal of the Experimental Analysis of Behavior, 47,* 5–16.

VOLLMER, T. R., & IWATA, B. A. (1992). Differential reinforcement as treatment for behavior disorders: Procedural and functional variations. *Research in Developmental Disabilities, 13,* 393–417.

VYGOTSKY, L. S. (1978). *Mind and society.* Cambridge, MA: Harvard University Press.

WAHLER, R. G., WINKEL, G. H., PETERSON, R. F., & MORRISON, D. C. (1965). Mothers as behavior therapists for their own children. *Behaviour Research and Therapy, 3,* 113–124.

WALKER, D., GREENWOOD, C. R., & TERRY, B. (1994). Management of classroom disruptive behavior and academic performance problems. In L. W. Craighead, W. E. Craighead, A. E. Kazdin, & M. J. Mahoney (Eds.), *Cognitive and behavioral interventions: An empirical approach to mental health problems.* Boston, MA: Allyn & Bacon.

WALKER, H. M., & BUCKLEY, N. K. (1972). Programming generalization and maintenance of treatment effects across time and across setting. *Journal of Applied Behavior Analysis, 5,* 209–224.

WALLACE, I. (1971). *The writing of one novel.* Richmond Hill, Ontario: Simon & Schuster (Pocket Books).

WALLACE, I., & PEAR, J. J. (1977). Self-control techniques of famous novelists. *Journal of Applied Behavior Analysis, 10,* 515–525.

WANDZEL, L., CZABALA, C. Z., & TYRA, T. (1991). Current state of behavioral and cognitive therapy in Poland. *Behavior Therapist, 14,* 77–78.

WARD, W. D., & STARE, S. W. (1990). The role of subject verbalization in generalized correspondence. *Journal of Applied Behavior Analysis, 23,* 129–136.

WATSON, D. L., & THARP, R. G. (1972). *Self-directed behavior: Self-modification for personal adjustment.* Monterey, CA: Brooks/Cole.

WATSON, D. L., & THARP, R. G. (1997). *Self-directed behavior: Self-modification for personal adjustment,* 7th ed. Monterey, CA: Brooks/Cole.

WATSON, J. B. (1913). Psychology as the behaviorist views it. *Psychological Review, 20,* 158–177.

WATSON, J. B. (1916). The place of the conditioned reflex in psychology. *Psychological Review, 23,* 89–116.

WATSON, J. B. (1930). *Behaviorism* (Rev. Ed). Chicago: University of Chicago Press.

WATSON, J. B., & RAYNER, R. (1920). Conditioned emotional reactions. *Journal of Experimental Psychology, 3,* 1–14 (reprinted in Ulrich, Stachnik, & Mabry, 1966, pp. 66–69).

WATSON, R. I. (1962). The experimental tradition and clinical psychology. In A. J. Bachrach (Ed.), *Experimental foundations of clinical psychology.* (pp. 3–25). New York: Basic Books.

WATSON, T. S., & GRESHAM, F. M. (1997). *Handbook of child behavior therapy.* New York: Plenum.

WEARDEN, J. H. (1988). Some neglect problems in the analysis of human operant behavior. In G. Davey & C. Cullen (Eds.), *Human operant conditioning and behavior modification* (pp. 197–224), Chichester, England: Wiley.

WEISS, R. L., & HALFORD, W. K. (1996). Managing marital therapy: Helping partners change. In V. B. Van Hasselt & M. Hersen (Eds.), *Sourcebook of psychological treatment manuals for adult disorders* (pp. 489–538). New York: Plenum.

WELCH, M. W., & GIST, J. W. (1974). *The open token economy system: A handbook for a behavioral approach to rehabilitation.* Springfield, IL: Charles C. Thomas.

WELCH, S. J., & PEAR, J. J. (1980). Generalization of naming responses to objects in the natural environment as a function of training stimulus modality with retarded children. *Journal of Applied Behavior Analysis, 13,* 629–643.

WELD, E. M., & EVANS, I. M. (1990). Effects of part versus whole instructional strategies on skill acquisition and excess behavior. *American Journal on Mental Retardation, 94,* 377–386.

WENRICH, W., GENERAL, D., & DAWLEY, H. (1976). *Self-directed systematic desensitization.* Kalamazoo, MI: Behaviordelia.

WHITAKER, S. (1993). The reduction of aggression in people with learning disabilities: A review of psychological methods. *British Journal of Clinical Psychology, 32,* 1–37.

WHITMAN, T. L. (1994). Mental retardation. In L. W. Craighead, W. E. Craighead, A. E. Kazdin, & M. J. Mahoney (Eds.), *Cognitive and behavioral interventions: An empirical approach to mental health problems.* Boston, MA: Allyn & Bacon.

WHITMAN, T. L., SCIBIK, J. W., & REID, D. H. (1983). *Behavior modification with the severely and profoundly retarded: Research and application.* New York: Academic Press.

WHITMAN, T. L., SPENCE, B. H., & MAXWELL, S. (1987). A comparison of external and self-instructional teaching formats with mentally retarded adults in a vocational training setting. *Research in Developmental Disabilities, 8,* 371–388.

WILLIAMS, C. D. (1959). The elimination of tantrum behavior by extinction procedures. *Journal of Abnormal and Social Psychology, 59,* 269.

WILLIAMS, J. E., & CUVO, A. J. (1986). Training apartment upkeep skills to rehabilitation clients: A comparison of task analysis strategies. *Journal of Applied Behavior Analysis, 19,* 39–51.

WILLIAMS, R. L., & LONG, J. D. (1982). *Toward a self-managed lifestyle* (3rd ed.). Boston: Houghton Mifflin.

WILLIAMSON, D. A., CHAMPAGNE, C. M., JACKMAN, L. P., & VARNADO, P. J. (1996). Lifestyle change: A program for long-term weight management. In V. B. Van Hasselt & M. Hersen (Eds.), *Sourcebook of psychological treatment manuals for adult disorders.* New York: Plenum.

WILSON, G. T. (1991). Chemical aversion conditioning in the treatment of alcoholism: Further comments. *Behavior Research and Therapy, 29,* 415–419.

WILSON, K. G., HAYES, S. C., & GIFFORD, E. V. (1997). Cognition in behavior therapy: Agreements and differences. *Journal of Behavior Therapy and Experimental Psychiatry, 28,* 53–63.

WISOCKI, P. A. (1991). *Handbook of clinical behavior therapy with the elderly client.* New York: Plenum.

WISOCKI, P. A., & POWERS, C. B. (1997). Behavioral treatments for pain experienced by older adults. In D. I. Mostovsky & J. Lomranz (Eds.), *Handbook of pain and aging.* New York: Plenum.

WITT, J. C., & WACKER, D. P. (1981). Teaching children to respond to auditory directives: An evaluation of two procedures. *Behavior Research of Severe Developmental Disabilities, 2,* 175–189.

WIXTED, J. T, MORRISON, R. L., & RINALDI, R. C. (1993). Psychiatric assessment and diagnosis: Adults. In A. S. Bellack and M. Hersen (Eds.), *Handbook of behavior therapy in the psychiatric setting* (pp. 73–98). New York: Plenum.

WOLF, M. M. (1978). Social validity: The case for subjective measurement or how applied behavior analysis is finding its heart. *Journal of Applied Behavior Analysis, 11,* 203–214.

WOLF, M. M., HANLEY, E. L., KING, L. A., LACHOWICZ, J., & GILES, D. K. (1970). The timer-game: A variable interval contingency for the management of out-of-seat behavior. *Exceptional Children, 37,* 113–117.

WOLF, M. M., RISLEY, T., & MEES, H. (1964). Application of operant conditioning procedures to the behavior problems of an autistic child. *Behavior Research and Therapy, 1,* 305–312.

WOLFE, V. F., & CUVO, A. J. (1978). Effects of within-stimulus and extra-stimulus prompting on letter discrimination by mentally retarded persons. *American Journal of Mental Deficiency, 83,* 297–303.

WOLFENSBERGER, W. (Ed.) (1972). *Normalization: The principle of normalization in human services.* Toronto: National Institute of Mental Retardation.

WOLPE, J. (1958). *Psychotherapy by reciprocal inhibition.* Stanford, CA: Stanford University Press.

WOLPE, J. (1969) *The practice of behavior therapy.* Elmsford, NY: Pergamon.

WOLPE, J. (1976). Behavior therapy and its malcontents, II: Multimodal electricism, cognitive exclusivism, and "exposure" empiricism. *Journal of Behavior Therapy and Experimental Psychiatry, 7,* 109–116.

WOLPE, J. (1982). *The practice of behavior therapy,* (3rd ed.). New York: Pergamon.

WOLPE, J. (1985). Requiem for an institution. *Behavior Therapist, 8,* 113.

WOLPE, J. (1990). *The practice of behavior therapy* (4th ed.). New York: Pergamon.

WONG, S. E., & LIBERMAN, R. P. (1996). Biobehavioral treatment and rehabilitation for persons with schizophrenia. In V. B. Van Hasselt & M. Hersen (Eds.), *Sourcebook of psychological treatment manuals for adult disorders* (pp. 233–256). New York: Plenum.

WOOD, L. F., & JACOBSON, N. S. (1985). Marital distress. In D. H. Barlow (Ed.), *Clinical handbook of psychological disorders: A step-by-step treatment manual* (pp. 344–416). New York: Guilford Press.

WOODS, D., & MILTENBERGER, R. (1995). Habit reversal: A review of applications and variations. *Journal of Behavior Therapy and Experimental Psychiatry, 26,* 123–131.

WOODS, D., & MILTENBERGER, R. (1996). Are persons with nervous habits nervous? A preliminary examination of habit function in a nonreferred population. *Journal of Applied Behavior Analysis, 29,* 123–125.

WOODS, D. W., MILTENBERGER, R., & FLACH, A. D. (1996). Habits, tics, and stuttering: Prevalence and relation to anxiety and somatic awareness. *Behavior Modification 20(2),* 216–226.

WRIGHTON, P. A. (1978). *Comparative effects of demerit tokens, response cost, and timeout to decrease self-stimulatory behavior during posture training with severely and profoundly retarded women.* Unpublished doctoral dissertation, University of Manitoba, Winnipeg, Manitoba.

WYATT, W. J., HAWKINS, R. P., & DAVIS, P. (1986). Behaviorism: Are reports of its death exaggerated? *Behavior Analyst, 9,* 101–105.

YAMAGAMI, T., OKUMA, H., MORINAGA, Y., & NAKAO, H. (1982). Practice of behavior therapy in Japan. *Journal of Behavior Therapy & Experimental Psychology, 13,* 21–26.

YANKURN, J., & DRYDEN, W. (1997). *Using REBT with common psychological disorders.* New York: Springer.

YATES, A. J. (1970). *Behavior therapy.* New York: John Wiley.

YU, D., MARTIN, G. L., SUTHONS, E., KOOP, S., & PALLOTTA-CORNICK, A. (1980). Comparisons of forward chaining and total task presentation formats to teach vocational skills to the retarded. *International Journal of Rehabilitation Research, 3,* 77–79.

ZARCONE, J. R., RODGERS, T. A., IWATA, B. A., ROURKE, D. A., & DORSEY, M. F. (1991). Reliability analysis of the Motivational Assessment Scale. *Research in Developmental Disabilities, 12,* 349–360.

ZEMAN, F. J. (1991). *Clinical nutrition and dietetics.* New York: MacMillan.

ZETTLE, R. D., & HAYES, S. C. (1982). Rule-governed behavior: A potential theoretical framework for cognitive behavioral therapy. In P. C. Kendall (Ed.), *Advances in cognitive behavioral research and therapy* (Vol. 1, pp. 73–118). New York: Academic Press.

ZIEGLER, S. G. (1987). Effects of stimulus cueing on the acquisition of groundstrokes by beginning tennis players. *Journal of Applied Behavior Analysis, 20,* 405–411.

ZIMMERMAN, E. H., & ZIMMERMAN, J. (1962). The alteration of behavior in a special classroom situation. *Journal of Experimental Analysis of Behavior, 5,* 59–60.

Author Index

Subject Index